Regional Policies and Comparative Advantage

Regional Policies and Comparative Advantage

Edited by

Börje Johansson

Professor of Economics
Jönköping International Business School
Jönköping University, Jönköping, Sweden

Charlie Karlsson

Professor of the Economics of Technological Change
Jönköping International Business School
Jönköping University, Jönköping, Sweden

Roger R. Stough

NOVA Endowed Professor of Public Policy
School of Public Policy
George Mason University, Fairfax, VA, USA

Edward Elgar
Cheltenham, UK • Northampton, MA, USA

Published by
Edward Elgar Publishing Limited
Glensanda House
Montpellier Parade
Cheltenham
Glos GL50 1UA
UK

Edward Elgar Publishing, Inc.
136 West Street
Suite 202
Northampton
Massachusetts 01060
USA

A catalogue record for this book
is available from the British Library

Library of Congress Cataloguing in Publication Data
Regional policies and comparative advantage / edited by Börje Johansson, Charles Karlsson, Roger R. Stough.
p. cm.
Includes bibliographical references and index.
1. Regional planning. 2. Regional economics. I. Johansson, B. (Börje) II. Karlsson, Charlie, 1945– III. Stough, Roger.

HT391 .R373 2002
307.12—dc21 2002020235

ISBN 1 84064 834 1

Printed and bound in Great Britain by MPG Books Ltd, Bodmin, Cornwall

Contents

List of Figures *viii*
List of Tables *x*
Contributors *xiii*
Acknowledgements *xv*
Preface *xvi*

1 Introduction: Regional Policy Evaluation in the New Economic Geography 1
Charlie Karlsson and Roger Stough

PART ONE REGIONAL POLICY AND LOCATION

2 Agglomeration, Economies of Scale and Dynamic Specialisation in a Central Place System 25
Charlie Karlsson and Rolf Nilsson

3 Regional Policy in the Internet Age: The Effects of Technological Change On Regional Development 49
Edward J. Malecki

4 Nomadic Firms in a Network Economy: Comparative Analysis and Policy Perspectives 77
Frank Bruinsma, Cees Gorter and Peter Nijkamp

5 Network Co-evolution with Cost–Benefit Rules: A Simulation Experiment 103
Kiyoshi Kobayashi, Makoto Okumura and Mehmet Ali Tuncer

6 Policies or Market Incentives? Major Changes in the Geographical Sources of Technology in the United States, 1945 –95 127
Luis Suarez-Villa

PART TWO EVALUATING REGIONAL POLICY

7 Regional Policy Evaluation and Labour Market Adjustment 153
Ian Gordon

8 The Evaluation of UK Regional Policy: How much Progress has been Made? 173
Jim Taylor

9 Counteracting the Counterfactual: New Evidence on the Impact of Local Policy from the Residuals 209
Paul Cheshire and Stefano Magrini

10 The Counterfactual Path: Defining the Non-Support Activity Level when Estimating Programme Effects 239
Jan Mønnesland

11 A Computable General Equilibrium Approach to the Ex Post Evaluation of Regional Development Agency Policies 253
Gary Gillespie, Peter G. McGregor, J. Kim Swales and Ya Ping Yin

12 Multi-level Regional Policies and Programmes in France: European Norms, Methods and First Applications 283
Maurice Baslé and Franck Pelé

13 Evaluation of the Employment Effects of United Kingdom Enterprise Zones: A Comparison of New Start-ups and Inward Investors 301
Barry Moore and Jonathan Potter

14 Rural Areas in Crisis? The Role of the Welfare State in Income Creation: The Case of Denmark 323
Chris Jensen-Butler, Bjarne Madsen and Søren Caspersen

PART THREE REGIONAL POLICY: METHODOLOGICAL APPROACHES

15 Methods for Identifying Functional Regions: Theory and Applications 367
Charlie Karlsson and Michael Olsson

16 European Integration and International Trade in Manufacturing: Productivity Considerations and Employment Consequences 391
Kingsley Haynes and Mustafa Dinc

17 Regional Development Potentials and Policy Options for Selected EU Regions 425
Jan S. Kowalski and Axel J. Schaffer

18 Deindustrialisation and Regional Productivity: Swedish Manufacturing Industry, 1970–90 441
Mats Johansson

PART FOUR NEW CONCEPTS AND PERSPECTIVES

19 Place Surplus, Exit, Voice and Loyalty 469
Roger E. Bolton

20 Capital and the Regions: Other Concepts in Need of Evaluation 489
John Rees

21 How can Regional Policies Influence the Location Advantages of a Region? 503
Börje Johansson

Index 515

List of Figures

2.1	The central place system according to strict definition	31
3.1	Principal Internet backbones in the USA	60
3.2	Number of redundant links of 33 backbone providers on the Internet for leading US cities	61
3.3	Bandwidth–weighted hierarchy of US cities, for 33 Internet backbones	62
3.4	Government actions that can enhance clusters	67
5.1	Initial equilibrium	117
5.2a	Final equilibrium after network evolution (case *A*)	118
5.2b	Final equilibrium after network evolution (case *B*)	119
5.2c	Final equilibrium after network evolution (case *C*)	119
5.3	Final utility levels (Benchmark Case)	120
5.4	Final equilibrium after network evolution (case *D*)	121
5.5	Final equilibrium after network evolution (case *C`*)	122
5.6	Final utility levels (Reference Case)	123
6.1	Regional divisions: Sunbelt, Northeast, Midwest	131
6.2	Regional patenting distribution, 1900–1995	132
6.3	Regional innovative capacity, 1900–1995	133
6.4	State innovative capacity, 1900–1995	135
8.1	The potential impact of foreign direct investment on the performance of UK firms	188
8.2	Modeling the effects of regional financial assistance	198
8.3	Ex post evaluation of business development projects supported by the Structural Funds: a case study of Scotland	202
10.1	The reference path, the path with programme implementation, and the programme effect, ex ante and ex post analyses	242
10.2	Growing and declining indicator development. Actual path and hypothetical alternatives without programme activities	243
10.3	Estimated support scheme effects	250
11.1	The time pattern of exogenous Hicks-neutral efficiency shocks in the manufacturing and non-manufacturing traded sectors, with an assumed 5-year decay	265
11.2	The estimated change in total employment in Scotland and the UK as a result of SE's business competitiveness strategic objective	266
13.1	The Location of enterprise zones within the UK	309

14.1	Disposable income 2010, initial effects of a transfer reduction, change with respect to baseline	330
14.2	Disposable income 2010, scenario 1	331
14.3	Disposable income per inhabitant by residence 1995, current prices	333
14.4	Average annual growth in disposable income 1980–95, by place of residence in current prices	334
14.5	The structure of LINE	340
15.1	The real wage less transportation costs between two centres (*i* and *j*)	369
15.2	The geographical interaction cost and the commuting frequency	372
15.3	The commuting frequencies to the two centers (*i* and *j*)	373
15.4	The number of local labour markets in 1986 and 1996	376
15.5	The rank–size distribution of the functional regions 1986 and 1996	377
15.6	A map of the core of the region	378
15.7	The Trollhättan and Lysekil functional regions	379
15.8	The Trollhättan, Lysekil and Uddevalla functional regions	380
15.9	The Trollhättan, Lysekil, Uddevalla and Vänersborg functional regions	381
15.10	The Uddevalla and Lysekil local labour markets (1996)	382
15.11	The Fyrstad region as two functional regions in 1996	382
15.12	The Trollhättan, Lysekil and Uddevalla functional regions	383
15.13	The Trollhättan, Lysekil and Uddevalla and Vänersborg functional regions	384
15.14	The Trollhättan, Uddevalla and Lysekil local labour markets in 1986	385
15.15	The Fyrstad region had parts in three counties	386
17.1	Classification of European regions	432
17.2	Classification of European regions into eight clusters	437
18.1	Sweden and the eight analysed regions	455
19.1	Good L	476
19.2a	Shift of demand for other goods (a)	476
19.2b	Shift of demand for other goods (b)	476
19.3	Demand curve shifts right	477
19.4	A case of a fixed quantity but zero-priced good	477
20.1	Major types of US non-profit organisations	495
20.2	Non-profit organisations by type and city, Piedmont Triad	500

List of Tables

2.1	Description of the regional classification	36
2.2	Number of CP industries with respect to their order in 1993 and 1996	37
2.3	Medium- and high-order industries in 1993 and 1996	38
2.4	Regression results for industry elasticity to population in 1996	39
2.5	Regression results for establishment elasticity to population in 1996	39
2.6	Average size in employment of establishments with respect to their order, in 1993 and 1996	40
2.7	Employment in CP industries with respect to rank	41
2.8	Description of industrial movement between orders in 1993 to 1996	42
3.1	Metropolitan area population effects on the number of central office switches	57
3.2	Presence of competitive telecom providers, by MSA size class	57
3.3	Digital telecommunications technologies, by metropolitan area size class	58
4.1	A typology of nomadic firms *vis -à-vis* other firms	84
4.2	Relocation of firms by country of origin and destination	85
4.3	List of interviewed nomadic firms	87
4.4	Distribution and features of nomadic firms	88
4.5	Multidimensional information table on the attributes of 21 nomadic firms	92
4.6	Data table on the occurrence and composition of minimal sets in rough set analysis	93
4.7	Results of the rough set analysis	93
4.8	Frequency of explanatory variables values included in the decision rules	94
4.9	Frequency of firms affected by variable values included in the decision rules	95
6.1	Regional innovative capacity, 1900–1994	134
6.2	Largest local sources of invention patenting, 1994	137
6.3	The technology-relevant policy context	139
7.1	Regressions of travel to work area non-employment rates, 1991	166
7.2	Regressions of regional non-employment rates, 1991	168

8.1	Estimated effect of region al policy instruments on the number of manufacturing establishments moving into assisted areas in Great Britain, 1960–81	178
8.2	Estimated effects of regional policy instruments on the movement of manufacturing establishments into each GB region, 1960–77	182
8.3	Foreign direct investment in UK regions: 1980–90 and 1991–97	183
8.4	Regional distribution of Japanese-owned plants in GB, 1996	184
8.5	Employment in Japanese-owned plants in the UK by type of assisted area, 1996	184
8.6	Reasons for the choice of a particular locality	185
8.7	Estimated effect of Regional Selective Assistance on jobs created in Scotland	199
9.1	The difference boundaries make: some NUTS regions which are cities	213
9.2	Definition of variables used in growth models 1 and 2	216
9.3	Model 1: 122 major European FURs: GDP growth (1978/80–1992/94)	219
9.4	The role of changing economic potential: estimated coefficients for different models	220
9.5	Residuals from model 1 – without policy units variable	223
9.6	Model 2: European FUR growth (1978/80–1992/4) including policy units	227
9.7	Residuals from model 2 – with policy units variable	229
9.8	Difference between residuals from models 1 and 2	231
11.1	A condensed version of the period-by-period variant of AMOSRUK	256
11.2	Scottish and UK effects in Period 3 of SE's business competitiveness strategic objective	268
11.3	The cumulative discounted Scottish and UK financial effects of SE's business competitiveness strategic objective	269
11.4	Period-by-period employment results for SE's business competitiveness strategic objective	270
13.1	Survey response	308
13.2	Key characteristics of sampled establishments	310
13.3	Types of establishments on EZs and associated employment	311
13.4	General characteristics of EZ establishments	312
13.5	Influences on the decision to locate or start-up on an EZ	313
13.6	Local impacts of EZ establishments: labour composition and local recruitment	315
13.7	Inward investor customer, supplier and competitor linkages	316
13.8	Types of establishment s on EZs and associated employment, by zone type	318

13.9	The main influences on location or start-up, by zone type	318
13.10	The main local impacts, by zone type	319
14.1	Disposable income per inhabitant by place of residence for different groups of rural municipalities in 1995, current prices	335
14.2	Overview of sequence of calculations in LINE in the isolated decomposition	352
14.3	Results of the isolated decomposition of growth in disposable income in Danish rural municipalities, 1980–95	354
14.4	Decomposition of changes in disposable income – cumulative approach	358
15.1	The number of functional regions at different self-sufficiency limits (1986 and 1996)	375
15.2	Summary statistics on the functional regions, 1986 and 1996	377
15.3	The estimated parameters, when 75 per cent self-sufficiency limit is used	377
15.4	The self-sufficiency in 1986 and 1996 in the larger Fyrstad region	379
15.5	The local labour markets in the Fyrstad region, 1996	381
15.6	The two-way flow measures in 1986 and 1996	386
16.1	Growth and employment EUR, USA and Japan	394
16.2	Geographical structure of extra- community trade (goods, extra-EC)	395
16.3	The regional structure of extra-EU imports of manufactured products	396
16.4	Export performance, total goods	397
16.5	Aggregated results	408
16.6	Employment change in the EU countries, shift– share results	409
17.1	Elasticities of the quasi –production function	430
17.2	Elasticities of German regions belonging to the industrial core	432
17.3	Region–type specific elasticities	434
17.4	Derivation of regional policy conclusions	436
17.5	Appropriate policy bundles	439
18.1	A schematic comparison between structure effects according to methods A and B	452
18.2	Employment in manufacturing industry (SN13) in Sweden and eight Swedish regions, 1970 snd 1990	456
18.3	Deindustrialisation in Sweden and eight Swedish regions, 1960–90	456
18.4	Labour productivity – thousands of SEK – within Swedish industry	461
18.5	Productivity development (%) 1970–1990	462
20.1	Current operating expenditures of US non-profit organisations, by type of organisation, 1989	497

Contributors

Maurice Baslé	University of Rennes, Rennes, France
Roger Bolton	Williams College, Williamstown, Massachusetts
Frank Bruinsma	Free University, Amsterdam, The Netherlands
Søren Caspersen	Institute of Local Government Studies, Copenhagen, Denmark
Paul Cheshire	London School of Economics, London, England
Mustafa Dinc	The World Bank, Washington, DC
Garry Gillespie	University of Strathclyde, Glasgow, Scotland
Ian Gordon	University of Reading, Reading, England
Cees Gorter	Free University, Amsterdam, The Netherlands
Kingsley E. Haynes	George Mason University, Fairfax, Virginia
Chris Jensen-Butler	University of St. Andrews, St. Andrews, Scotland
Börje Johansson	Jönköping International Business School, Jönköping, Sweden
Mats Johansson	Swedish Institute for Regional Research, Östersund, Sweden
Charlie Karlsson	Jönköping International Business School, Jönköping, Sweden
Kiyoshi Kobayashi	Kyoto University, Kyoto, Japan
Jan S. Kowalski	University of Karlsruhe, Karlsruhe, Germany
Bjarne Madsen	Institute of Local Government Studies, Copenhagen, Denmark
Stefano Magrini	London School of Economics, London, England
Edward J. Malecki	University of Florida, Gainesville, Florida
Peter McGregor	University of Strathclyde, Glasgow, Scotland
Jan Mønnesland	Norwegian Institute for Urban and Regional Research, Oslo
Barry Moore	University of Cambridge, Cambridge, England
Peter Nijkamp	Free University, Amsterdam, The Netherlands
Rolf Nilsson	Jönköping International Business School, Jönköping, Sweden
Makoto Okumura	Hiroshima University, Higashi –Hiroshima, Japan
Michael Olsson	Jönköping International Business School, Jönköping, Sweden
Franck Pelé	University of Rennes, Rennes, France

Jonathan Potter	Organisation for Economic Cooperation and Development, Paris
John Rees	University of North Carolina, Greensboro, North Carolina
Axel J. Schaffer	University of Karlsruhe, Karlsruhe, Germany
Roger R. Stough	George Mason University, Fairfax, Virginia
Luis Suarez-Villa	University of California, Irvine, California
J. Kim Swales	University of Strathclyde, Glasgow, Scotland
Jim Taylor	Lancaster University, Lancaster, England
Mehmet Ali Tuncer	Kyoto University, Kyoto, Japan
Ya Ping Yin	University of Hertfordshire, Hertfordshire, England

Acknowledgements

The authors thank Christina Green, Christine Pommerening, Irene Johansson and Kerstin Ferroukhin for their tireless work in making multiple rounds of edits on material in the book and for putting it all into the appropriate format for the publisher. Without their effort it would have been difficult to produce the book.

Preface

The contributions forming the different chapters in this book were first presented and discussed at an international workshop in June 1999 in Fiskebäckskil, Sweden. The workshop, which had the theme 'Evaluation of Regional Policies', was the second in a row of international workshops related to evaluating the effects of the application of the European Union structural funds.

The workshop was organised jointly by the Department of Economics and Business Administration, University of Trollhättan/Uddevalla, Sweden, Jönköping International Business School, Jönköping University, Sweden and the School of Public Policy, George Mason University, USA.

The workshop was sponsored by the European Union and by the Swedish Saving Bank. We thank them for their generous sponsorship.

1. Introduction: Regional Policy Evaluation in the New Economic Geography

Charlie Karlsson and Roger Stough

INTRODUCTION

The conceptions of economic development in modern regions have gone through a fundamental change since the beginning of the 1980s. Today, regions are increasingly looked upon as independent market places that are connected via interregional and international trade and not as administrative units embodied in a national unit. Two different but complementary theoretical frameworks explain the economic specialisation of regions. The traditional but insufficient framework assumes that the comparative advantages of regions depend upon differences in the supply of lasting resources.

The new complementary framework known as the new economic geography assumes that the dynamic interaction between geographical market potentials and rational firms in its own way creates the comparative advantage of regions. These comparative advantages take the form of localised increasing returns to scale, for example the formation of highly competitive and rapidly growing industrial clusters. In this framework the role of regions as market places and as carriers of specialisation advantages is stressed. Economic development in a country is no longer a question of national specialisation and competitive power but of regional specialisation often based on clusters and geographical competitive advantages.

The new framework puts regional policy in a new perspective. Of course, regional policy can still stimulate the development of dynamic comparative advantages through investments in lasting resources such as infrastructure capital, human capital and R&D. However, according to the modern theories of endogenous regional economic growth, regional growth comes in major part from internal conditions that can be influenced by policy and other processes. Internal conditions must be developed and implemented with specific local and regional knowledge. The new theoretical base for regional policy also means new challenges for evaluating the effects of regional policies. Evaluation of regional policies must be given a new focus, a new time perspective and new models. This, in summary, is the message from the papers collected in this book.

The purpose of this introductory chapter is to present the new theoretical framework for regional development and, hence, regional policy. It highlights the problems faced today in regional policy evaluation and it presents the chapters included in this volume.

A STYLISED MODEL OF THE NEW ECONOMIC GEOGRAPHY

Current research on the links between regional market potentials and scale economies has produced a rich variety of models. However, most of these models have a common theme. Some common aspects for many models related to the new economic geography are illustrated below.

Increasing returns is a common theme in these models. In the simplest case externalities emerge as a consequence of market interactions involving economies of scale at the level of the individual firm. To deal with this situation it is common to use a spatial version of the Dixit–Stiglitz model of monopolistic competition that allows for multiple locations and transport costs between different locations (Dixit and Stiglitz, 1977).

These models, in their most elementary form, contain two sectors: agriculture and manufacturing. The agricultural sector is perfectly competitive and produces a single homogenous good. On the other hand it provides a large variety of differentiated goods, is characterised by increasing returns and is hence imperfectly competitive. The number of potential manufactured goods is very large.

Production and consumption takes place at a specific location in a geographic space with discrete locations. All consumers have the same preferences and a taste for variety. Each variety of the manufactured good is produced in only one location. All varieties produced at a particular location are symmetric, having the same technology and price. Economies of scale arise for different levels of variety and no economies of scope are allowed.

Agricultural and manufactured goods can be shipped between locations and may incur shipment transport costs. Total sales of a specific variety depend on income in each location, the price index in each location, transport costs and the mill price. Because of increasing returns to scale, consumers' preferences for variety and the unlimited number of potential varieties of manufactured goods, no firm will choose to produce the same variety as another firm.

Hence, each variety is produced in only one location by a single specialised firm. This means that the number of firms is equal to the number of varieties. Here all scale effects work through changes in the variety of goods available. The number of firms in each location is related to the size of the manufacturing labour force in a location.

A location or region with a large manufacturing sector has a lower price index for manufactured goods, because a smaller proportion of this region's manufacturing consumption has to bear transport costs. The region with the larger home market has a more than proportionally larger manufacturing sector and therefore also exports manufactured goods. This phenomenon is known as the home market effect. Locations with large concentrations of manufacturing also tend to have a large demand for manufactured goods.

The basic model framework presented in this section is now expanded.

INCREASING RETURNS AND INTERNAL ECONOMIES OF SCALE

The idea of increasing returns is a basic ingredient in modelling approaches related to the new economic geography. Without increasing returns it is virtually impossible to explain the geographical concentration of firms, regional specialisation and the importance of the home market. Increasing returns is also a basic explanation for trade among regions. If the relationship between the scale of production and the average cost per produced unit is negative, scale advantages exist, which are synonymous with increasing returns to scale.

The major explanation for the existence of increasing returns is that some production factor in a firm is fixed and, hence, gives rise to a cost that is fixed and independent of whether production is small or large in a given interval. The most common explanations to the existence of fixed factors of production are indivisible resources and so called set-up costs, which consist of development, start-up, establishment, preparation and training costs. These latter costs are normally associated with labour and immaterial resources, while indivisible resources are most often associated with capital objects such as buildings, facilities, machines and material networks. Other examples of fixed factors are knowledge assets, brand names and non-material networks. A fixed production factor can be most closely compared to a catalyst, which must be present in production. As such it generates a cost – often a start-up cost – but the use of the resource is not dependent upon the volume of production or if the firm has many or few customers.

GEOGRAPHICAL INTERACTION COSTS

To deepen the analysis it is necessary to acknowledge the existence of geographical interaction costs. In the stylised model transportation costs were introduced in a simple way. However, geographical interaction costs include not only transportation cost but also geographical transaction costs. Furthermore, to make the concept of a functional region meaningful we have also to acknowledge that the geographical variation in interaction cost for many products is non-linear (see Johansson and Karlsson, 2000).

The interaction in the market place between demand and supply naturally gives rise to various forms of interaction costs, including transport costs. These costs include search costs, communication costs and other costs for exchanging information. When formulating a contract, the product (good or service) must be described, inspected and assessed by the seller as well as weighed and measured whenever this is possible. The good to be transferred must also be examined and accepted by the buyer. Other causes of transaction costs are negotiations, consultation of legal advisers, discussions with financiers and documentation of the agreement. Obviously, such costs are especially high when a product is not standardised. Such a product may be specially designed for a given customer or it may be in an early phase of its product life cycle when interaction with individual customers is particularly crucial for successful delivery. These contacts are usually distance sensitive, because they require face-to-face contact. The normal method to reduce transaction costs is to standardise the product as well as the transaction procedure. Standardisation is facilitated when demand becomes sufficiently large and the relevant technology is harnessed.

In a world with constant returns to scale in all production activities, neither high nor low geographical interaction costs can explain why regions grow more or are larger than other regions. If the geographical interaction costs are very high, it is of course most rational to split up and spread out the production and supply each regional market with local production via micro firms. If, on the other hand, the geographical interaction costs are very low then it does not matter whatsoever where production is located. But all this is true only if firms have constant returns to scale, for instance, when no internal economies of scale exist. Of course, there exist, in particular, some service industries delivering personal services that have almost no economies of scale. There are also industries that have relatively high geographical interaction costs due to the character of the services delivered. In these industries one finds a kind of micro firm that is located almost everywhere.

MARKET POTENTIALS AND INCREASING RETURNS

A region's market potential is determined by its accessibility to customers and the purchasing power of these customers. If the market potential of a region is small in relation to the efficient scale of a firm with increasing returns, then that firm cannot choose such a location. In particular, this holds if the demand per customer is small or if the customers seldom demand the actual product. In such a case the demand curve is below the average cost curve over its entire stretch, that is there is simply no production scale such that the cost per unit produced is lower than the customers' willingness to pay.

The full exploitation of increasing returns presupposes a market potential that is large enough, that is large market potentials become economically meaningful phenomena only when there are firms with internal economies of scale. A large regional market potential is attractive for firms with scale economies. Hence, such firms with internal economies of scale try to find regions that can offer larger market potentials. This observation represents a basic dynamic mechanism that generates regional growth and concentration in a self-reinforcing way. Having pronounced economies of scale, firms will locate in regions that have large market potentials and thus some large regional markets evolve because firms with economies of scale locate there. In this way, a cumulative relationship is established that is driven by the interaction between internal economies of scale, demand growth and geographical interaction costs. Internal economies of scale at the firm level in this way become a kind of external effect that is mediated by the market. In larger urban regions these internal economies of scale become a kind of collective agglomeration advantage, meaning that the urban milieu as a whole can be characterised by scale economies. It is only in a world with internal economies of scale that geographical interaction costs (in an interplay with the market forces) can give rise to cumulative processes and agglomeration advantages (Krugman, 1993). Furthermore, with internal economies of scale and cumulative processes it is possible to show that regions that basically have the same production resources may specialise in quite different ways.

With this view of the world, regional specialisation is to some extent an historical accident. The focus of a particular industry – with the exception of industries dependent upon natural resources – is to a large degree indeterminate and history-dependent. But once a pattern of specialisation is established for whatever reason such a pattern gets 'locked in' by the cumulative gains from interregional trade. There is a strong tendency towards 'path dependence' in the patterns of specialisation and trade between regions. In short, history matters.

As long as cumulative effects generate an increasing market potential in a region, a market place for an increasing number of industries and firms with internal economies of scale is created. For firms that are located in such a market place the regional market can be considered as their home market. If such firms get customers outside the home region, export to other regions is generated.

INCREASING RETURNS AND LARGE URBAN REGIONS

Without internal scale economies in most firms and/or external economies of scale, geographical concentrations and, in particular, large urban regions, become basically incomprehensible economic milieus. Large urban regions should simply not exist. Firms in large urban regions should not be able to cover those extra costs that arise due to the fact that costs for land and premises are often many times higher in large cities than in sparsely populated regions. Another related insight is that the more knowledge dependent manufacturing and service industries increase the prevalence of internal scale economies. With such a development the manifold of demand for specialised goods and services increases and the frequency of scale economies increases.

A concept that is related to internal economies of scale is economies of scope. Such economies exist in their simplest form when the total costs for producing two different products within one firm is lower than the sum of the total costs of producing the two products in two different firms. Economies of scope are basically the result of several products using the same fixed resource within in the firm. Hence, economies of scope are a basic motive for product differentiation within firms. Product differentiation often gives rise to large internal economies of scale and in practically all firms there are examples of economies of scope. In this connection the most important insight about economies of scope is that they, in the same way as ordinary internal economies of scale, give rise to cumulative market effects. This means that firms with economies of scope will try to locate in regions with a large market potential and that the market potential of these regions grows because such firms locate there.

If the theories about cumulative relationships with internal scale economies, geographical interaction costs and regional market potentials are taken seriously, they imply that larger regions are the home market for firms in many more niches and industries than small regions. Krugman (1992) shows theoretically, for example, that the number of products produced in a regional market is proportional to the size of its labour market. But this only holds if there exist internal economies of scale.

FUNCTIONAL REGIONS

A functional region is in a fundamental way characterised by its density of economic activities, social opportunities and interaction options (Ciccone and Hall, 1996). From the perspective of the individual firm, density is a positive factor to the extent that it creates accessibility to households, firms and other actors. The density may also relate to a specific industry. Such intra-industry density is also an important phenomenon in small and medium-sized functional regions. Industry-wide density exists mainly in metropolitan or other large regions with a large home market for local products.

Economic density can be interpreted as intra-regional accessibility, where 'region' is defined as a functional region. However, in the discussion here it is not density *per se* but accessibility to resources and economic agents that matters. Accessibility is obtained by an appropriate combination of density and infrastructure and it is the dynamic interaction between these three factors that forms the core of regional development. If density increases and the infrastructure remains unchanged, congestion and other tensions may follow. As a consequence, accessibility is reduced and the value of density declines. Infrastructure without matching density, on the other hand, represents only idle opportunities.

Economic density can be interpreted as intra-regional accessibility within a functional region, that is accessibility to resources and between economic actors. Central place systems and filtering-down models recognise density of purchasing power in a general sense. A dense region has an advantage in the production of goods and services with contact intensive sales. Location advantage and spatial product cycle models, on the other hand, focus on the density of firms producing similar or related products and of input suppliers and labour categories, which are specialised with regard to the cluster.

A particular geographical market will, according to the conceptualisation presented here, become equal to a functional region when the localised firms and households have very small geographical interaction costs. What factors will then delimit such a functional region? Basically it has to do with which primary resource has the largest geographical interaction costs and thereby establishes a geographical border for factor mobility. Disregarding fixed resources such as land and natural resources the major limiting factor is normally the labour force and its propensity to commute.

The geographical interaction costs between different market places for work are for households, in principle, equal to the total costs for moving between market places, that is between different labour markets. According to this conceptualisation, functional regions become equal to local labour markets. In the short and medium term it is only within such markets that the vast majority of the labour force is mobile between work places, firms and industries.

HOME MARKET EFFECTS

Given the existence of cumulative relationships between economies of scale, geographical interaction costs and regional market potentials, there exist economic advantages and incentives to concentrate production in the region with the largest home market, even if there exists a demand in other regions. This phenomenon is known as the home market effect and implies that regions will export those products for which they have the largest home market in relative terms (Krugman, 1990; Davies and Weinstein, 1997). To understand the significance of home market effects we study trade with goods and services between regional market places, that is functional regions. The different functional regions are separated by the geographical interaction costs and it is only these costs that meaningfully distinguish different functional regions. Within each functional region the interaction costs are assumed to be relatively small and in practice negligible.

Consider now the system of functional urban regions and we find that some functional regions are specialised due to the location of specific natural resources. Disregarding such location factors it is possible to identify two major types of endogenous specialisation. The first is a combination of home market size and internal economies of scale. The second is localisation economies, that is industry-specific external economies of scale.

Situations or regions with strong non-linear geographical interaction cost curves create a home market advantage for suppliers of contact-dependent products motivating the region to view these products as local products. If the number of potential buyers within the home market region is large and if their purchasing power is high then this creates a strong home market potential. Economic activities with strong internal economies of scale will enjoy a particular advantage from locating in a region with a large home market as defined here.

If internal economies of scale exist, the cumulative relationships imply that a functional region will export those products to other functional regions, which it has the largest home markets for. Hence home market effects should primarily be considered as effects of the size of the labour markets in different functional regions. This adds a new dimension to our discussion. A principal conclusion of the discussion to this point is that the variation in the number of industries in a functional region is mainly explained by the size of the labour markets, respectively. It is differences in size of local labour markets that determine the extent to which a functional region is characterised by versatility in the composition of its private sector and to what extent a functional region becomes a home market with exports to other functional regions.

The home market for products with high distance sensitivity (costs) ends at the border of the functional region. Such products are often called local commodities or even 'non-tradeables'. However, the design of product attributes as well as transaction procedures may, as a consequence of new technical solutions in combination with increased transaction volumes, change and lower the curve for geographical interaction costs. Infrastructure investments that lower the friction in the transportation and communication systems and/or bridge geographical barriers may have similar effects on these curves.

The curve for the geographical interaction costs for products with low distance sensitivity may, of course, have a steeply increasing section on the curve further away, for example, when the delivery passes a language and/or a cultural barrier. However, within such borders the home market is extended and there exist no significant home market effects for large urban regions, that is products with a small or no distance sensitivity normally have a much larger home market than products with a high distance sensitivity. Products with very low distance sensitivity may even be labelled global products.

Products with low geographical interaction costs can be located in a much less restricted way than products with high costs. In this case the location advantages will, in particular, depend upon the accessibility in the interregional transport networks.

Consider now a firm which sells much of its output in distant export markets, that is whose products have low distance sensitivity. However, this firm may have input supplier accessibility requirements. This latter type of accessibility concerns specialised labour inputs as regards skill and knowledge, specialised services including R&D services as well as current material inputs. Suppose now that these input suppliers have internal economies of scale. In that case the suppliers will have an incentive to locate in the same functional region as the exporting firm, if the demand in the region for their deliveries is large enough. If the exporting firm is not large enough, sufficient demand may be created if several firms of the same type locate in the same region. This would then represent a specialised demand density, which is big enough to match the internal scale economies of the input suppliers. The overall conclusion is that even firms with products with low distance sensitivity may be attracted to the larger urban regions by the large variation of inputs supplied by these regions.

DEMAND DYNAMICS AND HOME MARKET EFFECTS

To this point in the discussion the focus has been targeted at the importance of the size of the home market for taking advantage of internal economies of scale. Of course, it is not only the size of the market that determines the possibilities of taking advantage of internal economies of scale and, hence, the variation of firms and industries in a functional region. Besides the size of the market it is in particular the composition of demand and its rate of growth that stimulates cumulative geographical processes. This has been stressed by, for example, Sölvell, Zander and Porter (1991, 30):

> While home demand through its influence on economies of scale can confer static advantages, its more important influence is on the character and the rate of innovation by a nation's firms. Three broad characteristics of home demand are significant: the composition of home demand (or nature of buyer needs), the patterns of growth of home demand and the ability of domestic needs to be transmitted internationally.

For functional regions to create and maintain growth and renewal they must have customers – households and firms – that create a demand for the products of the future. As long as the demand per customer is very small there is a need for dense geographical markets with many customers so that they together can create a demand that gives enough scale advantages to one or several entrepreneurs. This is one of the most important explanations for large regions having external advantages for new products.

Often it is not enough with many customers. Customers that are sophisticated, knowledgeable and demanding are a particular asset in many large functional regions, since they can express early and future-directed demand. The nearness to such demand can in larger, functional regions very rapidly give rise to competitive advantages through internal scale economies and lead to home market effects. Such effects can be turned into real competitive advantages when firms that exploit early demand impulses in a regional market are able to move the products competitively to other regional and national markets.

Specialisation in an individual functional region does not primarily come from a large general demand. It builds upon idiosyncratic demand, in particular when products are young. With a dynamic perspective it also becomes critical that old and obsolete products are rapidly liquidated and that the firms in a functional region have the ability to find new possibilities using impulses, innovations, techniques, ideas, and so on, from other functional regions.

HOME MARKET EFFECTS AND EXPORT SPECIALISATION

A large demand density is synonymous with a functional region having a large home market for many own products (and for many imported products!). Such regional markets become an attractive location for both small and large firms with internal economies of scale. On the other hand, if a functional region has a thin structure and a small home market, then its economic growth must be based upon demand coming from other functional regions. In such a case the production in the region must be concentrated on products for which the geographical interaction costs rise very slowly when selling and deliveries take place over long distances. When the home market in a functional region is small the supply of products that demand a large home market will also be limited. Hence, functional regions whose firms are concentrating on products for which the geographical interaction costs increase very slowly with distance, will often be dependent upon firms that do not or rather can not demand goods and services from other firms located in the same region. The home market is simply not large enough for these kinds of products. Clearly this implies a strong limitation for the future development of these regions. This explains why regions with small home markets as a rule are characterised by a small number of export industries.

For functional regions with large home markets, on the other hand, home market effects often arise within many niches and industries, which implies that firms with such a home market as their base often also supply other functional regions. Under such circumstances firms can first build up their competitive power in their home market and then at a later stage widen their home market to nearby regions. But the critical decision comes when the firms decide to build up their competitive power interregionally and internationally. Early home market effects and the accompanying regional specialisation will then be turned into global competitive advantages. From this it follows that large regions as a rule have more international export industries than smaller regions.

SPECIALISATION AND CO-LOCATION

Internal economies of scale are not the only explanation why firms concentrate spatially and, hence, that certain functional regions become large. External economies of scale also play an important role. This phenomenon has to do with a qualitative change in a region's economic milieu that takes place when several firms with related activities (in the same industry) are located close to each other. In this case it is the external scale of an industry in a functional region in terms of the number of co-located firms that matters.

When there exist external economies of scale the unit costs for each firm in an industry in a functional region will decrease as the number of firms in the industry in the region increases. With decreasing costs co-located firms can increase their productivity and their factor rewards, that is wages and profits. The advantages coming from co-location is one of the reasons why there exist both small and large functional regions. In small functional regions firms get decreasing costs and increased productivity through co-location of one or a small number of industries, that is through specialised co-location (location economies).

In larger functional regions normally many firms within many different industries are co-located and together they form a complex and integrated milieu of co-located firms. The external economies generated by such economic milieus are known as urbanisation economies.

Firms that are dependent upon internal and external economies of scale will locate in functional regions, where there exist co-location advantages and when more firms locate in such a region the co-location advantage increases. Thus, we have a cumulative process, where internal and external economies of scale interact in a self-reinforcing way.

The analysis of external economies of scale was initiated by Marshall (1920). He showed how a regional economic milieu is created in a more or less self-organised way and in a manner that supports and expands a specialisation that has already begun. In principle there exist three primary explanations for the emergence of external economies of scale in a functional region:

- intra-regional spillovers of information and knowledge;
- the location of specialised supporting firms;
- the emergence of specialised labour markets.

Each of these three phenomena can develop and strengthen a specialisation and growth process in a functional region that has been initiated by internal economies of scale. In contrast to internal economies of scale, which are mediated by market forces, the external economies of scale are mediated outside the market in the form of so-called technological spillovers. Hence, to take full advantage of the external economies of scale in a functional region there is a need for meeting places outside the market place.

REGIONAL POLICY IN THE NEW ECONOMIC GEOGRAPHY

According to the modern theory for endogenous regional growth the growth of regions springs from internal conditions that can be influenced. With such a view regional development policy will deal with conditions that mainly must be developed and implemented with local and regional knowledge as a base even if a holistic view and financial support can come from 'above'. The list of political means, which can be used to stimulate economic growth at the regional level, is large and differentiated.

One overall problem in regional policy in all types of regions is to deal with processes that operate at different time scales. Product markets as a rule change rapidly and this demands that lasting capacities – human capital, real capital, infrastructure capital, and so on – be adapted. The problem is that such capacity adaptation processes are much slower processes and in particular processes connected with much more inertia than processes in the product markets. If the delay in the development of labour supply, built environment and infrastructure is large, the growth process can be retarded and rapidly turn into another phase. The opportunities to fight delays in capacity adaptations and to create sustainable growth are to be found in a long-term credible regional development policy that is able to reduce the market's uncertainty about the region's growth conditions.

One important conclusion from the literature on the new economic geography is that regional policies must be designed differently for regions of different size.

Large regions base their economic growth on a continuous introduction of new products and an early imitation of new products introduced in other large regions. Thus, the development of large regions is strongly dependent upon their innovation potential. The innovation potential is, on the one hand, a function of a large intra-regional market potential built up by demanding customers with a high willingness to pay for new advanced products; customers who often take an active part in the product development. On the other hand, the innovation potential is made up by rich and dense import networks, a large supply of R&D resources and a highly educated labour force. This implies that regional policies in large regions should focus in particular on interregional accessibility, R&D capacity and the capacity of institutions of higher education.

However, a strong innovation potential is not enough to secure economic growth in large regions. For new products and industries to develop, and in particular to grow, there must also exist mechanisms that secure that resources gradually are pressed out of maturing industries and made available for the new growth industries. This means in practice that growth in large regions is strongly related to the functioning of the relevant markets. Without well-functioning markets for labour, land, premises and housing large regions may never reach their full growth potential and resources might instead be kept too long in old industries. Hence, it is an important objective for regional policies in large regions to create and to preserve well-functioning markets for resources strategic for economic growth, and to avoid unnecessary regulations and red tapes.

The success of smaller regions is closely connected with the emergence and conservation of competitive clusters or, to use another concept, development blocks (Dahmén, 1988). Increased internationalisation driven by, among other things, an increased economic integration implies that it is important for smaller regions to support the conditions that are offered to important clusters in the region as well as to potential new clusters. Assuming perfect information the new economic geography framework motivates a cluster-specific regional policy. However, there are numerous problems associated with a cluster specific regional policy that have to do with risks for manipulation, lobbying and the existence of asymmetric information.

Due to the existence of positive external effects the existing clusters in a region will not achieve an optimal scale spontaneously. This situation opens a number of questions. How to determine the optimal scale of a cluster? How can existing clusters be stimulated to achieve an optimal scale? How to set priorities among different existing clusters when the resources for regional policy are limited?

In those cases where one or several existing clusters tend to lose competitive power and it is impossible from a long-term perspective to balance these losses with specific cluster policies, questions are naturally raised concerning new potential clusters. How to identify new potential clusters? How to make priorities between potential new clusters? How to get new clusters established? How to make sure that new clusters reach a large enough scale to function as a cluster and to assure that over time they reach an optimal scale?

Internal economies of scale are mainly outside the regional policy domain. However, policies that lead to reduced fixed costs for labour and capital reduce the firm's dependence on the size of the regional market. In particular, rents and real estate values that vary geographically play an important role for generating geographically varying costs for firms.

Geographical transaction costs are, among other things, determined by national and regional transport and communication policies. Lower geographical transaction costs widen the borders of functional regions and hence provide space for the development and growth of more industries and firms with internal economies of scale. The profitability of investments in infrastructure capital is higher in an economy with cluster mechanisms than in an economy without.

As industrial clusters consist of firms that are best able to profit from a region's market potential and its supply of lasting resources, regional development policy should primarily focus the possibilities to support, develop and expand existing clusters. To the extent that existing clusters are unable to carry a region's development there is a question about the possibilities of identifying and developing new expansive clusters. If a decision is made to try to establish new clusters it is important to identify their need for lasting infrastructure capacities. To support established as well as new industrial clusters it is important for regions to create optimal conditions for entrepreneurship, location of new firms and firm growth. Hence, regional policy should never focus on individual industries or firms except when they form strategic parts of an existing or a new cluster.

Large shares of the knowledge development in a region are characterised by collective characteristics. New knowledge that, for example, is developed in one firm will over time diffuse to other firms, other regions and other parts of the economy. Through such a process increasing returns is created in the economy as a whole. This means that the growth in a cluster and a region can be influenced by investments in knowledge and R&D.

EVALUATION OF REGIONAL POLICY IN THE NEW ECONOMIC GEOGRAPHY

With regional policy to an important degree motivated by principally new arguments it is obvious that the evaluation of regional policy also needs a new starting point. The central message of the new economic geography is that the dynamic interaction between geographical market potentials and rational firms in its own way creates the comparative advantages of regions in the form of localised increasing returns to scale. What does this mean for regional policy evaluation? It means a lot! The evaluation of regional policies must

- be based on a new theoretical framework,
- be based on dynamic models capable of dealing with increasing returns and interrelationships between regions,
- re-evaluate the demarcation of regional policies,
- re-evaluate the goals of regional policies,
- re-evaluate the means of regional policies,

- have a long time perspective,
- use new types of data,
- use new methodological perspectives.

Each of these points is fairly straightforward. The first and the second point follow directly from the theoretical discussion in the earlier sections. The need to re-evaluate the demarcation of regional policies from other policy fields is natural given the new view as regards what drives the growth of regions. It is, for example, given the importance of knowledge spillovers for generating increasing returns quite rational to argue that R&D and higher education policies must be defined as part of regional policies. As regional policies become more region-specific, evaluaters must consider that the goals of regional policy might differ among regions given, among other things, different initial conditions. In the same manner the means of regional policy might differ between regions due to different goals, different initial conditions and different information and knowledge about the specific conditions and economic mechanisms. As regional policies often try to influence conditions that only change slowly, evaluations normally must adopt a long time perspective. Evaluations of regional policy must also consider that much weight today is given to various types of knowledge spillovers. To trace knowledge flows and their importance policy evaluators need new types of data and to apply new methodological perspectives. This is, in particular, important since knowledge flows leave no paper trails (Krugman, 1991a).

THE CONTRIBUTIONS IN THIS BOOK

The book is organised in four parts that emphasise contributions to understanding the locational influences of regional policy, policy evaluation approaches, methodological contributions and conceptual contributions. Below we have briefly summarised the contributions in the sequence they appear in the book in an effort to provide the reader with a blueprint.

Part I Regional Policy and Location

The chapters in Part I all deal with regional policy and the location of economic activity. In the first chapter Charlie Karlsson and Rolf Nilsson note that there are two basic approaches to the study of industrial location: the central place systems approach and the locational advantage approach. They focus their analysis on the central place systems approach which argues that the location of firms in a specific industry is determined by the size of the regional market. They examine this endogenous oriented argument with central place system data from Sweden. With both static and dynamic analyses they show convincingly that the major determinants of the industrial distribution in the central place system is not just market size but the interplay between market size and economies of scale.

Chapter 3, by Ed Malecki, examines the effects of technological change through the Internet on regional development. The focus of this analysis is telecommunications infrastructure. Analysis finds that the highest level of telecommunications infrastructure and capability is increasingly concentrated at the highest levels of the urban hierarchy. These findings are consistent with those obtained by Karlsson and Nilsson.

Chapter 4 examines the concept of nomadic and highly footloose firms in the emerging knowledge or network economy. Bruinsma, Corter and Nijkamp rightly observe that modern multi-plant firms exhibit an increasingly more flexible mobility pattern. Interviews of 'nomadic firms' are summarised and subjected to rough set analysis. Firms that produce no goods, that is produce services, are capital-intensive and operate in an international freight transport trade network are more nomadic. The chapter concludes with an examination of policy relevant issues.

In Chapter 5, Kobayshi, Okumura and Tuncer use simulation analysis to examine the evolution of city systems in response to alternative network formation policies. The various simulations indicate that a city system will evolve with population clustering at dominant locations all of which depend upon geographical conditions and historical network improvement decisions. In short, policies that impact network formation will influence path dependency and therefore lock-in effects that produce and contribute to the maintenance of particular network configurations and population clusters.

The final chapter in Part I by Luis Suarez-Villa examines the major changes that have occurred in the geographical location of technology sources in the US during the last half of the twentieth century. This analysis shows that a remarkable change in geographical sourcing occurred whereby regions that were on the economic and technological periphery 50 years ago have emerged today as the most important sources of new technologies. The more recent concentration of technology sourcing in the US Sun Belt is attributed to market forces and the high level of physical mobility of a skilled population. Policies focused on infrastructure expansion and human capital, while lacking coordination in the large picture, are observed to be important.

Part II Evaluating Regional Policy

The first chapter in Part II by Ian Gordon makes a plea for regional policy analysis to give more attention to labour market outcomes. In particular, the author argues that the incidence of unemployment and the ways labour market processes respond to resource subsidies to assisted areas are crucial for achieving more appropriate evaluation results. The chapter empirically assesses the impacts of supply-side labour market adjustments and incorporates them into the evaluation of the impact of policy on unemployment. A conclusion of the chapter is that evaluation must focus not only on the immediate goals of regional policy, for example, job and income growth, but also on addressing structural problems in lagging regions, that is, unemployment.

Jim Taylor in Chapter 8 observes that the United Kingdom has a long tradition of regional policy. Further, and as a consequence, there has been considerable effort devoted to the development of regional policy evaluation techniques. Among the various elements of this review are particularly illuminating treatments of ex ante appraisal models and softer methods that have been more prominent in recent work.

Chapter 9 by Paul Cheshire and Stefano Magrini is concerned with the widespread prevalence of counterfactual analysis in regional policy evaluation. The counterfactual requires a technique or methodology for estimating what would have occurred in the absence of policy. This chapter proposes a new methodology focused on functional rather than administrative regions for estimating the counterfactual and applies it to Europe's largest city regions with convincing and robust results.

Chapter 10 by Jan Mønnesland also emphasises the importance and difficulties in using counterfactual analysis in regional policy assessment. Issues, methods and approaches for micro and macro level counterfactual estimation are examined in the context of both ex post and ex ante evaluations. This chapter offers guidelines and conclusions regarding the use of the counterfactual in regional policy evaluation.

In Chapter 11 Gillespie, McGregor, Swales and Yin develop and apply a two-region computable-general equilibrium model to evaluate the effects of the United Kingdom regional regeneration policy. The authors note the widespread use of the 'industrial survey' method for evaluating the effects of discretionary policy instruments and in particular strategic objectives of these instruments. The CGE approach is used to demonstrate that this approach can play a strong complimentary role to industrial surveys in evaluation research.

In the next chapter Maurice Baslé and Frank Pelé develop and apply a set of policy indicators for assessing the effect of regional decentralisation policies in France. The application is a case study of the Brittany region in France. The types of indicator vary from impact to risk, to physical condition, to financing and to timetable of implementation. Also, effort is devoted to measuring direct, indirect, *n*th level effects, and to unintended consequences.

A persistent problem confronting the inner city parts of urban areas is the underutilisation of physically derelict and vacant commercial or factory infrastructure. Barry Moore and Jonathan Potter evaluate the effect of various tax incentive policies for enterprise zones and their effect on business start-ups and inward investment. Notable findings from an analysis of enterprise zone new start ups (NSUs) and inward investment show that inward investment accounted for more job generation while NSUs have higher levels of skilled workers, are more likely to recruit locally and more likely to recruit from the unemployed. Further, NSUs are more likely to purchase locally.

The final chapter in Part II by Jensen-Butler, Madsen and Casperson examines the effect of welfare state income creation policies on lagging rural regions in Denmark. One effect of income maintenance policies is that low-income rural areas gain at the expense of other regions due to an income maintenance ceiling. The ceiling means that the unemployed who formerly had high incomes receive proportionately less than their opposites who are more densely represented in rural areas. In this way regional policy is being executed indirectly through national unemployment and social security insurance and income policy. This chapter is a good example of how the unexpected or unintended consequences of policies adopted at one level impact those at another level.

Part III Methodological Approaches

The chapters in this part of the book all contribute new methodological approaches for regional policy evaluation or apply existing methodologies in a new way. Chapter 15 by Charlie Karlsson and Michael Olsson focuses on techniques for defining functional regions. The first part of the chapter draws on the theoretical and practical literature that pertains to the definition of functional regions using labour market data. The middle part of the chapter applies these definitions in Sweden in an effort to define the functional regions there in 1986 and 1996. This analysis shows that there are fewer functional regions in 1996 and the size of the median region decreased over the study period. The authors conclude that the self sufficiency of Sweden's functional regions (municipalities) has been decreasing.

Chapter 16 by Kingsley Haynes and Mustafa Dinc employs an extended shift–share analysis to examine productivity and employment consequences of European integration in general and international trade in manufacturing in particular. The research results show that productivity changes positively effected employment growth rates most significantly in smaller economies. However, domestic demand was the most important factor impacting employment change in manufacturing, especially in the largest regional economies.

Jan Kowalski and Axel Schaffer develop a regional policy evaluation approach that establishes benchmarks that can be compared to regional input potentials. The input dimensions include agglomeration, infrastructure, education, nature and industrial sectors. Using a Cobb–Douglas approach the authors apply this potential analysis to NUTs 2 level regions in the European Union. With this analysis regions are sorted into average, above average and below average regions in terms of their achieved potential or performance. The authors offer policy recommendations for the three different types of regions thus illustrating the relevance of the regional potential approach for policy evaluation.

The final chapter in Part III by Mats Johansson examines the relationship between severe reindustrialisation in Sweden between 1970 and 1990 and productivity changes. Productivity change is measured with two alternative variants of the shift – share methodology. The analysis results in a conclusion that structural transformation of the industrial sector has had little if any effect on productivity change. It is primarily through branch plant activity that productivity improvements have been achieved. At the same time reindustrialisation has led to the elimination of companies with low productivity as well as renewal within branch plants which is where the positive productivity effects have originated from.

Part IV New Concepts and Perspectives

The final part of the book presents three chapters that introduce and explore concepts that promise to inform regional policy making and evaluation in the future. The first, by Roger Bolton, entitled 'Place surplus, exit, voice and loyalty', sees place surplus and related concepts as a measure of the net benefits derived from group action. A deductive model along with a numerical example is provided to illustrate how the concept may be used to evaluate regional policies.

In Chapter 20, John Rees examines the role of capital in its broadest definition in regional development. He is concerned with physical, financial, human and social capital as it contributes to regional production functions. The examination of social capital links nicely to the Bolton chapter and to the concept of 'place surplus'. Rees concludes that the concept of capital, in general, and social capital in particular, needs additional examination as it relates to the broader issue of regional policy evaluation.

In the final chapter, Börje Johansson asks the question 'How can regional policies influence the location advantages of regions?'. To answer this question he makes a synthesis of the contributions in this book. His synthesis highlights that regional policies and self-organised market adjustments usually combine and may be hard to separate, making assessments of regional policies difficult. But even if assessments are difficult, they are important to carry through since regional policies consume scarce resources. Assessments are also necessary parts of regional policy learning processes at the regional, national and supra-national level.

REFERENCES

Ciccone, A. and R.E. Hall (1996), 'Productivity and the density of economic activity', *The American Economic Review,* **86**, 54–70.

Dahmén, E. (1988), '"Development Blocks" in industrial economics', *Scandinavian Economic History Review,* **36**, 3 –14.

Davis, D. and D. Weinstein (1997), 'Economic Geography and Regional Production Structure: an Empirical Investigation', Harvard University and NBER.

Dixit, A.K. and J.E. Stiglitz (1977), 'Monopolistic competition and optimum product diversity', *American Economic Review,* **67**, 297–308.

Johansson, B. and C. Karlsson (2001), 'Geographic Transaction Costs and Specialisation Opportunities in Small and Medium-Sized Regions: Scale Economies and Market Extension', in Börje Johansson, Ch. Karlsson and R. Stough (eds), *Theories of Endogenous Regional Growth. Lessons for Regional Policies*, Berlin: Springer-Verlag, 150–180.

Krugman, P. (1990), *Rethinking International Trade*, Cambridge, MA: The MIT Press.

Krugman, P. (1991), 'Increasing returns and economic geography', *Journal of Political Economy,* **99**, 483–499.

Krugman, P. (1992), *A Dynamic Spatial Model*, Cambridge, MA; National Bureau of Economic Research, NBER Working Paper, 4219.

Krugman, P. (1993), 'First nature, second nature, and metropolitan location', *Journal of Regional Science*, **33**, 129-144.

Marshall, A. (1920), *Principles of Economics*, London: Macmillan

Sölvell, Ö., I. Zander and M.E. Porter (1991), *Advantage Sweden*, Stockholm: Norstedts.

PART ONE

Regional Policy and Location

2. Agglomeration, Economies of Scale and Dynamic Specialisation in a Central Place System

Charlie Karlsson and Rolf Nilsson

1 INTRODUCTION

It is a well-known fact that establishments and households are not spread evenly across space, but instead they concentrate in cities/regions of various sizes. One major reason for this concentration is the existence of scale economies. Without scale economies the establishments and their production would be more likely to be evenly dispersed over the geographical space. Compared to an evenly spread population and production, the clustering of establishments and households is generally beneficial for both producers and households. The concentration of households gives the firms a better opportunity to find an appropriate workforce and at the same time find a market that is large enough for their products. The concentration of establishments gives households a better chance in finding suitable jobs.

Furthermore, the concentration may even become self-reinforcing. Firms locate their business in regions with access to a large market, and access to the market tends to be good in regions where a lot of firms locate their business (Krugman, 1998).

However, these processes of self-reinforcing growth do not work in a positive direction in all regions. Many regions face problems with industrial decline, unemployment and out-migration of people. Instead of a positive spiral, these regions face a negative spiral, that is, unemployment and out-migration reduces the purchasing power which gives rise to more unemployment and out-migration and so on.

The major driving forces behind industrial/household concentration in regions are the interaction between factors such as trapped resources, for example raw-material sources, market size, transportation and transaction costs, different kinds of amenities and economies of scale.

Economies of scale are often divided into external and internal economies of scale. Internal economies of scale are primarily reaped by individual producers and arise when production is associated with fixed costs, that is, costs that are independent of the volume of production. External economies of scale, on the other hand, arise due to a concentration of mutually related firms in the same geographical area. Firms in such clusters are able to reduce costs through the proximity to each other. When the cluster consists of plants within the same industry, this is referred to as localisation economies, and when the cluster consists of plants from many different industries we talk about urbanisation economies (Marshall, 1920; Hoover, 1971, Mulligan, 1984). However, at some point these agglomeration economies can be offset by disagglomeration economies due to higher land rents, pollution and traffic congestion (Richardson, 1995).

When analysing why specific industries are located in a region two approaches are frequently used (Karlsson, 1999). On the one hand there is the central place system (CPS) approach and on the other hand there is the location advantage (LA) approach.

According to the location advantage approach, the location of an industry in certain regions is basically determined by the fact that these functional regions have a comparative advantage over other functional regions. One such advantage could be that a functional region hosts large and easily extractable natural resources. Firms and industries that are engaged in this type of production are characterised by supplying not only their products to their own region but also to other functional regions in the form of exports. Another feature is that these firms usually rely heavily upon economies of scale, in the form of either internal or external economies of scale.

According to the CPS approach, the location of firms in a specific industry is basically determined by the size of the regional market. If we assume that all production is associated with fixed set-up costs, a certain minimum level of demand must exist before any firm can start up a production that is profitable. The necessary demand needed to make production profitable is referred to as the threshold demand (Christaller, 1966). The total number of firms within an industry within a specific functional region will, amongst other things, depend upon the size of the actual product market and the size of the fixed set-up costs.

The CPS approach states that the larger the market in a functional region, the larger the number of different central place (CP) industries in the region (Christaller, 1966; Tinbergen, 1967; Beckmann, 1958). The reason for this is that only certain industries can cover their fixed costs in a region with a given size of market demand. For products where the spatial interaction costs are substantial, the production will take place only in those regions where the local market is large enough to make production profitable.

In this chapter, we will concentrate our discussion on the CPS approach, and hence to industries producing CPS products. To qualify as a CP industry, according to the strict definition, an industry must be present in all regions larger than the smallest region in which it is present. That is, if an industry is present in a functional region of size X, it should also be present in all functional regions larger than X.

Industries with very small fixed costs need a very small market demand in order to make production profitable. The larger the fixed costs of production are, the larger the demand must be in order to make production profitable. We should therefore expect that industries with very small fixed costs are likely to be present in every functional region. Industries with a certain amount of fixed costs will, ceteris paribus, not be present in the smallest functional regions, but in all functional regions larger than a certain threshold size. Finally industries that are associated with very large fixed costs are likely to find production profitable only in the largest regions.

Thus, location is not only determined by the size of the fixed costs needed to start up production but also by the demand for the actual products. Since the demand intensity differs between different products, certain industries with high fixed costs may still find production profitable even in the smallest regions, given that the demand intensity is sufficiently large. This can be the case for essential goods. Such goods have a high demand intensity in the sense that every consumer spends a large share of the budget on these goods. At the same time, certain industries with low fixed costs may not be able to produce with a positive profit, except in the largest regions, given that the per capita demand is sufficiently low. In all these cases the CP industries will be distributed over the system of functional regions in a hierarchical way.

One can observe that the distribution of CP industries in the system of functional regions does change over time. Important driving forces behind these changes are shifts in the demand intensity, in the costs for setting up production and in the technologies used in various industries. As the demand intensity of regional markets grow and/or as set-up costs go down, a general process of decentralisation of CP industries might take place. Such a decentralisation is known as a filtering-down process. However, the factors might work in the opposite direction, which give rise to a filtering-up process.

There are two objectives to this chapter. The first is to present a theoretical framework capable of explaining the distribution of CP industries in the system of urban regions and its dynamics. The second is to empirically analyse the distribution of CP industries in the Swedish system of functional urban regions and the changes over time of this distribution.

The rest of the chapter is divided into three sections. In Section 2 we outline our theoretical framework, that is the central place theory and its dynamic counterpart, namely the theory of the filtering-down and filtering-up processes. In Section 3 we describe the data as well as the empirical analyses. The chapter ends with Section 4, in which we present our conclusions and give some suggestions for further research.

2 DYNAMIC SPECIALISATION IN A CENTRAL PLACE SYSTEM

In the first part of this section we outline the theory of central places in a more formal way. We are interested in finding criteria to determine whether an industry should be classified as a CP industry or not. In the second part of the section we outline the theories of filtering-down and filtering-up processes, which provide dynamic aspects of the central place theory. Here we analyse how changes in technology and demand may affect the distribution of industries in the CP system over time. To do so we introduce a vintage index, which describes a product's degree of standardisation. We assume that as time goes by, production will become more and more standardised, which in turn induces changes in the hierarchical distribution of CP industries (Forslund-Johansson, 1997).

2.1 Industrial Location in a Central Place System

A national system of urban regions consists of a large number of small regions, a substantially smaller number of medium-sized regions and only a very limited number of large regions. The market size in a large region is usually considerably larger than the market size in a medium-sized region, which in turn usually is substantially larger than the market size in the smallest regions (Christaller, 1966; Tinbergen, 1967; Beckmann, 1958). Given this, we should expect industries with large economies of scale to find it favourable to locate in larger functional region with a large home market. This is especially true for products where the interregional transaction costs are substantially higher than the intraregional transaction costs.

According to the theory of central places, the urban system of regions can be ranked according to the market size in the following way $M_1 > M_2$ ...$> M_{m-1} > M_m$. M_1 is the market size in region(s) of rank 1 and M_m is the market size of regions of rank m. In a similar fashion we are also able to rank the goods produced in the urban system. Industries and their products denoted as 1 are for instance those that, due to for instance large fixed costs and/or small per capita demand, will be produced only in regions of rank 1. Products of rank 1 are thus only produced in the largest regions and exported to regions of lower ranks. These types of products are referred to as high-order products. Products of rank *m* are produced only in regions of ranks larger and equal to rank *m*. If we assume that rank *m* is the lowest rank in the urban system these products will be produced in every region in the urban system. Products that are produced in every region are referred to as low-order products (Christaller, 1966).

Hence, a central place system can be interpreted as a hierarchical system of functional regions, where the industrial composition in a region varies with its position in the hierarchy of functional urban regions. When analysing the industrial composition within the CP system it is natural to begin with the following question: What activities will the smallest functional regions of rank *m* contain? This will be determined by three factors:

- the fixed costs associated with starting the production;
- the size of the market in regions of rank *m*;
- the presence of agglomeration economies, which are assumed to be a function of the number of industries (*n*) located in regions of rank *m*.

An industry will be located in a region of rank m with at least one establishment if the following condition holds:

$$\pi_m = \{p - AVC\,[1 - A(n_m)]\}\, f(p) M_m - FC \geq 0 \qquad (2.1)$$

$$0 < A(n_m) \leq 1$$

where π_m is the profit made by an establishment, in a given industry, in a region of rank *m* and *p* is the price of the product. AVC is the average variable costs and FC the total amount of fixed set-up costs, $f(p)$ is the individual or the per capita demand, M_m is the market size in regions of rank *m*. $A(n_m)$ is a variable describing the agglomeration economies, in the form of urbanisation economies, in regions of rank *m*. It is assumed that the larger the number of industries, *n*, in a region, the larger the agglomeration effect. Hence, $A(n_m)$ is an increasing function of n_m. It is assumed that through the agglomeration economies firms are able to reduce their average costs. This is caused by spillover effects from R&D investments made by firms in related industries, by cheaper/better inputs from downstream companies and lower transportation costs, and so on. From equation (2.1) we can also see that, given constant prices and variable costs, the larger the fixed costs, the larger the market size must be in order to make production profitable.

If m is the rank of the smallest regions, this means that industries that satisfy criterion (2.1) will be represented in all regions in the CP system. The industries that produce these low-order products are usually characterised by small internal economies of scale as well as small urbanisation economies and/or are facing a large individual demand. Hence, these are products that more or less everybody needs and demands on regular basis.

For regions of rank $(m - 1)$, that is, the second smallest regional rank, we find a similar condition:

$$\pi_{m-1} = \{p - \text{AVC}\,[1 - A(n_{m-1})]\}\, f(p) M_{m-1} - \text{FC} \geq 0 \qquad (2.2)$$

Following the reasoning above, we have that regions of rank $(m - 1)$ will contain all industries present in regions of rank m. But, due to the larger market size they will also contain a number of additional industries. Since regions of rank $m - 1$ will contain more industries than regions of rank m we also have that $A(n_{m-1}) > A(n_m)$. M_{m-1} is larger than M_m since it not only contains the demand from the home region but also from the surrounding regions of rank m that it services. A larger market size in combination with larger agglomeration economies will thus make it possible for a number of industries that could not operate with positive profit in regions of rank m to do so in regions of rank $m - 1$. Industries that satisfy condition (2.2) will be represented in all functional regions of rank $m - 1$ and higher in the CP system. The criteria for profitable production in regions of rank larger than $(m - 1)$ follows analogously with equation (2.2).

Suppose that we have a hierarchical system with three ranks. According to the strict definition of the central place system such an urban system is illustrated in Figure 2.1.

From equation (2.2) above, we can also see that through the effects of the urbanisation economies, the variable costs of production will be smaller in regions of rank $m - 1$ compared to regions of rank m. This is consistent with the law of market areas (LMA) (Parr, 1995). The LMA states that the lower price in the larger regions will lead to a larger market area for the products produced there. If the price differentials are sufficiently large, the market area of the larger region can in fact cover the whole market area of the smaller region. In this case one or more low-order industries will not produce in the smaller region.

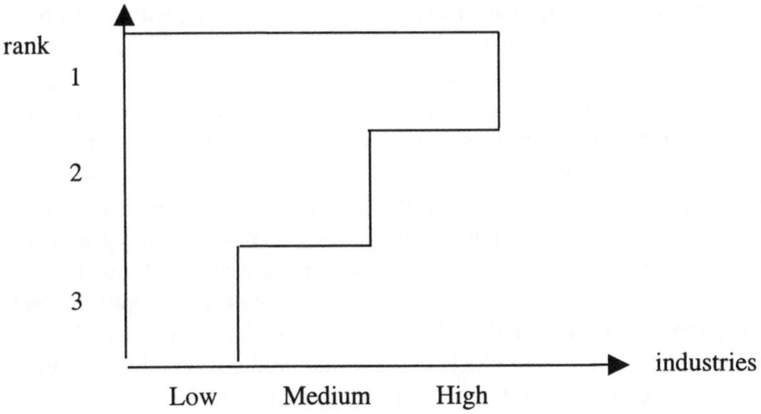

Figure 2.1 The central place system according to strict definition

The discussion above is of course not only confined to low-order industries and regions of rank $m - 1$ and rank m, but to all regions in all ranks. The only condition needed is price differentials between regions of different ranks. The effect is even further strengthened if the accessibility to regions of higher ranks is good, and if we introduce the possibility that consumers from smaller regions are able to buy products that cannot be produced in low rank regions (Parr, 1995). For example, a consumer from a small region is able to buy low-order products at the same time as he is going to the larger region for high-order products. This will give rise to gaps in CP system.

From the standard central place theory we can draw the rather obvious conclusion that the number of CP industries represented in a region will grow with the size of the region. But, what type of industries can we expect to belong to the different categories of CP industries?

To answer this question it is fruitful to separate manufacturing industries and service industries. The service sector can further be divided into two sectors, namely the household service sector and the business service sector.

Services usually have one common feature that distinguish them from manufactured goods, namely that the 'production' and the 'consumption' usually are carried out at the same place and at the same time. However, due to the increasing use of telecommunications there exist exceptions to this statement. For instance, some services can nowadays be provided via the Internet. In these cases the producer of the service and the consumer of the service could be located in separate parts of the world. But for most services, production and consumption include a certain amount of close interaction between the producer and the consumer, usually in the form of face-to-face contacts. Hence, many services are not as easily transported over long distances as manufactured goods are, which give rise to considerable spatial interaction costs between functional regions. Compared to manufacturing industries, service industries, and perhaps especially industries in the household service sector, are more likely to be categorised as CP industries (Keeble and Tyler, 1995).

What determines whether an industry is a low- or a high-order industry is the interplay between the amount of fixed costs needed to set-up production and the size of the market demand. Low-order industries will thus have no or very small fixed costs and/or consist of industries that supply products that are demanded frequently. High-order industries usually supply non-standardised products or products that are seldom demanded by consumers and/or products whose production requires large fixed costs, and this gives raise to strong internal economies of scale.

Thus in the standard model, the CP system will form a hierarchical pattern where every industry that is present in a region of a certain rank will also be present in all regions with a higher rank. However, the distribution of CP industries in the urban system is not static over time. How changes in technology and demand affect the distribution over time will be analysed in the next section.

2.2 Filtering Processes in a Central Place System

The dynamic framework associated with the central place theory is the filtering-down and the filtering-up processes. In these processes the major driving forces are technological change[1] and changes in demand (Camagni, Diappi and Leonardo, 1986). A major consequence of these processes is a gradual change in the hierarchical distribution of industries in the central place system. In the filtering-down process industries gradually decentralise to regions of successively lower rank. The filtering-up process works in the opposite way.

The dynamics of the filtering process are closely related to the product life cycle (Erickson, 1976). The product life cycle consists of three phases. The first phase is referred to as the innovation phase, the second one is the growth phase and the third phase is the mature phase (Hirch, 1967).

In the innovation phase the product is introduced to the market. In this stage the product is going through continuous improvements and developments. Hence, firms do not compete with prices as much as with the attributes of the product itself. This phase is usually associated with a high degree of R&D, which in turn demands a highly skilled workforce. In combination with a relatively limited demand for the product, production in this stage is usually concentrated in the largest functional regions.

In the growth phase knowledge about the new product increases among consumers in a wider area, and this tends to rapidly increase the demand for the product. Another reason for increased market demand is that the product gradually becomes more standardised and that the production process becomes increasingly more routinised.

During the mature phase the market demand for the product usually increases, but at a decreasing rate. The main reason for the slower growth rate is the introduction of newer and better products, which in accordance with the product life-cycle thinking tends to enter the economy in the largest regions.

Given the product life-cycle hypothesis, we should expect products and their associated industries to spread, or filter-down in the urban system over time. According to the filtering-down hypothesis this is a gradual process in which the products first spread from the largest functional regions to the medium-sized functional regions and finally to the smallest functional regions.

In this chapter we are interested in analysing how the standardisation process of products affects the distribution of industries in the central place system. In order to do so we introduce a vintage index, τ, which assumes the value of 0 when a new product is introduced to the market, and increases towards 1 the more standardised the product and the more routinised the production process, becomes.

Rewriting equation (2.1), taking the vintage index into account and changing the subscript from rank m to rank k gives.

$$\pi_k(\tau) = \{p - AVC(\tau)\,[1 - A(n_k)]\}\, f(p) M_k - FC(\tau) \geq 0 \qquad (2.3)$$

The regional rank k is here assumed to be the lowest regional rank in which production is profitable. Over time the product will become more and more standardised, that is, the vintage index will increase from τ to $\tau + \mu$. We assume that the technological change process results in decreasing fixed costs, that is $FC(\tau + \mu) < FC(\tau)$, but that it does not affect the variable costs (at least not positively), that is $AVC(\tau + \mu) \leq AVC(\tau)$. As the product becomes standardised, production becomes profitable in regions of successively lower rank. Given these assumptions industries will filter down to gradually smaller and smaller functional regions over time. This process can, at least partly, be offset if the industry relies heavily on the agglomeration economies arising from proximity to other industries.

However, in reality it is perhaps more likely to assume that when a product becomes more standardised and routinised the fixed costs will in fact increase and the variable costs will decrease as μ increases. In particular this might be the case for manufacturing industries. The reason for this is that firms are able to engage in large-scale production as the product gets more standardised and as the production processes becomes more routinised. From equation (2.4) below it is clear that the resulting dynamic process is ambiguous. If

$$\{p - AVC(\tau + \mu)\,[1 - A(n_k)]\}\, f(p) M_k > FC(\tau + \mu) \qquad (2.4)$$

the industry will filter down through the urban system. But if the inequality sign in equation (2.4) is reversed the industry will filter up through the urban system, due to the relatively larger impact of the increasing fixed costs compared to the decreasing variable costs the industry will need a successively larger market to make production profitable. Hence, technological changes may induce a process of gradual filtering down, but there is at least a theoretical possibility that the technological changes give rise to a filtering-up process (Camagni, Diappi and Leonardo, 1986). However, it is reasonable to assume that the standardisation process in combination with increased price competition will reduce prices, which in turn will induce an increase in the individual demand that is large enough to offset the filtering up process.

3 EMPIRICAL ANALYSES

3.1 The Data

The definition of a functional region used in this chapter is the one developed in NUTEK (1998). According to that classification Sweden is divided into 81 functional regions.

The data used in this chapter is collected by Statistics Sweden and consists of employment and establishment data at the 5-digit level for 737 different industries in 1993 and 741 different industries in 1996. Comparable data for years before 1993 does not exist because of changes in the industrial classification.

3.2 Classification of CP Industries

First, we are interested in finding out what type of industries follow the CP system according to a strict definition. That is, industries should be present in every region larger than the smallest one in which they are present. In order to study this we rank the functional regions according to size, measured by total population. The industries are ranked according to the number of functional regions in which they are present by at least one establishment. In Appendices 2.1 and 2.2 the results for the years 1993 and 1996 are shown.

Although the plots are hard to analyse in detail, we see that the number of industries that follow the strict definition of central place industries is very low. In both years they only add up to 42 industries (see Appendices 2.3 and 2.4). Most of the industries are related to utilities, building activities, private services, public services and retail sale. One common feature of these industries is that they supply products that are demanded frequently by the public, that is, necessities. Another feature is that most products have substantial spatial interaction costs, that is, they are not transported easily or at low cost over a long distance. These facts are not surprising since almost all of the industries are low-order industries. Another observation that can be made is that the distribution of CP industries is quite constant over time, that is, out of the 42 pure CP industries in 1993, 35 fulfil the strict criteria also in 1996.

However, according to Appendices 2.1 and 2.2 we can clearly see that regional size matters for location of industries. The rank correlation between the number of industries and the regional rank, measured by regional population, is 0.99[2] in 1996. However, the correlation between the actual number of industries and actual population in a region is 0.62 in 1996. Still the number of industries that follow the CP system according to the strict definition is relatively low. There are a few plausible reasons for this. One is that regional size measured by population is an unsatisfactory proxy for market size. Other studies have used employment or income as a proxy for market demand (Burns and Healy, 1978). Harris (1954) suggested a technique for the calculation of the market potential as the sum of retail sales for each county divided by the distance (Krugman, 1998). Other possible explanations for the 'gaps' in the CP system are that the market area for some industries in some regions is reduced due to price differentials between regions and/or proximity to denser and larger regions as described in Section 2.1. Other possibilities include regional differences regarding the infrastructure and the demographic composition. Furthermore, the gaps can to some extent be explained by the fact that some industries concentrate in a limited number of regions to capitalise on localisation economies or internal scale economies. The latter outcome is a possibility when products are only modestly sensitive to distance.

3.3 Analysis of the Swedish CP System

We will now change our approach to classifying the functional regions into size classes. The regional classification can be made in several ways (Gunnarsson, 1976). The regional classification used in this chapter is based upon the classification made by NUTEK (1998). In this classification are the 81 functional regions divided into three groups. The first group contains the three metropolitan regions, the second group contains the medium-sized regions, which are regional centres. In this group we also find all regions which have universities, apart from the metropolitan regions. And finally we have the group which contains the smaller regions in Sweden. A description of the classification is presented in Table 2.1.

Table 2.1 Description of the regional classification

Rank	Number of regions	Description	Year	Max. size	Min. size	Median size
1	3	Metropolitan	1993	1 750 793	601 828	856 067
		regions	1996	1 809 813	618 348	881 181
2	26	Regional	1993	294 619	81 059	152 452
		centres	1996	299 301	79 720	152 128
3	52	Small regions	1993	71 057	3 480	29 225
			1996	71 442	3 337	28 697

Note: Regional size refers to the population of the regions.

Despite the short time period, we are able to identify some of the effects of an ongoing urbanisation. In rank 1, all three functional regions show an increasing population. Out of the 26 regional centres, 19 increased their population from the year 1993 to 1996, but only 8 out of the 52 smallest functional regions exhibited population growth.

So, what type of industries is present in all functional regions? That is, what industries can be classified as low-order industries? What type of industries is present in every functional region apart from the functional regions in rank 3? That is, what industries can be classified as medium-order industries? And, what type of industries is present in the three metropolitan regions but not in rank 2 or rank 3?[3] That is, what industries can be classified as high-order industries? An industry is said to be present in a given rank if at least one establishment dwells in every region of that rank.

Given the above method of classifying CP industries in different orders, we obtain the results presented in Table 2.2:

Table 2.2 Number of CP industries with respect to their order in 1993 and 1996

	1993	1996	Number of industries that stay in the same order from 1993 to 1996
Number of low-order industries	37 (37)	37 (37)	33
Number of medium-order industries	100 (137)	117 (154)	80
Number of high-order industries	209 (346)	206 (360)	175

Note: Numbers in brackets show the total number of CP industries in rank 3, 2 and 1. For example, the total number of CP industries in the largest regions are 37 + 117 + 206 = 360 in 1996.

From Table 2.2 we can see that the number of CP industries that are present in large regions is higher than in small regions. The major reason for this is that the market in regions of rank 3 is too thin to host industries with large fixed costs and/or industries producing other things than necessities. We can also see that the number of CP industries is increasing but at a decreasing rate, as we move upward in the CP system.

As can be seen from Table 2.2 the total number of CP industries increases in the two largest size classes during the studied time-period. For the largest regions the number of CP industries increased from 346 to 360 and for the regional centres the number of CP industries increased from 137 to 154. This is probably a reflection of the increased population and/or increased purchasing power in those regions.

As stated above, industries classified as low-order industries are basically related to production of necessities. But what can be said regarding medium-order and high-order industries?

Almost two-thirds of the medium-order industries belong to wholesale, retail sales and business services (see Table 2.3). Furthermore, it seems as if these two types of industries are related to each other. Without a sufficient number of industries engaged in manufacturing, wholesale and retail sales the demand for business services will be too low to make separate production of services profitable. Thus, when the market for wholesale and retail sales increases, the threshold demand is not only exceeded for those industries but also for related service industries, for example security activities and cleaning of premises.

Table 2.3 Medium- and high-order industries in 1993 and 1996

Type of industry	Number in medium-order industries		Number in high-order industries	
	1993	1996	1993	1996
Manufacturing	7	7	55	51
Wholesale and retail sale	40	45	51	52
Business services	22	24	29	27
Public administration /services	6	5	10	12
Education & health services	7	8	10	8
Private/household services	8	13	17	17
Other industries	10	15	37	39

Many of the business service activities are of course present in low-order industries but they are then performed in house. This process of specialisation through division of labour (Stigler, 1951) becomes even more obvious if we study the industrial composition of high-order industries. Here, we see a substantial increase of industries in the manufacturing sector as well as in the wholesale and retail sales industries. The demand for services from these industries is reflected by the increase in specialised business services, such as consultancy activities. We also see that the number of household services is increasing, due to the larger demand in the largest regions.

To analyse if we are able to find any differences in how the employment in CP industries changes with regional size we run the following regression for the three orders of industries.

$$\text{Ln}(\text{Emp}_j) = \text{Ln}(A_j) + B_j\text{Ln}(\text{Pop}),$$

where Emp_j is total employment in industries of order j in each functional region, Pop is the population in each functional region. Ln(A) and B are parameters to be estimated. Table 2.4 presents the results.

Table 2.4 Regression results for industry elasticity to population in 1996

	Low-order	Medium-order	High-order
Ln(A)	– 1.421	– 5.163	– 8.526
	(– 10.7)	(– 22.0)	(– 20.2)
B	0.941	1.238	1.435
	(76.6)	(57.0)	(36.7)
R^2(adj)	0.987	0.976	0.944

Note: t-values are presented in parenthesis.

The estimated parameters B_j in the above regressions can be interpreted as the elasticity of employment in each order with respect to regional population. An increase in population of 1 per cent gives rise to a 0.941 per cent increase in employment in low-order industries, a 1.238 per cent increase in employment in medium-order industries and a 1.435 per cent increase in employment high-order industries.

To analyse how the number of establishments in each order changes with regional size, a similar model is estimated.

$$\mathrm{Ln}(\mathrm{Est}_j) = \mathrm{Ln}(\mathrm{A}_j) + \mathrm{B}_j\mathrm{Ln}(\mathrm{Pop}),$$

where Est_j is the number of establishments in industries of order j in each region, Pop is the population in each functional region. Ln(A) and B are parameters to be estimated. Estimated B_j values can be interpreted as the elasticity of the number of establishment in each order to population. The results are presented in Table 2.5.

Table 2.5 Regression results for establishment elasticity to population in 1996

	Low-order	Medium-order	High-order
Ln(A)	– 2.436	– 5.464	– 7.549
	(– 12.0)	(– 40.0)	(– 29.9)
B	0.883	1.087	1.144
	(47.0)	(86.0)	(49.0)
R^2(adj)	0.965	0.989	0.968

Note: t-values are presented in parenthesis.

A 1 per cent increases in the population increase the number of establishments in low-order industries by 0.883 per cent, the number of establishments in medium-order industries by 1.087 per cent and the number of establishments in the high-order industries by 1.144 per cent.

If we compare Table 2.4 and Table 2.5 we can see that the elasticities increase at a slower rate in Table 2.5. A reasonable explanation for this is that medium-order industries and especially high-order industries are able to increase their production within existing establishments to meet an increased demand due to increased population. This means that to a greater extent they are able to capitalise from the internal economies of scale.

To further analyse whether economies of scale are a crucial factor in the distribution of CP industries we also study the average size of establishments, with respect to whether the industry is a low-, medium- or a high-order industry (see Table 2.6). If economies of scale are an important factor we would expect the average size of an establishment to increase when we move upwards in the CP system.

Table 2.6 Average size in employment of establishments with respect to their order, in 1993 and 1996

	1993	1996
Low-order industries	6.06	5.96
Medium-order industries	9.89	8.32
High-order industries	16.53	17.08

We see that the average size of establishments in high-order industries is almost twice as large as establishments belonging to the medium-order industries, which in turn is around 50 per cent larger than the average size of low-order establishments. This is a clear indication that economies of scale are more prominent in high-order industries compared to both medium-order and low-order industries.

Demand for products produced in medium-order industries does not depend only on the demand in the region where they are produced but also on the demand from smaller regions, where these products are not produced. Likewise, the demand for high-order products also depends on the demand from smaller and medium-sized regions. We should therefore expect to find the employment ratio in CP industries (total employment in CP industries/total employment) to increase when we move from smaller regions to larger regions (see Table 2.7).

Table 2.7 Employment in CP industries with respect to rank

	Employment	1993	1996
Employment in regions of rank 3	In CP industries	220 384	208 038
	In all industries	547 511	562 814
	Share in CP industries	0.4025	0.3696
Employment in regions of rank 2	In CP industries	982 429	947 963
	In all industries	1 544 173	1 584 940
	Share in CP industries	0.6362	0.5981
Employment in regions of rank 1	In CP industries	1 150 780	1 197 664
	In all industries	1 318 287	1 412 376
	Share in CP industries	0.8229	0.8480

Note: Top figure shows total employment in CP industries in each rank. Middle figure shows total employment in each rank. Bottom figure shows the share of employment in CP industries.

As expected we find that the employment share of CP industries increases as regional size increase. For instance the employment share of CP industries more than doubles between the smallest regions and the largest regions.

In order to separate the effects of urbanisation economies from the internal economies of scale we would need to have an input–output table describing the links between the industries. Since we do not have this, the analysis is done by studying the industries in the different orders.

In Table 2.3, we saw that when demand for certain industries exceeded its threshold, the threshold demand for other industries was exceeded as well. This was especially the case in the largest regions but we were also able to identify some of these tendencies in regions of rank 2. However, in order to do a more thorough test regarding the role of urbanisation economies we would need more information about the linkages between different industries.

Turning to the changes over time we saw in Table 2.2 that a number of industries is not present in the same order in both 1993 and 1996. Table 2.8 indicates what has happened to the CP industries during the actual time period.

Due to the short observation period we find that the system is rather invariant over time. The most interesting feature in Table 3.8 is the filtering down of the 24 industries from high-order in 1993 to medium-order in 1993 and the filtering up of the nine industries from medium-order industries in 1993 to high-order in 1996.

Table 2.8 Description of industrial movement between orders in 1993 to 1996

		1996				
		LOI	MOI	HOI	Other	Sum
	Low-order industries	33	2	0	2	37
1993	Medium-order industries	1	80	**9**	10	100
	High-order industries	0	**24**	175	10	209
	Other	3	11	22	356	391
	Sum	37	117	206	377	737

Note: LOI, MOI and HOI are abbreviations for low-order, medium-order and high-order industries.

Regarding the nine industries that were classified as medium-order industries in 1993 and became high-order industries in 1996 none showed any greater tendencies to filter up, that is they only exited from a small number of medium-sized regions.

When it comes to the 24 industries that show tendencies to filter down, eight industries entered more than three regions of rank 2. Three industries entered more than eight of the rank 2 regions. These are retail sale in telecommunication equipment, courier services and educational services. However, to study the tendencies of filtering up and filtering down in more depth we should need a longer time period. But, the results give a clear indication that the process of filtering down is stronger than the filtering up process.

4 CONCLUSIONS AND SUGGESTIONS FOR FURTHER RESEARCH

In this chapter we analyse the Swedish CP system. This is done for the static case as well as for the dynamic case. In the static case we argue that the major determinant of the industrial distribution of the CP system is the interplay between market size and economies of scale.

We have shown that CP industries are distributed in a hierarchical manner. This means that some industries will be present in all functional regions. Other industries will be present in all functional regions except the smallest, and finally some industries will only be present in the largest functional regions.

Our regressions show that industries are more sensitive to population changes the higher their order, that is, high-order industries are more sensitive than medium-order industries and medium-order industries are more sensitive than low-order industries. This is also true for the number of establishments, but the differences in sensitivity are smaller which can be explained by high-order industries being able to increase production more within existing establishments compared to medium- and low-order industries.

Other findings are that the number of CP industries increases as we move upward in the CP system. Since the number of CP industries is increasing with regional size, we should also expect to find that the CP industries will be more important for larger than for smaller regions when it comes to employment. We show that this is the case and that the share of employment in CP industries amounts to over 80 per cent in the metropolitan regions.

During the short time period analysed in this chapter, the CP system is rather stable. However, we find indications of both filtering-up and filtering-down processes. From our study it seems evident that the filtering-down process is the dominating one. The results here are unfortunately a bit uncertain.

The results presented in the chapter can be improved in future research. One might, for example, consider other variables as determinants of the urban system. In this chapter we have implicitly assumed that preferences and per capita incomes are the same in all regions. It would also be of interest to study the effects of regional differences in infrastructure and geographical location. These factors might explain why regions of equal size might have a different industrial mix as regards the CP industries.

APPENDIX 2A

Appendix 1: The urban system in 1993

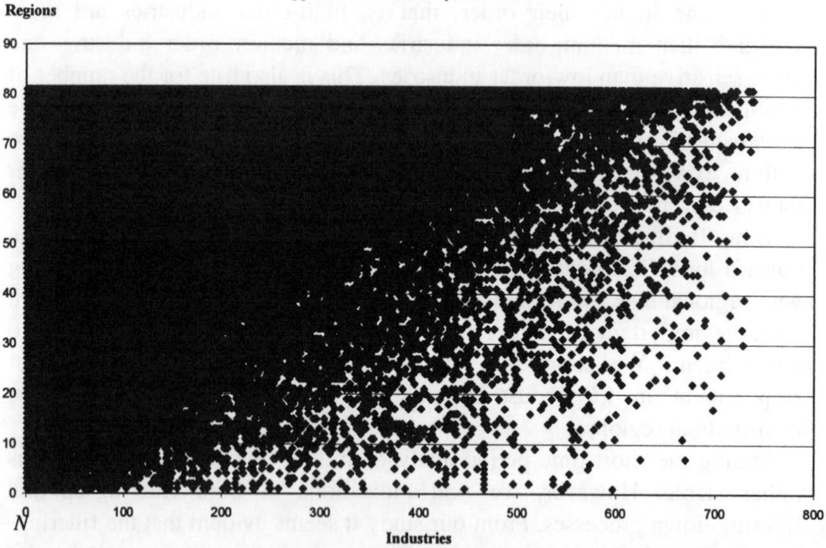

Appendix 2: The urban system in 1996

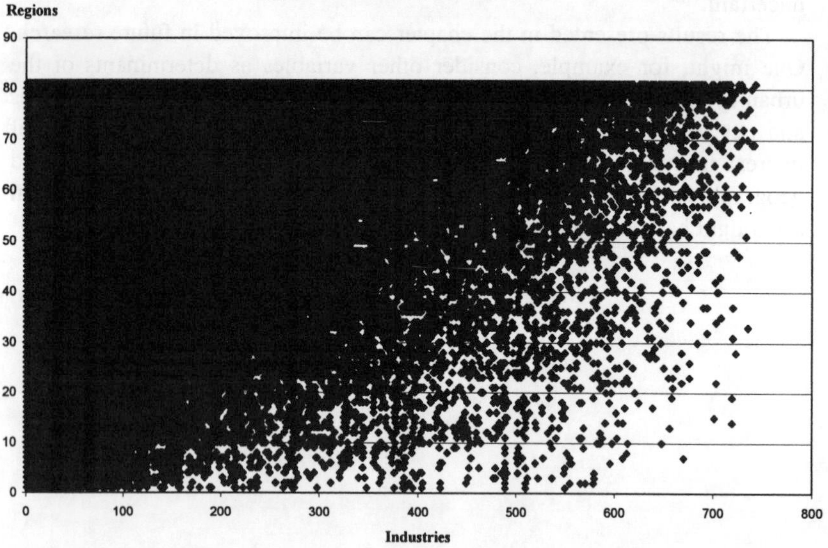

Note: On the y-axis regions are ranked according to their size measured as total population. Industries are ranked according to how many regions they exist in. Each black dot indicates that the industry is present by at least one establishment in that region. From the figure above we see that the larger a region gets, the more industries it can host.

APPENDIX 2A.3: CP INDUSTRIES ACCORDING TO STRICT DEFINITION, 1993

SIC code	Description	Order
1300	Growing of crops combined with farming of animals (mixed farming)	Low
2010	Sawmilling and planing of wood, impregnation of wood	Low
17230	Worsted-type weaving	High
24410	Manufacture of basic pharmaceutical products	High
24640	Manufacture of photographic chemical material	High
40100	Production and distribution of electricity	Low
45110	Demolition and wrecking of buildings; earth moving	Low
45211	General construction of buildings	Low
45230	Construction of highways, roads, airfields and sport facilities	Low
45310	Installation of electrical wiring and fittings	Low
45331	Installation of heating and sanitary equipment	Low
45441	Painting	Low
50201	Non-specialised maintenance and repair of motor vehicles	Low
50500	Retail sale of automotive fuel	Low
52112	Retail sale in other non-specialised stores with food, beverages and tobacco predominating	Low
52250	Retail sale of alcoholic and other beverages	Low
52310	Dispensing chemists	Low
52452	Retail sale of radio and television sets	Low
55111	Hotels with restaurant, except conference centres	Low
55300	Restaurants	Low
55521	Catering for the transport sector	High
60220	Taxi operation	Low
60240	Freight transport by road	Low
64110	National post activities	Low
64201	Network operation	Low
65120	Other monetary intermediation	Low
70201	Letting of dwellings	Low
74120	Accounting, book-keeping and auditing activities; tax consultancy	Low
74500	Labour recruitment and provision of personnel	Low
75211	Administration of foreign affairs	High
75300	Compulsory social security activities	Low
80100	Primary education	Low

80424	Activities of adult education associations	Low
85120	Medical practice activities	Low
85130	Dental practice activities	Low
85311	Care for residents in service homes and homes for the aged	Low
85321	Pre-primary school activities	Low
91310	Activities of religious organisations	Low
91330	Activities of other membership organisations n.e.c.	Low
92621	Sportsmen's and sports clubs activities	Low
92729	Various other recreational activities	Low
93021	Hairdressing	Low

APPENDIX 2A.4: CP INDUSTRIES ACCORDING TO STRICT DEFINITION, 1996

SIC code	Description	Order
1300	Growing of crops combined with farming of animals (mixed farming)	Low
2011	Growing of standing forest and standing timber	Low
2013	Logging	Low
40100	Production and distribution of electricity	Low
45110	Demolition and wrecking of buildings; earth moving	Low
45211	General construction of buildings	Low
45230	Construction of highways, roads, airfields and sport facilities	Low
45310	Installation of electrical wiring and fittings	Low
45331	Installation of heating and sanitary equipment	Low
45441	Painting	Low
50201	Non-specialised maintenance and repair of motor vehicles	Low
50500	Retail sale of automotive fuel	Low
51530	Wholesale of wood, construction materials and sanitary equipment	Low
52112	Retail sale in other non-specialised stores with food, beverages and tobacco predominating	Low
52250	Retail sale of alcoholic and other beverages	Low
52310	Dispensing chemists	Low
52410	Retail sale of textiles	Low
52452	Retail sale of radio and television sets	Low
52487	Retail sale of flowers and other plants	Low
55111	Hotels with restaurant, except conference centres	Low
55300	Restaurants	Low

55521	Catering for the transport sector	High
60220	Taxi operation	Low
60240	Freight transport by road	Low
64110	National post activities	Low
64201	Network operation	Low
65120	Other monetary intermediation	Low
70201	Letting of dwellings	Low
74120	Accounting, book-keeping and auditing activities; tax consultancy	Low
74500	Labour recruitment and provision of personnel	Low
75300	Compulsory social security activities	Low
80100	Primary education	Low
80424	Activities of adult education associations	Low
85120	Medical practice activities	Low
85130	Dental practice activities	Low
85311	Care for residents in service homes and homes for the aged	Low
85321	Pre-primary school activities	Low
85323	Day care activities for the aged and handicapped	Low
91310	Activities of religious organisations	Low
92511	Public library activities	Low
92621	Sportsmen's and sports clubs activities	Low
93021	Hairdressing	Low

NOTES

1. Even though technological change is not driven by demand as such it is difficult to oversee these changes over time.
2. Here the largest region is given number 1 and the second largest region number 2 and so on. The same principle is applied to the industries. That is, the region that holds the largest number of industries has been given a 1, the region with the second largest number industries a 2 and so on.
3. It should be pointed out some industries classified as medium-order industries are present in some of the smaller regions. Likewise, some of the industries classified as high-order industries are present in some medium and smaller regions.

REFERENCES

Beckmann, M.J. (1958), 'City hierarchies and the distribution of city sizes', *Economic Development and Cultural Change,* **6**, 243-248.

Burns, L.S. and R.G. Healy (1978), 'The metroplitan hierarcy of occupations. An Economic Interpretation of central place theory', *Regional Science and Urban Economics,* **8**, 381–93.

Camagni, R., L. Diappi and G. Leonardi (1986), 'Urban growth and decline in hierarchical systems– A supply-oriented dynamic approach', *Regional Science and Urban Economics*, **16**, 145–60.

Christaller, W. (1966), *The Central Places of Southern Germany*, Englewood Cliffs: Prentice-Hall.

Erickson, R.A. (1976), 'The filtering-down process: industrial location in a nonmetropoltitan area', *Professional Geographer*, **28** (3).

Forslund-Johansson, U. (1997), 'Studies of Multi-Regional Interdependencies and Change', Stockholm: Division of Regional Planning, Royal Institute of Technology (Licentiate Thesis).

Gunnarsson, J. (1976), 'Produktionssystem och tätortshierarki - om sambandet mellan rumslig ochekonomisk struktur', Doktorsavhandling Nr 56, Göteborgs universitet.

Harris, C.D. (1954), 'The market as a factor in the location of industry in the United States, *Annals of the Association of American Geographers*, **44**, *315–348*.

Hirch, S. (1967), *Location of Industry and Industrial Competitiveness*, Oxford: Oxford Press.

Hoover, E. (1971), *An Introduction to Regional Economics*, New York: Knopf.

Karlsson, C. (1999), *The Spatial Dynamics of Rapidly Declining Non-Urban Industries in Sweden*, Jönköping: JIBS.

Keeble, D. and P. Tyler (1995), 'Enterprising Behaviours and the Urban-Rural Shift', *Urban Studies*, **32** (6).

Krugman, P. (1998), 'Space: The final frontier', *Journal of Economic Perspective*, **12** (2), 161–175.

Marshall, A. (1920), *Principles of Economics*, London: Macmillan.

Mulligan, G.F. (1984), 'Agglomeration and central place theory: A review of the literature', *International Regional Science Review*, **9** (1), 1–42.

NUTEK (1998), Småföretag och regioner i Sverige 1998 - med ett tillväxtperspektiv för hela landet, NUTEK B 1998:10, Stockholm.

Parr, J.B. (1995), 'Alternative approaches to market-area structure in the urban system', *Urban Studies*, **32** (8), 1317–1330.

Richardson, H.W. (1995), 'Economies and Diseconomies of Agglomeration', in H. Giersch (ed.), *Urban Agglomeration and Economic Growth*. Berlin: Springer.

Stigler, G.J. (1951), 'The division of labor is limited by the extent of the market', *Journal of Political Economy*, **59**, 185-193.

Tinbergen, J. (1967), 'The hierarchy model of the size distribution of centres', *Papers of the Regional Science Association*, **20**.

3. Regional Policy in the Internet Age: the Effects of Technological Change on Regional Development

Edward J. Malecki

1 INTRODUCTION

This chapter focuses on the Internet and its implications for regional policy. The Internet is a remarkable convergence or fusion of information types (news, entertainment, data, pictures, voice), information media and information operators (Kellerman, 1997; Schiller, 1999). An 'accidental' rather than a planned technology (Anderson, 1995), it has in only a few years become identified as a *general-purpose technology* (Lipsey, Bekar and Carlaw, 1998), the leading sector of the fifth Kondratiev wave (Freeman, 1996), and a *key industry*, providing productivity gains in a large number of industries (Antonelli, 1997). Lipsey, Bekar and Carlaw (1998) list only a small number of technologies as general-purpose technologies (GPTs); these include lasers, the Internet, the factory system, mass production and flexible manufacturing. Historical precedents of GPTs are few, but include writing, printing and electricity. GPTs have scope for improvement, a wide variety of uses, a wide range of uses and strong technological complementarities. The Internet is changing scale and scope economies, causing integration of product markets, increasing the demand for skilled labour, and affecting productivity growth in several ways (Globerman, 1996).

Some see the Internet as less than a pure blessing; Schoenberger (1998) argues that in many instances the Internet is a 'time sink'. *Bandwidth*, of course, is the solution to that problem. Bandwidth is the term commonly used to designate transmission speed, measured in bits per second (*Boardwatch*, 1999). A simple 'rule of thumb is that good video requires about a thousand times as much bandwidth as speech. A picture is truly worth a thousand words' (Mitchell, 1995: 180, note 28). *Broadband* generally refers to transmission speeds above 64kbps, the base normal speed of a voice call (Huston, 1999: 160–71). Higher bandwidths generally are made possible by multiplexing the base line.

Several points are important at the outset. First, the Internet and its stimulus of a new infrastructure–parallel but not identical to the public switched telephone network (PSTN) – deserves more attention and analysis than it has received. Geographical inequalities, such as urban–rural contrasts, are not disappearing in the Internet age. The few analyses of the geography of telecommunications infrastructure suggest that inequalities will persist rather than vanish (Malecki 1997a, 1997b, 1998; Salomon 1996). Distance will not 'die' but become less important as other forms of proximity become more significant. It is evident that there are inequalities equally, if not more, pronounced than under the older plain old telephone service (POTS) technology (Arnum and Conti, 1998). The Internet has significant concentration in cities connected by 'backbones' or linked closely to them (Gorman, 1999). While Internet traffic travels by fibreoptic cable, problems remain the greatest at the local loop (Morgan, 1998).

A second impact of the Internet is the acceleration of the pace of change. That product life cycles have become shorter is well-known, but the rate at which strategic decisions are deemed successes or failures has dramatically quickened. *Competing on Internet Time*, the title of Cusumano and Yoffie's (1998) recent book, suggests that the usual time horizons for firms in the knowledge portion of the economy are very short indeed. Quinn's (1992) graph of these time horizons suggested a relatively leisurely pace for most industries, and under a year only for fashions, toys and financial services.

Third, the combination of spatial change and of temporal change places very different demands on regional policy. In addition to the rethinking necessitated by accommodating 'Internet time', the 'space of flows' (Castells 1989, 1996) and a switch 'from places to spaces' (Kelly, 1998), policy-makers must grapple with the essence of the knowledge economy (Foray and Lundvall, 1996; OECD, 1996). The concept of a knowledge economy has been around for at least a decade (Eliasson, 1988; Eliasson et al., 1990), recently transformed into the 'learning economy' (Foray and Lundvall, 1996; Lundvall and Johnson, 1994).

Fourth, the effects of the Internet are not unidirectional. Simplified models are able to conclude that its effects are spatially homogenizing, lowering agglomeration economies, facilitating mobility of services and of skilled labour, and reducing productivity differentials between large and small countries (Harris, 1998). However, more open-minded writers such as Moss (1998) and Kitchin (1998) see shades of grey: the Internet is both centralising and decentralising (Peitchinis, 1992). IT convergence has led to centralisation of activities involving codified information; at the same time, facilitation of communication between sites has enabled decentralisation of knowledge-creation activity – quite the reverse of what appeared to be the effect of information systems a decade ago (Hepworth, 1989). For research to answer questions regarding the effects of the Internet, there are both too many 'Internet indicators' and not enough (Paltridge, 1998a).

The remainder of this chapter reviews some of the emerging and still evolving features of the telecommunications infrastructure. It also presents empirical evidence of the uneven geographical structure of capabilities in the public switched telephone network in the US. There are indications that the highest level of technological capability is becoming increasingly concentrated at the highest levels of the urban hierarchy. In the case of the Internet and the connectivity of urban nodes, the evidence is clearly of an emerging hierarchy that focuses on a small set of the largest markets. The following sections of the chapter present some details of this work, first in Section 3 on CO switches and then in Section 4 on the Internet network. Section 5 contemplates the continued significance of location in the Internet Age. Finally, Section 6 assesses the notion of regional policy.

2 BACKGROUND: TECHNOLOGICAL AND REGULATORY CHANGE IN TELECOMMUNICATIONS

The Internet represents a surprising break in the evolution of telecommunications for several reasons (Kavassalis, Solomon and Benghozi, 1996; Nguyen and Phan, 1998). First, its origins are rather recent and its reputation as an unregulated seamless network operated by research-oriented geeks and nerds remains dominant. Second, the private nature of the Internet has evolved outside the view of most observers – in large corporations that, early on, developed internal computer intranets to exploit new computer technology. However – and this is where the private backbone providers entered the scene – corporations wanted to connect their many operations at different sites within a seamless network, for which they turned to private firms. Sometimes these were leased lines from existing telecommunications providers, such as AT&T and British Telecom; increasingly, they were new firms such as MCI, Sprint and UUNET (Langdale, 1989). The individual corporate networks and their spatial systems that evolved (Hepworth, 1989) became linked during the 1990s into the Internet – both to unite together their internal operations and to link better with other firms in the growing trend of interfirm collaborations and alliances (Schiller, 1999). Third, data transmission in general and thus the Internet have remained outside the purview of regulators in the US, a practice that has spread to Europe and elsewhere (Leo and Huber 1997; Schiller 1999).

New technologies and services related to telecommunications have proliferated only since the 1960s (Arnold and Guy, 1989). The technology that has attracted most attention is the fibreoptic network, but these cables also require new digital capabilities in the central office (CO) switches to enable new services, such as call waiting, caller ID and broadband transmission. The role of central office switches in the telephone network is well-documented (Flamm, 1989; Schoen et al., 1998). However, all capabilities are not implemented in all switches, and the geography of switch capability – and, therefore, the geography of digital telecommunications capability – is very uneven.

The importance of this issue is that, increasingly, firms and individuals demand high-end (high-speed, broadband) telecommunications access. Companies of all types are choosing locations in part on the capabilities of local telephone infrastructure. Several recent examples bear this out. Lawless and Gore (1999) found that firms in Sheffield, England, rated telecommunications as the most decisive factor in choosing a location. New buildings that incorporate the newest technologies and the necessary architecture have transformed the formerly concentrated Financial District of New York City into a 'doughnut' (Longcore and Rees, 1996). Richardson, Texas, a city midway between Dallas and Fort Worth, has attracted transnational companies, such as Alcatel, Ericsson, Nokia, and Bosch Telecom, Fujitsu and Samsung, on the strength of its telecommunications infrastructure – its 'Telecomcorridor'.

The largest firms, of course, can bypass the local network but only at substantial cost. More significantly, perhaps, new firm formation or entrepreneurship increasingly can be viable only in places where competitive telecommunications infrastructure is available. Small firms cannot afford bypass. Therefore, they are completely dependent on the local switched network, and this network is not geographically uniform. The lack of uniformity in the network was scarcely an issue in the days of AT&T's monopoly and universal service. However, in the late 1960s, when MCI and Sprint began to invest in parallel, competing networks, the focus of their attention was on the large cities where large numbers of customers were to be found. The research of Langdale (1983) on this evolution has not been replicated, although the generalisation is repeated in recent reviews (Salomon, 1996). The deregulation resulting from the Telecommunications Act of 1996 also has engendered new investment in selected (urban) locations (O'Keefe, 1998).

2.1 The First 100 Feet

The quality of *local* telecommunications service – and of an individual customer's service – depends critically on the capabilities of the local central office (CO) switch, and the customer's distance to it, rather than on the availability of fibreoptic trunk lines. Fibre to the home (at $3000) is not yet a realistic option, and the 'first 100 feet' to the customer remains unresolved (Akimaru, Finley and Niu, 1997; Hurley and Keller, 1999). Although there are exceptions, generally speaking rural areas are at a disadvantage when it comes to telecommunications technologies. Being unable to muster the demand needed to justify or amortise large infrastructure investments, rural areas are less likely to see the complete set of telecommunications innovations. In turn, the quality of service in local areas will suffer, as new technologies are increasingly needed for access to the latest broadband (multimedia) transmissions (Akimaru, Finley and Niu, 1997; Lu et al., 1998; O'Malley, 1999).

Since the 1960s, the technologies of computers and electronics have converged with those of broadcasting and wire-based telecommunications. Most applications have been driven by a growing set of information technologies for business applications, such as computer-aided design, remote sensing devices, management information systems and data bases. For individuals the ability to send and receive data and images, in addition to voice, effectively merged computer and telecommunications technologies in the form of the Internet and the World Wide Web. The Internet and personal computers require digital capability, and preferably broadband, which is not universally available, especially in rural areas where the cost of upgrading voice or dial-tone lines to broadband service would be prohibitive. Urban and suburban (metropolitan) areas have been the principal markets for new telecommunications services, because their customer base includes larger numbers of customers – especially large business customers – who are willing to adopt new services. The much smaller number of rural customers in any service area, as well as nationwide, means that rural areas are certain to be late in the service provision sequence (Egan, 1998; Gillespie and Cornford, 1996; Malecki, 1998). This is as true of cable modem service through cable television firms as it is of conventional telcos. Indeed, acquisitions and mergers increasingly blur the conventional lines between sectors.

2.2 Digital Technology: Switches and Why they are Important

Bandwidth and other aspects of quality of service are dependent on the capabilities of the CO switch. Digital technology as yet has not changed the overall architecture of the telephone system. Despite the information superhighway, 'the basic core of telecommunications is still voice-grade telephony' (Crandall, 1997: 163), but this is rapidly giving way to data-based Internet protocol (or IP) networks and the growth of data transmission over voice transmission as users take advantage of dial-up access to the Internet. As a type of 'modular technical change', digital switches can be added individually within a firm's network. Digital signalling permits the clear transmission of data and enables higher data rates, characteristics not possible in an analogue system. Digital switches, combined with fibreoptic lines, also give rise to system-scale economies and network effects, because these systems reduce the cost of training, maintenance and spare parts (Majumdar, 1997). Perhaps more significant than the cost savings is the capability to add value-added services such as custom-calling, which can bring a carrier additional revenue (Majumdar, 1995). Many other points of convergence between public switching and the Internet remain to be exploited (Schoen et al., 1998)

The radically different method of networking represented by packet-switching poses huge challenges for the telephone network, with which the Internet has co-evolved. In this regard, the infrastructure of the telephone system, particularly the central office (CO) switch, is a key piece in widespread Internet access (Schoen et al., 1998). A switch is needed even in wireless networks.

2.3 Deregulation

Deregulation has had large but unanalysed impacts on telecommunications inequality. Few analysts have examined the potential or actual spatial impacts of deregulation. The neoliberal push in the USA of the 1990s has affected the rest of the world, especially in telecommunications (Schiller, 1999). The story of the effects of deregulation and the strategies of new competitors told in this section is repeated by Gillespie and Cornford (1996) and Graham and Marvin (1996) in the UK.

In the US context, the greatest impact of telecommunications deregulation has been the entry of new providers of telecommunications services. The former AT&T monopoly, the American equivalent of a PTT, was broken up into nine 'Baby Bells' or Regional Operating Companies (RBOCs). The incumbent local exchange carriers (ILECs) – a category that includes the RBOCs as well as independent carriers such as GTE and Sprint and hundreds of small firms and coops – are now joined by hundreds of competitive local exchange carriers (CLECs). This group includes wireless carriers, competitive access providers (CAPs) of advanced fibre networks (which predated the 1996 Act) and personal communications services

(PCS). Several states had permitted local competitors in advance of the federal Telecommunications Act of 1996. 'Unbundling' allows CLECs to buy access to the 'network elements' (local loops, network interface devices, switches, transmission facilities, signaling and call-related databases, operation support systems and directory assistance facilities) of ILECs rather than build their own facilities. Unbundling may be slowing the development of network infrastructure by discouraging investment because it is so easy for a CLEC to resell services through an ILEC's network (Aron, Dunmore and Pampush, 1998). The reliance of the CLECs on the ILECs' central offices has led those CLECs that can afford it to install their own switches, if only co-located at the same CO site as the ILEC. Co-location of switching equipment, therefore, is both common and troubling (Chen, 1999).

There also is an emerging trend for CLECs to acquire Internet service providers (ISPs) or, alternatively, for ISPs to become CLECs within their service area. Such 'ISPCLECs can offer much more than local phone service' by providing Internet access, helped by hardware firms such as Nortel (Northern Telecom, 1998a). Indeed, a recent US Supreme Court decision makes ISPCLECs the growth segment of the industry, in part because of the minimal investment required for facilities (Geist, 1999).

Despite the AT&T breakup in 1984, a new oligopoly is evolving in US telecommunications. Soon, 171 million households will be served by one of the 'big four': AT&T/TCI, Bell Atlantic/GTE, SBC/Ameritech, and MCI WorldCom. These large players are unlikely to serve rural areas, small cities, and even large cities where state regulation thwarts competition (Mehta 1999). In long-distance, the three large networks (AT&T, MCI WorldCom, and Sprint) have been joined by Qwest/GTE, IXC, Williams, Frontier and Level 3 (King, 1999). These new firms are pushing broadband technologies that are in high demand by Internet users. MCI/WorldCom already is the largest CLEC, through its acquisition of MFS, which had 23 per cent of the US CLEC market in 1997.

3 SPATIAL VARIATION IN SWITCH LOCATION AND CAPABILITY

This section reports on an analysis of a data set of 33 273 switches in the US. Telcordia Technologies (formerly Bellcore – Bell Communications Research, Inc.) compiles and updates regularly a Local Exchange Routing Guide (LERG) for the entire North American region. An earlier analysis of the 493 switches in Tennessee presented a hierarchy of switches according to degree of digitalisation (Malecki and Boush, 1999).

The number of telecommunications providers in the US is mind-boggling. Of the 2300 operating companies in the Bellcore data base, 866 (37.7 per cent) are CLECs; the remaining 62.3 per cent are Baby Bells or Independents. Both groups are comprised predominantly of small companies; over 400 firms in each group operate only a single CO switch. The Baby Bells or RBOCs are the largest firms, three of them with over 1000 switches each. The size of the large firms is actually understated in the Bellcore database, because state regulation means that any firm operating in more than one state tends to register separately in each one. Thus, the 2300 firms are barely one-half of the 4445 operating company listings, many of which are unused but presumably have been applied for in anticipation of future market entry.

The most profitable market for telecommunications (or any economic activity) is where the costs of provision can be minimised and the revenues can be maximised. Agglomerations of large customers tend to be found in central business districts and in business parks on the periphery of urban areas (Gillespie and Cornford, 1996: 341). *The switches within urban or metropolitan statistical areas (MSAs) or, where applicable, consolidated MSAs (CMSAs) were identified.* A model of the location of CO switches takes the following form:

$$\# \text{ switches} = a + b\,\text{Pop} + c\,\text{Pop}^2 + d\,\text{PopDen} + e,$$

where Pop is the population of the MSA or CMSA, and PopDen is MSA/CMSA population density.

Table 3.1 (first column) shows that the number of switches is closely related to population and density, which together closely mirror market potential. The nonlinear relationship with metro area population is robust, and is enhanced by the addition of the (negative) quadratic term, which captures the effect of large metro areas where switches are less dense.

A second important area for analysis is the distribution of the new competitive operating companies, or CLECs. These firms are under no obligation to provide universal service and, instead, provide new services to markets that justify the investment. Although there is some sharing of facilities, as discussed above, many CLECs install their own switches. Overall, 53.3 per cent of all US switches, and 78.6 per cent of CLEC switches, are in metro areas. The pattern seen in the second column of Table 3.1 is that the number of CLEC switches is slightly more closely related to metro area population than is the case for all switches. The set of all switches analysed above included firms (such as telephone coops) whose purpose is often to serve rural areas with few customers.

Table 3.1 Metropolitan area population effects on the number of central office switches

	All switches	CLEC switches
Constant	– 23.041	– 0.065
Metropolitan area population (MSA or CMSA)	0.0834 ** (27.611)	0.011645 ** (16.028)
(State population)^2	– 000001497 ** (7.837)	– 0.0000000049 ** (0.122)
Metro area population density	246.999 ** (6.466)	0.0109 ** (3.829)
Adjusted R^2	0.900	0.902
degrees of freedom	268	268

Notes:
Values in parentheses are t-values.
* significant at the 0.05 level
** significant at the 0.01 level

CLECs, by contrast, have been free to focus on the most profitable markets. As in the situation of all switches, a nonlinear relationship holds with metro area population. The number of CLEC switches is significantly affected (nonlinearly) by population and population density (Table 3.1, column 2).

Table 3.2 Presence of competitive telecom providers, by MSA size class

MSA population size class	Mean population	Mean no. of CLECs	Mean no. of ILECs	Ratio of CLECs/ ILECs
>5 000 000 (n = 8)	9 328 060	37.8	9.5	3.97
2 500 000 – 5 000 000 (n = 10)	3 283 340	22.0	8.9	2.47
1 000 000 – 2 499 000 (n = 29)	1 422 289	14.2	6.8	2.09
500 000 – 1 000 000 (n = 29)	713 991	8.1	4.5	1.83
250 000 – 500 000 (n = 64)	362 795	5.1	4.0	1.26
150 000 – 249 999 (n = 52)	187 242	3.2	3.9	0.82
50 000 – 149 999 (n = 80)	114 881	2.3	2.9	0.77

The market-driven nature of telecommunications competition was established by Langdale's (1983) pathbreaking work. He demonstrated that the process of spread of the earliest competitive services in US telecommunications during the 1970s followed a pattern of decreasing metropolitan market size. Using the LERG data, all CO switches – but, even more, CLEC CO switches – are found where market demand (or its surrogate, population) warrants their location. Tables 3.2 and 3.3 show clearly the bias toward the upper end of the urban hierarchy. Larger numbers of new competitors (CLECs) have concentrated in the larger urban areas (Table 3.2). Similarly, a larger concentration of packet switches, which facilitate data transmission, have been implemented in the larger urban size categories (Table 3.3).

Table 3.3 Digital telecommunications technologies, by metropolitan area size class

MSA population size class	Mean population	Mean number of packet switches	Packet switches as % of all switches	Mean number of ISDN switches	ISDN switches as % of all switches
>5 million (n = 8)	9 328 060	136.6	24.4	22.0	3.9
2.5 – 5 million (n = 10)	3 283 340	78.9	26.1	12.0	4.0
1 – 2.49 million (n = 29)	1 422 289	19.7	17.1	5.0	4.3
500 000 – 1 million (n=29)	713 991	9.8	15.0	2.3	3.5
250 000 – 500 000 (n = 64)	362 795	3.5	9.9	1.7	4.7
150 000 – 249 999 (n = 52)	187 242	2.6	9.8	1.5	5.6
50 000 – 149 999 (n = 80)	114 881	1.2	6.9	1.0	5.8

Table 3.3 also shows, however, that integrated services digital network (ISDN) has been implemented most in small, rather than large, metropolitan areas. ISDN, formerly the technology of choice for upgrading of local telephone lines for high-speed digital service, has fallen back to various digital subscriber line (DSL) technologies in recent years. It was noted several years ago that the US was slow to implement ISDN relative to Europe (Gregg, 1992). DSL highlights the importance of the CO switch. Because it requires certain types of switching equipment, DSL service is constrained to a shorter distance from the switch than are lower-frequency signals. This is especially true of the Very High Rate DSL (VDSL) which is planned for initial deployment in 1999. In effect, VDSL allows telcos to provide cable television via copper phone lines, yet another example of convergence among technologies. Its highest speed, 51.84 Mbps, operates only within 1 000 feet of a switch, and declines to 12.96 Mbps from 3000 to 4500 feet (that is less than one mile) from the switch (Northern Telecom, 1998b). Clearly, such distance-constrained technologies will be located at first in high-density neighbourhoods, especially those with a high density of business customers willing to pay for premium service. These services

generally are available only in the biggest cities and in dense high-tech regions such as the Research Triangle (O'Keefe, 1998).

4 THE SPATIAL CONCENTRATION OF THE NTERNET'S NETWORKS

The Internet is supposedly eliminating geographical variation, providing people in all locations equal access. The 'death of distance' (Cairncross, 1996) and the 'end of geography' (O'Brien, 1992) are familiar summaries of the Internet's effects. It is difficult to understand why the Internet – the network of networks – has not been subjected to conventional network analysis. Instead, there are innumerable 'Internet infrastructure indicators' that focus on domains and other aspects of Internet use and demand, but not the structure of the network (Paltridge, 1998a). Network structure was a common analysis for transportation networks (Haggett and Chorley, 1969), but this has not been common for telecommunications networks. As Hepworth (1989: 63) notes, 'network topology receives relatively little attention in the technical literature, which is primarily concerned with architectural solutions to distributed processing and the roles of individual technologies'. The principles of network topology reduce a network to a graph of nodes and links, from which measures of nodal connectivity can be calculated, including the number of 'hops' a packet of data would have to travel between nodes and weights to account for different bandwidths available on each route.

Moss and Townsend (1998) have examined the pattern of 29 fibreoptic Internet 'backbones' in the USA, which shows clearly the bias of these private-sector providers towards the major urban centers (Figure 3.1).

As in the case of the CLECs, the bias of any individual firm providing Internet connections is compounded by the *redundancy* stemming from the networks of other providers. As Gillespie and Robins (1989) pointed out a decade ago, telecommunications is being built predominantly as a set of private networks rather than a public one.

While the individual networks have different structures, for all of them the market is in the largest urban areas. The degree of connectivity is so great in the 'Big Seven' metro areas – San Francisco, Washington, Chicago, New York, Dallas, Los Angeles and Atlanta – that they have 62 per cent of the nation's backbone capacity. The next 14 metropolitan areas together account for only an additional 25.5 per cent of the nation's backbone capacity (Moss and Townsend, 1998).

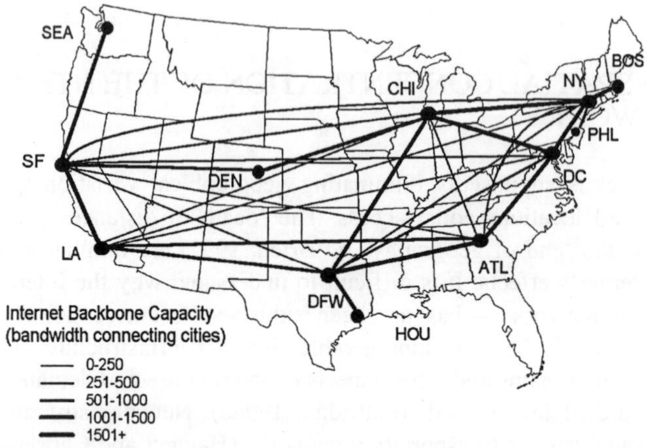

Source: Based on data in Moss and Townsend (1998).

Figure 3.1 Principal Internet backbones in the USA

Gorman (1999) has done a more comprehensive network analysis of 33 provider networks serving 60 urban areas in the US. Gorman's analysis confirms that the US urban hierarchy has been distorted by the Internet and its networks. The most-connected urban areas in simply the number of binary connections (1 if a connection is present, 0 if not) are Chicago, San Francisco (whose CMSA includes Silicon Valley), and Washington, DC; Atlanta, New York and Dallas-Fort Worth form a second tier of cities with lower connectivity.

The overlap or redundancy of the various Internet providers further affects urban connectivity, and sets out seven cities above the others as preeminent in connectivity: Washington, Chicago, San Francisco, Dallas, New York, Atlanta and Los Angeles (Figure 3.2). Note that this order is slightly different from that identified by Moss and Townsend, and is far from that based on population where the seven largest urban areas are New York, Los Angeles, Chicago, Washington, San Francisco, Philadelphia and Boston. The shuffling of cities indicates several things: the historical importance of Washington as the origin of the Internet as a military invention, the centrality of San Francisco's Silicon Valley in Internet technologies, and the importance of nodes in the centre of the country (Chicago, Dallas, Atlanta) as hubs for routing Internet traffic from the East Coast to the West Coast..

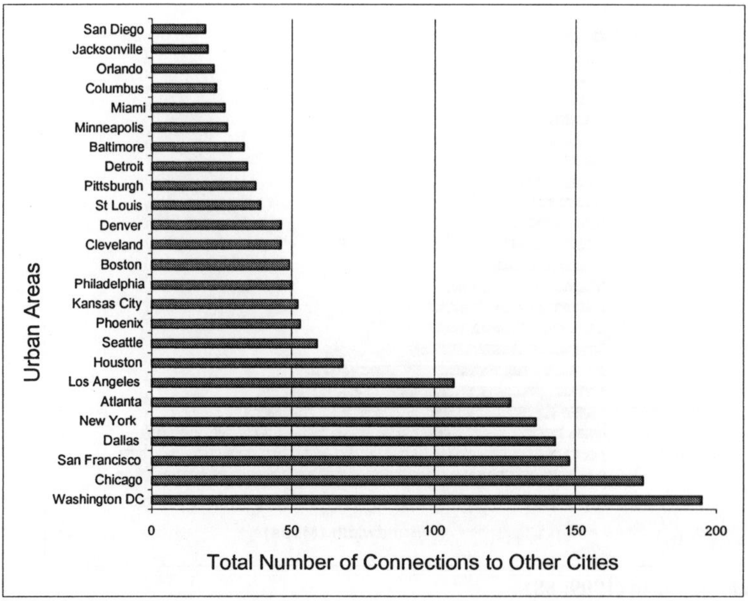

Source: Gorman (1999: 85).

Figure 3.2 Number of redundant links of 33 backbone providers on the Internet for leading US cities

Bandwidth is a critical element in the transmission of data, which is increasingly in the form of graphics, videos, and sound clips. A relatively simple 'Web page' can contain 1 megabyte (Mb) or more of data. Demand by more users for more Internet content of all kinds means that a larger number of 'packets' are traversing the fibreoptic cables of the network. There are several reasons why an individual's 'download' might be slow, including modem and processor speed, but the most likely reason is the capacity of the telephone line to the Internet provider's point of presence (POP) and the capacity of, and degree of congestion on, the fibreoptic connections from there to the provider's backbone. All major backbone providers are installing high-bandwidth links on key routes. Gorman's (1999) analysis of the 60 US cities in a bandwidth-weighted matrix identifies a distinct three-tier urban hierarchy (Figure 3.3). Neither New York nor Los Angeles is in the top tier, and Boston ranks only thirteenth – far lower than its status as a high-tech region would suggest.

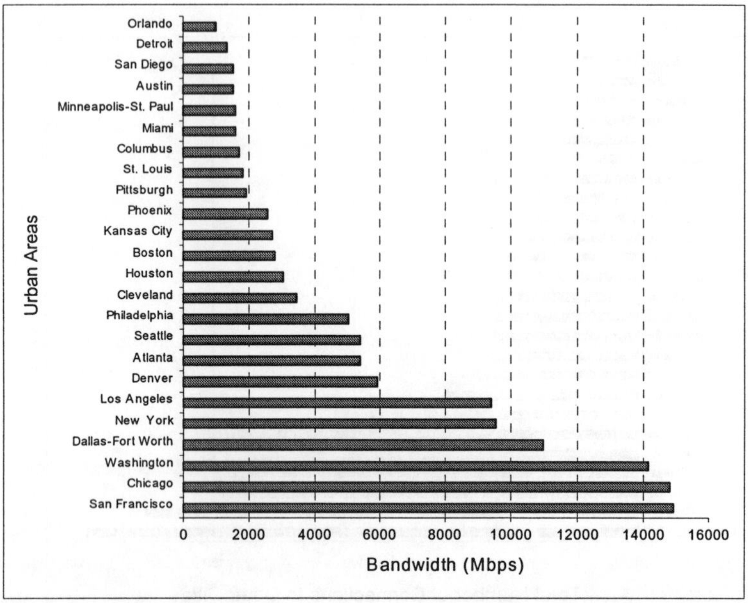

Source: Gorman (1999: 88).

Figure 3.3 Bandwidth-weighted hierarchy of US cities, for 33 Internet backbones

Many backbone providers, such as UUNET, MCI, Cable & Wireless, also provide international connections. The overall result to date, however, is an Ameri-centric network. Intra-Asian and intra-European data packets typically travel through the USA to reach their destination. This is caused by the fact that connections are better to the USA from most places than they are internally (Paltridge, 1998b). Bandwidth, rather than distance, is the determinant of the travel time of data packets. And bandwidth tends to be added to routes to North America rather than internally (Paltridge, 1998b, Annex 2).

The implications of the network analyses of this section centre on persistent spatial inequality. Although some shuffling attributable to competition among Internet backbone providers and competitive telecommunications providers is taking place, new technologies are being put in place in the usual list places – those that constitute large markets – and not as rapidly in smaller markets.

5 THE PARADOX OF THE INTERNET AGE: THE ENDURING IMPORTANCE OF LOCATION

Corporate spatial systems, interconnected by the Internet, give firms the ability to transcend space, interconnecting their operations with broadband, high-speed links that often are barely utilised but are there for when they are needed (Odlyzko, 1998). These links, formerly dedicated lines connecting only intracorporate sites, began to require links to collaborators and alliance partners, and that necessitated adhering to Internet (TCP/IP) data transmission protocols (Schiller, 1999).

As a result, firms became flexible in a global manner, exploiting pools of knowledge and labour in many locations. Incorporating that far-flung knowledge, however, was more difficult (Howells and Wood, 1993). It has become apparent that telecommunications alone can tap knowledge but does not facilitate its understanding and implementation. Recent research on multinational firms makes clear that in order to fully integrate localised knowledge, firms must become 'locals' in each locale (Blanc and Sierra, 1999; Gassmann and von Zedtwitz, 1999). Moreover, it is not clear which organisational form works best, because it is not the structure of the firm that is critical, but rather the set of connections the firm has to external knowledge, both tacit and codified – much, but not all, of which can be obtained from outside the firm (Antonelli, 1999; Chesbrough and Teece, 1996; Teece, 1998). Indeed, the nature of competition has changed dramatically, where time specificity and knowledge specificity are equally critical (Sampler, 1998). Amin and Cohendet (1998) suggest that there are now five competencies that are critical for globalised firms:

1. integrate the firm internally,
2. exploit advantages of proximity at many locations,
3. integrate fragmented pieces of localised learning,
4. ongoing investment in access to knowledge, and
5. focus on a small number of core competencies.

This suggests three aspects to the structure of an 'information age' organisation: decentralisation, information practices that promote both an awareness of external information and information-sharing within the organisation, and a network structure for the outsourcing of non-core activities (Mendelson and Pillai, 1999).

The importance of 'being there', not just being linked remotely, has become recognised as critical (Porter, 1998b; Gertler, 1995; Maskell and Malmberg, 1999). The reason is that tacit knowledge, on which localised capabilities are based, is 'sticky' and difficult to transfer within or between organisations (Brown and Duguid, 1998; Teece, 1998; von Hippel, 1994). In essence, as firms attempt to become closer to their customers in a world of short product cycles and mass customisation, the locus of problem-solving tends toward users because of 'sticky' local information that must be transferred a number of times (von Hippel, 1998). These transfers of knowledge represent the externalisation or transformation of tacit knowledge into codified knowledge to transmit it within the firm. Externalisation does not replace, but instead complements, local knowledge.

One hypothesis that has gained attention is that *clusters*, if we can agree to use Porter's term, reflect the 'enduring competitive advantages' of agglomeration (Porter 1998a: 237). Proximity and face-to-face communication provide 'thicker' information, resulting from 'sequential efficiency' and quick turnaround. The benefits appear to be greatest in the context of complex information such as that embedded in innovation and new technology (Boden and Molotch, 1994).

> The enduring competitive advantages in a global economy are often heavily local, arising from concentrations of highly specialized skills and knowledge, institutions, rivals, related businesses, and sophisticated customers. Proximity in geographic, cultural, and institutional terms allows special access, special relationships, better information, powerful incentives, and other advantages in productivity and productivity growth that are difficult to tap from a distance. Standard inputs information, and technologies are readily available via globalization, then, while more advanced dimensions of competition remain geographically bounded. (Porter, 1998a: 237)

The regional outcome is that of a mosaic of localised capabilities and competences (Scott, 1998). Just as no firm can know everything or master all necessary knowledge, regions have particular strengths or competences, based on set of relationships that emerge from social interaction. Some systems of interaction are better than others, whether for exchanging internal knowledge or accessing external knowledge. A region with 'thick' or 'deep' competences can compensate for – or add to – relatively thin competences in a firm (Lawson, 1999; see also Malmberg, Sölvell and Zander, 1996). Experiments are taking place, especially in Europe, that attempt to incorporate clusters and learning regions into regional policy initiatives (Lagendijk, 1999). However, it is not clear whether policies can create the characteristics of a learning region: institutional learning, institutional reflexivity and regional associationalism. Cooke and Morgan (1998) believe that these are found only in Germany's Baden-Württemberg and in Italy's Emilia-Romagna, and even there not without adjustments and adaptations. Learning also is likely to maintain regional inequalities rather than to remove them (Hudson, 1999).

But proximity does not guarantee interaction or 'automatically' generate linkages and networks. This has been made clear in a number of studies in a number of places, most recently by Lawton Smith (1998). Hardill, Fletcher and Montagné-Villette, (1995) likewise showed that it may be complex cultural forces that determine the degree of networking within an area. The typology of areas is still evolving, however, since we can see that industrial districts are not all the same; some of them generate not only a dense web of ties but also a culture of learning that is the hallmark of an innovative milieu (Maillat, 1995, 1998). Exactly *how* knowledge grows and is shared in an agglomeration is beginning to be teased out in detailed studies (Henry, Pinch and Russell, 1996; Pinch and Henry, 1999; Porter, 1998a). The process that makes geographically localised learning happen (or not happen) is not merely knowledge spillovers, but an array of *untraded interdependencies* that represent opportunities for a region to be able to build and keep its distinctive competence (Storper, 1995).

The strength of the local learning system depends greatly on competent governments and firms working to understand and support one another for the benefit of the region and its population. This mutual support system hinges on trust and social capital, and is exhibited in unique ways in different places, as Cooke and Morgan (1998) illustrate. Learning regions, local environments, and regional competitiveness have become central, rather than peripheral, to research in the field of regional development (Eskelinen, 1997; Maskell et al., 1998). Localised capabilities translate into sustainable competencies, which enable firms to survive and thrive in spite of an unfavourable local cost structure (Maskell et al., 1998; Maskell and Malmberg, 1999).

Telecommunications enables a number of elements of flexibility or, more properly, agility. Flexibility primarily involves exploiting three dimensions of a firm's operations: technology, labour and interfirm relationships (Malecki, 1996). The technological aspects involve both flexible automation for computer-integrated manufacturing and mass customisation, as well as services related to relationship marketing, customised information, push technology and other nonlocal electronic commerce. It has become evident that the Internet has changed the nature of competition for many industries (Cusumano and Yoffie, 1998; Evans and Wurster, 1997; Shapiro and Varian, 1998).

6 IS THERE A PLACE FOR REGIONAL POLICY IN A PLACELESS WORLD?

Regional policy has fallen into disrepair, if not disrepute, because of globalisation, glocalisation and, generally, of reterritorialisation (Brenner, 1999; Swyngedouw, 1992). Humphries (1996) provides a good overview of the key functions of national and regional policy:

(a) setting long-term vision, goals and targets,
(b) animating and resourcing strategic partnerships to achieve their share of these goals and targets,
(c) empowering partnerships to shape local policies,
(d) monitoring and managing and evaluating these partnerships, and
(e) supporting national and international networking of strategic partnerships to aid their learning.

In general, these and other lists of policy ideas of the 1990s tend to omit infrastructure investment, leaving that more and more to the private sector. Emphasis has been on trying to understand and facilitate networking and regional innovation systems, essentially relegating to the private sector the provision of infrastructure.

The telecommunications context poses additional problems. For example, the policy objective of 'universal service' has become more difficult to attain than when the technologies were fewer and simpler (Ypsilanti and Kelly, 1994). Policy choices are made more difficult because of the fact that telecommunications networks are a non-standard infrastructure, made up of juxtaposed sub-networks, based on different hardware, software, and standards (Bar et al., 1989: 52). The lack of standardisation may be coming to an end, converging on the standards and protocols of the Internet (Schiller, 1999).

Deregulation immediately shifts priorities in decision making from equity and universal service to new criteria that favour economic efficiency and profitability. Thus, it is large cities, where large firms (and large telematics customers) are found, as well as concentrations of small businesses, organisations and households (Carey, 1999; Graham and Marvin, 1996). The attraction of a market size will not diminish as increasingly sophisticated technologies are developed to attract customers who can afford them. In this context, the role of government in the Internet age must go beyond merely that of infrastructure provider and lead adopter. The complex interaction of systems in a world of positive feedbacks and increasing returns is for government to be a 'nudging hand', rather than a heavy hand or an invisible hand (Arthur, 1999). Government programmes seem to be necessary to counteract the tendency for urban market bias of private firms.

There is, of course, a need for national policies to promote learning, particularly institutional learning (Dalum, Johnson and Lundvall, 1992). Porter (1998a: 245–66) finds a great deal that governments can do to enhance the formation and operation of clusters. (Porter also makes recommendations which apply mainly to the national level. There, government's roles include maintaining macroeconomic and political stability, improving general microeconomic capacity (through infrastructure and institutions, among other things), establishing microeconomic rules and incentives governing competition, and facilitating development and upgrading of all clusters through long-term actions.) At the cluster level, Porter suggests reinforcing and building upon existing clusters, perhaps seeded and reinforced by inbound FDI, and removing obstacles and eliminating inefficiencies that impede cluster productivity and innovation. Some specific possibilities for government include: creating specialised education and training programmes, enhancing specialised transportation and communications infrastructure, and acting perceptively to respond to cluster needs for testing and other cluster-specific services (Figure 3.4).

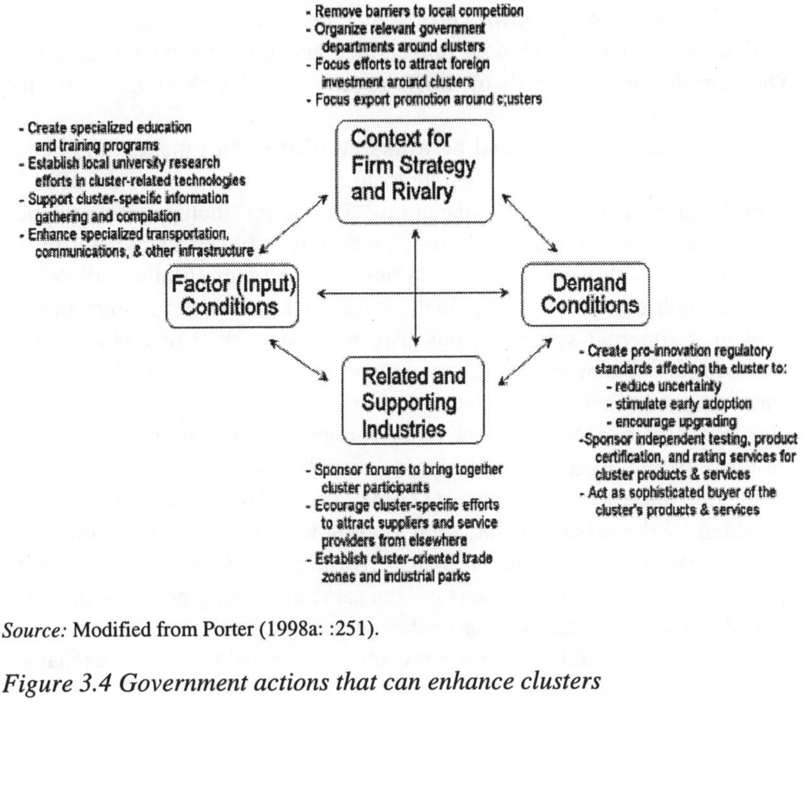

Source: Modified from Porter (1998a: :251).

Figure 3.4 Government actions that can enhance clusters

Porter emphasises that government policy will be unable to be influential alone; both the local private sector and trade associations and other collective bodies must work together – constructing what Cooke and Morgan (1998) call an associative economy. Perhaps the most difficult challenge is simply for governments to understand and recognise what a cluster is – more like a filière than a standard sector for which data allow easy identification (Porter, 1998a: 199–208). As Rosenfeld (1997: 9) puts it, describing the *synergy* found in a working cluster, 'the social ecology is as important as the agglomeration economies'. Rosenfeld (1997) suggests several policies to strengthen the synergy of local clusters, including learning how businesses interact and clusters work, improving the technical support services, and empowering and listening to cluster private-sector leaders.

Jacobs (1998) sees four government roles: providing infrastructure, organising social and political processes, providing an intellectual framework, and setting the overarching ambition for the nation. Although these are put in the context of science, technology and innovation policies, the greatest future policy need may be for national differentiation building on the upgrading of proven industrial strengths. Many of those strengths are likely to be local or cluster-specific. Nielsen's (1996) prescription is for a *technological service infrastructure*, which he sees as an integral part of the innovation system, along with universities and government research labs. The complex service needs of SMEs requires a polytechnological institute and networks.

Combining knowledge and networks, Maillat (1996) makes suggestions for policies to create the appropriate local milieu that recognise the need for both local and nonlocal connections. The latter include the technical environment and the market. A milieu can only maintain its dynamism if it is 'in phase' with market needs and new technologies (Maillat, 1996: 76). The strength of any local, regional, or national innovation system lies not only in its internal synergies, but also in its high level of connections to knowledge elsewhere (Oinas and Malecki, 1999). While telecommunications is less necessary locally, because the dynamics of informal, face-to-face communication dominate, telecommunications is the best way to be plugged into the external world.

In our increasingly privatised times, some infrastructures must be provided by the private sector, such as commercial and service support and multimodal transportation systems (Kasarda and Rondinelli, 1998). However, moving information is not the same as moving goods or products. Infrastructures for information exchange include conference facilities and other *interaction and learning sites* where knowledge can be exchanged (Crevoisier, 1999).

7 CONCLUSION

As interactions using the Internet and digital technologies change the ways in which the societies and economies operate, it is important to understand better the infrastructure on which those technologies depend. This chapter has drawn on a diverse set of literatures to show that geography has not died, and that it is asserting itself both through the evolving infrastructures and through the sustained competitiveness of places. It is too late to focus on only one geographical scale. A global awareness and action are needed, as are horizontal links to other places and other regions. And neither of these should take precedence over maintaining and enhancing the synergy of local economies and societies, for it is on these that development ultimately rests.

REFERENCES

Akimaru, H., M.R. Finley and Z. Niu (1997), 'Elements of the emerging broadband information highway', *IEEE Communications Magazine*, **35** (6), 84–92.

Amin, A. and P. Cohendet (1999), 'Learning and adaptation in decentralised business networks', *Environment and Planning D: Society and Space*, **17**, 87–104.

Anderson, C. (1995), 'The accidental superhighway: a survey of the internet', *The Economist*, July 1.

Antonelli, C. (1997), 'A regulatory regime for innovation in the communications industries', *Telecommunications Policy*, **21**, 35–45.

Antonelli, C. (1999), 'The evolution of the industrial organisation of the production of knowledge', *Cambridge Journal of Economics*, **23**, 243–60.

Arnold, E. and K. Guy (1989), 'Policy Options for Promoting Growth Through Information Technology', in OECD, *Information Technology and New Growth Opportunities*, Paris: Organisation for Economic Co-operation and Development.

Arnum, E. and Conti, S. (1998), 'Internet Deployment Worldwide: the New Superhighway Follows the Old Wires, Rails, and Roads', URL: http://www.isoc.org/inet98/ proceedings/5c/5c_5.htm (accessed October 28, 1998).

Aron, D.J., K. Dunmore, and F. Pampush (1998), 'Worldwide wait? How the Telecom Act's unbundling requirements slow the development of the network infrastructure', *Industrial and Corporate Change*, **7**, 615–21.

Arthur, W.B. (1999), 'Complexity and the economy", *Science*, **284** (2 April), 107–9.

Bar, F., M. Borrus, S. Cohen, and J. Zysman (1989), 'The evolution and growth potential of electronics-based technologies', *Science Technology Industry (STI) Review*, **5**, 7–58.

Blanc, H. and C. Sierra (1999), 'The internationalisation of R&D by multinationals: a trade-off between external and internal proximity", *Cambridge Journal of Economics*, **23**, 187–206.

Boardwatch (1999), *Maximum Dedicated Bandwidths*, URL: http://boardwatch.internet.com/isp/summer99/bandwidth. html

Boden, D. and H.L. Molotch (1994), 'The Compulsion of Proximity', in R. Friedland and D. Boden (eds), *NowHere: Space, Time, Modernity*, Berkeley: University of California Press.

Brenner, N. (1999), 'Globalisation as reterritorialisation: the re-scaling of urban governance in the European Union', *Urban Studies*, **36**, 431–51.

Brown, J.S. and P. Duguid (1998), 'Organizing Knowledge', *California Management Review*, **40** (3), 90–111.

Cairncross, F. (1996), *The Death of Distance*, Boston, MA: Harvard Business School Press.

Carey, J. (1999), 'The First 100 Feet for Households: Consumer Adoption Patterns', in D. Hurley and J.H. Keller (eds), *The First 100 Feet: Options for Internet and Broadband Access*, Cambridge, MA: MIT Press.

Castells, M. (1989), *The Informational City*, Oxford: Blackwell.

Castells, M. (1996), *The Rise of the Network Society*, Oxford: Blackwell.

Chen, K. (1999), 'OK, You Can Come In, But You Can't Use the Bathroom Alone', *Wall Street Journal*, March 5, A1.

Chesbrough, H.W. and D.J. Teece (1996), 'When is virtual virtuous? Organizing for innovation', *Harvard Business Review*, **74**, (1), 65–73.

Cooke, P. and K. Morgan (1998), *The Associational Economy: Firms, Regions, and Innovation*, Oxford: Oxford University Press.

Crevoisier, O. (1999), 'Innovation and the City', in E.J. Malecki and P. Oinas (eds), *Making Connections: Technological Learning and Regional Economic Change*, Aldershot: Ashgate.

Cusumano, M.A. and D.B. Yoffie (1998), *Competing on Internet Time*, New York: Free Press.

Dalum, B., B. Johnson and B.-Å. Lundvall (1992), 'Public Policy in the Learning Society', in B.-Å. Lundvall (ed.), *National Systems of Innovation: Towards a Theory of Innovation and Interactive Learning*, London: Pinter.

Egan, B.L. (1998), 'Improving Rural Telecommunications Infrastructure', in D. Freshwater (ed.), *Rural America at the Crossroads: Networking for the Future (OTA Follow-Up Report)*, Lexington, KY: TVA Rural Studies, URL: http://www.rural.org/workshops/rural_telecom/egan/

Eliasson, G. (1988), *The Knowledge Base of an Industrial Economy*, Stockholm: Industrial Institute for Economic and Social Research.

Eliasson, G., S. Fölster, T. Lindberg, T. Pousette and E. Taymaz (1990), *The Knowledge Based Information Economy*, Stockholm: Industrial Institute for Economic and Social Research.

Eskelinen, H. (ed.) (1997), *Regional Specialisation and Local Environment – Learning and Competitiveness*, Copenhagen: NordREFO.

Evans, P.B. and T.S. Wurster (1997), 'Strategy and the new economics of information', *Harvard Business Review*, **75** (5), 71–82.

Flamm, K. (1989), 'Technological Advance and Costs: Computers Versus Communications', in R.W. Crandall and K. Flamm (eds), *Changing the Rules: Technological Change, International Competition and Regulation in Communications*, Washington, DC: Brookings Institution.

Foray D. and B.-Å. Lundvall (1996), 'The Knowledge-Based Economy: From the Economics of Knowledge to the Learning Economy', in OECD, *Employment and Growth in the Knowledge-Based Economy*, Paris: OECD.

Freeman, C. (1996), 'The Factory of the Future and the Productivity Paradox', in W.J. Dutton (ed.), *Information and Communication Technologies: Visions and Realities*, Oxford: Oxford University Press.

Gassmann, O. and M. v. Zedtwitz (1999), 'New concepts and trends in international R&D organization', *Research Policy*, **28**, 231–50.

Geist, R.J. (1999). 'Supreme Court decision hands RBOCs defeat, makes ISP-CLEC status even more fundamental', *Boardwatch Magazine*, **13** (4), 32–6.

Gertler, M.S. (1995), 'Being there: proximity, organization, and culture in the development and adoption of advanced manufacturing technologies', *Economic Geography*, **71**, 1–26.

Gillespie, A. and J. Cornford (1996), 'Telecommunications Infrastructures and Regional Development', in W.H. Dutton (ed.), *Information and Communication Technologies: Visions and Realities*, Oxford: Oxford University Press.

Gillespie, A and K. Robins (1989), 'Geographical inequalities: the spatial bias of the new communications technologies', *Journal of Communication*, **39** (3), 7–18.

Globerman, S. (1996), 'The Information Highway and the Economy', in P. Howitt (ed.), *The Implications of Knowledge-Based Growth for Micro-Economic Policies*, Calgary: University of Calgary Press.

Gorman, S.P. (1999), 'Network Analysis of the Internet and Its Provider Networks', Unpublished Master's thesis, University of Florida, Department of Geography.

Graham, S. and S. Marvin (1996), *Telecommunications and the City: Electronic Spaces, Urban Places*, London: Routledge.

Grant, R.M. (1996), 'Toward a knowledge-based theory of the firm', *Strategic Management Journal*, **17** (Winter), 109–22.

Gregg, K.M. (1992), 'The status of ISDN in the USA', *Telecommunications Policy*, **16**, 425–39.

Haggett, P. and R. Chorley (1969), *Network Analysis in Geography*, London: Methuen.

Hardill, I., D. Fletcher and S. Montagné-Villette (1995), 'Small firms' "distinctive capabilities" and the socioeconomic milieu: findings from case studies in le Choletais (France) and the East Midlands (UK)', *Entrepreneurship and Regional Development*, **7**, 167–86.

Harris, R.G. (1998), 'The Internet as a GPT: Factor Market Implications', in E. Helpman (ed.), *General Purpose Technologies and Economic Growth*, Cambridge, MA: MIT Press.

Henry N., S. Pinch and S. Russell (1996), 'In pole position? Untraded interdependencies, new industrial spaces and the British motor sport industry', *Area*, **28**, 25–36.

Hepworth, M. (1989), *Geography of the Information Economy*, London: Belhaven Press.

Howells, J. and M. Wood (1993), *The Globalisation of Production and Technology*, London: Belhaven Press.

Hudson, R. (1999), 'The learning economy, the learning firm and the learning region: a sympathetic critique of the limits to learning', *European Urban and Regional Studies*, **6**, 59–72.

Humphries, C. (1996), 'The Territorialisation of Public Policies: The Role of Public Governance and Funding', in OECD, *Networks of Enterprises and Local Development: Competing and Co-operating in Local Productive Systems*, Paris: Organisation for Economic Co-operation and Development.

Hurley, D. and J.H. Keller (eds) (1999), *The First 100 Feet: Options for Internet and Broadband Access*, Cambridge, MA: MIT Press.
Huston, G. (1999), *ISP Survival Guide*, New York: John Wiley.
Jacobs, D. (1998), 'Innovation policies within the framework of internationalization', *Research Policy*, **27**, 711–24.
Kasarda, J.D. and D.A. Rondinelli (1998), 'Innovative infrastructure for agile manufacturers', *Sloan Management Review*, **39** (2), 73–82.
Kavassalis, P., R.J. Solomon and P.J. Benghozi (1996), 'The Internet: a paradigmatic rupture in cumulative telecom evolution', *Industrial and Corporate Change*, **5**, 1097–126.
Kellerman, A. (1997), 'Fusions of information types, media and operators, and continued American leadership in telecommunications', *Telecommunications Policy*, **21**, 553–64.
Kelly, K. (1998), *New Rules for the New Economy*, New York: Viking.
King, R. (1999), 'Too much long distance', *Fortune*, **139** (5) (March 15), 106 – 10.
Kitchin, R.M. (1998), 'Towards geographies of cyberspace', *Progress in Human Geography*, **22**, 385–406.
Lagendijk, A. (1999), 'The emergence of knowledge-oriented forms of regional policy in Europe', *Tijdschrift voor Economische en Sociale Geografie*, **90**, 110–16.
Langdale, J.V. (1983), 'Competition in the United States long distance telecommunications industry', *Regional Studies*, **17**, 393–409.
Langdale, J.V. (1989), 'The geography of international business telecommunications: the role of leased networks', *Annals of the Association of American Geographers*, **79**, 501–22.
Lawless, P. and T. Gore (1999), 'Urban regeneration and transport investment: a case study of Sheffield 1992–96', *Urban Studies*, **36,** 527–45.
Lawson, C. (1999), 'Towards a competence theory of the region', *Cambridge Journal of Economics*, **23,** 151–66.
Lawton Smith, H. (1998), 'Barriers to technology transfer: local impediments in Oxfordshire', *Environment and Planning C: Government and Policy*, **16**, 433–48.
Leo, E. and P. Huber (1997). 'The incidental, accidental deregulation of data and everything else', *Industrial and Corporate Change*, **6**, 807–28.
Lipsey, R.G., C. Bekar and K. Carlaw (1998), 'What Requires Explanation?' in E. Helpman (ed.), *General Purpose Technologies and Economic Growth*, Cambridge, MA: MIT Press.
Longcore, T. and P. Rees (1996), 'Information technology and downtown restructuring: the case of New York's financial district', *Urban Geography*, **17**, 354–72.
Lu, H.-L., I. Faynberg, A. Toubassi, F. Lucas and F. Renon (1998), 'Network evolution in the context of the global information infrastructure', *IEEE Communications Magazine*, **36** (8), 98–102.
Lundvall, B.-Å. and B. Johnson (1994), 'The Learning Economy", *Journal of Industry Studies*, **1** (2), 23–42.
Maillat D. (1995), 'Territorial dynamic, innovative milieus and regional policy', *Entrepreneurship and Regional Development*, **7**, 157–65.
Maillat D. (1996), 'Regional Productive Systems and Innovative Milieux', in OECD, *Networks of Enterprises and Local Development: Competing and Co-operating in Local Productive Systems*, Paris: OECD.

Maillat D. (1998), 'From the industrial district to the innovative milieu: contribution to an analysis of territorialised productive organisations', *Recherches Economiques de Louvain*, **64** (1), 111–29.

Majumdar, S.K. (1995), 'Does technology adoption pay? Electronic switching patterns and firm-level performance in US telecommunications', *Research Policy*, **24**, 803–22.

Majumdar, S.K. (1997), 'Modularity and productivity: assessing the impact of digital technology in the U.S. telecommunications industry', *Technological Forecasting and Social Change*, **56**, 61–75.

Malecki, E.J. (1996), 'Technology, Competitiveness, and Flexibility: Constantly Evolving Concepts', in D.C. Knudsen (ed.), *The Transition to Flexibility*, Boston: Kluwer Academic.

Malecki, E.J. (1997a), 'Telecommunications Technology and Business Location: A Review', in J. Schmidt (ed.), *Rural Infrastructure as a Cause and Consequence of Rural Economic Development and Quality of Life* (SERA-IEG-16), Mississippi State, MS: Southern Rural Development Center.

Malecki, E.J. (1997b), 'Technology in the Process of Regional Development: Issues Raised by Telematics', in B. Jaeger and K. Storgaard (eds), *Telematics and Rural Development*, Bornholm, Denmark: Research Centre of Bornholm.

Malecki, E.J. (1998), 'Telecommunications Technology and American Rural Development in the 21st Century', in D. Freshwater (ed.), *Rural America at the Crossroads: Networking for the Future*: *OTA Follow-Up Conference Report*, Lexington, KY: TVA Rural Studies, URL: http://www.rural.org/workshops/rural_telecom/ malecki/

Malecki, E.J. and C.R. Boush (1999), 'Digital Telecommunications Technologies in the Rural South: An Analysis of Tennessee', in P. Stenberg (ed.), *Proceedings of the Workshop on Rural Telecommunications*, Corvallis, OR: Western Rural Development Center.

Malmberg, A., Ö. Sölvell and I. Zander (1996), 'Spatial clustering, local accumulation of knowledge and firm competitiveness', *Geografiska Annaler*, **78B**, 85–97.

Maskell, P., H. Eskelinen, I. Hannibalsson, A. Malmberg and E. Vatne (1998), *Competitiveness, Localised Learning and Regional Development: Specialisation and Prosperity in Small Open Economies*, London: Routledge.

Maskell P. and A. Malmberg (1999), 'Localised learning and industrial competitiveness', *Cambridge Journal of Economics*, **23**, 167–85.

Mehta, S.N. (1999), 'In Phones, the New Number is Four', *Wall Street Journal*, March 8, B1, B10.

Mendelson, H. and R.R. Pillai (1999), 'Information age organizations, dynamics and performance', *Journal of Economic Behavior and Organization*, **38**, 253–81.

Mitchell, W. (1995), *City of Bits: Space, Place and the Infobahn*, Cambridge, MA: MIT Press.

Morgan, S. (1998), 'The Internet and the local telephone network: conflicts and opportunities', *IEEE Communications Magazine*, **36** (1), 42–8.

Moss, M.L. (1998), 'Technology and Cities', *Cityscape* **3** (3), 107–27.

Moss, M.L. and A.M. Townsend (1998), 'Spatial Analysis of the Internet in U.S. Cities and States', paper prepared for the 'Technological Futures – Urban Futures' Conference, Durham, England, April 1998; URL: http://urban.nyu.edu/research/newcastle/newcastle.html

Nguyen, G.D. and D. Phan (1998), 'Learning and the Diffusion of the Digital Paradigm in Information and Communication Technology', in S. Macdonald and G. Madden (eds), *Telecommunications and Socio-Economic Development*, Amsterdam: Elsevier.

Nielsen, N.C. (1996), 'The Concept of Technological Service Infrastructures: Innovation and the Creation of Good Jobs', in OECD, *Employment and Growth in the Knowledge-Based Economy,* Paris: OECD.

Northern Telecom (1998a), *Nortel Networks ISP Partner Program:storming the local exchange: strategies and options for becoming a CLEC,* URL: http://www1.nortelnetworks.com/pcn/isp/goals/goals.htm

Northern Telecom (1998b), *Nortel Networks ISP Partner Program: high-speed access: xDSL and other alternatives for last mile access,* URL: http://www1.nortelnetworks.com/pcn/isp/goals/hispeed.htm.

O'Brien, R. (1992), *Global Financial Integration: The End of Geography*, London: Pinter.

O'Keefe, S. (1998), 'While RBOCs drag their heels, CLECs, ISPs mean business', *Telecommunications Online*, December, URL: http://www.telecommagazine.com/issues/199812/tcs/okeefe.htm

O'Malley, C. (1999), 'The Digital Divide: Small Towns That Lack High- speed Internet Access Find it Harder to Attract New Jobs', *Time*, March 22, URL: http://cgi.pathfinder.com/time/magazine/articles/0,3266,21491,00.

Odlyzko, A. (1998), 'The Internet and other networks: utilization rates and their implications', URL: http://www.research.att.com/~amo/doc/internet.rates.pdf

OECD (1996), *Employment and Growth in the Knowledge-based Economy*, Paris: OECD.

Oinas, P. and E.J. Malecki (1999), 'Spatial Innovation Systems", in E.J. Malecki and P. Oinas (eds), *Making Connections: Technological Learning and Regional Economic Change*, Aldershot: Ashgate.

Paltridge, S. (1998a), *Internet Infrastructure Indicators*, Paris: OECD, URL: http://www.oecd.org/dsti/sti/it/cm/prod/ tisp98-7e.htm

Paltridge, S. (1998b), *Internet Traffic Exchange: Developments and Policy*, Paris: OECD, URL: http://www.oecd.org/dsti/sti/it/cm/prod/traffic.htm

Peitchinis, S.G. (1992), 'Computer technology and the location of economic activity', *Futures*, **24**, 813–20.

Pinch, S. and N. Henry (1999), 'Discursive aspects of technological innovation: the case of the British motor-sport industry, *Environment and Planning A*, **31**, 665–82.

Porter, M.E. (1998a), 'Clusters and Competition: New Agendas for Companies, Governments, and Institutions', in M.E. Porter, *On Competition*, Boston: Harvard Business School Press.

Porter, M.E. (1998b), 'Competing Across Locations: Enhancing Competitive Advantage Through a Global Strategy', in M.E. Porter, *On Competition*, Boston: Harvard Business School Press.

Quinn, J.B. (1992), *Intelligent Enterprise*, New York: Free Press.

Rosenfeld, S. (1997), 'Bringing business clusters into the mainstream of economic development', *European Planning Studies*, **5**, 3–23.

Salomon, I. (1996), 'Telecommunications, cities and technological opportunism', *Annals of Regional Science*, **30**, 75–90.

Sampler, J. (1998), 'Redefining industry structure for the information age', *Strategic Management Journal*, **19**, 343–55.

Schiller, D. (1999), *Digital Capitalism: Networking the Global Market System*, Cambridge, MA: MIT Press.

Schoen, U., J. Hamann, A. Jugel, H. Kurzawa and C. Schmidt (1998), 'Convergence between public switching and the internet', *IEEE Communications Magazine*, **36** (1), 50–65.

Schoenberger, E. (1998), 'Science and everyday life', *Environment and Planning A*, **30**, 575–76.

Scott, A.J. (1998), *Regions and the World Economy: The Coming Shape of Global Production, Competition, and Political Order*, New York: Oxford University Press.

Shapiro, C. and H.R. Varian (1998), 'Variationing: the smart way to sell informationi, *Harvard Business Review*, **76** (6), 106–14.

Storper, M. (1995), 'The resurgence of regional economies, ten years later: the region as a nexus of untraded interdependencies', *European Urban and Regional Studies*, **2**, 191–221.

Swyngedouw, E.A. (1992), 'The Mammon Quest: "Glocalisation", Interspatial Competition and the New Monetary Order: The Construction of New Scales', in M. Dunford and G. Kaflakas (eds), *Cities and Regions in the New Europe*, London: Belhaven.

Teece, D.J. (1998), 'Capturing value from knowledge assets: the new economy, markets for know-how, and intangible assets', *California Management Review*, **40** (3), 55–79.

von Hippel, E. (1994), 'Sticky Information and the locus of problem solving: implications for innovation', *Management Science*, **40**, 429–39.

von Hippel, E. (1998), 'Economics of product development by users: the impact of "Sticky" local information', *Management Science*, **44**, 629–44.

Ypsilanti, D. and T. Kelly (1994), 'Fostering Telecommunications Development: the Role of the OECD', in C. Steinfield, J.M. Bauer and L. Caby (eds), *Telecommunications in Transition: Policies, Services and Technologies in the European Community*, Thousand Oaks, CA: Sage.

4. Nomadic Firms in a Network Economy: Comparative Analysis and Policy Perspectives

Frank Bruinsma, Cees Gorter and Peter Nijkamp

1 INTRODUCTION

The location behaviour of modern multi-plant firms appears to exhibit increasingly a flexible mobility pattern with a strong tendency towards footlooseness. The spatial–economic dynamics – often across the border – of such firms is sometimes encapsulated in the term 'nomadic firms'. This chapter addresses the issue of nomadic behaviour of firms against the background of an emerging network economy. It sets out to formulate and test a series of relevant hypotheses of spatial relocation behaviour of international firms in a globalising network economy.

The analytical framework is examined by means of empirical data originating from a field study among actual or potential nomadic firms, in both The Netherlands and abroad. Infrastructure quality and geographical accessibility appear to play an important role in spatial relocation decisions, but also opportunity-seeking behaviour of multinational firms has a prominent place in nomadic behaviour. The results of the structured interview rounds among various international firms are next more rigorously analysed by using a recently developed method for qualitative classification and explanation, namely rough set analysis. The results from the latter method confirm to a large extent our previous findings. The chapter concludes with lessons for infrastructure policy.

2 SETTING THE SCENE

The past decade has witnessed an avalanche of changes in industrial organisation, both locally and globally. The face and position of modern industry has drastically altered. Business linkages have since the 1980s increasingly assumed the form of internationally (or interregionally) operating industrial networks (see for a review Von Raesfeld Meyer, 1997; Schachar and Öberg, 1990). The drive towards a network economy has exerted a profound impact on the volume and structure of international trade and service delivery (containerisation, outsourcing, back to core business and so on). In addition to shifts in the internal–external *network* configurations of modern firms, we also observe that the role of transaction costs for intermediate deliveries and intra-firm decision-making is gaining much more importance (see Williamson, 1979, and, for a more recent review, Castells, 1996).

The economic organisation of modern industries can, in principle, be characterised by three alternative archetypes, namely *market*, *hierarchy* and *networks* (see for an overview Lagendijk, 1993; Nijkamp and Vermond, 1996). A market configuration takes for granted that a firm buys its necessary inputs in a competitive way from other producers as intermediate goods on the market, thus incurring high risks and transaction costs of ad hoc contracts. A hierarchy is an organisational structure where (a significant part of) the industrial production is carried out under the control or inside the own corporation. And finally, a network is an organised industrial structure characterised by exchange relations between actors based on business interactions and mutual linkages (see for an extensive description Hakansson, 1987). In recent years we have seen a significant shift towards network structures at different geographical levels, ranging from local to global, largely as a result of ICT forces (see Button, Nijkamp and Priemus, 1998; Dicken, 1986).

Network theory and analysis have recently become also a fashionable research topic in geography, regional science and transportation science (see also Nagurney, 1993). Networks are essentially an intermediate form between the market and the hierarchical industrial structure (see Davidson, 1995). The benefits of an industrial network to the actors involved originate from value-added creating synergy as a result of economic complementarity in the activities of firms and their interactions (see also Nijkamp and Reggiani, 1998). Efficiency is then enhanced by a combination of both competition and cooperation inside the network, supported by high quality communication potentials and regular interactions among interdependent partners (see also Kamann and Nijkamp, 1993). Thorelli (1986) and Hakansson (1987) emphasise in particular the long-lasting structural effects of a network, even though the individual firms' position in a network may change; this position is a market asset built up by investments in manpower, communication time and scarce financial means (see also Hinterhuber and Levin, 1994). It should be added here that networks may exhibit different structural forms: vertical, horizontal or diagonal, depending on the firm's internal organisation and competence as well as on the external market conditions (see also Storper, 1996).

The drive towards an industrial network economy has been accompanied by a drastic change in the spatial–economic position of cities, regions and nations all over the world. There has been a complex and turbulent movement induced by indigenous growth and spatial connectivity, which has influenced the internal functioning of cities and regions and which has also placed network infrastructure in the centre of spatial dynamics (see also Castells, 1985). Consequently, structural change and differential dynamics (a simultaneous occurrence of slow and fast motion) have become a major feature of modern economies at all spatial levels, while stability is nowadays increasingly substituted for spatial–temporal transformation. Structure is increasingly replaced by fluidity.

After the era of the Industrial Revolution in the second part of the nineteenth century which was marked by new ways of organising production and transport on the basis of new technological innovations favouring large-scale production for an opening world market, we observe in the last part of the twentieth century a new phase in the history of our developed world, namely a *Network Revolution* marked by interconnected modes of production and by transport and communication processes based on neo-Fordist types of production (see for a review Lagendijk, 1993). As a result, we observe nowadays drastic changes in the spatial–economic, sectoral and organisational structures of modern industries, especially in sectors dominated by technological innovation (compare also Dicken, 1986; Storper, 1996; Thwaites, 1978).

Fluidity and mobility have become the landmark of modern networked firms in a Schumpeterian era, where innovation and economic transformation are the characteristics of competitive opportunity seekers. As a result, research in industrial dynamics has gained much popularity in the past decade (see for a review also Bertuglia, Lombardo and Nijkamp, 1997).

Particularly in a European context this industrial transformation process has a pronounced meaning, as the European unification process and the opening up of Central and Eastern Europe as low-wage countries have shaped the conditions for a mobile and fluid network economy. The increasingly free exchange of persons, commodities and capital has far-reaching implications for intra-European trade and transport. The introduction of the European Monetary Union will reinforce the tendency toward further spatio-economic integration (see Fischer and Nijkamp, 1999). Recent policy documents show that trade and transport in Europe may be looked at from three partly complementary, partly competing policy angles: the need for *competitive efficiency*, the need for *geographical accessibility* of all regions in Europe, and the need for an *environmentally sustainable development* (see also Reggiani, Nijkamp and Bolis, 1997). These three issues will now be discussed succinctly.

Competitive efficiency is at the heart of current European transport policy, where massive investments in Trans European Networks (TENs) and in missing European links serve to support the goal of economic and geographical integration. But also at local, metropolitan and regional scales formidable investment efforts are foreseen in order for main players to survive in a competitive world market based on global networks. Efficiently operating transport networks in the former segmented European space-economy are critical success factors for the competitive edge of Europe in a global setting. This European network policy will undoubtedly stimulate more mobility, both of persons and of goods.

There is also a major concern on geographical accessibility of less central regions in Europe. The low density of transportation in many rural and peripheral areas has been a permanent source of concern for public authorities, from the viewpoint of both the service quality offered by public transport operators and the objectives set for regional development. A look at the historical development of European infrastructure networks (road, rail, air, waterways) makes immediately clear that the most important links were first constructed between major centres of economic activity. The connections with rural and peripheral areas were in all cases delayed and usually less developed. This situation still holds true for most Central and East European regions. This is a clear case where efficiency motives and equity motives are in conflict with one another. In the emerging European welfare states, however, the rights of the rural and peripheral areas have been recognised as legitimate claims, even though the economic feasibility of such low density connections was often debatable. Clearly, the equity argument – often reinforced by the 'generative' argument (that is an infrastructure – once constructed – will attract new activities) – has played a major role in the political debate on subsidies for transport for the 'mobility deprived' in remote areas.

And finally, there is a more recent major policy concern on the question of whether transport will be devastating for environmentally sustainable development. Our mobile society fulfils many socio-economic needs, but calls at the same time for social and political change in order to attain sustainable mobility (see for a review Nijkamp, Rienstra and Vleugel, 1998). Both passenger and goods transport have increased rapidly in the past years, and for the time being there is no reason to expect a change in this trend. Some European scenarios even forecast a doubling of transport flows in one generation. This development provokes intriguing questions on the external (social) costs of transport, such as congestion, pollution and safety issues (see Verhoef, 1996). Apart from local problems such as congestion or noise, the global environmental implications of transport are increasingly becoming a source of major concern (see Nijkamp, Rienstra and Vleugel, 1998).

After the above sketch of the scene which shows that industrial dynamics and transport policy are increasingly based on network developments (sometimes material, sometimes immaterial), the question arises: what is the likely mobility pattern of modern industries in the era of innovation, globalisation and networking? Will fluidity and mobility become a dominant feature in modern spatial industrial networks? After the scene offered above, the present chapter will address the issue of spatial relocation of firms from the viewpoint of internationalisation of business life. The aim of this chapter is to trace and investigate the origins of dynamic location behaviour of firms and to analyse in particular the possible implications of nomadic firm behaviour for Dutch – and European – infrastructure policy. More specifically, this research addresses on two major policy concerns: (i) what are the locational motives of footloose – and more particular – nomadic companies; and (ii) can such firms be encouraged to locate or to stay inside a country by means of an improvement of the supply of infrastructure facilities? In the present chapter, the Dutch scene will act as a background.

Important in the relationship between relocation decisions of footloose or nomadic firms and infrastructure policy is the question whether a spatial shift of such companies – often comprising the most dynamic, internationally operating, and cost-sensitive companies – does offer an early warning or signal to infrastructure planners that (part of) the transport or communication infrastructure in the overall location profile of a region or country might be sub-optimal compared to locations elsewhere (that is, abroad). The relocation behaviour of dynamic firms may also offer strategic information about future developments in the volume and direction of transport flows, about the expected transport modes to be used, and finally also about structural changes in industrial heartlands. On the basis of careful monitoring and analysis of such trends it may be possible to identify the need for new infrastructure investments as part of a regional industrial development policy.

After these introductory background observations, we will start the chapter with a concise review of evidence on footloose and nomadic (re)location behaviour of firms (Section 3). We will then proceed with a description of a microeconomic-based survey of foreign companies in The Netherlands as well as of Dutch firms with subsidiary plants abroad (Sections 4 and 5). Based on this information, the relationship between nomadic behaviour and infrastructure of a selection of international firms is analysed in greater detail using a recent qualitative classification method, that is, rough set analysis (Section 6). And finally, we conclude the chapter with some relevant policy lessons and general conclusions (Section 7).

3 NOMADIC FIRMS IN AN INTERNATIONAL ECONOMY

Section 2 has described the emergence of spatial dynamic behaviour of firms operating in complex network configurations. Clearly, in the conventional economic location literature much attention has already been given to footloose firms whose location is less dependent on the physical geography of a given area. But in recent years the term '*nomadic*' firm has become popular.

'Nomadic location' behaviour is not yet a generally accepted or widely used expression in scientific literature. The phenomenon on repeated relocation is still underinvestigated. Nevertheless, several basic principles of nomadic location behaviour can be found in recent globalisation literature and in related publications (such as network theory). A nomadic firm is a potentially repeatedly moving firm which does not have a specific local commitment to the place in a certain country (that is, it has low transaction costs for international movement). It is commonly recognised that the most important reasons why firms move abroad or establish subsidiary plants elsewhere are market expansion (preferably in emerging markets) and cost reduction (in competitive markets). Worldwide deregulation (witness for example the World Trade Organisation) and technological harmonisation trends have greatly increased the possibilities of entering new foreign markets. However, it is also noteworthy that firms are increasingly confronted with foreign competitors on their own home markets. To survive in this global race characterised by international competition, firms are forced to economise and to grow in order to benefit from scale and scope advantages. Large firms are, for instance, able to reduce the share of their R&D expenditure per product by allocating them over larger product volumes (economies of scale). In view of severe competition, firms also have to optimise their production process by strict cost reduction strategies. This optimisation of the production process may also prompt a relocation of activities over space. Nowadays, international firms increasingly appear to reallocate their activities on a worldwide level as a result of competitive strategic behaviour. In this relocation process, firms are of course restricted by source-related and market-related activities, but an increasing number of activities becomes more and more footloose and can, in principle, be located almost anywhere between the source and the market place. Such footloose activities are eligible candidates for adopting nomadic location behaviour. Significant cost reductions can, for instance, be realised by outplacement of labour-intensive production processes towards low wage countries such as East European countries and various Asian countries (see also Amin and Thrift, 1994).

Clearly, nomadic behaviour may be different for a firm as a whole, the corporate organisation or headquarters, the manufacturing plant, the logistic or distributional activities and so on. Repeated migration of entire firms –

especially those with a large size – is internationally likely less plausible. This means that nomadic behaviour has to be explained from the firm specificity, the industrial structure and the market the firm is operating in. In the context of market-related activities, significant cost reductions can often be achieved by adopting sophisticated logistic principles or by introducing a large-scale distribution network such as European Distribution Centres (EDC). These activities may clearly show nomadic location behaviour: to reduce the logistics costs, the geographical location and mobility in the overall context of European infrastructure networks will then be of critical importance for their competitive position.

Nomadic firms will in general not be rooted deeply in a given area; their activities need not necessarily be regionally embedded. As a consequence, new fixed capital investments in a given place (which will usually reduce geographical mobility) will be kept at a minimum. This means that a company often prefers to start a new subsidiary instead of entering a market by a takeover or merger. It often also prefers to rent rather than to buy real estate. Finally, the company is usually less interested in offering its products for the local or regional market concerned.

In summarising the literature on nomadic behaviour, we find that international relocation behaviour may be considered to be 'nomadic', when:

- it is a temporary (re)location;
- few durable investments of a fixed or lumpy nature are involved;
- there are clear cost reductions at stake in the (re)location;
- the (re)located activities are footloose;
- the company is not clearly embedded in the local or regional economy;
- the company is part of an international industrial network producing for the international market.

Thus, nomadic companies can be characterised as 'spatial opportunity seekers'. To make a clear distinction between a nomadic (re)location and other international (re)locations, the following stylised typology of nomadic (re)locations may offer a meaningful analytical framework (see Table 4.1).

In summary, the characteristics of nomadic relocations can be categorised in a few prominent, mutually related attributes. The first aspect may be referred to as *footloose*. A limitation in the freedom to relocate at any time may stem from either large investments in real estate, education and so on (that is, high sunk costs), or from the specific nature of the production process (source- or market-related). A second feature centres around the notion of *regional embeddedness*. Nomadic companies tend to prevent regional embeddedness not only – as mentioned above – by low capital investments, but also by a low administrative or institutional embeddedness.

Table 4.1 A typology of nomadic firms vis-à-vis *other firms*

Nomadic relocation	Other relocation
– footloose company	– regionally-oriented company
– footloose activities	– source and market-related activities
– relocation across the border	– local, regional or national relocation
– creation of a new company or division	– take-over or merger
– cost reductions	– penetration into emerging market
– low capital investments	– high capital investments
– labour-intensive production	– capital-intensive production
– production for international market	– production for local/regional market
– international network orientation	– local/regional network orientation
– international transport flows	– local/regional transport flows

They often prefer to start a new company or division instead of a local or regional takeover or merger, as the latter strategy may have significant legal consequences (often constraints) in case of a next relocation. The third aspect concerns *cost reduction*. In contrast to the desire to penetrate emerging markets, cost reduction in a competitive environment is the decisive factor to relocate – part of – the company. For example, labour-intensive production processes are relocated towards low wage countries, or the assembly of final products may be concentrated in one particular location in each continent. By these means, standard products can be adjusted to continental standards (for example value added logistics in European Distribution Centres). And finally, there is the aspect of the *international* dimension. The firm is usually part of an internationally operating network of firms aiming at producing for a global market (see also Rietveld and Bruinsma, 1998).

Clearly, the above typology of attributes of nomadic firms is not entirely unambiguous; the difference between dynamic, footloose and nomadic firms is gradual. First, there is a number of *imprecisely demarcated classes*; a number of the characteristics is mutually related. Furthermore, most characteristics are not such pure contrasts as suggested in the above typology. For instance, the category 'cost reduction' is placed opposite to 'emerging markets'. In reality, a relocation may be caused by a mixture of both factors. Although cost reductions will usually be the driving relocation factor for a nomadic firm, that company will also respond to the advantages that emerging markets offer.

A second problem is the *timing of activities* in the process of international relocation decisions. In general, a company starts penetrating a market by hiring a local agent. After a number of sequential steps (outplacement of representatives, starting a sales and/or distribution network), in a final step (part of) the production activities of the company are relocated. It is reasonable to assume that also nomadic companies will use a similar strategy, while it seems unrealistic to expect that nomadic firms will spontaneously start up a new company in a completely unknown environment.

Using Table 4.1 as a starting point, we now aim to test the importance of nomadic behaviour in an international network economy by addressing the question whether there is evidence in recent (re)location behaviour of international firms that supports a rise in nomadic trends of firms. On the basis of this question infrastructure policy implications are also addressed. The next section is devoted to the provision of some empirical data on nomadic behaviour of firms.

4 SOME EMPIRICAL FACTS ON NOMADIC FIRMS

The existence and order of magnitude of nomadic behaviour cannot properly be identified and investigated by means of current statistics. One needs to investigate more thoroughly the determinants of firms' relocation behaviour from a micro perspective. This is the subject of the present section, in which first a systematic selection framework for nomadic firms is described. This framework is based on the observation that for meaningful relocation research on nomadic firms both the country of origin of the firm and its country of destination have to be considered (see Table 4.2).

Table 4.2 Relocation of firms by country of origin and destination

Country of destination / Origin of firms	The Netherlands	Abroad
Dutch companies	I	II
Foreign companies	III	IV

The first quadrant (I) concerns Dutch firms relocating within The Netherlands and is of no interest for the present research endeavour focused on multinational nomadic firms (except for the very rare cases of Dutch firms operating overseas that establish branches back in The Netherlands). Moreover, in the past years, abundant knowledge has already been gathered on such intra-country relocations. The second and the third quadrant concern Dutch companies moving towards a location abroad and foreign firms locating in The Netherlands, respectively. Not all these relocations are necessarily nomadic. For example, we might have a single relocation leading to a fixed settlement of the firm, and not necessarily followed by another cross-border relocation in a foreseeable period of time. This restriction does not hold for quadrant IV, which contains foreign firms migrating into The Netherlands but relocating after some time out of the country again. It should be noted, however, that in our empirical research we were able to trace only one such dynamic company belonging to this quadrant.

After the description of the analysis framework in Table 4.2, we shall now proceed with our empirical work. To examine the impacts of the relocation of foreign companies into The Netherlands and of Dutch companies abroad on cross-border transport flows and related infrastructure demands of these firms, various companies have been identified and interviewed. By using a structured questionnaire, a wealth of relevant systematic information could be collected. The following distribution of nomadic firms has been deployed for our empirical analysis (see Table 4.3).

The firms listed in Table 4.3 belong to quadrants II or III of Table 4.2. These are footloose firms with nomadic features and have been selected from the general business register of the Chambers of Commerce in The Netherlands. All selected companies were characterised by a recent relocation (after 1990). Clearly, the sample does not cover the whole population of nomadic firms, but contains at least important decisions, for example from American and Japanese firms and for Dutch firms moving to East Europe. The foreign companies in The Netherlands (that is, quadrant III) appear to be service-oriented firms located in the central urban area of The Netherlands (Randstad) and industrial firms located in areas in the vicinity of the Randstad (compare also Nijkamp and Rienstra, 1998). First, they were asked to fill out a survey questionnaire in which they could express their views on the importance of some 40 locational factors for their company as well as the attractiveness score for The Netherlands as a whole on these factors. The scores were given on a five-point scale, for both the time period of their initial location decision in The Netherlands and for the actual present situation. This double check was made, since the importance of some of the locational factors for the firm's activities might have changed since its location in The Netherlands. The same holds for the score of The Netherlands as a whole on these location factors. After the survey questionnaires were returned, the firms were personally interviewed. In the interviews the following items were addressed in particular: general company characteristics, the company network structure, location motives, development of transport flows (inward and outward), and the infrastructure use and demand by the company.

For quadrant II of Table 4.2, the attention was particularly focused on Dutch firms in Poland, as this country has recently begun to be regarded as a new springboard for Central and East Europe.

Table 4.3 List of interviewed nomadic firms

Foreign companies in The Netherlands
– 4 North-American service-oriented companies
– 2 North-American manufacturing companies
– 3 Japanese service-oriented companies
– 3 Japanese manufacturing companies
Dutch companies abroad
– 3 trade companies in Poland
– 2 transport companies in Poland
– 2 service-oriented companies in Poland
– 1 service-oriented company in England
– 1 service-oriented company in Ireland

The Polish pilot study was conducted to analyse the impact of Dutch firms relocating toward a region abroad. In addition, also some control telephone interviews were held with a foreign company (a truly nomadic company with repeated relocation behaviour) recently relocated from The Netherlands to England and a Dutch firm that had decided to relocate the majority of its activities to Ireland.

All Dutch companies interviewed in Poland are located in the Warsaw urban area, which is the major booming area in Poland. These firms were asked to fill out a similar questionnaire on the importance of 40 locational factors comparable to those completed by the foreign firms concerned in The Netherlands. The only difference is that they were asked to give the scores for both The Netherlands and Poland for all relevant factors at the time of relocation. In the personal interviews the same items were the subject of discussion, but greater emphasis was laid on the changes in transport flows (volumes and directions related to The Netherlands) caused by the firm's relocation to Poland.

Both the survey questionnaires and the structured interviews generated a wealth of relevant information, partly of a quantitative and partly of a qualitative nature. The main results will now be discussed in the next section.

5 RESULTS OF THE COMPANY SURVEYS

In our presentation of the results of both the survey questionnaires and the interview rounds we address in particular three issues, namely the *company structure*, the *transportation factors* and the *(re)location motives*, successively.

5.1 Company Structure

Seven of the twelve foreign companies located in The Netherlands and investigated in our empirical analysis appeared to concern European headquarters of the company. In Poland none of the Dutch firms under consideration is a European headquarter, although for six of the seven companies, the Dutch parent company forms the European headquarters.

Table 4.4 offers some interesting empirical insights. The network structure of all foreign companies is at least European; however, only two of the Dutch companies in Poland are part of a worldwide company network. From both types of firms in our survey (that is, quadrants II and III from Table 4.2) it turned out that the companies are completely new subsidiaries. Only one case concerns a takeover of an already existing company. Another common feature of firms in class II and III is the preference for rented premises. Only some 25 per cent of the firms possesses its own accommodation and real estate. These companies are either manufacturing companies or transport companies. It seems from our empirical investigation that more land-use extensive companies tend to posses their own company real estate. The land-use intensive companies, however, needing for example office buildings, seem to prefer to rent real estate.

Table 4.4 Distribution and features of nomadic firms

Company structure and feature	Foreign companies in The Netherlands	Dutch companies in Poland
European headquarters	7	0 (6)*
European network	12	7
World-wide network	12	2
New company	11	7
Rented premise	8	5

Note: In six cases the Dutch parent company is the European headquarters.

Most relocations are apparently the result of an expansion of existing activities abroad. This does not necessarily mean however, that those activities were discontinued in the country of origin. It is important to mention that firms from both classes II and III show that only minor adjustments are made to accommodate the product to the demands of the new market. Those minor adjustments consist mainly of regrouping, repacking or adding guidelines for use in the correct languages.

A major difference between classes II and III is that foreign firms in The Netherlands have hardly changed their activities, whereas Dutch companies in

Poland have increased the range of their activities to a large extent. Foreign companies in The Netherlands have to serve an apparently mature European market, whereas the emerging East European market in transition offers many unexploited opportunities. The wish of many Dutch companies to have their own – Dutch – management available to them and working with them in Poland, seems largely instigated by their wish to exploit these new opportunities which might not be judged to be sufficiently and effectively ensured by local managers in the host country.

5.2 Demand for Transport Systems

In our investigation of the relevance of transport systems for nomadic firms, both types of classes from Table 4.2 in our survey point in the same direction. Intercontinental freight flows are transported either by sea or by air. The distribution within Europe takes place by road, except for special deliveries, high value products, and/or spare materials which are often transported by air. Rail and inland waterway infrastructure seem to be of marginal importance for nomadic firms according to the results of our surveys. However, one should remember that none of the companies surveyed generates flows of low-value bulk products; for such products, rail and inland waterway infrastructures are often used.

There are, however, a number of differences between foreign companies located in The Netherlands and Dutch companies located in Poland. Whereas American and Japanese firms in The Netherlands largely generate their own activities and trade flows, Dutch companies in Poland are strongly linked to and dependent on their Dutch parent company. American and Japanese companies appear to develop their own trade flows for independent producers outside of their network structure. The Dutch companies in Poland however, are dependent on goods flows which are generated and directed by the parent company. Dutch parent companies appear to collect almost all inputs and components and distribute those goods to their subsidiary firms in Poland. This spatial pattern of collection and distribution by the parent company can partially be explained by the explicit company policy to keep stocks in Poland low, in particular since taxes and customs duties must be paid immediately at the Polish border.

Another important difference between American and Japanese companies in The Netherlands on the one hand and Dutch companies in Poland on the other is that the market area of the first class comprises all of Europe, whereas the market area of the latter is mainly in Poland and its East European neighbours. Only in the long term do the Dutch companies in Poland intend to expand their activities by opening new subsidiary firms in, for instance, Russia. Clearly, it is noteworthy that, in general, it may be difficult to attract and maintain internationally operating firms in The Netherlands, since the market area clearly exceeds clearly the small size area of The Netherlands. The large consumer markets for those internationally operating firms are predominantly Germany, France and the United Kingdom. However, a number of companies stated that from a strategic point of view, it is an advantage to be located in a relatively small consumer market in Europe: none of the large consumer markets can claim that the company is competitively located in their home markets; and even more importantly, none of the large consumer markets can complain that the company is located in another large consumer market instead of their own home market. Thus, from a strategic competitive viewpoint a small country may also have advantages for a nomadic firm.

5.3 Location Motives

In both case studies related to quadrants II and III of Table 4.2 the main aim of the companies investigated to relocate across the border is to expand their activities in an emerging market. All companies stated that both the expansion and the entrance into the new market have been successful; so there is apparently a low tendency to relocate the subsidiary firm once more. Apparently, nomadic tendencies are mitigated by market success.

The entrance of companies into the Northwestern European market is of a different magnitude compared to the entrance into the East-European market. The Northwestern European market is a developed, mature market close to the point of saturation for standard products, whereas the East European market is a young, undeveloped market in a phase of rapid transition. The particular advantages of the Polish market are the relatively stable economic and political climate. The Polish market is also a good frontier market for expanding into other East-European markets, although the recent recession in Russia tends to make Western firms more hesitant.

The entrepreneurial demands concerning the location profile of a region are rather diverse in the case studies related to quadrants II and III. In Poland the entrepreneurs require a stable political, economic, financial – notably currency exchange – climate and low wages. The underdeveloped infrastructure network, inefficient customs facilities and bureaucratic legislation and so on do not severely restrain Dutch companies from locating in Poland. In regard to the second class of case studies, that is, a location in The Netherlands, the prerequisites of American and Japanese companies are more stringent. They make their locational choice based on a favourable locational profile like legislation, accessibility to various types of infrastructure networks, fast customs facilities offered, and so on. Clearly, if The Netherlands were unable to fulfil such wishes, these companies would decide relatively easily to relocate to another country within North-western Europe. The decision to relocate from The Netherlands to countries such as Belgium, Luxembourg, Germany, and even France and the United Kingdom, seems to be easier than the decision to relocate from Poland to a Baltic state, Russia or the Ukraine.

In conclusion, locational motives of nomadic firms are rather diverse. There are common elements (such as market expansion and cost-minimising behaviour in a competitive global economy), but there are also country-specific, site-specific and sector-specific motives. This analytical issue will be further addressed in Section 6.

6 A ROUGH SET ANALYSIS FOR A COMPARISION OF LOCATIONAL DETERMINANTS OF NOMADIC FIRMS[1]

The sample of nomadic firms investigated in our field work is rather small (21). Furthermore, many of their statements on the importance of infrastructural and other factors of their locational decision – as expressed during intensive interview rounds – appeared to be rather 'soft' in nature. As a consequence, standard statistical techniques (such as logit analysis) cannot be applied here. Therefore, we will resort to a rather new mathematical approach which is suitable for small samples and which has recently been used for another comparative study of 'soft' locational factors (see Nijkamp and Rienstra 1998).

Rough set analysis is essentially a decision support tool from operations research which tries to formulate decision rules of an 'if...then' nature. Based on a multidimensional survey table of objects (alternatives, individuals, phenomena), it aims to find out which combinations of a classified set of values characterising these objects are consistent with the occurrences of a class value of a response variable. Clearly, there may be multiple decision rules that fulfil this consistency requirement. So rough set analysis seeks to trace these decision rules (based on some sort of combinatorial logic) and to identify which background variables (or attributes) are showing up in these decision rules and with which frequency. These variables are then the critical determinants of the phenomenon under investigation. More details on rough set analysis can be found in the Appendix.

In the framework of our empirical research we start with the specification of the multidimensional information table (see Table 4.5), which we have constructed on the basis of the survey questionnaires and interviews among all nomadic firms. The variables $x1$ to $x10$ are the 'explanatory' factors (attributes) which for each nomadic form determine its response variable, namely the degree of footlooseness (in contrast to source- or market-orientation) as an indicator for the question whether the firm concerned is in principle nomadic in nature. The total number of interval classes per item is 2, 3 or 4. Clearly, for each firm in our sample this information table can now be filled out by using the qualitative ('soft') information from the survey questionnaires and the interviews. Clearly, this codified table may be subject to sensitivity analysis.

Table 4.5 Multidimensional information table on the attributes of 21 nomadic firms

		Class 1	Class 2	Class 3	Class 4
Country of origin	*x1*	US	Japan	Netherlands	Other
Economic sector	*x2*	Services	Industry	Trade	Trans-port
Investment level	*x3*	– – –/– –/–	+	++/+++	
New vs. take-over/merger	*x4*	Takeover	New		
Cost reduction versus market penetration	*x5*	– – –/– –	–/0	++/+++	
Labour intensity	*x6*	–	0	+/++/+++	
Int'l production	*x7*	– –	0	+/++	+++
Int'l network	*x8*	0/+	++	+++	
Int'l freight transport	*x9*	– – –/– –/–	+/++	+++	
Goods flows	*x10*	– – –	+	++/+++	
Nomadic character	*Y*	– – –/– –/–	+	++/+++	

Following the rough set approach (see Appendix), we can now draw up the table containing all information on the minimal sets (see Table 4.6), which indicate which combination of attributes do unambiguously lead to a certain class allocation of the dependent variable, that is, nomadic behaviour. The country of origin appears to show up in the core of the decision rules, so that this is a common explanatory variable for nomadic behaviour in all cases.

Other explanatory variables with a high frequency in the decision rules are the sector comprising the firm concerned, international freight transport, the size of goods flows, the labour intensity and the degree of international production (see Table 4.7).

Table 4.6 Data table on the occurrence and composition of minimal sets in rough set analysis

Minimal sets			
{*x*1, *x*6, *x*9, *x*10}	{*x*1, *x*3, *x*5, *x*9, *x*10}	{*x*1, *x*2, *x*6, *x*7}	{*x*1, *x*2, *x*4, *x*6, *x*9}
{*x*1, *x*5, *x*7, *x*10}	{*x*1, *x*3, *x*6, *x*7, *x*10}	{*x*1, *x*2, *x*5, *x*7}	{*x*1, *x*2, *x*3, *x*4, *x*5, *x*9}

Table 4.7 Results of the rough set analysis

		Minimal set	Variable value in decision rule	Average per set	No. of classes
Country of origin	*x*1	8 (core)	86	10.8	4
Economic sector	*x*2	4	51	12.8	4
Investment level	*x*3	3	13	4.3	3
New versus take-over/merger	*x*4	2	5	2.5	2
Cost reduction vs. market penetration	*x*5	4	20	5.0	3
Labour intensity	*x*6	4	25	6.3	3
International production	*x*7	4	25	6.3	4
Int'l network	*x*8	0	–	–	3
Int'l trade	*x*9	4	23	5.8	3
Goods flows	*x*10	4	32	8.0	3

Although the country of origin is the only core variable in the model (and hence essential in explaining nomadic behaviour), it appears to need in all cases quite a few additional attributes to explain the variance in the footlooseness of firms (as is the case for economic sectors). In other words, there seems to be no simple and straightforward relationship between any country of origin and nomadic behaviour. More information about the underlying relationships can be derived from Table 4.8 by looking at the values of the explanatory variable included in the decision rules. For instance, it appears that American companies are either footloose or not. This might be explained by the fact that half of the American firms are industrial in nature, while the other half is service-oriented.

Table 4.8 Frequency of explanatory variables values included in the decision rules

		y = – – –/– –/–				y = +				y = ++/+++			
		1	2	3	4	1	2	3	4	1	2	3	4
86	Country	17		25			12			13	5	6	8
51	Sector	8	5	4	3		2			25	4		
13	Investments	1	1	5						1	2	3	
5	New/take-over						2			2	1		
20	Costs/market	6	4	5						5			
25	Labour	2	8	4						3	7	1	
25	Int'l production			2	4			4		2	2	7	4
0	Int'l network												
23	Int'l freight	1	5				2	2		3	4	6	
32	Goods flows		2	8			2	2		12		6	

As can be seen from the sectoral findings, the industry is rather inert from a spatial mobility perspective, whereas services are highly footloose. The Dutch firms in Poland are rather inert. This can also be explained by the sector composition; the Dutch firms in Poland are mainly trade and transport sector companies.

Another interesting result is that market-oriented firms are inert and that firms that produce no goods are footloose. The latter result implies that the infrastructural needs of footloose companies are low from the viewpoint of the inflow and outflow of goods.

The results of Table 4.8 appear even more pronounced in Table 4.9, in which the frequency of firms affected by the specific variable values included in the decision rules are given. For instance, it can be seen that the American, Dutch and market-oriented firms are more inert and that Japanese firms, service sector firms and firms producing no goods are even more footloose than suggested at first glance by Table 4.8.

Table 4.9 Frequency of firms affected by variable values included in the decision rules

		y = ---/--/-				y = +				y = ++/+++			
		1	2	3	4	1	2	3	4	1	2	3	4
141	Country	25		41			32			16	9	6	12
72	Sector	8	9	12	6		2			31	4		
13	Investments	1	1	5						1	2	3	
5	New/take-over						2			2	1		
27	Costs/market	6	10	5						6			
33	Labour	2	11	8						3	8	1	
40	Int'l production			2	4			16		2	2	10	4
0	Int'l network												
34	Int'l freight	1	7				6	2		4	4	10	
46	Goods flows		2	9			6	2		20		7	

Some additional findings are that labour-intensive firms are relatively established, while firms operating in an international freight transport trade network tend to be more nomadic.

The results of the rough set analysis confirm our findings (see Table 4.1) about the relationships between nomadic behaviour and the characteristics of firms. Having now discussed in mainly qualitative terms the findings from our empirical investigation of nomadic firms, it is important to suggest policy-relevant conclusions. This will be the subject matter of the next section.

7 NOMADIC BEHAVIOUR AND POLICY LESSONS

The relationship between nomadic companies and transport infrastructure has to be seen from two angles. The supply side of infrastructure is of critical importance in convincing and attracting foreign firms to locate in a specific country. More important, however, is the fulfilment of the business demand for efficient transportation of goods. For an efficient handling of the input and output of transport flows of internationally operating companies, the quality of interregional and international infrastructure networks are of critical importance. Admittedly, for commuting trips, business services and daily deliveries, the local – urban – infrastructure networks are also of primary importance. Although the quality of local infrastructure networks did not receive particular attention in our case studies, a number of Japanese and American companies stated that the accessibility of urban areas is of utmost importance for their decision to stay in The Netherlands. In particular, metropolitan accessibility seems to be a critical location factor in severely congested areas.

An efficient infrastructure policy appears to be in line with the demands of the Japanese and American companies located in The Netherlands. Several of these companies appear to constantly evaluate critically their geographical location and accessibility with a view to their access to European markets.

The trade flows of Dutch companies in Poland continue to be directed by the parent company in The Netherlands. The transport flows to Poland mainly use the road network, even though the Polish road infrastructure is of a poor quality. Only high-value goods are transported by air. However, the Dutch parent companies often buy their inputs on the world market, while the distribution towards the subsidiary companies abroad then usually takes place afterwards by road transport. This observation underlines the importance of efficient road transport corridors from The Netherlands towards the rest of Europe.

Most firms interviewed in our field work intend to expand their activities in Central and Eastern Europe in the near future, assuming that the 'Russian disease' will not affect trade significantly. If the transport flows continue to be organised by parent companies, one might expect a rapid increase in the volume of the transport flows towards Central and Eastern Europe; these flows may especially pass through the eastern area of The Netherlands. We may thus conclude that both foreign companies in The Netherlands and Dutch firms abroad highlight the importance of an effective Dutch infrastructure policy, in which much emphasis is laid on the quality of mainports and their hinterland connections.

Both case studies related to quadrants II and III of Table 4.2 show the importance nomadic companies attach to the development of the European road network. From a company perspective, in the short term a further development of the road network seems to be of utmost importance. It should be added, however, that in our empirical work no heavy industries were included, since these are not footloose. It is highly possible that for such industries, inland waterways and rail may also be important transport modes (next to pipelines).

An interesting finding of our study is that really footloose or nomadic companies exist only rarely in a pure form. There will always be some kind of physical linkage to existing transport infrastructure. Relocation of activities is only desirable when the costs of a new location – in terms of infrastructure costs – are lower than those at the old location. Next to this, the transition and sunk costs caused by the relocation might be prohibitive. Therefore, in reality there will only be a small fraction of companies operating in a purely contestable market with zero entry and exit costs which might instigate a frequent relocation of company activities. The chance of finding nomadic companies that are both footloose and have negligible transition and sunk costs is thus small. This means that even in an international network economy, pure nomadism will probably not become a phenomenon of considerable size in terms of entire physical company relocations. However, a development that may be expected is a flexible relocation in several phases. Firms may open subsidiary companies which, over time, expand their activities and gain in economic importance. In the longer term, this process will have the impact of a nomadic relocation, and can only be measured in an evolutionary sense. Research on relocations should therefore pay more attention to those incremental relocation processes. In other words, ultimately it is not the question whether pure nomadism exists that is important, but rather to what extent – given a number of relocations of certain activities – there is a process of nomadic tendencies.

Finally, transport infrastructure is only one of the important determinants of relocational decisions and of nomadism, next to other location factors, such as quality of life, labour market conditions, cost levels, and so on. Even though in some cases it may seem that the quality of the transport infrastructure network is of decisive importance, the actual location decision is normally based on a broad set of locational factors which determine the entrepreneur's choice. This is also confirmed by the results of our rough set analysis. In a saturated competitive market, 'soft' location factors such as local image and local policy might be particularly important. It might be attractive in such a market to link infrastructure advantages of a given geographical site to economic and psychological image factors of that particular location. In other words, the study of nomadic behaviour requires the analysis of a broad, multi-faceted portfolio of attributes and driving forces.

APPENDIX

Concise Description of Methodology of Rough Set Analysis

The total number of cases investigated in our study is 21 potentially nomadic companies. Clearly, this sample is not sufficient for applying standard statistical methods. Therefore, a recently developed nonparametric statistical method concerning data analysis is used. This is rough set analysis, developed by Pawlak (1991) and Slowinski (1992). We will offer here a concise introduction to rough set theory (for further details we refer to van den Bergh et al. (1997), Matarazzo and Nijkamp (1997), Baaijens and Nijkamp (1998) and Button and Nijkamp (1998)).

A rough set is a set for which it is uncertain in advance which objects belong precisely to that set, although it is in principle possible to identify all objects which may belong to the set at hand. Rough set theory takes for granted the existence of a finite set of objects for which some information is known in terms of factual (qualitative or numerical) knowledge on a class of attributes (features, characteristics). These attributes may be used to define *equivalence* relationships for these objects, so that an observer can classify objects into distinct equivalence classes. Objects in the same equivalence class are – on the basis of these features concerned – *indiscernible*. In case of multiple attributes, each attribute is associated with a different equivalence relationship. The intersection of multiple equivalence relationships is called the indiscernibility relationship with respect to the attributes concerned. This intersection generates a family of equivalence classes that is a more precise classification of the objects than that based on a single equivalence relationship. The family of equivalence classes that is generated by the intersection of all equivalence relationships is called the family of elementary sets. The classification of objects as given by the elementary sets is the most precise classification possible, on the basis of the available information.

Next, we will introduce the concept of a *reduct*. A reduct is a subset of the set of all attributes with the following characteristic: adding another attribute to a reduct does not lead to a more accurate classification of objects (that is, more granules), while elimination of an attribute from a reduct does lead to a less accurate classification of objects (that is, less granules).

Finally, the *core* of a set is the class of all indispensable equivalence relationships. An attribute is indispensable if the classification of the objects becomes less precise when that attribute is not taken into account (given the fact that all attributes have been considered until then). The core may be an empty set and is, in general, not a reduct. An indispensable element occurs in all reducts. The core is essentially the intersection of all reducts.

Based on the previous concepts, rough set theory is now able to specify various decision rules of an 'if then' nature. For specifying decision rules, it is useful to represent our prior knowledge on reality by means of an information table. An information table is a matrix that contains the values of the attributes of all objects. In an information table the attributes may be partitioned into *condition* (background) and *decision* (response) attributes. A *decision rule* is then an implication relationship between the description of the condition attributes and that of a decision attribute. Such a rule may be exact or approximate. A rule is exact if the combination of the values of the condition attributes in that rule implies only one single combination of the values of the decision attributes, while an approximate rule only states that more than one combination of values of the decision attributes corresponds to the same values of the condition attributes. Decision rules may thus be expressed as conditional statements ('if then').

In practice, it is possible to use both decision rules implied by the data contained in the information table and, if necessary, in further rules supplied and suggested by experts. The former may be accompanied by an indicator of their 'strength', for example, the frequency (absolute or relative) of events in agreement with each decision rule. Moreover, both the former and the latter rules may be based on suitable and different sets of condition attributes, containing a larger or smaller number of attributes (even a single attribute). This latter case implies that the value assumed by an attribute is sufficient to guarantee that the decision attribute (or attributes) will assume certain values, whatever the values of the other condition attributes.

Decision rules, that constitute the most relevant aspects of rough set analysis, may be directly applied to problems of *multi-attribute sorting*, that is, in the assignment of each potential object (action, project, alternative, and so on) to an appropriate predefined category according to a particular selection criterion. In this case, the classification of a new object may be usefully undertaken by a comparison between its description (reflected in the values of the condition attributes) and the values contained in the decision rules. These are more general than the information contained in the original information table and also allows a classification of new objects more easily than would be possible by using a direct comparison between the new and the original objects. In general, decision rules in rough set analysis allow conditional transferable inferences to be made, as the 'if' conditions specify the initial conditions, while the 'then' inference statements highlight the logical valid conclusions for cases outside of the initial set of objects. In this way, rough set analysis can also be used as a tool for conditional transferability of results from some case study to a new situation.

NOTE

1. The authors wish to thank Maurice Ursem for his statistical support in the rough set analysis.

REFERENCES

Amin, A. and N. Thrift (eds) (1994), *Globalisation, Institutions and Regional Development in Europe,* Oxford: Oxford University Press.

Baaijens, S., P. Nijkamp and K. Van Montford (1998), 'Explanatory meta-analysis for the comparison and transfer of regional tourist income multipliers', *Regional Studies*, **32**, 839–849.

Bergh, J.C.J.M., van den, K. Button, P. Nijkamp and G. Pepping (1997), *Meta- analysis in Environmental Economics*, Dordrecht: Kluwer.

Bertuglia, C.S., S. Lombardo and P. Nijkamp (eds) (1997), *Innovative Behaviour in Space and Time*, Berlin: Springer-Verlag.

Bruinsma, F.R., C. Gorter and P. Nijkamp (1997), *En de karavaan trok verder...*, Rotterdam: Adviesdienst Verkeer en Vervoer.

Button, K. and P. Nijkamp (1998), 'Environmental policy assessment and the usefulness of meta-analysis', *Socio-economic Planning Sciences*, **31**, 231–40.

Button, K., P. Nijkamp and H. Priemus (eds) (1998), *Transport Networks in Europe*, Cheltenham: Edward Elgar.

Castells, E. (ed.) (1985), *High Technology, Space and Society*, New York: Sage.

Castells, E. (ed.) (1996), *The Rise of the Network Society*, Oxford: Oxford University Press.

Davidson, P. (1995), 'Netwerkvorming in de Vliegtuigindustrie', Master's Thesis, Dept. of Economics, Free University, Amsterdam.

Dicken, P. (1986), *Global Shift*, London: Harper & Row.

Fischer, M.M. and P. Nijkamp (eds) (1999), *European Monetary Integration and Regional Industrial Development*, Berlin: Springer-Verlag.

Hakansson, H. (ed.) (1987), *Industrial Technological Development; A Network Approach*, Andover, Hants: Croom Helm.

Hinterhuber, H.H. and B.M. Levin (1994), 'Strategic Networks', *Long Range Planning*, June, 43–58.

Kamann, D.J. and P. Nijkamp (1993), 'Technogenesis', *Technological Forecasting and Social Change*, **39**, 35–46.

Lagendijk, A. (1993), *The Internationalisation of the Spanish Automobile Industry*, Amsterdam: Thesis Publishers.

Matarazzo, B. and P. Nijkamp (1997), 'Methodological complexity in the use of meta-analysis for empirical environmental case studies', *Journal of Social Economics*, **34**, 799–811.

Nagurney, A. (1993), *Network Economics*, Boston: Kluwer.

Nijkamp, P. and A. Reggiani (1998), *The Economics of Complex Spatial Systems*, Amsterdam: Elsevier.

Nijkamp, P. and S. Rienstra (1998), Research Chapter, Department of Spatial Economics, Free University Amsterdam.

Nijkamp, P., Rienstra and J. Vleugel (1998), *Transportation Planning and the Future*, Chichester/New York: John Wiley.

Nijkamp, P. and N. Vermond (1996), 'Scenarios on opportunities and impediments in the Asian Pacific rim', *Studies in Regional Science*, **11** (3), 1–46.

Pawlak, Z. (1991), *Rough Sets*, Dordrecht: Kluwer.

Raesfeld Meyer, A. von (1997), *Technological Cooperation in Networks*, PhD Thesis, Twente University of Technology.

Reggiani, A., P. Nijkamp and S. Bolis (1997), 'The role of transalpine freight transport in a common European Market', *Innovation*, **10** (3), 259– 275.

Rietveld, P. and F. Bruinsma (1998), *Is Transport Infrastructure Effective?: Transport Infrastructure and Accessibility; Impacts on the Space Economy*, Berlin: Springer-Verlag.

Schachar, A.. and S. Öberg (eds) (1990), *The World Economy and the Spatial Organization of Power*, Aldershot: Avebury

Slowinski, R. (1992), *Intelligent Decision Support*, Dordrecht: Kluwer.

Thorelli, H.B. (1986), 'Networks: between markets and hierarchies', *Strategic Management Journal*, **7**, 37–51.

Thwaites, A.T. (1978), 'Technological change, mobile plants and regional development', *Regional Studies*, **12**, 445–61.

Verhoef, E. (1996), *The Economics of Regulating Road Transport*, Cheltenham: Edward Elgar.

Williamson, O.E. (1979), *Markets and Hierarchies*, New York: Free Press.

5. Network Co-evolution with Cost–Benefit Rules: A Simulation Experiment

Kiyoshi Kobayashi, Makoto Okumura and Mehmet Ali Tuncer

1 INTRODUCTION

Seemingly insignificant events in history may create an urban system different from the one that exists today. In particular, the locational patterns of interaction-intensive activities such as service, finance, knowledge production, and so on follow paths that depend upon history (Kobayashi, Batten and Anderson, 1991). Agglomeration economies introduce an indeterminacy; when agents and firms want to congregate where others are located, one or a few locations may end up with the large share of the entire population. If we bypass this indeterminacy by arguing historical accidents for dominant locations, we must define historical accidents and how they act to select the winning locations.

The spatial economic literature finds the spatial ordering of cities as the economic response to geographical endowments, especially transport possibilities and firms' needs. Many authors have analysed general equilibrium effects of inter-city transportation investment (for example, Kanemoto and Mera, 1985; Sasaki, 1992). These studies specify *a priori* the industrial structure of each city and trade pattern, which is a restrictive assumption for city size distribution. Urban economists have developed models explaining how the city size of each city is determined in the system of cities (for example, Henderson, 1985; Abdel-Rahman, 1990). However, these models have not considered spatial factors at the inter-city level, such as location of cities, distance, or transport costs between them. In this tradition, the locational pattern is an equilibrium outcome of individual agents' decisions. From this point of view, development history is not an issue to the extent that the equilibrium outcome is unique. The urban system is deterministic and predictable.

Recently, it has also been proposed that city development is path-dependent, much like an organic process, with new agents laid down upon and very much influenced by inherited locational patterns. Geographical differences and transport possibilities were important, but here the main driving forces were agglomeration economies: the benefits of being close to other agents. Later-comers might be attracted to these same places by the presence of these early locators, rather than geography (Batten, Kobayashi and Mori, 1989; Kobayashi, Batten and Andersson, 1991; Krugman, 1991; Fujita, 1993; Arthur, 1994; Fujita, Krugman and Mori, 1995; Matsuyama, 1995). Krugman (1991) analysed industrial location by incorporating transport costs in the multi-region model of interregional trade with scale economy. Concentration of production activities may occur even when all regions are homogeneous and no comparative advantage exists.

Several authors further developed the model so that the economy has multiple industrial sectors, and analysed a dynamic process of city formation and development (Fujita, Krugman and Mori, 1995; Matsuyama 1995). They demonstrated that as an economy's population increases, the city system organises itself into a Christaller-type hierarchical system. There are an increasing number of general equilibrium models, which allow increasing returns to explain the formation of city systems. Among others, Mun (1997) presented a tractable general equilibrium model with increasing returns caused by interactions between agglomeration economies and transport network structure in city systems. Kobayashi and Okumura (1997) investigated dynamic multi-regional growth models with spatial agglomeration, where a major concern is interregional knowledge spillover.

In the previous literature, two types of externalities have been discussed in shaping spatial agglomeration: peculiar and technological externality. The former is the externality, which appears through market transactions. For example, more and more population agglomerates because of the various factors that allow a greater diversity and a wider array of human interaction and consumption. Cities are typically associated with a wide range of products and a large spectrum of public services so that consumers can reach higher utility levels and have stronger incentives to migrate toward cities. The latter is associated with the advantage of proximity in communications. Setting up of new links in transport networks gives rise to new incentives for people to migrate because they may expect better business opportunities. This in turn makes the place more attractive to producers, who may expect the advantage of getting the knowledge and ideas they need. This idea has been well expressed by Marshall (1920).

As pointed out more recently by several authors (Romer, 1986; Lucas, 1988), human contact among individuals sharing common interests can be a vital input to creativity. It is well known that face-to-face communications are most effective. In this chapter, we exclusively focus upon the latter types of externality to describe how city systems will evolve in response to increasing possibilities of face-to-face communications due to railway network improvements. A simple general equilibrium model is presented to provide some insights into the impacts of decreasing distances among cities upon economic geography. The model tries to highlight one of the major sources of increasing returns, that is spatial agglomeration generated through technological externalities in production. The model is designed to exclusively simulate how the structure of city systems will evolve in response to railway network improvement. Compared with the previous studies the model is rather simple, but sufficient to simulate how interactions via railway transportation lead to the endogenous formation of dominant cities on the networks.

The spatial ordering is not unique when scale economies function in locational fields. Early agglomeration and/or link formation are established by historical accident on the network; the subsequent locational and investment decisions are regulated by their presence. A different set of early events could have steered the network pattern into a different outcome, so that development history is crucial. Because of the existence of multiple equilibrium states, minor changes in historical events, for example, the sequence of network improvement, may generate dramatic changes in the equilibrium network geography in the long run. This suggests that historical matters explain actual city patterns and that circular causation generates a snowball effect that leads city systems to be locked in within the same region for long time periods (Arthur, 1994).

Path-dependency is omnipresent for the evolutionary patterns of city systems. Given that cities grow largely due to the self-enforcing advantages of agglomeration economies, their very presence generates the lock-in effect. The lock-in effect is the reason why a city can still prosper even after the disappearance of distance friction. The structure of the city system is not determined freely; rather due to the lock-in effect of the city systems as a whole, its structure tends to follow the power of inertia. However, the strong presence of inertia in the structure of the city system does not necessarily deny the chance of the structural change in the long run. The transport network is the means to keep the power of inertia, but it may also provide chances for the city system to change its structure.

The task of network formation requires coordination of a large number of activities, performed by a large number of people. It is the problem of discovering a pattern of formation of links that brings about a better outcome for the urban system as a whole. The major part of this problem is to find out which combination of nodes should be coordinated to open up new links. Finding the efficient link would be relatively easy if we knew that every link comprised a network. The problem is much harder to find an efficient formation process. One would have to evaluate welfare improvement across an entire formation process along all possible paths. And yet, the number of all possible formation processes would grow exponentially with the number of links. This is difficult to solve, as anyone who has tackled the combinatorial problem may know. Due to the large number of possibilities, it is practically impossible to check all possible paths, but there is no way of reducing the entire problem into a number of separate problems of a manageable size.

The discovery of new links by its nature cannot be designed nor even anticipated; all we can do is to design a better search mechanism or discovery procedure. A decision maker tries to discover a better way of network formation by applying cost–benefit rules, and yet, due to fundamental complexity of combinatorial problems, there are general tendencies in which the network pattern evolves into one of a large number of inefficient ones. There is the circular causation between spatial agglomeration of population and network improvement decisions through forward-linkages (increased interactions due to network improvement enhances spatial agglomeration) and backward-linkages (spatial agglomeration needs more network investment). Through these linkage effects, scale economies at a certain location start to function, and are transformed into increasing returns at the level of the city system as a whole. In the presence of linkage effects, a small change in the initial network could start a long chain reaction of subsequent link formation.

We do not have full knowledge of the optimal network structure. This means that there is no way of knowing all feasible paths; the only available method of discovering a better link formation sequence is an heuristic one that leads us to a local optimum. There is no way of verifying that the selected link is indeed the globally efficient one. Even if we are sure as a matter of conviction that there must somewhere be a link better than the selected one, it is still not clear where this search process should start.

The cost–benefit rule is a way to find an efficient solution for local coordination. Their success in local coordination may indeed block the possibility of achieving a better way of coordinating at a global level. An attempt to write down such a procedure itself has the danger of conditioning us into certain prescribed patterns of thinking. Nothing can be more dangerous than an attempt to design such a mechanism in a collective way, and to put an economy into the straitjacket of a bureaucratic framework, as any attempts to organise, categorise, and even classify search efforts would restrict the directions of the search.

This chapter attempts to provide some experimental examples for the path-dependent agglomeration by revealing how city systems may evolve through time in response to policy initiatives for network formation. In particular, it examines the dynamics of population location using a simple general equilibrium model with increasing returns that permits a description of lock-in effects associated with existing agglomerations. By assuming that the government applies slightly different decision rules (cost–benefit rules) and that it improves transport, especially railway, networks one by one in the order that the links with the largest values of benefit–cost ratios are given the highest priority to be improved. This chapter tries to demonstrate that city systems will evolve in such a manner that the population will indeed cluster in some dominant locations, and that they depend both on the geographical conditions and historical orders of network improvement. In Section 2, a general equilibrium model for the simulation experiments is formulated. Section 3 explains the structure of the simulation experiments, and Section 4 summarises the results of our experiments.

2 THE MODEL

2.1 Assumptions

An economic system of n cities, indexed by $i = 1,2,...,n$, is considered, where the cities are connected by a railway transportation network. The economy produces one type of homogeneous good consumed by the whole population and the transportation sector. Perfect competition is assumed to prevail in goods markets both within each city and between cities. To avoid unnecessary complications, we consider economies without capital. This assumption, together with the assumption of a single-good economy, is strong since it is implicitly assumed that respective cities form their own autarky economies; no trade occurs between cities. By sacrificing the trade possibility, we can gain analytical tractability and investigate solely the interactions between city formation and face-to-face interactions via railway transport. The population is homogeneous and freely mobile among cities, whereas multi-habitation and inter-city commuting are not allowed. The assumption of perfect free mobility will be relaxed in Sections 3 and 4. Furthermore, the total population of the whole system is given exogenously at any point in time, and is assumed to be constant throughout the whole period.

Each city is geographically monocentric *à la* Alonso (1964), and consists of two parts, the central business district (CBD) and residential area. The city residents commute to the single CBD by intra-city railway systems, and pay for the commuting cost. For simplicity, we assume that each CBD is a point and all production activities are concentrated in the CBD of the respective cities. Production agents employ only the labour force, and local labour force is fully employed in their respective markets. The land area of a city is assumed to be collectively owned by all local residents through shares in a local land bank. The local land bank pays out dividends to local residents which normally equal the average per-capita land rent paid out. There is no agricultural land available, which means that the land price is zero at the edge of the city. The residential area is divided into land lots (Henderson, 1985), whose areas are fixed to the same size regardless of their location. In the spatial equilibrium, given the railway network, the households achieve the same utility level regardless of the city and location in which they live. The central government controls the travel costs between cities by improving the existing railway connections according to cost–benefit selection rules. The government does levy uniform lump-sum taxes on all households to fully finance network improvement. The intra-city railway systems are assumed to be operated by foreign firms; the revenue of these firms leaks from the respective city economies. The foreign ownership of intra-railway firms may be unrealistic in developed countries, but is a necessary assumption to describe congestion diseconomies driven by agglomeration in a simple way.

The model formulated below comprises an urban economics model to describe urban land use patterns of the respective cities and a general equilibrium model to characterise the whole economy of the city system. The size, land use patterns, and production capacities of respective cities, the so-called economic geography, is endogenously calculated at each step given the spatial distribution of population of the whole economy. This formulated model is extremely simple compared with the previous general equilibrium models of city systems with increasing returns, but it is sufficient to describe the fundamental features of path-dependent network evolution.

2.2 Households

Consider the representative household residing at a point with distance u_i from the CBD of city i. The utility function is regulated by both composite commodity consumption $x_i(u_i)$ and housing lot size $l_i(u_i)$, being fixed to $l_i(u_i)=1$. With a budget constraint, the composite commodity consumption is given by

$$x_i(u_i) = y_i - p_i(u_i) - c_i u_i - \tau , \quad (5.1)$$

where y_i is income, $p_i(u_i)$ is the land rent per unit lot size at point u_i, and c_i is the cost of commuting per unit distance that is constant everywhere in the city, τ is the lump-sum tax to be levied by the government to finance the network improvement. The tax is uniformly levied across the whole system. With the Cobb–Douglas utility function $x_i(u_i)l_i(u_i)^{\iota}$ where ι is a parameter, the indirect utility function is

$$V_i(u_i) = y_i - p_i(u_i) - c_i u_i - \tau . \tag{5.2}$$

Since all households will get the same utility regardless of their location, the spatial equilibrium condition gives us $\partial V(u_i)/\partial u_i = 0$. From equation (5.2) it can be seen that increased commuting costs are offset by reduced rents, thus we have $p_i(u_i)/u_i = -c_i$. From the assumption that there is no agricultural land use, there holds $p_i(L_i) = C_0 - c_i L_i = 0$ at the edge of the city where $u_i = L_i$. Integrating the equation $\partial p(u_i)/\partial u_i = -c_i$ we have the land gradient given by

$$p_i(u_i) = c_i(L_i - u_i). \tag{5.3}$$

The utility level of the household at the city edge, $u_i = L_i$, is

$$V_i = y_i - c_i L_i - \tau , \tag{5.4}$$

which is also equal to the utility level for all households regardless of their location within the city. Given the fixed lot size in the economy, the size of city i can be defined by the area of urban land use. Thus,

$$N_i = \int_0^{Li} 2\pi u_i \, du_i = \pi L_i^2. \tag{5.5}$$

By integration, the aggregate demand function, F_i can be described by

$$F_i = \int_0^{Li} 2\pi u_i x_i(u_i) \, du_i = N_i(y_i - c_i \pi^{-\frac{1}{2}} N_i^{\frac{1}{2}}). \tag{5.6}$$

Similarly, we can get the aggregated land rents, P_i, and commuting costs, T_i, over the population of city i by

$$P_i = \int_0^{Li} 2\pi u_i p_i(u_i) \, du_i = \frac{1}{3} c_i \pi^{-\frac{1}{2}} N_i^{\frac{3}{2}} , \tag{5.7}$$

$$T_i = \int_0^{Li} 2\pi c_i u_i^2 \, du_i = \frac{2}{3} c_i \pi^{-\frac{1}{2}} N_i^{\frac{3}{2}} , \tag{5.8}$$

respectively. The equilibrium utility level of the representative household V_i can be fully characterised by the four parameters, y_i, N_i, c_i and τ:

$$V_i = y_i - c_i \pi^{-\frac{1}{2}} N_i^{\frac{1}{2}} - \tau . \tag{5.9}$$

2.3 Firms

Let us next define the behaviour of the firms. We will assume a constant return to scale technology and use the production function of the form in equation 5.10 (Kobayashi and Okumura, 1997)

$$Y_i = N_i^{\alpha}\left\{\sum_j N_j\left(\frac{R_{ij}}{N_j}\right)^{\xi}\right\}^{\gamma}, \tag{5.10}$$

where Y_i is the total output, R_{ij} is the inter-city communication frequency between city i and j, and α, ξ, γ are parameters satisfying $\alpha + \xi\gamma = 1$. The production function, (5.10), indicates that the cities have identical production technology but different potential for human contacts. The frequencies of interaction among cities are endogenous in the model. Since the factor demands for production are determined by perfect competition, equating the marginal products of the labour force and the frequency of inter-city communication respectively to the wage rent, w_i, and the transportation cost between nodes i and j, d_{ij}, we get the following conditions:

$$w_i = \alpha\frac{Y_i}{N_i}, \tag{5.11}$$

$$d_{ij} = \frac{\gamma\xi Y_i}{R_{ij}}\frac{N_j\left(\frac{R_{ij}}{N_j}\right)^{\xi}}{\sum_k N_k\left(\frac{R_{ik}}{N_k}\right)^{\xi}}. \tag{5.12}$$

From (5.12), we directly see that

$$R_{ij} = \left\{\frac{\gamma\xi Y_i}{d_{ij}}\frac{N_j^{1-\xi}}{\Phi}\right\}^{\frac{1}{1-\xi}}, \tag{5.13}$$

$$\Phi = \sum_k N_k\left(\frac{R_{ik}}{N_k}\right)^{\xi}. \tag{5.14}$$

By substituting equation (5.13) into equation (5.14) we have

$$\Phi = (\gamma \xi Y_i)^{\xi} \left\{ \sum_k N_k d_{ik}^{-\frac{\xi}{1-\xi}} \right\}^{1-\xi}. \qquad (5.15)$$

Thus, from equations(5.14) and (5.15), we see that the inter-city communication frequency, R_{ij}, is described by a gravity model:

$$R_{ij} = \gamma \xi Y_i \frac{N_j d_{ij}^{-\frac{\xi}{1-\xi}}}{d_{ij} \sum_k N_k d_{ik}^{-\frac{\xi}{1-\xi}}}. \qquad (5.16)$$

From equations (5.7) and (5.12), the household income is given by

$$y_i = w_i + \frac{P_i}{N_i}. \qquad (5.17)$$

Within the model, the transportation sector is included implicitly. Both inter-city and intra-city transportation sectors are assumed to be run by non-profit firms. Transportation sectors do not utilise labour and they produce transportation services by utilising economies' outputs. The firms pay for the consumption of the inter-city transportation services, while the households do the same for intra-city commuting. The revenue of the interregional transportation sector is balanced with its factor payments. On the contrary, the revenue of intra-city transportation services leaks from the economy. The more population concentrates to a single city, the more leakage of the revenue occurs due to the increase of city size. This is the negative effect of agglomeration upon the economy of the city system. The central government also consumes economies' outputs to improve the inter-regional railway network. The improvement cost is fully financed by the tax revenue from the households.

2.4 Equilibrium Conditions

The wage rate w_i of a particular city is determined by the general equilibrium conditions so that the supply and demand for the labour force is brought into equilibrium. The population distribution among cities can be brought into equilibrium when no household has an incentive to move. According to the above statement the equilibrium of population distribution is characterised by

$$V_i = \overline{V} \quad \text{if } N_i > 0 \tag{5.18}$$

$$V_i \leq \overline{V} \quad \text{if } N_i = 0,$$

for i (i = 1,...,n), where $\overline{V}$ is the equilibrium utility level. Utility level calculations are only made for the cities that have positive population. Other cities, in which people cannot attain the equilibrium utility level, die. The city population satisfies the adding-up constraint:

$$\sum_{i=1}^{n} N_i = N, \tag{5.19}$$

where N is the exogenously given total population of the system, and N_i is the population of city i that is updated at every time step in order to reach the above mentioned equilibrium conditions. In the model described above, N, c_i, and d_{ij} are the exogenous variables that remain constant throughout the simulation process, whereas $\overline{V}$, V_i, u_i, P_i, y_i, N_i and R_{ij} are the endogenous variables updated at each time step.

3 STRUCTURE OF SIMULATION EXPERIMENTS

3.1 The Objectives

The major objective of this study is to investigate through simulation experiments how the network evolution is regulated by the history of policy initiatives for network improvement. The network evolution refers to the dynamic change of the city systems driven by the successive construction of new links, or of improvement to the existing links that connect the cities. Throughout the whole evolution period, the quality of intra-city transport remains unchanged. We focus on the cost–benefit evaluation rules and use them as the policy initiatives to determine the successive order of network improvement. As explained in Section 1, when the circular causation between locational and investment decision works, the decision rules to select new links play decisive roles in directing the network evolution. In our experiments, we will illustrate how a network will end up with a quite different network structure in the long run when slightly different cost–benefit evaluation rules are applied throughout the network evolution process.

3.2 Cost–benefit Evaluation Rules

The central government, which controls the travel costs between the cities by improving the existing transportation links, acts as the decisionmaker in selecting the links to be improved. At this point we introduce the discrete time system. Each investment decision is supposed to be made at the beginning of each time period. At each period, only one link with the largest value of the benefit-cost ratio is improved as far as the ratio exceeds the (predetermined) reservation level. Throughout the whole period, the same decision rule is mechanically applied by taking the values of benefit–cost ratios as the only criteria for the link improvement. In the simulation experiments, we consider three kinds of cost–benefit evaluation rules. In the order of complexity, the rules are named as follows: (1) the *naive* rule (case A), (2) the *intermediate* rule (case B), and (3) the *sophisticated* rule (case C). As its name implies, the *naive* rule is the simplest one. In applying this rule, the government only calculates the aggregated change in the consumer surplus provided that O-D trip demands and population distribution of the whole system remain unchanged. The overall benefit by using the consumer surplus is simply calculated by applying the formula:

$$B^{*} = \sum_{i=1}^{n} \sum_{j \neq 1}^{n} R_{ij}(d_{ij} - d'_{ij}), \qquad (5.20)$$

where B^{*} is the *naive* measure of benefits gained by the improvement, R_{ij} is the current O-D trip volume, d_{ij} is transportation cost between node i and j before the improvement is made, and $d^{`}_{ij}$ is transportation cost after the improvement. In calculating the benefit from the *intermediate* rule, the changes of O-D trip demands are taken into account whereas the demand functions are assumed to remain unchanged. The *intermediate* measure of benefits B^{**} is approximated by

$$B^{**} = \sum_{i=1}^{n} \sum_{j \neq 1}^{n} \frac{1}{2}(R_{ij} + R'_{ij})(d_{ij} - d'_{ij}). \qquad (5.21)$$

The demand function is defined by equation (5.16). In calculating the change in R_{ij}, we only consider the change in d_{ij} in equation (5.16), while regional output Y_i and population distribution N_i are supposed to remain the same. In case of the *sophisticated* rule, we make the calculations by both considering the changes in the O-D trip patterns and the shifts in the demand function. The *sophisticated* measure B^{***} is practically defined as the overall change in the equilibrium utility level, which is driven by the network improvement, summed up over the whole population of the whole system. Measured in monetary terms it is given as follows:

$$B^{***} = (\overline{V}' - \overline{V})N, \tag{5.22}$$

where $\overline{V}'$ and $\overline{V}$ indicate the equilibrium utility levels after and before the link improvement respectively, and N is the total population of the whole system. The *sophisticated* rule reflects the full benefits of the network improvement.

3.3 Adjustment Speed

As will be explained in Section 4, the initial conditions are highly decisive in determining the resulting evolution path. Once the city system starts its evolution from a certain initial condition, it becomes difficult to control spatial agglomeration process. Our model assumes that the city system adjusts itself immediately to a change in the network structure. Due to this assumption, any improvement made on the network through the application of cost–benefit evaluation rules does reinforce the ongoing agglomeration process. In reality, the city system can adjust itself only with time lags. If the system is staying at a disequilibrium state, being far from the equilibrium state, the spatial agglomeration processes could be partly controlled by the network improvement. Thus, the adjustment speed (the migration speed of the population) is another significant ingredient, which may regulate the evolution processes along with the cost–benefit evaluation rules. The disequilibrium dynamics of a city system can be characterised by the following population dynamics (Smith, 1982; Hofbauer and Sigmund, 1988):

$$s_{t+1}(i) = s_t(i) + \lambda \frac{(V_t(i) - \overline{V}_t)s_t(i)}{\overline{V}_t}, \tag{5.23}$$

where $s_t(i)$ is the share of population of the ith city to the total population at the beginning of period t, λ is the adaptation parameter reflecting the adjustment speed of convergence, $V_t(i)$ is the utility level of the i-th city at period t, and $\overline{V}_t = \Sigma_i s_t(i) V_t(i)$ is the average utility level of the whole system calculated by taking the average of the utility levels of all the cities weighted by their share of population. Population dynamics, given by equation (5.23), satisfies the adding-up constraint. In fact, by summing up both sides of equation (5.23), we see that

$$\Sigma_i s_{t+1}(i) = \Sigma_i s_t(i) + \lambda\{\Sigma_i V_t(i) s_t(i) / \overline{V}' \, \Sigma_i s_t(i)\} = 1, \text{ if } \Sigma_i s_t(i) = 1.$$

Provided $\Sigma_i s_0(i)=1$, there holds $\Sigma_i s_t(i)=1$ for all periods. The total population of the system is assumed to be constant N over the whole evolution period. The population dynamics defined above simply imply that the population moves toward locations with above-average utility levels and away from those with below-average utility levels.

4 COMPUTATIONAL SIMULATIONS

4.1 Description of Simulations

The network that is simulated is assumed to be a simple grid system, which lies on a flat ground, where the cities are located at the node points of the grid and are connected with railway lines. The network simulated consists of 10 x 10 = 100 cities. All the links are assumed to have the same length and the cost of improvement for each link is same. The central government improves existing transportation connections by introducing a higher-level transportation system. At one stage of the network evolution the government improves only one link which is selected according to the cost–benefit evaluation rule. The links that have been improved once cannot be improved further. This assumption is made so that the degree of the concentration on the network can simply be compared with respect to the number of links that have been improved. This assumption is very restrictive in exploring the properties of evolution process of a network. If reimprovement of a single link is allowed, evolution patterns may end up with more concentrated networks, with fewer but highly improved links. The improvement costs are fully financed by the tax revenue within the respective periods. The government is assumed to leave no debt for the future.

The network evolution is simulated as follows: (1) given the initial populations, we bring the system into equilibrium before any link improvement is made; (2) the urban economic submodel is simulated and benefits are calculated for all of the unimproved links; (3) if link improvement is justified, the link chosen by the cost–benefit evaluation rules is improved by decreasing the transportation cost on that link from its initial value of $d_{ij}=1.0$ to $d'_{ij}=0.7$; (4) then, evolution proceeds to the next period; (5) the system is brought into the new equilibrium by using the general equilibrium model starting from the equilibrium state at the end of the previous period. This process is repeated until no network improvement is justified by the cost–benefit evaluation rules. The case where the system can instantly adjust itself to the network improvement are taken up as the benchmark case.

The main technical assumptions for simulations are as follows: A total system population of 500 000 has been assumed. The population is allowed to migrate freely throughout the evolution process, and the cities whose population becomes zero at one point during the evolution process are assumed to die and are not allowed to be reborn. Besides the given assumptions, the cities that have died are not included in the calculations for utility equilibrium. Other important factors in designing the simulation experiments are the choice of the parameters α, ξ, γ, and the initial distribution pattern of city populations. In our simulations, the parameter values are set to: $\alpha = 0.7$, $\xi = 0.6$, $\gamma = 0.5$, and the tax value is taken as $\tau = 0.023$. Given these parameter values, the production technology exhibits the property of constant returns to scale. The interactability across the whole network forms the external economies of production in cities. At the very initial stage, given the initial network pattern, the city system is assumed to reach its initial equilibrium state.

4.2 Multiplicity of Equilibrium

The population distribution at the initial equilibrium stage highly influences the equilibrium states at each point in time as well as the evolution process of the city system. By selecting a different initial equilibrium state the city system may end up with a completely different final network pattern at the end of the evolution processes, and this choice is crucial in regulating the evolution processes. To observe this influence upon the network evolution process, we ran different simulations with different initial equilibrium states. For this purpose, different hypothetical patterns of population distribution were artificially generated and then they were brought into initial equilibrium states. The system can be characterised by the multiplicity of initial equilibrium states. Figure 5.1 illustrates an initial equilibrium population among other possible equilibrium states. In this figure, the size of the population in a city is indicated by the size of the circle located at the node point and the numbers inside them. The population figures are divided by 100 and then rounded off (values less than 1 are rounded up) for the ease of presentation and readability.

Figure 5.1 exhibits a symmetric equilibrium pattern along both the vertical and horizontal axes passing through the centre of the network, which was obtained by starting from an initial hypothetical pattern of an evenly distributed population. For the case shown in Figure 5.1 initial population was distributed evenly, with 5000 for every cities. Other initial population distribution patterns, such as skewed and concentrated distribution patterns, were also tested and different states have been achieved at the end of the initial equilibrium. Thus, we know that at the beginning of period 0 before the evolution starts, there exist many initial equilibrium states. In what follows, simulation experiments based upon the symmetric initial equilibrium state will be investigated.

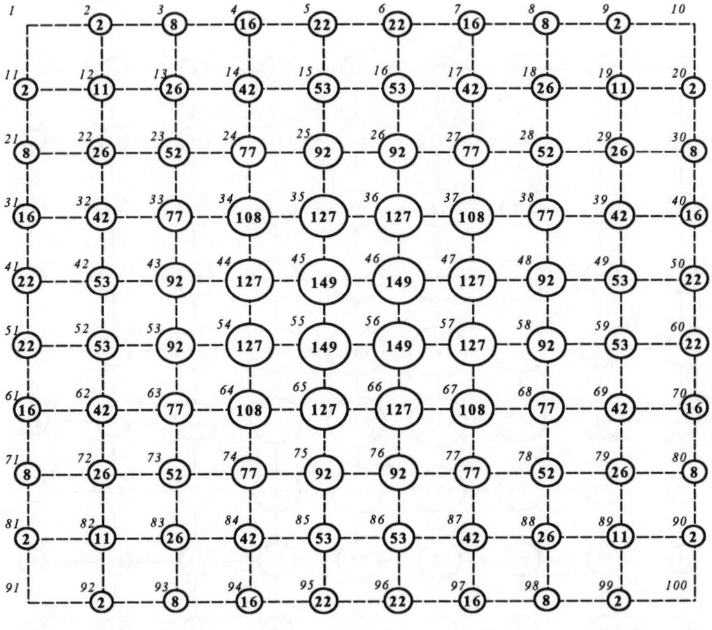

Figure 5.1 Initial equilibrium

4.3 Results

We start our investigation of the cases from the benchmark case. In the benchmark case the population in the system moves freely without any friction and the system comes to full equilibrium at the end of each period after each link improvement. The simulation results for the benchmark case indicate that there exist a number of different evolution patterns when different cost benefit rules are applied. Figures 5.2a, 5.2b and 5.2c illustrate the final network patterns and population distributions when the investments are terminated with the respective cost–benefit rules. In the figures, the numbers in the small squares next to the links show the order of link improvement, whereas the size of the population in a city is indicated by the same way as in Figure 5.1. Node points without any circle show the dead cities with zero population. Dotted lines indicate the initial connection between cities, whereas solid lines show the links that have been improved according to cost–benefit evaluation rules. Figures 5.2a, 5.2b and 5.2c refer to the cases where the *naive*, *intermediate*, and *sophisticated* rules are applied, respectively. Cases *A*, *B* and *C* also refer to the *naive*, *intermediate*, and *sophisticated* benefit calculations, respectively.

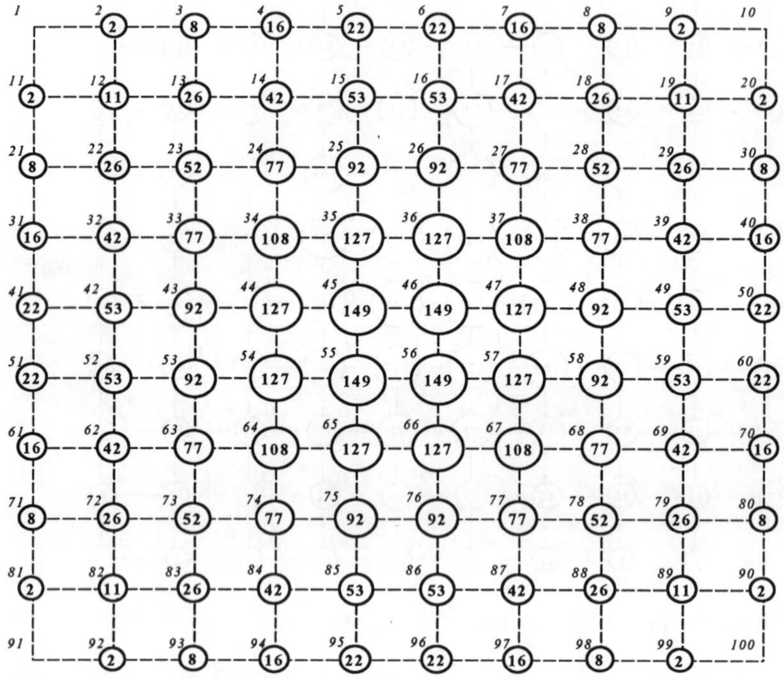

Figure 5.2a Final equilibrium after network evolution (case A*)*

In Figure 5.2a, we see that there are only 14 links improved when the *naive* rule is applied, however the number of link improvements becomes 18 (Figure 5.2b), and 24 (Figure 5.2c) for the *intermediate* and *sophisticated* rules, respectively.

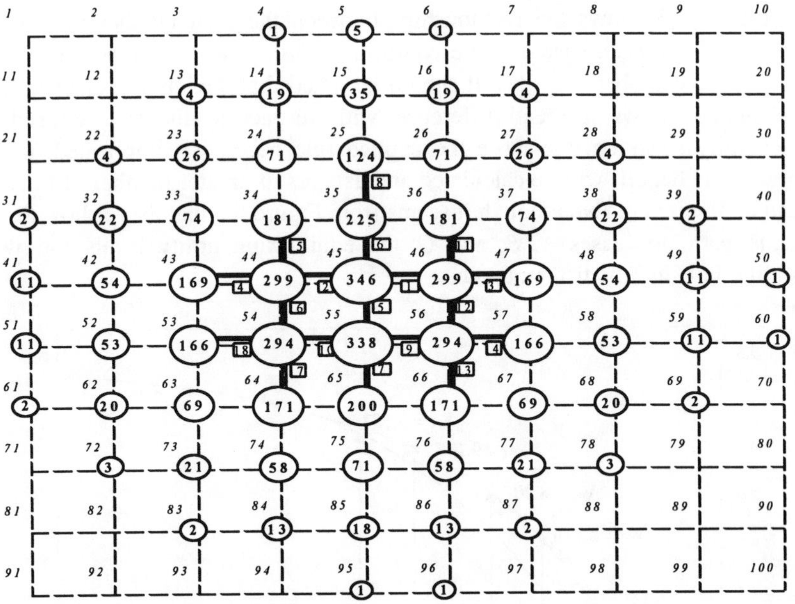

Figure 5.2b Final equilibrium after network evolution (case B*)*

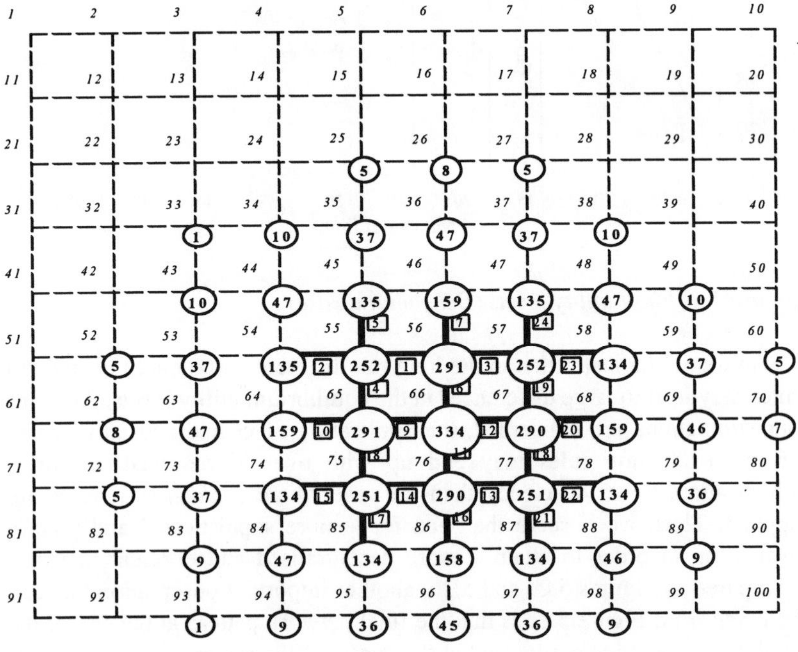

Figure 5.2c Final equilibrium after network evolution (case C*)*

Figure 5.3 shows the relationships between the total number of links improved for each case and the equilibrium utility levels attained by the respective cost–benefit rules. It should be noted that the amount of benefit calculated shows a great difference with respect to the rule utilised. Generally speaking, the more the applied rule becomes complicated, the higher the benefit will be calculated and as a result greater number of links can be improved. Even though it seems from Figure 5.3 that they follow the same path, for cases *A*, *B*, and *C*, the equilibrium utility levels follow similar but slightly different paths.

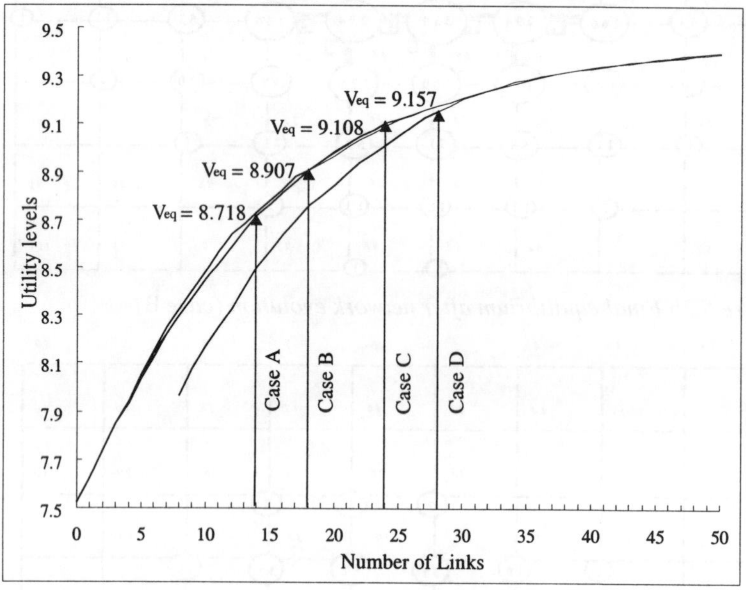

Figure 5.3 Final utility levels (Benchmark Case)

Figure 5.3 indicates that in the long run different cost–benefit evaluation rules may lead to large differences in the equilibrium utility levels. As far as our simulations are concerned, the application of coarse and *naive* cost–benefit evaluation rules may end up with over-concentrated networks, which attain lower efficiency than the case where *sophisticated* rules are applied. Thus, we observe the need for a more sophisticated and precise evaluation in order to attain a more decentralised and efficient network. Compared to Figures 5.2a and 5.2b, another important observation that can be made from Figure 5.2c is that the final network pattern at the end of the evolution process is not located at the centre of the system even though the evolution starts from one of the central links of the network that has a completely symmetric initial population distribution.

The selection of the link in case *C* is of course decided by the cost–benefit rule. In order to see the effect of the initial link formation upon the subsequent network evolution, an independent simulation (case *D*) is also made. In this case we assume that the decision maker exercises its initiative by making a policy decision and improves links so that the resulting network pattern will remain around the centre of the network. In order to achieve this, at the initial period of simulation, we improve eight links at once and force the system population to move toward the centre and start the evolution process with cost–benefit rules from this point on. The initially selected links for this case are marked with 0 on Figure 5.4, which shows the final network pattern for this case. A selection of links as such creates an initial inertia that will provide the final network pattern to build around the initially decided links.

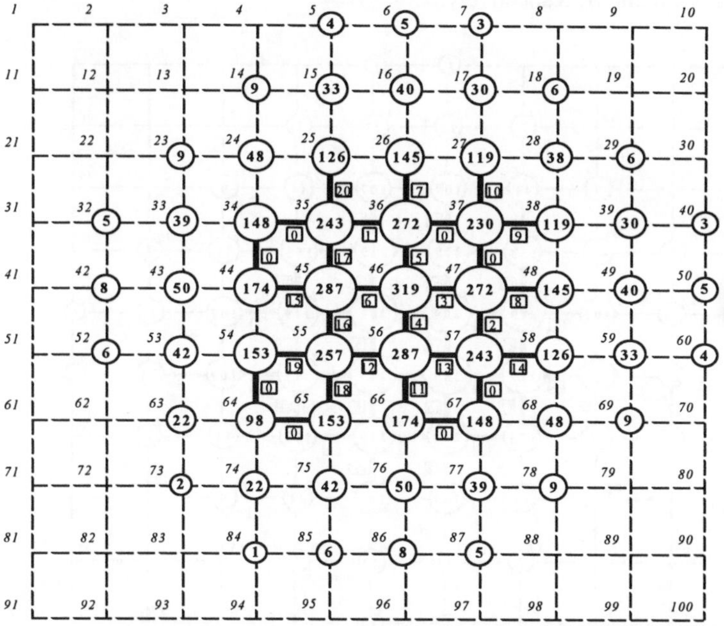

Figure 5.4 Final equilibrium after network evolution (case D*)*

Comparing Figure 5.4 to Figure 5.2c, we see that the final patterns of the network and the population distributions are quite different from each other. The comparison of the two cases shows the drastic effect such policy decisions can have on the resulting network depending on the selection of the initial link(s). Once the selection of the initial links is made, subsequent link improvements are very conditional to those links. Every other link improved on the network strengthens the inertia of the network pattern around which the subsequent evolution continues. As can be observed from Figure 5.3, when the eight initial links are chosen by political initiatives, the equilibrium utility levels achieved at the end of network evolution are higher than the case where the first link is decided by the *sophisticated* rule. Furthermore, in the former case, the final network structure becomes larger than the latter case. These findings imply that the initial links should not be solely designed by the cost–benefit evaluation rule; rather the inertia that builds around the already improved links and the spatial expansion capability of the network should also be taken into account in selecting the initial links to be improved. Considering that the initial equilibrium utility of the system before link improvements was 7.521, the amount of increase in case D is about 3.1 per cent, 18.0 per cent and 36.7 per cent higher than in cases C, B and A, respectively.

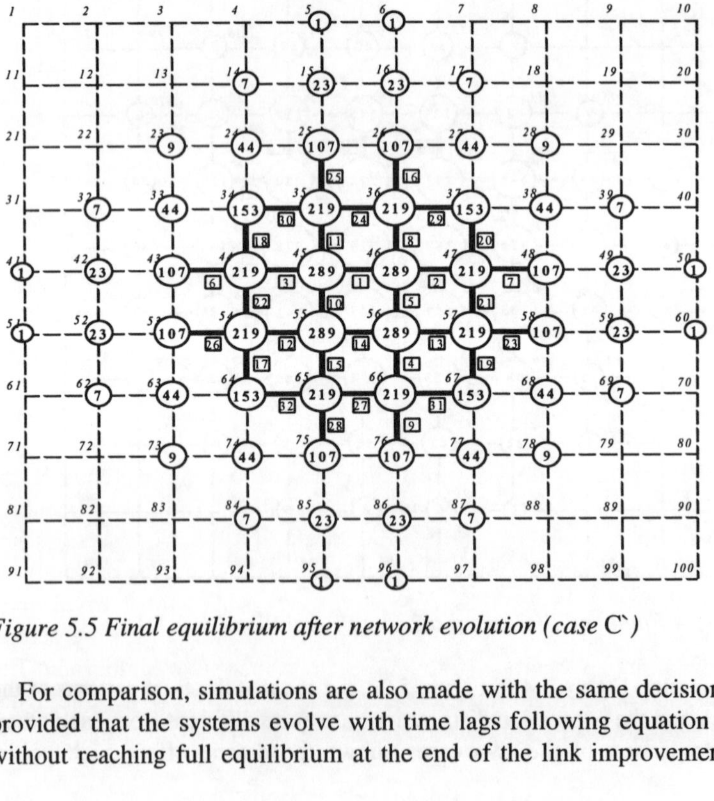

Figure 5.5 Final equilibrium after network evolution (case C`*)*

For comparison, simulations are also made with the same decision rules provided that the systems evolve with time lags following equation (5.23) without reaching full equilibrium at the end of the link improvement. For this case, the migration speed, λ, is taken as 0.5 and the population is moved at five steps with this given migration speed, rather than allowing for instant adjustment. Here, again, cases *A*`, *B*`, and *C*` correspond to the evolution patterns applying, *naive*, *intermediate* and *sophisticated* benefit rules, respectively. Figure 5.5 illustrate the final equilibrium in case *C*`.

Figure 5.6 shows the average utility levels right after the termination of the network evolution and the equilibrium utility levels achieved in the long run. For these cases we can easily see that the total number of link improvements is higher than the case with full equilibrium.

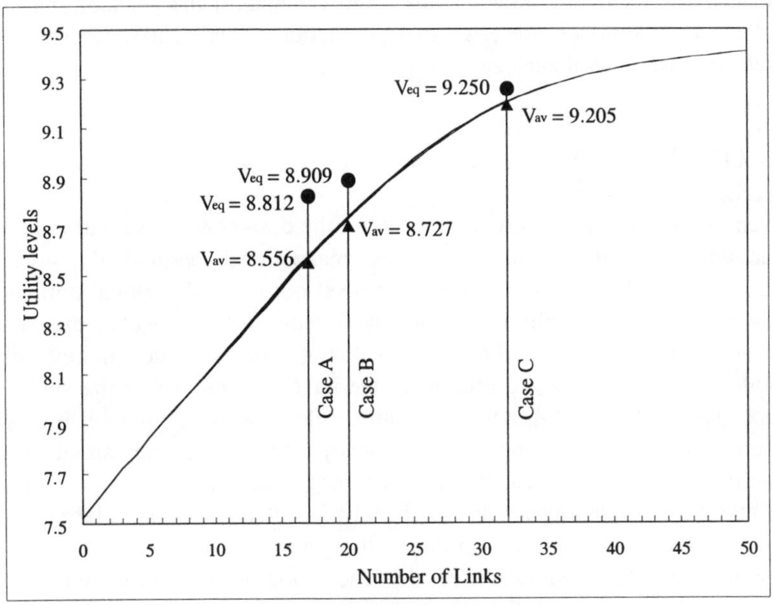

Figure 5.6 Final utility levels (Reference Case)

If we compare Figure 5.6 with Figure 5.3, we see that the equilibrium utility levels in the case of *C*` follow a flatter path, until the very final link improvement is complete. The reason for this is that the system is not necessarily brought into full equilibrium at the end of each period and there is a time lag for the system to adjust itself as a result of the newly formed network structure. After network improvement is terminated at some certain point, the utility levels are still moving toward a long-term equilibrium. The average and long-term utility levels are indicated with V_{av} and V_{eq} in Figure 5.6. The long-term equilibrium utilities, V_{eq}, are higher than the average utility levels, V_{av}, for all the cases $A`$, $B`$ and $C`$. Average utility levels for these three cases seems to follow the similar but slightly different paths, just like the equilibrium utility levels in the benchmark cases shown by Figure 5.3. Comparing the long-term equilibrium levels of cases $A`$, $B`$ and $C`$ with each other, we see that the increase in the equilibrium utility level (regarding that the initial equilibrium utility was 7.521) achieved in case $C`$ is about 24.6 per cent and 33.9 per cent higher than in cases $B`$ and $A`$, respectively. With the existing results we can say that the final network pattern is very sensitive to the values of population adjustment speed. This finding implies that more rigorous cost–benefit evaluations are needed to decide the order of the network link improvements, if the decision maker wishes to contemplate the effects of population adjustment speed on the results of cost–benefit analysis.

5 CONCLUSION

Given the history of the network evolution, the cost–benefit evaluation rule guarantees that the government may make local optimal decisions. Successive local optimal improvements need not reach the global optimal network. This is especially true if the city system is inherently characterised by the multiplicity of equilibria. Even though only a limited number of simulation experiments are presented, we have illustrated that the simple succession of the cost–benefit evaluation rules may end up with highly centralised systems having low efficiency. As far as our simulation experiments are concerned, this becomes especially clear when decisions are made by coarse and *naive* cost–benefit calculations. It must be noted, however, that it is dangerous to derive the general conclusion based upon the limited number of simulated results. The evolution possibility with cost–benefit evaluation rules still needs further scrutiny from various angles.

The simulation model presented in this chapter still remains at a prototype level. The model should be improved to make more careful investigation. Among others, the following revisions should be made for further research: (1) rebirth of cities that have died along the evolution process should be considered (policy initiatives may lead to the formation of new city); (2) simultaneous improvement of multiple links during the cost–benefit analysis should be discussed; (3) multiple quality ranks allowing for gradual link improvement must be considered; (4) the factors neglected in the model, for example knowledge, capital and trade should be implemented. In particular, growth modelling is the most important direction of further development because changes in the population may inject new equilibrium points and higher inertia and lock-in effects into the existing city system. The issues around lock-in effects in the dynamic setting remain unsolved. Although awaiting further development and sophistication, our simulation experiments are encouraging in that they seem to capture the essential mechanism controlling the evolution process of the city systems with cost–benefit evaluation rules.

REFERENCES

Abdel-Rahman, H.M. (1990), 'Agglomeration economies, types, and sizes of cities', *Journal of Urban Economics*, **27**, 25–45.

Alonso, W. (1964), *Location and Land Use*, Cambridge: Harvard University Press.

Arthur, B. (1994), *Increasing Returns and Path Dependence in the Economy*, Ann Arbor: The University of Michigan Press.

Batten, D.F., K. Kobayashi and Å.E. Andersson (1989), 'Knowledge, Nodes and Networks: An Analytical Perspective', in Å.E. Andersson, et al. (eds), *Knowledge and Industrial Organization*, Berlin, Heidelberg: Springer Verlag.

Fujita, M. (1993), 'Monopolistic competition and urban systems', *European Economic Review*, **37**, 308–315.

Fujita, M., P. Krugman and T. Mori (1995), 'On the evolution of hierarchical urban systems', Discussion Paper 419, Institute of Economic Research, Kyoto University.

Henderson, J. (1985), *Economic Theory and The Cities*, New York: Academic Press.

Hofbauer, J. and K. Sigmund (1988), *The Theory of Evolution and Dynamical Systems*, Cambridge: Cambridge University Press.

Kanemoto, Y. and K. Mera (1985), 'General equilibrium analysis of the benefits of large transportation improvements', *Regional Science and Urban Economics*, **15**, 343–63.

Kobayashi, K., D.F. Batten and Å.E. Andersson (1991), 'The sequential location of knowledge-oriented firms over time and space', *Paper of Regional Science*, **70**, 381–97.

Kobayashi, K. and M. Okumura (1997), 'The growth of city systems with high-speed railway systems', *Annals of Regional Science*, **31**, 39–56.

Krugman, P. (1991, 'Increasing returns and economic geography', *Journal of Political Economy*, **99**, 483–99.

Lucas, R.E. (1988), 'On the mechanics of economic development', *Journal of Monetary Economics*, **22**, 3–22.

Marshall, A. (1920), *Principle of Economics*, 8th edition, London: Macmillan.

Matsuyama, K. (1995), 'Complementarities and cumulative process in models of monopolistic competition', *Journal of Economic Literature*, **33**, 701–29.

Mun, S.I. (1997), 'Transport network and system of cities', *Journal of Urban Economics*, **42**, 205–21.

Romer, P.M. (1986), 'Increasing returns and long-run growth', *Journal of Political Economy*, **94**, 1002–37.

Sasaki, K. (1992, 'Trade and migration in a two-city model of transportation investments', *Annals of Regional Science*, **26**, 305–17.

Smith, J.M (1982), *Evolution and the Theory of Games*, Cambridge: Cambridge University Press.

6. Policies or Market Incentives? Major Changes in the Geographical Sources of Technology in the United States, 1945–95

Luis Suarez-Villa

1 INTRODUCTION

Technology has received relatively little attention in most regional policymaking over the years. Most regional policies have tended to address socioeconomic disparities or development issues, leaving technology and its key components, invention and innovation, out of their scope. This neglect has become all the more noticeable in recent years, because of the increasing importance of technology in most advanced economies and in everyday life.

There are several reasons for the neglect of technology in regional policymaking. For many in the policymaking community, technology has often been seen as something that is beyond the usual policy concerns, because of its complexity and the lack of an obvious link with the more pressing socioeconomic issues. Another factor has been the difficulty in understanding technology's connection with a region's or nation's socioeconomic well-being or with their economic competitiveness. Also, a less noticed but perhaps important reason is that technological development requires long periods of time, which are usually beyond the scope of most politicians' typically short-term concerns or their careers.

In the American case, it can be argued that the market has had substantial influence in shaping national and regional technological development. American regional policymaking has been very limited over the years, in a comprehensive sense, even on socioeconomic issues. What regional or local policymaking has occurred has been very fragmented, being typically limited to an aspect or a few facets of a problem. In many cases, policies have tended to cancel each other's effects, because of the lack of coordination or a unified approach to their implementation. Even when policies have had some effect on technological development, their benefits have been mostly indirect and have either been very difficult or impossible to assess.

What is remarkable in the American case is that the nation's technological achievements and the radical changes in the geographical sourcing of technology seem to have occurred in a very fragmented policy context. It is impossible to point to any single federal, regional or local policy mechanism that has had a direct or major effect on technological development over the years. The development of new technologies has instead occurred through an enormous variety of private actors and, in some cases, many public agents. Most of the time, market forces seem to have been the driving force behind new developments in technology, leaving little for governments to do in that regard, except in the regulation of unforeseen effects or the licensing of new products for consumption.

This chapter will discuss the major changes that have occurred in the geographical sourcing of technology over the past 50 years, considering the American policy context and the role of market forces in the outcomes that have been achieved. While it is tempting to think that market forces may have produced far better results than what could otherwise have been achieved, that assertion will be resisted in this chapter. The fact is that we do not know what a comprehensive, unified or sustained policy approach could have produced in the area of technological development, simply because such an approach has never existed in the American case, at least not over the past 50 years. At best, what can be done is to assess the outcomes, and to try to understand the developmental context in which they occurred.

The following section will provide an overview of the most important changes that have occurred in the United States' geographical sourcing of technology. Precise definitions of invention, innovation and R&D will be provided, to avoid the sort of confusion that frequently involves these terms in the literature. Twentieth century data on the regional sourcing of new inventions will be examined, with emphasis on the period 1945–95. That section will then be followed by a discussion of the policy context, and the kinds of forces that have affected the radical redistribution of technological sourcing. The objective will be to provide a broad overview of the policy context rather than to consider the micro-analytic details. Finally, the conclusions will place the topic and discussions of this chapter in perspective, in a way that may allow comparisons with the experiences of other nations.

2 THE RADICAL CHANGE IN TECHNOLOGICAL SOURCING

The past 50 years have witnessed a remarkable change in the geographical sourcing of American technology. Regions that were undeveloped or backward six decades ago have emerged as the most important sources of new technologies. In contrast, the regions and states that were the most important sources of new technologies five decades ago have generally declined or given up their leading roles. This radical change in the sourcing of new technologies has no parallels in other advanced nations, at least not to the same degree or intensity as in the American case.

The sourcing of technology will refer in this chapter to the generation of newly patented inventions at any given place and time. Invention patent data are compiled geographically in the United States, and are available in historical series. Such data are related to the location of the first-named inventor in all patent awards, regardless of whether they are retained by an individual or assigned to a firm or institution (see U.S. Patent and Trademark Office, 1997). Patenting information is considered to be among the most reliable historical data available, because of its consistency over time, and the kinds of criteria that are applied to evaluate new ideas or products in the patent review process (see, for example, Griliches, 1990; Scotchmer and Green, 1990; Griliches, Pakes and Hall, 1987; Suarez-Villa, 1990, 2000). Innovation will then refer to the application of inventions in any given activity. R&D (research and development) activities typically include both invention and innovation. However, most R&D activities involve much more innovation than invention, even in high technology firms, because of the high costs of invention and the need for expediency in marketing new products. R&D data are therefore much less reliable as indicators of new technologies than patenting information.

A causal relationship is implicitly assumed by these definitions, leading from invention to innovation, to the use of new technologies and, eventually, to economic change. Invention is therefore assumed to be the root source of new technologies and of innovation. Innovation and new technologies, in turn, result in economic change through productivity increases, and the myriad qualitative changes which make individuals and production more effective. However, the relationship between invention, innovation and economic change is not as linear as might be imagined. Existing technologies have often been the source of ideas for new inventions (see, for example, Kealey, 1996). Thus, a strong feedback connection between new technology, innovation and invention has existed historically, and must be taken into account when considering the relationship between invention, innovation, new technologies and economic change.

Unfortunately, the importance of invention has all too often been ignored in the literature. We have often assumed capital accumulation to be the prime source of economic change, when in fact new ideas and technologies are at the root of long-term economic progress (see, for example, Schmookler, 1966; Hagerstrand, 1967; Mensch, 1979; Kleinknecht, 1987; Griliches, 1990; Malecki, 1991; Dosi, Giannetti and Toninelli, 1992). The fact that invention and technological change have often been relegated to the status of a 'black box' in standard economic theory, have prevented them from being adequately considered in most analyses of economic progress. Also, in part, the lack of long-term perspectives on economic progress and its relationship with technological change has contributed to this neglect.

Invention patent data will be used to illustrate regional changes in American technological sourcing in this chapter. Patent data cannot capture all invention in an absolute or totally complete way, but it can be argued that such data are possibly a more complete and reliable indicator than some of the more commonly used economic variables, such as gross domestic product (GDP), value added, or even personal income. Patenting provides a property right that is unequalled in the legal protection it provides to inventors. The kind of situation when patenting of an invention may not occur is when a firm has a monopoly on its sector or market. In such cases, a firm might forego patenting, since it would have no competitors that could use its invention. However, in the United States monopolies are illegal, and anti-trust or anti-monopoly laws have been carefully enforced. Moreover, the globalisation of technology has created a powerful incentive to patent inventions, even where firms can monopolise specific niches in a national or regional market.

The radical change in the geographical sourcing of new technologies is part of a larger process of *regional inversion* that has overtaken the United States over the past five decades (see, for example, Sale, 1975; Abbott, 1981; Schulman, 1990; Suarez-Villa, 1997a, 2000). This process of inversion has brought many social and economic indicators, in areas that were previously peripheral or undeveloped, up to the levels of the most advanced regions, surpassing them in some cases. This remarkable process of radical change has received limited attention in the literature, and its technological dimension has perhaps been the most neglected of all aspects.

The process of regional inversion is most noticeable when comparing the so-called Sunbelt states with those of the Northeastern and Midwestern regions. The Northeastern and Midwestern states have been the industrial heartland of the United States. Those two regions became the core of

American industrial capitalism, holding its most important industries and its most advanced technologies over the first seven decades of the twentieth century. Although the territorial size of the Sunbelt is substantially greater than that of the Northeastern and Midwestern regions, as shown in Figure 6.1, the total population of the Sunbelt states did not approach that of the two combined heartland regions until the early 1980s (U.S. Bureau of the Census, 1980–1997). By the early 1990s, the total population of the Sunbelt was only 14 per cent larger than that of the combined Northeastern and Midwestern regions (U.S. Bureau of the Census, 1980–1997). This was in stark contrast with the situation in 1900, when the total population of the Sunbelt amounted to only 72 per cent of the combined population of the Northeast and Midwest, despite its much larger territorial size.

Figure 6.1 Regional divisions: Sunbelt, Northeast, Midwest

The rapid rise of the Sunbelt as a source of new technologies, and the relative decline of the Northeastern and Midwestern regions, is probably best represented by its rising proportion as a source of new invention patents (see Figure 6.2). Between 1935 and 1995, the Sunbelt states' proportion rose from 16 to 48 per cent of the total number of patents awarded in the United States, while the combined proportions of the Northeastern and Midwestern regions declined from 83 to 48 per cent. By 1995, the Sunbelt had in fact converged with the combined Northeastern and Midwestern levels, as shown in Figure 6.2. It is difficult to find any other indicator that changed, and converged, as fast as the proportion of invention patenting between those regions.

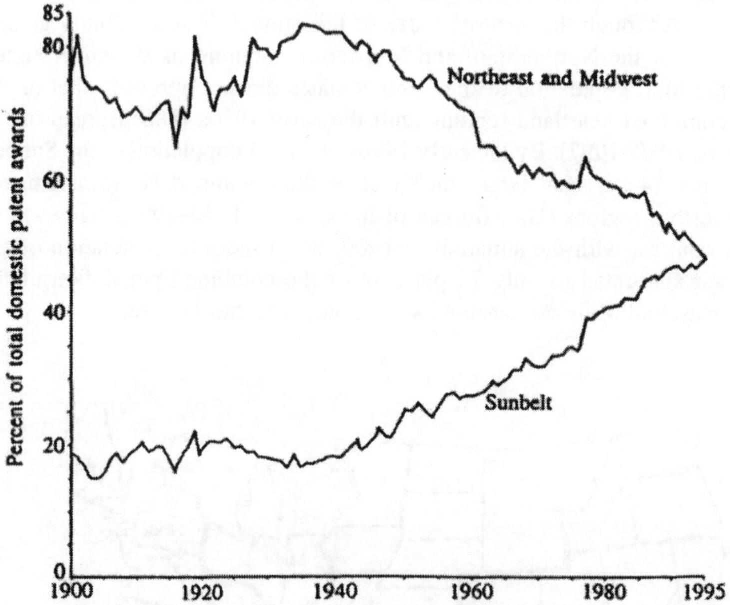

Figure 6.2 Regional patenting distribution, 1900–1995 (U.S. Patent and Trademark Office)

A cumulative measure of invention, the *innovative capacity* indicator, was developed to compare the accumulation of invention patents between regions. This indicator cumulates all the invention patent awards that are legally valid in any given year. In the United States, invention patent awards have had a legal life term of 17 years since the early nineteenth century, with extensions of this term being very rare. The innovative capacity indicator therefore provides a moving annual estimate of the total number of invention patents that are valid in any given region or geographical area. Additional details and applications of this indicator can be found in Suarez-Villa (1990, 1993a, 1996, 1997a, 2000), and will therefore not be discussed in this chapter. By and large, the innovative capacity indicator provides a measure of inventive accumulation which is non-monetary, and is strictly limited by the evaluation criteria on which patent awards are based. Such criteria typically emphasise novelty as the single most important aspect of any idea, product or process in determining whether a patent can be awarded.

The innovative capacity estimates shown in Figure 6.3 illustrate the regional trajectories over most of the twentieth century. The Northeastern region was the predominant source of inventions in the United States between 1900 and 1940. The Midwestern region, a relative latecomer to industrialisation, followed behind, with a trend similar to that of the Northeast. Both regions were the most industrialised in the United States over the first half of the century, and they provided much in the way of invention and new technologies. The Great Depression and the Second World War had the greatest impact on the Northeastern and Midwestern innovative capacity trends, perhaps because those two regions had the most to lose from economic calamity and war, since they had the largest concentrations of inventors and of economic activities at that time.

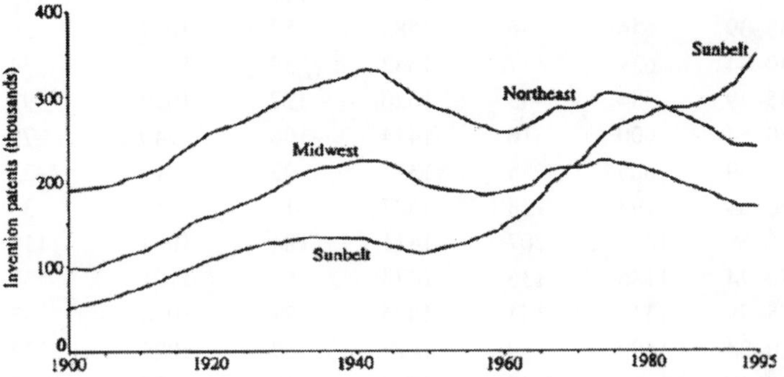

Figure 6.3 Regional innovative capacity, 1900–1995 (U.S. Patent and Trademark Office)

By the late 1940s, however, a new regional division of labour for invention was beginning to unfold. It was hard for almost anyone then to imagine that some of the peripheral or relatively backward states of the west and south would eventually emerge as the most important sources of new inventions and technology in the American economy. The Northeastern and Midwestern regions had until then concentrated most invention in the United States, as well as the nation's most cherished educational institutions, most of its manufacturing activities, investment capital, infrastructure and urban population, to mention only a few aspects. In Table 6.1, the changing fortunes of the heartland regions can be noted in the negative interval changes for innovative capacity after the late 1940s, compared with the equivalent data for the Sunbelt region.

Table 6.1 Regional innovative capacity, 1900–1994

	Sunbelt		Northeast		Midwest	
Years	Interval total[a]	Interval change[a]	Interval total[a]	Interval change[a]	Interval total[a]	Interval change[a]
1900–04	276	–	953	–	487	–
1905–09	326	50	990	37	552	65
1910–14	395	69	1065	75	625	73
1915–19	488	93	1206	141	739	114
1920–24	558	70	1309	103	825	86
1925–29	617	59	1407	98	909	84
1930–34	652	35	1524	117	1023	114
1935–39	646	–6	1583	59	1077	54
1940–44	639	–7	1642	59	1111	34
1945–49	584	–55	1520	–122	1019	–92
1950–54	600	16	1414	–106	940	–79
1955–59	665	55	1321	–93	919	–21
1960–64	793	128	1307	–14	954	35
1965–69	1000	207	1411	104	1064	110
1970–74	1186	136	1474	63	1101	37
1975–79	1340	154	1496	22	1098	–3
1980–84	1409	59	1427	–69	1026	–72
1985–89	1449	40	1315	–112	937	–89
1990–94	1586	137	1242	–73	888	–49

Note: [a] 10^3

Source: US Patent and Trademark Office.

By the late 1960s, the Sunbelt's innovative capacity had passed the Midwest's, and by the early 1980s it had surpassed the Northeast's. In contrast, the two heartland regions' innovative capacity trends had started to decline swiftly after the early 1970s (see Figure 6.3).

State-level innovative capacity estimates, shown in Figure 6.4, provide more detailed evidence on the rising importance of some Sunbelt states as major sources of new inventions and technology. The rise of California as a major source of new inventions was obviously fundamental for the growth of the Sunbelt's innovative capacity after the late 1940s. The contrast between California and New York could not be more obvious, and it reflects the rising fortunes of the Sunbelt and the decline of the state that was the United States' most important source of new inventions and technology over the first half of the twentieth century. Although Texas' and Florida's innovative capacities also began to rise after the late 1950s, California was undoubtedly the prime force behind the Sunbelt's rapid gains throughout the second half of the twentieth century. All of the Northeastern or Midwestern states shown in Figure 6.4 to a great extent follow New York's decline, revealing little or no difference in the general path of decline within each of the two heartland regions. Those states (Illinois, Pennsylvania, Ohio, Michigan and Massachusetts) were by far the other most important sources of invention and new technology in America's heartland regions.

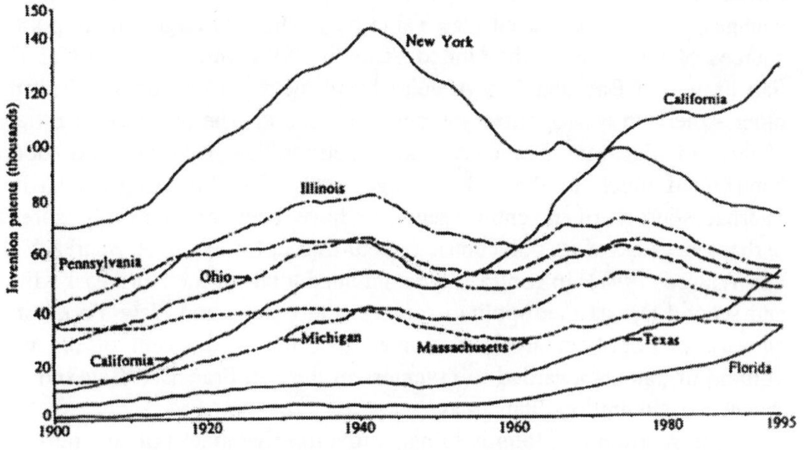

Figure 6.4 State innovative capacity, 1900–1995 (U.S. Patent and Trademark Office)

The shift toward Sunbelt states shown by the innovative capacity indicator is partly due to the rise of new activities and industries, such as electronics, information services and, more recently, biotechnology. Some of those new industries, such as electronics, started in California, expanding later to other Sunbelt states, such as Texas, North Carolina, Virginia and Florida. Entirely new firms grew up in the Sunbelt with those industries and some, such as Hewlett Packard or Intel, expanded to become global companies. Much of the Sunbelt's increase in the innovative capacity indicator is undoubtedly linked to those industries.

Less important for the Sunbelt's rising role was the so-called deindustrialisation of the Northeast and Midwest, which occurred mainly over the 1970s and early 1980s. The deindustrialisation of the heartland regions may have caused some displacement of inventors and other highly skilled individuals toward the Sunbelt, but there is practically no evidence showing that it contributed in any significant way to the rise of the Sunbelt as a major source of invention. Also, the migration of industrial firms from the Northeast or Midwest toward the Sunbelt was quite limited, since the flight of the old, traditional industries tended to be more toward low-cost nations. More important for the growing technological profile of the Sunbelt was the rise of entirely new industries or activities within its boundaries and cities (Suarez-Villa, 2000).

Unfortunately, historical data on invention patenting are not available for cities, counties or metropolitan areas, but some recent information on the local sources of new invention patents can provide additional details on the changes that have occurred (see Table 6.2). The two largest metropolitan sources of invention in the United States in 1994 were in California. The San Francisco Bay and Los Angeles basin metropolises surpassed all the other American metropolitan sources of invention. The presence of Silicon Valley in the San Francisco Bay metropolitan estimates no doubt contributed much to that area's large totals. The Los Angeles basin's internal sources of invention seem to have been more evenly spread, perhaps because of its polycentric structure (see, for example, Suarez-Villa and Walrod, 1997). In contrast, the combined totals of the Northeast's first- and second-largest metropolitan sources (the Boston and New York City–Newark metropolitan areas) amounted to only 61 per cent of the total volume of patents awarded to inventors in the San Francisco Bay and Los Angeles basin metropolitan areas.

The proportion of patent holdings in the top five metropolitan areas was relatively more concentrated in the case of the Midwest, with over 56 per cent of the region's total number of invention patent awards going to those five metropolises in 1994 (see Table 6.2). The Northeast followed, with almost 50 per cent of all its 1994 patent awards going to its top five metropolises. The Sunbelt, on the other hand, had the lowest level of concentration (41 per cent), although California's three major metropolitan areas took a significant proportion of the top five metropolises' total.

From Table 6.2, it seems clear that California and Texas accounted for much of the Sunbelt's importance as a source of metropolitan-based invention, although the region's territorial size and diversity may have contributed to spread the sourcing of invention patents over a larger number of cities.

Table 6.2 Largest local sources of invention patenting, 1994

Region/Metropolitan area (counties)	Invention patents
Sunbelt	
San Francisco–Oakland–San Jose (10)	3786
Los Angeles basin (5)	3493
Houston (8)	1408
Dallas–Fort Worth (12)	1232
San Diego (1)	935
Total	10854
Percentage of Sunbelt's total	41.0%
Northeast	
Boston (10)	2474
New York City–Newark (13)	1978
Philadelphia (9)	1425
Rochester (6)	1381
New Haven (2)	924
Total	8182
Percentage of Northeast's total	49.7%
Midwest	
Chicago (13)	2334
Detroit–Ann Arbor–Flint (10)	1932
Cleveland–Akron (8)	916
Cincinnati (12)	724
Milwaukee (5)	517
Total	6423
Percentage of Midwest's total	56.5%

Source: U.S. Patent and Trademark Office.

There is no evidence showing that any nation has experienced the sort of radical shift that occurred in the United States over the past five decades. Very few studies exist that trace the geographical distribution of invention over long periods of time in other countries. Even within the North American context, the changes that occurred in the United States were not replicated, for example, in Canada. In what is obviously a deep contrast with the United States, Canada's geographical sourcing of invention and new technologies remained stable over the twentieth century (see Ceh and

Hecht, 1990). The Toronto region still accounts for the vast proportion of new inventions produced in Canada, much as it did at the start of the twentieth century. This is remarkable, since the Canadian economy is often thought to mirror the American economy, or to be highly linked to its patterns of change.

In general, the changes that occurred in the American regional sourcing of invention and new technologies are quite radical. It is impossible to find any other nation where the process of regional inversion in this area went as fast or as far as it did in the American case. Overturning the predominance of heartland regions in any national context is something that would normally be expected to occur over centuries, if at all, for most any economic aspect or activity. The American experience therefore begs for explanations regarding the role of policies in this rapidly changing dynamic.

3 THE POLICY CONTEXT AND THE FORCES OF CHANGE

This section will provide an overview of the policy context, by taking into account the most important forces favouring change in America's regional sourcing of technology. It must be acknowledged, however, that the policy context in which those changes occurred is an extremely fragmented one. No one knows precisely the effects of the multitude of measures that have been implemented, at various levels of government and through the numerous policy programmes that have been undertaken. Moreover, there is a pervasive feeling that many policy efforts affecting technology have not only not been effective, but have been wasteful or even counterproductive. There is also a widespread notion that many policy measures undertaken by different levels of government or by various government agencies have tended to cancel each other out frequently, or have at least obstructed each other, because of the lack of any national overarching coordination or planning.

To organise the discussion of this section, Table 6.3 provides a listing of the policy areas relevant to regional technological development in the United States, and a simple indication of the levels of government or policymaking to which they are more closely related. The main forces that have favoured radical change in the regional sourcing of new technology will be related to each policy area listed in Table 6.3, to provide an overview of their contribution and significance over the long term. It is important to stress that the varying effects of the policy programmes, and of the forces which affected regional change, can only be adequately understood from a long-term perspective. It is precisely because of this requirement that it is so difficult to quantify the effects and significance of those policy areas and the forces which they affected.

Table 6.3 The technology-relevant policy context

	Government levels		
Policy Area	Federal	State	Local[a]
Tax policies	X		
Infrastructural development	X	X	X
Human capital development		X	
Special projects	X		X
Defence	X		

Note: [a]Municipal, county, metropolitan.

Two policy areas were catalytic for the rise of the Sunbelt as a major source of new technologies: infrastructural and human capital development. Those two policy areas led market forces, since they set the conditions and made it easier for private capital to be deployed in the Sunbelt. The other policy areas listed in Table 6.3 pretty much followed market forces, supporting or making it easier for them to work, usually in peripheral ways. It must therefore be kept in mind that the weight of the various policy areas was very uneven, with some having catalytic roles while others were mainly followers or supporters of processes that were already functioning.

Infrastructural development was a very important force supporting the rise of the Sunbelt as the most important source of new technologies. The accumulation of expenditures on infrastructure by the federal government over the past six decades has not been fully accounted for, but it seems clear that much spending went to projects in Sunbelt states (see U.S. Bureau of the Census, 1975, 1981; American Public Works Association, 1976; Suarez-Villa and Hasnath, 1993; Gramlich, 1994; Suarez-Villa, 1997a, 2000). The most important types of infrastructure support affecting the Sunbelt's technological base were federal contributions to the educational and scientific infrastructure, such as the construction of laboratories, testing facilities and educational buildings, along with their equipment and physical resources. Many universities and scientific institutions in the Sunbelt received much federal support over the years. Also, for example, efforts aimed at exploring outer space concentrated most facilities in Sunbelt states, such as the launch complex (Cape Canaveral in Florida) and main tracking stations (Johnson Space Center in Texas and the Jet Propulsion Laboratory in California), or the space shuttle's landing site (in California). All of those facilities depended on a constellation of local or regional laboratories, research facilities and private technology firms which developed much scientific and technological talent.

A second important type of infrastructural support was the development of the Sunbelt's communication infrastructure at all levels. The construction of the vast interstate highway system over the 1950s and 1960s opened up the Sunbelt to road accessibility as never before. Before the rapid expansion of the communications infrastructure, the establishment of basic utility networks made it possible for many areas of the west to be urbanised or farmed (see, for example, American Public Works Association, 1976; Hughes, 1993). In this regard, for example, the completion of the Colorado River's Hoover Dam in the 1930s, for several decades the world's largest hydroelectric project, made it possible for Southern California and Phoenix to become urbanised through the provision of water and electricity. When all of these projects and expenditures are considered, it seems fair to state that infrastructural development was possibly one of the most effective policy roles supporting the rise of the Sunbelt as a source of new technologies.

State and local governments also contributed much to build infrastructure that supported the technological development of the Sunbelt. All public universities in the United States receive substantial state-level support, and many also receive significant support from local governments. In the case of most Sunbelt states, public higher education carried more weight than those of the Northeastern or Midwestern states, because there are fewer private universities and the public institutions had to rise fast qualitatively, in order to be competitive at the national level (see Graham and Diamond, 1997; Geiger, 1993; Webster, 1986; Vesey, 1965). State and local governments also provided substantial support for the educational infrastructure at the primary and secondary levels. Primary and secondary school construction and maintenance are mainly a local or state responsibility in the United States. The development of the transport infrastructure, in road construction, ports and airports, for example, also depended greatly on local and state government programmes. No single national, regional or local policy programmes was targeted at comprehensive (or broad-ranging) infrastructural development, however. Rather, much of the enormous progress made in infrastructural development over the years was largely due to the efforts of many fragmented state and local actors, sometimes helped by federal aid.

It is important to note that the policy context of infrastructural development was, by and large, to support market forces and the private economy, rather than to meet any self-determined, long-term objectives. This means that the programmes and policies which supported infrastructural development were subordinated to the market. This is in sharp contrast with the experiences of many nations, where infrastructural development has been justified or based on overarching policy objectives, such as the reduction of interregional disparities or the dispersion of industry to the hinterland (see, for example, Rodwin and Sazanami, 1991; Suarez-Villa and Karlsson, 1996). Making the market function more efficiently was, if anything, the real objective of the sort of infrastructural development which allowed the Sunbelt to rise as a source of new technologies. It should therefore not come as a surprise that the rapid development of infrastructure in the Sunbelt made it easier for the private sector to invest in the region, by making access to skilled personnel, communications and transactions more efficient and less costly.

Perhaps the infrastructural development programmes owed much of their effectiveness to the fact that they were subordinated to market forces. This narrow perspective may also explain why coordination between the different levels of government involved in infrastructural construction was more effective than those of most other efforts. Infrastructural development efforts, though fragmented, therefore tended to obstruct or interfere less with each other than in most other policy programmes. A contributing factor may have been the fact that infrastructure tends to be more visible and costly than the objects of most other policy programmes, and any costly obstructions, mutual cancelling of outcomes, or other obstacles can be more embarrassing or politically damaging to those who are responsible for their implementation. Among many American policymakers there is a belief that no 'white elephant' is as embarrassing as that which is tangible and visible to the public (the term 'white elephant' being commonly used to refer to wasteful or useless projects).

Another major force supporting the rise of the Sunbelt as a source of new technology was the massification of education that occurred at all levels, but particularly so in higher education. This process started in the late 1940s, and over the span of four decades it contributed much to raise the level of technical skills of the population. A large proportion of Sunbelt residents thus became the first in their families to gain access to a university education, even in some of the poorest states. Technical and scientific university education boomed over the 1950s, 1960s and 1970s, providing many of the skills needed by the rapidly expanding Sunbelt economy. This massive human capital development was also highly fragmented, with individual states being mostly responsible for its support, with significant federal aid.

The enormous expansion of public university enrollment, coupled with the equally impressive development of the physical infrastructure of higher education, noted previously, also resulted in substantial increases in the quality of many universities (see Graham and Diamond, 1997; Geiger, 1993; Haynes and Stough, 1988). To a great extent, therefore, quality was not compromised by quantity, mainly because physical resources and budgets were increased along with enrollment. Also, a great deal of competition between universities for resources, prestige and capable students forced many institutions to adjust or correct flaws, in order to raise their level of recognition and to be able to compete for greater support and better faculty. This sort of competition was very much a product of the fragmented character of human capital development programmes, where each state had considerable flexibility in designing their own strategy, and the sort of resources that would be made available for that purpose. Thus, even though much federal aid was provided to states and to specific institutions, strategic and resource decisions, along with implementation, were left up to each individual state.

Such fragmentation also resulted in many disparities between states. Some Sunbelt states simply supported their existing public institutions, for example, while others, such as California, developed grand long-range expansion plans for their public universities (see Smelser and Almond, 1974; OECD, 1990). California, the most successful of the Sunbelt states, developed a division of labour in public higher education, designed to accommodate almost any individual who could qualify for admission. A three-tier public university structure was developed, to provide different levels of quality and educational standards. Thus, the University of California system, with 9 campuses, was oriented toward research, especially in science and technology, emphasising advanced graduate education as its distinctive feature, while admitting only the top 12 per cent of secondary school graduates at the basic college level (see, for example, Stadtman, 1970; Smelser and Almond, 1974). The second tier was then made up by the California State University system, with 20 campuses, emphasising teaching, professional education and public service, limited to provide only masters' degrees at the graduate level, and with more open admissions at the college level. The California community colleges then made up the third tier, with over 100 campuses, providing two-year college certificates, open admission, and entry level education for the least qualified, with remedial education, labour force retraining and community service as its main objectives. Other states adopted very different strategies, equipping their public universities to undertake all of those functions within each individual campus. Fragmentation therefore led to substantial disparities in human capital development strategies across states.

Such massive human capital development efforts were also subordinated to market forces. A review of states' master plans for higher education would show that improving the economic 'competitiveness' of each state and its local areas was by far the most frequently articulated goal (see Graham and Diamond, 1997; Geiger, 1993; Trow, 1991; El-Khawas, 1976). This subordination of educational policies to the real or anticipated needs of the market placed much emphasis on providing technically skilled personnel for private capital. The hope was that such skills, in addition to meeting the needs of growing indigenous businesses, would also help attract out-of-state or even foreign capital investment. In the case of various Sunbelt states, such as California, Texas, Florida, North Carolina, Georgia and Virginia, for example, such efforts would yield substantial benefits over time. Much external investment, and a more dynamic environment for local businesses, helped promote the rise of new high-technology activities. Higher incomes from those and other activities then attracted much technically skilled personnel from other regions.

Such in-migration of skilled personnel also helped the Sunbelt to become a major source of new technologies. The in-migration of skilled personnel helped many Sunbelt states avoid additional expenditures for education, since most training and skills had already been paid for by the states from which they migrated. Although little data exists on this aspect, it is known that the migration of highly educated individuals from the Northeastern and Midwestern regions to some Sunbelt states was significant over the years. At the start of the twentieth century, for example, almost all members of the National Academy of Sciences, the United States' most prestigious scientific organisation, were found in Northeastern or Midwestern states. By the late 1980s, membership in the National Academy was almost equally divided between the Sunbelt and the industrial heartland regions, with California concentrating a large proportion of the Sunbelt's total (National Academy of Sciences, 1990, 1997). Members from western states gained significant influence over the Academy, inducing it, for the first time in its history, to look away from Washington and set up a west coast headquarters in Southern California.

In general, however, population migration by itself cannot be considered a major force in the rise of the Sunbelt as a source of invention. Invention is, after all, an elite activity, undertaken by very few individuals in the population. It is therefore a mistake to assume that population redistribution can automatically result in more invention wherever population settles. There are many regions around the world that have received substantial populations, without any appreciable rise in invention, even when highly skilled individuals joined such migrations.

Tax policies are often mentioned as mechanisms to sustain or develop technology. In the United States, the most important tax measure for invention and innovation is possibly the R&D credits provided by federal tax laws to many industries or producers. Related to this aspect was the legislation passed by Congress in the 1980s to motivate firms to pursue cooperative R&D projects, which resulted in the creation of the Microelectronics and Computer Technology Consortium, comprising over 20 firms which targeted basic research, and the Semiconductor Research Consortium, for product development. Capital depreciation allowances included in the tax laws also provide some support for new technology, by allowing firms to write off their equipment and receive credits as it is replaced with new technology. The regulatory and tax systems have therefore provided indirect support for technology policies over some periods (see, for example, Nester, 1998; Malecki, 1991; Rees, 1986). These measures are difficult to assess in terms of their contribution to the rise of the Sunbelt as a source of new technology. They help, perhaps, only after a firm is established in a Sunbelt state or relocates there, or if depreciation allowances in some way help a relocation toward the Sunbelt, by making it less costly to move when capital equipment is almost fully depreciated and is about to be replaced.

Tax measures perhaps helped the Sunbelt more by their absence at the state level. Most Sunbelt states do not have corporate income taxes, in contrast with their counterparts in the Northeast and Midwest. California is a notable exception, with significant corporate income taxes, but it can be argued that those taxes are more than offset by other advantages, such as the concentration of highly skilled personnel and of technology firms. At the local level, property taxes tend to be lower in the Sunbelt than in many Northeastern and Midwestern states. Such taxes, however, are not usually considered to be significant in attracting external investment, although some communities have occasionally voided them temporarily in order to motivate some firms to relocate. In general, lower tax levels may have helped the Sunbelt's economic development, but they were not a decisive factor in its rise for invention.

By and large, the tax measures, limited as they are, have also been subordinated to the market. In their scope and implementation, such mechanisms aim to stimulate businesses to adopt new technologies, as a means to increase productivity. Improving competitiveness is also implicit in the kinds of changes they induce, since firms that are more productive are also more likely to be profitable and expand their markets at home and abroad. As firms become more profitable they will also contribute more to tax revenues, thereby enlarging the government's coffers. Thus, the tax measures are intertwined with market incentives and with the interests of the private sector. This is perhaps a classic feature of the American approach to taxation, in contrast with the approaches taken in many other nations, where tax policies are kept distant or separate from market considerations.

Special projects undertaken by federal agencies, on their own, have also pursued new technologies in the Sunbelt. Such projects cannot be considered policy programmes in the usual sense of the term, but they nevertheless deserve to be mentioned. One example was the federal Department of Energy's pursuit of solar energy in various projects that were funded in the Sunbelt. The federally-funded national laboratories have also occasionally undertaken civilian projects dealing with new technologies, in the areas of energy, communications and transportation, among others. The National Institute of Standards and Technology has also sponsored projects dealing with new technologies, more recently in trying to find commercial applications for military technologies. In general, however, the federal agency projects have not had any significant impact on the rise of the Sunbelt as a major source of new technologies, because of their isolated, very limited and fragmented character.

The American defence establishment has sometimes been mentioned as a force behind the growth of new technologies in the Sunbelt. There have been many defence installations and private contractors in some Sunbelt states, such as California, Texas and Florida (see, for example, Gansler, 1980; Koistinen, 1980; Malecki and Stark, 1988; Markusen et al., 1991). However, there is little evidence that many military technologies have trickled down to commercial applications over the years, in the Sunbelt or elsewhere (see Suarez-Villa, 1997b; Lynch, 1987). Even the substantial efforts at defence conversion sponsored after the end of the Cold War were largely unsuccessful in developing commercial applications, out of an enormous array of military technologies that were released for civilian use (see, for example, Suarez-Villa, 1997b). Also, military inventions cannot be patented, unlike commercially-oriented inventions.

The main impact of defence spending on the Sunbelt's rise as a source of new technologies may have been through the number of highly skilled personnel, that the region's defence contractors and installations attracted over the years. Even then, a large number of those skilled individuals would have had to switch to commercial invention in order to have any effect on the Sunbelt's capacity to produce new technologies. It is unknown to what extent such dislocation occurred, if it ever had any significant effects. Also, within defence contracting establishments that were engaged in both military and commercial production, there is little verifiable evidence about whether some of their military inventions in any way influenced or were used in their commercial operations. Defence contracting usually obstructed such synergies, requiring some separation between defence and commercial operations. Any transfer of new technologies from defence production to the commercial side of a firm would have required substantial scrutiny and review from defence authorities, and might have jeopardised future contracts if the transfer led to any revelation of military secrets.

The argument that defence contracting by Sunbelt firms subsidised their commercial activities is also largely unproven. Many, if not most, defence contractors were not engaged in commercial production of new technologies. This situation became more obvious at the end of the Cold War, when severe cutbacks in defence spending caused many contractors to go out of business or to retrench and remain solely dedicated to defence work. Other contractors simply merged with similar firms in order to reduce competition for reduced defence contracts, and to remain exclusively dedicated to defence work (see Suarez-Villa, 1997b). Thus, the argument for any significant impact by defence spending on the Sunbelt's rise as a major source of new technologies remains a doubtful one, with little supporting evidence. Also, defence policies aimed at developing new military technologies did not interact or become entwined with market mechanisms, as occurred with the other policies discussed before, for obvious reasons. The development of new defence technologies did not take into account market considerations since their primary purpose was not commercial to begin with. That characteristic alone made it very difficult for them to be converted for commercial use later on, or to help the Sunbelt's rise as a major source of commercial inventions and technology.

4 CONCLUSIONS

The radical changes that occurred in the regional sourcing of invention and new technology have been one of the most interesting features of the past five decades. The rise of the Sunbelt as the United States' most important source of new technologies over a relatively short period has no parallels in any other advanced nation. The role of market forces in this process was undoubtedly very important. Government's role in this process of change was subsidiary to the market. The high level of fragmentation and split functions in the policy programmes that affected the rise of the Sunbelt are probably the best indication of government's subsidiary role. Fragmentation also meant that it is practically impossible to point to any single policy or measure that had a decisive effect on the rise of the Sunbelt as a major source of new inventions and technology. Rather, what emerges is a collection of policy measures split between various levels of government, often implemented without any overarching coordination or planning.

The policy programmes and projects that contributed more to the Sunbelt's rise as a source of new inventions and technology were obviously those which had strong links with market forces. Being coupled to or entwined with the market was obviously a vital prerequisite for effectiveness, in the context of American market capitalism. The high physical mobility of the skilled population also helped, but it is important to note that migration to the Sunbelt typically occurred in response to market-driven opportunities. Also, it seems that the policy programmes which were both linked to market forces and were geographically sensitive (or location-specific) were the most effective. In that regard, infrastructural and human capital development were significant for their long-term contribution to the rise of the Sunbelt. Less effective, if not largely irrelevant, were the programmes which were more distant from market forces and from the territorial context. In that regard, tax policies, defence and the isolated special projects of some federal agencies seem to have been less important for the development of new inventions and technology in the Sunbelt.

It is difficult to present this case as a model for rapid regional change, because of the peculiar characteristics of the American economic and political context. Market incentives, supported by a highly fragmented policy context, worked in concert with many other factors to produce a remarkable change in the regional sources of new technology. The American experience in this regard is very different from that of most other advanced nations, where government has usually taken a leading role in promoting regional change, with market forces being secondary or less significant actors. What is most interesting about the American experience is that this market-led process of regional change resulted in convergence and in a reduction of disparities, between what were the more advanced industrial heartland areas and a large region that was largely backward or undeveloped barely five decades ago. If recent trends are any indication, the process of convergence is giving way to one of inversion, where the Sunbelt becomes the most important domestic source of new technologies, while the industrial heartland recedes into a subsidiary or less significant role.

REFERENCES

Abbott, C. (1981), *The New Urban America: Growth and Politics in Sunbelt Cities*, Chapel Hill: University of North Carolina Press.

American Public Works Association (1976), *History of Public Works in the United States, 1776–1976,* Washington, DC: U.S. Government Printing Office.

Ceh, S.L.B. and A. Hecht (1990), 'A Spatial Examination of Inventive Activity in Canada: An Urban and Regional Analysis Between 1881 and 1986', *Ontario Geography,* **35**, 14–24.

Dosi, G., R. Giannetti and P.A. Toninelli (eds) (1992), *Technology and Enterprise in Historical Perspective,* Oxford: Oxford University Press.

El-Khawas, E. (1976), *Public and Private Higher Education: Differences in Role, Character and Clientele,* Washington, DC: American Council on Education.

Gansler, J. (1980), *The Defense Industry,* Cambridge, MA: MIT Press.

Geiger, R.L. (1993), *Research and Relevant Knowledge: American Research Universities since World War II,* New York: Oxford University Press.

Graham, H.D. and N. Diamond (1997), *The Rise of American Research Universities: Elites and Challengers in the Postwar Era,* Baltimore, MD: Johns Hopkins University Press.

Gramlich, E.M. (1994), 'Infrastructure investment: a review essay', *Journal of Economic Literature,* 22, 1176–96.

Griliches, Z. (1990), 'Patent statistics as economic indicators: a survey', *Journal of Economic Literature,* **28**, 1661–707.

Griliches, Z., A. Pakes and B. H. Hall (1987), 'The value of patents as indicators of inventive activity', in P. Dasgupta and P. Stoneman (eds), *Economic Policy and Technological Performance*, Cambridge: Cambridge University Press.

Hagerstrand, T. (1967), *Innovation Diffusion as a Spatial Process,* Chicago: University of Chicago Press.

Haynes, K.E. and R.R. Stough (1988), 'Infrastructure Investment for Basic Research: U.S. Patterns in University Science and Technology', in L.J. Roborgh, R.R. Stough and T.A.G. Toonen (eds), *Public Infrastructure Redefined,* Leiden: Leiden University Press.

Hughes, T. P. (1993), *Networks of Power: Electrification in Western Society, 1880–1930*, Baltimore, MD: Johns Hopkins University Press.

Kealey, T. (1996), *The Economic Laws of Scientific Research,* New York: St. Martin's.

Kleinknecht, A. (1987), *Innovation Patterns in Crisis and Prosperity,* London: Macmillan.

Koistinen, P.A.C. (1980), *The Military–Industrial Complex: An Historical Perspective*, New York: Praeger.

Lynch, J.E. (ed.) (1987), *Economic Adjustment and Conversion of Defence Industries*, Boulder, CO: Westview Press

Malecki, E.J. (1991), *Technology and Economic Development,* New York: Longman

Malecki, E.J. and L. Stark (1988), 'Regional and Industrial Variation in Defence Spending: Some American Evidence', in M.J. Breheny (ed.), *Defence Expenditure and Regional Development*, London: Mansell

Markusen, A.R., P. Hall, S. Campbell and S. Deitrick (1991), *The Rise of the Gunbelt,* New York: Oxford University Press.

Mensch, G.O. (1979), *Stalemate in Technology,* Cambridge, MA: Ballinger.

National Academy of Sciences (1990, 1997), *Organization and Members,* Washington, DC: National Academy of Sciences.

Nester, W.R. (1998), *A Short History of American Industrial Policies*, New York: St. Martin's.

OECD (1990), *Higher Education in California,* Paris: OECD.

Rees, J. (ed.) (1986), *Technology, Regions and Policy,* Totowa, NJ: Rowman and Littlefield.

Rodwin, L. and H. Sazanami (eds) (1991), *Industrial Change and Regional Economic Transformation: The Experience of Western Europe,* London: Harper Collins Academic.

Sale, K. (1975), *Power Shift: The Rise of the Southern Rim and its Challenge to the Eastern Establishment,* New York: Random House.

Schmookler, J. (1966), *Invention and Economic Growth,* Cambridge, MA: Harvard University Press.

Schulman, B.J. (1990), *From Cotton Belt to Sunbelt: Federal Policy, Economic Development and the Transformation of the South, 1938–1980,* New York: Oxford University Press.

Scotchmer, S. and J. Green (1990), 'Novelty and disclosure in patent law', *Rand Journal of Economics,* **1**, 131–46.

Smelser, N.J. and G. Almond (1974), *Public Higher Education in California,* Berkeley, CA: University of California Press.

Stadtman, V. (1970), *Origin and Development of the University of California,* New York: McGraw-Hill.

Suarez-Villa, L. (1990), 'Invention, inventive learning, and innovative capacity', *Behavioral Science,* **35**, 290–310.

Suarez-Villa, L. (1993), 'The dynamics of regional invention and innovation: innovative capacity and regional change in the twentieth century', *Geographical Analysis,* **25**,147–64.

Suarez-Villa, L. (1996), 'Innovative capacity, infrastructure, and regional policy', in D. Batten and C. Karlsson (eds), *Infrastructure and the Complexity of Economic Development,* Berlin and New York: Springer-Verlag.

Suarez-Villa, L. (1997a), 'Innovative capacity, Infrastructure and Regional Inversion: Is there a Long-term Dynamic?', in C.S.Bertuglia, S. Lombardo and P. Nijkamp (eds), *Spatial Effects of InnovativeBehaviour,* Berlin and New York: Springer-Verlag.

Suarez-Villa, L. (1997b), 'California's Recovery and the Restructuring of the Defence Industries', in R.D. Norton (ed.), *Regional Resilience and Defence Conversion in the United States,* Greenwich, CT: JAI Press.

Suarez-Villa, L. (2000), *Invention and the Rise of Technocapitalism,* Lanham, MD: Rowman & Littlefield.

Suarez-Villa, L. and S.A. Hasnath (1993), 'The effect of infrastructure on invention: innovative capacity and the dynamics of public construction investment', *Technological Forecasting and Social Change,* **44**, 333–58.

Suarez-Villa, L. and C. Karlsson (1996), 'The development of Sweden's R&D-intensive electronics industries: exports, outsourcing, and territorial distribution', *Environment and Planning A,* **28**, 783–817.

Suarez-Villa, L. and W. Walrod (1997), 'Operational strategy, R&D, and intra-metropolitan clustering in a polycentric structure: the advanced electronics industries of the Los Angeles Basin', *Urban Studies,* **34**, 1343–80.

Trow, M. (1991), 'American Higher Education: Exceptional or Just Different?', in B.E. Shafer (ed.), *A New Look at American Exceptionalism,* Oxgord: Clarendon Press.

U.S. Bureau of the Census (1975), *Historical Statistics of the United States,* Washington, DC: U.S. Government Printing Office.

U.S. Bureau of the Census (1980–1997), *Statistical Abstract of the United States,* Washington, DC: U.S. Government Printing Office.

U.S. Bureau of the Census (1981), *Construction Reports: Value of New Construction Put in Place in the United States, 1964 to 1980*, Washington, DC: U.S. Government Printing Office.

U.S. Patent and Trademark Office (1997), *Annual Report,* Washington, DC: U.S. Government Printing Office.

Vesey, L.R. (1965), *The Emergence of the American University*, Chicago: University of Chicago Press.

Webster, D.S. (1986), *Academic Quality Rankings of American Colleges and Universities,* Springfield, IL: Thomas.

PART TWO

Evaluating Regional Policy

7. Regional Policy Evaluation and Labour Market Adjustment

Ian Gordon

1 INTRODUCTION

Regional policy is commonly conceived as a response to effects of uneven spatial development on individuals' job prospects, and/or earnings from employment. In evaluating the successes and failures of policy, however, curiously little attention has been given to labour market processes, or to the final impacts on individuals flowing from policy's immediate effects on investment and so on.. This is a curiosity both in respect of the academic literature and (perhaps even more) in relation to the concerns of government agencies active in commissioning evaluations of spatial economic policies. Indeed in the latter case it might even lead one to question the real objectives of policy.

Despite a wide range of objectives which are cited for regional policy, evaluations have tended to focus explicitly or implicitly on net additions to employment in the areas concerned as the key performance indicator. And, indeed, in terms of the evaluation of performance, as distinct from that of projects or processes, this is a quite reasonable position, since job creation is a key intermediate variable in most strategies, and more readily measurable than most final outcomes. As with all performance indicators, however, there is a real danger of goal displacement, with action being oriented to the measured variable, irrespective of the achievement of underlying objectives.

The aim of this chapter is to demonstrate the need for regional policy evaluations to give more attention to labour market outcomes – particularly in terms of the incidence of unemployment – and to the ways in which labour market processes respond to injections of new activity into assisted areas. It approaches this task via a review of the different roles which evaluation may be expected to play, and some of the key issues associated with each (in Section 2), followed by a discussion of the objectives against which regional policies should be evaluated (in Section 3). The main section of the chapter (4) then examines how impacts of supply-side labour market adjustments may be incorporated in evaluations of the impact of policy on unemployment, in particular.

2 THE OBJECTIVES OF EVALUATION

Given the objective-directed character of this activity, one starting point is to consider what policy evaluation itself is intended to achieve. In fact, within the general policy evaluation literature three rather distinct objectives and contexts for the process are distinguishable, highlighting different questions and raising rather different methodological problems. For convenience we shall refer to these as project, performance and process evaluation respectively, though these labels are somewhat arbitrary. Academically they tend to be associated with different disciplinary backgrounds, and practically they often imply different ways of proceeding with the task of evaluation, which can be mutually incompatible.

The first of these forms of evaluation is concerned with the question of whether a specific *project* is worthwhile, in relation to a set of objectives and associated costs. As such, whether asked before a decision is taken or retrospectively (*ex ante* or *ex post*), it is essentially an economic question, with an answer which is either binary (yes/no) or at least ordinal (that is a number allowing the project to be ranked alongside competitors/ substitutes). Conceptually then, project evaluations belong to the family of cost–benefit and cost–effectiveness analyses. One key variation within this family is in terms of whether an absolute standard of worthiness is to be set, commensurable across all projects, or just one permitting relative evaluation among those with related objectives. The second important source of variation is in terms of the status given to those objectives, as between a highly specific objective function with weightings supplied by the policymaker, and (at the other extreme) a criterion of social benefit based on the preference functions of those affected. Between these extremes, the key issue is how far expressed or implicit objectives are to be taken as given, or as open to question in relation to some more general criterion, via analyses of actual causal links and evidence on preferences. Within this form of evaluation, a central problem is that of counterfactuals, that is of what could be expected to happen in the absence of this project. In ex ante studies this appears essentially in terms of opportunity costs, to be set against expectations of the benefits accruing from the project. Ex post, the issue tends to be that of what part of the observed outcomes has actually been caused by the project (especially when there is no independent control that can be used as a benchmark). Both of these issues are particularly important where the potential for direct and indirect market responses is strong (as in the labour market).

A second form of evaluation is focused on *performance* in implementing projects or other tasks. This tends to take for granted the worthwhileness of the projects or programmes themselves, at the level of principle, while asking questions about how well they are actually being delivered in practice by particular institutions, individuals, areas, or political regimes – and the specific instruments or tactics which they employ. This approach is essentially managerial, with implications being drawn about the competence of those concerned, and frequently about the way in which they should be rewarded, whether individually or in terms of future resourcing. As such, a key requirement is to develop performance indicators which are objective (especially being independent of those being evaluated), regularly available for the units concerned, and as consistent as is practicable in their substantive meaning. In practice, these requirements imply a considerable gap between what is measured and what is really valued (by policymakers or consumers), encouraging goal displacement and potential distortion of operations toward activities allowing measured performance to be improved with least effort. Fairness and control (that is reliability) tend to be more important criteria in designing evaluations of this sort than either purpose or scientific truth (that is validity).

The third approach to evaluation is concerned less with testing worthwhileness or performance than with trying to analyse *processes* affected by a policy, in order to diagnose the factors associated with better/worse outcomes and discover ways of improving on these (Deutscher, 1976). The set of relevant concerns are those revealed as important in this analysis, including ones ignored in the originally stated objectives. The emphasis on processes rather than outcomes alone could be seen as extending and complementing other forms of evaluation. However, in practice there are substantial tensions between pursuit of this approach and (particularly) implementation evaluation, since the latter tends to discourage openness about what lies behind measured performance and treats operational goals as given. Process evaluation generally requires cooperation between practitioners and analysts in a task which is perceived as mutually beneficial, implying that self-evaluation may be best – whereas this appears quite inappropriate in relation to performance evaluation (Wildavsky, 1972). Against the former view, it is argued that self-evaluation encourages self-justification, allowing the perpetuation of inefficient management structures. On the other hand, there is an argument that (necessarily) uninformed external evaluation lacks understanding of how projects interact with their environment, permitting the persistence of ineffective policies/programmes – or sometimes their arbitrary abandonment. when measured performance is declining everywhere for reasons that are not understood.

Some of these tensions have been highlighted in a debate over the relationship between instrumental and contextual uses of evaluation. In the former case, evaluation is supposed to feed directly into a 'rational' decision-making process, while the latter involves a more indirect effect, via changes in the way that policymakers think about the problem, possible approaches and outcomes (Alback, 1989–90).[1] While the initial 1960s upsurge in evaluation studies was framed almost entirely in instrumental terms, this has been followed by increased interest (among researchers) in contextual applications, due to the lack of any convincing evidence that policymakers made direct use of evaluations, and growing scepticism about rational models of the decision-making process (Rist, 1995).[2] In particular, research indicated that policy goals were *normally* vague, unspecified (even unspecifiable) or disguised, often because of the need to cover-up a lack of real consensus about these (Alback, 1989–90). From the perspective of Braybrooke and Lindblom's (1963) theories of administration as disjointed incrementalism, this need not be a problem, so long as there is an array of effective interest groups (each able to draw on their own evaluations), but this is often not the case with the redistributive policies on which much evaluation effort has focused. Furthermore, organisational research has shown that administrative and operational policies are often dependent on sets of underlying assumptions that escape in-depth probing (Rist, 1995). In the fields on which American evaluation studies had been concentrated, Weiss[3] concluded that further studies would be a waste of time, since what they all showed was the ineffectiveness of policies that failed to address the social, economic and cultural roots of problems. The need now was to focus on questioning basic assumptions and goals in order to design better policies, rather than to continue measuring degrees of failure.

For the practitioner, a focus on each of these forms of evaluation highlights issues which are of more general relevance. These include the importance of:

- establishing counterfactuals;
- looking critically at stated objectives;
- paying attention to final outcomes (as well as more readily available activity indicators); and
- investigating the processes through which these outcomes are produced.

When these issues are attended to, there is a greater chance, than with concentration on single predefined measures, of contributing productively to policymaking–and also that core measures will not be seriously misleading.

3 THE OBJECTIVES OF REGIONAL POLICY

Evaluation of any of these kinds presupposes a view as to what policy is *for*, whether this is couched in terms simply of:

- what policymakers say or believe to be important; or
- open to critique in the light of evidence about how those affected actually behave and what they experience as being of significant value;

and operationalised in terms of:

- a set of fixed, quantifiable indicators, or
- in a more open-ended fashion to accommodate changing understandings of how processes operate.

In relation to regional policy there are a number of different broad formulations of what the underlying policy concerns might be, varying in terms of:

- whether they are primarily related to reducing (spatial) inequalities in welfare; or to enhancing productivity, competitiveness and factor utilisation at a national/European level;
- whether they primarily involve direct short/medium-term effects on employment, income, costs and productivity, or longer-term strategic shifts in regional productive capacities and potential competitiveness; and
- how far they are directed at the welfare of those in the weakest labour market situation (the present and future unemployed in particular) or that of other, more mainstream groups.

The position taken on each of these dimensions can be seen to involve both value and reality judgements, though it is rarely explicit how far a policy concern is really dependent on assumptions about particular causal processes, or simply buttressed by these, in a more or less opportunistic way.

To take an example, efficiency arguments for regional policy in the UK have tended to draw on three sorts of proposition:

(a) That in the absence of policy an uneven development of certain relatively immobile resources (including various kinds of labour potential, as well as infrastructural and social capital), implies lower levels of overall productivity, given conventional assumptions about the diminishing marginal productivity of capital.
(b) More specifically, that excess demand for some of these factors in the more developed regions during periods of growth engendered inflationary pressures, spreading through the whole economy and requiring restraining macroeconomic policies to be introduced while substantial spare capacity still existed elsewhere in the economy.
(c) That over-development in certain regions imposed higher levels of negative social externality (including various sorts of congestion cost) than would obtain with a more even pattern of development.

Very limited evidence is actually available in relation to any of these assumptions, including that about regionally-based inflation, which dates back to a speculation of Keynes in the late 1930s and was inconclusively investigated during the 1960s and 1970s.

In relation to the equity arguments, particularly those focused on the welfare of groups in or at risk of unemployment, two critical assumptions are:

(d) That policy initiatives in the assisted regions will significantly alter the balance between labour supply and demand, overcoming any structural constraints to re-employment, so that the benefits are substantially concentrated within the region, with limited leakage elsewhere.
(e) That on welfare grounds (leaving aside any national efficiency gains) it is preferable for any given level of unemployment to be more evenly spread geographically–perhaps because this reduces the likelihood of prolonged (or repeated) individual spells, or because social externality effects increase rapidly beyond some threshold level in local or regional unemployment.

Again, supporting evidence is thin. In the first case there is relevant research (to be discussed in the following sections), but in the second case there is a notable lack of attempts even to address the question.

As a third example, the issue of whether policy is to be justified, and hence judged, by its direct effects and/or in terms of a longer-term transformation of economic potential involves not only value judgements about whose welfare is of prime concern, but also analytic judgements about:

(f) The extent to which current regional disparities (or at least the unacceptable elements in these) reflect the impact of specific shocks which will *eventually* be resolved through one form or another of factor mobility, or rather involve structural weaknesses (maybe induced by a long series of 'shocks') which can, only, be addressed through strategic interventions.
(g) The capacity to identify appropriate policy instruments (and performance indicators) for the quite different objectives of: mitigating the immediate impacts of shocks on those most groups and places most severely affected; *or* catalysing the development of new sources of competitive advantage.

In practice, official statements about regional policy tend to be a good deal more opaque about underlying value judgements and factual/theoretical assumptions, not simply through ignorance or carelessness, but through the political exigencies of building and maintaining support. From this perspective, advocacy of policies in terms of multiple, loosely defined objectives is a very positive feature. In relation to implementation and evaluation, it is much more problematic, however, since ambiguities then have to be resolved, usually at the cost of some of the more difficult objectives, as well as to the overall coherence of the policy. In the specific case of regional policy, a particular factor is the presence of latent, unstated objectives. Sometimes these may have been deliberately repressed in order to disguise otherwise unacceptable policies, as when 'regional' policy measures have been used to pursue essentially *national* economic or industrial policies (subsidising export activities, inward investment projects, or industrial restructuring) in ways generally unacceptable to GATT, the EU or the labour movement (Pickvance, 1981). More commonly the motive is one of political management. Thus the EU's concern with 'social and economic cohesion' is better seen as involving *political* cohesion, with side-payments to potential losers intended to secure their attachment to a European project of economic liberalisation. At a national level, in the UK at least, the crucial issue (for governments of both major parties) seems to have been one of maintaining the hegemony of an essentially national party system, organised around a single class/ideological dimension of competition/cleavage (Gordon, 1990).

Despite such sophistications, there do appear to be two central foci to regional policy:

1. Reduction of unemployment in areas where this is associated with relatively weak economic performance (not simply concentrations of disadvantaged groups), whether as a welfare problem to be addressed on some sort of equity ground, or because of efficiency concerns about under-used resources and inflationary pressures.
2. A strategic concern with building up the long-term competitive strength of old or under-developed regions, whether in the national interest or to counter a spatial division of labour which leaves these regions with a subordinate role and inferior types of opportunity.

For the first of these, the impact of regional policy on unemployment rates is an absolutely crucial indicator to use in evaluations, although the appropriate measure of unemployment may well vary according to the reasons why this is thought to be significant. Thus, where the concern is welfarist in nature or concerned with under-use of human resources an inclusive measure including various groups who would like a job though they are not currently engaged in search is appropriate. On the other hand, where the concern is with short-term demand management and inflationary pressures it would be appropriate to focus on those actively engaged in search (that is the ILO unemployed rather than Beatty et al.'s (1997) 'real unemployed') – and possibly only with the shorter term unemployed, if it is their numbers alone which affect wage bargaining outcomes (Layard et al., 1986; Blackaby and Manning, 1990). In relation to the second concern, there are no such obvious single indicators, since the relevant outcomes are long-term ones, and since regional development theory does not yet provide the basis for confident judgements about the crucial mediating variables. But it is clear, as with the unemployment concern, that overall measures of jobs created, or investment attracted must be an unsatisfactory proxy for real indicators of progress towards the policy goal.

The use of measures of additional regional employment as an evaluation criterion has, however, been defended by Armstrong and Taylor (1993) on two grounds. First, they claim that this is 'one of the major objectives of regional policy' (p. 330), though it could only be justified as such in relation to its expected consequences of employment creation. Among these consequences, they do highlight the reduction of regional disparities in unemployment rates as representing the 'prime purpose of regional policy' (p. 331). But (as their second, pragmatic line of argument) they argue that: 'attempting to estimate the effect of regional policy on unemployment in the assisted areas is a *pointless exercise*' (p. 333, emphasis added) on the grounds that there is no simple link between changes in unemployment and: 'those variables which regional policy is meant to affect directly, such as employment, investment and the movement of industry into assisted areas' (p. 333). In particular, they recognise a number of ways in which supply adjustments are to be expected, that will be discussed in relation to wider labour market processes in the next section. But these are precisely *the point* of directing evaluation toward final outcomes – either directly, or at least indirectly through analyses of the processes intervening between the immediate effects of policy and the socially valued outcomes – *because* this link is an uncertain one.[4]

4 LABOUR MARKET RESPONSES TO REGIONAL MEASURES

Almost all of the plausible regional policy objectives are linked to the labour market in some way, and thus may potentially be affected by how regional labour markets respond to the direct impacts of policy. Labour market adjustments are a particular issue since spatial labour markets are open, in the sense that neither purchasers nor suppliers of labour are necessarily restricted to operating in a particular geographically defined sub-market – nor indeed in a specific occupational sub-market either. Some at least of those involved can shift their activity elsewhere in response to changing patterns of opportunity and advantage. On the supply side of the market this particularly involves labour migration (that is household moves involving changes in workplace as well as residence) and shifts in the direction of commuting. Some such moves are occurring all the time, reflecting the incidence of specific opportunities relevant and available to particular people, so the issue of spatial supply adjustment can be as much one of the redirection or inhibition of movement as of immobile individuals being stimulated into locational shifts. A large proportion of these moves may be over rather short distances (especially in the case of commuting changes), but redirection of such moves in the face of a shifting surface of opportunities can effect significant changes in the balance of flows for quite broad, clearly separated regions indirectly as these moves alter local supply–demand balances. Both geographically and in occupational space, key adjustments may thus take the form of ripples through overlapping sets of labour markets, rather than direct shifts between areas with conspicuous disparities in opportunities. Even when the latter kind of movement seems unlikely to be substantial it is important therefore to consider the possibility of strong supply adjustments to new opportunities created through regional policy interventions in evaluating their effects on target variables.

These adjustments may come about both through 'price' and quantity signals. In this context, 'price' effects involve responses to varying expected streams of real income (including social and environmental as well as financial factors) associated with taking up specific job/search opportunities, as against remaining in a current workplace (or area of search). Particularly when employment opportunities are differentiated, quantity signals also come into play in the sense that probabilities of making moves to other locations depend on the spatial distribution of opportunities (that is here on the flow of relevant vacancies) as well as the ratings of representative opportunities in different areas. Indeed in a competitive labour market, with minimal disparities in real income, this will be the dominant mode of spatial redistribution of labour supply – rather than responses to potentially short-lived disparities in rewards. In those (secondary) occupational sub-markets where turnover rates tend to be high, there will be a flow of vacancies in most places, and labour migrants who may well have to move speculatively in order to search may be stimulated by a generalised expectation of opportunities, and reward levels. In mainstream jobs with low turnover rates, and migrants able to await contracts before actually moving, however, the rate of creation of new jobs is going to be much more crucial to the incidence of migration opportunities, and thus a more direct influence on the balance of movement between sub-labour market areas.

In the first instance this means that jobs created directly through regional policy initiatives may be taken up by in-migrants (including returners), or new in-commuters into the area, or by people who would otherwise have moved their workplace (at least) elsewhere. The latter group are harder to identify, but probably the minority at least among migrants, in the context of a 'pull' effect, and a reasonable approximation to the *initial* degree of 'leakage' of the benefits of regional policy jobs out of the area might be gained by surveying recruits to work on identifiable projects. But, given that jobs tend to be filled by people already in employment, rather than by the unemployed, each job filled by a local person leaves another vacancy which also has some probability of being filled by an induced in-mover, or a diverted out-mover. New job creation thus sets in motion a chain of vacancies, terminating either with recruitment of an unemployed person or an incomer, with multiple chances of 'leakage' occurring, and more substantial difficulties in monitoring how many jobs eventually accrue to locally unemployed (or inactive) persons. Some form of modelling is therefore required to evaluate the impact of – even a known number of – new jobs on regional unemployment levels.

The potential scale of the gap between local/regional employment and unemployment effects, together with the main factors likely to modify this in particular situations, can be examined with a simple model incorporating responses of net migration and commuting change to spatial disparities in unemployment levels and employment changes (Burridge and Gordon, 1981). This starts from an accounting identity relating changes in unemployment within a sub-market to changes in various components of labour supply and demand:

$$\Delta U_i \equiv \Delta S_i - \Delta E_i + M_i + \Delta C_i + W_i . a_i . \Delta p_i \qquad (7.1)$$

where:

ΔU = change in numbers unemployed;
ΔS = natural change in labour supply (consequent on ageing and deaths);
E = numbers in employment;
M = net migration of economically active persons;
C = net commuting;
W = the working age population;
a = an age factor, weighting population proportions in each age group by age-specific specific participation rates;
p = an age-standardised participation rates; and
the subscript i identifies zones.

Employment change and natural change in labour supply are treated as endogenous; while both migration and commuting are responsive to the distribution of opportunities; and participation rates to the level of open unemployment. Starting from a gravity model approach to labour migration, an area's balance on this account is represented as a function of differences between local conditions and those in its migrational hinterland:

$$\frac{M_i}{(E_i)} = f(U_n) \sum_j \left[E_j f(D_{ij}) \left(-\alpha (u_i - u_j) + \beta (g_i - g_j) + \chi (X_i - X_j) + \gamma (C_i - C_j) \right) \right] \qquad (7.2)$$

where:

u = the unemployment rate (defined as U/E);
g = an employment growth rate;
X = a vector of valued zonal characteristics;
C = a vector of population characteristics;
$f(D_{ij})$ = an inverse function of the distance between zones i and j);
$f(U_n)$ = an inverse function of national unemployment; and
α, β, χ, γ are (positive) parameters.

With this function, the scale of net migration is conditioned both by an area's accessibility, and by a national mobility factor reflecting the current tightness of the national labour market. All estimates of the responsiveness of migration to employment and unemployment differentials are therefore conditional on the areas and time periods involved.

The commuting change equation is similarly specified in term of differentials, although in this case only employment growth rates are assumed to be significant influences and the relevant hinterland is more tightly defined.

$$\Delta C_i = \phi o_i E_i (e'_i) \qquad (7.3)$$

where: o_i = a measure of the openness of area i to commuting ($0 > o_i > 1$);

e'_i = the difference between the rate of employment change in area i and the average for its commuting hinterland; and ϕ is a parameter.

Finally, age standardised participation rate changes are represented as a function of time and of local unemployment rates:

$$\Delta p_i = f(t) + \pi \, \Delta u_i \qquad (7.4)$$

where: t = time; and π is a parameter.

In the form specified above, with no time lags in responses, this model yields an equilibrium unemployment equation of the form:

$$u_i = \overline{\Pi}(u_i) + \alpha^{-1}\left[\frac{s_i - e_i}{f(U_n)\Pi(E_i)} + \beta\tilde{g}_i + \chi\tilde{X}_i + \gamma\tilde{C}_i + \phi o_i e'_i + f(t)\right] \qquad (7.5)$$

where:

$\overline{\Pi}(u_i)$ = a weighted average unemployment rate for the migrational hinterland of area i;

s = the rate of natural increase of labour supply (S/E);

e = the rate of growth of employment;

$\Pi(E_i)$ = a measure of migrational accessibility (employment potential);

and tildes denote differences between local values and a weighted average for the migrational hinterland.

Introducing a single period time lag in the response of migration to unemployment – so that adjustment involves both an initial response to employment differentials and a continuing one to unemployment relativities

– yields a disequilibrium version where current values of independent variables are replaced by distributed terms (with longer mean lags for inaccessible areas and in periods of slack labour demand).

Initial applications of this model to cross-sectional data for British sub-regions (Burridge and Gordon, 1981) and to time series for Scotland (Gordon, 1985) confirmed the importance of supply adjustments even in the case of large regions.[5] A short (one year) lag was evident in the response of migration to differential unemployment changes, but the strength of this response was such that the effects of one-off employment changes were short-lived, and prevailing unemployment relativities were generally close to the equilibrium pattern.[6] However, these generalisations related to years preceding the sharp upsurge in unemployment at the end of the 1970s, and it was evident that the responsiveness of migration was substantially reduced at higher levels of overall unemployment.[7] Subsequent research has shown that this diminution of mobility (primarily affecting those in high turnover labour markets) specifically involves a much weakened response to unemployment differentials[8] (Gordon and Molho, 1998), implying longer-lasting effects from one-off employment shocks and stronger disequilibrium elements in the observed pattern.

In order to explore the impact of a changing economic context on the link between regional employment and unemployment, a (slightly simplified) version of equation (7.5) has been used for a cross-sectional regression analysis of 1991 Census unemployment rates across the 322 British Travel To Work Areas. As compared with the earlier analyses, two clear shifts were evident. The first involves the size of the effective hinterland areas within which equilibriation is concentrated: as indicated by the best-fitting distance decay functions, these now appear to be much more intraregional than interregional in scale.[9] The second is that there is now little evidence of employment effects falling off over time: the best specification of an employment growth variable involved an unweighted sum of changes over the previous 10 years.[10] And, as the regression results in Table 7.1 show, there is further evidence of persistence via the unemployment rate prevailing 10 years previously. In relation to open unemployment half of 1981 differentials were still extant 10 years later, while this proportion rises to two thirds when concealed unemployed groups, such as the permanently sick, are also included.

Elements of continuity in the results, as compared with earlier periods, include the fact that even for TTWAs a substantial part of the unemployment disparities is structural in character, associated with disadvantaging personal/household characteristics, and clear evidence of spillovers between each area and its hinterland.

Table 7.1 Regressions of travel to work area non-employment rates, 1991

Dependent variable	Unemployment rate			Unemployed plus permanently sick		
	1	2	3	4	5	6
Constant	–16.2***	–17.2****	–7.44**	–47.9****	–46.9****	–22.4***
Differential employment change 1981–91: manual sectors	–0.061***	–0.065****	–0.077****	–0.084****	–0.095****	–0.105****
Differential employment change 1981–91: non-manual sectors	–0.005	–0.019	–0.017	–0.024	–0.032	–0.019
Hinterland unemployment rate 1991		0.271****	0.727****		0.474****	0.988****
Differential unemployment rate 1981			0.559****			0.652****
Differential permanent sickness rate 1981						0.690****
% Asian	–0.045	–0.058	–0.052	–0.087	–0.115	–0.060
% Black	0.107	0.218	0.158	–0.039	0.102	0.134
% Public housing	0.208****	0.203****	0.039	0.415****	0.392****	0.125**
% House-owners	0.129***	0.136****	0.003	0.324****	0.309****	0.071
% With limiting illness	1.638****	1.463****	0.592****	3.062****	2.695****	0.766***
% Non-married males	0.210***	0.195***	0.145***	0.366***	0.346***	0.254****
% Non-married females	0.152***	0.156***	0.009	0.115	0.130	–0.037
% Aged 16-19	0.583***	0.578***	0.263*	0.831**	0.835**	0.567***
% semi-skilled (SC4)	0.052	0.052	–0.037	0.108	0.109	0.007
% Unskilled (SC5)	0.268**	0.223*	0.031	0.547***	0.436**	–0.040
Adjusted R^2	0.694	0.711	0.872	0.760	0.778	0.921

Notes:

1 Both unemployment and sickness rates are expressed as percentages of the numbers economically active (though the permanently sick are classed as economically inactive); all compositional variables relate to the economically active population, except for ethnicity and housing tenure which relate to all residents/households.
2 Observations are the 322 1981-based Travel to Work Areas in Great Britain.
3 'Hinterland' values relate to averages of other observations, using weights proportional to the volume of employment in each and an inverse distance function [exp(–0.06)*distance in miles].
4 Rates of employment change in (non-)manual sectors are measured as percentages of *total* employment in 1991;
5 Differential employment changes are measured relative to the overall national average, except in columns 3 and 6 where they are relative to hinterland averages; similarly, 1981 unemployment rates are measured as differences from the national average, except in columns 3 and 6 where the base is the hinterland average.
6 All regressions are weighted, using as weights the square root of numbers employed in each TTWA.
7 Stars indicate significance levels (* = 5%, ** = 1%, *** = 0.1%, **** = 0.01%).

Sources: 1991 Census of Population, and 1981/1991 Censuses of Employment (for employment change only).

In terms of the crucial relationship between employment changes and unemployment, much depends on the sectors involved, but typically, only 2 per cent of employment changes in non-manual sectors and 7 per cent of those in manual sectors[11] are reflected in levels of unemployment, while including the permanently sick as the most significant of the groups of hidden unemployed only raises the proportion to 10 per cent for changes in the manual sectors. As we should expect, there is some evidence of a size effect, with small travel to work areas showing even weaker effects of employment change on local unemployment, but for most provincial cities the estimated effects are not substantially greater than the average figures cited here.[12].

Shifting the level of analysis up that of standard regions does, however, almost double the effect of manual employment changes on open unemployment, but without adding anything further to the effect on 'concealed unemployment' (see Table 7.2). Focusing on the largest of all regions, the South East, with a third of national employment, a time series analysis (over the years 1972–94) does, however, suggest a much stronger first year effect, with 1000 less jobs in manufacturing adding 530 to open unemployment in the region, while a similar change in other sectors added 160.

Potentially as important as such estimates of average impacts of employment changes on unemployment, is the guidance which a model of this sort can provide about likely sources of variation. Three of these which have already been noted are in terms of broad sectors of employment, the size/accessibility of areas of interest, and the impact of macroeconomic circumstances. In the first case, though differences have emerged for industrial sectors, our theoretical expectations really relate to occupational variations, with those in higher levels being more readily able to afford mobility costs, more able to benefit from national advertising/ employer support, and likely to require specialised vacancies unavailable locally.

Table 7.2 Regressions of regional non-employment rates, 1991

Dependent variable	Unemployment rate	Unemployed plus permanently sick and so on
Constant	–9.4	–12.2
	(18.8)	(8.8)
Differential employment change 1981–91: manual sectors	–0.143	–0.177
	(3.7)	(1.7)
1981 value of dependent variable	0.381	0.880
	(6.9)	(8.3)
Adjusted R^2	0.909	0.898

Notes:

1. The observations are the 11 standard statistical regions of Great Britain, with a further division between Devon/Cornwall and the rest of the South West.
2. The dependent variable in column 3 includes as well as the unemployed, those who are permanently sick, on government schemes or prematurely retired, all expressed as a proportion of the economically active population.
3. In both equations non-employment rates have been standardised for the effects of personal/household characteristics, using the estimated coefficients for each in the TTWA regressions (columns 3 and 6 of Table 7.1).
4. Bracketed values are t statistics.

This expectation is substantially confirmed when the TTWA regressions are recast with measures of employment change differentiated by social class, when a clear distinction emerges between professional and managerial jobs, which appear to have no impact on local unemployment, while for other jobs in the 'manual' sectors impacts are a bit larger than the sectoral average figures presented in Table 7.1. The impact of macroeconomic circumstances, via the encouragement or discouragement of long-distance mobility, also appears to be very important, with the significant implication that any regional policy jobs which can be secured during periods of generally high unemployment will be of substantially greater value in reducing differential unemployment than is the case in boom periods when labour market adjustment processes operate more effectively. A related point involves an asymmetry between the effects of job gains and job losses. Though the model above is cast in terms of responses to overall rates of employment change, the emphasis on mobility as a response to discrete employment opportunities implies that migration rates in particular should be influenced by gross (rather than net) rates of employment growth, with the implication that unemployment is much more heavily influenced by (involuntary) job losses. This hypothesis is not readily tested with British data, although one time series analysis for London did show that differential redundancy rates had a much more substantial impact on unemployment than other employment changes even within the manufacturing sector (Gordon, 1988). Fitting a version of equation (7.5) to US state data, with a differentiation of components of employment change, however, provides clear evidence of the asymmetry, with unemployment rates apparently being determined essentially by rates of job loss (whether through closure or plant-level contractions), and with no evidence of effects from job gains, at least after the first year (Gordon, 1995). Such disparities have potentially great importance in relation to the relative salience of job creation versus job retention policies, and (for this reason) would seem to be among the key topics for investigation in regional policy evaluation studies.

The approach to evaluating policy impacts on unemployment outlined here involves a very aggregative view of labour market adjustment, assuming a substantial degree of interconnection across all sub-markets within a region, despite varying degrees of 'distance' between them. Thus probabilities of employment are seen as essentially the product of two separate factors: one reflecting the overall pressure of demand for labour; and the other representing potential workers' 'competitiveness' in relation to generalised preferences of employers. What is omitted is any specific consideration of 'mismatch' between more specific characteristics of workers ('skills') and the particular requirements of a local employment structure. Theoretically the justification for this simplification lies in a deep scepticism about the fixity and specificity of both requirements and competences, together with an emphasis on the indirect connection of all sub-labour markets. Actual mismatches are thus expected to be resolved through *many* small adjustments by participants in linked sub-markets – via changing standards, personnel development practices, and pay relativities – rather than requiring (improbably) large adaptations by those in sub-markets with conspicuous shortages and surpluses. Empirically, this simplification is supported by the high proportions of spatial variances in unemployment rates which are explicable via overall indicators of demand-pressure and job-competitiveness – together with evidence of strong interactions between even broad skill groups when spatial unemployment in these is modelled separately (Gordon, 1981).

Against this, it is clearly possible to hypothesise situations where some more specific mismatch is involved (and more where this would be the case if activities actually located in inappropriate areas). But these are not at all typical and the real danger of the mismatch perspective is that it diverts attention from processes actually operating within the labour market. In an evaluation context it suggests a need to focus on the characteristics of jobs directly created through regional policy, in relation to characteristics of the unemployed, but in isolation from the processes connecting these to wider labour markets. And in a policy context it encourages an overemphasis on the provision of entry-level jobs, coupled with over-optimism about the unemployment impact which can be expected from feasible levels of job creation.

5 CONCLUSIONS

The central argument of this chapter is that regional policy evaluations need to concern themselves not simply with performance measures reflecting the immediate effects expected from the policy instruments which are being used, but with some measures closer to the valued outcomes, *and* with understanding more clearly the processes which link these. In terms of the general typology of approaches to policy evaluation this involves a synthesis between project, performance and process evaluation as the most fruitful approach to securing actual improvements in policy. In the case of regional policy this presents some particular difficulties given pervasive ambiguities as to exactly what the underlying objectives are. One of the two strategic objectives, however, always appears to be a reduction of unemployment rates in economically backward areas, and is probably often the central concern, as well as the more operationalisable of the strategic objectives. In this case regional policy evaluations ought to focus on the unemployment impacts, rather than resting content with measuring direct effects on employment or investment. This is important because strong labour market adjustment processes can drive a very large wedge between employment and unemployment effects. Consequently assessments of unemployment impact may well be disappointing, but this is a good reason for looking hard at the intervening labour market processes and the circumstances in which a greater or lesser share of the benefits accrue to unemployed people within the region. Given that much of the residue from industrial restructuring and the recessions of the 1980s and 1990s will now take the form of structural unemployment it is also very important to relate evaluations of what can be achieved through demand-side regional policies to the effects achievable through other initiatives to improve the competitive position of unemployed and marginal workers in the assisted areas. More generally, it is crucial that evaluators recognise the fluidity and inter-connectedness of labour markets, and not assume that impacts of regional policy can simply be read off from numbers of jobs 'created', even when accompanied by information on the characteristics and occupants of those specific jobs.

NOTES

1. A third possibility, in practice, is a purely symbolic, legitimising use (Alback, 1989–90).
2. Noting the survival capacity of this model in the face of contradictory research findings, Gordon , Lewis and Young, (1977) suggest that it has the status of a 'dignified' myth, both for policymakers and researchers, who it 'helps towards a comfortable life: [enabling them] to appear to engage in direct debate with the policy-makers on the basis that information provided by the researchers will be an aid to better policy-making'.
3. Quoted in Bamberger (1991).
4. This argument applies as much when benefits are seen in terms of additions to production as in terms of social welfare or income objectives, since the opportunity costs depend crucially on the extent to which net additions to employment accrue to workers who would not otherwise have been productive (notably the unemployed).
5. This is significant, since the model entails much stronger responses for smaller, more open sub-labour market areas.
6. Not surprisingly, these conclusions also apply in the US context, where levels of spatial mobility are generally much higher, especially for manual workers (Gordon, 1995).
7. The estimated mobility function was inversely proportional to unemployment over rates up to about 6 per cent after which it flattened out (Gordon, 1985).
8. The response to the quantity signal of employment change rates remains strong, however, and notably stable over a 30 year period.
9. The best fitting parameter in an exponential distance function was –0.06 with 1991 data, as compared with –0.005 with 1971 data.
10. In part at least this may reflect the particular circumstance of falling national unemployment through the second half of the 1980s.
11. The manual sectors as defined here include all production industries together with wholesale distribution and transport/communications.
12. For example, confining the analysis to the 10 per cent of TTWAs with labour forces over 150 thousand raised the coefficients on each of the employment change variables by about 0.03.

REFERENCES

Alback, E. (1989–90), 'Policy evaluation: design and utilization', *Knowledge in Society*, **2**, 6–19.

Armstrong, H. and J. Taylor (1993), *Regional Economics and Policy*, 2nd ed, Hemel Hempstead: Harvester.

Bamberger, M. (1991), 'The politics of evaluation in developing countries', *Evaluation and Program Planning*, **14**, 325–39.

Beatty, C., S. Fothergill, T. Gore and A. Herrington (1997), *The Real Level of Unemployment*, Centre for Regional Economic and Social Research, Sheffield Hallam University.

Blackaby, D.H. and D.N. Manning (1990), 'The north–south divide – earnings, unemployment and cost of living differences in Great Britain, *Papers of the Regional Science Association*, **69**, 43–55.

Braybrooke, D. and C. Lindblom (1963), *A Strategy of Decision: policy evaluation as a social process*, New York: Free Press.

Burridge, P. and I.R. Gordon (1981), 'Unemployment in the British metropolitan labour areas', *Oxford Economic Papers*, **33**, 274–97.

Deutscher, I. (1976), 'Toward Avoiding the Goal-trap in Evaluation Research', in C.C. Abt (ed.), *The Evaluation of Social Programs*, Beverly Hills: Sage, pp. 249–68.

Gordon, I.R., J. Lewis and K. Young (1977), 'Perspectives on policy analysis', *Public Administration Bulletin*, **25**, 26–30.

Gordon, I.R. (1981), 'Social class variations in the effects of decentralisation in the London metropolitan region', paper for the Third International Workshop on Strategic Planning, University of Dortmund.

Gordon, I.R. (1985), 'The cyclical interaction between regional migration, employment and unemployment: a time series analysis for Scotland', *Scottish Journal of Political Economy*, **32**, 135–58.

Gordon, I.R. (1988), 'Evaluating the impact of employment changes on unemployment', *Regional Studies*, **22**, 135–47.

Gordon, I.R. and I. Molho (1998), 'A multi-stream analysis of the changing pattern of interregional migration in Great Britain, 1960–91', *Regional Studies*, **32**, 309–23.

Gordon, I.R. (1990), 'Regional policy and national politics', *Environment and Planning C: Government and Policy*, **8**, 427–38.

Gordon, I.R. (1995), 'Accounting for inter-state unemployment disparities in the United States', Discussion Chapter 26, Geography Department, University of Reading.

Layard, R. and S. Nickell (1986), 'Unemployment in Britain', *Economica*, **53**, S121–S169.

Pickvance, C.G. (1981), 'Policies as chameleons: an interpretation of regional policy and office policy in Britain', in M. Dear and A.J. Scott (eds), *Urbanization and Urban Planning in Capitalist Society*, Andover: Methuen, pp. 231–65

Rist, R.C. (1995), 'Introduction', in R.C. Rist (ed.), *Policy Evaluation: linking theory and practice*, Aldershot: Edward Elgar.

Wildavsky, A. (1972), 'The self-evaluating organisation', *Public Administration Review*, **32**, 509–20.

8. The Evaluation of UK Regional Policy: How much Progress has been Made?

Jim Taylor

1 INTRODUCTION

The UK has a long tradition of regional policy dating back to the late 1920s when attempts were made to relocate unemployed coal miners to areas where job prospects were better. Since the creation of the Special Areas in the 1930s, however, the primary purpose of regional policy has been to create jobs in areas suffering from persistently high unemployment rates rather than to encourage out-migration from high unemployment areas (Armstrong and Taylor, 1993). It has been argued consistently that such a policy yields benefits not only to the areas designated for assistance, but also to the nation as a whole (Taylor and Wren, 1997). The benefits to the assisted areas obviously include better job prospects for the unemployed and a consequent improvement in living standards. In addition, reducing an area's unemployment rate is likely to confer benefits on all residents since high unemployment rates are associated with geographically concentrated social problems and poor quality infrastructure as well as economic malaise. All residents of the assisted areas therefore benefit from policies which reduce the unemployment rate. The national benefits include an increase in the utilisation rate of the economy's resources, giving rise to a higher level of national output.[1] The residents of the non-assisted areas may also be expected to benefit from regional policy since income transfers into high unemployment areas will be reduced if the economic performance of the assisted areas can be improved. In addition, there will be less incentive for people to migrate out of the assisted areas and into areas which may already be experiencing an excess demand for land, housing and other fixed factors of production.

Given the long tradition of regional policy in the UK, it is not surprising to find that there has been considerable interest in developing evaluation methods (Foley, 1992). This interest in policy evaluation essentially began in the 1960s (Needleman and Scott, 1964; McCrone, 1969) and accelerated in the 1970s following the seminal articles by Moore and Rhodes (1973, 1976), who made the first serious attempt to quantify the effect of regional policy on key economic variables such as employment and the transfer of industry into the assisted areas. Since these early attempts at evaluation, many different approaches based upon different time periods and different data sets have been used. Some researchers have focused on estimating the effect of regional policy instruments on the individual recipients of financial assistance while others have attempted to assess the effect of regional policy on the assisted areas as a whole. More recently, attention has turned to the evaluation of entire regional development programmes, particularly those supported by the EU's Structural Funds.

The primary concern of this chapter is to review the development of policy evaluation techniques in the UK. It begins, in Section 2, by reviewing the attempts to estimate the effect of regional policy on employment levels in the assisted areas. Section 3 turns to the effect of regional policy on the location decisions of domestic manufacturing firms, while Section 4 examines cross-sectional models of interregional movement of industry. Section 5 focuses specifically on the extent to which regional policy has been successful in steering foreign inward investment into the assisted areas. Section 6 discusses the importance of distinguishing between the net and gross effects of regional financial assistance, while Section 7 reviews some recent developments in the construction of *ex ante* appraisal techniques, the aim of which is to predict the effect of regional policy over some future time period. Section 8 discusses some of the 'softer' methods which have been introduced to evaluate regional development programmes supported by the EU. Finally, Section 9 concludes with a summary of progress made in UK regional policy evaluation.

The papers selected for review in this chapter represent only a fraction of the research into policy evaluation in the UK. They provide a flavour, however, of the wide variation in approaches used to evaluate regional policy.

2 THE EFFECT OF REGIONAL POLICY ON AGGREGATE EMPLOYMENT TRENDS IN THE ASSISTED AREAS

Several attempts have been made to estimate the effect of regional policy on employment trends in the UK's assisted areas. The earliest, and one of the most ambitious, attempts to estimate the effect of regional policy on employment in the assisted areas was by Moore and Rhodes (1973). Their aim was to estimate the impact of regional policy as a whole by comparing actual employment in the assisted areas with the employment level that would have occurred if the policy had not existed. This counterfactual approach was based primarily on the assumption that trends in employment are primarily determined by a region's industry mix, but may change direction if a 'shock' such as regional policy is introduced. Trends discerned during a previous policy-off period are then used to estimate the counterfactual in a subsequent policy-on period. Dissatisfaction with this trend-based approach led researchers to construct economic models designed to explain the time path of employment rather than relying simply on extrapolation from policy-off periods into policy-on periods.

These subsequent studies used regression analysis to estimate the effect of a number of potential explanatory variables on employment changes over time, including the effect of regional policy. The dependent variable in these models is the annual change in employment in those industries eligible for assistance (that is, manufacturing). The change in employment in the manufacturing sector is regressed on a number of explanatory variables which include quantitative indicators of the strength of regional policy. A variable believed to be of key importance is a region's industry mix, the influence of which can be taken into account by calculating the growth in employment that would have occurred if all industries in the region had grown at national growth rates per industry.[2] Finally, a range of other possible influences on a region's employment growth are added to the model.

The first of these studies, by Moore, Rhodes and Tyler (1986), attempted to estimate the effect of capital and labour subsidies on employment trends in the UK's assisted areas during 1950–81. Their model is as follows[3]:

$$\Delta e_t = \mathrm{f}\,(\,\Delta e_t{}^*, \mathrm{PVGRANT}_t\,, \mathrm{GRANTEXP}_t\,, \mathrm{LSUBSIDY}_t\,)$$

where:

Δe = annual change in manufacturing employment in assisted areas

Δe* = expected annual change in manufacturing employm. in assisted areas

PVGRANT = present value of automatic Regional Development Grants per £100 expenditure

GRANTEXP = total annual expenditure on Regional Selective Assistance at constant prices (discretionary investment grants)

LSUBSIDY = total annual expenditure on the Regional Employment Premium at constant prices.

Regression analysis is then used to estimate the relationship between employment change and each explanatory variable. It was found that the three regional policy instruments had a substantial effect on employment growth in the assisted areas during the study period.

A problem with such highly aggregated studies of the effect of regional policy on changes in employment is that they may conceal effects of policy instruments which can only be revealed in more disaggregated studies. The effect of policy instruments on employment trends, for example, is likely to vary between regions and between industries. For example, regional investment incentives were designed to modernise older industries by making them more capital-intensive (the consequence being a decline in employment) whereas in other cases the incentives were intended to induce entirely new industries to move into the assisted areas. In view of the criticisms levelled against highly aggregated studies of employment change, Wren and Taylor (1999) estimated a model disaggregated by industry and by region. This model allows for employment trends to be affected by a range of other variables, such as the growth in demand for each regional industry's output, in addition to the following three regional financial incentives:

RDG = regional development grant expenditure (an automatic investment grant taken up mainly by large firms)
RSA = regional selective assistance (a discretionary investment grant directed at inward investors)
REP = regional employment premium (a labour subsidy operating during 1967–76).

(These three policy instruments were expressed in terms of expenditure per capita in the regression model.)

A panel data set was constructed to estimate the model, which consists of 14 manufacturing industries and 12 regions for the period 1973–94. The findings of this analysis were mixed. Automatic investment grants were found to be associated with a decline in employment levels, the probable explanation being that the Regional Development Grant has been used to improve efficiency and productivity. By contrast, labour subsidies had the expected positive effects on employment, while discretionary grants (Regional Selective Assistance) had positive effects in some industries and negative effects in others. For example, automatic investment grants are estimated to have had a negative impact on employment levels in the chemical industry, whereas discretionary grants and labour subsides had a positive impact.

The purpose of these highly aggregated studies of regional policy is to estimate the jobs created by each specific regional policy instrument in the assisted areas. Their main strength is that they provide an estimate of the overall effect of regional policy on employment trends. They suffer, however, from two significant shortcomings. First, they fail to focus on those firms which have actually received financial assistance. The dependent variable in these aggregate studies is the sum of many different decisions reached by many different firms, the vast majority of which have not received regional financial assistance. The aggregated nature of the data does not allow us to identify the potential impact of the underlying determinants of employment change. Researchers have consequently attempted to overcome this problem by shifting their focus to the recipients of the financial aid themselves (see Section 7 below). The second problem with highly aggregated studies of the effect of regional policy instruments is that they do not allow for the wider effects of financial incentives on the competitiveness of the regional economy as a whole. These two criticisms suggest the need for more disaggregated microeconomic investigations of the effects of regional policy on a wide range of economic variables rather than focusing simply on jobs created. We will return to this point later in the chapter.

3 THE EFFECT OF REGIONAL POLICY ON THE INTERREGIONAL MOVEMENT OF INDUSTRY

In the 1960s and 1970s, UK regional policy relied heavily on steering manufacturing industry from non-assisted areas to assisted areas, the main policy instruments being location controls and subsidies on both capital and labour. Two approaches have been used to estimate the effect of these policy instruments on the movement of manufacturing industry into the assisted areas. The first approach, based on time series data of industrial movement, attempts to identify the role of policy instruments on the movement of industry over time. The second approach utilises cross-section data in order to estimate the effect of regional policy instruments on the interregional movement of industry.

3.1 Time Series Models of Industrial Movement

The time series approach attempts to estimate the effect of regional policy on the movement of industry into the assisted areas over time. In the earliest study using this approach, Moore and Rhodes (1976) argue that the movement of industry into the assisted areas has been influenced by four main variables:

- national business conditions
- investment incentives
- labour subsidies
- controls on the location of industry in non-assisted areas.

A measure of national business conditions is included in the model to allow for the fact that the movement of industry is likely to be higher during booms than during recessions. All three regional policy instruments are expected to have a positive effect on the aggregate movement of industry into the assisted areas.

After estimating a regression model with the movement of industry into the assisted areas as the dependent variable, the effect of each policy instrument is then estimated by 'switching off' each policy instrument in turn in order to estimate the number of plants that would have moved into the assisted areas in the absence of each policy instrument. A similar method is used by Moore, Rhodes and Tyler (1986), who estimate that the three policy instruments together caused nearly 2000 manufacturing establishments to move into the UK's assisted areas as a direct result of regional policy during 1960–81 (see Table 8.1). One problem with this approach is that the policy intruments may actually work in an interactive way. They may only be effective if they are used in combination with each other and so estimating the independent effect of each instrument may give a misleading picture of their individual effectiveness.

Table 8.1 Estimated effect of regional policy instruments on the number of manufacturing establishments moving into assisted areas in Great Britain, 1960–81

Period	Investment incentives	Location controls	Regional employment premium	Total effect
1960–65	288	228	–	516
1966–71	246	246	240	732
1972–77	258	102	180	540
1978–81	176	24	–	200
Total 1960–81	968	600	420	1988

Source: Moore, Rhodes and Tyler (1986).

An alternative approach to modelling the movement of industry is taken by Ashcroft and Taylor (1977, 1979). They argue that the movement of industry is best treated as a two-stage process. In stage one, the aggregate movement of industry to all regions is assumed to be determined primarily by the national level of investment. In addition, regional policy may have some effect on the aggregate movement of industry since location controls in non-assisted areas together with the availability of input subsidies in assisted areas may induce more industrial movement than would have occurred in the absence of policy. In stage two, the geographical distribution of industrial movement is determined by the relative economic attractiveness of alternative locations, including the effects of regional policy instruments. This two-stage model is as follows:

$$M_t = f(INV_t, LC_t, GRANTS_t)$$

$$\frac{M_{a,t}}{M_t} = g\left(\frac{W_{a,t}}{W_t}, \frac{U_{a,t}}{U_t}, LC_t, GRANTS_t\right)$$

where:

M = total number of firms moving between regions
M_a = number of firms moving into assisted areas
INV = national level of investment
LC = strength of location controls in non-assisted areas
$GRANTS$ = value of investment incentives to firms in assisted areas
W_a = wage rate in assisted area
W = national wage rate
U_a = unemployment rate in assisted area
U = national unemployment rate
t = time (in years).

This model is based on the notion that industrial movement is first generated at national level and is then distributed between regions according to the relative economic pulling power of each region. Estimates of the effect of regional policy on the movement of industry into the assisted areas based on this approach indicate that over 50 per cent of the moves during 1960–71 could be attributed to the existence of regional policy instruments.

As with the attempts to estimate the effect of regional policy on employment trends in the assisted areas, the early investigations of industrial movement were highly aggregated and consequently suffer from the same sorts of problems. Attempts were subsequently made to use a more disaggragated approach and these included investigations of the movement of industry between all regions, not simply the movement of industry into the assisted areas. This interregional approach is discussed in the next section.

4 CROSS-SECTIONAL MODELS OF THE INTER-REGIONAL MOVEMENT OF INDUSTRY

Cross-sectional data of the number of manufacturing establishments moving between regions provides an alternative way of modelling the interregional movement of industry. It has been argued that the movement of industry between any two regions will depend upon three main factors (Twomey and Taylor, 1985; Taylor and Twomey, 1988):

i. *The size of the origin and destination regions*
Larger regions are not only likely to generate more moves than smaller regions, but are also likely to attract more moves than smaller regions because of the existence of scale economies and larger markets.

ii. *The distance between regions*
Firms will normally have more information about locations nearer to their existing operations and will also prefer short-distance moves to long-distance moves in order to maintain close contact with existing manufacturing operations and existing suppliers.

iii. *The relative economic attractiveness of each region*
This is determined by any factors affecting the expected net profitability of locational choice, including the effect of regional policy on economic attractiveness.

The model based upon these hypotheses is as follows:

$$M_{ij} = f(P_i, P_j, \text{DIST}_{ij}, \text{ATTRACT}_{ij})$$

where:

M_{ij} = number of establishments moving from region i to region j
P_i = number of plants in region i
P_j = number of plants in region j
DIST_{ij} = distance between region i and region j
ATTRACT_{ij} = relative economic attractiveness of regions i and j (for example regional differentials in the price of factor inputs between i and j).

This model argues that the movement of industry between any pair of regions is positively related to the stock of plants in both the origin region and the destination region, and is negatively related to the distance between them. The model also incorporates variables which measure differences in the relative economic attractiveness of the origin and destination regions, which surveys of industrial location indicate is likely to be determined by factors such as the availability and cost of labour, financial incentives, controls on the location of industry, transport links, access to markets, and the availability of industrial sites and industrial buildings (Munday, 1990; PACEC, 1995).

Once these potential determinants have been identified, multiple regression techniques are then employed to estimate the effect of each variable on the movement of industry between each pair of regions (M_{ij}). To estimate the overall effect of regional policy on M_{ij}, the policy instruments are simply 'switched off' in order to provide an estimate of what M_{ij} would have been in the absence of regional policy. The results of this exercise indicated that about 42 per cent of all manufacturing moves in Great Britain during 1960–77 were due to regional policy. Table 8.2 shows the estimated effect of location controls and investment incentives separately. Analyses at county level produce similar results. Once again, however, there are problems with estimating the effects of individual policy instruments since the effectiveness of any single instrument may be conditional on the coexistence of other (complementary) policy instruments.

In view of the relative success of these various investigations of the effect of regional policy on the movement of industry into the UK's assisted areas, it is perhaps surprising that this approach has not been followed up in subsequent research work. There are several reasons for this. First, regional policy has switched away from encouraging firms to move from non-assisted areas to assisted areas since this job diversion was thought to be too costly for the benefits likely to be gained. Secondly, regional policy has focused more directly on stimulating indigenous growth within the assisted areas themselves. Thirdly, creating jobs by attracting foreign investors into the assisted areas would mean that the economy as a whole would gain rather than there simply being a geographical redistribution of jobs as in the case of diverting industry from non-assisted areas to assisted areas. Fourthly, the interregional movement of industry database has not been maintained.

Table 8.2 Estimated effect of regional policy instruments on the movement of manufacturing establishments into each GB region, 1960–77

Region	% of GB manufacturing employees in 1970	Total number of moves	Estimated effect of location controls on inward moves	Estimated effect of investment incentives on inward moves	Combined effect of location controls and investment incentives
South East	27.0	124	0	0	0
East Anglia	2.6	359	110	0	110
South West	5.3	333	100	16	116
East Midlands	7.7	251	33	0	33
West Midlands	14.0	71	9	0	9
Yorksh./Humb.	10.0	143	71	8	79
North West	14.6	217	65	29	94
North	5.9	250	76	80	156
Wales	4.3	331	110	57	167
Scotland	8.6	264	104	109	213
GB	100	2343	678	299	977

Source: Twomey and Taylor (1985).

5 REGIONAL POLICY AND FOREIGN INWARD INVESTMENT

The sharp decline in the movement of industry from non-assisted areas to assisted areas in the 1980s led to a switch in regional policy strategy. Policymakers in the UK turned their attention to foreign inward investment. Since regional investment incentives have been extensively used to attract foreign direct investment (FDI) into the assisted areas, policymakers have been keen to discover (a) the extent to which investment incentives have affected the location decisions of inward investors, and (b) the effect of FDI on the economic performance of the assisted areas. We first consider the methods used to estimate the effect of regional policy on the location decisions of foreign inward investors.

5.1 The Effect of Regional Financial Incentives on the Location of Foreign Inward Investment

Foreign direct investment (FDI) has played a substantial part in the UK's regional development policy, especially since the mid-1980s (Hill and Munday, 1994; Stone and Peck, 1996). This is clearly indicated by the continuing success of the UK's assisted areas in attracting almost 50 per cent of all manufacturing FDI during 1991–97 (see Table 8.3) even though these regions have only 20 per cent of the UK's manufacturing employment.

Table 8.3 Foreign direct investment in UK regions: 1981–90 and 1991–97

Region	Estimated jobs associated with inward investment in manufacturing (1981–90)	Number of inward investors (1991-97)			
		Manufacturing		Non-manufacturing	
	%	Number	%	Number	%
South East	9.0[1]	86	5.4	161	24.7
East Anglia	–	29	1.8	76	11.7
South West	3.5	79	5.0	20	3.1
East Midlands	4.4	68	4.3	46	7.1
West Midlands	17.4	255	16.0	91	14.0
Yorkshire/Humber	4.8	122	7.7	43	6.6
North West[2]	11.6	176	11.0	68	10.4
North	8.7	179	11.2	48	7.3
Wales	13.6	242	15.2	42	6.5
Scotland	17.6	269	16.9	85	13.1
Northern Ireland	9.3	88	5.5	11	1.7
UK	100.0	1593	100.0	651	100.0

Notes: 1. Includes East Anglia. 2. North West includes Cumbria for the number of moves.

Source: *Office of National Statistics* (1998) *Regional Trends*, 33, p.158.

By contrast, the South East region attracted a mere 5 per cent of manufacturing FDI despite its 24 per cent share of UK manufacturing employment. A similar picture is obtained from the regional distribution of Japanese-owned manufacturing plants: around 50 per cent of the jobs are located in Scotland, Wales and the North (Table 8.4), and nearly 75 per cent of all jobs in Japanese manufacturing plants are located in an assisted area (Table 8.5).

Table 8.4 Regional distribution of Japanese-owned plants in GB, 1996

Region	Number of Japanese plants	Number of employees in Japanese plants	% of total employees in Japanese plants
Greater London	12	1 420	1.8
Rest of South East	45	6 180	7.9
East Anglia	6	1 310	1.7
South West	14	4 120	5.3
West Midlands	32	13 280	17.0
East Midlands	22	5 880	7.5
Yorkshire and Humber	13	4 550	5.8
North West	19	2 840	3.6
North	29	11 720	15.0
Wales	41	15 860	20.3
Scotland	34	10 780	13.8
GB	267	77 940	100.0

Source: Data obtained from the Invest in Britain Bureau, Department of Trade and Industry.

Table 8.5 Employment in Japanese-owned plants in the UK by type of assisted area, 1996

Type of assisted area	Japanese firms		All firms
	Number of employees in Japanese plants	%	% of total GB employment in area
Development area	26 500	34	16
Intermediate area	29 800	39	19
Non-Assisted area	21 100	27	64
Total	77 400	100	100

Source: Data obtained from the Invest in Britain Bureau, Department of Trade and Industry.

To what extent have regional financial incentives influenced the relative success of the UK's assisted areas in attracting foreign inward investors? Several empirical studies have been undertaken in an attempt to answer this question (Munday, 1990; Hill and Munday, 1992, 1994; Taylor, 1993;

PACEC, 1995). These fall into two groups. First, direct surveys of inward investors have been undertaken with the aim of discovering the importance of financial incentives compared to other potential influences on the location decision. PACEC (1995), for example, found that financial incentives were considered to have been a 'very important' factor in 20 per cent of the firms surveyed, ranking way below the availability of a suitable site or premises (see Table 8.6). In an earlier survey, Munday (1990) found that 25 per cent of inward investors considered financial incentives to have been 'important' in their choice of location, ranking well below factors such as the availability of a suitable site, the reliability of suppliers and the availability of labour.

Table 8.6 Reasons for the choice of a particular locality

Reason given for actual choice of location in UK	% of firms replying 'very important'
Site/ premises availability	53
Availability of labour	33
Presence of pre-existing company (acquisitions)	33
Availability of skilled labour	30
Low-cost labour	20
Financial incentives	20
Utilities available (water/energy)	20
Road/rail connections	13
Proximity to customers	13
Air connections	10
Training provision	7
Good industrial relations	7
Proximity to suppliers	7
Image of location	3

Source: PA Cambridge Economic Consultants (1995).

The relatively high rank for the availability of a suitable site is not surprising, especially since it may reflect the influence of local development agencies in providing a range of attractions to lure investors into their particular locality. The effect of regional financial incentives may therefore be underestimated by responses to questionnaires since it is likely to be the entire package on offer that is important rather than simply financial incentives *per se*.

Secondly, several statistical analyses have been undertaken in order to identify the main determinants of the location decision of inward investors. In one such study, Taylor (1993) investigates the number of Japanese manufacturing firms locating in each county during 1972–91. Since a wide range of factors can be expected to influence the locational choice of mobile investors, multiple regression methods are used to estimate the influence of a range of potential determinants. Following similar work in the US (Friedman, Gerlowski and Silberman, 1992; Coughlin, Terza and Arromdee, 1990, 1991), these determinants might be expected to include:

- access to markets: road links, access to ports and airports
- labour market conditions: labour costs, labour availability and labour relations
- availability of financial incentives
- promotional activities of the region
- land and site availability and construction costs
- industrial structure at the new location: access to local suppliers.

The main findings from UK studies of the spatial distribution of Japanese inward investors indicate that financial incentives have played a critical role in inducing firms to locate in assisted areas. The UK's assisted areas have attracted far more Japanese plants than would have been expected on the basis of their relative size. Additional factors include: the availability of labour, the proportion of the workforce employed in manufacturing and a good transport infrastructure. Other variables such as wage costs appear not to have had much effect.

Some assisted areas, however, have been far more successful in attracting Japanese plants than others, one possible reason for this being that 'success breeds success'. Once an area is successful in attracting foreign investment, it is easier to attract further foreign investment in the future. There is, in fact, substantial evidence that inward investors are attracted to locations where there is already a concentration of firms in the same industry. This suggests the presence of agglomeration economies which arise as a direct consequence of the clustering of industries in particular geographical areas (O'Huallachian and Reid, 1997). The high level of clustering of Japanese plants in the same industry in particular locations in the UK provides some support for this hypothesis. Examples of this clustering process (based on 1996 data) are as follows:

- 101 of the 266 Japanese manufacturing plants are located in 8 of the 64 counties. These 101 plants employ 43 per cent of the total workforce of Japanese manufacturing plants.
- 44 of the 107 Japanese plants in electrical engineering are located in 7 of the 64 counties. These 44 plants employ 56 per cent of the workforce of inward investors in this industry.
- 22 of the 42 Japanese plants in the motor industry are located in just 5 of the 64 counties. These 22 plants employ 65 per cent of the workforce of inward investors in the motor industry.

This clustering of foreign investors has direct implications for regional policymakers since it suggests that once the initial breakthrough of attracting a major inward investor has been made, it will then be easier to attract further foreign investors into the area in the future.

5.2 The Impact of Foreign Inward Investors on UK Firms

Although the primary purpose of encouraging inward investment is to create jobs and income in the destination region, especially in areas where it is most needed, there is ample evidence from several empirical studies that inward investment has a far wider impact (Munday, 1990; Munday, Morris and Wilkinson, 1995; PACEC, 1995). Inward investors may have some effect, for example, on the management practices and economic performance of domestic firms. There are several ways in which these impacts can occur (see Figure 8.1). First, inward investors may introduce new management practices which domestic firms decide to imitate. Secondly, domestic firms may have to work to higher standards and introduce new management practices if they are to win new business from inward investors. Thirdly, inward investors which acquire or form practices on these firms. Fourthly, domestic firms in competition with inward investors may have to become more efficient in order to maintain their market share. The impact of inward investors on UK firms has been investigated by PA Cambridge Economic Consultants (1995). Three main types of impact are identified: the impact on suppliers, the impact on competitors, and the impact on the local economy.

Impact on competitors

Views about the impact of inward investment on competitors diverged considerably between the inward investors and their major competitors in the UK.

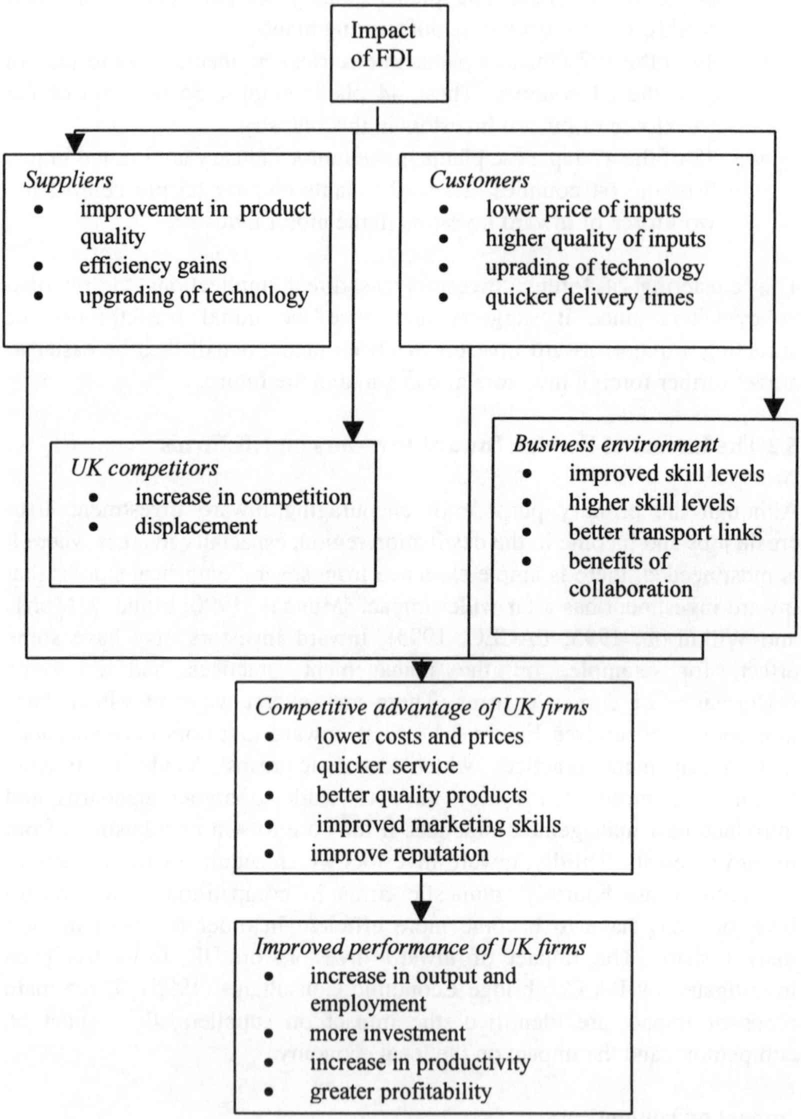

Figure 8.1 The potential impact of foreign direct investment on the performance of UK firms

While the inward investors believed that their presence had beneficial effects on product quality, product design and production costs, the competitors themselves claimed that many of these improvements would have occurred anyway. Domestic competitors did agree, however, that the impact of inward investors had been positive and not negative.

Impact on suppliers

A majority of inward investors were found to have an explicit strategy for developing supply networks in the host country. They are particularly keen that domestic suppliers have appropriate quality assurance systems and are active in product development. Many inward investors take the view that domestic suppliers have responded to the challenge by improving product quality while simultaneously improving their competitiveness by reducing costs. Very similar views were expressed by the suppliers themselves, many of whom claimed to have changed their practices to meet the expectations and requirements of the inward investors. Many domestic suppliers, for example, stated that their association with inward investors had resulted in higher sales, higher employment and higher profits and there was little evidence of negative impacts.

Local impact of inward investment

The impact of inward investors has obviously been highly visible in some localities and regions simply because of the sheer size of some plants and the number of firms locating in some relatively small local economies. The 'knock-on' effects of this direct impact through local supply chains varies from area to area, however, and depends upon the quality and range of the local supply network. The largest quantitative impact on other local industries was found to be in business services; and the smallest impact has been on capital goods which are imported not just into the locality but also into the UK, often from the inward investor's country of origin. On average over all the firms investigated, it was found that for every 100 direct jobs created by the inward investor, about 30 extra jobs were created in the UK as a whole. In addition to this impact on jobs, the areas in which inward investors have located have benefited from increased visibility and a general improvement in their image. This has helped to generate further inward investment through a lagged migrant stock effect. Local development agencies have also reported an increase in the supply of labour due to an increase in labour force participation rates as more jobs have become available, and labour force quality has improved as a result of increased investment in education and training.

The PACEC survey therefore indicates that inward investment leads to benefits to the economy more generally in addition to the direct jobs created in the localities in which they decide to locate. Both suppliers and competitors appear to have gained from the inflow of foreign direct investment and there can be little doubt that overseas firms locating in the UK have had positive effects on the competitiveness of domestic firms.

6 NET VS. GROSS EFFECTS OF REGIONAL FINANCIAL ASSISTANCE

Several attempts have been made to estimate the effectiveness of regional financial incentives through collecting information directly from the recipients themselves. An early example of the use of detailed firm by firm enquiries into the effectiveness of regional financial incentives is provided by Robinson, Wren and Goddard (1987), who surveyed 201 manufacturing establishments located in north-east England which had received some form of financial assistance either from central government or local government. Asking firms whether they have been affected, and in what way, by regional incentives has the distinct advantage that those to whom the incentives are directed are asked for their views about the effect of these incentives on their own operations. The obvious drawback of such surveys is that so many factors affect a firm's operations that they may not know themselves what effect investment incentives have had. Moreover, the recipients may be economical with the truth if they believe that their answers could affect the future availability of government grants. Despite these problems, surveys are thought to provide useful feedback information for the evaluation process.

Industrial surveys have focused on three main questions:

1. To what extent have financial incentives affected a recipient firm's investment and employment?
2. Would the investment have occurred if financial incentives had not been available?
3. What is the cost per job of financial incentives?

Although there have been several attempts to estimate the impact of financial incentives on variables such as profitability, productivity and R&D spending (Wren 1987, 1988), attention has focused primarily on just two outcomes: the jobs created and the cost (to the government) of each job created. Several new concepts have consequently been introduced in order to improve the accuracy of estimates of these two crucial outcomes.

6.1 Additionality, Displacement and Multiplier Effects: Estimating the Jobs Created

A question lying at the heart of the effectiveness of regional financial incentives is how many extra jobs are created in an assisted area as a consequence of this financial assistance. We need to know:

- the extent to which the direct jobs created exceed the number that would have been created if financial incentives had not been available (to identify the extent of *deadweight* spending and hence to estimate the *additionality* of the project)
- whether the increase in employment is at the expense of other firms in the same locality (that is are there *displacement* effects?)
- the extent of any *multiplier* effects on the local economy through supply linkages or through the household sector.

To calculate the expected impact of financial incentives on employment, estimates are required of additionality, displacement and local multiplier effects. Additionality is simply the probability that a project takes place as a direct consequence of the financial assistance. It can also take into account the extent to which a project is larger than it otherwise would have been or occurs sooner than it otherwise would have done. If the project would have gone ahead without financial assistance, then additionality is obviously zero. Displacement is the extent to which the project displaces output (and hence employment) from other firms in the same region due to taking away market share from existing firms or through attracting labour from other firms which consequently have to reduce their output. Finally, the multiplier effects of the project on the local economy are calculated from information about the supply linkages of the firm receiving the grant and from estimates of the regional multiplier.

The importance of deadweight spending (and hence additionality) in regional financial assistance has been investigated by several researchers. In a comprehensive *ex post* evaluation of UK regional policy, PACEC (1993) estimates that the degree of additionality is about 50 per cent for a typical project. In another detailed empirical investigation of regional financial assistance, Wren (1987, 1988) finds that deadweight spending was far higher for local authority financial assistance and for automatic investment grants than for discretionary investment grants linked to the number of jobs created. Deadweight spending was also found to be higher for start-ups than for existing firms, which is not surprising since start-ups have a high death rate. The lower percentage of deadweight spending for discretionary grants is because firms that qualify for assistance have to establish that they cannot obtain finance elsewhere.

An alternative way of estimating the job creation effects of regional financial assistance is to compare the employment trends of assisted firms with those of a sample of comparable non-assisted firms. A control group is established by selecting a matching set of firms which have similar characteristics to the assisted firms. The employment trends of the assisted firms are then compared with the control group in order to obtain an estimate of the impact of the assistance. In effect, the comparison with the control group allows the deadweight loss to be estimated since the experience of the control group is assumed to indicate what would have happened to the assisted firms in the absence of the financial assistance. This method is used by Hart and Scott (1994) for assessing the employment impact of financial assistance provided to small firms in Northern Ireland.

Despite its obvious attraction in producing estimates of what would have happened in the absence of policy, the control group approach suffers from a serious drawback: the non-assisted firms are unlikely to be a reliable control group (Storey, 1990). One obvious way in which the assisted firms differ from the control group of non-assisted firms is that the control group did not apply for (or obtain) financial assistance. This could mean that they did not desire to expand their activities whereas the assisted firms clearly did intend to expand their operations. The behaviour of the control group would not, in this case, provide any guidance to what would have happened to the assisted firms in the absence of policy.

6.2 The Cost per Job of Regional Financial Incentives: Gross vs. Net Effects

Governments are rightly keen to evaluate the effectiveness of financial incentives. One very simple device is to calculate the cost to the exchequer of the jobs created as a result of the grant expenditure. For individual projects, this means calculating the *gross* costs per *direct* job created. These cost per job estimates can then be used not only to compare the cost per job of different types of financial assistance but also to compare the effectiveness of regional financial incentives for different types of firms.[4]

The measure of cost per job based on the gross costs per direct job created, however, has two potentially severe disadvantages. First, gross exchequer costs are likely to differ from the net costs to the exchequer (Moore and Rhodes, 1975). If, for example, regional incentives create jobs that would not have existed in the absence of the policy, the exchequer will benefit not only from tax clawbacks due to more people having jobs but also from reduced expenditure on unemployment and related benefits.

Secondly, the *gross* jobs created may differ substantially from the net jobs created because of additionality, displacement and multiplier effects. This suggests that we require a measure of the net exchequer costs per net job created.

One of the first studies to attempt to estimate net costs per net job created was undertaken by King (1990), who used this revised cost per job measure to evaluate the effectiveness of the UK's Regional Selective Assistance policy.[5] Calculating the net jobs created or safeguarded in RSA-supported projects is not, however, the end of the story. It is also necessary to estimate how long the jobs will last. King makes the simple (but plausible) assumption that the jobs will last as long as the capital assets are in use, which means that the lifetime of the capital assets has first to be estimated. It is then possible to express this time stream of employment in terms of the total job years of employment which the project generates.[6] The main finding of King's study is that 'RSA did indeed have the effect of raising the level of employment in the Assisted Areas – and by substantial amounts' (King, 1990, p. 85).

The purpose of King's study, however, was not simply to estimate the overall net cost per net job created. A further reason for undertaking the study was to discover whether the gross cost per direct job created could be used as a performance indicator for individual projects. On examining the differences between projects, it was discovered that there was little correlation between the gross costs per direct job created and the net costs per net job created. The gross measure cannot therefore be used with any confidence as an indicator of the net measure. For example, gross cost per job was higher for foreign firms than for domestic firms, yet the net cost per job was very similar for these two groups of firms. The more favourable net cost per job for foreign firms (compared to gross cost per job) is the result of smaller displacement effects for foreign firms, many of whom would not have located in an assisted area without financial assistance. Indeed, some foreign firms would not have located in the UK without financial assistance.

7 EX ANTE EVALUATION OF REGIONAL FINANCIAL INCENTIVES

Although policymakers need to evaluate regional financial assistance *ex post*, they also have to make judgements about the worthiness of projects *ex ante*. Two quite different approaches have been suggested. First, Swales (1997a, 1997b) argues that the evaluation of individual projects should be based on the cost–benefit decision rule (see Schofield, 1976, 1989a and

1989b for earlier applications of cost–benefit analysis to the evaluation of regional policy). He shows that a formula can be constructed that can be used for deciding whether a project is likely to be worthwhile. The second approach is to use large-scale economic models for predicting potential policy impacts.

7.1 Adapting the Cost–Benefit Decision Rule

The UK Treasury requires government agencies to use the *gross cost per net job created* to evaluate individual applications for selective financial assistance. The underlying assumption is that regional financial incentives do not lead to any positive macroeconomic effects and so it is the gross costs of a project which are appropriate, not the net costs. The longstanding Treasury view is that jobs are simply 'diverted' and not 'created'. The purpose of estimating the *gross* cost per *net* job created for individual projects is to assess whether or not the taxpayer is getting 'value for money'.

The problem with this value for money indicator is that it does not provide policymakers with a clear cut decision rule. In its present form, its use is limited to comparing value for money across projects. It is consequently possible for a project to be rejected even though it may have a positive net present value to the economy. It has been shown by Swales (1997a, 1997b), however, that this value for money indicator can be converted into a decision rule which can be used for identifying all projects which have a positive net present value. An important feature of this decision rule is that it takes into account the real resource cost of each individual project. Specifically, it takes into account the extent to which a project results in unemployed labour being re-employed as a consequence of the project going ahead. A 'shadow wage' is used to estimate the opportunity cost of creating jobs in the assisted area. The higher the shadow wage, the lower the value added by the project.

The great advantage of Swales' decision rule is that it is embedded in cost-benefit analysis, which argues that a project is worthwhile provided the social benefits outweigh the social costs. In practice, it is not possible to measure all the costs and benefits associated with individual projects and so the decision rule is based upon only those costs and benefits that are measurable. Swales starts by defining the components of the net present value of a project as follows:

Net present value of project	=	Value added by project	–	Costs of applying for and administering the project	–	Subsidy

The value added by the project (V) to the assisted area is defined as follows:

$$V = R_n \alpha L(1-d)(1+m)(w-w^*)$$

where:

R_n = present value of a £1 income stream discounted over n years
α = additionality factor ($0 < \alpha < 1$)
L = direct jobs created by project
d = displacement of other jobs in locality ($0 < d < 1$)
m = additional jobs created in locality through the supply chain and household income effects
w = average market wage in locality for the type of workers employed by the project
w^*= shadow wage (an estimate of the opportunity cost of employing extra workers in the locality).

Swales then derives the following decision rule[7]:

$$\frac{\text{Cost per job}}{\text{Wage}} = \frac{\text{Subsidy}/L(1-d)}{w} = \frac{R_n[\alpha(1-\lambda)(1+m)]}{\alpha + c}$$

where:

λ = ratio of the shadow wage to the market wage
c = administration costs/subsidy ratio.

The left-hand side of the above equation is simply the cost per net job created (allowing for displacement effects) divided by the wage. This equation gives the *maximum* cost per job/wage ratio consistent with the net present value being greater than zero. Hence, provided the ratio of the cost per job to the market wage is less than the numerical value of the right-hand side of the equation, the subsidy will result in positive net benefits and the project will be worthwhile.

Using plausible values for the parameters on the right-hand side of the above equation, Swales estimates that the cost per job/wage ratio must not exceed approximately 2.3 for a project to be worthwhile. For example, with a real interest rate of 6 per cent, R_n is 7.8. Assuming an additionality factor (α) of 0.5, a ratio of the shadow wage to the actual wage of 0.7, a multiplier of 1.3 and a value for c of 0.15, gives a value of 2.3. With these parameter values, the cost per job/wage ratio would have to be less than 2.3 for the subsidy to be worthwhile. It can be shown that this decision rule is very sensitive to small variations in the shadow wage/market wage ratio (λ) and to the number of years the project is expected to last (and hence R_n). For example, if $\lambda = 0.5$ the maximum cost per job/wage ratio consistent with $NPV > 0$ increases to 3.9. It is much less sensitive to small changes in the other parameters. Since the parameters themselves will vary between projects and between assisted areas, this means that the maximum value of the cost per job/wage ratio will vary (in some cases substantially) between projects and between assisted areas. For example, the value of λ will vary inversely with the unemployment rate, which means that a much higher cost per job/wage ratio will be relevant in high unemployment areas. A useful extension to Swales' decision rule would be to construct a simple method of predicting the value of λ for different local labour market areas.

It is worth reiterating the two primary advantages of Swales' decision rule. First, it is directly related to the cost-benefit decision rule, which is the optimal approach to evaluating public expenditures. Second, it is easy to operationalise provided the appropriate data can be obtained.

7.2 Using Large-scale Regional Models to Estimate Potential Policy Impacts

The use of large-scale models of the regional economy to estimate the potential impact of policy instruments has become increasingly popular in recent years. A prime example is provided by the annual updating of the Scottish Input–Output Tables in order to provide policymakers with a tool for estimating policy impacts, such as the effect of inward investment on Scotland's income and employment (Alexander and Whyte, 1995; Alexander and Martin, 1997). The great advantage of input-output models is that they are able to provide detailed estimates of the economy-wide effects of exogenous shocks to the regional economy. These economy-wide impacts include not only the output and employment effects on other industries, but also the effect on household income and expenditure.

A problem with the input–output approach to measuring impacts, however, is that it is based upon unrealistic assumptions of how the regional economy operates. It assumes, for example, that the regional economy has an unlimited supply of labour at the going market wage, and that the market wage is unaffected by any change in the demand for labour in the region. More complex regional models have been developed, however, which are able to incorporate more realistic assumptions about the response of the labour and product markets to exogenous shocks. Harrigan, McGregor and Swales (1996), and Harrigan et al. (1996), for example, construct a computable general equilibrium (CGE) model of the Scottish economy which allows different assumptions to be made about the response of the labour and product markets to exogenous shocks. They also introduce a time dimension to the predicted effects of these shocks on the main economic variables of the regional economy. This allows the researchers to estimate the time path, for example, of the impact of financial incentives on investment, output and employment over a period of years.

An illustration of the way in which the CGE model takes into account the response of the labour and product markets to a demand injection is shown in Figure 8.2. The first stage is to calculate the amount of 'additionality' provided by the project. This involves estimating the deadweight loss and the initial displacement of jobs due to increased competition resulting from the expansion of the assisted firm. The net additional jobs provided in the assisted firm will now have multiplier effects in the assisted area due to supply chain effects and through increases in household income which result in an increased demand for non-traded goods. It is at this point at which the labour market effects 'kick in'. The CGE model allows wages (and hence prices) to increase as a result of the increased demand for labour. Firms in the traded goods sector lose some of their competitiveness and this results in job losses. The net employment effects on the regional economy of financial assistance are therefore somewhat less than they would have been if wages were set nationally and were unrelated to conditions in the local labour market.

Gillespie et al. (1997, 1998) demonstrate that the estimated effects of regional financial assistance vary substantially according to the assumptions made about the responsiveness of the regional labour market to an increase in the demand for labour. Even allowing for the fact that an increase in labour demand will induce net in-migration and an increase in the regional participation rate (thereby relieving the labour shortage to some extent), the negative feedback from increased wages can substantially reduce the net effect of financial incentives on employment in the long run. For example, the estimated impact of regional selective assistance (in a particular year) on Scotland's employment level obtained from (a) an input–output model is compared with (b) a CGE model in which wages are determined in the Scottish labour market. This simulation shows that the ultimate employment level after ten years estimated by the CGE model is 77 per cent of the employment level predicted by the input–output model. When the present value of the job years is estimated, the difference between the two models is even greater (see Table 8.7).

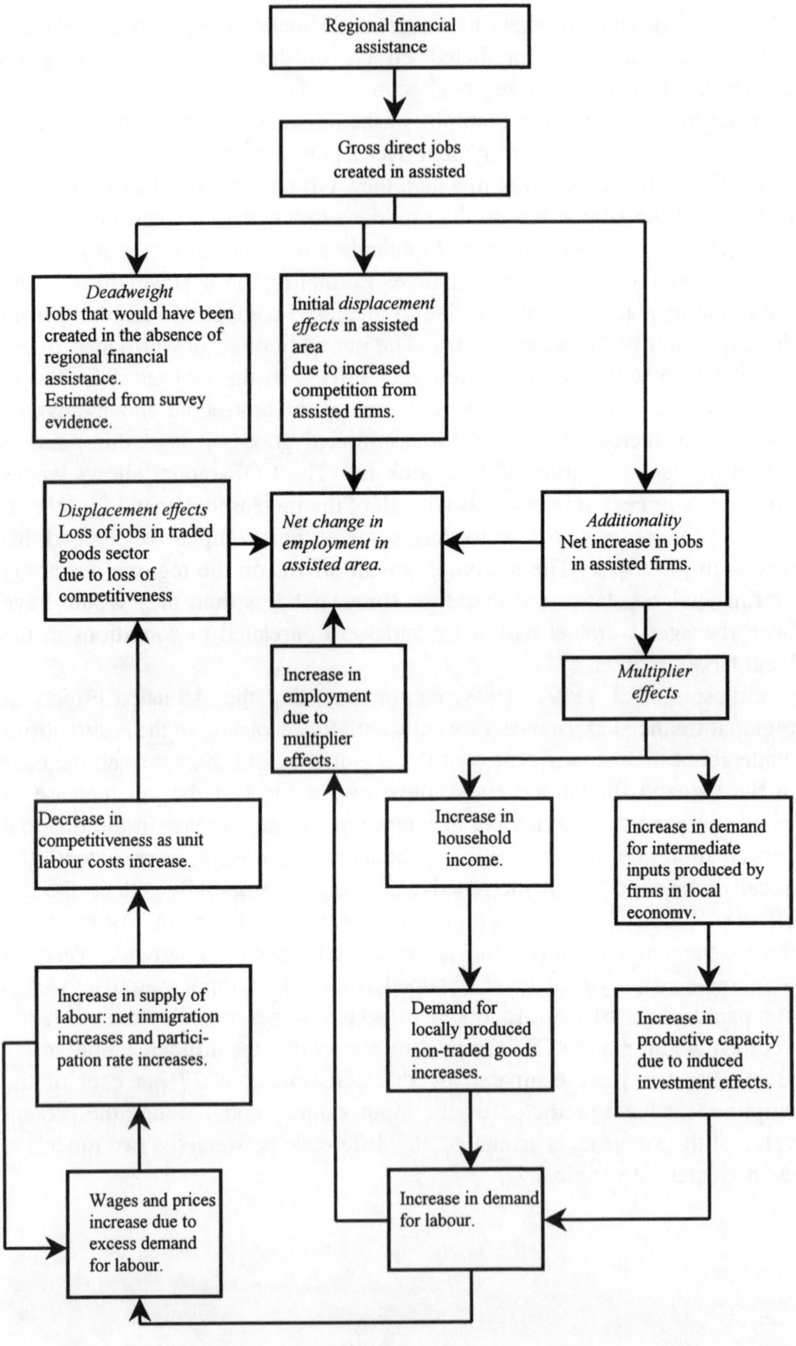

Figure 8.2 Modeling the effects of regional financial assistance

Table 8.7 Estimated effect of Regional Selective Assistance on jobs created in Scotland

Model	Estimated number of jobs created after 10 years	Present value of job years
Input–output	9 260	59 400
Computable General Equilibrium Regional bargaining + endogenous population	7 140	37 200

Note: The present value of job years (PVJY) is calculated by summing the number of *net* jobs created over a ten year period, discounted at an annual rate of 6 per cent as follows:

$$\text{PVJY} = \sum_{t=1}^{10} [E_t/(1.06)^t].$$

Source: Gillespie et al. (1998).

8 EVALUATION OF REGIONAL DEVELOPMENT PROGRAMMES: THE EU'S STRUCTURAL FUNDS

The increasing financial commitment of the EU to regional policy during the 1990s has led to demands for a more thorough evaluation of this expenditure. Is the money being spent efficiently and effectively? Are the taxpayers of the EU getting value for money? Are there more efficient ways of achieving regional policy objectives? Answers to such questions are needed if confidence in an EU-wide regional policy is to be maintained and strengthened. Policymakers have been keen to improve evaluation methodology in order to win support for regional policy at both local and national levels (Bachtler and Mitchie, 1997).

A major aim of EU regional policy during the 1990s has been to stimulate the growth and development of small and medium enterprises (SMEs). This aim is typically pursued through wide-ranging regional development programmes designed to tackle the problems arising from structural weaknesses, such as job losses in manufacturing. SMEs have been deliberately targeted because they are believed to have considerable potential for revitalising the economic performance of depressed regions. This increasing emphasis on SMEs stems from two factors. First, there was a switch in policy, during the early 1980s, from relying on diverting industry from non-assisted to assisted areas to one based upon stimulating indigenous growth within the assisted areas themselves. Second, the balance of EU regional policy has switched away from funding infrastructure projects towards providing more support for business enterprise. Regional development programmes funded by the EU have consequently focused increasingly on supporting SMEs located in assisted areas (Turok, 1997).

In view of the increasing expenditure on regional policy in the EU, the European Commission has recognised the need for more comprehensive methods of evaluation. This is indicated by the creation of a common set of guidelines for monitoring and evaluating these expenditures (Bachtler and Michie, 1995). In addition to Monitoring Committees being set up in each region and the submission of annual reports to the European Commission, all projects are subject to both *ex ante* and *ex post* evaluation of regional development programmes. Attempts have also been made to impose a common framework for evaluating regional development programmes in general. For example, a research programme (Methods for Evaluating Actions of a Structural Nature, or MEANS) was established in 1993 to develop common evaluation methods and to improve the quality of the techniques used to evaluate the Structural Funds.

There are, however, immense problems in evaluating regional development programmes in their entirety. These include:

- programmes have many different objectives
- many different organisations are usually involved in any single programme
- a wide range of policy instruments are used to achieve the objectives of a programme
- the outcomes of the programme are affected by many factors and it is difficult to isolate the effects of the programme from the influence of these other factors
- adequate and appropriate data are often not available for undertaking a comprehensive evaluation since this would ideally require a detailed social cost–benefit analysis.

These difficulties of evaluating regional development programmes have led to evaluations being dominated by financial considerations and by a tendency simply to measure what is easily measurable. For example, targets such as the number of firms contacted, the number of businesses receiving some form of assistance, or the number of training places taken up are all easy to measure and have therefore been used as indicators of a programme's degree of activity. But such measures fall a long way short of what is needed. The aim should be to find out more about *how* the policies work since this is crucial for designing future policies. Some policies will work better in some local economic environments than others and such diversity needs to be taken into account in the evaluation process.

Given the difficulties of evaluating entire regional development programmes, Turok (1997) argues that it would be more fruitful to concentrate on evaluating well-defined components of programmes. This would improve the quality of evaluations and make it easier to compare the effectiveness of specific policy instruments across programmes. An example is provided by Turok, who evaluates the funding of business development projects designed to stimulate indigenous growth in two Scottish regions which received financial support under Objective 2 of the EU's Structural Funds during 1989–93. The purpose of this evaluation exercise was to assess the quality of the planning and implementation of the projects receiving funding, and to estimate the economic effects of the projects on the performance of individual businesses. This was done in three stages (see Figure 8.3).

Stage 1

The initial applications for funding were appraised in order to obtain an overall picture of the types of projects receiving assistance. What were the objectives of the projects? What targets were set? How many jobs were expected to be created or safeguarded?

Stage 2

Information was obtained from the project managers in order to assess the quality of the planning and implementation of the projects. Were the targets realistic and appropriate? Were the projects distinctive? How effective were the project managers in implementing the projects? Were the projects well planned? Was the funding from the EU necessary for the projects to go ahead?

Stage 3

The effect of the financial and other support on the businesses themselves was estimated by collecting information from the businesses receiving support. To what extent did the support received by firms affect their profitability, turnover, marketing activities, productivity or the competence of the firm's management?

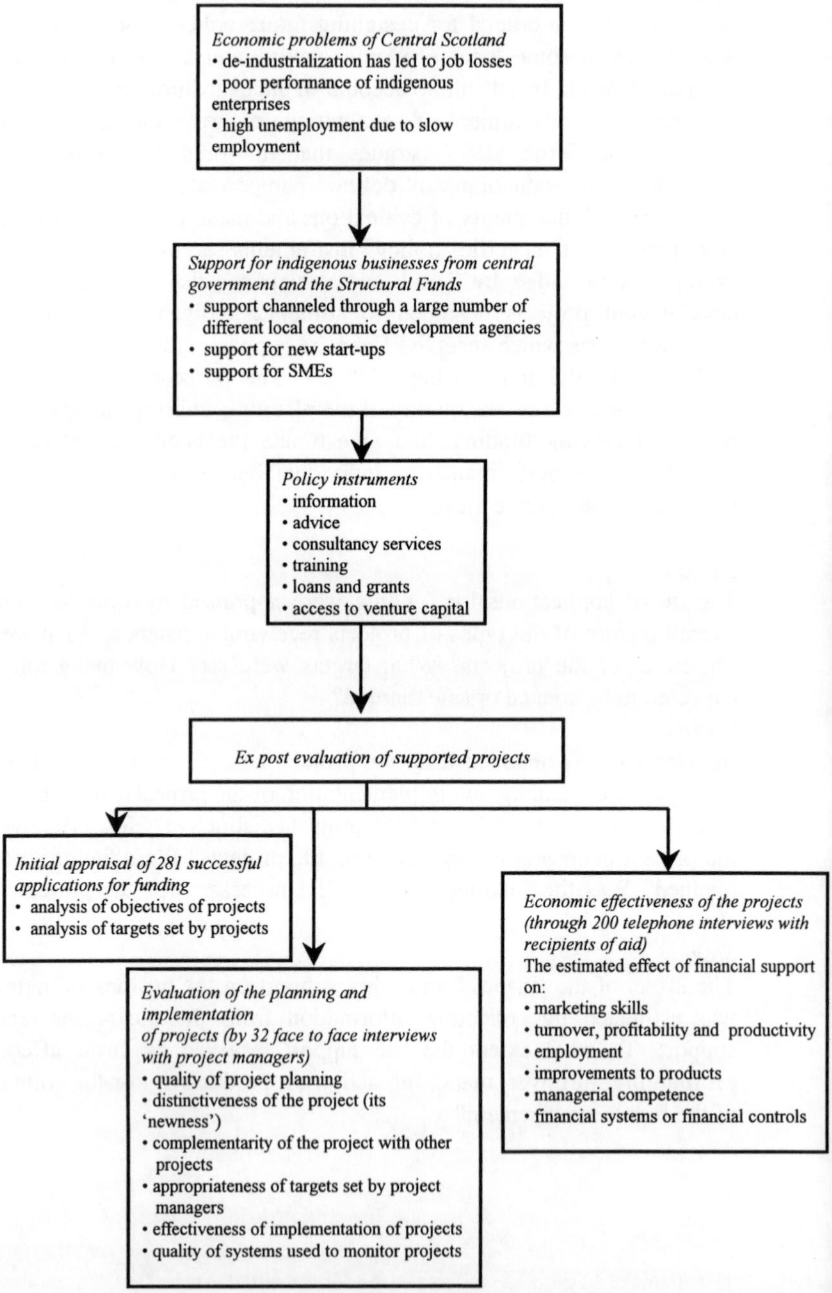

Figure 8.3 Ex post evaluation of business development projects supported by the Structural Funds: a case study of Scotland

This example of a recent evaluation supported by the EU's Structural Fund demonstrates the qualitative end of the evaluation spectrum. It is clear that these qualitative evaluations rely heavily upon the subjective judgement of the evaluator, with the consequent danger that the results of the evaluation will be subject to wide variation depending upon who does the evaluating. This potentially damaging criticism is particularly relevant for evaluations which rely heavily on extracting qualitative information from managers, especially since the latter may have an incentive to give a favourable impression about the value of financial and other government support to their businesses.

9 CONCLUSION

The primary aim of this chapter was to assess whether any progress has been made in developing methods of evaluating UK regional policy since the seminal articles by Moore and Rhodes in the mid-1970s. This partial, but hopefully representative, review of the regional policy evaluation literature suggests that the answer is positive.

Progress has been made in several directions. First, many surveys of recipients of government aid have drawn attention to the potential importance of obtaining accurate estimates of additionality, displacement and multiplier effects. This has important implications not only for the estimated effects of regional policy on employment, but also for estimating the exchequer cost per net job created. Second, the development of large-scale models of the regional economy allows the full system-wide effects of government financial assistance to be estimated. This means that the feedback effects from the region's factor and product markets can be taken into account as well as providing a time dimension to the estimated policy impacts. Third, evaluation has become more broadly based and includes the impact on the competitiveness of the regional economy more generally rather than focusing narrowly on the output and employment effects of specific policy instruments. Fourth, regional development agencies at all levels of government have become far more serious about adopting best practice methods of evaluation in order to improve the quality of their regional development programmes.

Although substantial progress has been made in the construction of methods of evaluating regional policy in the UK during the past two decades, this does not mean that there is no room for further research. It is not simply a matter of tying up the loose ends and encouraging the government to provide more and better data so that the techniques that have been developed can be more readily used. Several fundamental questions which seem to have been avoided by researchers because of their obvious complexity need to be addressed. The 'big' question is whether regional policy yields economic benefits for the economy as a whole. We need to know, for example, whether the *non*-assisted areas benefit from regional policy and, if so, to what extent. Do the non-assisted areas gain from not having to accommodate a continuous net inflow of migrants from high unemployment regions? Would it be economically more efficient to allow firms to locate wherever they believe to be the most efficient location for their plant? We therefore need to know whether regional policy can be justified on economic efficiency grounds as well as on social equity grounds. In other words, we need to know whether, and to what extent, regional policy benefits the economy as a whole. These questions will not be easy to answer, but the increasing importance of regional policy, especially in the EU, suggests that more research into regional policy evaluation is essential and should be encouraged.

NOTES

1. This is disputed by the UK Treasury, which has traditionally assumed that regional policy simply re-allocates jobs between regions and does not create jobs in the economy as a whole (Treasury, 1991, 1995). The Department of Trade and Industry (1995), on the other hand, argues that increasing the competitiveness of the assisted areas has beneficial effects on the economy as a whole by raising national productivity.
2. The expected change in employment is calculated by applying national growth rates per industry to the industry mix of the assisted areas. In other words, each industry in the assisted area is assumed to grow at the same rate as the same industry in the nation as a whole. The expected employment in each industry is then summed across all industries to give the employment level that would have occurred if each industry had grown at national growth rates per industry (e^*).
3. Employment in indigenous industries (non-inward investors) is used for the two employment variables since the aim is to estimate the effect of regional policy on industries already located in the assisted areas. The effect of regional policy on the movement of industry is estimated separately.
4. Wren (1989), for example, finds that cost per job is greater on average for large firms than for small firms.
5. RSA is a selective grant paid towards investment projects which are judged likely to provide new jobs or to safeguard existing jobs in the assisted areas. In addition, the projects must be financially viable, be necessary for the project to go ahead, and be of benefit to the national economy as well as to the regional economy.
6. King estimates that the net cost per net job year was under £600 (at 1988 prices), which is an excellent return compared to paying out unemployment and related benefits.
7. This is a simplification of the decision rule obtained by Swales but captures its essential characteristics and determinants.

REFERENCES

Alexander, J. and S. Martin (1997), '1994 Scottish input-output tables', *Scottish Economic Bulletin*, 55, 45–50.

Alexander, J.M. and T.R. Whyte (1995), 'Output, income and employment multipliers for Scotland', *Scottish Economic Bulletin*, 50, 25–40.

Armstrong, H. and J. Taylor (1993), *Regional Economics and Policy*, London: Harvester and Wheatsheaf.

Ashcroft, B. and J. Taylor (1977), 'The movement of manufacturing industry and the effect of regional policy', *Oxford Economic Papers*, **29**, 84–101.

Ashcroft, B. and J. Taylor (1979), 'The effect of regional policy on the movement of manufacturing industry in Great Britain', in D. Maclennan and J. Parr (eds), *Regional Policy: Past Experience and New Directions*, Oxford: Martin Robertson.

Bachtler, J. and R. Mitchie (1995), 'A new era of regional policy evaluation? The appraisal of the Structural Funds', *Regional Studies*, **29**, 745–51.

Bachtler, J. and R. Mitchie (1997), 'The interim evaluation of EU regional development programmes: experiences from Objective 2 regions', *Regional Studies*, **31**, 849–58.

Coughlin, C.C., J.V. Terza and V. Arromdee (1990), 'State government effects on the location of foreign direct investment', *Regional Science Perspectives*, **30**, 194–207.

Coughlin, C.C., J.V. Terza and V. Arromdee (1991), 'State characteristics and the location of foreign direct investment within the United States', *Review of Economics and Statistics*, **73**, 675–83.

Department of Trade and Industry (1995), *Regional Industrial Policy*, Cm.2910. London: HMSO.

Foley, P. (1992) Local economic policy and job creation: A review of evaluation studies', *Urban Studies*, **29**, 557–98.

Friedman, J., D.A. Gerlowski and J. Silberman (1992), 'What attracts foreign multinational corporations? Evidence from branch plant location in the United States', *Journal of Regional Science*, **32**, 403–18.

Gillespie, G., P. McGregor, K. Swales, and Y.P. Yin (1997), 'The regional impact of inward investment: product market displacement, labour market effects and efficiency spillovers', Discussion Paper 97/2, Department of Economics, University of Strathclyde.

Gillespie, G., P. McGregor, K. Swales and Y.P. Yin (1998), 'The displacement and multiplier effects of Regional Selective Assistance: A computable general equilibrium analysis' Discussion Paper 98/3, Department of Economics, University of Strathclyde.

Harrigan, F., P. McGregor and K. Swales (1996), 'The system-wide impact on the recipient region of a regional labour subsidy', *Oxford Economic Papers*, **48**, 105–33.

Harrigan, F., P. McGregor, N. Dourmashkin, R. Perman, K. Swales and Y.P. Yin (1991), 'AMOS: a macro-micro model of Scotland', *Journal of Economic Modelling*, **8**, 424–79.

Hart, M. and R. Scott (1994), 'Measuring the effect of small firm policy: some lessons from Northern Ireland', *Regional Studies*, **28**, 849–59.

Hill, S. and M. Munday (1992), 'The UK regional distribution of foreign direct investment: analysis and determinants', *Regional Studies*, **26**, 535–44.
Hill, S. and M. Munday (1994), *The Regional Distribution of Foreign Manufacturing Investment in the UK,* London: Macmillan.
HM Treasury (1991), *Economic Appraisal in Central Government: A Technical Guide for Government Departments,* London: HMSO.
HM Treasury (1995), *A Framework for the Evaluation of Regeneration Projects and Programmes*, London: HMSO.
House of Commons (1995), *Regional Policy*, Fourth Report of the Trade and Industry Committee, Session 1994-95, HC 356, I and II, London: HMSO.
King, J. (1990), *Regional Selective Assistance 1980–84*, London: HMSO.
McCrone, G. (1969), *Regional Policy in Britain*, London: George Allen and Unwin.
Moore, B. and J. Rhodes (1973), 'Evaluating the effects of British regional policy', *Economic Journal*, **83**, 87–110.
Moore, B. and J. Rhodes (1975), 'The economic and Exchequer implications of British Regional Economic Policy', in J. Vaizey (ed.), *Economic Sovereignty and Regional Policy*, Gill and Macmillan.
Moore, B. and J. Rhodes (1976), 'Regional economic policy and the movement of manufacturing industry to Development Areas', *Economica*, **43**, 17–31.
Moore, B., J. Rhodes and P. Tyler (1986), *The Effect of Government Regional Economic Policy*, London: HMSO.
Munday, M. (1990), *Japanese Manufacturing Investment in Wales*, Cardiff: University of Wales Press.
Munday, M., J. Morris and B. Wilkinson (1995), 'Factories or warehouses? A Welsh perspective on Japanese transplant manufacturing', *Regional Studies*, **29**, 1–17.
Needleman, L. and B. Scott (1964), 'Regional problems and location of industry policy in Britain', *Urban Studies*, **1**, 153–73.
O'Huallachian, B. and N. Reid (1997), 'Acquisition versus greenfield investment: the location and growth of Japanese manufactures in the United States', *Regional Studies*, **31**, 403–16.
PACEC (1993), *Regional Selective Assistance 1985–88,* London: HMSO.
PACEC (1995), *Assessment of the Wider Effects of Foreign Direct Investment in Manufacturing in the UK*, London: Department of Trade and Industry.
Robinson, F., C. Wren and J.B. Goddard (1987), *Economic Development Policies: An Evaluative Study of the Newcastle Metropolitan Region*, Oxford: Clarendon Press.
Schofield, J.A. (1976), 'Economic efficiency and regional policy', *Urban Studies*, **13**, 181–92.
Schofield, J.A. (1989a), *Cost–Benefit Analysis in Urban and Regional Planning*, London: Unwin Hyman.
Schofield, J.A. (1989b), 'Federal regional development policies in Canada: employment impact in Quebec and the Atlantic Provinces', *Review of Urban and Regional Development Studies*, **1**, 65–79.
Scottish Enterprise (1997), *Output Measurement Framework Guidelines*, Glasgow: Scottish Enterprise.
Stone, I. and F. Peck (1996), 'The foreign-owned manufacturing sector in UK peripheral regions, 1978–93: restructuring and comparative performance', *Regional Studies*, **30** (1), 55–68.
Storey, D. (1990), 'Evaluation of policies and measures to create local employment', *Urban Studies*, **27**, 669–84.

Swales, J.K. (1997a), 'The *ex post* evaluation of Regional Selective Assistance, *Regional Studies*, **31**, 859–66.

Swales, J.K. (1997b), 'The cost–benefit approach to the evaluation of Regional Selective Assistance', *Fiscal Studies*, **18** (1), 73–85.

Taylor, J. (1993), 'An analysis of the factors determining the geographical distribution of Japanese manufacturing investment in the UK, 1984–91', *Urban Studies*, **30**, 1209–24.

Taylor, J. and J. Twomey (1988), 'The movement of manufacturing industry in Great Britain: an inter-county analysis', *Urban Studies*, **25**, 228–42.

Taylor, J. and C. Wren (1997), 'UK regional policy: an evaluation', *Regional Studies*, **31** (9), 835–48.

Turok, I. (1997), 'Evaluating European support for business development: evidence from the structural funds in Scotland', *Entrepreneurship & Regional Development*, **9**, 335–52.

Twomey, J. and J. Taylor (1985), 'Regional policy and the inter-regional movement of manufacturing industry in Great Britain', *Scottish Journal of Political Economy*, **32**, 257–77.

Wren, C. (1987), 'The relative effects of local authority financial assistance policies', *Urban Studies*, **24**, 268–78.

Wren, C. (1988), 'Closure rates for assisted and non-assisted establishments', *Regional Studies*, **22**, 107–19.

Wren, C. (1989), 'Factors underlying the employment effects of financial assistance policies', *Applied Economics*, **21**, 497–513.

Wren, C. and J. Taylor (1999), 'Industrial restructuring and regional policy', *Oxford Economic Papers*, **51**, 187-98.

Wren, C. and M. Waterson (1991), 'The direct employment effects of financial assistance to industry', *Oxford Economic Papers*, **43**, 116–38.

9. Counteracting the Counterfactual: New Evidence on the Impact of Local Policy from the Residuals

Paul Cheshire and Stefano Magrini

INTRODUCTION

It is a commonplace of regional policy evaluation – indeed of policy evaluation in general – that the single most significant obstacle to obtaining accurate results is the problem of the counterfactual. Sometimes we know what the policy intervention was. We can hope to be able to estimate what the situation was in the region before the policy intervention. We can hope to be able to observe the situation in the region after the policy has come into effect. The problem is to estimate what the situation in the region would have been in the absence of the policy intervention so that the actual impact of the policy can be isolated

It is often unclear what the policy intervention actually was; or at least difficult to measure the policy intervention on a comparable basis in different regions. That is a particular problem in the present context which is focused on the impact of local interventions or *territorially competitive* policies. A range of agencies may be active with a different mix of agencies in different territories or cities. Such agencies typically operate within different institutional contexts, derive their resources from varying sources and offer policies which combine visible expenditures, 'rule bending' and help in kind in different combinations. There is also an intrinsic difficulty in defining what constitutes a policy intervention. For example infrastructure is a component of local public expenditure in almost all cities, although the extent to which it is a local, a regional, a national or even an international responsibility, varies radically from context to context. Sometimes, however, at least a proportion of infrastructure expenditure is directed towards boosting local economic activity. It is to an extent an instrument of territorial competition. The problem is to estimate the proportion of infrastructure spending that is being applied in this way.

The availability of regional data – especially in Europe – and especially for meaningful and consistently defined regions is also a problem. This may significantly impede the observers' ability to estimate accurately the pre- and post-policy situation in the region concerned.

These problems are as nothing compared to that of the counterfactual, however. This requires the development of some technique for estimating what would have happened in the absence of the policy. Most frequently the technique employed rests on some process of aggregative modelling. The techniques used have ranged from the simplistic but simple shift-share analysis (Moore and Rhodes, 1973) to regional modelling using some sort of adaptation of national forecasting models or input–output models (Beutel, 1995). Other efforts have relied on building up from the behaviour of individual economic actors, such as firms or establishments, using questionnaires or less commonly economic modelling approaches (see Moore, Rhodes and Tyler, 1986 or Armstrong and Taylor, 1993, for a summary). All of these approaches are data intensive, some, such as input–output modelling, almost prohibitively so. Most, also, are one-off studies that do not yield a basis for either general comparisons or continuing routine evaluation. This chapter proposes an alternative method and explores its application to the largest city regions (defined as Functional Urban Regions – see below) of the EU.

Resources devoted to standard top-down regional policies may be estimated with a reasonable degree of accuracy; or if not, they may perhaps be assumed to be applied to all qualifying regions with a reasonable degree of even-handedness (which lends some plausibility to proxying such policy with a dummy variable). The same is manifestly not the case with policies applied for purposes of territorial competition. By 'territorial competition' is meant a process through which groups, acting on behalf of a regional or sub-regional economy (typically a city-region's), seek to promote it as a location for economic activity either implicitly or explicitly in competition with other areas. This competitive activity is often addressed to the attraction of mobile investment, sometimes with discrimination between more and less desirable activities. But it may equally be concerned with enhancing the share of existing local businesses in the markets they serve and generating new businesses and markets. Territorial competition may use national programmes or European Structural funds but, in contrast to traditional regional policy, it is bottom-up in motivation and is concerned with economic efficiency (conceived purely locally) not with spatial equity. Its origins and nature necessarily imply, therefore, that its instruments and form vary from region to region as does the energy and level of resources devoted to it. Thus it is all but impossible to derive systematic quantitative indicators which would measure its intensity in a consistent way across the regions of the EU.[1]

Instead it is proposed that information may be obtained from the residuals of a growth model: that is from the variance in regional growth rates that the model does not 'explain'. Such residuals reflect random error and the influence of those variables which were not included in the model. So long as the model performs well statistically and the estimated parameters are not biased, then the residuals may yield information. If it is reasonable to assume that the most important of the omitted variables is the influence of local territorially competitive policy then the residuals should reflect the impact of such policy. Building on earlier work in this vein (Cheshire, 1990; Cheshire and Gordon, 1998) this chapter examines the residuals from an improved model, applied to an updated and extended data set, for the largest urban regions of the EU. The results are largely consistent with those of the earlier work and support the conclusion that territorially competitive policies can have an impact on urban growth.

Building on hypotheses set out in Cheshire and Gordon (1996)[2] a variable is then proposed which should capture one of the most important sources of variation in the capacity of city regions to develop effective territorially competitive policies. This variable is added to the model and greatly improves its performance. The residuals from this modified growth model are then examined to see how far their pattern supports the use of residuals to counteract the counterfactual. This analysis provides new insights into the growth performance of individual cities and supports many of the conclusions about the determinants of their performance reached in Cheshire and Gordon (1998). It does, however, suggest that there are additional factors in the conditions of any city region which influence its capacity to develop effective local development policies beyond the simple proxy for transactions costs involved in forming a territorially competitive 'club' the new variable is designed to provide.

The underlying theoretical framework for the growth models presented in this chapter might be described as modified endogenous growth theory. Economic theory focuses on long-run outcomes but data is only available for European regions on at best a medium-run period. Certainly within the span of the period it is presently possible to analyse, some 16 years from 1978 to 1994,[3] actual growth performance is the outcome of a multivariate process. If this is accepted several points follow. It will only be possible to provide credible estimates of the influence of a particular variable if one has as fully specified a model as possible and has paid careful attention both to the data and to the performance of the model. As is argued below studies of regional growth typically have paid careful attention to neither of these practical issues. A second consequence of actual growth outcomes being the result of multivariate processes is that there are likely to be significant variables contributing to convergence in regional incomes (such as technological diffusion) and others contributing to a divergence of regional incomes (such as agglomeration economies). Indeed, as is argued by Magrini (1997), the same variables could contribute to either divergence or convergence in different contexts.

SOME PRELIMINARIES

Criticisms have been raised with respect to the use of OLS models with which to analyse growth. It is our contention that, in the main, careful modelling and testing can resolve such problems for practical purposes and OLS can yield valuable insights into the causes of differences in growth rates. The main problems result from failure to ensure that OLS models are robust and appropriate. In the context of regional growth a more serious problem – but one which gets scant attention perhaps because of its lack of intrinsic technical complexity – is the use of inappropriate data. Table 9.1 bears witness to the fact that the choice of data is vital. In a US context data is widely available off the shelf for metropolitan regions – the Metropolitan Statistical Areas (MSAs). These are self contained and relatively independent local economic systems. Economic shocks are relatively contained within them and have homogeneous impacts. Moreover they have identifiable economic structures which are meaningful.

Some economists interested in growth and with backgrounds in macroeconomics have simply not considered the issue of what spatial units are most appropriate for regional analysis. For example Blanchard (1991) goes so far as to claim that 'macroeconomists have rediscovered regional economics' for the reason that there are so many more 'cities, states and regions' and so more degrees of freedom, as if these spatial units were interchangeable. Researchers have also frequently transferred models and ideas developed in a US context to analyse European regional growth taking available data from Eurostat. Unfortunately regions, states and cities are far from interchangeable concepts. The data in Table 9.1 illustrate one very important, if extremely basic, reason for this. They contrast values taken from Eurostat data for the official European regions (the 'NUTS' regions)[4] with values for the same variables estimated for functionally defined urban regions (FURs) broadly similar in conception to MSAs.[5]

The normal dependent variable in studies of (regional) economic growth is the rate of growth of GDP per capita. Output, however, is measured at workplaces while people are measured where they live. Unless boundaries are defined so that they identify regions which are self contained in labour market terms – that is there is minimal across boundary net commuting – GDP per

Table 9.1 The difference boundaries make: some NUTS regions which are cities

Region (L) / Functional Urban Region (F)	Population '000s 1991		% Change 1981–91			GDP pc @ PPS % Change 1981–91		
	F	L	F	L	F–L	F	L	F–L
Bremen	1 272	682	2.3	-1.8	4.1	58.2	80.7	–22.5
Hamburg	2 806	1 645	3.4	0.4	3.0	64.2	84.7	–20.5
Ile de France/ Paris	10 624	10 740	5.5	6.9	-1.4	102.1	87.1	15.0
Brussel/ Bruxelles	3 399	960	0.6	-4.0	4.6	73.4	92.9	–19.5
Greater London /London	8 757	6 871	-3.2	0.3	-3.5	114.0	95.2	18.8

Note: L = NUTS Region; F = FUR.

Source: Eurostat and Urban Estimates

capita will be misrepresented. Not only do many of the regions used by Eurostat for statistical reporting have substantial net inflows of commuters but also the regions that do have such net inflows are systematically those with the highest measured per capita income. This is partly because they tend to be large cities but more obviously because they have large-scale net inward commuting and therefore upwardly biased measured GDP per capita.

As the measures of growth reported in columns 7 to 9 of the table show there is not only bias in the measurement of levels of per capita income as a result but also in the measurement of its growth. This is because if there is population (re)decentralisation over time relative to the location of employment, the misrepresentation of GDP per capita at the end of the period will be (less) greater than at the start. As can be seen in the case of Bremen, which for historical reasons is a separate Land within the German Federal system, the difference between the growth rate measured for the NUTS region and the FUR can be as much as 39 per cent within one decade. Thus analysis of economic growth using Eurostat regional data will involve systematic measurement bias affecting the richest regions.

Another problem is that some NUTS regions (such as the Ile de France) correspond very closely to functionally defined metropolitan regions whereas others (such as the Nord-Pas de Calais or Andalucia) are extensive and economically very heterogeneous and contain two or more very distinct metropolitan regions within them. In the case of self contained regions such as the Ile de France it is possible to obtain consistent measures of their economic structure and other characteristics which may influence the growth of the region as a whole. In the case of very heterogeneous regions, however, no such consistent variables, exerting an influence on the economic performance of the region as a whole, may even exist.

The analysis reported in this chapter therefore relates to the major Functional Urban Regions of the EU of 12 member countries. FURs are defined on the basis of core cities representing concentrations of employment and hinterlands defined by patterns of commuting. They therefore approximate the spheres of economic influence of urban economies and are definitionally as self-contained as possible. 'Major' is defined as having a total population of one third of a million or more in 1981 and having had a core city of at least 200 000 people at some point since 1951. In addition considerable care has been taken throughout to define variables and obtain measures of them which are appropriate to the underlying conceptualisation of growth processes rather than just conveniently available.

THE MODEL

As was noted above the focus of this analysis is on those factors which contributed to regional growth during the period under study in order to throw light on the influence of local policy on growth. Having identified the best model in terms of underlying theory and fit of the data, the focus then shifts to analysing the role of local policy in influencing regional growth. The basic model has the following form:

$$\frac{1}{14}\ln\left(\frac{y_{i,1993}}{y_{i,1979}}\right) = \alpha_0 + \alpha \mathrm{E}_i + \varepsilon_{i,1993} \tag{9.1}$$

where

$y_{i,t}$ = level of per capita GDP at time *t* (3-year average centred in *t*) in FUR *i*
E = vector of explanatory variables
ε_{1993} = vector of random error terms

In general form the model follows that reported in Cheshire and Carbonaro (1995, 1996). The variables are defined in Table 9..2. Rather than use national dummies, the effects of the different temporal incidence of the economic cycle and underlying differences in policy, institutions and behaviour that influence differential national rates of growth are represented with a continuous variable, the rate of growth in the area of each country outside its major FURs. As with many other analysis of patterns of development in Italy there are apparently substantial differences between the North and the South. Rates of growth of FURs in Northern Italy exceed those of other Italian urban regions but experimentation (and some data improvement) shows that it is only the performance of three urban regions in the North East that was significantly exceptional once the influence of other variables was allowed for. These were Padua, Venice and Verona for which a dummy variable is included in the model.

The variables reflecting the regional economic structure, as reported in Cheshire and Carbonaro (1996) continue to perform as expected. To meet the criticism that the use of a dummy variable to measure the importance of port activity implicitly imposes a functional form on the variable, however, data has now been obtained on the actual volume of trade through each port in 1969. That date was chosen since it is early enough to still capture the importance of port activity within city economies before the transformation of port activity was complete. As can be seen from the results reported in Table 9.3 the estimated co-efficient for the new port variable is non-linear. This formulation satisfied tests of appropriateness of functional form.

The spatial concentration of some declining industries, including that of the port industry but especially coal, can be expected to blight the growth performance of the local host economy for a considerable period after the industry concerned has ceased to account for a substantial share of local employment and output. In the case of coal, other industries which have developed because of its local availability tend to decline or disappear, land has to be reclaimed if it is to be redeveloped, the environment has been damaged, local skills are inappropriate and perceived industrial relations problems may act as a disincentive for inward investment. By 1977, the first date for which the FUR data on GDP per capita can be calculated, the coal industry had entirely disappeared from Belgium and the Netherlands and all but disappeared from northeastern France and the Ruhr. The historic influence of the coal industry is measured in this model, therefore, by a dummy variable related to the physical coincidence of coal measures with the area of FURs; if the whole of a FUR was located within the area of a coalfield (as defined in the *Oxford Regional Economic Atlas*, 1971) it had a value of 2; if a part was within a coalfield area it had a value of 1; and otherwise it had a value of 0. There are then two measures reflecting the industrial structure of the wider region within which the FUR is located: the proportion of the labour force in agriculture and in industry in 1975. There is little correlation between these two measures.

Table 9. 2 Definition of variables used in growth models 1 and 2

Variable	Description
Dependent Variable	
FUR growth 1978/80–1992/4	Annualised rate of growth of GDP per capita (constant $US at Purchasing Power Parity): start and end dates 3-year means
Independent Variables	
Macroeconomic factors	
Growth in National Reminder 1978/80–1992/4	Annualised rate of growth in per capita GDP in area of country outside major FURs
Dummy for NE Italy	Dummy variable for Padua, Verona and Venice
Structural factors	
Coal Mining Dummy	Dummy variable measuring the physical extent of coal field within the FUR: 0, 1 or 2
Port (1969)	Trade – in '000s of tons – through port in 1969
Industry (1975)	% of labour force in Industry in wider NUTS Level 2 region 1975
Agriculture (1975)	% of labour force in Agriculture in wider NUTS Level 2 region in 1975
Spatial economic factors	
Change in Economic Potential	Measure of the economic impact of European integration on FUR resulting from elimination of tariffs and reduced transport costs
Population Density (1981)	Population density of FUR in 1981
Sum of Differential Growth (1979–86)	Sum of difference in growth rate of a FUR and growth rates of FURs within 150 minutes divided by distance
Research & Human Capital	
University Students (1977)	Total enrolled university students in universities, higher and further education institutions 1976–77 ('000s)
R&D Laboratories (1980)	R&D Laboratories of Fortune top 500 companies per million population – 1980
Capacity to Develop Policy	
Policy Units (1981)	Ratio of population of central administrative unit of FUR to total population of FUR in 1981

Forces for economic integration are global but in Europe they have been given an explicit policy directed boost. At least since the work of Clark, Wilson and Bradley (1969) the potential effects of European integration on regional incomes and output have been on the agenda. The Single European Market was one more marker on a path towards integration established by the Treaty of Rome in 1957 and most recently marked by European monetary union.

The concept of *economic potential* (defined as the accessibility to total income at any location allowing for distance, transport costs and tariffs) as put forward by Clark, Wilson and Bradley (1969) is an *ad hoc* one in theoretical terms. Various theoretical reasons why it might be associated with regional growth differentials and justifications for the use of changes in it as a measure of the spatial impact of European integration are possible. Despite any concern as to its *ad hoc* nature, however, there is no alternative measure of the systematic effects of integration. Since the object of the present analysis is *growth*, the appropriate indicator is *change* in economic potential brought about by tariff reductions, falling transport costs and EU enlargements. This is calculated from Clark, Wilson and Bradley, (1969). This study derived measures for the regions of a Europe of 10, including Norway but excluding Greece. These estimates have been supplemented with one derived from Keeble, Offord and Walker (1988) for the regions of Spain. These have been scaled to Clark's values. Values for Athens, Lisboa, Porto and Saliniki have been interpolated.

The theoretical arguments as to why integration should favour core regions do not imply that the relationship measured for the 1980s or the 1990s should necessarily be linear. Clark's calculations are for different hypothetical states of the world but with data for 1966. Induced growth might have been fastest where economic potential increased most in the initial stages of integration and falling transport costs. But such growth would tend to bid up land and labour costs and produce additional congestion, other things equal. In turn this would tend, over time, to produce deconcentration from the core to surrounding regions. So if the integration force remained constant, by the 1980s the relationship between differential urban growth and Clark, Wilson and Bradley's (1969) estimates of the change in economic potential should be quadratic. The introduction of the Single European Market and then of monetary union might be expected to have given additional impetus to the spatial impact of European integration. Thus with the extension of the observations into the 1990s there might be a reinforcing of the influence of the change in economic potential on FUR growth. Such an increase in the influence of European integration on local growth would be reflected in an increased significance of the estimated coefficient of the change in economic potential variable and a reversion to a linear functional form. This would reflect a re-concentration of the strongest impact in the inner core regions.

The variables designed to reflect other spatial factors are also formulated as in Cheshire and Carbonaro (1995; 1996). Their impact should be expected to remain unchanged. Population density in 1981 is included on the grounds that it should be a proxy for the price of land and congestion costs once all other factors had been allowed for. Other things being equal it might be expected to reflect differences between cities in policy and topographical constraints on land supply. Land use planning in British cities as well as in those of Germany and elsewhere may have a significant constraining effect on land supply.

The inclusion of the sum of the lagged growth differential with neighbouring FURs is to capture the interaction effect between local growth performances. The reasons to expect this were set out in Cheshire and Carbonaro (1996). If a FUR has one or more contiguous neighbours and grows faster than its neighbour(s) it would be expected that it should suck in additional commuters, an issue also considered by Gordon (Chapter 7, this volume). This will have three effects. First its employment will rise relative to its resident population causing its measured growth rate to increase relative to its neighbours on constant boundaries. Secondly there may be a favourable composition effect on the human capital of its workforce since long distance commuters tend to be more skilled than short distance commuters are. And thirdly there may be dynamic agglomeration economies as it grows relative to its neighbours. Although not the subject of the present chapter, tests show that the interaction effect cannot be explained to any significant extent in terms of measurement, that is the first of the effects identified above. There is a real economic impact of localised differential growth – or a 'growth shadow' effect.

The results reported for this growth shadow effect for the extended period are essentially the same as those reported previously. It may be noted that since the growth differential is measured only over the first half of the period no significant problem of endogeneity should exist. As Quah (1993) demonstrated the correlation between growth in successive periods, at least at a national level, is surprisingly weak. Given the economic mechanisms hypothesised as giving rise to the relationship some lag in effect is to be expected. While it might be argued that ideally the differential growth should be measured over a period such as 1975 to 1985 data do not permit this.

Finally the model includes two measures of local human capital as a spatialised modification of an endogenous growth model. This applies the theoretical insights of Magrini (1997) to re-formulate measures of the accessibility of intellectual capital and tacit knowledge in a region.

Overall the model reported in Table 9.3 performed well. The adjusted R^2 using 122 observations was 0.66 compared to 0.60 for the model reported in

Cheshire and Carbonaro (1996) using 118.[6] Diagnostic tests revealed no problems of functional form, non-normal residuals or spatial autocorrelation.

The only significant difference from the results reported in Cheshire and Carbonaro (1996) is that the fading influence of the change in economic potential for the 1980s, compared to earlier periods, ceased. Indeed the influence of the variable increased and also its functional form reverts to being linear. A comparison with previous results obtained from different models of urban development is provided in Table 9.4.

Table 9.3 Model 1: 122 major European FURs: GDP growth (1978/80–1992/94)

Adjusted R^2		0.6553
Constant		0.01234*
	t-ratio	2.37
Growth in National Reminder (1979-93)		0.05752**
	t-ratio	10.72
Dummy North-East Italy		0.007029**
	t-ratio	3.09
Change in Economic Potential		0.00224*
	t-ratio	1.92
Agriculture (1975)		0.0003352*
	t-ratio	2.35
Agriculture (1975) squared		-0.000009457*
	t-ratio	-2.47
Coal Mining Dummy		-0.002159**
	t-ratio	-3.28
Port (1969)		-0.0008685*
	t-ratio	-2.45
Port (1969) squared		0.00003888*
	t-ratio	1.72
Industry (1975)		-0.0001019*
	t-ratio	-1.95
Population Density (1981)		-0.000002165**
	t-ratio	-4.07
Sum of Differential Growth (79-86)		0.178**
	t-ratio	4.74
University Students (1978)		0.00003081**
	t-ratio	3.30
R&D Laboratories (1980)		0.0005849
	t-ratio	2.25

Notes: * = Significant at 10%, ** = Significant at 1%.

Table 9.4 The role of changing economic potential: estimated coefficients for different models

	Period over which Dependent Variable was Measured							
	1961–71	1971–81	1977/81–1985/7	1971–78[a]	1975–83[a]	1975–88[a]	1979–90	1978–94
	Dependent Variable of Model							
Measure of European Integration Effect	% Population Change[b]		Change in Unemplmt[c]	Change in Urban Welfare Index			% Change in GDP p.c.[f]	
Change in Economic Potential following :								
(i) Treaty of Rome	+0.0038*							
(ii) All changes		+0.0038**	–1.1621	+1.0780*	+1.3291*	+5.6145**	+10.2756[a]	0.00368**
(iii) All changes squared						–2.6290**	–5.5536[a]	

Notes: * Significant at 5% , ** Significant at 1%
[a] Calculated as a moving average so periods are not precise and overlap,
[b] Reported in Cheshire and Hay (1989), [c] Reported in Cheshire (1991), [d] Reported in Cheshire (1995),
[e] A linear form was reported for the whole period 1971–88 in Cheshire (1990), [f] Reported in Cheshire and Carbonaro (1996),
[g] Significant and nearly significant at 10% respectively,

Source: adapted from Cheshire and Carbonaro (1996)

The appropriate interpretation of this series of results would appear to be that while between 1975 and about 1988 the impact of European integration on differential regional growth had been becoming less important and the areas most favoured had been spreading outwards from the core towards the 'near-periphery', the impact intensified again in the late 1980s and early 1990s and the most favourable impacts returned to the innermost core regions. It may be coincidence but it seems plausible that this re-focusing and intensification of the spatial impact of European integration in the late 1980s and early 1990s resulted from the Single European Act. Monetary Union might, in that case, maintain a strong spatial influence of integration on patterns of spatial growth and the concentration of the positive effects on the innermost core of the EU into the twenty-first century.

These results seem to provide empirical support for the ideas of the 'new economic geography' as represented in the work of Krugman (1991), Krugman and Venables (1990, 1993) or Venables (1996). The evidence presented here supports their general conclusions in that it suggests that integration 'shocks' in the EU since 1961 have favoured core regions although over time the effect of any specific integration 'shock' has tended to be dissipated. Maleki's (Chapter 3, this volume) evidence on how new technology in information transfer creates new forms of agglomeration economy in the largest cities provides a different but complementary type of supporting evidence for the way in which integration favours the strongest regions at the expense of the poorer and creates now forms of 'peripherality'.

THE IMPACT OF POLICY

Following the methodology first suggested in Cheshire (1990) and outlined in the introduction, we may ask whether the residuals from Model 1 reveal any insights into the efficacy of local territorially competitive policy. These residuals, ranked, are shown in Table 9.5. Residuals from a similar model applied to data for the period 1979/81–1987/90 are shown as Appendix Table 9A.1. This appendix table also suggests some FURs where there is independent information suggesting that local policy promoting economic development was particularly active and effective or inactive and/or ineffective. This listing was not intended to be exhaustive since only those FURs which had substantial residuals were identified.

It will be seen that the pattern of the larger residuals closely follows that reported in Appendix Table 9A.1 for the 1980s. Edinburgh has joined Frankfurt, Barcelona and Saarbrücken as a city with one of the largest four positive residuals. Those for Murcia, Venezia (now with a more specific dummy), Taranto and Paris are far smaller: indeed that for Paris suggests underperformance in strong contrast to the 1980s. Other cities identified earlier as having positive local policy effects likely to be reflected in the residuals from the model, such as Glasgow, Leeds or Strasbourg, continue to have substantial positive residuals. At the other end of the table cities identified as having poor local policy and with substantial negative residuals were Liverpool, Malaga, Brussels, Napoli, Sheffield and Torino. In an earlier analysis (Cheshire, 1990) Kobenhavn, London and Dublin had also been identified as having negative local policy effects. Of these only Napoli has a substantial positive residual from Model 1 and, except for Dublin[7] and perhaps London, all the rest have amongst the largest negative residuals.

At least two strands of related literature conclude that the capacity to develop effective local policy, especially strategic policy to promote economic growth, is not a random variable but is conditioned by a number of factors of which the most commonly cited is the structure of local governance – or administrative capacity. Both Cheshire and Gordon (1996) and Hochman, Pines and Thisse, (1995) draw on the ideas of Olson (1965) to reach this conclusion. The argument stems from the recognition that the promotion of local economic development can be viewed as the provision of a quasi-public good. It is likely to suffer, therefore, from the usual problems of such goods: how are they to be provided effectively? The usual solution is by some form of 'club' of actors, those actors consisting of representatives of potential beneficiaries of economic growth. Different classes of actor will systematically benefit to differing extents, depending on the incidence of the benefits from economic growth within the territory. Broadly such benefits will disproportionately accrue to those whose incomes derive from locally generated (economic) rents or quasi-rents; most obviously local property owners, franchise owners (including utilities), those whose incomes are dependent on local revenues (such as providers of business services to the local economy) and those whose skills are in inelastic supply to the local economy (such as specific skills or those who are immobile and presently not in employment). Others may lose from local economic development – such as those who do not own property and are on fixed incomes. Examples would include retired people in rented social housing.

Table 9.5 Residuals from model 1 – without policy units variable

Model 1: Without policy units			
FUR	Residual	FUR	Residual
Edinburgh	0.012556	St Etienne	0.001758
Frankfurt	0.007926	Bremen	0.001725
Barcelona	0.007041	Venezia	0.001660
Saarbrücken	0.006931	Palermo	0.001608
München	0.006071	Coventry	0.001578
Madrid	0.005548	Karlsruhe	0.001158
Mannheim	0.005464	Taranto	0.001083
Saloniki	0.005452	Bristol	0.001015
Palma de Mallorca	0.005211	Cordoba	0.000961
Utrecht	0.005114	Duisburg	0.000863
Hamburg	0.004371	Bilbao	0.000724
Antwerpen	0.004300	Lille	0.000697
Zaragoza	0.004285	Catania	0.000691
Toulouse	0.004233	Essen	0.000504
Kassel	0.004049	Nice	0.000456
Augsburg	0.003917	Derby	0.000361
Belfast	0.003857	Murcia	0.000300
Genova	0.003570	Dublin	0.000296
Aachen	0.003534	Clermont Ferrand	0.000144
Messina	0.003500	Brescia	0.000081
Granada	0.003408	Dortmund	–0.000102
Sunderland	0.003301	Bochum	–0.000125
Strasbourg	0.003164	Wiesbaden	–0.000165
Valencia	0.002864	Bari	–0.000174
Grenoble	0.002774	Rotterdam	–0.000291
Cagliari	0.002496	Mönchengladbach	–0.000363
Roma	0.002495	Sevilla	–0.000428
Valenciennes	0.002432	Milano	–0.000432
Leeds	0.002416	Aarhus	–0.000443
Braunschweig	0.002362	Brighton	–0.000476
Cardiff	0.002260	Stuttgart	–0.000491
Glasgow	0.002225	Verona	–0.000557
Napoli	0.002223	Newcastle	–0.000577
Birmingham	0.002211	Nürnberg	–0.000682
Lyon	0.001827	Amsterdam	–0.000687
Nantes	0.001768	Hannover	–0.000737

Table 9.5 Continued

Model 1: Without policy units			
FUR	Residual	FUR	Residual
Portsmouth	–0.000795	Marseille	–0.002729
Hull	–0.000823	Bordeaux	–0.002788
Nottingham	–0.000940	Dijon	–0.002939
Vigo	–0.001011	Le Havre	–0.003121
Porto	–0.001048	Liverpool	–0.003144
Bologna	–0.001067	Krefeld	–0.003164
Southampton	–0.001102	Athens	–0.003174
Padova	–0.001103	Montpellier	–0.003300
Mulhouse	–0.001282	Aviles	–0.003527
Bonn	–0.001463	Bruxelles	–0.003547
Charleroi	–0.001583	Teesside	–0.003597
Leicester	–0.001631	Wuppertal	–0.003663
Valladolid	–0.001674	Toulon	–0.003770
Rennes	–0.001675	Alicante	–0.004460
London	–0.001744	Düsseldorf	–0.004755
Munster	–0.001806	Rouen	–0.004807
Liège	–0.001913	La Coruña	–0.005057
Stoke on Trent	–0.002174	Nancy	–0.005174
Bielefeld	–0.002283	Sheffield	–0.005501
s'Gravenhage	–0.002326	Torino	–0.005940
Firenze	–0.002384	Kobenhavn	–0.006323
Manchester	–0.002510	Köln	–0.006795
Paris	–0.002555	Lisboa	–0.007109
Plymouth	–0.002619	Malaga	–0.007130
Orleans	–0.002644		

Economic actors in local economies may be potential club members on an individual basis (for example as active members of public–private partners in growth-promoting agencies) or they may be represented through local or regional government. Viewed in this way the probability that a local territorially competitive (growth promoting) policy will develop, and the efforts that are likely to be devoted to it, are likely to be conditioned by the expected net benefits such a policy is expected to produce for the 'club' participants. In turn these are likely to depend on the potential scope for increasing local economic activity and the costs of so doing. The costs will be a function of the actual resource costs the circumstances of the territory require to achieve a given increment to it is growth and the transactions costs of forming an effective club.

The costs of achieving a given increment to local growth are likely to vary from FUR to FUR depending on local circumstances. The representation of rent earners in local government may vary likewise, as may the potential scope for increasing the local growth rate (or avoiding loss). But these are extremely difficult to observe other than on the basis of a case-by-case, detailed evaluation. An important conditioning variable is much easier to observe, however, and that is one of the primary determinants of the transactions costs involved in forming a territorially competitive 'club' to promote strategically co-ordinated development policies. If, as was argued in Section 2, FURs are a reasonable representation of meaningful local economies, then their structure of government is likely to be influential in determining the transactions costs in forming a growth club. The more units of government there are that have to co-operate and the less obvious is the existence of a 'leader' public actor with the financial and/or political resources necessary to provide the catalytic power around which a club can coalesce, then the higher the transactions costs are likely to be, other things being equal. As was concluded in Cheshire and Gordon (1996):

> Territorial competition is more likely to be engaged in, and will be more energetically pursued where:
>
> 1) There are a smaller number of public agencies representing the functional economic region, with the boundaries of the highest tier authority approximating to those of the region;

Such a variable – the *policy units* variable – can be specified and measured relatively easily. The ratio of the total population of the largest relevant unit of government representing the FUR to the population of the FUR as a whole, was calculated using explicit rules which varied from country to country depending on the structure of government powers. These 'rules' were:

Belgium	The central communes for all except Bruxelles for which the capital region (Arrondissement) was taken;
Denmark	Central Municipality;
Germany	The Kreisfreie Stadte except for Bremen and Hamburg where the Land (a NUTS 1 region) was taken and Frankfurt where the Umlandverband was taken;
France	Since there is a NUTS 1 region, the Ile de France, which has significant powers, that was taken for Paris. Elsewhere in France the central Commune was selected except for those FURs for which a Communité Urbaine exists;

Greece	The central Municipality;
Ireland	The County Borough (of Dublin);
Italy	The central Commune was selected in all cases. Unlike the situation in France (Paris) or Germany (Bremen and Hamburg) there is no NUTS 1 or 2 region corresponding to any city nor is there any city region with a city-wide tier of government (such as the Communité Urbaine);
Netherlands	The central Municipality (as Italy);
Portugal	The central Municipality (as Italy);
Spain	Where there was one major FUR in a Communidad Autonoma (a NUTS 2 region), the Communidad Autonoma was taken; where there was more than one major FUR in the Communidad Autonoma but only one in the Provincia (a NUTS 2 region), the Provincia was taken; where there was more than one major FUR within a Provincia then the central Municipio was taken;
United Kingdom	In England the District was taken except in London where Inner London was used; in Scotland the regions of Lothian and Strathclyde were taken and for Belfast the NUTS 1 region of Northern Ireland.

The only fudge, therefore, was in the case of London where there was no obvious way to select the largest relevant governmental unit. The City of London, with a population of only about 4000, would have been unrealistically small; so, too, would any individual London Borough. The larger unit – Greater London – was abolished in 1985, however, so that would also have been unrepresentative. The choice of Inner London represented no more than a compromise.

Any relationship should be expected to have a quadratic (or possibly log) functional form. As the size of the representative unit rises towards that of the FUR then transactions costs should fall and the leadership capacity of the central unit should rise. The financial and political power of the representative unit should continue to increase and transactions costs fall as its size gets bigger relative to that of the FUR. This increasing positive impact should continue until the influence of the interests of the FUR begins to get dissipated in the larger unit. Where the relevant unit is very large relative to the FUR then the interests of the FUR may get lost or displaced by those of other elements of the larger unit. An example of this might occur in a case such as Aviles/Gijon. This is a twin core FUR in northern Spain within the Communidad Autonoma of Asturias. It is the only major FUR within Asturias so the Communidad Autonoma was taken as the governmental unit. However the municipio of neither Aviles nor Gijon is very large individually and they are both politically outweighed by the regional capital, Oviedo. But Oviedo is not a 'major' FUR. The decision rule seems to have produced an appropriate outcome therefore. One would expect considerable difficulties for Aviles/Gijon in forming a successful local territorially competitive agency reflecting their interests.

Table 9.6 Model 2: European FUR growth (1978/80–1992/4) including policy units

Adjusted R^2		0.7194
Constant		0.005009
	t-ratio	1.00
Growth in National Reminder (1979-94)		0.05817**
	t-ratio	12.24
Dummy North-East Italy		0.006642**
	t-ratio	3.28
Coal Mining Dummy		-0.002354**
	t-ratio	-3.95
Port (1969)		-0.0009162**
	t-ratio	-2.90
Port (1969) squared		0.000041*
	t-ratio	2.05
Industry (1975)		-0.0000848*
	t-ratio	-1.78
Agriculture (1975)		0.0004078**
	t-ratio	3.17
Agriculture (1975) squared		-0.0000094**
	t-ratio	-2.75
Change in Economic Potential		0.003683**
	t-ratio	3.28
Population Density (1981)		-0.0000014*
	t-ratio	-2.57
Sum of Differential Growth (1979-86)		0.175**
	t-ratio	5.24
University Students (1978)		0.0000228**
	t-ratio	2.70
R&D Laboratories (1980)		0.0007258**
	t-ratio	3.11
Policy Units (1981)		0.01198**
	t-ratio	4.28
Policy Units (1981) Squared		-0.004642**
	t-ratio	-3.63

Notes: * = Significant at 10%, ** = significant at 1%.

The results of including the policy units variable in the growth model are reported in Table 9.6. The variable is significant and the estimated functional form is quadratic (both a linear and a logarithmic form were experimented with but the quadratic form dominated). The estimated values of the coefficients imply that the positive impact on FUR growth is maximised if the representative governmental unit is about 1.6 times the size of the urban region. Not only is the variable significant but the whole performance of the model improves. The R^2 rises from 0.66 to 0.72 and the t values of the other parameters increase but the estimated values of the co-efficients are stable.

Table 9.7 shows the residuals from this model while Table 9.8 shows the difference between the residuals from Models 1 and 2. The pattern of residuals is modified rather than transformed. The difference between the two residuals (Table 9.8) should reflect a quadratic transformation of the policy units variable although the R^2 between the value of the policy units variable and the difference in residuals is in fact only 0.72. The difference in the residuals from the two models, therefore, can be interpreted as a measure of the contribution to a FUR's growth of the most obvious factor determining its intrinsic capacity to evolve effective growth policy – the transactions costs in forming a growth 'club'.

If this is accepted then we see that an important element in the consistent 'excess' growth performance of FURs such as Frankfurt, Palma de Mallorca, Glasgow, Edinburgh, Barcelona or, indeed, Venezia, is their advantageous governmental structure. Equally the adverse governmental structure of FURs such as Valenciennes, London, Nancy, Kobenhavn or Manchester appears to be a factor in their undeperformance of Model 1's prediction. They are hampered in the development of effective policies to promote their growth.

Governmental structure is not the only factor in explaining the consistent (that is apparently non-random) pattern of residuals from the growth models, however. It is an obvious fact that there are likely to be other variables omitted from the growth models as well as the capacity to develop effective local policy.

Nevertheless the evidence of Tables 9.7 and 9.8 is consistent with there being particular problems in developing policy in Torino, Sheffield, Bordeaux or even Liverpool and Brussels beyond their governmental structure.They have substantial negative residuals from both the growth models despite having a favourable impact from their governmental structure on their capacity to develop policy. Conversely governmental structure and its impact on local policy fails to explain the particular outperformance of FURs such as Frankfurt, Edinburgh, München or Saarbrücken. Even allowing for the advantages of their governmental structures they still substantially outperformed the predictions of both models.

Table 9.7 Residuals from model 2 – with policy units variable

Model 1: With policy units			
FUR	Residual	FUR	Residual
Edinburgh	0.009938	Roma	0.001276
Saarbrücken	0.006828	Lyon	0.001223
München	0.005522	Bristol	0.001181
Kassel	0.005394	Genova	0.001089
Valenciennes	0.005152	Sunderland	0.000922
Barcelona	0.005040	Aachen	0.000857
Saloniki	0.004951	Bari	0.000720
Madrid	0.004905	Clermont Ferrand	0.000693
Frankfurt	0.004845	Dublin	0.000662
Utrecht	0.004771	Munster	0.000617
Grenoble	0.004599	Wiesbaden	0.000530
Messina	0.004389	London	0.000508
Antwerpen	0.004039	Porto	0.000462
Hamburg	0.004012	Belfast	0.000461
Valencia	0.003901	Taranto	0.000428
Cagliari	0.003790	Sevilla	0.000178
Toulouse	0.003713	Padova	0.000164
Mannheim	0.003711	Duisburg	0.000120
Nantes	0.003475	Derby	0.000054
St Etienne	0.003303	Nottingham	0.000045
Augsburg	0.003170	Portsmouth	0.000043
Leeds	0.002971	Bochum	0.000037
Braunschweig	0.002915	Verona	0.000016
Birmingham	0.002828	Hannover	0.000015
Strasbourg	0.002774	Stuttgart	0.000007
Granada	0.002518	Nürnberg	–0.000027
Cardiff	0.002505	Brighton	–0.000070
Palma de Mallorca	0.002482	Nice	–0.000128
Karlsruhe	0.002034	Mulhouse	–0.000153
Newcastle	0.001810	Southampton	–0.000174
Catania	0.001738	Venezia	–0.000180
Brescia	0.001606	Rotterdam	–0.000223
Napoli	0.001513	Cordoba	–0.000282
Zaragoza	0.001452	Amsterdam	–0.000372
Bremen	0.001442	Glasgow	–0.000440
Palermo	0.001389	Aarhus	–0.000722

Table 9.7 Continued

Model 1: With policy units			
FUR	Residual	FUR	Residual
Manchester	–0.000734	Dijon	–0.002679
Bielefeld	–0.000868	Liverpool	–0.002927
Bonn	–0.000883	Marseille	–0.002971
Leicester	–0.001086	Firenze	–0.003004
Coventry	–0.001112	Paris	–0.003005
Rennes	–0.001311	Bruxelles	–0.003020
Liège	–0.001327	Toulon	–0.003088
Vigo	–0.001339	Lille	–0.003098
Mönchengladbach	–0.001395	Nancy	–0.003140
Milano	–0.001514	Plymouth	–0.003164
Teesside	–0.001668	Bordeaux	–0.003340
Rouen	–0.001745	Montpellier	–0.003347
Orleans	–0.001757	s'Gravenhage	–0.003460
Stoke on Trent	–0.001823	Valladolid	–0.003571
Charleroi	–0.001836	Le Havre	–0.003761
Hull	–0.001903	Wuppertal	–0.004012
Bilbao	–0.001908	La Coruña	–0.004484
Bologna	–0.002149	Kobenhavn	–0.004491
Athens	–0.002242	Lisboa	–0.004870
Essen	–0.002321	Düsseldorf	–0.004887
Murcia	–0.002353	Sheffield	–0.006593
Dortmund	–0.002395	Köln	–0.006684
Aviles	–0.002405	Malaga	–0.006956
Alicante	–0.002409	Torino	–0.007515
Krefeld	–0.002415		

Table 9.8 Difference between residuals from models 1 and 2

Residual 1 – Residual 2			
FUR	Difference	FUR	Difference
Lille	0.003795	Nice	0.000584
Belfast	0.003396	Bordeaux	0.000552
Frankfurt	0.003081	München	0.000549
Zaragoza	0.002833	Plymouth	0.000546
Essen	0.002825	Toulouse	0.000520
Palma de Mallorca	0.002730	Saloniki	0.000501
Coventry	0.002691	Paris	0.000450
Aachen	0.002677	Strasbourg	0.000389
Glasgow	0.002665	Hamburg	0.000358
Murcia	0.002652	Wuppertal	0.000349
Bilbao	0.002632	Utrecht	0.000342
Edinburgh	0.002619	Vigo	0.000328
Genova	0.002481	Derby	0.000307
Sunderland	0.002379	Bremen	0.000283
Dortmund	0.002293	Aarhus	0.000279
Barcelona	0.002000	Antwerpen	0.000261
Valladolid	0.001897	Charleroi	0.000252
Venezia	0.001840	Marseille	0.000243
Mannheim	0.001753	Palermo	0.000218
Torino	0.001575	Düsseldorf	0.000131
Cordoba	0.001243	Saarbrücken	0.000103
Roma	0.001219	Montpellier	0.000047
s'Gravenhage	0.001134	Rotterdam	–0.000067
Sheffield	0.001091	Köln	–0.000111
Bologna	0.001082	Bochum	–0.000162
Milano	0.001082	Bristol	–0.000165
Hull	0.001080	Malaga	–0.000171
Mönchengladbach	0.001032	Liverpool	–0.000216
Granada	0.000890	Cardiff	–0.000245
Augsburg	0.000747	Dijon	–0.000261
Duisburg	0.000744	Amsterdam	–0.000315
Napoli	0.000710	Stoke on Trent	–0.000352
Taranto	0.000655	Rennes	–0.000364
Madrid	0.000643	Dublin	–0.000366
Le Havre	0.000640	Brighton	–0.000406
Firenze	0.000620	Stuttgart	–0.000498
Lyon	0.000604	Bruxelles	–0.000527

Table 9.8 Continued

Residual 1 – Residual 2			
FUR	Difference	FUR	Difference
Leicester	–0.000545	Catania	–0.001048
Clermont Ferrand	–0.000549	Aviles	–0.001122
Braunschweig	–0.000553	Mulhouse	–0.001130
Leeds	–0.000556	Padova	–0.001267
La Coruña	–0.000573	Cagliari	–0.001295
Verona	–0.000573	Kassel	–0.001345
Bonn	–0.000580	Bielefeld	–0.001415
Liège	–0.000586	Porto	–0.001510
Sevilla	–0.000606	Brescia	–0.001525
Birmingham	–0.000617	St Etienne	–0.001544
Nürnberg	–0.000655	Nantes	–0.001707
Toulon	–0.000681	Manchester	–0.001776
Wiesbaden	–0.000695	Grenoble	–0.001825
Krefeld	–0.000749	Kobenhavn	–0.001832
Hannover	–0.000752	Teesside	–0.001929
Portsmouth	–0.000848	Nancy	–0.002034
Karlsruhe	–0.000876	Alicante	–0.002051
Orleans	–0.000887	Lisboa	–0.002239
Messina	–0.000889	London	–0.002251
Bari	–0.000894	Newcastle	–0.002387
Southampton	–0.000928	Munster	–0.002423
Athens	–0.000932	Valenciennes	–0.002719
Nottingham	–0.000984	Rouen	–0.003062
Valencia	–0.001037		

5 SOME CONCLUSIONS

The evidence presented in this chapter strongly supports the conclusion that the use of administratively defined regions (such as NUTS) for analysing patterns of regional growth in Europe leads to misleading and perhaps biased results. The present investigation of growth processes uses data for consistent urban regions defined on functional criteria (FURs). In terms of understanding urban growth processes it confirms the results reported in Cheshire and Carbonaro (1996) but significantly extends them. One aspect of this extension is that the variables included in the earlier model appear to perform in a way which is robust. They continue to have similar estimated effects on urban growth differentials with additional observations, over an extended time period and with a more fully specified model. One new result is that extending the data forward from the mean of 1987/90 (the end point used in the earlier analysis) to 1992/94 suggests a reinforcement of the spatial impact of European integration and a re-focusing of the strongest gains on an innermost core of regions. This is consistent with the impact of the Single European Market.

The analysis of the residuals from the growth model is consistent with some part of urban growth differentials being accounted for by the impact of local (territorially competitive) policy. A factor identified in previous studies as likely to have a conditioning influence on the capacity of urban regions to develop effective growth policy is the structure of local government. This may systematically influence the transactions costs involved in forming successful 'clubs' to promote effective growth policy. The greater is the leadership capacity of the central government unit representing the urban region the lower these costs should be expected to be. The results strongly support this hypothesis. Even allowing for such systematic differences in the capacity of FURs to develop effective growth policy the pattern of residuals still suggests that there remain other systematic influences on the success of policy in particular cities: both for outperforming the models' predictions and for underperforming them. The residuals from the augmented Model 2 still fail fully to account for the consistent good growth performance of cities such as Frankfurt or Edinburgh just as they also fail fully to account for the outstandingly poor performance of cities such as Brussels, Bordeaux, Liverpool or Sheffield.

APPENDIX

Table 9A.1 Residuals from growth model[1] for 1980s

	Growth > Expected					Growth = Expected					Growth < Expected			
	FUR	% G^2	R^3	Ex^4		FUR	% G^2	R^3	Ex^4		FUR	% G^2	R^3	Ex^4
1	Murcia	77.2	13.5	*P	41	Wiesbaden	60.1	2.7		81	Belfast	64.8	–3.0	...
2	Palma Mallorca	75.5	13.0	*	42	Toulon	53.3	2.3		82	Sunderland	53.7	–3.1	...
3	Strasbourg	66.9	11.0	*P	43	Amsterdam	54.7	2.0		83	Orleans	51.5	–3.1	...
4	München	76.1	10.5	*	44	Edinburgh	70.2	2.0		84	Firenze	59.4	–3.1	...
5	Venezia	71.8	9.7	*	45	Brescia	64.2	1.9		85	Bochum	49.2	–3.1	...
6	Saarbrucken	58.3	9.4	*P	46	Antwerpen	56.5	1.7		86	Toulouse	55.6	–3.2	...
7	Leeds	75.6	9.0	*P	47	Montpellier	59.0	1.3		87	Kobenhavn	62.9	–3.4	...
8	Taranto	65.3	8.8	*P	48	Bonn	56.0	1.3		88	Aviles/Gijon	46.9	–3.4	...
9	Coventry	69.0	8.5	?	49	Hull	86.7	1.0		89	Lille	48.1	–3.8	...
10	Bristol	74.6	7.8	*	50	Karlsruhe	58.0	0.9		90	Cordoba	58.1	–3.9	...
11	Mannheim	60.0	7.7	?	51	Glasgow	64.3	0.8		91	Essen	40.3	–4.0	...
12	Granada	63.3	7.0	*	52	Grenoble	56.1	0.8		92	Sevilla	65.6	–4.5	?
13	Cardiff	72.3	6.7	*P	53	Bremen	54.7	0.4		93	Augsburg	54.5	–4.7	?
14	Valencia	74.7	6.6	*P	54	Marseille	52.3	0.4		94	Portsmouth	62.1	–4.9	?
15	Cagliari	62.4	6.5	*	55	Hamburg	57.5	0.4		95	Bordeaux	50.1	–5.3	*
16	Leicester	78.6	6.3	*	56	Clerm't-Fe'd	56.7	0.3		96	Bilbao	57.9	–5.7	*
17	s-Gravenhage	53.8	6.1	?	57	London	74.5	0.2		97	Vigo	46.0	–6.0	*
18	Paris	67.5	5.7	P	58	Nottingham	59.5	0.0		98	Alicante	56.3	–6.3	?

19	Mön'gladbach	57.5	5.7	*	59	Nantes	54.7	–0.1	99	Plymouth	61.3	–6.6	?
20	Aachen	55.1	5.6	*	60	Hannover	61.3	–0.2	100	Rennes	52.0	–6.6	?
21	Barcelona	72.1	5.6	*P	61	Charleroi	48.6	–0.3	101	Valladolid	56.7	–6.7	*
22	Frankfurt	71.1	5.5	*P	62	Southampton	62.1	–0.4	102	Mulhouse	45.9	–6.8	*
23	Duisburg	41.5	5.4	P?	63	Kassel	60.5	–0.6	103	La Coruña	46.9	–6.9	*
24	Rotterdam	55.0	5.2	P	64	St. Etienne	46.7	–0.7	104	Torino	61.4	–7.0	*(P)
25	Roma	75.0	5.1	*	65	Milano	64.5	–0.9	105	Bielefeld	53.8	–7.2	*
26	Padova	71.6	4.6	*	66	Manchester	62.8	–0.9	106	Sheffield	47.5	–7.2	*(P)
27	Nürnberg	67.3	4.3	*	67	Dublin	67.5	–1.2	107	Nice	54.8	–7.4	*
28	Zaragoza	76.7	4.1	...	68	Derby	64.8	–1.2	108	Napoli	55.1	–7.7	*(P)
29	Stuttgart	63.4	4.1	...	69	Le Havre	45.8	–1.4	109	Münster	54.0	–7.8	*
30	Verona	71.5	4.0	...	70	Birmingham	65.4	–1.4	110	Düsseldorf	62.2	–8.0	*
31	Brighton	78.1	4.0	...	71	Wuppertal	54.4	–1.4	111	Köln	56.3	–8.2	*?
32	Stoke on Trent	74.2	3.8	...	72	Dijon	53.6	–1.7	112	Brussel/Bruxelles	57.7	–8.4	*(P)
33	Braunschweig	60.3	3.8	...	73	Utrecht	49.3	–1.7	113	Berlin	45.3	–8.7	*
34	Bari	65.1	3.7	...	74	Lyon	57.6	–1.8	114	Nancy	42.1	–8.8	*
35	Madrid	75.6	3.6	...	75	Liège	51.3	–1.9	115	Newcastle	55.1	–9.6	*?
36	Palermo	59.8	3.5	...	76	Teesside	59.5	–2.3	116	Bologna	57.5	–9.9	(?P)
37	Messina	58.6	3.2	...	77	Dortmund	46.9	–2.4	117	Malaga	55.7	–1.2	*(P)
38	Aarhus	67.2	3.2	...	78	Genova	59.7	–2.4	118	Liverpool	44.6	–12.7	*(P)
39	Valenciennes	48.1	3.0	...	79	Rouen	49.0	–2.5					
40	Catania	59.8	2.7		80	Krefeld	53.5	–2.5					

Notes to Table 9A1:

1 See p. 221.
2 % Growth in GDP p.c. @ PPS 1979/82 to 1987/90.
3 Residual between growth predicted by model and actual.
4 Explanation of residual: * = Identifiable local factors; P, (P) = positive or (negative) local policy for economic development; ? = uncertain; = residual too small to speculate.

NOTES

1. An interesting attempt to measure the intensity of local development efforts at the city level in the much more homogeneous context of the US was devised and applied with some success in Stough (1999)
2. This analysis was developed independently of the work of Hochman, Pines and Thisse (1995), but its implications are broadly consistent with the conclusions of that more technical theoretical treatment of the problem.
3. There are regional GDP data available from 1977 to 1996. Those for 1977 and 1978 appear to be substantially less reliable than for more recent dates. Those for 1995 and 1996 are currently being integrated into the FUR database, but not only were there changes to the boundaries of the regions for which Eurostat reported their data from 1995, but there were also some significant revisions to data for past years. These data problems have delayed the incorporation of the data for 1995 and 1996.
4. The data are taken from Eurostat's REGIO database. NUTS stands for *Nomenclature des Unités Territoriales Statistiques*.
5. For a detailed discussion of the definition of these Functional Urban Regions (FURs) see Cheshire and Hay (1989). They are defined on the basis of core cities identified by concentrations of employment and hinterlands from which commuters flow to the employment core.
6. Athens, Lisboa, Porto and Saloniki have been added to the data set.
7. Dublin is an interesting case. It was identified in Cheshire (1990) as having adverse local policy effects because, in common with London, it had a local administration with little power and less fiscal capacity and had the additional disadvantage of having a separation of physical planning from financial provision. This resulted in large scale planning blight as physical projects were announced but substantial delays were experienced with finance.

REFERENCES

Armstrong, H. and J. Taylor (1993), *Regional Economics and Policy*, Harvester Wheatsheaf.

Beutel, J. (1995), 'The Economic Impacts of the Community Support Frameworks for the Objective 1 Regions 1994–99', Report to the Directorate General for Regional Policies, Commission of the European Communities.

Blanchard, O. (1991), 'Convergence across states and regions: discussion', *Brookings Papers on Economic Activity I*, 183–92.

Cheshire, P.C. (1990), 'Explaining the recent performance of the European Community's major urban regions', *Urban Studies*, **27** (3), 311–33.

Cheshire, P.C. (1991), 'Problems of Regional Transformation and Deindustrialisation in the European Community', in L. Rodwin and H. Sazanami (eds), *Industrial Change and Regional Economic Transformation: the case of Western Europe*, London: Harper Collins Academic.

Cheshire, P.C. and D.G. Hay (1989), *Urban Problems in Western Europe: an economic analysis*, London: Unwin Hyman.

Cheshire, P.C. and G. Carbonaro (1995), 'Convergence–Divergence in Regional Growth Rates: An Empty Black Box?', in Armstrong, H.W. and R.W. Vickerman (eds), *Convergence and Divergence Among European Regions*, London: Pion.

Cheshire, P.C. and G. Carbonaro (1996), 'Urban economic growth in Europe: testing theory and policy prescriptions', *Urban Studies*, **33**, 1111–28.

Cheshire, P.C. and I.R. Gordon (1996), 'Territorial competition and the logic of collective (in)action', *International Journal of Urban and Regional Research*, **20**, 383–99.

Cheshire, P.C. and I.R. Gordon (1998), 'Territorial competition: some lessons for policy', *The Annals of Regional Science*, **32**, 321–46.

Cheshire, P.C. and S. Magrini (1999), 'Endogenous Processes in European Regional Growth: Implications for Convergence and Policy', paper presented at the symposium on *Endogenous Growth Policy and Regional Development*, held at the Tinbergen Institute, Amsterdam, February.

Clark, C., F. Wilson and J. Bradley (1969), 'Industrial location and economic potential in Western Europe', *Regional Studies*, **3**, 197–212.

Hochman, O., D. Pines and J.-F. Thisse (1995), 'On the optimal structure of local governments', *American Economic Review*, **85** (5), 1224–40.

Keeble, D., J. Offord and S. Walker (1988), *Peripheral Regions in a Community of Twelve Member States*, Luxembourg: Office of Official Publications.

Krugman, P. (1991), 'Increasing returns and economic geography', *Journal of Political Economy*, **99**, 483–99.

Krugman, P.R. and A.J. Venables (1990), 'Integration and the competitiveness of peripheral industry', Centre for Economic Policy Research, Discussion Paper Series, 363.

Krugman, P.R. and A.J. Venables (1993), 'Integration, specialization and adjustment', Centre for Economic Policy Research, Discussion Paper Series, 886.

Magrini, S. (1997), 'Spatial Concentration in Research and Regional Income Disparities in a Decentralised Model of Endogenous Growth', Research Paper in Environmental and Spatial Analysis No. 43, London School of Economics.

Moore, B. and J. Rhodes (1973), 'Evaluating the effects of British regional economic policy', *Economic Journal*, **83**, 87–110.

Moore, B., Rhodes, J. and P. Tyler (1986), *The Effects of Government Regional Economic Policy*, London: HMSO.

Olson, M. (1965) *The Logic of Collective Action, Public Goods and the Theory of Groups*, Cambridge, Mass: Harvard University Press

Quah, D.T. (1993), Galton's fallacy and tests of the convergence hypothesis'. *Scandinavian Journal of Economics*, **95**, 427–43.

Stough, R.R., S.V. Lall and M.P. Trice (1999), 'Regional Endogenous Growth and Policy', paper presented at the symposium on *Endogenous Growth Policy and Regional Development*, held at the Tinbergen Institute, Amsterdam, February.

Venables A.J. (1996), Localization of industry and trade performance, *Oxford Review of Economic Policy*, **12**, 52–60.

10. The Counterfactual Path: Defining the Non-Support Activity Level when Estimating Programme Effects

Jan Mønnesland

INTRODUCTION

The chapter focuses on the need to generate a counterfactual path when the effect of policy actions, programmes and so on are carried out.

The comparison between the path with and without policy actions has a long history in ex ante analysis. Here, both levels need to be estimated. In ex post analysis, the path including the policy actions will often be the observed path. As a result, it is in ex post analysis that problems often emerge, and where conclusions may be misleading due to a non-explicit assumption about the contrafactual path.

Methods used for measuring the counterfactual activity level in micro-based evaluations are examined. The approach used most often is to ask respondents about additional programme contributions according to their own activity level.

In macro-based analysis, the counterfactual path will often have to be generated through methodological assumptions. The estimated effects will then rely on the quality of the methodology applied. Examples are shown where different assumptions lead to great differences in the estimated effect of regional policy support schemes.

ANALYSING EFFECTS: AN EXERCISE WITH TRADITIONS

The aim of public activity will normally be to influence society in a way seen as beneficial, given the political priorities upheld by the authorities. The very legitimacy of the public sector is that without this sector activity, society will be losing qualities.

As the public sector gradually expanded its ambitions, the need for more systematic knowledge about the effect of various types of public action became greater. From the early postwar years, systems of macroeconomic planning based on analytical methods were gradually used in most industrialised countries. Keywords are national budgets, long-term programmes, programme budgets and, in the later years, impact analyses. Both the effects of an activity as such, as well as the secondary effects imposed on the national economy, were normal elements in the national economic planning process. Also national multi-sector planning models were developed, using econometric tools in order to grasp the overall effects resulting from the expected sector developments in the different parts of the economy.

The tradition may vary somewhat in style from country to country. In the Norwegian tradition, the planning process normally took the form of public reports, either regularly in the form of Long Term Programmes and National Budgets (see Bjerve, 1959, for an early overview), or ad hoc when important decisions were on the agenda, for instance on activity levels in the oil extraction sector, building of hydro power plants, implementation of emission quotas in the environmental policy and so on. Such reports often included analytical prediction paths, set up by the macroeconomic econometric models used for short-term or long-term predictions (Larsen, 1997 could serve as an example of the long list of such reports, most of them only in Norwegian). Here, alternative paths were normally developed. One path used to be called the reference path, describing the future if no special actions were taken. The other paths were deviations from this reference path, showing the effect of decisions or possible external impulses.

Using such analytical methods was not at all a universal routine to be implemented for all actions to be taken by different public units. Only the more important decisions seen from a macroeconomic point of view were undertaken in such an analytical way. The reason for focusing on this topic here is to underline that calculating the effects of political actions is not a new phenomenon, neither is it confined to evaluations. In the last half century, quite elaborate techniques have been in more or less regular use to deal with the estimation of policy effects. The main difference, however, is that the tradition up to the recent past has mostly focused on ex ante analysis, what the effects are expected to be in the short- and long-term future, while evaluations normally deal with ex post analysis, what the effects have proved to be in the past.

Another important difference is that traditional ex ante approaches mostly were carried out for greater projects with significant macro impacts.

Evaluations are now often expected to take place also for minor programmes and projects.

The growing demand for impact analyses and evaluations, involving minor as well as macro type of activities, has led to a new wave of reports from a lot of different milieus, using a multitude of techniques of quantitative as well as qualitative type. The quality of those reports varies, from skilled approaches to more consultant-based guestimates in a nice layout.

In my opinion, to estimate activity effects ex post and ex ante will involve a great deal of similar challenges. Therefore, the experiences from the developed tradition of ex ante analysis should also be utilised for evaluation methodology.

THE REFERENCE PATH: NON-ACTION DEVELOPMENT

Often, evaluation reports are presented which include mainly a pure description of the activity in question. Also so-called effect indicators are often described in a purely statistical manner. Although it is important to have a statistical picture of the ongoing devcelopment, doing this one will often be distant from a real estimation of the programme effects.

In impact analyses and other types of ex ante analyses of the potential future with and without different policy actions, the available statistics are only valid before the activities to be analysed have begun. Then, it will be obvious that indicators of a purely statistical type cannot tell the full story about the effects of the future actions. Confusing the effects with the experienced development is something only seen in unskilled ex post evaluations, or in unskilled comments to evaluations.

The basic challenge, to distinguish between the development with and without the actions, and then to let the difference alone and not the development itself be the effect indicator, is rather similar in ex post and ex ante analysis. A schematic illustration is provided in Figure 10.1.

As seen in Figure 10.1, it is only in ex ante analyses that the path including programme activities needs to be estimated, this is a realised and then observable path in the ex post analyses, that is the evaluations. As will be commented on below, this is both an advantage as well as a disadvantage for the evaluation analyses.

Often, in ex ante analysis, the actual paths estimated for the future development without the programme activities (often called the reference path) will not influence so much on the effect estimation. The reason is that most estimation methods deal directly with the activity effects.

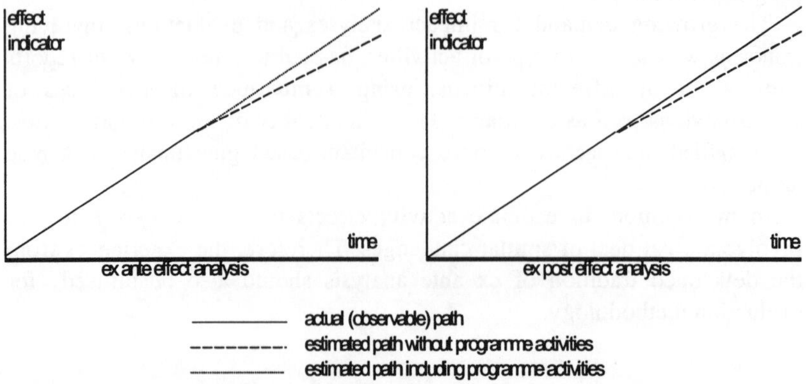

Figure 10.1 The reference path, the path with programme implementation, and the programme effect, ex ante and ex post analyses

The normal technique is to establish a reference path, then to use the applied method to end up with an estimation of effects, and then to add the effects and the reference path to get the development including programme activities.

This way, the reference path is used for scaling. To say something about the effects of, say, new emission quotas on production and employment at the national level, it is important to know the production level of the influenced industries. It is also important to know if the influenced industries are facing a positive or negative future development regardless of the changing quotas, to know if the future effects may be greater or smaller than the actual expected effects. Anyway, the results presented will normally focus on the effects as such, that is the difference between the paths with and without the activities. What could differ in the level of elaboration will mostly be to what extent a distinction between actual and future effects is made.

There is, then, no great danger involved when analysts in ex ante analyses do not keep the model of Figure 10.1 clearly in mind, and maybe ignore the concept of the reference path. A statement of the type 'the effect will be x man-year reductions in this and/or that industry', will be interpreted in a situation where the actual operating level of these industries is expected to be known. Interpreted in the framework of Figure 10.1, the statement will be judged as valid for a future date where the total effect has got time to emerge, and the implicit reference path may be interpreted as a zero growth path from today up to that future date. The type of reference path adopted will normally not have a great influence on the reliability of the estimated effects.

In the ex post analyses, the actual level of today will normally be a situation where the programme activity is ongoing. Here, a much more dangerous situation will appear if the development without programme activities is not seriously estimated.

Evaluations of ongoing programmes will have to obtain some timespan limits. This may be the total programme period, for instance for temporary programmes, or a time limit set up for the evaluation period for more long lasting activities. In any case, the evaluation will concentrate on a specific timespan, from time A to time B, where B is the actual date or the date of the latest available statistical information.

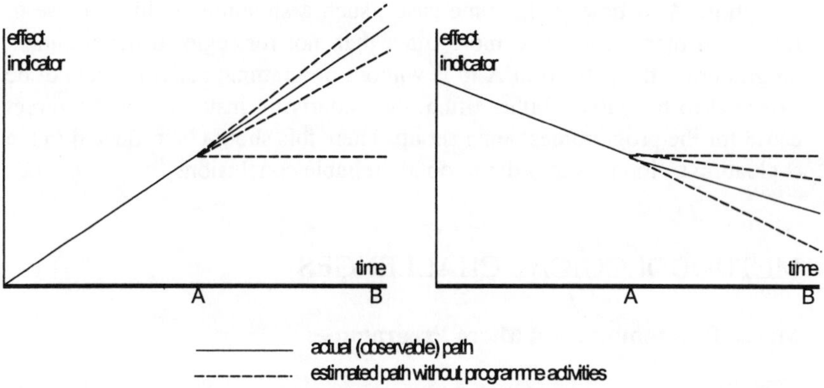

Figure 10.2 Growing and declining indicator development. Actual path and hypothetical alternatives without programme activities

In Figure 10.2, two situations are illustrated, showing the development of an effect indicator (as employment, production, value added and so on, and could be regarded for the whole economy or only for the units involved, depending on the type of the programme). In both situations, it is expected that time A, the starting date of the evaluation period, is also the starting date for the programme activity.

If the evaluator does not have the concept of the reference path clearly in mind, important mistakes may be made about the programme effects. In a situation with growing indicator values, the evaluator may conclude that the programme is a success. In a situation with declining indicator values, the evaluator may similarly conclude that the programme is a failure. None of these conclusions is obvious. Depending on the level of the reference path, the programme effect could in both cases be either positive or negative. Without estimating the contrafactual path describing what the non-programme indicators could have been, it is impossible to know the dimension as well as the direction of the programme effect.

It is more the rule than the exception to see evaluations that do not distinguish between the total indicator development and the programme effect. Then, in a situation of general growth, most programmes will tend to get a positive evaluation, and in a situation of general decline they will tend to get a negative evaluation, when unskilled evaluators are engaged to do the job. Interpreted in the framework of Figures 10.1 and 10.2, the unskilled evaluator will implicitly analyse as if the counterfactual reference path (the path without the programme activity) would have been a zero growth path from time A to time B. In some cases, such a situation could be close to reality. In other cases, and more often than not for regional development programmes, the path from A to B without programme activities cannot be expected to be stable. Rather often, the underlying instability is the direct cause for the programmes being set up. Then, this should be reflected in the evaluation techniques in order to obtain reliable conclusions.

METHODOLOGICAL CHALLENGES

Macro Programmes and Micro Programmes

The methodological challenges for ex post evaluations are primarily connected to the estimation of the reference path, that is the counterfactual development showing what would have been the path if the programme activities were not operating. Here, a distinction should be made between macro programmes where secondary effects may be significant, and smaller programmes that mainly affect the participating actors with non-significant external effects.

An example of the first category is the firm-directed support programme operated for the designated support zones. The programme consists of grants and loans to be used for investment purposes as well as for business development (soft type investments). The firms have to claim for support to the State Industrial and Regional Fund, who decide the level of grant and/or loan to be approved if they accept the project (see Mønnesland, 1997, for a closer description). The programme is on such a level that the production and employment effect should not be restricted to the receiving firms alone.

Secondary effects are important, that is the general activity level generated (or upheld) in the total regional economy due to the support. It is mainly through these secondary effects that the scheme is expected to contribute to better employment and population development in the designated areas.

An example of the second category, where the secondary effects may be ignored in the evaluations, is Interreg cross-border programmes. Here also, the intention of the programmes is to support a style of cross-border activities to be significant also beyond those actors taking active part in programme activities, although the economic level of the programmes is moderate relative to the total economy in the border region. It is difficult, then, to generate a counterfactual path of behaviour for the actors not included in the programme. Effect indicators based on general regional statistics will therefore be of minor relevance. For the involved actors, however, statistical effect indicators may be constructed. It will also be relevant to estimate counterfactual indicator levels showing what the actors would have done if the programme were not established (see Mønnesland et al., 1998, for an evaluation along these lines for three Interreg programmes).

The analytical challenge will deviate between the two abovementioned categories. In the first category, an analytical model will be needed to generate indicators where the secondary effects are included. The counterfactual path will also have to be generated through such a model. In the second category, project information alone should be sufficient to end up with effect indicators. The challenge is to estimate the counterfactual (non-programme) behaviour of the programme actors.

Estimating the Additionality on Micro Level

Several programme evaluations are based on questionnaires to the participating actors. They are asked about their opinion of the programme, in what way the programme has been useful for them, and often to what extent they have reached different targets in their activities. They may be asked to set up some indicator values showing the employment effect, value added effect and so on which they regard as programme dependent.

If the programme operate through projects, the data reported will normally be project data. In the investment support scheme, the firms will report on the effect of the supported investment activities. In the Interreg case, they will report on the activity projects which are included in the programme.

There may be problems connected to the validity of the reported project data. In particular, if a programme is ongoing and the transfers to the projects are expected to continue, a positive bias in the reported effect indicators may be expected. The experience is that the answers are more reliable if collected ex post, that is after the termination of the projects, than by reports collected underway. Also, the reports seem to be more reliable if collected by evaluation milieus being regarded to be independent of the programme operating units. Several questionnaire techniques are developed to deal with the validity problem. This is often a problem able to be overcome if the evaluations are carried out in a skilled way.

The challenge of estimating the counterfactual path is not overcomed by getting valid project data and reliable project effect estimates. To find the counterfactual path, it is necessary to estimate the additionality, that is what would have happened if the support scheme had not existed.

Normally, several of the projects supported by the programmes under evaluation also could have taken place without the programme. As mentioned, investments supported by the support scheme could to some extent have been financed by alternative sources without the programme. Some of the Interreg activities are cross-border-linked activities that at least partly would have taken place without the programme, but maybe with looser cross-border ties. Then, the cross-border target may have been dependent on the programme, while the employment indicator may have a low degree of additionality.

Measuring the additionality will often have to be done by questionnaires. The normal method is to include additionality questions in the questionnaire used to estimate the project indicators. If the project indicators are obtained by other sources, such as project registers, accounting figures and so on, questionnaires will still be needed to generate the additionality information.

The straightforward way to measure additionality is to ask the support receivers and/or project actors what they would have done if the support were not given or they were not involved in the programme. The alternatives offered in several evaluations (see Mønnesland et al., 1998; Berge, Hærvik and Johnsen, 1993; Brein and Hærvik, 1996), have used these answer categories:

- would have effectuated the project in the same way
- would have postponed the project
- would have scaled down the project
- would have cancelled the project.

The first option is given the additionality factor of 0, the two next options a factor of 0.5 and the last option a factor of 1. The method is then to multiply the estimated project effect indicator values by this additionality factor in order to find the programme effect.

The reliability of the answers on additionality questions will have some of the same characteristic as the other information collected in the questionnaire. The questions should preferably be asked after the project financing is terminated, and/or by a milieu regarded as independent of the programme administration. It is also of great importance how the questions are formulated and what methods are used to collect the answers. As the questions are of a counterfactual character, the respondents will not always know the correct answers themselves. In most cases, however, the actors have considered some strategies on what to do if the programme application should be turned down.

In addition to the variance caused by the validity problem, another problem is caused by the category division used. In reality, the additionality factor will lie on a continuous scale from 0 to 1. It is difficult to construct answer alternatives reflecting this continuum, and if done, the respondents will probably understand such a graduation differently. For this reason, one will have to stick to the rather crude categories mentioned above. Even as the variance of the estimates might be significant, this is a better situation than using estimates being systematically biased upwards, as will be the case when additionality is not taken into consideration.

Such respondent-based estimation methods will normally lead to positive effect estimates. The difference between methods dealing with additionality and those which ignore this aspect, will be the size of the estimated effects, not the direction. This is not a problem, it reflects reality. Money granted through different types of programmes will normally generate positive effects. It is difficult to generate reduced investment activities by providing loans and grants, when measured at the respondent level. As long as secondary effects may be neglected, the results are normally bound to be positive.[1]

Such evaluations are often criticised as measuring the popularity of Santa Claus. Respondents will tend to report that they are satisfied to have received money, and for that reason, the evaluator may conclude that the programme has been beneficial and should continue.

If serious work is conducted in the estimation of the indicators, including serious treatment of the additionality problem, the result should be that Santa Claus is popular. The problem is whether the relevant questions have been brought into the evaluation. To measure the benefits alone may be relevant, but it may be more relevant if such benefits are also related to the costs. If cost efficiency is brought into the analyses, the result will often be that a programme may benefit the clients but other types of programmes may bring more benefits for the society per money unit. To include the relevant questions into an evaluation project, to remember the relative aspect and to compare with alternative methods for money channelling, are aspects of evaluation quality. These questions, however, are not genuinely connected to the challenge of estimating the counterfactual path.

Estimating the Counterfactual Path for Macro Programmes

When the relevant indicators include secondary effects, some type of analytical models will be needed to link the programme information with the relevant indicator levels. The programme information may be of the type of total budgets or other observable realised figures, or questionnaire-generated estimates of actor behaviour. When the relevant project information is generated, then it is through the model calculation that the programme effect indicators will be generated.

In the ex ante analysis referred to in Figure 10.1, the method will often be to start with a reference path developed as a straightforward prolonging of the trends existing independent of the programme activities. Then, the relevant exogen input generated from the study of the programme activity is put into the model, and the model will generate the alternative path for the effect indicators when the programme is operating.

In the ex post evaluations, the same method will have to be used, but now with a negative sign. The model must be calibrated to reflect the actual observed development. Then, the relevant exogen input generated from the study of the programme should be put into the model with negative signs, and the model will then generate the alternative path for the effect indicators if the programme had not been operating.

If the programme information used is reflecting real deviation from a non-programme situation, such a method will give the non-programme development of the effects. If the programme information used does not reflect real deviations from a non-programme situation, the method will generate a misleading counterfactual path.

The above-mentioned example with the evaluation of the firm-oriented regional support may illustrate this point (Mønnesland, Hervik and Dale, 1993).

It may be assumed that the money put into the scheme is of a real net character, that is that the money would not have been used differently in a way affecting the indicators if the programme were not operating. The major fluctuations in state budget balances make it reasonable to expect that the balance will be effected more than the other state budget elements. The alternative path will be a situation where these state budget transfers of the scheme are non-existent, while all other public budget streams are regarded as unaffected. If the state budget is under a more heavy stress, such a reasoning may be questionable, and then it could be needed to generate a reference path where other state expenditures were affected.

The investments to be supported would, however, not only be net investments. Some firms would have drained other resources if grants and loans were not provided through the programme. The net effect will then depend partly on the alternative investment behaviour of the firm, and partly from what type of funds the alternative financial sources would allocate to the region in the non-programme situation. Some types of alternative funding will lie within the region and the effect will only be of a redistributional type, while others will imply additional funding to the region in focus.

For macro programmes, it will often be necessary to base the calculations in effect on counterfactual assumptions for the involved programme actors. The method to do this is the same as described above for the micro level. Different models may be set up to estimate the macro effects where the secondary effects are also included. There are several classes of models that do not use the micro-based respondent information in the analyses.

Two different approaches have been used in the evaluation of the regional investment support scheme in Norway.

First, is the shift–share type of analysis (Dale, Ellingsen and Espedal, 1993). The scheme is operating within the designated support zone. The hypothesis is that the scheme should have generated better development within the zone than outside the zone. Differences in the industrial structure are taken care of by using the shift–share method on a disaggregated sector level. The effect of the support scheme is then measured as the higher investment intensity at the disaggregated sector level within the zone compared to outside the zone. The total effect is measured by aggregating the sector differentials. Similar measurements are also made on other indicators as production and employment.

The second approach has been a respondent-based method (Berge, Hervik and Johansen, 1993). A representative sample of respondents is asked about the investment level, production effect and employment effects generated by the support. They are also asked about the additionality, that is to what degree the investment would have taken place without the support. The sample respondent figures are then expanded to the level of the total support receivers, giving the estimated effect of the support scheme on the direct receiver level. Ordinary multiplicator models of the cross-section type are then used to include the secondary effects.

Figure 10.3 shows the results for the evaluation estimates. The shift–share approach found the effect to be close to zero (a–b in Figure 10.3), while the respondent based method estimated the effect to be substantial (a–c in Figure 10.3).

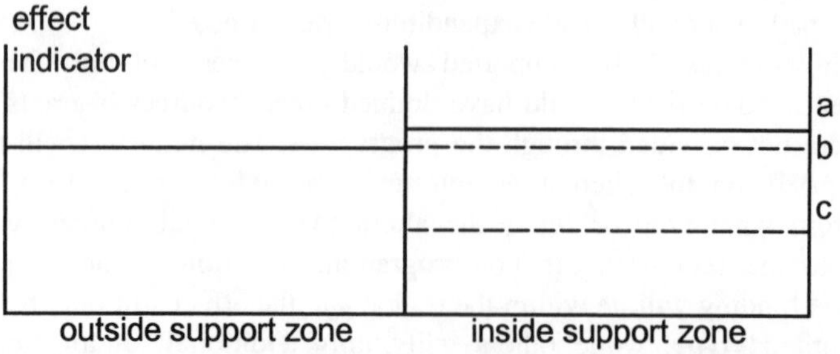

Figure 10.3 Estimated support scheme effects (see text for explanation)

In the shift–share method, the counterfactual level, that is the estimated level if the scheme did not exist, was supposed to be similar to that outside the support zone when corrected for different industrial structure. In the respondent-based method, the counterfactual level was estimated based on the respondent replies, adjusted for the additionality factor and included secondary effects.

Similar types of evaluations took place on two occasions, one in the early 1980s and one in the early 1990s, giving the same striking differences in estimated effects as shown in Figure 10.3. On both occasions, a methodological debate occurred. Those being in favour of the shift–share method claimed that you cannot trust respondent answers. Those in favour of the respondent method claimed that the shift–share method underestimated the disadvantageous conditions operating in the support zone.

What, then, is the relevant counterfactual path within the support zone? If the only disadvantage were an unfavourable industrial structure, then the b line in Figure 10.3 could be a relevant estimate of the non-support level, and the shift–share method would have been appropriate. But as other disadvantage factors no doubt exist in the zone, and are in fact important reasons behind the generating and upholding of the support scheme, the b line will lie above the real counterfactual level. Such factors are long distance to the greater market network; the weaker level of the labour market at the different segments making the recruitment of the optimal working staff more difficult; the weaker second-hand values of production assets giving more strict credit terms on private loans, and so on. A claimed argument for the schemes is that they aim at counteracting such periphery disadvantages. Then, an optimal scale of the support scheme would be to make an exact counteraction so that line b in Figure 10.3 could be the output of the programme, starting from a much lower counterfactual level.

It may be disputed whether the estimation of level c in Figure 10.3 is made by good enough methods, if level c is over- or underestimated and so on. Nevertheless, the very concept of a counterfactual level lying below the b line seems to be justified by the nature of the scheme. Whatever can be said about the respondent-based method, the shift–share method is based on a non-justified conception of the counterfactual level making this method generate a serious underestimation of the support scheme effect.

CONCLUSIONS

This chapter aims to illustrate the need for a clear idea of the counterfactual level when evaluations are executed.

Both ex post and ex ante analysis of the effect of public (or private) activities will need to compare the situation including the activity with a situation where the activity does not take place. However, it seems that ex post analysis to a greater extent than ex ante analysis often forgets to operate in this way, and for this reason often arrives at unjustified conclusions.

To estimate the counterfactual path in ex post analysis may often be complicated, and the methods used may be disputed. Quite often, the estimated programme effect will rely heavily on the method used to generate such a counterfactual path.

If not explicitly generated, an implicit counterfactual path will necessarily generate the base for the estimated effect calculations. Often, such an implicit counterfactual path will be some type of status quo. In a process of growth, then, all programmes tend to be evaluated positively, and in a process of decline they tend to be evaluated negatively if a more elaborate analysis of the counterfactual path is carried out.

In the actual debate, this effect is clearly seen. It is rather common among both politicians and among short-thinking academics, to claim that regional support schemes no longer have an effect. The argument is the observed ongoing centralisation process. There are strong and probably growing forces fueling such a process, and the schemes are not strong enough to counteract these forces. This is not to say that the schemes are without any effect, or that they are less effective than in earlier periods. On the contrary, there are reasons to believe that the effects of the schemes are even more important in a situation when other market forces work in a centralising direction. The role of regional scientists should be to address such questions, to focus on the differences between scheme effects and the observed indicator path. Then, it may at least potentially help to reduce the rather vast amount of unskilled evaluations delivered from more consultant-based milieus.

NOTE

1. This is not always the case for all effect indicators. For investment programs, it is possible to get negative effects on the employment indicator due to labour-saving productivity growth.

REFERENCES

Berge, D.M., A. Hervik and R. Johansen (1993), *DUs betydning for bedriftene*, Møreforsking Rapport nr. 9303, Molde.

Bjerve, P.J. (1959), *Planning in Norway 1947–56*, Amsterdam: North-Holland.

Bræin, L.A. and A. Hervik (1996), *Surveyundersøkelser av SNDs virkemidler*, Møreforsking Arbeidsrapport M 9602, Molde.

Dale, K., T. Ellingsen and K. Espedal (1993), *Næringsutvikling i regionalt perspektiv*, SNF-rapport 10/93, Bergen

Larsen, B.M. (1997), 'Economic Impacts of Reducing NO_x Emissions in Norway', *Environmental and Resource Economics*, **9**, 125–32.

Mønnesland, J., A. Hervik and K. Dale (1993), *Bedriftsrettet distriktsstøtte. Evaluering av Distriktenes Utbyggingsfonds virkemidler*, Molde: NIBR-Møreforsking- SNF.

Mønnesland, J. (1997), *Regional Policy in the Nordic Countries. Background and Tendencies 1997*, Stockholm: NordREFO 1997:2.

Mønnesland, J., T.L. Andersen, B. Moen and H. Westlund (1998), *Grenseregionalt samarbeid. Underveisevaluering av tre svensk-norske EU-program under Interreg IIA*, Oslo: NIBR Prosjektrapport 1998:26.

11. A Computable General Equilibrium Approach to the Ex Post Evaluation of Regional Development Agency Policies

Gary Gillespie, Peter G. McGregor, J. Kim Swales and Ya Ping Yin

1 INTRODUCTION

Within the UK and other European economies, policies for regional economic regeneration have become increasingly fragmented, discretionary and supply-orientated. The use of regional development agencies to provide flexible aid to local companies, attract inward investment and improve the working of the local labour market is a particularly good example. However, such policies are difficult to evaluate and the present official UK approach is to adopt a hybrid procedure. Different methods are used to capture the direct policy impact and the subsequent system-wide effects.

The direct policy impact is calculated via some 'industrial survey' method where recipient companies are asked, through interviews or questionnaires, to identify the extent of additionality and product-market displacement associated with the aided project.[1] However, the system-wide effects of such a policy are assessed in quite a different manner. The impact on local employment is calculated using a standard demand-determined multiplier of an Input–Output (I–O) or Keynesian type. But at the UK level there is assumed to be 100 per cent crowding out so that there is no net addition to national activity or employment (Alexander and Whyte, 1995; HM Treasury, 1995, 1997: McVittie and Swales, 1999; PA Cambridge Economic Consultants Ltd., 1993).

Because of the nature of present regional regeneration programmes, it is difficult to imagine an evaluation method which could capture the direct impact of individual policies without the use of 'industrial survey' methods.

First, typically there are numerous policies operating simultaneously in a given problem region and aided firms are often in receipt of assistance under a range of programmes. It is therefore difficult to isolate statistically the impact of one individual policy. Second, the flexible and discretionary nature of the aid and, in the UK at least, the attendant problems of confidentiality, render the modelling of direct effects problematic. However, the shift to the use of 'industrial survey' methods for the quantification of the direct impacts of policy has been accompanied by a relative neglect of system-wide effects. Essentially these are presently modelled in a very rudimentary fashion. In this chapter we illustrate a theoretically and empirically more satisfactory approach where the system-wide impacts of regional development agency policy, on both recipient region and the rest of the nation, are calculated using a multi-regional Computable General Equilibrium (CGE) model.

Specifically, we present an attempt to measure the cost effectiveness of the strategic objectives used to operationalise the goals of Scottish Enterprise (SE), a regional development agency located in Scotland.[2] We focus almost exclusively on one strategic objective, business competitiveness, but give some indication of how the method is adapted for other strategic objectives. We again use a hybrid model in which the direct impacts of the strategic objective are identified through microeconomic studies which have been either undertaken directly by SE or commissioned from outside consultants. These estimates of the direct effects then form the basis for the exogenous disturbance that is fed into our two-region Computable General Equilibrium model of the UK economy, AMOSRUK.[3] The approach is an extension of the single-region analysis in Gillespie et al. (1998). Multiregional CGE models have been used extensively for policy evaluation, especially in the US and Canada, but this is their first use in the UK (Buckley, 1992; Gazel, Hewings and Sonis, 1995; Harrigan and McGregor, 1989; Jones and Whalley, 1990; Kilkenny, 1998; Morgan, Mutti and Rickman, 1996; Mutti, Morgan and Partridge, 1989; Rickman, 1992).[4]

We organise the chapter in the following way. Section 2 gives a description of the AMOSRUK model. In Section 3 we detail: the expenditures made under the business competitiveness strategic objective; the estimated direct impacts, the way in which this disturbance is introduced into the AMOSRUK model; and the simulation results for this strategic objective. Section 4 is a very brief account of our attempts to model SE's other strategic objectives. Section 5 outlines the strengths of this evaluation approach. Section 6 presents extensions to this procedure: essentially ways in which the simulation accuracy could be improved. Section 7 is a short conclusion.

2 AMOSRUK

AMOSRUK is a computable general equilibrium model of the UK economy with two endogenous regions, Scotland and RUK, and one exogenous region, the Rest of the World (ROW). The model is calibrated on a Scottish–RUK Social Accounting Matrix for 1989. This is the last year for which full-survey I–O tables are available for both Scotland and the UK. In terms of relative scale, Scotland makes up a little less than 9 per cent of the UK population, employment and output. We treat each endogenous region in a similar manner to that adopted in our single-region Scottish model, AMOS (Harrigan et al., 1991; McGregor, Swales and Yin, 1996a). However, in the interregional variant the individual regions are linked by trade and potential migration flows generally determined by endogenous changes in prices, wages and activity in both regions.[5] The national economy is subject to certain macroeconomic constraints, though in the present analysis our treatment of these is extremely straightforward. Specifically, we assume that interest rates are exogenous to the national economy and that the government operates a fixed exchange-rate regime.[6] In this chapter we do not impose any national public sector budget or current account constraints, although we do track the impact of disturbances on the relevant financial deficits.[7] Nor do we impose any such financial constraints on either regional economy.[8]

AMOSRUK is a flexible CGE model which offers the user a wide range of time-period and labour-market options. In this chapter we concentrate on period-by-period simulations. In these simulations, in each individual time period the capital stock is fixed, both in aggregate and in its regional and sectoral composition, and the regional populations are constant. However, between periods capital stocks are updated by investment and the regional distribution of the national population is adjusted through interregional migration. (There are no natural changes in population or international migration.) Each regional labour market is characterised by endogenous participation and wage-setting functions. Whilst there are a number of regional wage-setting options available with AMOSRUK, in this chapter we adopt regional bargaining, where the real wage in each region is solely a function of the tightness of the regional labour market.

A condensed representation of the period-by-period variant of the AMOSRUK model used in this chapter is given in Table 11.1. In the equations presented in this table, the endogenous (UK) regions of the model are identified generically by superscripts X and Y and, where required, specifically by the superscript S for Scotland and R for RUK. The superscript W represents Rest of the World.

Table 11.1 A condensed version of the period-by-period variant of AMOSRUK

Variables	Equations
1. Value-Added Prices	$pv_i^X = pv_i^X(w_n^X, w_k^X)$
2. Commodity Prices	$p_i^X = p_i^X(pv_i^X, p_j^X, \underline{p}^Y, \underline{\overline{p}}^{W})\ \forall_{j \neq i}$
3. Consumer Price Index	$cpi^X = \sum_i \theta_i^{XX} p_i^X + \sum_i \theta_i^{XY} p_i^Y + \sum_i \theta_i^{XW} \overline{p}_i^{W}$
4. Capital Price Index	$kpi^X = \sum_i \gamma_i^{XX} p_i^X + \sum_i \gamma_i^{XY} p_i^Y + \sum_i \gamma_i^{XW} \overline{p}_i^{W}$
5. Labour Demand	$N_i^X = N_i^X(Q_i^X, p_i^X, pv_i^X, w_n^X)$
6. Capital Demand	$K_i^X = K_i^X(Q_i^X, p_i^X, pv_i^X, w_k^X)$
7. Regional Wage Bargaining	$w_n^X = w_n^X(u^X, cpi^X)$
8. Unemployment Rate	$u^X = \dfrac{L^X T^X - \sum_i N_i^X}{L^X T^X}$
9. Participation Rate	
10. Capital Rental	$K_i^X = K_i^{SX}$
11. Household Income	$Y^X = \psi_n^X N^X w_n + \psi_k^X K^X w_k + L^X T^X u^X f$
12. Commodity Demands	$Q_i^X = C_i^X + J_i^X + I_i^X + G_i^X + X_i^{XY} + X_i^{XW}$
13. Consumption Demand	$C_i^X = C_i^X(\underline{p}^X, \text{underline}p^Y, \underline{\overline{p}}^{W}, Y^X)$
14. Intermediate Demand	$J_i^X = J_i^X(\underline{Q}^X, \underline{pv}^X, \underline{p}^X, \underline{p}^Y, \underline{\overline{p}}^{W})$

15. Investment Demand
$$I_i^X = I_i^X\left(\underline{p^X}, \underline{p^Y}, \underline{\overline{p}^W}, \sum_j b_{ij}^X V_j^X\right)$$

16. Government Demand
$$G_i^X = \alpha_i^X \overline{G}^N$$

17. Interregional Export Demand
$$X_i^{XY} = X_i^{XY}\left(\underline{p^X}, \underline{p^Y}, \underline{\overline{p}^W}, Y^Y, \underline{Q^Y}, \underline{J^Y}, \overline{G}^N\right)$$

18. International Export Demand
$$X_i^{XW} = X_i^{XW}\left(p_i^X, pBAR_i^W, \overline{D}^W\right)$$

19. Capital Stock
$$K_{i,t}^{SX} = (1 - \delta_i^X)\, K_{i,t-1}^{SX} + V_{i,t-1}^X$$

20. Investment
$$V_{i,t}^X = \lambda(K_{i,t}^{*SX} - K_{i,t}^{SX}) + \delta_i^X K_{i,t-1}^{SX}$$

21. Desired Capital Stock
$$K_{i,t}^{*SX} = K_i^X\left(Q_i^X, p_i^X, pv_i^X, ucc_i^X\right)$$

22. User Cost of Capital
$$ucc_i^X = ucc_i^X(kpi)$$

23. National Population
$$\overline{L}^N = \sum_X L^X$$

24. Regional Population
$$L_t^S = L_{t-1}^S + m_{t-1}^S$$

25. Migration
$$m_t^S = m^S\left[\frac{w_t^S}{cpi_t^S}, \frac{w_t^R}{cpi_t^R}, u_t^S, u_t^R, L_t^S\right]$$

Notes:
Underlined variables are vectors whose elements are the sectoral values of the relevant variables.
A bar over a variable indicates exogeneity.
A starred variable indicates desired value.

Key

cpi: consumer price index
kpi: capital price index
m: Scottish inmigration
p: commodity price
pv: value-added price
u: unemployment rate
ucc: user cost of capital
w_n: nominal wage rate
w_k: capital rental rate
C: consumption
D: foreign demand
G: government expenditure
I: investment demand
J: intermediate demand
K: capital
L: population
N: employment
Q: output
T: participation rate
V: investment levels
X: exports
Y: household income

Parameters

b: capital coefficient
f: benefit payment per registered unemployed
α: government expenditure coefficient
δ: depreciation rate
ψ: regional share of factor income

Subscripts

i,j sectors
k capital
n labour
t time

Superscripts

R rest of the UK
S Scotland
W foreign (rest of the world)
X,Y generic regional identifiers

In this summary depiction of the model, many of the detailed income transfers between transactor groups are suppressed. Also suppressed are the time subscripts in equations 1 to 18.

Equation 1 in Table 11.1 gives the determination of commodity value-added prices where pv^X_i represents the value-added price in sector *i* in endogenous region *X*. We assume that in each region the three commodities in the model are all produced by perfectly competitive regional industries. These commodities/industries are: manufacturing, non-manufacturing traded and the sheltered sectors.[9] Given linear homogeneity in the production of value added and the implied assumption of cost minimisation and zero profits, value-added prices are determined by the corresponding industry cost functions. This means that the value-added price is a linear homogeneous function of the two regional factor prices, w^X_n and w^X_k, which are the wage rate and the capital rental rate respectively. Similarly, the regional commodity price, p^X_i, is a linear, homogeneous function of the value-added price and the vector of intermediate prices which comprises the vector of other commodity prices in the region, the vector of commodity prices in the second region, $\underline{p}^Y$, and the vector of the domestic currency prices of foreign imports, $\underline{\bar{p}}^W$. (A 'bar' above a variable indicates that this variable is taken to be exogenous in the simulations that we conduct in this chapter). This relationship is shown in equation (2). The regional consumer and capital price indices, cpi^X and kpi^X, are the weighted sums of all the commodity prices in the system. These are given by equations 3 and 4. Equations 5 and 6 are the cost-minimising factor demand functions. In each regional industry the demand for labour and capital, N^X_i and K^X_i is a function homogeneous of degree one in regional industry output Q^X_i and degree zero in the regional factor, value-added and commodity price.

Equation 7 gives the generic form of the regional-bargaining wage-setting option used in this exercise. In this labour-market closure, for each region the value taken by the real consumption wage is negatively related to the local unemployment rate, u^X. Essentially, wages are determined in accordance with a regional wage curve (Blanchflower and Oswald, 1994). The particular bargaining function adopted is the econometrically-parameterised relationship identified by Layard, Nickell and Jackman (1991) which takes the form

$$\ln\left[\frac{w^R}{cpi^R}\right] = \beta - 1.113\ln u^R$$

where β is a calibrated parameter.

Equation 8 is the definition of the regional unemployment rate. The regional labour force is the product of the regional population, L^X and participation rate, T^X. The regional unemployment rate is the difference between the regional labour force, $L^X\, T^X$, and regional employment, ΣN^X, expressed as a proportion of the regional labour force. The participation rate is taken to be a function of regional population and aggregate labour demand. This is represented generically in equation 9. The particular expression used is:

$$T^X = \phi + 0.25\frac{\sum_i N_i^X}{L^X}$$

This expression embodies the Treasury assumption (Alexander and Whyte, 1995) that 25 per cent of any increase in regional employment comes from increased local participation rather than reduced registered unemployment. ϕ is a calibrated parameter. The capital rental rate in each regional sector is set by equating capital demand, $K^x{}_i$ with the existing capital supply, $K^{SX}{}_i$, which is equation 10.[10]

Equation 11 gives regional nominal household income, Y^X, as the shares, $\psi^X{}_n$ and $\psi^X{}_k$ respectively, of the labour and capital income generated in the region plus the welfare transfers associated with unemployment. These transfers are given by the number of unemployed $L^X\ T^X\ u^X$ in the region multiplied by the unemployment benefit f. Equation 12 determines the regional demand for commodity i, $Q^X{}_i$. This is the sum of consumption, intermediate, investment, government, interregional export demand and international export demand, $C^X{}_i$, $J^X{}_i$, $I^X{}_i$, $G^X{}_i$, $X^{XY}{}_i$ and $X^{XW}{}_i$ respectively. These individual elements of commodity demand are identified in equations 13–18.

Consumption demand (equation 13) is a function linear in regional real income and homogeneous of degree zero in all nominal variables. Intermediate demand (equation 14) is a linear function of regional outputs and homogeneous of degree zero in regional value-added and all commodity prices. The first step in deriving investment demand (equation 15) is to calculate the level of investment $V^X{}_j$ undertaken in each regional industry j. This is discussed later in this section where we consider capital-stock updating between periods (equation 20). The vector of $V^X{}_j$ values is converted to the investment demand for the output of a sector i via a fixed-coefficient capital matrix whose elements are $b^X{}_{ij}$. The vectors of commodity prices are also included as an argument in the investment demand equation to determine the proportion of activity which goes to the region rather than interregional or international imports. Government demand (equation 16) is simply a fixed proportion $a^X{}_i$ of the total national government expenditure $\bar{G}^N$ which is exogenous in these simulations. Interregional export demand for industry i (equation 17) depends upon the relevant price vectors and consumption, intermediate, investment and government demand for industry i in the other region Y. International export demand (equation 18) is a homogeneous function of degree one in foreign demand $\bar{D}^W$ and zero in regional and foreign prices. Again, in the results presented here, foreign demand is taken to be exogenous.

The between-period updating of population and capital stocks is given by equations 19–25. In these equations, where appropriate, there is the addition of a time subscript. Equation 19 shows that the capital stock in regional industry i and time period t, $K^{SX}{}_{i,t}$, equals the capital stock in that industry in the time period t–1 minus depreciation and plus gross investment in period t–1. That is to say, investment implemented in time period t–1 augment capacity in time period t. The rate of depreciation is $\delta^X{}_i$ and the gross investment is $V^X{}_{i,t\text{-}1}$. Gross investment in industry i in time period t is a proportion, λ, of the difference between actual and desired capital stock plus the capital depreciation in the previous period. This is shown in the capital-stock-adjustment equation 20. To determine the desired capital stock, $K^{*SX}{}_{i,t}$, equation 21 indicates that we use the capital demand equation 6 but substitute the risk-adjusted user cost of capital (*ucc*) for the actual capital rental rate. This implies that where the capital rental rate is above the risk-adjusted user cost of capital, the desired capital stock is above the actual capital stock. In these circumstances, capital accumulation will continue until the risk-adjusted user cost of capital and the capital rental rate are brought back into equality. Therefore, in long-run equilibrium the capital rental rate in all sectors equals the appropriate risk-adjusted user cost of capital. The value of the user cost of capital depends upon the interest rate, the depreciation rate, relevant tax and subsidy rates and the regional capital price index. In the simulations performed here we hold the interest, tax and subsidy rates constant so that changes in the regional capital rental rate are determined solely by changes in the regional capital price index (equation 22)..

We assume that there is no natural population increase and that international migration can be ignored. This is formally represented by equation 23, where L^{-N} is the exogenous national labour force. In this specification of the model, the Scottish labour force is updated between periods by net inmigration, m^S. This is given by equation 24. Net inmigration is itself determined by a flow-equilibrium specification (equation 25) where the Scottish rate of net inmigration is positively related to the Scottish/RUK ratio of the real consumption wage and negatively related to the Scottish/RUK ratio of unemployment rates (Treyz, Rickman and Greenwood, 1993). The specific form of equation 25 used in these simulations is again derived from the work of Layard, Nickell and Jackman (1991), in this case their interregional migration function:

$$\ln\left[\frac{m^S}{L^S}\right] = \zeta - 0.08\,(\ln u^S - \ln u^R) + 0.06\left[\ln\left[\frac{w^S}{cpi^S}\right] - \ln\left[\frac{w^R}{cpi^R}\right]\right]$$

where ζ is a calibrated parameter. From equation 23, net inmigration to RUK is simply net inmigration to Scotland with the sign changed. Given that the parameterisation of the updating equations are based on annual data, periods are interpreted as years.

For these simulations the AMOSUK model is parameterised in the following way. We impose constant elasticity of substitution (CES) production functions in all sectors with the elasticity of substitution taking the value 0.3 (Harris, 1989). This is relevant for the price-setting functions (equations 1 and 2) and the factor demand equations (5 and 6). We use the Armington (1969) assumption for both interregional and international trade with the elasticity of substitution taking the value 2.0 (Gibson, 1990). This is required in the consumption, intermediate, investment and export demand functions (equations 13, 14, 15, 17 and 18). The rates of depreciation δ^{X}_{i} in equation 19 are calibrated on the original data set on the assumption that the economy is initially in long-run equilibrium. The speed of adjustment parameter λ in the investment equation 20 takes the value 0.5 following econometric work on the determination of investment in Scottish manufacturing. The model is run in a comparative static mode such that we assume that the regional economy is initially in long-run equilibrium at a zero growth rate. We therefore concentrate on comparative static adjustments to the policy innovations, ignoring any possible growth effects.

3 BUSINESS COMPETITIVENESS

The activities which are included under the business competitiveness strategic objective involve business support and/or technology and product development (Scottish Enterprise, 1998). They include specific schemes to promote technological advance in Scottish plants and to aid technologically sophisticated Scottish firms. Other initiatives covered under this strategic objective are the supply of venture capital and support for the development of multi-discipline 'clusters' of private sector companies and public sector service and infrastructure provision.

There are two challenges involved in attempting correctly to quantify the system-wide impacts of such initiatives. The first is to capture the qualitative changes that the policy generates in model variables or parameters which can be exogenously shocked The second is to calibrate the size of these shocks to produce the appropriate scale for the direct effects. In this example, we tackle the first problem by modelling the improvement in business competitiveness as an increase in company efficiency. This increase in efficiency simply means that the same output can be produced with less factor inputs. Therefore, with constant factor prices, profitability rises and/or commodity prices fall, so that Scotland becomes more competitive as a location for business activity and/or its products become more price competitive in extra-regional markets.

There are various standard characterisations of efficiency improvement. We here adopt the 'Hicks-neutral' form. This is where the efficiency of all factor inputs in the production of value added is increased equiproportionally. In this form of technical change there is no inherent capital or labour bias accompanying the improvement in technology so that, with factor prices constant, the cost-minimising capital/labour ratio remains unchanged. We also assume that there is a three-year linear build up of the direct effects. This is consistent with the views of SE staff concerning the direct impact of their policies. We have also had to make assumptions concerning the extent of policy decay. This is much more arbitrary. The central simulations are undertaken with an assumed linear 5-year decay. However experiments have also been undertaken where alternative patterns of policy decay are imposed.

A second problem here is calibrating the size of the assumed improvement in efficiency. For the business competitiveness strategic objective we do not have a direct estimate of the increase in business. Rather we have the estimated direct employment impact. This is taken from the Scottish Enterprise Operating Plan – Year End Report for 1997/8 which gives the direct employment under this strategic objective as 17475. A report by Cambridge Policy Consultants identifies the relationship between gross and net jobs at the Scottish level for this strategic objective for the year 1997/8 as 0.4571. This implies that deadweight and displacement claims just over 54 per cent of the direct employment identified under this objective so that the direct net increase in employment equals 7998. What we attempt to do is to calibrate the model so that the simulation results generate this net change in direct employment.

It is difficult in practice to identify the employment gains associated with supply-side efficiency improvements. With a sectoral increase in efficiency there are countervailing factors operating on employment within that sector. The increased competitiveness has an expansionary impact on sectoral output which, other things being equal, generates an increase in sectoral employment. On the other hand, the reduction in employment per unit of output simultaneously limits that increase. The net result is that the employment change in the sector that receives the efficiency stimulus can be low or even negative, especially in the early periods following an efficiency gain (McGregor, Swales and Yin, 1996c). Therefore, if we try to measure the employment impacts by concentrating on the sector that received the increase in efficiency and using a procedure of 'grossing up' using a simple employment multiplier, the results could be perverse.

Whilst the employment impacts on the sector receiving the efficiency shock are less than for a demand-side expansion which would generate the same increase in output, the employment impacts on other sectors can be greater. This is because the increased competitiveness of one sector tends to have expansionary impacts on other sectors which use its inputs as intermediate goods. Specifically, the reduced price in the sector whose efficiency has increased improves the competitiveness of other sectors in the regional economy. Also, because the ratio of output to employment has risen in the sector receiving the efficiency increase, the standard I–O employment multiplier will rise. The crucial point here is that for efficiency gains the direct employment effects may well be small whilst the multiplier effects are likely to be large.

What we have done in the simulations reported here is to calibrate the size of the efficiency shock to the manufacturing and non-manufacturing traded sectors so that it generates the same number of additional Scottish manufacturing and non-manufacturing traded jobs by year three as given in the SE estimates (as adjusted by Cambridge Policy Consultants). That is to say, with a three-year build up of direct efficiency gains, in period 3 the total increase in Scottish manufacturing and non-manufacturing traded employment is 7998. This represents a 0.58 per cent increase in Scottish manufacturing and non-manufacturing traded employment.

We used trial and error to identify the appropriate size of the Hicks-neutral efficiency change in the manufacturing and non-manufacturing traded sectors. This turned out to be an increase of 2.87 per cent which produces a combined increase in period 3 employment in Scottish manufacturing and non-manufacturing traded of 7995. We are therefore simulating the initial employment increase in these sectors to within 0.04 per cent accuracy. For the central set of simulation results, we also assume a 5-year policy decay, beginning in period 3. This implies that we model the direct impact of SE policy as a set of exogenous efficiency shocks to the manufacturing and non-manufacturing traded sectors that apply over periods 1 to 7. The particular pattern of these disturbances is given in Figure 11.1. Note that these are not cumulative changes but variations from the base-year values.

We focus on the simulation values for a number of key economic variables which measure the impact on economic activity in both Scotland and the rest of the UK (RUK) and on the UK national budget and balance of payments positions. We concentrate on this limited set of variables solely to render the analysis more manageable and easily comprehended. However, one cost of such a parsimonious approach is that it does not do full justice to the whole range of SE policy outputs. This observation holds particularly for those strategic objectives where goals such as social inclusion and environmental improvement are important.

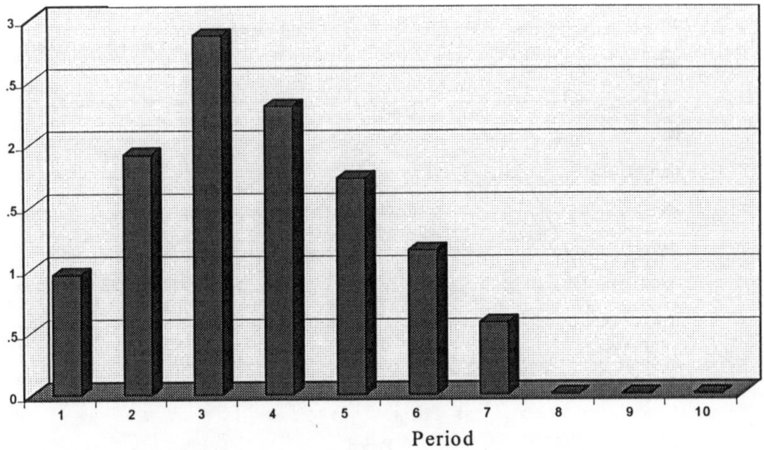

Figure 11.1 The time pattern of exogenous Hicks-neutral efficiency shocks in the manufacturing and non-manufacturing traded sectors, with an assumed 5-year decay

The exogenous efficiency disturbances identified in Figure 11.1 produce a time-path of simulated Scottish and UK total employment change which is given in Figure 11.2. Note first that there is increased employment in both Scotland and the whole of the UK over the full 10-year period. That is to say, the simulations do not reveal a situation where there is 100 per cent crowding out in RUK of this policy-induced employment change in Scotland. Also, up to period 3, the increase in UK employment is greater than the increase in Scottish employment. This implies that in the early policy periods the RUK economy experiences a positive net stimulus from the increase in efficiency experienced by the Scottish manufacturing and non-manufacturing traded sectors. After period 3 Scottish employment change is greater than UK employment change, so that there is some reduction in employment in RUK, as against the base-year level, but this reduction in RUK employment is much less than the increase in Scottish employment.

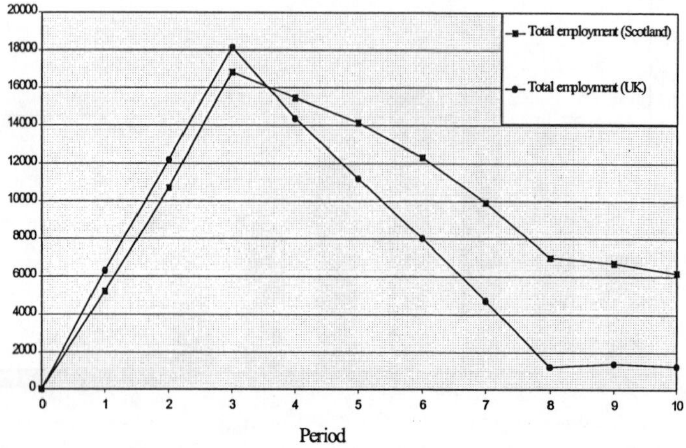

Figure 11.2 The estimated change in total employment in Scotland and the UK as a result of SE's business competitiveness strategic objective

The increase in efficiency in the manufacturing and non-manufacturing traded sectors enhances Scottish competitiveness in both RUK and ROW markets. The subsequent increase in output in these Scottish sectors has a positive impact on the derived demand for labour. This is greater than the reduction in labour demand resulting from the lower unit labour input associated with the efficiency improvement. Further, the increase in intermediate and consumption demand for the output of the Scottish sheltered sector produces an additional stimulus to labour demand within Scotland. The rationale for the expansion in Scottish employment is therefore rather straightforward.[11] For the RUK, the Scottish efficiency gain initially leads to an increase in exports to both ROW and Scotland, with a corresponding expansionary impulse to RUK activity. RUK competitiveness with ROW is increased through lower nominal wages and intermediate prices. Exports to Scotland rise, even though RUK competitiveness falls, because the increase in activity in Scotland stimulates consumption, investment and intermediate demand. However, over time outmigration from RUK to Scotland puts upward pressure on RUK wages, whilst easing wage pressure in Scotland, adversely affecting RUK employment.

At the UK level, the underlying rationale for increased activity as a result of the business competitiveness strategic objective comes through the labour market. The improvement in Scottish manufacturing and non-manufacturing traded efficiency allows a fall in the real product wage, measured in efficiency units, accompanied by a rise in the real consumption wage. Under these circumstances the quantity demanded and supplied of labour can rise simultaneously, increasing employment and economic activity. The Treasury 100 per cent crowding-out assumption does not apply in this case.

This change in activity in both Scotland and the UK also has impacts on GDP, tax receipts and benefit payments and the balance of payments. The period-3 values of these variables are shown in Table 11.2.[12] (The proportionate impact on a wider range of nominal and real variables over the full 10 years is given in Appendix 11A.1) With the balance of payments, a negative change represents an improvement. We report figures for the GDP and employment changes for both Scotland and the UK. For changes in government revenue and benefit payments and balance of payments, we only give the UK figures.

The first point to make about the simulation results is that the implied improvement in efficiency is very large and generates substantial aggregate effects. Scottish GDP increases by £ 107 9365 000 accompanied by an increase in total Scottish employment of 16 821. Secondly, note the sectoral distribution of employment change. The period-3 increase in Scottish sheltered employment is over 10 per cent higher than the increase in manufacturing and non-manufacturing traded employment combined.

The total UK impacts are similarly very large. UK GDP in period 3 is estimated to increase by £ 1 156 821 000. This implies that there is an increase in RUK GDP (calculated by subtracting the Scottish value from the UK value) of £ 77 456 000 which is 7 per cent of the Scottish figure, and RUK period-3 employment increases by 1324 which is 7.8 per cent of the change in employment in Scotland. It is clear that, rather than crowding out occurring, RUK benefits from the expansion in the Scottish economy, at least in the initial periods. These RUK benefits are concentrated in manufacturing. There are small falls in activity in RUK non-manufacturing traded and the sheltered sector.

We observe very significant increases in UK government savings in these simulations. By period 3, increases in government tax revenue are £ 390 791 000 and unemployment benefit savings are calculated as £ 7 285 000. This has to be offset against an initial public expenditure of £ 90 472 000 identified in the 1997/98 Operating Plan – Year End Report for the business competitiveness strategic objective.

Table 11.2 Scottish and UK effects in Period 3 of SE's business competitiveness strategic objective

	Scotland Period 3	UK Period 3
GDP (real), £million	1 079.365	1 156.821
Total Employment ('000s)	16.821	18.145
Manufacturing	2.167	3.870
Non-manu traded	5.828	5.697
Sheltered	8.826	8.579
Government tax revenue, £million	–	390.791
Expenditures on benefits, £million	–	–7.285
Balance of payments, £million	–	–157.883

Period-3 government savings are therefore over four times the initial public expenditure, and the expenditure in this strategic objective breaks even in period 1. Accompanying the increase in government savings is an improvement in the UK balance of payments of £ 157 883 000 (balance of payments improvements are identified by negative changes here). This is not surprising given the period-3 2.65 per cent and 3.75 per cent expansion in Scottish manufacturing and non-manufacturing traded exports to ROW and the 0.07 per cent and 0.10 per cent increase in RUK exports to the ROW in the same two sectors. There is a reduction in Scottish ROW exports from the sheltered sector, but these are very small in absolute terms so that the manufacturing and non-manufacturing traded sectors dominate the aggregate results.

Table 11.3 presents the cumulative sums of the monetary variables discounted using the Treasury-recommended rate of 6 per cent per annum. Calculations are made for a number of assumptions about decay. The size of these cumulated figures is large. Note especially that, even with the most rapid (sudden-death) decay after period 3, the discounted government revenue increase is just under eight times the value of the initial public expenditure. There are similarly substantial gains to the UK balance of payments. Table 11.4 gives Scottish and UK employment changes over the whole 10-year time span, under the same set of assumptions concerning policy-effectiveness decay.

Also shown in Table 11.4 is the cumulative discounted employment total for the ten-year period. This is the estimated total discounted jobs, measured in present value years (PVYs). Again we observe substantial employment gains both at the Scottish and UK level.

Table 11.3 The cumulative discounted Scottish and UK financial effects of SE's business competitiveness strategic objective

	Scot. GDP	UK GDP	UK tax revenue	UK expend. on benefits	UK balance of payments
Periods 1 to 3	1 973.691	2 134.584	720.367	–	-264.855
Periods 1 to 10				13.838	
5-Year Decay	4 297.213	4 168.752	1 402.652	-23.203	-891.462
10-Year Decay	6 018.799	5 945.095	2 005.855	-33.830	-1192.271
No Decay	8 120.200	8 135.425	2 749.210	-47.284	-1531.891

Moreover, if the relaxation of the national macroeconomic budget constraints identified in Table 11.3 led to a subsequent rise in government expenditure (or reduction in taxation), there would be a further expansion in economic activity so that, on this score, the results presented here for the increase in national employment are conservative.

4 EVALUATION OF THE OTHER STRATEGIC OBJECTIVES

In the evaluation of the impact of the six other strategic objectives pursued by Scottish Enterprise, we use exactly the same general method as adopted for business competitiveness. That is to say, we introduce an exogenous disturbance to the AMOSRUK model which qualitatively replicates the direct impacts of the policy initiative.

This disturbance is calibrated to generate a period-3 change in simulated activity in the relevant Scottish sectors which hits the estimated direct impacts from SE's independent evaluation methods. Again, typically we impose a three-year build up of effects.

Table 11.4 Period-by-period employment results for SE's business competitiveness strategic objective for a range of assumptions concerning policy decay

	Period 1	Period 2	Period 3	Period 4	Period 5	Period 6
Scotland						
5-Year Decay	5.188	10.686	16.821	15.452	14.128	12.313
10-Year Decay	5.188	10.686	16.821	16.994	17.335	17.395
No Decay	5.188	10.686	16.821	18.532	20.529	22.452
UK						
5-Year Decay	6.294	12.188	18.145	14.359	11.183	8.014
10-Year Decay	6.294	12.188	18.145	16.219	14.827	13.469
No Decay	6.294	12.188	18.145	18.075	18.459	18.900

cont'd.	Period 7	Period 8	Period 9	Period 10	Cumulative discounted employment total
Scotland					
5-Year Decay	9.923	6.983	6.698	6.171	83.100
10-Year Decay	17.093	16.438	15.458	14.182	112.313
No Decay	24.225	25.843	27.317	28.660	147.205
UK					
5-Year Decay	4.699	1.222	1.392	1.261	66.589
10-Year Decay	12.015	10.446	8.773	7.012	94.440
No Decay	19.296	19.623	19.890	20.100	128.891

The model is then run forward under various assumptions concerning effectiveness decay. The key information provided by the model is the change in activity in those sectors not directly stimulated by the strategic objective, including RUK sectors.

For some strategic objectives the nature of the disturbance is very straightforward. For example, one of the strategic objectives involves encouraging export growth. The effect of this strategic objective can be simulated very easily: all that is required is an exogenous shock to Scottish exports to the rest of the world (McGregor, Swales and Yin, 1998). However, with other strategic objectives it is more difficult for the model to capture the direct policy stimulus. For some (for example physical business infrastructure) considerable ingenuity is required to emulate the qualitative nature of the disturbance. For others (for example skills and knowledge) it is difficult to calibrate the model to achieve the appropriate scale of direct estimated effects. Finally, for strategic objectives where there is thought to be direct displacement in RUK activity (new business, inward investment) the exogenous shock has elements which apply to RUK industries as well as Scottish industries.

5 STRENGTHS OF THE CGE APPROACH

The major advantage gained from using this CGE approach, as against the conventional Keynesian or input–output multiplier models, is the ability to deal with supply-side disturbances and constraints. In terms of disturbances, many of the strategic objectives pursued by Scottish Enterprise have a supply-side orientation. That is to say, they aim to improve the efficiency and/or reduce the costs facing specific sectors of the Scottish economy. Such supply-side changes affect relative prices and competitiveness in other Scottish and RUK sectors. They also generally change the relationship between employment, value-added and gross output in the policy-targeted sectors. In these circumstances, the ratio of the change in activity in the sectors which are the focus of SE policy initiatives and the change in total activity is more complex than the standard Keynesian and I–O analyses allow. In short, traditional multiplier values may provide wildly inaccurate measures of the impact on other sectors. As Greenaway et al. (1993: 97) argue in their HM Treasury-commissioned report ‘when it comes to large scale models where interdependencies and feedbacks are important, and where insights into distributional changes are an objective, CGE probably represents “state of the art”.

In the evaluation of regional regeneration policies, a key issue is the nature of the national effects. At present, the UK Treasury view is that such policies have no overall expansionary impact on the national economy (HM Treasury, 1997). This rule applies specifically to employment. Such a position implies that an increase in employment in the region where policy is in operation will be fully offset by an equal and opposite reduction in employment in the rest of the UK: there is assumed to be 100 per cent displacement at the national level. This carries the implication that regional policy only has spatially redistributive effects. Also in calculating the exchequer cost of regional policy, HM Treasury argue that it is inappropriate to offset any of the subsidy cost with reduced payment of unemployment benefit or an increased tax take.

However, we have never seen an explicit defence of the Treasury position on complete national displacement.[13] Further, AMOSRUK clearly identifies national effects which accompany effective supply-side policies. Where such national impacts occur, regional policy potentially has positive efficiency and redistributive implications. Also the reduced welfare payments and the increased tax receipts should be set against the subsidy payments (and ideally also other public and private sector costs (Swales, 1997) in the evaluation of regional policy. AMOSRUK presents a much more sophisticated representation of the supply side of the national economy than that adopted by HM Treasury in their existing rules for the evaluation of spatial regeneration policy. As such it offers a means to engage in a more appropriate debate about the national implications of spatial policy.

Even where a strategic objective has direct impacts which are captured by an expansion in demand, CGE analysis, unlike I–O and Keynesian models, incorporates supply-side constraints in the subsequent regional and national adjustments.[14] One central constraint is represented by the operation of the labour market. Here there are two key considerations: the wage-setting mechanism and the regional migration function. If one believes that regional wages are sensitive to the tightness of the local labour market, any expansion in regional demand for labour will be partially offset by increased wages. This sensitivity to local labour market conditions can be motivated by wage curve, regional bargaining or competitive labour market arguments (Blanchflower and Oswald, 1994; Layard, Nickell and Jackman, 1991; Minford et al., 1994). Conventional demand-orientated multipliers fail to capture the substitution of capital for labour and the fall in regional competitiveness that accompanies such a wage increase.

The second important labour-market issue is interregional migration. The population movements that result from changing economic conditions have an impact both on the extent and the time path of adjustment to economic disturbances. In general, migration eases labour market pressure in the aided region (Scotland), so that the positive impacts on this region tend to rise over time. However, the opposite occurs in the non-aided region (RUK) where outmigration tightens the local labour market and leads to reduction in labour demand. These considerations are ignored in the conventional UK evaluation procedures.

A further supply-side constraint is posed by the short-run fixity of the capital stock. Here we expect capacity constraints to bind before they are eased through net investment. Again such capacity constraints have price and competitiveness implications which are neglected in the standard demand-driven approach. Also the relaxing of both short-run capital- and labour-supply constraints through investment and regional migration takes time. Our CGE analysis maps out not just the extent but also the time-path of adjustment of the regional and national economies to the policy disturbance.

A final advantage of the CGE analysis is that it provides an additional, indirect check on the accuracy of the estimate of the direct policy effect. That is to say, the size of the disturbance required to hit the estimated direct employment target might add support to, or cast doubt upon, the validity of this estimate. In the example which is the focus of this chapter, the business competitiveness strategic objective, we require a 2.87 per cent Hicks-neutral increase in efficiency in the manufacturing and non-manufacturing traded sectors in order to produce the period-3 direct employment effects. On the face of it, this increase seems too large and suggests that some iterative procedure, using both microeconomic and system-wide CGE results, would be desirable in determining the size of the direct impacts.

6 POTENTIAL EXTENSIONS

Our view is that the simulation results given in this chapter present a more accurate account of the regional and national operation of regional supply-side policy than the present official UK evaluation procedures. However, the validity and accuracy of these CGE results could be improved. There are three main sources for such improvement. These can be classified under the following headings: model calibration and parameterisation; identifying and modelling the direct effect; and model characteristics.

6.1 Model Calibration and Parameterisation

At present the model is calibrated to a 1989 data set whose core is an interregional social accounting matrix (SAM), which is built around an interregional input–output table. This interregional I–O table is itself constructed from two separate tables, one for Scotland and the other for the UK economy as a whole. The simulation results would be improved if we had a more up-to-date and reliable interregional SAM. One key requirement for interregional CGE analysis is the timely construction of interregional I–O tables. The availability of such information is not problematic for some countries but is for the UK, where no official interregional I–O tables have ever been constructed.

A standard criticism of CGE analysis is that simulation results can be sensitive to the values of key parameters which are sometimes at best 'guess estimates'. There is validity in this argument though our view is that CGE modelling is not very different from other modelling approaches on this score. After all, I–O analysis adopts particular (and extreme) parameter values in the use of fixed coefficients in production and consumption. Further, regional econometric modelling often imposes parameter restrictions (Minford et al., 1994). In our approach, wherever possible we use econometrically estimated parameter values, examples being in the wage-setting and migration functions. However, it is true to say that a lack of data makes reliable regional econometric work difficult in the UK. An improvement in UK regional data would again improve the accuracy of CGE simulations.[15]

6.2 Identifying and Modelling the Direct Effects

The accuracy of the regional and national impacts of SE's policies identified by AMOSRUK depends crucially on the accuracy of the estimates of the direct effects. Within a UK context such effects are conventionally measured through some sort of 'industrial survey' method (Armstrong and Taylor, 1993; Foley, 1992). In this chapter we do not question the validity of the estimates of the direct effects: the simulation results given here are presented as conditional on the accuracy of the estimates of the direct effects. However, it would be desirable to integrate more closely the processes involved in both the estimation of the direct effects and the simulation of the system-wide impacts. Crucially, the assumptions made in the calculation of the direct effects must be consistent with the assumptions implied in the parameterisation of the CGE model. Also, as argued in the previous section, attempts to model the estimated direct effect produce indirect evidence concerning the plausibility of the size of these effects.

A closely related issue is the propriety of the exogenous shocks chosen to emulate SE's policies. Close consideration of this topic can bring gains both to the policymaker and the economic modeller. The operation of the CGE model requires a precise specification of the way in which policy is expected to operate. Such a discipline can be useful for policymakers. But attempting appropriately to capture these supply-side policy effects also has major benefits for the modeller as it tests the policy-relevance of the model. Our view is that the interaction between the modeller and the policymaker should be a two-way process. The model provides information to the policymaker on the constraints imposed by system-wide effects operating in the economy. The policymaker provides information on the relevance of the model to current policy concerns.

6.3 Model Characteristics

We have used the two-region AMOSRUK model to investigate the impact of a supply-side disturbance in one region. The results are both quantitatively plausible and qualitatively consistent with standard economic theory. However, it would be useful to investigate more systematically the national characteristics of the model. That is to say, where we introduce an exogenous disturbance which does not vary across regions, how do the results from AMOSRUK compare with those derived from other econometric UK national models? It must be stressed here that we would not expect, nor necessarily want, the national behaviour of AMOSRUK to replicate the behaviour of national econometric models. AMOSRUK has a more fully-developed supply side which is explicitly regionally-disaggregated. However, major discrepancies should be investigated and explained.

In a similar vein, we have yet to fully investigate the regional characteristics of the model. That is to say, we have not compared the impact of the same disturbance when targeted on each of the two regions of the UK. The work presented in this chapter suggests that supply-side policies have national impacts and that those impacts are geographically concentrated in the areas where the supply disturbance occurred. However, it does not show that such policies should necessarily be focused on development areas. Moreover, we have yet to think closely about what the model implies about the nature of the underlying regional problem.

7 CONCLUSIONS

In the past decade the 'industrial survey' method has come to dominate the evaluation of UK regional regeneration policy (Foley, 1992; HM Treasury, 1995, 1997). This method relies on interview and questionnaire techniques to identify policy effectiveness. The prevalence of discretionary policy instruments, such as those operated by Scottish Enterprise, is at least part of the explanation of the popularity of this approach. It is difficult to know how government could quantify the effectiveness of certain elements of such a policy without a direct approach to firms (Swales, 1997). However, the focus on the 'industrial survey' method has been accompanied by a severe neglect of spatially disaggregated system-wide modelling. We believe that this is a mistake. 'Industrial survey' and modelling approaches can play complementary roles in the identification of policy impacts, at least in the context of models that possess a fully-specified supply side (Gillespie et al., 1998). This chapter hopefully lays some of the groundwork for such a marrying of techniques. Moreover the explicit modelling of national effects opens up the debate on the efficiency effects of spatial policy.

NOTES

1. Additionality is the extent to which the project would have gone ahead in the target area had the regional aid not been available. Displacement is the reduction in economic activity in unaided companies as a result of the expansion in activity in aided companies (HM Treasury, 1997).
2. Scottish Enterprise is a regional development agency located in Scotland but funded at the UK (national) level. Its broad aims are to create jobs and prosperity for the people of Scotland. These aims have been operationalised through seven Strategic Objectives: Business Competitiveness, New Business, Inward Investment, Exports, Skills and Knowledge, Physical Business Infrastructure and Access to Opportunity (Scottish Enterprise, 1998). The chapter is based on work undertaken by the present authors for Scottish Enterprise on the evaluation of the impact of all seven Strategic Objectives.
3. AMOSRUK is an acronym for *A Ma*cro-micro model *Of S*cotland and the *R*est of the *UK*.
4. For a review of regional CGE modelling see Partridge and Rickman (1998).
5. In the single-region version Scottish prices, wages and activity are endogenous, but prices, wages and activity in the rest of the UK are exogenous.
6. Numerous other macroeconomic options are possible for interest-rate and exchange-rate determination in a national CGE context. Some of these are discussed in McGregor, Swales and Yin (1996b).
7. This implies that the net acquisition of financial assets by the UK private sector (the excess of its savings over its investments) is typically non-zero in the equilibrium simulations below. The resultant changes in wealth would be expected to feedback onto expenditures and modify the equilibria. AMOSRUK can in fact be used to examine the ultimate effects of such changes through suspension of the relevant expenditure function to allow satisfaction of public-sector and current-account constraints.

8. This implies that the net acquisition of financial assets by the UK private sector (the excess of its savings over its investments) is typically non-zero in the equilibrium simulations below. The resultant changes in wealth would be expected to feedback onto expenditures and modify the equilibria. AMOSRUK can in fact be used to examine the ultimate effects of such changes through suspension of the relevant expenditure function to allow satisfaction of public-sector and current-account constraints.
9. The sheltered sector is made up of service sectors which undertake very low levels of extra-regional trade. Manufacturing comprises sectors 12-89; non-manufacturing traded sectors 1–10, 91–97, 99, 109–111; and sheltered sectors 11, 90, 98, 103–108 and 112–114 in the 1989 Scottish I–O Tables (Scottish Office Industry Department, 1994).
10. In this equation, and also in the capital updating equations 19–21, the superscript *SX* represents stock in region *X*. In these cases the superscript *S* does not stand for Scotland.
11. However, it is important to note that if the elasticity of labour demand is low, employment can fall with an increase in labour productivity (McGregor, Swales and Yin, 1996c).
12. AMOSRUK is calibrated on a 1989 data set. We have converted nominal values to 1997 prices using the UK GDP deflator (Office of National Statistics, 1997).
13. It might be that this rule has been adopted for strategic purposes in order to reduce influence costs from areas seeking assistance or as a convenient assumption under circumstances where, up to now, it has been difficult to accurately identify the national effects of local regeneration policies.
14. An example would be the exports strategic objective. However, even here in our interregional CGE approach the primary way in which an expansion in exports operates is through the improvement in the terms of trade that it generates. This allows the real consumption wage to rise, thereby expanding labour supply, and the real product wage to simultaneously fall, expanding labour demand.
15. It is unlikely that appropriate econometric estimation and testing of regional CGEs will prove feasible in the foreseeable future. Accordingly, it is inevitable that some degree of uncertainty will attend the values of key parameters and some aspects of market structure. Where this is true, sensitivity analysis can shed light on the likely policy significance of this uncertainty.

APPENDIX

Appendix 11.A1 Percentage change in key Scotland and RUK variables as a result of SE's business competitiveness strategic objective

SCOTLAND	Period 1	Period 2	Period 3	Period 4	Period 5
GDP (real)	0.751	1.526	2.334	1.981	1.614
Consumption (real)	0.383	0.792	1.223	1.059	0.872
Nominal before tax wage	-0.108	-0.207	-0.321	-0.294	-0.297
Real take-home wage	0.120	0.261	0.397	0.328	0.221
Total employment (000's)	0.230	0.475	0.747	0.687	0.628
Manufacturing:	0.122	0.254	0.411	0.409	0.413
Non-Manu traded:	0.202	0.428	0.690	0.673	0.651
Sheltered:	0.322	0.652	1.003	0.866	0.735
Total labour supply (000's)	0.052	0.162	0.319	0.436	0.495
Unemployment rate	-1.751	-3.078	-4.221	-2.459	-1.305
Population (000's)	0.000	0.070	0.194	0.362	0.455
Price of value added:					
Manufacturing	-0.957	-1.905	-2.852	-2.350	-1.848
Non-Manu traded	-0.835	-1.681	-2.539	-2.144	-1.728
Sheltered	0.065	0.096	0.083	-0.080	-0.214
Price of commodity output:					
Manufacturing	-0.434	-0.867	-1.301	-1.072	-0.842
Non-Manu traded	-0.599	-1.207	-1.826	-1.540	-1.241
Sheltered	0.059	0.085	0.073	-0.075	-0.196
Consumer price index	-0.229	-0.465	-0.715	-0.620	-0.516
Value-added:					
Manufacturing	1.049	2.116	3.211	2.654	2.098
Non-Manu Traded	1.093	2.223	3.397	2.859	2.302
Sheltered	0.269	0.560	0.881	0.801	0.710
Exports to the other region:					
Manufacturing	0.768	1.548	2.349	1.954	1.556
Non-Manu Traded	0.843	1.716	2.627	2.230	1.816
Sheltered	0.189	0.405	0.654	0.644	0.615
Exports to ROW:					
Manufacturing	0.875	1.756	2.653	2.179	1.706
Non-Manu Traded	1.210	2.459	3.753	3.152	2.528
Sheltered	-0.117	-0.170	-0.146	0.150	0.393
Real income (CPI deflator):					
Households disposable	0.384	0.792	1.222	1.058	0.872
Firms disposable	0.706	1.376	2.042	1.580	1.181

SCOTLAND	Period 6	Period 7	Period 8	Period 9	Period 10
GDP (real)	1.220	0.796	0.346	0.325	0.297
Consumption (real)	0.667	0.447	0.211	0.194	0.178
Nominal before tax wage	-0.288	-0.259	-0.211	-0.212	-0.195
Real take-home wage	0.113	0.013	-0.079	-0.092	-0.086
Total employment (000's)	0.548	0.442	0.311	0.299	0.275
Manufacturing:	0.399	0.361	0.299	0.290	0.269
Non-Manu traded:	0.600	0.517	0.403	0.384	0.355
Sheltered:	0.586	0.418	0.230	0.221	0.203
Total labour supply (000's)	0.511	0.490	0.438	0.389	0.350
Unemployment rate	-0.359	0.479	1.251	0.892	0.729
Population (000's)	0.500	0.504	0.475	0.416	0.372
Price of value added:					
Manufacturing	-1.328	-0.787	-0.225	-0.222	-0.210
Non-Manu traded	-1.285	-0.814	-0.314	-0.296	-0.274
Sheltered	-0.305	-0.357	-0.375	-0.327	-0.280
Price of commodity output:					
Manufacturing	-0.605	-0.359	-0.102	-0.100	-0.094
Non-Manu traded	-0.922	-0.583	-0.224	-0.211	-0.195
Sheltered	-0.278	-0.323	-0.340	-0.297	-0.254
Consumer price index	-0.400	-0.272	-0.132	-0.120	-0.108
Value-added:					
Manufacturing	1.522	0.924	0.303	0.293	0.274
Non-Manu Traded	1.712	1.089	0.434	0.409	0.379
Sheltered	0.591	0.447	0.280	0.256	0.228
Exports to the other region:					
Manufacturing	1.140	0.705	0.249	0.239	0.222
Non-Manu Traded	1.370	0.893	0.385	0.360	0.329
Sheltered	0.551	0.454	0.328	0.295	0.258
Exports to ROW:					
Manufacturing	1.222	0.721	0.205	0.201	0.189
Non-Manu Traded	1.869	1.175	0.449	0.423	0.391
Sheltered	0.558	0.651	0.682	0.596	0.509
Real income (CPI deflator):					
Households disposable	0.667	0.447	0.212	0.194	0.178
Firms disposable	0.795	0.409	0.020	0.052	0.059

RUK	Period 6	Period 7	Period 8	Period 9	Period 10
GDP (real)	-0.009	-0.014	-0.019	-0.018	-0.018
Consumption (real)	0.001	-0.007	-0.013	-0.013	-0.013
Nominal before tax wage	0.008	0.017	0.024	0.021	0.018
Real take-home wage	0.034	0.031	0.026	0.021	0.017
Total employment (000's)	-0.020	-0.024	-0.026	-0.024	-0.023
Manufacturing:	-0.004	-0.014	-0.021	-0.020	-0.019
Non-Manu traded:	-0.024	-0.028	-0.029	-0.027	-0.026
Sheltered:	-0.024	-0.026	-0.026	-0.023	-0.021
Total labour supply (000's)	-0.039	-0.040	-0.039	-0.034	-0.031
Unemployment rate	-0.304	-0.253	-0.202	-0.152	-0.135
Population (000's)	-0.044	-0.045	-0.042	-0.037	-0.033
Price of value added:					
Manufacturing	-0.012	-0.008	-0.002	0.002	0.004
Non-Manu traded	-0.010	-0.001	0.008	0.009	0.010
Sheltered	-0.010	0.000	0.010	0.011	0.012
Price of commodity output:					
Manufacturing	-0.019	-0.012	-0.003	-0.001	0.001
Non-Manu traded	-0.018	-0.007	0.005	0.006	0.007
Sheltered	-0.012	-0.003	0.006	0.008	0.009
Consumer price index	-0.027	-0.015	-0.002	0.000	0.002
Value-added:					
Manufacturing	0.002	-0.006	-0.013	-0.014	-0.015
Non-Manu Traded	-0.019	-0.022	-0.024	-0.024	-0.023
Sheltered	-0.019	-0.021	-0.022	-0.021	-0.019
Exports to the other region:					
Manufacturing	0.285	0.150	0.015	0.021	0.023
Non-Manu Traded	0.179	0.099	0.017	0.017	0.017
Sheltered	0.076	0.018	-0.036	-0.032	-0.027
Exports to ROW:					
Manufacturing	0.039	0.024	0.007	0.002	-0.002
Non-Manu Traded	0.035	0.013	-0.009	-0.011	-0.013
Sheltered	0.024	0.006	-0.012	-0.016	-0.018
Real income (CPI deflator):					
Households disposable	0.000	-0.007	-0.013	-0.013	-0.013
Firms disposable	0.002	-0.010	-0.020	-0.017	-0.014

REFERENCES

Alexander, J.M. and T.R. Whyte (1995), 'Output, income and employment multipliers for Scotland', *Scottish Economic Bulletin*, **50**, Winter 1994/95.

Armington, P. (1969), 'A theory of demand for products distinguished by place of production', *IMF Staff Papers*, **16**, 157–78.

Armstrong, H. and J. Taylor (1993), *Regional Economics and Policy* (2nd edition), Brighton: Harvester Wheatsheaf.

Blanchflower, D.G. and A.J. Oswald (1994), *The Wage Curve*, Cambridge, MA: MIT Press.

Buckley, P.H. (1992), 'A transport-orientated interregional computable general equilibrium model of the United States', *The Annals of Regional Science*, **26**, 331–48.

Foley, P. (1992), 'Local economic policy and job creation', *Urban Studies*, **29**, 557–98.

Gazel, R., G.J.D. Hewings and M. Sonis (1995), 'Trade, Sensitivity and Feedbacks: Interregional Impacts of the US-Canada Free Trade Agreement', in J.C.J.M. van den Bergh, P. Nijkamp and P. Rietveld (eds), *Recent Advances in Spatial Equilibrium Modelling*, New York: Springer.

Gibson, H. (1990), 'Export Competitiveness and UK Sales of Scottish Manufactures', paper delivered to the Scottish Economists' Conference, The Burn, 1990.

Gillespie, G., P.G. McGregor, J.K. Swales and Y.P. Yin (1998), 'The Displacement and Multiplier Effects of Regional Selective Assistance: A Computable General Equilibrium Analysis', Strathclyde Papers in Economics, No. 98/3, Department of Economics, University of Strathclyde.

Greenaway, D., S.J. Leybourne, G.V. Reed and J. Whalley (1993), *Applied General Equilibrium Modelling: Applications, Limitations and Future Development*, London: HMSO.

Harrigan, F. and P.G. McGregor (1989), 'Neoclassical and Keynesian perspectives on the regional macroeconomy: a computable general equilibrium approach', *Journal of Regional Science*, **29**, 555–73.

Harrigan, F., P.G. McGregor, N. Dourmashkin, R. Perman, J.K. Swales and Y.P. Yin (1991), 'AMOS: A Macro–Micro Model of Scotland', *Economic Modelling*, **10**, 424–79.

Harris, R.I.D. (1989), *The Growth and Structure of the UK Regional Economy 1963-85*, Aldershot: Avebury.

HM Treasury (1995), *A Framework for the Evaluation of Regeneration Projects and Programmes*, London: HMSO.

HM Treasury (1997), *Appraisal and Evaluation in Central Government: Treasury Guidance*, London: The Stationary Office.

Jones, R. and J. Whalley (1990), 'Regional balance sheets of gains and losses from national policies', *Regional Science and Urban Economics*, **20**, 421–35.

Kilkenny, M. (1998), 'Transport costs and rural development', *Journal of Regional Science*, **38**, 293–312.

Layard, R., S. Nickell and R. Jackman (1991), *Unemployment: Macroeconomic Performance and the Labour Market*, Oxford: Oxford University Press.

McGregor, P.G., J.K. Swales and Y.P. Yin (1995), 'Regional Public Sector and Current Account Deficits: Do They Matter?' in J. Bradley (ed.), *The Two*

Economies of Ireland: Public Policy, Growth and Employment, Dublin: Oak Tree Press.

McGregor, P.G., J.K. Swales and Y.P. Yin (1996a), 'The system-wide impact on the recipient region of a regional labour subsidy', *Oxford Economic Papers*, **48**, 105–33.

McGregor, P.G., J.K. Swales and Y.P. Yin (1996b), 'AMOSRUK: An Interregional Computable General Equilibrium Model of Scotland and Rest of the UK', paper presented at the 5th World Congress of the Regional Science Association, Tokyo, May, 1996.

McGregor, P.G., J.K. Swales and Y.P. Yin (1996c), 'The Impact of an Increase in Regional Efficiency', paper presented at the ESRC Urban and Regional Study Group, Queen's University, Belfast, December, 1996.

McGregor, P.G., J.K. Swales and Y.P. Yin (1998), 'The Scottish and UK Effects of the Promotion of Scottish Exports: An Inter-Regional CGE Analysis', paper presented at the Regional Science Association International, British and Irish Section, York, September, 1998.

McVittie, E. and J.K. Swales (1999), 'Sector-Specific Factor Subsidies and Employment in a Regional Price-Endogenous Export-Base Model', *Environment and Planning A*, forthcoming.

Minford, P., P. Stoney, R. Riley and B. Webb (1994), 'An econometric model of Merseyside: validation and policy simulations', *Regional Studies*, **28**, 563–75.

Morgan, W., J. Mutti and D. Rickman (1996), 'Tax exporting, regional economic growth and welfare', *Journal of Urban Economics*, **39**, 131–59.

Mutti, J., W. Morgan and M. Partridge (1989), 'The incidence of regional taxes in a general equilibrium framework', *Journal of Public Economics*, **39**, 83–107.

Office of National Statistics (1997), *United Kingdom National Accounts: The Blue Book*, London: The Stationery Office.

PA Cambridge Economic Consultants Ltd. (1993), *Regional Selective Assistance 1985–88*, London: HMSO.

Partridge, M.D. and D.S. Rickman (1998), 'Regional computable general equilibrium modelling: a survey and critical appraisal', *International Regional Science Review*, **21**, 205–48.

Rickman, D.S. (1992), 'Estimating the impacts of regional business assistance programs: alternative closures in a computable general equilibrium model', *Papers in Regional Science*, **71**, 421–35.

Scottish Enterprise (1998), *Annual Report, 1997–98*, Glasgow: Scottish Enterprise.

Scottish Office Industry Department (1994), *Scottish Input–Output Tables for 1989*, Edinburgh: HMSO.

Swales, J.K. (1997), 'The *ex post* evaluation of regional selective assistance', *Regional Studies*, **31**, 857–63.

Treyz, G.I., D.S. Rickman and M.J. Greenwood (1993),' The dynamics of U.S. internal migration', *Review of Economic and Statistics*, **75**, 209–14.

12. Multi-level Regional Policies and Programmes in France: European Norms, Methods and First Applications

Maurice Baslé and Franck Pelé

1 INTRODUCTION

Evaluation of the impact of private or public action is a great problem and a basic problem in the human and social sciences. In fact, a scientific approach is, by definition, an evaluation of the state of the world and of the influence of human action. In evaluation of regional public policies, this general methodological approach and this type of knowledge is necessary and specific knowledge of the regional economy and its dynamics has to be produced.

The production of this specific knowledge can be assured by an organisational device (for example, statistical offices). Such devices are not always regional in centralised or unitary states. In France, only national statistical information is geared to meet the needs of the various official or private users. But, among those needs is a new objective to evaluate public policies. Evaluation is induced by necessity: from the pressure of financial constraints on national or local public expenditure. However, there is also a desire for more information and greater transparency. Further, the modernist movement within the French administration over the last five years has contributed to a need for information on public policies and their effects. But, with the development of numerous co-financed policies by multi levels of government and the necessity to co-ordinate their action, these needs are being felt at both the national and regional levels and thus there is a need for the production of knowledge at the regional level.. Fortunately, an experiment in decentralisation has occurred over the past ten years which enables the production of shared knowledge about the impact of regional policies.

The institutional context was a national one. At the national level, the institutional context for evaluation in France has for five years been marked by the decree of 22 January 1990 on the evaluation of public policies, the circular of 9 December 1993 on the implementation of evaluation in contractual procedures (plan contracts, city contracts), and the Prime Minister's circular of 13 July 1994 on the plan for modernising financial procedures for the purpose of devolution (Baslé, 1994). A new National Council of Evaluation (decree of 18 November 1998) has been installed. The main objective is to develop an assessment of efficacy of national public policies.

The problem is that statistical and qualitative information has remained very much national and, among other things, the regional development of evaluation brings with it a growing need for regional statistical information. So, for many and various reasons, not only for evaluation purposes, the small quantity and poor quality of regional statistical information in France will have to be tackled: improvements will therefore have to be proposed. In our view, those improvements should in particular make use of certain general ideas on the need to make more interregional comparisons in Europe. It is our contention here that they should also be useful for evaluating regional policies. We will be showing here how it might be possible to draw on the experience of specific regional work that has been done in the field of evaluating public policies, bearing in mind that such work often starts with a statistical phase that consists of information on the policy and the context, the field where the action takes place. The experiment consists of making selected crucial indicators of evaluation of regional policies. The domain is that of co-ordinated French territorialised policies embedded in contracts between several levels of governments.

The intention of this chapter is also to make a first assessment of policy evaluation of what is called in France 'new generation of plan contracts' (1994–99), and especially of the regional policies of plan contracts (Baslé, 1994). Despite the attempts at co-ordination made by the Commissariat Général Du Plan (General Planning Commission) (CGP, 1995), the exercise is in fact little known and little analysed. We will then look at the case of Brittany, because it is probably the best example to illustrate current practice and arrive at recommendations on the needs for regional statistical mechanism for evaluating public policies, for the purpose of conducting and implementing evaluations. A memorandum of agreement between State and Region signed in September 1991 set out the principles for a structure comprising a Committee and a Scientific Commission, which were set up in 1992 after two years of experimentation. In January 1995, this memorandum of agreement was amended with the establishment of a new body, the Consultative Committee on Evaluation, which brought in the four

Breton departments (General Councils and prefects). The inclusion of evaluation in the 1994–98 plan contract helped to give the mechanism a new dimension by encouraging its organisational and functional development. The original memorandum was strengthened and complemented by the signing, by the State and the Region, of an implementing agreement setting out the conditions for implementation of the evaluation provided in the 1994/1998 State–Region Plan Contract.[1] A new direction was chosen in 1993: the implementation of 'light' evaluations of all the programmes in the plan contract. Encouraged by the new obligation to evaluate contractual procedures (plan contracts, city contracts), the State and the Region of Brittany decided to put a light evaluation mechanism in place. As conceived and implemented in Brittany, light evaluation (that is production of crucial indicators of impact) has several aims. Upstream, its aim is to encourage better public coordinated management of contract programmes and actions: it sees itself as a tool for enhancing the work of the services responsible for the programmes so as to provide them with data that will enable them to keep elected representatives and partners better informed about the actions undertaken and the impact they are having. Downstream, the light evaluation mechanism is intended to help in the preparation of feasibility studies and tender specifications for in-depth evaluations. The desire to set up and/or perfect a statistical information system justified an approach aimed at increasing the 'evaluation feasibility' of public policies by means of new, jointly produced (State and Region) information and an improvement in the quality of existing information.

We will begin by presenting the difficulties of evaluation of cooperative regional policies and programmes (Section 2) then, we will present examples of real indicators used in the light evaluation mechanism for the French plan contract between the State and the region of Brittany with the utilisation of European norms of impact indicators (Section 3). We will then conclude (Section 4) from this initial review that regional statistical information needs to be considerably strengthened and that new surveys will have to allow for the possibility that at least some of the regional statistical information collected might be used for evaluation. Evaluation of cooperative regional policies could only be developed if we have sufficient basic knowledge about spatial, economic and social contexts of public action.

2 SOME DIFFICULTIES IN THE EVALUATION OF REGIONAL POLICIES AND PROGRAMMES IN FRANCE

2.1 Qualitative or Quantitative Materials

For choosing and using quantitative and qualitative, there is *a priori* no difference between national policy evaluation and regionalised policy evaluation. Scientific norms, knowledge and know-how are homogeneous and standards of monitoring the evaluation converge. The main difference is probably the effect of smaller budgets, necessity of some local proximity and relational networks, and the choice of smaller consulting teams.

2.2 Specific Evaluation Problems at a Regional Level

From the point of view of the 'evaluation feasibility', the smaller the area concerned with the effects of a public policy, the more problematic is the inventory of local incidence: externalities of public actions are looked for and spillovers are numerous. For example, one may have a local assessment of the monitoring of a local programme to purify water. But you cannot have knowledge of the combined effects of different programmes and water policies in the larger area. Systemic effects are impossible to assess by addition of local effects. Intermediary efficacy indicators are to be used.

2.3 Regional Instance

For regional evaluation, a necessity of regional partnership emerges. Good local governance is a cooperative game between financing local authorities and monitoring local actors. In France, this cooperative game is very difficult to apply at a national level. But a local level, with the existence of spatial proximities and corresponding local networks, we could have a better probability of acceptance (Baslé, 1999).

3 REGIONALISED KNOWLEDGE AND THE IMPACT OF INDICATORS FOR EVALUATING REGIONAL POLICIES

In the case of light evaluation of a regionalised plan contract we propose to make *a grid of impact indicators*. The procedure breaks down into four stages. The first involves making the range of proposed indicators as wide as possible. In the second stage, we must select from each type of indicator those crucial or warning indicators which are considered the most relevant, representative and operational with regard to the characteristics of each programme or each line of action within those programmes. In the third stage, the Scientific Commission uses its expertise to select the indicators. Finally, in a fourth stage, the proposals for indicators incorporating the Scientific Commission's observations and suggestions are returned to the services of the State and Region for final validation before actually being put into use.

The elaboration procedure is thus the prior production of *a cognitive oriented frame of reference* (some would say, a model). The data and the transformation of a collection of facts and figures into an information product that is useful for public action must be considered.

3.1 Stage 1: The Creation of the Different Types of Impact of Indicators

The creation of the different types of indicators is a practical operation: it depends on the inherent characteristics and conditions of the programme in question, but also on the how far the follow-up procedures are advanced. The announced priorities (official objectives), the nature of the objectives to be achieved (quantitative or qualitative), the means of action or even the modes of intervention are therefore important elements to be taken into account.

In Brittany, with some debt to European methodological considerations (MEANS programme, that is 'Méthodes d'évaluation des actions de nature structurelle'), the various types of theoretical indicators fall into 12 categories:

1. Physical monitoring indicators
2. Financial monitoring indicators
3. Indicators of programme timetable
4. Indicators of the achievement of the intermediate objectives
5. Indicators of the achievement of official objectives in the quantitative or qualitative reference units
6. Indicators of the first order impact or effects on the beneficiaries, non-beneficiaries or third parties (effects include the official objectives)
7. Indicators of the higher rank effects of the programme
8. Indicators of unintended effects
9. Indicators of beneficiary satisfaction
10. Indicators of satisfaction of eligible non-beneficiaries
11. Indicators of satisfaction of third parties with respect to public actions (local or regional public opinion)
12. Indicators of the relevance of the programme's objectives to needs (these indicators may be combined indicators constructed at the highest level, by elected representatives or politicians).

3.2 Stage 2: Choice of Crucial or Warning Indicators

The variety of potential indicators of impact is very great. The initial selection process, by appealling to a frame of reference, has some consequences for the final information and evaluative judgement. But collecting the information necessary for producing those indicators obviously has a cost and, in any case, not all information has the same value for the conduct of an action. A selection of indicators has to be made by experts. The question is what type of experts? In Brittany, the answer is services, *ad hoc* groups (monitoring groups) of the Scientific Commission.

Within each type or class of indicators, the choice of existing or potential indicators is made *pro rata* to the information that exists (data banks on the progress of the programmes) or that will be created to satisfy the priority needs and objectives of the light evaluation of the action programmes in the State–Region Plan Contract. The possibility of further work to add to the information already available may be useful in some cases. The general idea underlying the procedure is to select from among the existing or potential indicators those that seem best able to render account of the programme's performance (efficiency, effectiveness).

The choice, that is the selection of indicators from within each type, is made in consultation between the Regional Evaluation Committee and the services of the State and the Region responsible for implementing the programmes. In a spirit of Cupertino, collaboration and adaptability, meetings were organised with those services in order to discuss, on the basis of proposals, the relevance and feasibility of information channels for the potential indicators. After a back and forth process between State and Region in which the indicators were discussed, a genuine consensus was reached; resulting in a common choice of the light evaluation indicators that would be used.

Ultimately, the grid of potential indicators that was provided served as a *frame of reference* for the formation and/or operational fine-tuning of the computerised databases. The various types of theoretical indicators developed fall into the preceding twelve categories. We provide some details in the next section.

3.2.1 Physical monitoring indicators

The physical monitoring indicators proposed could not be applied to all the programmes in the Plan Contract. They were largely conditioned by the nature of the programme(s) to be developed and especially by the populations affected by their implementation.

The definition of such indicators requires a quantification in advance of the objective of the physical work expected from the programmes to be implemented under the State–Region Plan Contract for 1994/1998. The *target value* so defined must then be capable of comparison with a *base or reference value* justifying the objective to be achieved. This assumes a prior diagnosis designed to target, on the basis of their real needs, the populations or territorial areas that will be affected by the action programme(s). Among the physical monitoring indicators, we can distinguish:

- Physical execution indicators (planned/actual)
- Capacity indicators (proposed/achieved)
- Target population identification indicators
- Indicators characterising the territories of application

Examples of physical execution indicators
Number and type of public projects to be implemented (target value)
Number and type of private projects to be supported (estimate of the population satisfying the specific criteria for public intervention)
Number of specific amenities created
Number of amenities or specific structures renovated or rehabilitated

Examples of hypothetical capacity indicators
Maximum demand relative to existing capacity
Maximum demand relative to increased capacity (for example transport infrastructure programme)
Resources or ability to fund the programme
Human resources mobilised to carry out the programme
Organisational resources put in place for the application of the programme

Example of indicators for identifying the populations targeted by the programme
Number of beneficiaries (proposed/actual)
For individuals (professional situation, place of residence, age, gender, family situation, number of children, income, education)
For enterprises (sector of activity, specialisation, legal status, workforce, turnover, location)
For public or collective organisations (composition, status, vocation or functions, resources, number of members)

Example of indicators identifying the territory where the programme will apply
Demographic context: population density, population growth by age and gender, migratory balance, natural balance
Socio-economic context: state of the labour market (sectoral breakdown of employment,proportion of wage earners, proportion of female workers,

unemployment rate), economic activities, wealth of local authorities, wealth of residents, supply of services and businesses
Environmental context: natural, cultural, architectural, touristic assets
Spatio-organisational context: territorial structures and group dynamics (levels of intermunicipal solidarity, networks)

3.2.2 Financial monitoring indicators

Financial monitoring indicators are essentially quantitative and include:

- Indicators of budgetary resources with their origin (State, budget heading)
- Ratios
- Indicators of financial costs (totals, by origin)
- Indicators of the use of credits

Examples of indicators in absolute value
Basic indicators of budgetary resources:
Overall cost of the programme
Overall financing plan for the programme (State, Region, other)
Overall budget allocated by action and line of action
Breakdown of credits allocated by action and line of action (State, Region, other)
Breakdown of aids by type of investment (tangible, intangible)

Basic indicators of budget appropriations
Total cost of operations or projects financed
Total cost of subsidies granted
Amount of subsidizable expenditure by operation or project financed
Consumption of credits by programme, action and line of action
Consumption of credits by financier

Examples of ratios
Concerning budgetary resources:
Structure of the breakdown of budget funds by action and line of action of the programme
Each investor's share in the overall funding of the programme (State, Region, other)
Structure of the breakdown of aids by type of investment (tangible, intangible)
Concerning budget appropriations:
Rate of subsidy of actions relative to total cost, including tax

Rate of subsidy of actions relative to the amount of subsidisable expenditure, including tax
Rate of consumption of credits by programme and line of action
Rate of consumption of credits by programme financier
Rate of consumption of credits by the appropriate time
Amount of credits allocated to the programme relative to the number of its beneficiaries (credit per capita)

The periodicity of monitoring these indicators may be annual or more frequent (quarterly, half-yearly)

3.2.3 Indicators of keeping to the programme timetable

A programme may have as a stated priority the strict adherence to a timetable for its implementation. Indicators allowing adherence to the timetable to be monitored must therefore be preferred here.

- Programme timetable (date of commencement, date of completion of planned work)
- State of progress on the programme relative to the timetable (late, on time, ahead)

3.2.4 Indicators of the achievement of the programmes' intermediate objectives

Construction of these indicators requires the clear and precise identification of the intermediate objectives serving the achievement of final objectives or of the programmes drawn up.

Examples:

- Increasing capacity to meet the increase in numbers of university students (the final objective being to increase the level of higher education)
- Number of additional university institute of technology departments opened
- Increased tourist accommodation capacity to satisfy tourists' demand for accommodation
- Improving the quality of the accommodation (so as to improve the supply of services)

3.2.5 Indicators of the achievement of the official objectives (results compared with the announced objectives)

The effectiveness or performance of a programme of action depends on its ability to meet the set objectives. However, the development of indicators to monitor a programme's objectives requires the prior fulfilment of a number of conditions of measurability. If the objectives are to be capable of assessment, they must in fact be *standardized*, that is quantified or linked to a reference value (the 'height' of the target serves here as a reference standard for assessing the results obtained).

In the absence of numerical objectives (as is the general rule), we need to be able to say how the initial situation justifying public intervention has been changed. Finally, even though measurement of the discrepancies between the aims in view and the objectives achieved is an essential process of evaluation, it is nonetheless insufficient. We need to be able to complete the information (with a view to a 'heavier' evaluation) so as to give the persons concerned the means of determining the factors behind any discrepancies found or the processes behind the results observed.

Some examples of quantified indicators of official targets to be achieved:

- Modernisation of some 1000 craft and commercial enterprises (target value)
- Improving the competitiveness of 300 enterprises
- Encouraging the creation of a Commercial Union per canton (collective actions)
- Facilitating access to employment for young persons aged 16 to 25 in an enterprise following a six-month course

3.2.6 Indicators of the first order impact, results or effects on the beneficiaries, non-beneficiaries or third parties

Indicators of impact or effect only have real meaning in relation to the precise measurement of a basic environmental context that is to be corrected, which justifies public intervention. A programme's impact is by definition *differential*. The indicators describe the difference observed between an initial situation, which is to be changed, and a final situation. Measuring the impact of a programme in the field where it is applied means taking account of the value of indicators describing the initial environment that is to be transformed (diagnosis or analysis of the situation at point zero, that is before the intervention begins) and monitoring how they change as time goes on in order to judge the level of the effects produced by the implementation of an action scheme. Most often, this will require an in-depth evaluation (as we go along or afterwards).

Example of absolute value indicators

- Initial capacity (reference value)/Capacity expected after completion (target value)/Capacity achieved (final value)

- Impact on regional development (sectoral diversification). Differential between an initial state and a final state
- Impact on the environment (*ex post* appraisal of the situation in the zone concerned)
- Economic profitability of the project assisted
- Leverage effect in terms of private investment (amount of investment made/amount of subsidy granted)
- Leverage effect in terms of public investments
- Return on investment
- Indices of existing capacity (in terms of employment, accommodation available)
- Increased capacity (in terms of employment, accommodation available)
- Jobs created, unemployment reduced
- Impact on the accommodation available in the context of a tourism policy

Example of ratios

- Survival rate of the companies or enterprises assisted
- Rate of growth in initial capacity resulting from public intervention (difference between an initial state and a final state)
- Rate of growth in employment in the enterprises assisted
- Change in the percentage of nitrates or phosphates in water
- Incentive rate of aids on the decision to invest and the date, quality or quantity of investments (incentive effect of public aid)
- Rate of participation in collective activities or dynamics
- Rate of penetration or awareness of a programme among the target public (number of applications for aid/population potentially eligible for aid)

This list is only an indication and could be expanded or varied according to the announced characteristics of each programmes in the State–Region Plan Contract.

3.2.7 Indicators of the higher order effects of the programme

An action programme may have (knock-on) effects on agents or sectors of activity other than those targeted by its implementation. Such higher order spillover effects may in some cases be felt in the monetary and financial spheres through the creation of additional markets.

A sectoral programme may have indirect effects on other sectors of activity that were not originally in view. The potential spin-offs may be economic, social, environmental or even psychological (renewed optimism). Here again, only additional surveys will throw light on such knock-on or *n*th order effects:

- The building sector from a programme to assist in the creation or modernisation of physical structures (for production or accommodation)
- On other sectors of activity resulting from public intervention (business or architectural consultancy
- Effect of aid to an enterprise for the purpose of preserving employment feeding through into the amount of business tax collected locally
- Effect of imitation or contagion from one sector to another
- Effect of image or reputation

3.2.8 Indicators of unintended effects

The main purpose of indicators of unintended effects (beneficial or otherwise) is to highlight certain observable but unexpected phenomena by analysing the interactions between the programme and its environment (the vision is systemic). Among the effects encountered, we often find:

- Opportunist behaviour (seeking to get as much financial aid as possible for investments that were planned at lower cost).
- Production of positive or negative external consequences (map of the pollution resulting from the implementation of a transport infrastructure programme, for example).
- Disruption to the operational mechanism of competition on the market.
- Acquisition by certain interest groups of the income created by the regulations (capture of the 'regulator').

3.2.9 Indicators of satisfaction of the target populations (beneficiaries)

Measuring *the degree of satisfaction* of the beneficiaries of a public action programme is a commonly accepted approach. Opinion polls are the rule here. We can also imagine heavier questionnaires including a description of hypothetical situations of the offer or non-offer of such and such public policy and the formalisation of questionnaires on the expectations and demands of the agents targeted (including in terms of performance to be paid for and performances expected).

- Rate of beneficiary satisfaction with the systems of aid and their operation (collection of views or opinions on the way applications are dealt with, aids are granted or, more precisely, on the service rendered by a particular public policy)

- Rate of beneficiary satisfaction with the investments made (link between expectations and results)
- Rate or degree of satisfaction with the general interest structures or bodies through which action programmes are applied (for example opinion of the consultancy or technical assistance provided)
- Monitoring such indicators would require further investigations in the field (specific surveys and methodologies)

3.2.10 Indicators of satisfaction of eligible non-beneficiaries

It may also be useful and relevant to survey categories of the population (public bodies, associations, enterprises, individuals) that are not beneficiaries but would be eligible for a particular public incentive scheme so as to ascertain their attitudes towards or their images of public aid systems or procedures. Here, too, surveys will have to be carried out to measure the reactions of non-beneficiaries, asking more or less leading questions in order to uncover views, opinions or value judgements on the public actions potentially concerning them but which they did not want to take part in or did not know how to. One might, for example, seek for the reasons or motivations for not making use of a particular aid procedure (lack of information on the mechanisms available, no need for it, coming at the wrong time, refusal of any outside interference.

3.2.11 Indicators of satisfaction of third parties

It may also be interesting to conduct surveys or opinion polls of third parties about the policies or programmes implemented. Satisfaction indicators can be constructed and monitored to measure and assess the effects of action programmes as they may be perceived locally in the places where they apply through the outside eyes of persons with resources (elected representatives, presidents of various structures, technical assistants of chambers of commerce, traders, artisans, restaurant owners). In this case, the indicators measure mainly qualitative dataand the collection of information depends largely on the characteristics or specific features of the programmes put in place. For example, in the case of a policy to assist the rural tourism, measurement of the degree of third party satisfaction may be combined with consideration of opinions on various aspects of the policy:

- general opinion of the policy
- opinion of the economic, social and political spin-offs
- opinion of the structures through which the policy is applied
- opinion of which actions should be given priority
- opinion of the 'Cupertino Spirit' between various agencies involved

3.2.12 Indicators of the relevance of objectives to needs

The indicators of the *relevance* of a public intervention relate to the needs actually felt by the populations targeted by the action programme. It may nevertheless be difficult to ascertain both the characteristics of those whom the action is intended to benefit (and therefore to analyse whether the mechanism meets their expectations and needs) and to take account of the characteristics of the social and economic environment and to assess whether the programme is geared to the specific nature of that environment. The work to evaluate relevance is therefore a final task that can and must be carried out at the highest level of policy implementation (that is, at the level of elected representatives or of central government). This explains why this final class of indicators is not effective in Brittany.

Examples:

- Can we judge the relevance of an objective seeking to modernise 1200 craft trade and commercial enterprises without knowing the potential number of enterprises with real needs for modernisation or renovation?
- Can we enlist young people in a vocational retraining scheme without first studying the local employment market?
- Can we encourage a local development project in a rural canton without placing it in a wider national or European spatio-economic context?

This means that it must be possible for *indicators of need* to be constructed *beforehand* so that the relevance of any objective can be assessed. They are generally constructed on what economists call the political market.

3.3 Stage 3: Expert Report by the Scientific Commission on Indicators Chosen by State and Region

The Scientific Commission of the Regional Evaluation Committee, which guarantees the scientific nature of the work undertaken, then has to use its expertise to make a scientific appraisal of the indicators. It gives its opinion on the relevance, quality and performance (in the light of the programmes' stated objectives) of the indicators developed jointly by the State and the Region.

3.4 Stage 4: Final Validation of the Indicators by the State and the Region and their Implementation

Lastly, in the final stage the proposed indicators are reformulated on the basis of the Scientific Committee's observations and suggestions and returned for final validation in the services of the State and the Region. This final stage signals the actual implementation of the indicators.

3 INCORPORATING LIGHT EVALUATION NEEDS INTO THE NEW SURVEYS AND DATA COLLECTION

The evaluation of regional policies in the French plan contracts can be light, in the sense described above, or in-depth. In both cases, they always require the following statistical information:

- background information,
- statistical information on policies carried out (their cost and timescale), and more specific statistical information on one of the policy's given target groups (the beneficiaries: households, enterprises, territories),
- (quarterly, six-monthly or annual) monitoring of this information to see how long it takes for the effects of the regional policies to appear.

In view of the information we have just provided on the methodology and results of Brittany's experiences with evaluation, we could advance the following proposals:

For background statistical information, it is necessary to gain a firm grasp of the basic data relating to the existing infrastructure (roads or motorways already constructed before the new road plan, for example), or the surface areas of educational or other buildings in order to calculate the ratio of new investment to existing stock. It should be possible to do the same for employment statistics (for example trends in employment in the craft or commercial sectors) or production statistics, turnover (for example the trend in turnover by commercial or craft enterprises compared with the trend in turnover by enterprises assisted by a specific target policy). The abovementioned statistics – investment, employment, turnover and others – are the most frequently requested. They are also requested at various geographical levels: regional, regional authority action area, areas defined by zoning policy (for European cross-financing policy, these may be Objective 5b areas; for other policies, employment areas or urban agglomerations)

For statistical information on the policies carried out in the region, it is necessary to call on public authority finance departments, computerised procedures for dealing with applications and the minutes of discussions on eligibility and the granting of loans to this or that operation or beneficiary. In this case, the national statistical institutes need to be relayed information by the public authorities' statistical departments.

Information which allows one to monitor and assess the impact and various direct, indirect, intentional and unintentional effects is often the same as the abovementioned background information. It can, however, also include a vast range of information which is not produced or collected regularly under the standard surveys conducted by the national statistical institutes. The statistical departments of the various public authorities can, in certain cases, be asked to contribute without any new research – for example the Ministry of Agriculture or Regional Directorate for Industry, Research and the Environment. However, in a number of cases where the information has to be created, there are two possible scenarios: it can be done at low cost, or not at all. In some cases, the public authorities, in their role as lead managers or awarding authorities, should lay down the conditions regarding information feedback more authoritatively and more professionally: non-responses could be punished by the suspension of aid. This could allow savings to be made on additional surveys, which are expensive and generally unpopular. One problem with these 'return-ticket' operations, even when carried out professionally, is that certain information can be manipulated by the respondent, especially when there is a link between certain responses on the effects of aid and the granting of the final instalment, or further instalments, of this aid.

5 CONCLUSION

New ideas about 'light' evaluation performance indicators should be of greater use in devising and selecting relevant and useful indicators. In the new information society, at all territorial levels, we need to be more effective in providing efficient, reliable, useful and accessible information: knowledge and know-how for better evaluation indicators of regionalised policies. The challenge is harder when we want to analyse regionalised co-financed policies. But it is not impossible to also consider that when multiple levels of government want to know something about their common agency and action, cooperation and co-production of information is a preamble to the working of the game.

NOTES

1. Regional Public Policy Evaluation Committee (Brittany) 1995, *'The regional public policyevaluation mechanism and what it has achieved'*, September, 3 rue du Général Guillaudot, 35000 Rennes.

BIBLIOGRAPHY

Albaek, E. (1989–90), 'Policy Evaluation: design and utilisation', *Knowledge in Society,* **2** (4), 6–19.

Baslé, M. (1994a), 'Problèmes de méthodes pour l'évaluation d'une politique européenne relayée par l'Etat et la région en France: le cas du FEDER', Colloque de l'Association de Science régionale de Langue française. Tours, 30 août 1993, *Revue d'Economie Régionale et Urbaine*, 1994, **4**.

Baslé, M. (1994b), 'Questions de méthodes et évaluation des politiques touristiques: les leçons d'une étude de cas', *Revue Française des Finances Publiques*, **48**, 45–57.

Baslé, M. (1994c), 'Some problems of causality in ex-post European evaluation: a case study for European objectif 2 of industrial restructuration', Founding Conference of European Evaluation Society, La Haye, 1–2 décembre 1994, en collaboration avec Béatrice Floc'hlay.

Baslé, M. (1995a), 'Problèmes de transposition de la méthode d'évaluation contingente au cas desservices collectifs publics et sociaux', *Politiques et Management Public,* **13** (2), juin, 1–19, Paris.

Baslé, M. (1995b), 'Essai sur les jugements de valeur et les méthodes d'évaluation', in M. Baslé, D. Dufourt, J.A. Heraud and J. Perrin (eds), *Changement institutionnel et changement technologique,* Paris: Editions du Centre National de Recherche Scientifique.

Baslé, M. (1996), *Petit guide de l'évaluation des politiques publiques,* en collaboration au sein du Conseil Scientifique de l'évaluation, Commissariat général du plan, La documentation française, 180 pp., mars 1996.

Baslé, M. (1998a), 'Politique régionale de formation et d'insertion d'adultes à la recherche d'emploi: évaluation quantitative et qualitative ex-post du chèque-force en Bretagne, 1989-1996',*Conférence européenne sur les pratiques d'évaluation en matière de politiques structurelles*, Séville, 17–16 mars 1998, Centre européen d'expertise en Evaluation, DG XVI Commission Européenne, Politique régionale et cohésion.

Baslé, M. (1998b), 'Contexte et méthodes pour l'évaluation partenariale des politiques publiques territoriales en France: quelques leçons de l'évaluation des contrats de plan Etat-Région et du cas breton', *Revue d'Economie Régionale et Urbaine*, **1**, Numéro spécial sur l'Evaluation des Politiques Territoriales.

Baslé, M. (1998c), 'Théories de la coordination d'agents : de l'interdépendance faible à l'interdépendance forte', Conférence invitée, Séminaire européen des doctorants en Economie Régionale, Bordeaux, juin, à paraître.

Baslé, M. (1999), 'Lévaluation territorialisée des politiques publiques en France : organisation, constat et problèmes spécifiques', Premier congrès de la Société française d'Evaluation, Marseille, 4–5 juin 1999, ronéoté.

Baslé, M. and F. Pelé (1994), 'L'évaluation des politiques et des contrats de plan Etat-Région en France: la situation en France en fin 1994', *Cahiers Economiques de Bretagne,* **39** (4), 1–29, Rennes.

Baslé, M. et al. (1998), 'Analyse comparative des méthodes quantitatives et qualitatives et des résultats obtenus par l'évaluation de trois programmes français de formation visant l'insertion professionnelle d'adultes en difficulté sur le marché du travail', XVIIIème Colloque de l'association d'Economie Sociale, septembre, Université de la Méditerranée, Marseille, sur l'initiative du LEST-CNRS et du CEREQ, à paraître, L'harmattan.

Commissariat Général du Plan, (1995), Rapport sur le colloque de Toulouse d'octobre 1994, roneoté.

Conseil Scientifique de l'Evaluation (1993, 1994, 1995), *L'Evaluation en Développement. Rapport sur l'évolution des pratiques d'évaluation des politiques publiques,* Paris: La Documentation Française.

Conseil Scientifique De L'evaluation (1996), *Petit Guide de l'Evaluation des Politiques Publiques,* Paris: La Documentation Française.

Gaudy, C. (1996), 'Bilan des expériences en matière d'évaluation des programmes européens, objectif 2 et 5b', Centre d'études de projets, une étude financée par la Délégation française à l'aménagement du territoire.

Rist, R.C. (ed.) (1995), *Policy Evaluation. Linking theory to practice,* Cheltenham: The International Library of Comparative Public Policy, Edward Elgar.

13. Evaluation of the Employment Effects of United Kingdom Enterprise Zones: A Comparison of New Start-Ups and Inward Investors

Barry Moore and Jonathan Potter

INTRODUCTION

A persistent problem confronting many inner city and other urban localities in the United Kingdom and other advanced industrialised countries seeking to tackle concentrations of economic and social distress, is the physical dereliction and decay of unutilised vacant factory/office space and public infrastructure. Such problems arise for a variety of reasons but are often associated with major factory closures and loss of economic activity, much of which has been linked to the restructuring of traditional manufacturing industries. The environmental problems associated with contaminated land, physical dereliction and blight and the presence of localised concentrations of long-term unemployment are closely interrelated and create a situation where markets fail to resolve the problems even in the very long run. The sources of market failure are well known and include for example negative externalities resulting from dereliction; information deficiencies and assymetric risk relating to site conditions; costs of renewal and refurbishment; ownership barriers, economies of scale and indivisibilities in land and infrastructure renewal activities; planning controls and bureaucratic inflexibilities which increase uncertainty and costs; and labour market immobility and restricted access of unemployed to jobs. In areas experiencing severe economic and social distress, problems associated with market failure are compounded by the dynamics of adjustment that tend to reinforce and sustain the competitive disadvantage of these areas. Physical dereliction, run-down infrastructure, unattractive vacant offices and factory floorspace discourages inward investment and the start up of new small firms. This in turn undermines the confidence of developers and increases their assessment of the risk of funding major new developments in the area. Existing firms located in the area seek alternative locations as the area continues to experience relative decline.

To address this complex mix of problems, governments have increasingly sought to target and concentrate policy initiatives on tightly defined geographical areas and to orchestrate policy programmes which both recognise the different and interactive sources of market failure and the need for a more holistic approach. The Enterprise Zone (EZ) 'experiment' introduced in the UK in the early 1980s aimed at regenerating tightly targeted local areas (up to 450 hectares) rather than the more widely defined geographical areas typically associated with traditional regional policies. It also provided a policy package which simultaneously addressed the need to stimulate the local commercial property market, the need to improve public infrastructure and service provision whilst at the same time meeting the floorspace and locational requirements of inward investors and new start-ups. The government consultative paper published in 1980 asserted that:

> the purpose of these zones is to test as an experiment, and on a few sites, how far industrial and commercial activity can be encouraged by the removal of certain fiscal burdens and by the removal or streamlined administration of certain statutory or administrative controls.

Two yardsticks were established against which the EZ experiment could be judged. The first was the extent to which EZs have maintained and/or generated additional economic activity and employment both on zones and in their local areas. The second was the extent to which EZs have contributed to the physical regeneration of their local ares through the provision of infrastructure, environmental improvement, and stimulation of the property market.

Although EZ policy could be expected to have some benefits for the survival or expansion of pre-existing firms on the zones, it was anticipated that the attraction of inward investment and new enterprise development would be the key mechanisms by which the EZ experiment would secure its objectives. However, whilst several studies have investigated the impact of the EZ policy, relatively little is known about the nature and impact of different types of policy-induced economic activity. Two of the most important sources of information on UK EZs are the reports by PA Cambridge Economic Consultants on the mid-term and final evaluations of Enterprise zone policy (PA Cambridge Economic Consultants, 1987, 1995). The final evaluation provides the data on which this chapter is based. These evaluations assessed the extent to which the zones had generated additional economic activity and physical regeneration in their local areas midway through their operation and then at the end of their ten year designation. It was estimated that total employment on the surveyed zones was originally some 29 400 in 1250 companies, had risen to 63 300 in just over 2800 firms by the mid-point of the programme and to nearly 126 000 people in an estimated 5000 firms at the time of de-designation. After allowing for deadweight and displacement and including short-term multiplier effects, about 58 000 jobs were thought to be additional to the local areas. This chapter explores more closely the distinctive features associated with inward investment induced economic activity and new start-ups (NSUs) and compares their relative impact on the zones and their local areas.

Although the Enterprise Zone (EZ) concept was among the first of this type of targeted local area policy to be developed, similar special zone initiatives include the 'Zones Franches Urbaines' in France, 'Area Contracts' in Italy and EZs are now an active component of local economic development policy in other European countries (including Ireland, Hungary, Poland, Russia), and countries such as Israel, Australia, China, Japan the Philippines and Vietnam. EZs are particularly widespread in the United States, where by the early 1990s over 3000 had been designated in 38 states and the District of Columbia (Gunn, 1993). The zones cover not just inner city areas but also suburban and rural areas in economic difficulties. In 1994 the concept was extended to a federal programme called 'Empowerment Zones' which is now a keystone of urban policy in the United States, offering grants for social programmes as well as powerful tax incentives for business.

It is clear that the use of locally targeted tax incentive-based policies is being actively used as a way of tackling pockets of severe economic disadvantage. Moreover, the current interest in this type of policy tool is demonstrated, for example, in the recent Rogers report on the future of urban regeneration policy in the United Kingdom, which concluded that a key instrument should be the creation of Urban Priority Areas where special regeneration measures would apply, including a streamlined planning process, accelerated compulsory purchase powers and fiscal incentives (Urban Task Force, 1999). The research findings presented here from the operation of United Kingdom Enterprise Zone policy provide some important lessons for the design of this type of policy in the United Kingdom and in other countries.

THE AIMS AND INSTRUMENTS OF UK ENTERPRISE ZONE POLICY

The first 11 UK EZs were set up in 1981/82 for a ten-year period, followed by a second round of 14 new zones and 2 extended zones designated in

1983/84. All have now lost their EZ status. However, new zones were designated in the late 1980s and the 1990s, with some recent adjustments to the tax regulations and restrictions on certain types of industry. Some have been set up near to de-designated zones in order to sustain the momentum achieved whilst others have been set up to tackle new problems in areas of coal, steel and shipbuilding closures. The zones are each managed by a Zone Authority, such as the local council or Development Corporation, which may undertake site and inward investment promotion or appoint an agency to promote the zone. The main instruments of EZ policy are:

- Exemption from Local Authority business rates (property taxes).
- Enhanced capital allowances at the rate of 100 per cent for the year of expenditure against corporation tax (income tax for the self employed) for expenditure on industrial and commercial buildings and hotels.
- Exemption from Development Land Tax (DLT) on the development value realised from disposals of interest in land on an EZ within 10 years of the EZ designation. DLT was abolished in 1985.
- Exemption from Industrial Training Board Levies, which are important in construction, engineering and haulage.
- A Simplified Planning Regime for each zone specifying activities for which planning permission is not required plus speedy permission for non-qualifying activities.
- Speedier administration requiring delays of not more than 14 days for planning and other decisions (land availability, highways access, utilities availability and so on).
- Exemption from government statistical requirements.
- Enhanced public expenditure on infrastructure and land renewal.

These benefits were available to firms located on the zones during the whole of the ten-year zone designation period. By focusing on tightly targeted geographical areas the policy has aimed to steer public expenditure into the areas of greatest need and to try and ensure that jobs are created that local residents will have geographical access to.

ENTERPRISE ZONES AND INWARD INVESTMENT

Although it was recognised that one important way in which EZ policy would work would be by attracting inward investment, a number of reservations were raised at the outset about its likely effectiveness in stimulating local regeneration. The concerns included the view that the zones would not provide the proper sorts of incentive to attract firms because they would not directly address their fundamental locational needs, such as for good transport and communications and labour supply; that EZ land would be absorbed by local relocations of firms simply transferring jobs from adjacent areas; that the structure of incentives would favour capital-intensive rather than labour-intensive investment, thus limiting the number of jobs created; and that the quality of inward investment attracted could be poor in terms of the skills and remuneration of jobs offered, poor links to local suppliers or significant displacement of other local firms (Glickman, 1984; Butler, 1981; Massey, 1982; Clarke, 1982). A further concern was that unemployed people living in the areas surrounding the zones may form a relatively small proportion of those winning jobs with inward investors.

In the UK relatively little work has been done on the factors influencing inward investment to EZs. The PA Cambridge Economic Consultants (1995) study examined the question of establishment status and history but did not make a direct assessment of the importance of inward investment to the zones. At the time of de-designation, 23 per cent of establishments on the zones were new branches or subsidiaries of firms headquartered elsewhere and 38 per cent were transfers of entire firms onto the zones. The nature of the investment varied significantly between different zones in the UK. For example in Telford the emphasis was on attracting inward manufacturing investment, in Dudley and Newcastle there has been a strong focus on new retailing and leisure activity and in the Isle of Dogs (London) commercial activity was encouraged (Tyler, 1993). We extend this original analysis here by examining features of 185 firms that claim to have been influenced to locate on EZs from alternative locations outside of their local areas as a result of EZ designation. All of these establishments therefore appear to have been induced to locate on the zones by EZ policy.

ENTERPRISE ZONES AND NEW START-UPS

At the outset of the EZ experiment the government stated that one important objective was the encouragement and stimulus of enterprise. Support for new start-ups and encouraging the growth and survival of small businesses were considered to be central to achieving the enterprise objective of EZs. At the same time, however, support for enterprise involves measures which influence the innovative capabilities of small business and risk taking, elements which are largely absent from the basket of EZ measures.

Although few of the EZ measures directly aimed to encourage enterprise in the sense of providing support for innovative activity or encouraging risk taking, indirectly a number of the EZ measures could be expected to stimulate enterprise. First, enterprise might be strengthened through the impact of EZ measures on the commercial property market leading to the development of premises suitable for new start-ups and more efficient small business activity. Secondly enterprise benefits could arise as a result of reduced bureaucracy and faster planning regimes, both of which are likely to improve the efficiency of small businesses as they develop and grow. Thirdly the EZs provide a potential location for establishing clusters of small businesses with resulting benefits from agglomeration and opportunities for cooperation and collaboration. Finally the financial benefits derived from an EZ location might be expected to support enterprise.

There is a dearth of research on the impact of EZ policy on the stimulation of enterprise. Perhaps the most comprehensive study is that by PACEC (1995) which noted that the nature of establishments on the EZs was heavily weighted towards new and small companies and identified approximately one-third of companies on the EZs as new start-ups. An estimated 42 per cent of companies in the PACEC survey claimed that an EZ location benefited their start-up. It is also clear from this survey that many of the new start-ups would have located off the EZ in the absence of designation. Thus 68 per cent would have located off the zone and 18 per cent would have cancelled or delayed their start-up. The bulk of the NSU activity on the zones can therefore be directly attributed to EZ policy.

THE RESEARCH OBJECTIVES AND APPROACH

Objectives

The principal objective of this chapter is to compare the scale, characteristics and impacts of inward investment attracted to UK EZs with new start-ups (NSUs) on EZs and to assess the relative importance of the various forms of policy assistance offered to these two types of firms. The following key research questions are addressed:

- How important has EZ-attracted inward investment been as a component of total economic activity on EZs by comparison with NSUs?
- What are the key distinguishing characteristics of inward investors compared with NSUs?
- What have been the key policy and non-policy factors that have influenced inward investors and NSUs to locate on EZs?

- What have been the relative impacts of inward investment and NSUs on local area regeneration in terms of local employment opportunities and economic linkages?
- Are there differences between types of inward investor in their reasons for locating on the zones or in their local impacts?
- Are there differences between types of zone (Urban, Remote, Accessible) in the relative scale, characteristics and impacts of inward investors and NSUs?

In answering these questions the aim is to help inform strategies for targeted local area regeneration.

The Database and Sample Characteristics

The findings presented relate to surveys undertaken on 22 of the UK EZs; nine Round One zones de-designated in 1991/92 and 13 Round Two zones de-designated in 1993/94. It does not include the Isle of Dogs zone in London Docklands or the Belfast zone, which were evaluated separately, nor does it include zone extensions or new zones designated since 1985. The surveys were carried out at the time of zone de-designation, in 1991/92 for Round One zones and in 1993/94 for Round Two zones. Overall, 492 face-to-face interviews were completed, over 4500 postal questionnaires were sent out and 596 were returned completed. The postal questionnaire included all the core questions from the face-to-face survey in exactly the same format, providing comparable data for 1088 zone companies. All known firms on the zones were approached and responses were obtained from 23 per cent of the estimated population. The breakdown of responses by zone is shown in Table 13.1.

To reflect differences in the geographical context of the zones they were classified into those in inner cities (Urban Core Zones), those outside urban centres but easily accessible from major population centres (Accessible zones) and those in remote areas (Remote Zones). The composition of the groups is as follows:

Urban Zones: Dudley, Salford/Trafford, Speke, Tyneside, Swansea, Clydebank.
Accessible Zones: Corby, Hartlepool, Wakefield, Glanford, Middlesbrough, North East Lancashire, North West Kent, Rotherham, Scunthorpe, Telford, Wellingborough, Delyn, Tayside.
Remote Zones: Allerdale, Milford Haven, Invergordon.

Table 13.1 Survey response

	Postal returns	Face to face	Total surveyed	Sample size	Response rate
Round One zones:					
Corby	33	19	52	183	28.4
Dudley	33	56	89	407	21.9
Hartlepool	17	15	32	143	22.4
Salford/Trafford	37	54	91	516	17.6
Speke	10	8	18	69	26.1
Tyneside	74	81	155	882	17.6
Wakefield	2	15	17	90	18.9
Swansea	19	36	55	248	22.2
Clydebank	44	36	80	384	20.8
Total	269	320	589	2922	20.2
Round Two zones:					
Allerdale	26	14	40	133	30.1
Scunthorpe	10	9	19	63	30.2
Rotherham	34	14	48	177	27.1
NW Kent	77	47	125	494	25.3
Wellingborough	10	14	24	71	33.8
Invergordon	8	4	12	42	28.6
Middlesbrough	31	11	42	113	37.2
Delyn	12	4	16	67	23.9
Telford	24	6	30	112	26.8
NE Lancs	33	14	47	193	24.4
Tayside	24	10	34	124	27.4
Glanford	4	5	9	37	24.3
Milford Haven	34	20	54	211	25.6
Total	327	172	499	1835	27.2
Total	596	492	1088	4757	22.9

Figure 13.1 shows the location of the zones studied. As with all surveys of this type there is the possibility of sampling bias, which may arise if the sample frame is not fully comprehensive or if certain types of firm are more likely to respond. The sampling frame for the study is considered to be very comprehensive, being derived from the Department of Employment databases used for the national Census of Employment and updated by the relevant zone authorities.

Figure 13.1 The location of enterprise zones within the UK

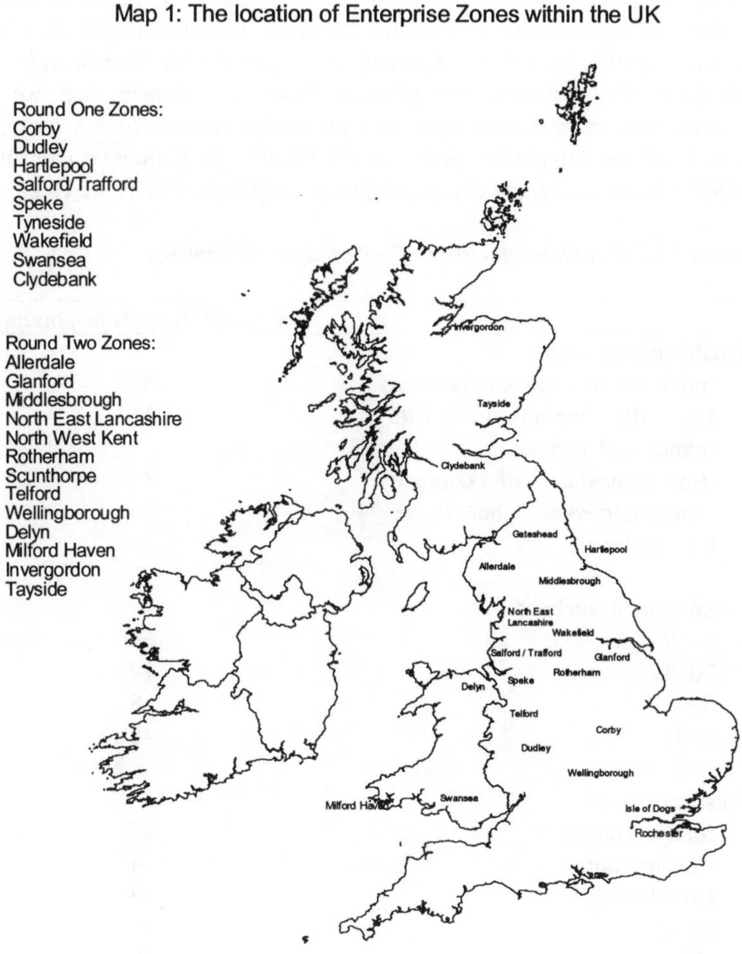

In order to examine whether there is a skew in survey responses sample firms have been compared with basic information on the population of establishments collected independently by the Department of the Environment in 1991 and 1993, which covered more than 75 per cent of known establishments (Department of the Environment, 1995). This comparison suggests that there is some bias towards large establishments (34 per cent of employment in sample firms compared with only 23 per cent of establishments) and the manufacturing sector (45 per cent of the sample compared with 37 per cent of the population). This may be associated with some over-representation of inward investors. The main implication of this is that although inward investors can be compared with other firms in terms of their characteristics and impacts there is a danger that we may overestimate inward investment as a proportion of total zone activity. Full details of the sample are given in PA Cambridge Economic Consultants (1995). Some of the key characteristics are highlighted in Table 13.2.

Table 13.2 Key characteristics of sampled establishments

	% establishments responding
Establishment status	
Independent single site business	55
Head office/main business with branches elsewhere	11
Branch/subsidiary of a company headquartered elsewhere in the UK or abroad	34
Employment sizeband	
1–19	66
20–49	19
50–99	8
100+	8
Business sector	
Manufacturing	45
Construction	4
Distribution	17
Retail	16
Other services	19

RESULTS

How Important has EZ-attracted Inward Investment been as a Component of Total Activity on EZs by Comparison with NSUs?

The presence in the sample database of 185 establishments that came onto the zones following designation but claim they would have located outside of the local area of the EZs (within a 10 mile radius) in the absence of EZ policy demonstrates that EZ policy has had some success in attracting inward investment, even when bearing in mind the possibility of an over-representation of inward investors amongst survey respondents. They accounted for approximately 11 600 jobs at the time of de-designation. By comparison NSUs accounted for 235 establishments (22.6 per cent of the sample) and 3399 jobs, equal to 9 per cent of the total jobs on the EZs and only 29 per cent of the jobs generated directly by inward investors (see Table 13.3).

Table 13.3 Types of establishments on EZs and associated employment

	No. establishments	No. employees	Percent of establishments	Percent of employees
Inward investors	185	11 637	17.8	31.0
New start	235	3 399	22.6	9.0
Not locally additional	619	22 560	59.6	60.0
Total	1 039	37 596	100.0	100.0

Note: 'Not locally additional' comprises EZ-influenced short distance transfers, immobile operations and pre-designation operations

What are the Key Distinguishing Characteristics of Inward Investors Compared with NSUs?

Table 13.4 provides the basic information on the sector and size of the two types of companies on the EZs. There are no significant differences in the sectoral characteristics of inward investors and NSUs. Both inward investors and NSUs are relatively concentrated in manufacturing industries with about one-half of their establishments in this sector. Retail and distribution services together account for between one-quarter and one-third of establishments, and other services make up the remainder, approximately one-fifth of establishments, for both inward investors and NSUs. However there are statistically significant differences in the size of inward investors and NSUs. Thus NSUs are typically smaller than inward investors, with 81.5 per cent of NSUs employing less than 20 workers compared with only 51.1 per cent of inward investors. This of course is likely given that the inward investor establishments involve either relocations of previously existing activities and jobs or the establishment of new activities by mature firms already operating outside of the local area.

Table 13.4 General characteristics of EZ establishments

	% of each establishment type	
Variable description	Inward investors	New starts
Industrial sector		
Manufacturing	53.3	49.4
Distribution	14.4	16.3
Retail	11.1	14.6
Services	21.1	19.8
Total	100.0	100.0
No. respondents	(180)	(233)
Employment size		
1–19 employees*	51.1	81.5
20–49 employees*	24.2	12.4
50–99 employees	7.9	3.9
100+ employees*	16.9	2.1
Total	100.0	100.0
No. respondents	(178)	(233)

Note: * Significant difference at 5% level (Chi-square test of independence between inward investors and new starts).

At the other end of the size distribution of EZ inward investors and NSUs only 2.1 per cent of the latter employ more than 100 employees compared with 16.1 per cent of inward investors. This suggests that even after a decade of EZ status the contribution of the average NSU to job creation on the designated areas is significantly less than that of the inward investor.

What have been the Key Policy and Non-policy Factors that have Influenced Inward Investors and NSUs to Locate on EZs?

Table 13.5 sets out survey responses on what attracted inward investors and NSUs to locate on EZs. For both inward investors and NSUs the EZ policy instruments have been an important locational influence and the most important policy instrument has been tax relief benefits on business rates. Rates relief was an important influence on 62 per cent of firms, providing them with long-term operating cost benefits. Capital tax allowance benefits, reducing the costs of initial project development on the EZ, were an important influence on 33 per cent of inward investors but only 12.5 per cent of NSUs. Only a minority of inward investors and NSUs tended to regard the EZ planning and 'red tape' initiatives as important. A number of non-policy factors have also influenced the location of inward investors and NSUs on the zones. For inward investors, both land and labour availability influenced 27 per cent of establishments, a significantly higher proportion than in the case of NSUs (5.4 per cent and 13.8 per cent respectively).

Table 13.5 Influences on the decision to locate or start-up on an EZ

Variable considered important to location or start-up on the zones	% establishments	
	Inward investors	New starts
Zone instruments:		
Rates relief	62.5	62.1
Capital allowance tax benefits*	33.0	12.5
Relaxation of normal planning procedures and controls*	10.8	8.0
Reduced statistical requirements	5.1	5.4
Other zone measures	8.5	4.9
Other factors:		
Non-EZ government incentives*	14.2	10.7
Premises availability*	19.3	57.6
Land availability*	26.7	5.4
Supply opportunities to other businesses on the EZ*	2.8	8.9
Purchasing opportunities from other businesses on the EZ*	0.6	1.3
Opportunities for cooperation with other businesses on the EZ	2.3	5.4
Attractive physical environment	18.2	12.5
Available labour force*	26.7	13.8
No. respondents	(176)	(224)

Note: * Significant difference at 5% level (Mann-Whitney U test of differences in ranked scores between inward investors and new starts). The percentages identify establishments giving a factor a score of 4 or 5 on a scale where 1 is of no importance and 5 is of great importance.

The other major difference between inward investors and NSUs relates to the importance of premises availability. Thus 57.6 per cent of NSUs regarded the availability of premises as an important locational attribute of

EZs compared with 19.3 per cent of NSUs. Inward investors were also more likely to have been influenced by non-EZ government incentives than NSUs.

The fact that inward investors put more emphasis on capital tax allowances, other government incentives, land availability and labour availability may partly be linked to their larger average size and investment than NSUs. NSUs were more likely to emphasise the possession of existing premises on the zones or being able to obtain new premises.

As well as demonstrating the relative importance to inward investors of different policy and non-policy factors, Table 13.5 also shows that local clustering effects on EZs have been relatively less important in attracting inward investors onto the zones than for NSUs. Very low proportions of establishments were attracted by supply or purchasing opportunities to other firms on the zones but these factors were more important for NSUs than for inward investors.

What Have Been the Relative Impacts of Inward Investment and NSUs on Local Area Regeneration in Terms of Local Employment Opportunities and Economic Linkages?

There are important differences between inward investors and NSUs in the scale and nature of their local labour market impacts. Table 13.6 presents the analysis of the type of labour employed by the two groups of firms and the extent to which they recruited their labour locally. With respect to the former the evidence shows that new start-ups typically employed a much higher proportion of managers, professionals and technologists than inward investors. If skilled workers are also included the same conclusion emerges. Thus managers, professionals, technologists and skilled workers account for just under 60 per cent of the workforce in NSUs compared with 43 per cent of the workforce of inward investors. In part this reflects the smaller number of employees in the typical NSU compared with the inward investor. Employment of professional and more skilled workers would be unlikely to increase *pari passu* with the expansion of the firms workforce more generally. In addition, inward investors are often branch plants or subsidiaries which can have a tendency to employ mainly routine back-office and administrative staff and assembly workers with more skilled workers remaining in or close to the companies headquarters.

It is also apparent from Table 13.6 that NSUs are more likely to recruit a much higher proportion of their managers, professionals and technologists locally than are inward investors. This may reflect the potential for the inward investment project to be staffed by key more senior and skilled workers transferred from plants or offices located outside the local area but it may also be linked to the relocation or commuting costs which NSUs may be less well placed (or willing) to bear than more mature and larger inward investors.

Table 13.6 Local impacts of EZ establishments: labour composition and local recruitment

	Inward investors	New starts
Labour composition		
Median % of managers, professionals and technologists in workforce*	22.9	30.2
Median % of managers, professionals/ technologists and skilled manual/technical in workforce*	42.9	59.7
No. respondents	(169)	(230)
Local recruitment		
% of firms recruiting the majority of managers locally**	33.3	70.9
No. respondents	(174)	(213)
% of firms recruiting the majority of professionals and technologists locally**	36.4	68.6
No. respondents	(99)	(70)
% of firms recruiting the majority of their administrative and clerical staff locally	87.4	92.5
No. respondents	(151)	(159)
% of firms recruiting the majority of their skilled manual and technical workers locally	81.8	85.5
No. respondents	(110)	(117)
% of firms recruiting the majority of their semi-skilled manual workers locally	94.5	90.7
No. respondents	(91)	(118)
% of firms recruiting the majority of their unskilled workers locally	95.2	91.9
No. respondents	(104)	(86)
% of local recruits who were unemployed*	33.7	44.6
No. respondents	(145)	(175)

Notes: * Significant difference at 5% level (Mann–Whitney U test of differences between inward investors and new starts).

** Significant difference at 5% level (Chi-square test of independence between inward investors and new starts).

It is also likely that the latter may be more accustomed to advertising and searching for labour at a regional and national level than NSUs, whilst NSUs have greater knowledge and awareness of local labour market recruitment opportunities for senior managers, professionals and technologists compared with firms coming from outside the local area. For the less skilled groups in the labour market recruitment tends to be primarily local and there are no significant differences between inward investors and NSUs.

From a policy perspective it is important to note that both inward investors and NSUs recruit a significant proportion of their labour from the pool of unemployed. Moreover, NSUs are more likely than inward investors to recruit unemployed (44.6 per cent) than inward investors (33.7 per cent), although it should be recalled that the absolute number of jobs created locally by inward investors is much higher than for NSUs.

A second important way in which firms attracted to locate on EZs contribute to local area regeneration and employment creation is through their collaborative links with and purchasing from local suppliers. Table 13.7 shows that the proportion of local purchases by NSUs is about twice that of inward investors. However this relatively greater local economic impact from local purchases may be partly offset by the greater displacement effects of NSUs on local competitors by comparison with inward investors. Thus 36 per cent of NSUs claimed to have competitors in the local area compared with just over 20 per cent of inward investors.

Table 13.7 Inward investor customer, supplier and competitor linkages

Variable Measure	Inward investors	New starts
% of competitors located within the local area*	20.4	36.0
No. respondents	(171)	(207)
% sales to customers abroad*	13.1	4.2
No. respondents	(181)	(226)
% sales to customers outside of the local area*	86.2	61.6
No. respondents	(181)	(226)
% of purchases by value made from local suppliers*	13.3	27.5
No. respondents	(172)	(221)

Note: * Significant difference at 5% (Mann–Whitney U test of differences between inward investors and new starts).

On the demand side the main distinction between inward investors and NSUs is the greater dependence of NSUs on the local market, but even so, NSUs make over 60 per cent of their sales outside the local area, although neglible sales to customers abroad. This greater 'export' orientation of inward investors suggests that they may be an important source of export-led growth for the local economy in which the EZs are located even though their local supply linkages may be relatively weak.

Are There Differences Between Types of Zone (Urban, Remote, Accessible) in the Relative Scale, Characteristics and Impacts of Inward Investors and NSUs?

Although the above analysis has identified some important differences between inward investors and NSUs in their impact on the local economy of the EZ, it should be recognised that these impacts may vary across the different types of EZ. The starting point for investigating this possibility is the analysis of the distribution of inward investors and NSUs across the three EZ types – Rural EZs, Accessible EZs and Urban Core EZs. Table 13.8 shows that inward investors accounted for a relatively high proportion of employment on Accessible EZs compared with their importance on Urban Core Zones where NSUs made a relatively large contribution to employment.

If locational factors vary in their relative importance across the different types of zones for each of the two types of firms, this may have significant implications for how the EZ managing authorities shape their policy package and target and market to firms that might locate on the EZ. The evidence shows that the main factors influencing the location or start-up does differ across the different types of EZ in a number of important respects. Thus capital allowance tax benefits are more likely to be an important locational policy factor for Rural and Accessible Zones.

Equally the availability of labour is more frequently cited as an important locational factor for inward investors on Rural and Accesible EZs by comparison with Urban Core Zones. Land availability emerges as a relatively important locational factor for inward investors on Accessible EZs. Suitable available premises remains a key locational factor for the majority of NSUs irrespective of the type of zone.

It is also important for policy-makers concerned with different zone types to know whether the impacts of NSUs and inward investors vary according to the type of zone on which they are located. If NSUs or inward investors are particularly beneficial for a certain zone type then it may make sense to weight the zone development strategy towards this type of firm.

Table 13.8 Types of establishments on EZs and associated employment, by zone type

	Rural Zones		Accessible Zones		Urban Core Zones	
	% ests	% empl.	% ests	% empl	% ests	% empl.
Inward investors	12.9	15.8	24.6	43.6	8.5	14.1
New start	20.1	8.6	22.7	8.1	33.0	25.1
Not locally additional	67.0	75.6	52.7	48.3	58.5	60.8
Total	100.0	100.0	100.0	100.0	100.0	100.0

Note: 'Not locally additional' comprises EZ-influenced short distance transfers, immobile operations, pre-designation operations.

Table 13.9 The main influences on location or start-up, by zone type

	% of inward investors		% new starts	
	Rural	Accessible	Urban Core	Rural
Rates relief	62.5	62.3	63.0	63.6
Capital allowance tax benefits*	37.5	37.7	22.2	9.1
Premises availability	2.9	67.6	29.4	51.5
Land availability*	12.5	34.2	13.0	6.1
Available labour force*	37.5	33.3	11.1	6.1
No. respondents	(9)	(117)	(59)	(33)

Note: * Significant difference at 5% level (Kruskal–Wallis test of differences in ranked scores between inward investors and between new starts on different zone types) The percentages identify establishments giving a factor a score of 4 or 5 on a scale where 1 is of no importance and 5 is of great importance.

There is also the issue of whether EZ policy itself is likely to be more successful in one type of location compared with another. Table 13.10 examines some of the main impacts by zone type.

In terms of impacts on labour and recruitment, there are no statistically significant differences across types of EZs in the skill composition of labour recruited by either inward investors or NSUs. However, there are significant differences in the recruitment of the unemployed across zone types. Thus the percentage of unemployed recruited by inward investors is much higher on rural zones than on other types of zone. No significant differences across types of zone emerge for NSUs.

Table 13.10 The main local impacts, by zone type

	Inward investors			New starts		
	Rural	Acces-sible	Urban Core	Rural	Acces-sible	Urban Core
Impacts on labour an recruitment						
Median % of managers, profes-sionals, technologists and skilled labour in the workforce	50.0	42.1	44.4	62.5	56.4	60.0
No. respondents	(7)	(107)	(55)	(35)	(106)	(89)
% recruiting the majority of managers locally	57.1	28.8	39.3	83.9	70.3	66.7
No. respondents	(9)	(117)	(59)	(31)	(101)	(81)
% of local recruits who were unemployed*	55.0	37.9	23.4	50.6	43.8	43.4
No. respondents	(9)	(117)	(59)	(24)	(84)	(67)
Impacts on customer and suppliers						
% of competitors located within the local area*	17.9	9.2	42.2	38.8	23.1	51.3
% sales to customers abroad*	14.4	15.1	8.9	2.8	6.9	1.6
% sales to customers outside local area*	87.5	91.3	76.1	46.2	71.7	55.3
% of purchases made from local suppliers*	11.4	13.7	12.8	32.6	18.3	36.6
No. respondents	(9)	(117)	(59)	(34)	(105)	(87)

Note: * Significant difference at 5% level (Kruskal-Wallis test of differences between inward investors and between new starts on different types).

In terms of economic linkages, the inward investment attracted by EZ policy appears to be relatively less beneficial on Urban Core Zones than on other zone types. Thus, potential displacement of local competitors is higher and the proportion of exports out of the local area is lower on Urban Core than on Accessible or Rural Zones. This is probably linked to the sectoral structure of inward investment on Urban Core Zones and the relatively greater density of local economic activity. For NSUs, the picture is more complicated. As with inward investors, potential displacement of competitors is relatively high in Urban Core Zones. However, NSU exports are greater on Urban Core Zones than on Rural Zones, although both are lower than on Accessible Zones, and the level of local purchases by NSUs on Urban Core Zones is relatively important. This suggests that perhaps NSUs are a better target for policy than inward investment in the case of Urban Core Zones.

CONCLUSION

The EZ experiment in the UK aimed to address the problem of severe local concentrations of economic and social distress and physical dereliction of factory/office space and public infrastructure through locally targeted tax incentives and the removal or streamlined administration of certain statutory or administrative controls. One of the major aims was to generate additional economic activity and employment in the zones and the local areas. The attraction of inward investment and new enterprise development were key mechanisms by which the EZ experiment would secure the objectives.

Evidence on the relative impact of the two firm types shows that whilst there appear to have been a greater number of NSUs than inward investors on the surveyed zones (22.6 per cent of establishments compared with 17.8 per cent), inward investors were much more important for job creation, accounting for approximately 31.0 per cent of jobs at the time of de-designation compared with only 9.0 per cent in NSUs. Clearly, NSUs are typically smaller than inward investors, with 81.5 per cent of NSUs employing less than 20 workers compared with only 51.1 per cent of inward investors.

For both NSUs and inward investors the most important influence on location or start-up on the zones has been tax relief on business rates. However, there are certain differences in the aspects of EZ policy that influenced the start-up of NSUs on the zones compared with inward investors. These should be taken into account in future policy design. Thus capital tax allowance benefits, land and labour availability were relatively important to inward investors, whilst NSUs were more influenced by premises availability.

In terms of local labour market impacts, whilst inward investors accounted for a much greater volume of job generation, NSUs typically have more highly skilled occupational profiles than inward investors, are more likely to recruit their managers and skilled workers locally and are more likely than inward investors to recruit from the unemployed. There are also differences in the impacts of the two types of firm on linked suppliers and competitors. NSUs are more likely to purchase locally than inward investors but also seem to have greater displacement effects on local competitors. By contrast, inward investors have a greater export orientation.

The investigation has also identified some differences between zones located in different types of area – Rural, Accessible, Urban Core – in terms of the local impacts of NSUs and inward investors. Thus inward investors are relatively numerous on Accessible and Rural EZs, whilst NSUs are more numerous on Urban Core EZs. Moreover, inward investors appear to be relatively less beneficial on Urban Core Zones in terms of their economic linkages, with higher local displacement and lower non-local sales than other zone types. Policies aiming to tackle the problems of inner city areas may therefore find it more fruitful to stress instruments that favour NSUs, in particular premises availability.

REFERENCES

Butler, S. (1981), *Enterprise zones: Greenlining the Inner Cities*, London: Heinemann Educational.

Clarke, S. (1982), 'Enterprise zones: seeking the neighbourhood nexus', *Urban Affairs Quarterly*, **18** (1), 53–71.

Department of the Environment (1995), *Enterprise zone Information 1981–1994*, London: HMSO.

Glickman, N. (1984), 'Economic policy and the cities: in search of Reagan's real urban policy', *Journal of the American Planning Association*, **50**, 471–8.

Gunn, E. (1993), 'The growth of Enterprise zones: A policy transformation', *Policy Studies Journal*, **21** (3), 432–49.

Massey, D. (1982), 'Enterprise zones: a political issue', *International Journal of Urban and Regional Research*, **6** (3), 429–34.

PACEC (PA Cambridge Economic Consultants) (1987), *An Evaluation of the Enterprise zone Experiment*, London: HMSO.

PACEC (PA Cambridge Economic Consultants) (1995), *Final Evaluation of Enterprise Zones*, London: HMSO.

Tyler, P. (1993), 'Enterprise zones: the British experience', International Economic Insights, May/June, 42–3.

Urban Task Force (1999), *Towards an Urban Renaissance. Final Report of the Urban Task Force,* Chaired by Lord Rogers of Riverside, London: Department of the Environment, Transport and the Regions.

14. Rural Areas in Crisis? The Role of the Welfare State in Income Creation: The Case of Denmark

Chris Jensen-Butler, Bjarne Madsen and Søren Caspersen

1 INTRODUCTION

Many West European states are facing the prospect of undertaking substantial changes in welfare state provisions for their citizens. These changes arise from the political goal of limiting growth of public expenditure or even reducing public expenditure in the face of what are perceived to be increasing demands on the welfare state. The implementation of such policies leads to interesting regional economic questions concerning the role of the welfare state in creating regional income growth and interregional income convergence. There is a body of evidence that suggests that welfare states in general create a geographical redistribution of income to the advantage of poorer regions, but little work has been done to estimate the magnitude of these effects. The main weight of earlier studies has been on comparative static analysis and examination of the direct effects of welfare state expenditure.

Rural areas in West European countries have generally lower income levels than more urbanised areas within the same country, and it can be expected that transfer incomes and public consumption play a greater role in income creation in such areas. This chapter examines the role of the welfare state in Denmark in income creation in rural areas. Rural areas are grouped into types and the effect of the welfare state on income creation as well as the effects of other income-generating factors in the different types of rural area are examined. The results indicate the need to differentiate between types of area in order to understand the process of income creation in rural areas.

Denmark is a particularly interesting example because of the relative importance of the welfare state in the Danish economy. Both public consumption and transfer incomes are very large, as a percentage of GDP. The development of disposable income in the period 1980–95 in different types of Danish rural area is examined and decomposition techniques are used to assess the relative importance of different components of income creation, including welfare state expenditure and taxation, on changing patterns of disposable income. This chapter takes further an earlier study on the regional economic impact of the Danish welfare state undertaken by Hansen and Jensen-Butler (1996).

Section 2 examines the literature on the regional economic consequences of the welfare state. Section 3 describes changes in disposable income in Denmark in the period 1980-95, both by region and by type of rural area, in order to set the scene. In this period there has been convergence in levels of disposable income per capita between rural and more urbanised areas in Denmark. In Section 4 decomposition analysis is discussed in some depth and the model, LINE, used in the decomposition, is presented. Section 5 outlines the methodology of cumulative decomposition, this being one of the two approaches to decomposition used, seen in relation to LINE. Section 6 describes the second approach used, single component decomposition, again in relation to LINE. The results of both types of decomposition are presented in Section 7 which permits evaluation of the effects of both the welfare state and other factors on income creation for rural areas as a whole and also by type of rural area. Finally, Section 8 draws conclusions from the analysis and examines policy prescriptions with respect to income creation in rural areas.

2 THE REGIONAL ECONOMIC CONSEQUENCES OF THE WELFARE STATE

There is a growing body of work on the relationship between welfare state expenditure, revenues that finance welfare state expenditure and central regional macroeconomic variables such as gross factor incomes, disposable income and employment.

Most studies examine only the direct effects of the welfare state on regional income and employment levels, though some attempts have been made to include indirect and induced effects, as well as dynamic effects, in a broader macroeconomic framework.

Work on these questions can be loosely grouped under three headings: studies of financial flows between regions; studies of the effects of welfare state expenditure on disposable income; and modelling approaches to the regional economic effects of welfare state expenditure.

It should be noted that the definition of what constitutes welfare state expenditure is in itself ambiguous. There is a primary distinction between public sector consumption and transfer incomes, the sizes of which, in relation to GDP, vary considerably between different countries. In 1988 income transfers were 27.6 per cent of Danish GDP at factor cost, whilst in the Netherlands this reached 30.9 per cent. In 1987 public consumption constituted 30.1 per cent of GDP at factor cost in Denmark, whilst in Germany the corresponding figure was 22.1 per cent and in the UK 24.4 per cent. In Denmark the education and health sectors would be regarded as a part of the welfare state, as would significant elements of such activities as recreation and culture, which may not be the case in other countries.

2.1 Studies of Income Creation and the Welfare State

Examples of studies of financial flows between regions are for the case of the UK, Short (1978, 1984), and for Sweden, NUTEK (1994). A general result from these studies is that net flows of welfare state expenditure in per capita terms favour poorer and more peripheral regions when direct effects alone are considered. Whether or not these effects are sufficient to create regional economic convergence over time between regions in a country depends on both changes in welfare state provision and taxation over time in relation to other factors such as the regional distribution of employment and productivity growth. Everything else being equal, it is changes in welfare state provision and taxation, which create changes in disposable income.

The regional direct effects of welfare state expenditure on per capita disposable incomes follow from the conclusions concerning financial flows. A number of authors in different countries have pointed out that interregional flows of social security-related expenditure in quantitative terms by far exceed expenditures related to regional policy. Hence, it is argued, the regional economic effects of (net) social security expenditure are potentially much more substantial than expenditure occurring under regional policy. Thus, policies which are not explicitly spatial in their conception, may well have more substantial regional economic impacts than specifically spatial economic policies (Oosterhaven and Stoffelsma, 1990; Disney, 1984; Groes, 1994, 1997; Hansen and Jensen-Butler, 1996).

Stoffelsma and Oosterhaven (1989) examined the regional distribution of welfare state expenditure in the Netherlands in the period 1979–86 and concluded that social security benefits led to a 40 per cent reduction in the inequality of regional primary incomes per capita in the period. In general, the poorer and more peripheral regions received above average per capita welfare state expenditure, whilst the core regions received lower per capita expenditure. However, there were important anomalies: a core region such as Noord-Holland received above average expenditure per capita, probably explained by the urban problems of the Amsterdam conurbation, whilst a few poorer and peripheral regions, such as Overijssel, had under average per capita expenditure. Their study also undertook a decomposition of welfare state expenditure in order to examine the overall pattern as well as the anomalies. They used a cumulative decomposition technique (discussed below) in order to identify the relative influences of:

1. Regional differences in numbers of recipients per inhabitant in each region, as compared with the national proportion.
2. Differences in average benefit per recipient by region as compared with the national level.
3. Interaction effects between 1. and 2.

They also analysed the regional economic effects of different welfare state programmes, further decomposing 2 into:

4. The relative contribution of high and low benefit per recipient programmes in each region.
5. The contribution of high or low benefit levels within each programme in each region.
6. Interaction between 5 and 6.

They conclude that: 'The core regions have less benefit recipients per capita and a lower average benefit per recipient than the Netherlands as a whole. The peripheral regions, on the other hand, have relatively more recipients and higher benefit levels than the national average. The intermediate regions show a more diverse pattern' (p. 239). Decomposition techniques are the central methodology used in the present study. However, their 1989 study of income generation involved only welfare state related expenditures.

Oosterhaven and Stoffelsma (1990) undertook an analysis of interregional net financial flows in the Netherlands, examining both revenue and expenditure flows, documenting that the seven Dutch provinces which had a net inflow of public expenditure in the period 1979–86 received net expenditure amounting to 1.1 per cent of Dutch GNP. These provinces were all poorer and more peripheral. The major net contributor was Zuid-Holland, a core region, whilst the other three net contributors were in regional economic terms less clearly core. They conclude that these net flows reduce differences in per capita incomes between the richest and poorest regions by up to 24 per cent. The study of net flows reinforces the conclusions from the study of expenditures alone. Hansen and Jensen-Butler (1996) document similar core to periphery flows of net expenditure in Denmark, using data from the Local Authorities' Research Institute (AKF). They then go on to examine the role of social security payments in income creation at municipal level in the Danish peripheral region of West Lolland, showing clearly the growing share of social security payments in disposable income in the region during a period of economic crisis, whilst in Denmark as a whole and also in Greater Copenhagen, this share was stable.

In addition to the work of Hansen and Jensen-Butler, a number of Danish studies have examined public expenditure flows and the role of the welfare state in regional income creation. One of the first studies of the regional economic effects of changes in taxation and public expenditure was undertaken in connection with a general economic reform of the welfare state proposed by the then conservative-liberal government in 1989 (Madsen 1989). The results showed that the effects on regional disposable income per inhabitant were positive for Greater Copenhagen whilst they were negative in the more peripheral regions in Denmark. The main reason for this pattern was that a principal element in the reform was a reduction in average levels of income tax, a change that favoured the richer regions. Reductions in public expenditure and increases in user payments and specific elements of taxation, such as environmental taxes, did not exhibit major regional variation. Methodologically, the study was a straightforward analysis of the spatial impact of taxation and expenditure changes at regional level, using the national–regional economic database of AKF.

This was followed by a number of studies of the consequences of taxation and public expenditure for regional disposable income in Danish regions. A study of flows of revenue and expenditure for the peripheral island of Bornholm (Madsen and Rasmussen, 1991) demonstrated that there was a considerable net financial inflow to the island through the public sector, despite the fact that tourism is an important element in the island economy. Also, at the same time an incipient independence movement for the island was claiming that the island was de facto economically independent of Denmark and therefore could opt to join a Baltic community instead. The study revealed that this was not the case. A more general study of interregional financial flows in the public sector for the 16 Danish regions followed (Nørskov, 1991). This revealed the same general pattern, namely that the richest regions (principally Greater Copenhagen) had a net deficit in relation to public finances whilst poorer regions had a net surplus. Another study, undertaken at the level of municipalities (275 in all) provided results which exhibited the same pattern at a lower level of spatial disaggregation (Hansen, 1991).

2.2 Beyond the Direct Effects

There are four main problems associated with these studies. First, the derived effects (indirect and induced) of the public sector financial flows are not examined. Second, the dynamic effects of changes in welfare state provision working through their effects on factor supply and prices are not included. Third, the studies tend to mix the problems of identification of the absolute magnitude of financial flows in the space economy (and changes in other key variables, such as population and employment) with the question of the extent to which the flows contribute to regional income convergence or divergence. Fourth, the studies are generally cross-sectional, providing a static picture at one point of time.

Two recent Danish studies have attempted to remedy these deficiencies. Dam et al. (1997) have undertaken an analysis of the regional economic effects of a reduction in welfare state-related expenditure and changes in taxation in Denmark which includes the derived and dynamic effects on the regional and local economy. Madsen and Caspersen (1998) and Ekspertudvalget (1998) have analysed changes in disposable income per inhabitant in the period 1980–95 for Danish regions and municipalities.

The study by Dam et al. (1997) attempted to get beyond identification of the direct effects of changes in welfare state expenditure, drawing in both derived and dynamic effects of such changes. The basis of the study was a national level forecast of central macroeconomic variables, derived from the national macroeconomic model ADAM built by Statistics Denmark (Dam, 1996). This model was used to create a forecast for 2010 by extrapolating existing trends. The forecast was then used as a baseline to examine the regional and local economic effects of two scenarios involving changes in welfare state expenditure for the year 2010. The macroeconomic model LINE (described below) was utilised to model these regional and local economic effects. The first scenario involved a reduction of current welfare state expenditure of DKr 20 billion (3 billion ECU) in the period 1997–2000. This was divided into a reduction of DKr 6 billion in government final demand, involving in turn a reduction of the public sector labour force by 20 000 and a reduction in government transfers of DKr 14 billion, or about 7 per cent, spread evenly over the four-year period. The second scenario involved the same expenditure reduction, accompanied by a corresponding reduction in taxation of DKr 20 billion.

The initial or direct effects of a reduction in transfers on disposable income can be seen in Figure 14.1. The hardest hit areas are the most peripheral and the poorest: the southern islands of Lolland-Falster, Northern Jutland, remoter parts of eastern Jutland, some of the smaller islands, South-West Jutland and North-West Zealand. The areas least affected are the richer Copenhagen suburbs and its periphery as well as the manufacturing areas in central and western Jutland. In the 1970s and 1980s Denmark experienced substantial relocation of manufacturing employment from Greater Copenhagen and to a lesser extent other cities, to rural areas in Jutland, where agriculture was and is still relatively important (Maskell, 1986; Jensen-Butler, 1992)

However, when the full derived and dynamic effects of reductions in welfare state expenditures are included, as shown in relation to changes in disposable income in Figure 14.2, then it is clear that the rural areas are not, in general, affected negatively. The hardest hit areas are the larger cities, both provincial cities and Copenhagen as well as some very peripheral areas. Again, the richer suburbs of Greater Copenhagen perform relatively well. This pattern reflects the distribution of manufacturing and service activity and indicates that the simple idea that peripheral areas will be hardest hit by reductions in welfare state expenditure must be treated with caution when derived and dynamic effects are taken into account. In particular, industrial exports seem to benefit from reductions in public expenditure. Reduction in public sector employment increases unemployment and lowers wages through labour market reactions. This cost reduction improves competitiveness in foreign export markets. Growing exports create expansion of economic activity in manufacturing industries, which is to the advantage of industrial areas, which in Denmark are in part at least rural and peripheral. Spillover effects will have a positive influence on the economies of the more urbanised regions.

The studies by Madsen and Caspersen (1998) and Ekspertudvalget (1998) of changes in disposable income by municipality leads directly into the present study and introduce the issues of ex ante and ex post analysis.

2.3 Ex Ante and Ex Post Approaches

Model-based analysis of the role of the welfare state in income creation by region, as exemplified above, is often ex ante in its approach, providing answers to what-if questions, embodied in scenarios. Such questions can address changes in financial flows between regions, the direct effects of changes in welfare state expenditure on disposable income or analyses of direct, indirect, induced and dynamic effects.

An alternative modelling approach is ex post, where historical data can be used to identify the relative contributions of different causal variables in income creation.

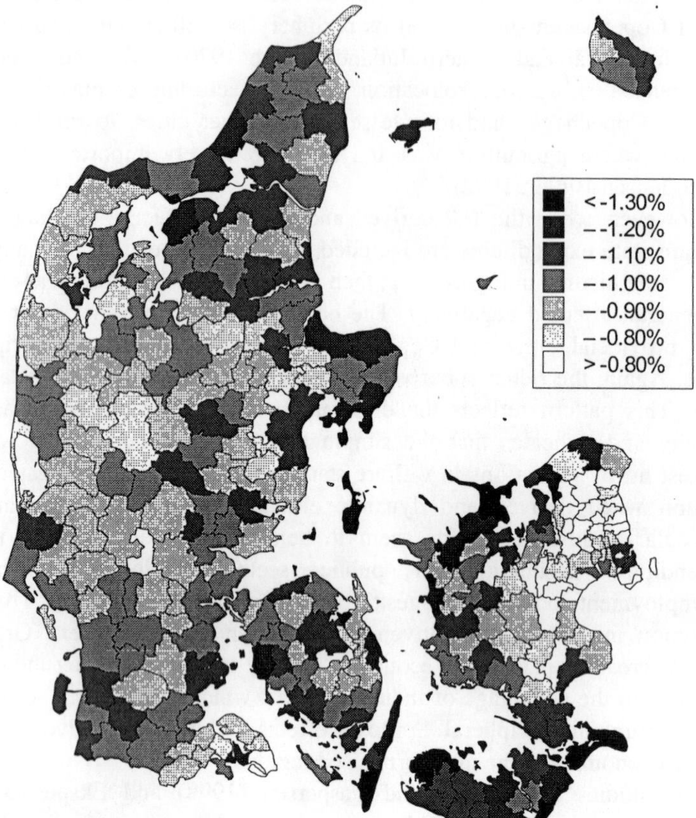

Figure 14.1 Disposable income 2010, initial effects of a transfer reduction, change with respect to baseline

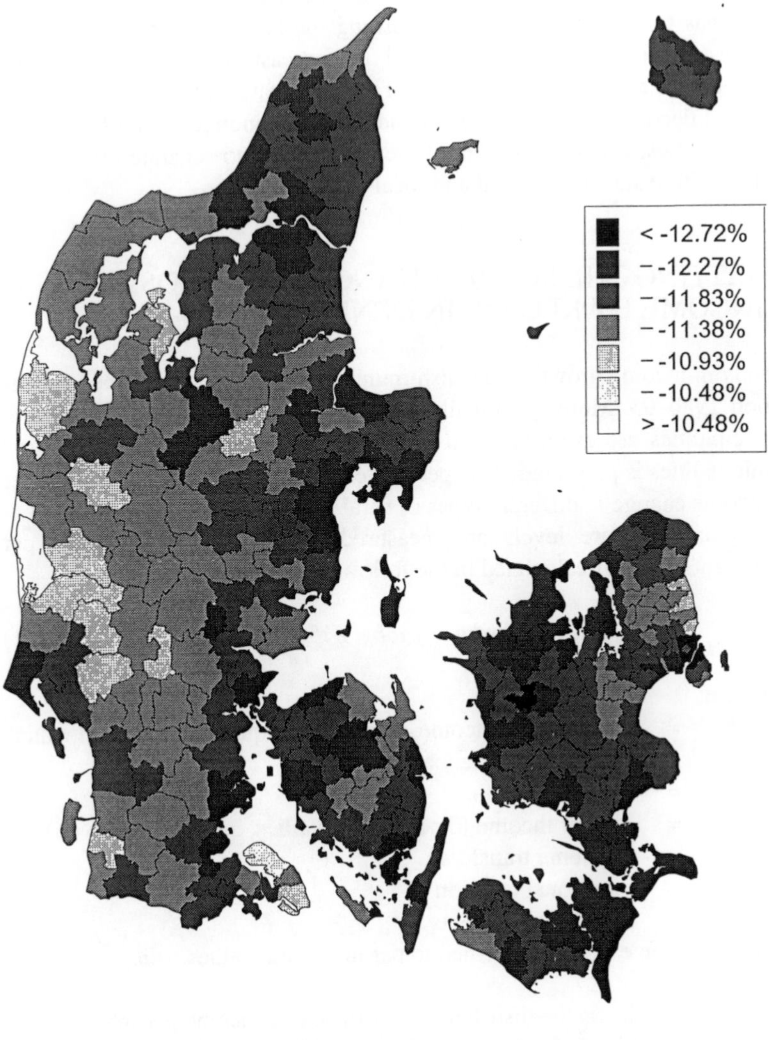

Figure 14.2 Disposable income 2010, scenario 1

Time series econometric analysis is a standard tool and increasingly, decomposition techniques are being used to undertake ex post analysis of changes in disposable income over a period where data exist for one year at the beginning and one at the end of the period. Both approaches require specification of an underlying explanatory model. The present study utilises decomposition techniques based on a regional economic model. The real role of the welfare state in the process of regional economic convergence, which has taken place in Denmark during the last 20 years, is examined. The lessons of history can be used to forecast future local economic development and to assess the role of welfare state in this process. Using different decomposition techniques and a local economic model for Danish municipalities, it is possible, in a time perspective, to separate out the role of the welfare state in regional and local income creation.

3 SETTING THE SCENE: CHANGES IN DISPOSABLE INCOME BY REGION IN DENMARK, 1980-95

Trends in income growth in Danish municipalities are first outlined for the period 1980–95. More specifically, changes in disposable income for rural municipalities are examined and for this purpose a classification of rural municipalities is presented. This permits examination of patterns and causes of income change in different types of rural area.

Regional welfare levels are measured using disposable income per inhabitant, which is calculated in the following manner:

$$ydibg = ylorbg + yaobg + tbg - sbg - ysfrbg \tag{14.1}$$

where:

ydibg	=	disposable income, persons with qualification level *g* and place of residence *b*
ylorbg	=	earned income
yaobg	=	other income (dividends, royalties, interest, and so on)
tbg	=	income transfers
sbg	=	personal taxation
ysfrb	=	interest payments

ydibg is then easily transformed to per inhabitant values, *ydibgq*.

Figure 14.3 shows the distribution of disposable income per inhabitant in all of Denmark's 275 municipalities in 1995. The figure shows that disposable income is highest in Greater Copenhagen and in the major cities as well as municipalities with a high level of industrial activity. In the peripheral areas, the larger islands and in West Lolland (the extreme southwestern part of the island south of Zealand where Copenhagen is located), disposable income is especially low. Figure 14.4 shows growth in disposable income 1980–95 in current prices and it can be seen that rural areas in Jutland have in many cases experienced above average growth in disposable income, whilst the cities, Greater Copenhagen, Århus, Odense and Ålborg, have experienced below average income growth.

For rural areas the pattern is as shown in Table 14.1, where the classification of rural municipalities can also be seen. For the 109 rural municipalities as a whole, disposable income in 1995 lies about 10 per cent under national average (column 2). Rural municipalities are defined as municipalities where the largest town has less than 3000 inhabitants. For agricultural municipalities, defined as having at least twice the national share of income arising from agriculture, disposable income is a little more than 10 per cent under national average.

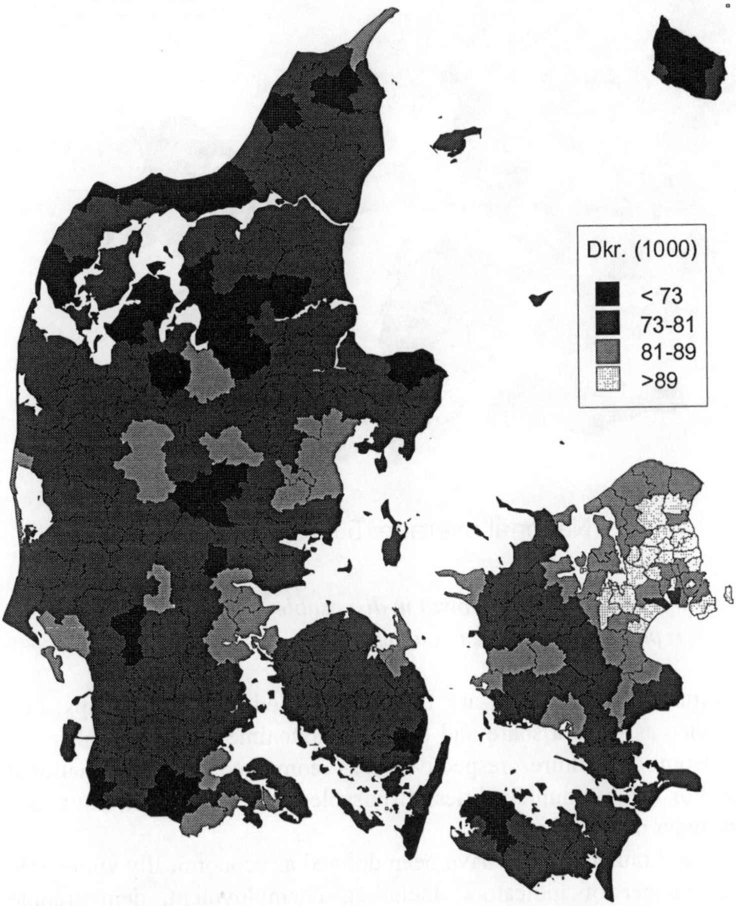

Figure 14.3 Disposable income per inhabitant by residence 1995, current prices

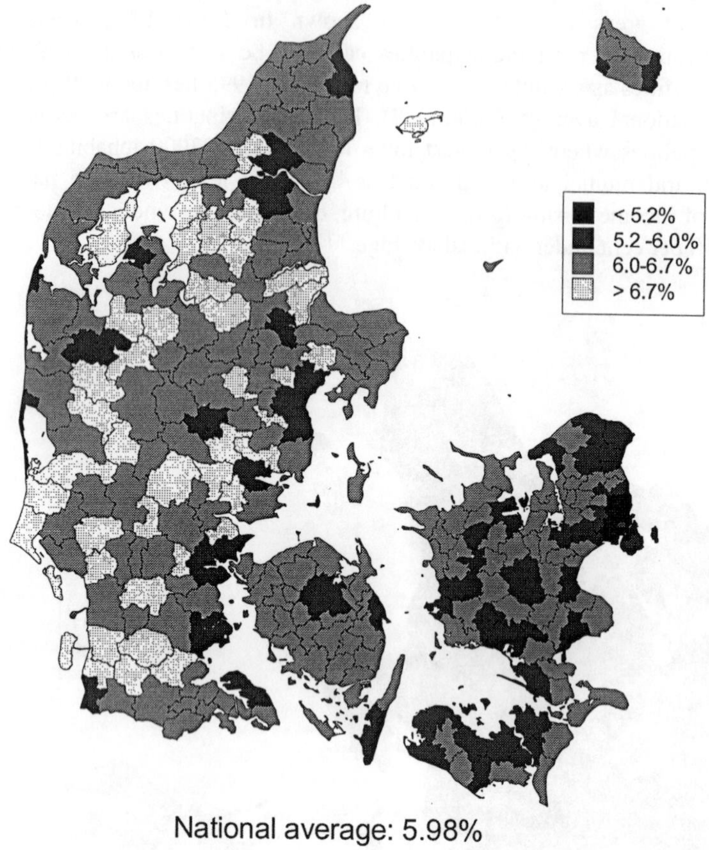

Figure 14.4 Average annual growth in disposable income 1980–95, by place of residence in current prices

Agricultural municipalities are further classified into two groups, one having twice as large a share and the other four times as large a share of income from agriculture, respectively, as compared with the national average. For fishing municipalities, disposable income is higher, but still 5 per cent under national average.

Some rural municipalities have been defined as economically vulnerable using a number of indicators, including unemployment, demographic decline and small tax base. These municipalities have been further subdivided into three subgroups with different degrees of vulnerability.

Table 14.1 Disposable income per inhabitant by place of residence for different groups of rural municipalities in 1995, current prices

	DKr per capita				Percentage	
	1980	1995	Absolute growth	Absolute difference in growth	Growth per year	Difference in growth rate
Rural mun.	29 163	75 847	46 684	–1 087	6.58	0.60
Agricultural mun. (2)	29 086	75 886	46 800	–9 71	6.60	0.62
Agricultural mun. (4)	28 222	74 093	45 871	–1 900	6.65	0.67
Fishing mun.	31 713	77 332	45 619	–2 152	6.12	0.14
Vulnerable mun.:						
– lowest	28 696	73 816	45 120	–2 651	6.50	0.52
– middle	28 832	73 987	45 155	–2 616	6.48	0.44
– highest	29 992	76 271	46 279	–1 492	6.42	0.44
Peripheral mun.	29 251	74 790	45 539	–2 232	6.46	0.48
Large islands	29 739	75 050	45 311	–2 460	6.37	0.39
West Lolland	31 686	74 196	42 510	–5 261	5.84	–0.14
Bornholm	30 305	74 238	44 930	–2 838	6.25	0.27
Denmark	34 368	82 139	47 771	0	5.98	0.00

The most vulnerable have a level of disposable income 12 per cent under national average whilst the least vulnerable are 9 per cent under. A further group is defined as peripheral, having a weak urban centre located at a considerable distance to a strong urban centre. These have a disposable income 11 per cent under the national average.

Finally, three specific groups of contiguous peripheral municipalities have been defined, these three groups being highly peripheral with a weak urban centre, forming in each case a sub-region. These are Bornholm, the larger islands, and West Lolland. It should be noted that in general (except for these three last groups with respect to each other), the groups of rural municipalities are not mutually exclusive.

Table 14.1 also shows that in terms of income growth, rural municipalities have been performing better than Denmark as a whole (6.58 per cent pa as compared with 5.98 per cent). Furthermore, as the final column shows, all classes of rural municipalities have been performing better than the national average, except for one of the three highly peripheral groups, West Lolland. Both Bornholm and the large islands perform less strongly, though still better than the national average. The more vulnerable rural municipalities have also performed less strongly, as have fishing municipalities, though their level of disposable income was higher in 1980.

4 DECOMPOSITION OF INCOME GROWTH IN DANISH RURAL MUNICIPALITIES

In the most general sense, economic models are used to decompose growth into components explained by causal variables. Decomposition is a form of ex-post analysis that involves an underlying theoretical model, requiring data for two points of time, both for the dependent and independent variables, in this case 1980 and 1995. The model is applied in steps and the contribution of the causal variables entered at each step to changes in the dependent variable are assessed. A number of problems arise from different approaches to decomposition which are discussed below and the methodological choices that have been made in the present study are examined.

Decomposition techniques have been used extensively in regional economics. Reviews and applications have been provided by Wolff (1985), Dietzenbacher (1997) and Andersen (1998). The best-known decomposition technique in regional economics is shift-share analysis, where growth is decomposed into a national component, a structural component and a residual or regional component. A well-developed tradition for decomposition is to be found in input-output modelling (Rose and Casler, 1996). Here the principal and most simple division into components is between changes in total demand, final demand and intermediate consumption. (For a Danish example of decomposition of energy consumption using national inputoutput models, see Wier (1998) and for a decomposition of regional income growth see Madsen, Jensen-Butler and Dam (1997).

In the following section general principles concerning decomposition are discussed. In Section 4.2 the model underlying the decomposition analysis is presented.

4.1 General Principles

Decomposition can, in principle, be undertaken in two different ways. Cumulative decomposition involves the successive inclusion of the effects of different components, starting with the first set of factors, then adding the second set to explain the residual arising from application of the first set, followed by application of a third set of factors to explain the residual arising from the application of the second set and so on. In principle, total growth is explained after application of the last set of explanatory factors and the model reproduces the growth pattern at the end of the period. Cumulative decomposition faces the basic problem that the magnitude of the effects of the individual elements is affected by the order in which the factors are applied. This is because the difference between the 1980 and 1995 level of any one factor may influence the calculation of the effects of succeeding factors.

In order to avoid the problem of order, decomposition can be undertaken as a set of isolated, or single component, calculations, where the exogenous variables are given their 1995 values and the calculations are performed on the 1980 values for each step, starting at the beginning each time. One set of changes therefore does not affect calculation of any other set of changes. The disadvantage of this method is that the sum of the isolated components of the decomposition will not necessarily (and not usually) be equal to the total growth in the variable in question, here disposable income. It is difficult to interpret the positive or negative residual appearing from this type of analysis. In this study both types of decomposition have been applied and a major divergence between the two would be a cause for concern.

The two approaches can be described at a general level as follows, using variables to explain changes in disposable income that can be classified into two broad groups:

- Exogenous market-related variables, E^m
- Exogenous non-market related variables, E^{nm}

Cumulative decomposition can be expressed as follows:

$$\Delta ydibgq = \left[M(E^m_{t1}, E^{nm}_{t1}) + (\text{model error } t1)\right] - \left[M(E^m_{t0}, E^{nm}_{t0}) + (\text{model error } t0)\right]$$
$$= \left[M(E^m_{t1}, E^{nm}_{t1}) - M(E^m_{t0}, E^{nm}_{t1})\right] + \left[M(E^m_{t0}, E^{nm}_{t1}) - M(E^m_{t0}, E^{nm}_{t0})\right] \quad (14.2)$$

where:

M: model specified variables

t0 and *t1* are points of time at period start and finish, respectively

The first element inside the first square brackets of equation (14.2) is the market-induced change and the second element is the non-market induced change.

Isolated decomposition can be expressed as follows:

$$\Delta ydibgq = \left[M(E_{t1}^{m}, E_{t1}^{nm}) - M(E_{t0}^{m}, E_{t1}^{nm})\right] \quad (14.3a)$$

$$\Delta ydibgq = \left[M(E_{t1}^{m}, E_{t1}^{nm}) - M(E_{t1}^{m}, E_{t0}^{nm})\right] \quad (14.3b)$$

Equation (14.3a) represents market-induced change and equation (14.3b) non-market-induced change.

The causal model

An underlying causal model should determine the sequence of decomposition in a cumulative decomposition. In some cases (for example, shift-share analysis) the decomposition sequence represents an underlying theoretical hierarchy of causality. In other cases, the sequence reflects the structure of the economic model lying behind. For example, the Keynesian demand-driven model will start with demand which generates production, whilst a supply-side growth model will start with factors of production which are used to generate income. In the present study LINE is a Keynesian demand-driven model, which starts with production, which generates income, which in turn generates demand. In an isolated decomposition the model determines which causal variables are included, but their sequence of inclusion is without significance.

A further consideration is whether to use a single or multiple equation model. Other things being equal, a multiple equation model is a model in structural form, whilst a single equation model can be regarded as a many equation model in reduced form. In the present study a multiple equation model (LINE) has been used. The Danish regional research tradition has typically employed single equation models (see for example Groes and Heinesen, 1997 and Kristensen and Henry, 1998, who use a two-equation model). A general discussion of the advantages of using models in structural form is provided by Lucas (1976). In the case of Danish regional models, Madsen and Jensen-Butler (1999) argue for a formulation in structural form rather than reduced form multiplier models.

Model error

The actual growth can be decomposed in the following manner:

$$y_{1995}^{a} - y_{1980}^{a} = y_{1995}^{a} - y_{1995}^{m} + (y_{1995}^{m} - y_{1980}^{m}) + (y_{1980}^{m} - y_{1980}^{a})$$

where:

y is income, a is actual and m is model = model error 1995 + model calculated growth 1980/95 + model error 1980.

As can be seen from the expression, before decomposition can be carried out, a model calculation has to be made for 1980 and 1995, in order to exclude model error from the analysis. In the case of LINE, because of the simple linear structure of the model, the model error is zero.

Forward or backward

Decomposition can, in principle, be undertaken forwards or backwards in time. In this study, as in the previous section, a forward procedure has been used, starting in 1980.

4.2 LINE – a Model for the Danish Local Economy

Given the pattern of income growth in Table 14.1, the next task is to identify the different components of change, which can be used to explain the pattern of income growth. A simple version of the LINE model has been used to decompose growth in disposable income for the period 1980–95 for different types of rural area in Denmark. The structure of LINE is shown in Figure 14.5. This shows that economic activity is determined in the municipality where the labour force is employed, where earned income is calculated on the basis of the number of places of employment in the municipality and earned income per employed person in each sector.

After this, earned income and employment is allocated to the municipality of residence using a commuting model. In the next step earned income and employment by sector are calculated by socio-economic group based on qualification. Given the total labour force and the calculated employment, unemployment can be determined. Income transfers are calculated using demographic information and social security data covering such elements as unemployment and numbers of social security recipients.

Taxation is calculated using incomes. Finally, disposable income is calculated by adding earned income, other income and income transfers and substracting taxes paid and interest payments (see equation (14.1)). In Figure 14.5 the location in the model where changes are made in order to estimate the individual factor's contribution to income growth are indicated, both for the isolated and the cumulative decomposition.

In the following, the model relations are described in some detail. This version of LINE contains no behavioural equations, only input–output type relations and institutionally-determined relations.

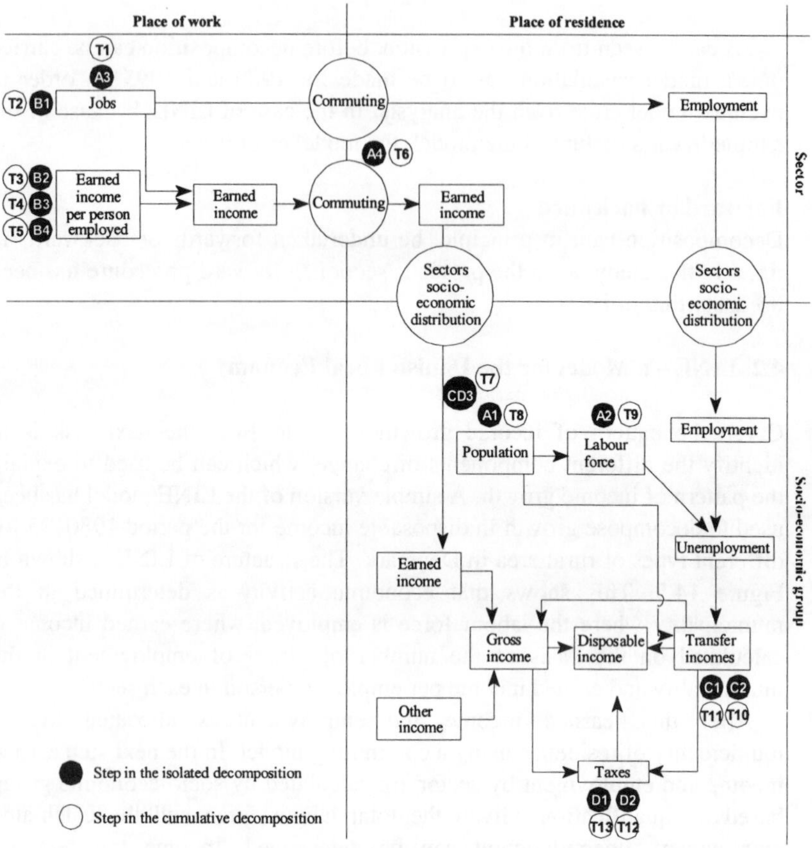

Figure 14.5 The structure of LINE

The starting point for LINE is the number of jobs in each municipality. For each of the 12 sectors in the model, earned income is calculated by multiplying the number of jobs with the average earned income per person employed. For all municipalities and sectors earned income by place of employment is calculated as follows:

$$ylorae = YLORAEQ * qae \qquad (14.4)$$

where:

ylorae = earned income by municipality of employment *a* and sector *e*
YLORAEQ = earned income per person employed by municipality of employment and sector
qae = number of jobs by municipality of employment and sector

Earned income and employment is distributed to municipality of residence using a simple commuting model:

$$qbe = \sum_a QABEQ \cdot qae \qquad (14.5)$$

$$ylorbe = \sum_e YLORABEQ \cdot ylorae \qquad (14.6)$$

where:
qbe = employment in municipality of residence *b* and sector *e*
QABEQ = employment in municipality of residence *b* as a share of the number of jobs in municipality of employment *a*, for sector *e*
ylorbe = earned income in municipality of residence band sector e
YLORABEQ = earned income in municipality of residence *b* as share of earned income in municipality of employment *a*, for sector *e*

Earned income and employment is then transformed from sector to socio-economic group by qualification. There are seven qualification groups (*g*) and for each the following calculation is made:

$$qbg = \sum_a QBEGQ \cdot qbe \qquad (14.7)$$

$$ylorbg = \sum_a YLORBGEQ \cdot ylorbe \qquad (14.8)$$

where:
qbg = employment for persons in socioeconomic group *g* in municipality of residence *b*
QBGEQ = employment for persons in socioeconomic group *g* as a share of total employment, for sector e and municipality of residence *b*
ylorbg = earned income for persons in socioeconomic group g in municipality of residence *b*
YLORBGEQ = earned income for persons in socioeconomic group *g* as a share of total earned income for sector *e* and municipality of residence *b*

The supply of labour depends on the number of persons in the age group 18–59 years and the activity rate:

$$usbg = USBGQ * u1859bg \qquad (14.9)$$

where:

usbg = labour force for people in socioeconomic group *g* and municipality of residence *b*

USBGQ = labour force as a share of the total number of 18–59-year-old persons, for socioeconomic group *g* and municipality of residence *b*

u1859bg = population between 18 and 59 years in socioeconomic group *g* and municipality of residence *b*

On this basis unemployment is calculated:

$$ulbg = usbg - qbg \qquad (14.10)$$

where:

ulbg = number of unemployed in socioeconomic group *g* in municipality of residence *b*

In the following steps disposable income is calculated as shown in equation (14.1). The general model for the group of other income (defined by a number of types of other income) is as follows:

$$y<type>bg = Y<TYPE>BGQ * ubg \qquad (14.11)$$

where:

y<type>bg = other income by type for persons in socioeconomic group *g* and municipality of residence *b*

Y<TYPE>BGQ = other income by type per person in socioeconomic group *g* and municipality of residence *b*

ubg = total population in socioeconomic group *g* in municipality of residence *b*.

Income transfers consist of a number of different types, for example unemployment support, pensions of different types, housing subsidies, income support, child allowance, educational grants and early retirment subsidies. Two types of equation are used to calculate income transfers:

$$t<type>bg = T<TYPE>BGQ\ A\ UT<TYPE>BGQ * u<alder>bg \qquad (14.12)$$

$$t<type>bg = T<TYPE>BGQ * Au<alder>bg \qquad (14.13)$$

where:

t<type>bg = income transfers by type for persons in socioeconomic group *g* and municipality of residence *b*

T<TYPE>BGQ = income transfers by type per recipient (equation (14.12)) or per person (equation (14.13)) for persons in socioeconomic group *g* by municipality of residence *b*

UT<TYPE>BGQ = persons who receive income transfers as a share of the number of persons in the relevant age group, for socioeconomic group *g* and municipality of residence *b*

u<alder>bg = number of persons in the relevant age group in socioeconomic group *g* by municipality of residence *b*.

In general, equation type (14.12) is preferred, though the choice of equation is determined by data availability.

Personal taxation consists of a number of different types of taxation for persons in socioeconomic group *g* and municipality of residence *b*. In general, tax is calculated using taxable income multiplied by a rate of taxation:

$$s<type>bg = S<TYPE>BGQ * yti<type>bg \qquad (14.14)$$

where:

s<type>bg = tax payments by type of tax for persons in socioeconomic group *g* and municipality of residence *b*

S<TYPE>BGQ = tax rate for type of tax for persons in socioeconomic group *g* and municipality of residence *b*

yti<type>bg = taxable income by type of tax for persons in socioeconomic group *g* and municipality of residence *b*

Taxable income is composed of different elements of income and tax deductions and is calculated as follows:

$$yti<type>bg = y<type>bg - yf<type>bg \qquad (14.15)$$

where:

y<type>bg = sum of taxable income for type of tax for persons in socioeconomic group *g* and municipality of residence *b*

yf<type>bg = sum of before-tax deductions for the tax type in question for persons in s socioeconomic group *g* and municipality of residence *b*

In general, before-tax deductions for each type of tax are determined as follows:

yf<subtype>bg = *YF<SUBTYPE>BGQ* * *ubg* (14.16)

where:

yf<subtype>bg = before-tax sub-type of deduction for each type of tax for persons in socioeconomic group *g* and municipality of residence *b*

YF<SUBTYPE>BGQ = before-tax sub-type of deduction for each type of tax for persons in socioeconomic group *g* and municipality of residence *b*

5 CUMULATIVE DECOMPOSITION USING THE SIMPLE VERSION OF LINE

Decomposition of the growth of disposible income per inhabitant using LINE involves a model circuit from income calculated by place of production and sector through commuting to income calculated by place of residence and socioeconomic group and onward through taxes and income transfers to disposible income, as shown in Figure 14.5. In technical terms the cumulative decomposition is performed by sucessively setting LINE's exogenous variables equal to 1995 values in order to calculate the consequences for earned income and disposible income of these changes. For example, the effects of setting the tax rates for 1980 equal to the 1995 values can be calculated. In the following, decomposition is outlined in 13 steps.

Step 0

Before the decomposition begins 1980 prices are converted to 1995 prices. Productivity is raised by the national deflator for GDP at factor prices (*pyf* = 1.9312 for 1980–95). Other nominal variables in LINE are raised by consumer price index (*pcp* = 1.9146 for the same period).

Step 1 (T1 in Figure 14.5)

In the first real step employment in the first year is scaled so that it is the same as in the last year. This gives a municipality distribution effect:

$$qae_{start} \Leftarrow qae_{start} \cdot \frac{qa_{fin}}{qa_{start}} \quad (14.17)$$

where:

qae_{start} = employment in of place of work (municipality) *a* and sector *e* for the first year

qa_{fin} = employment by place of work (municipality) for all sectors for the final year

qa_{start} = employment by place of work (municipality) for all sectors for the first year

Step 2 (T2)

In the second step employment by place of work and sector in the first year is replaced by the value for the final year, which allows estimation of the marginal effect of developments in industrial structure:

$$qae_{start} \Leftarrow qae_{fin} \quad (14.18)$$

Step 3 (T3)

In the third step the effect of price changes in each sector is estimated. Productivity in 1980 is multiplied by the national sector-specific deflators borrowed from ADAM:

$$YLORAEQ'_{start} \Leftarrow YLORAEQ_{start} \cdot \frac{pyf_e}{pyf} \quad (14.19)$$

where:

pyfe = the national sector-specific deflator for GDP at factor prices for sector *e*

YLORAEQ` = earned income per person employed, by place of production a and by sector *e*, corrected for national sectoral changes in GDP at factor cost.

Step 4 (T4)

In step 4 the effect of the real growth in productivity in each sector is estimated. Productivity in 1980 is multiplied by the national sector-specific deflators borrowed from ADAM and the national real growth in productivity:

$$YLORAEQ''_{start} \Leftarrow YLORAEQ'_{start} \cdot \frac{\sum_a YLORAEQ_{fin}'}{\sum_a YLORAEQ_{start}'} \quad (14.20)$$

where:

YLORAEQ'' = earned income per person employed, by place of production a and by sector *e*, corrected for national sectoral changes in GDP at factor cost and for real labour productivity growth.

Step 5 (T5)

In this step earned income in the first year is replaced with earned income in the final year. In this way the residual in relation to steps 3 and 4 is obtained:

$$YLORAEQ_{start} \Leftarrow YLORAEQ_{fin} \qquad (14.21)$$

Step 6 (T6)

Here the effects of changed commuting patterns on the local economy is calculated by replacing the 1980 with the 1995 commuting matrix:

$$QBAEQ_{start} \Leftarrow QBAEQ_{fin} \qquad (14.22)$$

$$YLORBAEQ_{start} \Leftarrow YLORBAEQ_{fin} \qquad (14.23)$$

Step 7 (T7)

In this step the effects of a changed distribution of socioeconomic groups by sector is estimated by replacing the distribution by socioeconomic group in the first year with that of the final year:

$$QBGEQ_{start} \Leftarrow QBGEQ_{fin} \qquad (14.24)$$

$$YLORBGEQ_{start} \Leftarrow YLORBGEQ_{fin} \qquad (14.25)$$

Step 8 (T8)

In step 8 population by age group in the final year replace the same values for the first year. In this way the effects of a changed population are assessed:

$$u0017b_{start} \Leftarrow u0017b_{fin} \quad u1825b_{start} \Leftarrow u1825b_{fin}$$
$$u2659b_{start} \Leftarrow u2659b_{fin} \quad u6066b_{start} \Leftarrow u6066b_{fin}$$
$$u6700b_{start} \Leftarrow u6700b_{fin} \qquad (14.26)$$

where:

$u0017b_{start/fin}$ = the number of persons between 0 and 17 years residing in municipality *b* in the start or finish year

$u001825_{bstart/fin}$ = the number of persons between 18 and 25 years residing in municipality *b* in the start or finish year and so on by age group.

Step 9 (T9)

In step 9 the activity rate of the labour force in the first year is replaced with that of the final year. Here the effects of a changed activity rate are estimated:

$$USBGQ_{start} \Leftarrow USBGQ_{fin} \tag{14.27}$$

Step 10 (T10)

In the tenth step the age dependent socio-economic composition and share of transfer income recipients in each recipient group for the final year are used to calculate the effects of transfer incomes:

$$U0017BGQ_{start} \Leftarrow U0017BGQ_{fin} \tag{14.28}$$
$$U1825BGQ_{start} \Leftarrow U001825BGQ_{fin} \tag{14.29}$$

where:

U0017BGQstart/fin = Share of 0–17 years-olds with qualification *g* in municipality of residence *b* in either start or finish year receiving unemployment insurance.

U1825BGQstart/fin = Share of 0–17 years-olds with qualification *g* in municipality of residence *b* in either start or finish year receiving unemployment insurance.

There are a further 15 categories of recipients of transfer incomes, some age-dependent, other not, including recipients of different types of pension (see Madsen et al., 1997, for a detailed description).

Step 11 (T11)

In this step the rates for transfer incomes for the final year are entered:

$$TAUBGQ_{start} \Leftarrow TAUBGQ_{fin} \tag{14.30}$$
$$TDPBGQ_{start} \Leftarrow TDPBGQ_{fin} \tag{14.31}$$

where:

$TAUBGQ_{start/fin}$ = rate for unemployment insurance in municipality of residence *b*, with qualification *g* in either start or finish year.

$TDPBGQ_{start/fin}$ = part-time pension level per recipient in municipality of residence *b*, with qualification *g* in either start or finish year.

There are a further nine categories of rates for transfer incomes (see Madsen et al., 1997, for a detailed description)

Step 12 (T12)

In this step all tax variables for the final year are entered, except for tax rates:

$$YLORBGQ_{start} \Leftarrow YLORBGQ_{fin} \qquad (14.32)$$

$$YLOSBGQ_{start} \Leftarrow YLOSBGQ_{fin} \qquad (14.33)$$

where:

$YLORBGQ_{start/fin}$ = coefficient linking the labour and income registers

$YLOSBGQ_{start/fin}$ = share of earned income in total income for persons in qualification group *g* and municipality of residence *b* in either start or finish year

There are a further 24 categories of income which constitute the structure of taxable income. (See Madsen et al., 1997, for a detailed description).

Step 13 (T13)

In this step the tax rates are replaced:

$$S12BGQ_{start} \Leftarrow S12BGQ_{fin} \qquad (14.34)$$

where:

$S12BGQ_{start/fin}$ = income tax paid at the 12 per cent rate as a share of personal income in municipality of residence *b* for qualification group *g* in either start or finish year

A further ten categories of tax rates are used (see Madsen et al., 1997, for a detailed description).

6 ISOLATED OR SINGLE COMPONENT DECOMPOSITION USING LINE

In Section 5 the methodology used in the cumulative decomposition is presented. In the single component decomposition, which is dealt with in this section, the individual steps are treated separately, setting the exogenous variables from the other steps equal to the 1980 value. In the analysis of economic development by municipality using isolated or single component decomposition, four groups of factors are identified.

Step A. Changes in number of jobs and population
The municipalities have experienced changes in numbers of jobs and the size and composition of the population. Estimation is made of the extent to which these changes have contributed to changes in earned income and disposable income per inhabitant.

Step B. Changes in earned income per person employed
Changes in earned income per person employed, calculated by place of work, has consequences for growth in disposible income per inhabitant accounted for by place of residence. A more even distribution of earned income per inhabitant will create conditions for convergence in levels of disposible income. Changes in earned income per inhabitant can either be the result of an unfavourable development in industrial structure in the municipality or a high growth in earned income per employee in the municipality as compared with the rest of the country. Changes in primary income per employed person are in turn the results of sectorally dependent differences in growth in productivity, changes in sectoral terms of trade and a locally determined development of productivity.

Step C. Changes in transfer incomes
A third contribution to a positive development in disposible income per inhabitant could arise from changes in transfer incomes. Here changes in income transfers per person and changes in the share of the population receiving income transfers are examined. For example, average income transfers per recipient may have grown more rapidly than in the rest of the country. Only changes not related to automatic adjustments to unemployment levels are included. Automatic adjustments of transfer incomes to changes in employment and unemployment are included under A and B.

Step D. Changes in taxation

A fourth element in explanation of income convergence could be changes in taxation. If taxation levels in a municipality have been decreasing relatively, average disposible income will increase. Again, only non-automatic changes in taxation are included.

All four groups of factors can contribute to explanation of the development of disposible income. In order to estimate the contribution of each of these factors to income level convergence, the isolated decomposition model is used to estimate the consequences of changes in these factors on disposable income (and earned income) per inhabitant in the period 1980–95.

The calculations are undertaken for all four groups of explanatory variables. These four groups are again subdivided into 13 elements, corresponding to the 13 steps in the cumulative decomposition. An overview over the 13 steps in the decomposition is to be found in Table 14.2. The first column shows the 13 elements of the decomposition. For each element is indicated which variable or variables are equated with the 1995 values and the number of the equation where the change can be observed. In the first row of the table the different results from the model calculations are shown. Inside the body of the table for each element is shown whether the variable in question is changed exogenously, remains constant or is endogenously determined. The location of the step in Figure 14.5 is also shown in the first column of the table.

The calculation of the sectorally dependent changes in earned income per employee (steps B2, B3 B4) and the effects of employment changes are performed cumulatively. This cumulative calculation of the effects of development in earned income per person employed is undertaken in steps 3, 4 and 5 in the cumulative decomposition.

7 RESULTS OF DECOMPOSITION

Both an isolated and a cumulative decomposition were undertaken, providing similar results. In the following section the results of the isolated decomposition analysis are presented. The results from the cumulative decomposition are discussed briefly in Section 7.2.

7.1 Results of the Isolated Decomposition

As noted earlier, in the period 1980–95 there has been a reduction in differences in disposable income between rural areas and the rest of Denmark. Disposable income in Danish rural (and generally more peripheral) areas grew faster than at national level However, for the most peripheral rural areas, growth in disposable income has only been marginally above the national average, whilst for certain problem areas, notably West Lolland, divergence has actually occurred.

In Table 14.3 the results of the isolated decomposition are presented. As can be seen from the table, the individual elements of the decomposition have been grouped into four main categories, corresponding to those identified in Section 6:

(a) employment and population
(b) earned income per person employed
(c) income transfers
(d) taxation

The vertical dimension of the table shows the four main components referred to above, subdivided by individual elements of the decomposition. The horizontal dimension shows the grouping of rural municipalities described in Section 3. The figures in the table show negative or positive growth in relation to the national average, measured in percentage points. The third row in the table shows that rural municipalities have experienced a growth in disposable income that is 8–12 per cent over the national average, considering the entire period. However, some of the problem areas have experienced a weaker income growth than other rural areas and West Lolland has actually experienced decline in relation to the national average.

A: Employment and demographic change

Rural areas have, compared with the rest of Denmark, experienced a positive development, both in employment and population. Changes in population size and composition (A1) have provided a positive contribution to the above-national growth of 1–2 per cent. This has arisen because of favourable changes in population composition and emigration from the most peripheral areas.

Changes in activity rates (A2) have contributed with 1–2 per cent higher real growth in most rural municipalities. The most peripheral areas have, however, experienced declining activity rates, which have contributed negatively to income growth.

A favourable growth in employment in rural municipalities has contributed positively to income growth whilst negative growth in employment (A3) in the most peripheral areas has had the opposite effect. Changes in commuting patterns (A4) have been neutral, or perhaps even marginally negative, for rural areas.

Table 14.2 Overview of sequence of calculations in LINE in the isolated decomposition

Changes: Model variables:	Population size and composition (residence)	Labour force activity rate	Jobs (place of work)	Earned income/ employed (place of work)
A Jobs and population				
A1 Population size and composition. *U*xxxx*bg* is changed in equations (14.9), (14.11), (14.12) and (14.13)	Changes 1980=1995	Constant	Constant	Constant
A2 Labour force acivity rate *USBGQ* changed in equation (14.9)	Constant	Changes 1980=1995	Constant	Constant
A3 Local employment change *qae* changed in equation (14.4)	Constant	Constant	Changes 1980=1995	Constant
A4 Commuting QABEQ and *YLORABEQ* Changed in equations (14.7) and (14.8)	Constant	Constant	Constant	Constant
B Earned income per employed person				
B1 Industrial strcuture *qae* changed in equation (14.4)	Constant	Constant	Changes 1980=1995	Constant
B2 National GDP deflator *YLORAEQ* changed in equation (14.4)	Constant	Constant	Constant	Changes 1980=1995
B3 National growth in earned income/employed person *YLORAEQ* changed in equation (14.4)	Constant	Constant	Constant	Changes 1980=1995
B4 Resuidual (local earned income/ employed person B2-B3) *YLORAEQ* changed in equation (14.4)	Constant	Constant	Constant	Changes 1980=1995
C Income transfers				
C1 Rates *T<TYPE>BGQ* changed in equations (14.12) and (14.13)	Constant	Constant	Constant	Constant
C2 Structure *UT<TYPE>BGQ* changed in equations (14.12) and (14.13)	Constant	Constant	Constant	Constant
D Taxation				
D1 Tax levels *S<TYPE>BGQ* changed in equation (14.14)	Constant	Constant	Constant	Constant
D2 Structure *Y<TYPE>BGO* and *YF<TYPE>BGQ* changed in equations (14.11) and (14.16)	Constant	Constant	Constant	Constant
C3/D3 Sectors' socio-economic composition Changes in equations (14.7) and (14.8)	Constant	Constant	Constant	Constant

Commuting co-efficients	Employment (residence)	Sectors' socio-econom. distrib. (resid.)	Unemployment (residence)	Earned income (residence)	Transfers and tax rates (residence)	Disposable income/ inhabitant (resid.)
Constant	Constant	Constant	Endogeous	Constant	Constant	Endogen.
Constant	Constant	Constant	Endogen.	Constant	Constant	Endogen.
Constant	Endogen.	Constant	Endogeous	Endogen.	Constant	Endogen.
Changes 1980=1995	Endogen.	Constant	Endogeous	Endogen.	Constant	Endogen.
Constant	Endogen.	Constant	Endogen.	Endogen.	Constant	Endogen.
Constant	Constant	Constant	Constant	Endogen.	Constant	Endogen.
Constant	Constant	Constant	Constant	Endogen.	Constant	Endogen.
Constant	Constant	Constant	Constant	Endogen.	Constant	Endogen.
Constant	Constant	Constant	Constant	Constant	Changes 1980=1995	Endogen.
Constant	Constant	Constant	Constant	Constant	Changes 1980=1995	Endogen.
Constant	Constant	Constant	Constant	Constant	Changes 1980=1995	Endogen.
Constant	Constant	Constant	Constant	Constant	Changes 1980=1995	Endogen.
Constant	Constant	Changes 1980=1995	Endogen.	Constant	Constant	Endogen.

Table 14.3 Results of the isolated decomposition of growth in disposable income in Danish rural municipalities, 1980–95. Deviations from the national average in percentage points by component and by type of municipality

	Rural mun.	Agri. mun. (2)	Agri. mun. (4)	Fish-ing mun.	Vulner mun. (low)	Vulner mun. (mid)	Vulner mun. (high)	Peri-pher. mun.	Lge. Islands	West Lolland	Born-holm	DK= Nat. effect
Disposable income/inhab DKr 1980 (95 prices)	56 739	56 626	54 953	61 858	55 851	56 110	58 378	56 929	57 819	61 589	58 922	66 842
Disposable income/inhab DKr 1995 (95 prices)	75 847	75 886	74 093	77 332	73 816	73 987	76 271	74 790	75 050	74 196	75 238	82 139
Local growth divergence	11	11	12	2	9	9	8	9	7	–2	5	0(23)
A Jobs and population												
A1 Population size and composition	1	1	1	2	1	1	1	1	1	2	1	0(23)
A2 Labour force activity rate	1	1	1	2	–1	0	2	–1	0	–2	0	0(–2)
A3 Local jobs	1	1	0	1	–2	0	1	–1	–2	–7	–1	0(1)
A4 Commuting	0	0	–1	–1	–1	0	–1	0	0	–1	0	0(0)
B Earned income/ employed person												
B1 Changes in industrial structure	0	0	0	–5	–1	0	–1	–1	–1	0	–3	0(–1)
B2 National GDP deflator	–2	–2	–3	–2	–3	–3	–1	–2	–2	–2	–2	0(7)

B3 National growth in earned income/ employed	6	6	8	6	7	6	2	5	3	1	3	0(15)
B4 Residual (local earned income/employed B2–B3	0	–1	–1	–4	–1	–1	–1	–1	–1	–1	–3	0(0)
C Income transfers												
C1 Rates	1	1	1	0	2	2	2	2	2	3	2	0(7)
C2 Structure	2	2	3	-1	2	1	-1	2	1	0	2	0(7)
D Taxation												
D1 tax levels	0	1	1	1	1	1	0	1	1	1	1	0(–7)
D2 Tax structure	2	2	3	0	3	2	2	2	1	2	1	0(–3)
C3/D3 Sectors' socio-economic distribution	0	0	0	0	0	0	–1	0	0	–1	0	0(1)

B: Changes in earned income per person employed

Changes in earned income per person employed, which reflect changes in labour productivity, have had substantial effects on growth in disposable income. A more even distribution of earned income per employed person is the primary factor underlying the observed convergence in disposable income, though this varies between different types of rural area. Growth in earned income per employed person has been in net terms positive for most rural areas. Only fishing municipalities and the very peripheral areas have remained neutral or are only marginally positive. The favourable development can be a result both of an improvement in industrial structure in rural areas (B1) and a growth in earned income per employed person inside each sector which is above the national average (B2–B4). The growth in labour productivity (B2–B4) is a result of the difference of differences in sectoral income growth (B3) and changes in terms of trade between sectors (B2) together with the local development (B4). The table shows that changes in sectoral composition are without consequences for income growth (B1). Only fishing municipalities and Bornholm have had losses because of this factor.

Changes in labour productivity have, on the other hand, had a significant effect. The consequences of changes in sectoral terms of trade (B2) are negative for rural areas, which have lost 1–3 per cent. This is due to the fact that agricultural prices have grown slowly. National sectoral growth rates for productivity have contributed positively to income growth (B3), which is due to substantial increases in productivity in agriculture and some industrial sectors (5–7 per cent growth). Only West Lolland and some of the larger islands and Bornholm have had small advantage of this factor, which is due to their specific sectoral composition.

Finally, the residual (B4) is negative for rural areas (–1 per cent). The residual can be interpreted as that part of growth in labour productivity that cannot be attributed to changes in terms of trade or sectoral composition.

C: Changes in income transfers

A third contribution comes from changes in income transfers. In this analysis changes in transfer incomes per recipient and changes in share of the population that receives income transfers, are included. Thus, changes alone, which are not associated with automatic adjustments related to unemployment (unemployment support) and demographic changes (pensions), are considered.

Changes in average rates for income transfers (C1) have contributed positively to income growth in rural areas (1–3 per cent). This is mainly because changes in rates for income transfer have been weaker in high-income areas (such as Greater Copenhagen) and stronger in low-income areas (such as West Lolland).

Changes in the structure of income transfers (C2) (share of persons who receive income transfers in each socio-economic group) have also had positive effects for rural areas (1–3).

D: Changes in taxation

A fourth element in explanation of income convergence is taxation. Limited increases in taxation levels will be an advantage for rural areas. Again only non-automatic changes in taxation are considered. Changes in taxation levels (D1) have given rural areas a positive contribution (0–1). Changes in unearned income and the tax structure (D2) have also contributed positively (1–3)

Conclusions from the isolated decomposition

The positive and convergent development in disposable income per inhabitant in rural areas is strongly related to a favourable development of labour productivity in these areas (B3), whilst a positive growth in numbers employed has only contributed marginally (A3). The positive income growth in rural areas has also developed because of non-automatic changes in income transfers and taxation.

A little more than 50 per cent of the income growth in rural areas can be allocated to market-based mechanisms (A and B), whilst a little less than 50 per cent can be allocated to the role of the public sector in rural areas (C and D). In the more vulnerable and peripheral rural areas the public sector plays a more important role in income creation. For the most peripheral areas the non-convergent growth in income is because of a negative growth in employment whilst growth of labour productivity has been around the national average. This negative market-determined development is more than compensated for by a favourable development in income transfers and taxation. However, for West Lolland, the negative effects from decline in employment have not been fully compensated for by the positive effects arising from the public sector, a finding that is in agreement with the work of Hansen and Jensen-Butler (1996).

7.2 Results of the Cumulative Decomposition

Table 14.4 shows the results of the cumulative decomposition. In broad terms, the pattern of effects arising from the decomposition of growth in disposable income corresponds to that arising from the isolated decomposition which can be taken as a confirmation of the reliability of the method.

Table 14.4 Decomposition of changes in disposable income – cumulative approach

Steps Type of rural Municipality	1980 in 80 prices	1980 in 95 prices	Step 1 Local jobs % (A3)	Step 2 Industrial structure % (B1)	Step 3 Natl. GDP-deflator % (B2)	Step 4 Natl. growth earned income/ employee % (B3)	Step 5 Residual local earned income/ employee % (B4)
Rural municipality	29163	56739	0.6	-0.2	-1.1	4.3	0.8
Agricultural municipality (2)	29086	56626	0.6	0.1	-1.2	4.5	0.2
Agricultural municipality (4)	28222	54953	-0.0	0.1	-1.8	5.1	0.1
Fishing municipality	32019	61858	0.5	-4.7	-2.6	5.0	0.3
Vulnerable municipality:							
– lowest	28696	55851	-1.6	-0.6	-2.8	3.1	0.3
– middle	28832	56110	-0.1	-0.1	-1.7	3.4	0.9
– highest	29992	58378	0.6	-0.5	-0.4	2.0	1.2
Peripheral mun.	29251	56929	-1.1	-0.9	-2.4	2.9	1.2
Large islands	29661	57819	-1.5	-1.4	-3.0	0.8	1.1
West Lolland	31686	61589	-6.6	-0.3	-3.0	-4.4	-3.1
Bornholm	30305	58922	-1.2	-2.6	-2.7	1.4	0.3
Denmark	34368	66843	0.0	0.0	0.0	0.0	0.0

Table 14.4 continued

Step 6 Com-muting % (A4)	Step 7 Socio-econom. group distbn % (C3/D3)	Step 8 Pop size and compo-sition % (A1)	Step 9 Labour force activity rate % (A2)	Step10 Transfer incomes structure % (C2)	Step 11 Transfer incomes rates % (C1)	Step 12 Tax structure % (D2)	Step 13 Tax levels % (D1)	Differ-ential growth %
0.6	0.2	1.7	1.1	0.2	1.8	1.0	-0.2	10.8
0.6	0.2	1.3	1.0	0.2	1.7	1.7	0.2	11.1
0.2	0.4	1.7	0.8	-0.3	2.7	2.5	0.4	11.9
0.3	-0.1	3.1	1.9	-2.2	0.5	-0.9	0.9	2.1
0.2	0.1	2.9	-0.3	0.6	3.0	3.4	1.1	9.3
-0.2	0.4	1.6	-0.2	-0.2	2.6	2.0	0.5	9.0
-1.1	-0.4	1.5	2.0	-0.4	2.3	1.5	-0.8	7.8
-0.1	0.1	2.6	-0.4	0.6	3.0	1.9	1.1	8.5
0.6	-0.5	3.4	0.0	1.1	2.7	2.2	1.5	6.9
2.0	-0.6	3.6	-1.7	0.3	3.4	5.8	2.2	-2.4
0.0	-0.5	3.0	0.0	1.5	1.4	3.0	1.1	4.8
0.0	0.0	0.0	0.0	0.0	0.0	0.0	0.0	0.0

8 CONCLUSIONS AND CONSEQUENCES FOR POLICY

The study has illustrated the importance of differentiation between different types of rural area. Patterns of income growth vary between different types of rural area, as does the contribution of the different causal factors.

It is useful to divide the components of change into two broad groups: those which are determined primarily by market forces rather than public policy (elements A–B) and those which change more directly because of policy decisions (elements C–D).

8.1 Market Forces and the Future of Rural Areas in Denmark

A number of market-based factors will affect the future growth of income in rural areas in Denmark.

A: Employment

Danish industrial production, which is strongly represented in rural areas (Jensen-Butler, 1992), will face increasing competition from Eastern Europe. In rural Jutland four sectors are particularly important: clothing and textiles, wood and furniture, food and beverages and metal products. As none of these sectors is especially high-tech or knowledge-intensive then growing competition is clearly a threat to number of jobs (Engelstoft and Jensen-Butler 1997). Already in the textile and clothing sector much routine production has already moved to countries such as Poland and the Herning area in Jutland is attempting to retain the high value-added components of production.

B: Productivity

It seems probable that the favourable development of real productivity in rural areas will continue in the future, this being an important component in regional income convergence. Industrial and agricultural productivity has grown rapidly since 1980 and will probably continue to do so. On the other hand, it seems likely that prices will continue to rise slowly for agricultural and some Danish industrial products that will have negative consequences for income growth.

The industrial structure of most – but not all – rural areas will probably remain sound. This structure in terms of sectors is traditional, with a strong representation of industries such as food and beverages, wood and furniture, textiles and clothing as well as some metal products. Process rather than product innovation has characterised much industrial growth in rural and peripheral areas in Denmark. However, if the vision of a transformation of the Danish economy to a competitive, knowledge-based and high-tech economy is realised (Erhvervsministeriet, 1997), then it is clear that the industrial structure of rural areas in Denmark will be less favourable than it is today.

The three specific types of peripheral area, West Lolland, Bornholm and some of the larger islands do face problems of industrial structure, which will probably continue to exist. These are the true peripheral and poorer regions in Denmark.

Finally, there is an unexplained and negative residual pertaining to local economic conditions. This at present has a limited role in income development, but could change in the future.

8.2 Policy and Income Growth in Rural Areas in Denmark

The potential for policy to influence the above market-based components is limited. Local and regional industrial development policy does exist in rural areas in Denmark and many central actors in economies of rural areas feel the need to transform their industrial structure more in the direction of knowledge-based production (Engelstoft and Jensen-Butler, 1997; Jensen et al., 1997). However, resources devoted to this type of policy are limited and their efficacy doubtful. Furthermore, these areas do not in general have the conditions that promote the growth and development of positive externalities related to knowledge and information. They also lack highly qualified labour.

C and D: Public finances and policy

A number of the components of income growth do, however, fall more directly into the policy sphere.

An important element of social policy is related to distributional questions. Unemployment support in Denmark is, in principle, at a level of 90 per cent of former wage or salary. However, there is also a ceiling in terms of absolute levels of support. This means that unemployed persons who formerly had a high income receive compensation which is proportionally less than those who had a lower income. The reasons for this are to be found in national-level policy concerning income redistribution. One effect of this policy is that low-income areas gain disproportionately from the existence of the ceiling. In a sense, regional income policy is being conducted through national policy concerning unemployment insurance, social security and income distribution. National level policy concerning distribution will continue to dominate regional policy considerations. On the other hand, a policy option to compensate for these automatic effects could be to reduce block grants to rural areas.

A second policy component is changes in the system of public finance, which transfers income between the state and municipalities, functioning as regional policy. There is an in-built bias in this system to support poorer municipalities. As regional income convergence seems to be occurring in Denmark then political pressures may build to reduce or even eliminate this redistribution effect, in which case, peripheral regions will be especially hard hit.

REFERENCES

Andersen, A.K. (1998), *Decomposition of the change in the annual commuting in Denmark 1980–95*, Denmark: AKF Forlag.

Dam, P.U. (ed.) (1996), *ADAM–En model af dansk økonomi, marts 1995*, Copenhagen: Danmarks Statistik.

Dam, P.U., B. Madsen, T. Jensen and N. Groes (1997), 'Modelling national and local economic consequences of changes in the Danish welfare system',paper presented to the 28th Conference of the British and Irish Section of the Regional Science Association International, Falmouth UK, September 1997.

Dietzenbacher, E. (1997), 'An intercountry decomposition of output growth in EC countries', paper presented at the 44th North American Meeting of Regional Science Association International, Buffalo, November 6–9, 1997.

Disney, R. (1984), 'The regional impact of unemployment insurance in the United Kingdom', *Oxford Bulletin of Economics and Statistics*, **46** (3), 244–54.

Ekspertudvalget (1998), *Markedskræfter og politisk styring*, Ekspertudvalget nedsat af Regeringens Hovedstadsudvalg.

Engelstoft, S. and C.N. Jensen-Butler (1997), *'Industrial dynamics in two Danish regions'*, Manuscript, Department of Geography, University of Copenhagen.

Erhvervsministeriet (1997), *Erhvervsredegørelse,* Copenhagen: Erhvervsministeriet.

Groes, N. (1994), *Uligheder i Danmark,* Memo, Copenhagen: AKF-Forlaget.

Groes, N. (1997), 'Inequalities and Mobility in the Danish Welfare State', in K. Peschel (ed.), *Regional Growth and Regional Policy within the Framework of European Integration,* Heidelberg: Physica-Verlag, pp. 142–175.

Groes, N. and E. Heinesen (1997), *Uligheder i Danmark–noget om geografiske vækstmønstre*, Copenhagen: AKF-Forlaget.

Hansen, A.C. (1991), *Den geografiske omfordeling*, Copenhagen: AKF-Forlaget.

Hansen, F., C.N. Jensen-Butler (1996), 'Economic crisis and the regional and local effects of the welfare state: The case of Denmark', *Regional Studies*, **30** (2), 167–187.

Jensen-Butler, C.N. (1992), 'Rural industrialization in denmark and the role of public policy', *Urban Studies*, **29** (6), 881-904.

Jensen, T.P., P. Maskell, S. Arnberg, M.B. Hansen and T. Ranis (1997), *Erhvervslokalisering og vækst*, Copenhagen: AKF-Forlaget.

Kristensen, K., and M. Henry (1998), *Lokaløkonomisk vækst i Danmark – en rumlig analyse*, Copenhagen: AKF-Forlaget.

Lucas, R.E. Jr. (1976), 'Econometric Policy Evaluation: a Critique', in K. Brunner and A.H. Meltzer (eds), *The Philips Curve and Labour Markets,* Amsterdam: North-Holland, pp. 14–46.

Madsen, B. (1989), 'Planens regionale virkninger', *AKF-Nyt 1989/2*, Copenhagen.

Madsen, B. and L.E. Rasmussen (1991), *Offentlige betalinger mellem Bornholm og det øvrige Danmark*, Copenhagen: AKF-Forlaget.

Madsen, B. and S. Caspersen (1998), *Økonomien i landkommunerne – status og udvikling*, Copenhagen: AKF-Forlaget.

Madsen, B. and C.N. Jensen-Butler (1999), 'The commodity balance and make and use approaches to interregional modelling', *Economic Systems Research*, June.

Madsen, B., C.N. Jensen-Butler and P.U. Dam (1997), 'The LINE Model', Working Paper, Local Governments' Research Institute, Copenhagen: AKF-Forlaget.

Maskell, P. (1986), *Industriens flugt fra storbyen. Årsager og konsekvenser*, Copenhagen: Nyt Nordisk Forlag, Arnold Busch.

NUTEK (1994), *Statsbudgetens regionale fördelning*, Swedish Board for Industrial and Technical Development B, 1994:3, Stockholm.

Nørskov, L. (1991), *Offentlige og mellem-regionale pengestrømme i Danmark i 1988*, Copenhagen: AKF-Forlaget.

Oosterhaven, J. and R.J. Stoffelsema (1990), 'The Net Effect of Social Security on the Dutch Interregional Income Distribution', in L. Anselin and M. Madden, *New Directions in Regional Analysis*, London: Belhaven Press, pp. 236–252.

Rose, A. and S. Casler (1996), 'Input-output structural decomposition analysis: a critical appraisal', *Economic Systems Research*, **8**, 33–62.

Short, J. (1978), 'The regional distribution of public expenditure in Great Britain 1969/70-1973/74', *Regional Studies*, **12**, 499–510.

Short, J. (1984), 'Public finance and devolution–Money flows between government and regions in the United Kingdom', *Scottish Journal of Political Economy*, **31** (2), 114–130.

Stoffelsma, R.J. and J. Oosterhaven (1989), 'Social security benefits and interregional income inequalities. The case of the Netherlands', *Annals of Regional Science*, **23**, 223–240.

Wier, M. (1998), 'Sources of change in emissions from energy: A structural decomposition', *Economic Systems Research*, **10** (2), 99–112.

Wolff, E.N. (1985), 'Industrial composition, interindustry effects and the US productivity slowdown', *Review of Economics and Statistics*, **67** (2) 268–277.

PART THREE

Regional Policy; Methodological Approaches

15. Methods for Identifying Functional Regions: Theory and Applications

Charlie Karlsson and Michael Olsson

1 INTRODUCTION

In Sweden, the daily mobility of persons has increased from a half kilometre in the year 1900 to an estimated fifty kilometres in the year 2000 (Andersson and Strömquist, 1988). Although the daily commuting region has expanded, economic activities are spatially concentrated. In particular, this is true for production activities. According to Krugman (1991), geographical concentration is the most striking feature of economic reality. Consumers' daily activities, including work, tend to be performed close to their residence. Companies hire workers living relatively close to the firm, buy services from firms located nearby and often sell their products in close proximity.

This means that short-distance spatial interaction dominates for most households and firms. For each centre of economic activities, there exists a hinterland dominated by interactions with the centre. In the subsequent analysis, an economic functional region consists of one or more centres and the appurtenant hinterland (Karlsson, 1994). A functional region is characterised by a high frequency of economic interaction (Johansson, 1998), such as intra-regional trade in goods and services, labour commuting and household shopping. Hence, the essence of a functional region is a system of highly connected smaller and larger places.

Given this rather general definition the question arises, how do we delimit functional regions in real geographical space? The answer to this question is of considerable interest, since it has important analytical and planning implications. Functional regions often contain several administrative regions. This creates tensions and causes planning problems, since in the generic case several local governments are responsible for the planning of the functional region as a whole. The administrative regions need to cooperate in order to support the functional region. For labour market analysis and infrastructure planning, the functional region is the relevant geographic concept.

The purpose of this chapter is to analyse various methods for identifying functional regions and to apply them, using Swedish data, with a focus on the Fyrstad region in western Sweden. In forming functional regions the aim is to aggregate areas with high economic interaction and there are many types of interaction that one may consider, such as population flows, trade in goods and services, communication, traffic flows, goods flows, service connections, newspaper circulation and financial flows (Vanhove and Klaassen, 1987). In this chapter, we make use of commuting data, since the pattern of daily interaction in the labour market is a good proxy for the functional region.

Theoretical and practical methods for identifying functional regions using labour market data are presented in Section 2. In Section 3 the methods presented in Section 2 are applied to Swedish data for the years 1986 and 1996. This general application is followed up in Section 4, where the same methods are applied to the Fyrstad region to determine the geographic area of the region using varying criteria. Conclusions and suggestions for future research are presented in Section 5.

2 METHODS FOR IDENTIFYING FUNCTIONAL REGIONS BASED UPON LABOUR MARKET DATA

The purpose of this section is to present and discuss alternative methods for identifying functional regions using labour market data.

2.1 A Theoretical Model Delineating Commuting Regions

In this first section, we analyse factors that determine where persons with a fixed place of residence choose to work. This is a reasonable framework for the short term. In the medium term, people may move and so the framework must be modified. In a short-run analysis, simplified assumptions can be used. All workers have perfect information about jobs, wages and travel costs. All jobs are concentrated to two centres, *i* and *j*. All wages are the same in *i* and the same applies to j, but wages in *j* are assumed to be higher than in *i*, that is $w_j > w_i$.

Wages can be higher in *j* due to higher productivity in *j*. All jobs are equal in terms of the skills they demand and all workers have the same skills. All workers are assumed to live on a linear strip between *i* and *j*. Travelling from any point between *i* and *j* is associated with travel costs, c_i and c_j , that increase with the distance to *i* and *j*, respectively.

Given this we now assume that the objective of the workers is to maximise the real wage (*w*) net of the generalised travel cost (*c*). This net wage we refer to as ω. The net wage that is obtained from working in centres *i* and *j*, respectively, is illustrated in Figure 15.1 below as ω_i and ω_j. The net wage at any location between the two centres is $\max\{\omega_i, \omega_j\}$.

Given that the net wage is higher than the reservation wage all workers to the left of k will commute to centre *i* and all workers to the right of *k* will commute to centre *j*. Workers living in k are indifferent since $\omega_i = \omega_j$. Hence, *k* is the border between the two functional regions, *i* and *j*. The two functional regions consist of the locations (*x*), which satisfy either Equation (15.1a) or Equation (15.1b).

$$FR_i = \{x : \omega_i(x) > \omega_j(x)\} \tag{15.1a}$$

$$FR_j = \{x : \omega_j(x) > \omega_i(x)\} \tag{15.1b}$$

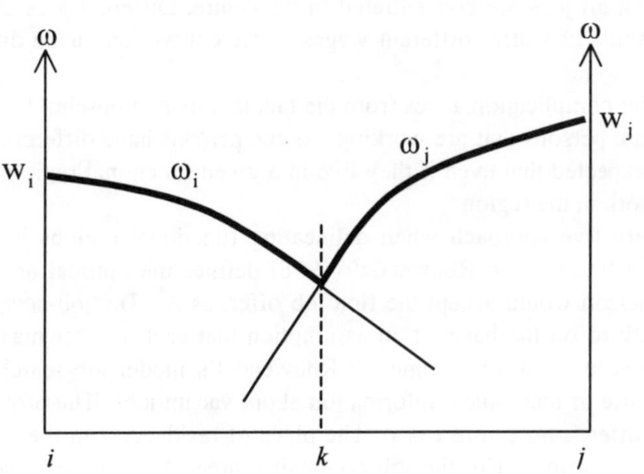

*Figure 15.1 The real wage less transportation costs between two centres (*i* and* j*)*

In the sequel, we will analyse what happens with the border *k* when the basic conditions change. First, we analyse what happens when there is a change in the commuting costs. Assume that travel costs to centre *j* decrease due to investments in infrastructure or improvements in the public transport system. This will lead to a shift upward in the function ω_i The border between the two functional regions in Figure 15.1 will shift to the left and hence functional region *j* will be extended and functional region *i* will become smaller. Moreover, there will be an increase in the net wages and thus an improvement in economic welfare, given that the tax cost of the improvements is lower than the wage increase. There will also be an increase in the supply of workers since fewer people will have reservation wages that are higher than the net wage.

In a second step we analyse what happens if the real wage in *j*, w_i, increases compared to the real wage in *i*, w_i. The driving force behind such an increase can be productivity improvements in *j* due to capital investments and/or an increase of agglomeration economies in *j*. The effects of a comparative real wage increase are the same as that of a reduction of the generalised travel costs. The reach of the region *j* will be extended as the border *k* is shifted to the left.

In reality, the border between two functional regions is always fuzzy. Workers do not have perfect information about job offerings in different centres. Not all jobs are concentrated in the centre. Different jobs demand different skills and offer different wages. Different workers have different skills.

A further complication arises from the fact that many households contain two or more persons that are working. As the persons have different skills, it can be expected that even if they live in a given functional region not all of them work in the region.

An alternative approach when delineating functional regions is to use commuting frequencies. Rouwendal (1998) defines the optimal area from which a person would accept the first job offer, as A^*. The job-acceptance area is defined on the basis of an assumption that each worker maximises the net present value of income. In Rouwendal's model job-search takes time, because of incomplete information about vacant jobs. The probability for a job offer from centre *i* is γ_i. The place of residence and the place of work are by definition in the job-acceptance area. As a consequence, the (conditional) probability of working in centre *i* is:

$$P_i = \gamma_i \Big/ \sum_{j \in A^*} \gamma_j , i \in A^* \qquad (15.2)$$

This probability can explain the empirical regularity (Bradford and Kent, 1981) that commuting frequencies to a centre decline with increasing distance to the centre in question (Figure 15.2). Assume that the household choice of location reveals the job-acceptance area in consideration. Assume that a household is located in a centre, since the members prefer to live and work in the same centre. A choice of living outside the large centre reveals that if the household members have to work in the centre they will do so, but they will not live there. The household located outside the centre has already accepted longer commuting (on average). The size of the job-acceptance area therefore increases with the distance from the centre in question. Outside the centre, there are small towns, with some job offers, which the household automatically takes into consideration. This enlarged job-acceptance area increases the sum of job-offer probabilities and causes the commuting probability (to centre *i*) to decline.

2.2 Taking the Models Closer to Empirical Observations

According to the first approach presented above, the net wage-functions identify the functional regions. Even if the real wages are not the only things valued by workers, they have a strong influence on behaviour. Hence, one can assume that commuting is attracted by the places with the highest net wage. The implementation of the local labour market approach has used existing commuting data.

The distance interval that is observed in everyday commuting for a majority of the working population in Sweden is 15–60 minutes. When the distance gets too long other solutions than everyday commuting are usually preferred, such as weekly commuting, moving or teleworking (some or all of the time).

Johansson (1998) uses a distance-dependent cost function to explain that the interaction frequency declines with the distance (Figure 15.2). The sum of all costs that depends on geography (distance) is called the geographical interaction costs. The geographical interaction costs include costs for transportation, communication and transactions.

Products differ in their distance-sensitivity. Non-standardised production such as service production is of a local nature and the cost curve is very distance-sensitive. Standardised products have very flat cost curves. According to Johansson, it is possible to identify the border of the functional region when a large share of all distance-sensitive products has approximately the same distance barrier (approximately the distance where the interaction frequency is significantly reduced).

In the labour market, such barriers exist because of friction in the transport system. The infrastructure and the functioning of the transport system give rise to discontinuous travel costs (including the value of time).

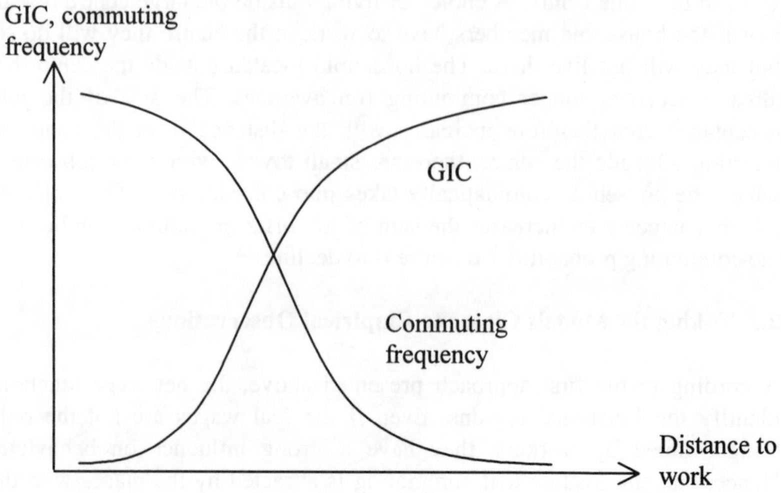

Figure 15.2 The geographical interaction cost and the commuting frequency (Johansson, 1998)

The tariff system, when crossing an administrative border, often causes the costs to take a leap. During commuting, a change of means of transport induces waiting time. The reliability of the transport system is important and a change of transport mode may lower reliability. The infrastructure may cause traffic congestion and the unpredictability of commuting time is costly.

There are three different levels of interaction that may be used in estimating the extension of a functional region. Assume two centres indexed *i* and *j* located in a region represented by a line. The left endpoint is signified by *i* and the right by *j*, as illustrated in Figure 15.3. Moreover, *x* denotes an intermediate point between *i* and *j*. At a location (*x*) the commuting frequency to centre *i* is $f_i(x)$. The functional region consists of all geographic locations (*x*) that satisfy one of the following three conditions (Equations (15.3a)–(15.3c)).

The first condition would be to include all locations (*x*) with any commuting to the centre *i*. The border of the region is seen at k_1. The extension of the functional region *i* is defined by:

$$FR_i = \{x : f_i(x) > 0\} \tag{15.3a}$$

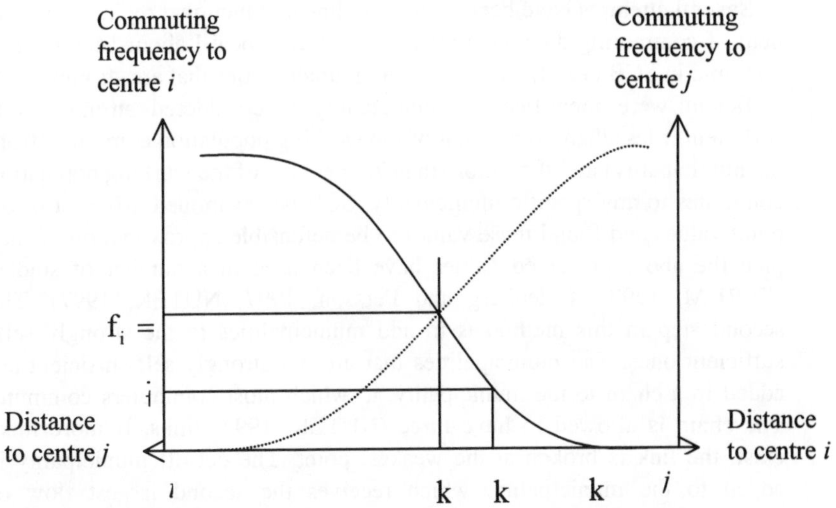

Figure 15.3 The commuting frequencies to the two centres (i *and* j)

A second alternative condition would be to use a cut-off frequency (larger than zero) for inclusion. The cut-off frequency gets rid of the very few long-distance commuters. This rule does not allow extremely low interaction and the border is at k_2. The functional region is smaller using the second condition than when using the first condition.

$$FR_i = \{x : f_i(x) \geq \bar{f}\} \tag{15.3b}$$

The third criterion for defining a functional region is to consider neighbouring central places and to calculate the break point between the different central places. A point on the border k_3 is found where the attraction is equal to both the closest cores.

$$FR_i = \{x : f_i(x) \geq f_j(x)\} \tag{15.3c}$$

In theory, the borders are exactly defined and the theoretical borders will not necessarily follow administrative borders. In practice, the functional region will consist of smaller areas aggregated. This means that the smallest geographical area, for which there exist commuting data (usually municipalities[1]) influence how close the estimated functional region will be to the theoretical functional region.

Several attempts have been made to delineate functional regions with the help of commuting data. One method to create Local Labour Markets can be found in SCB (1992). As a first step, municipalities that are strongly self-sufficient were identified. A municipality is considered strongly self-sufficient if less than 20 per cent of the working population commute (from the municipality) and if no more than 7.5 per cent of the working population commutes to any specific municipality. SCB has examined different break point values and found these values to be defensible approximations. Since then the above-presented values have been used in a number of studies (CERUM, 1993; Kullenberg and Persson, 1997; NUTEK, 1997). The second step in this method is to add municipalities to the strongly self-sufficient ones. The municipalities that are not strongly self-sufficient are added in a chain to the municipality, to which most commuters commute. The chain is allowed to have three (NUTEK, 1997) links. If more links exist, the link is broken at the weakest point. The cut-off municipality is added to the municipality, which receives the second largest flow of commuters. In SCB (1992) one more rule is presented, but not used. If two municipalities are not strongly self-sufficient, but the largest commuter flow in each municipality goes to the other, they themselves form a local labour market.

Killian and Tolbert (1993) estimate commuting zones. This approach is less focused on urban cores than the methods mentioned above. The commuting zones are built from the existing mutual dependency of municipalities, rather than one-way dependency. The number of commuters from municipality i (j) to municipality j (i) is measured by C_{ij} (C_{ji}) and P_i (P_j) measures the working population in municipality i (j). A measure of the strength of the two-way commuting ties is calculated by equation (15.4).

$$\left(C_{ij} + C_{ji}\right)/\min\left\{P_i, P_j\right\} \tag{15.4}$$

With such a measure, two municipalities with a large one-way commuter flow do not necessarily qualify as a region.

2.3 Conclusions

There are several ways to delineate functional regions. In this section, three somewhat different approaches have been presented. The first and second classification rule uses one-way commuter flows. First, a single criterion can be used to identify the regions. The use of commuting frequencies is an example. Second, a more complicated criterion for identification of the regions can be used. An example would be the definition of a local labour market above. The third criterion would be to calculate the connection among municipalities, using commuter flows in both ways. These differences in how to define regions have consequences for the outcome, which will be seen in the following sections.

3 FUNCTIONAL REGIONS IN SWEDEN

The purpose of this section is to describe the changes of Sweden's functional regions during the period from 1986 to 1996. The characteristics used are the number and sizes of the functional regions.

Statistics Sweden collects commuting data (ÅRSSYS), and in this application, data from 1986 and 1996 are used. In this section, the following rule is used for the separation of municipalities into self-sufficient and not self-sufficient municipalities. Self-sufficiency is defined as the share of persons employed that work in the municipality where they live. The result from identifying all and counting all municipalities with self-sufficiency over a chosen limit is illustrated in Figure 15.4 (and Table 15.1). In this case, the number of functional regions in Sweden is equal to the number of self-sufficient municipalities, since the municipalities that are not self-sufficient are added to the self-sufficient ones. This procedure has been repeated for 1986[2] and 1996. In Figure 15.4 the curve for 1986 lies above the curve for 1996 (except for extremely low self-sufficiency requirements). This shows that the number of functional regions has been decreasing from 1986 to 1996, using the above criteria.

Table 15.1 The number of functional regions at different self-sufficiency limits (1986 and 1996)

Self-sufficiency(%)	Number 1986	Number 1996
90	42	22
80	138	113
70	204	165
60	228	215
50	249	242
40	262	256
30	281	280
20	284	287

The size of a functional region is an important indicator of local market size, which is an important variable in the decision whether to start a firm or not. The threshold market size is different between industries and the bigger the local market, the more industries there are in the region. The size of the functional region also has implications for worker flexibility. A worker in a bigger functional region has more to choose from, regarding both workplace and type of occupation.

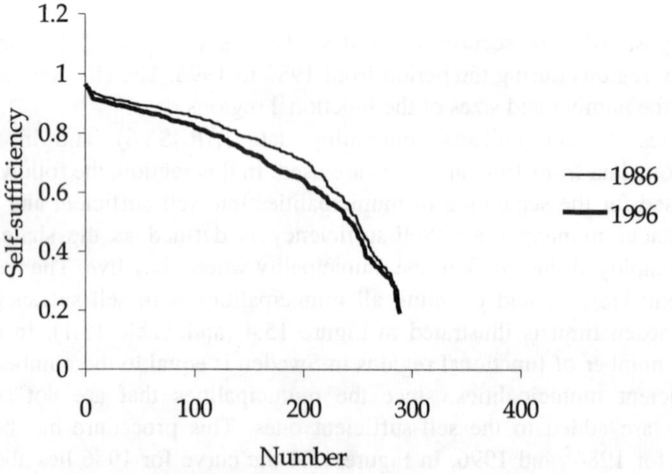

Figure 15.4 The number of local labour markets in 1986 and 1996

Hence, it is important to ask what has happened to the size of the functional regions in Sweden between 1986 and 1996. The number of persons working in the municipalities, belonging to a functional region, is here used as a measure of the size of a functional region (summary statistics are given in Table 15.2). Here we define a self-sufficient municipality[3] as a municipality with less than 25 per cent out-commuting, that is the self-sufficiency limit is set to 75 per cent. The rank-size distribution of functional regions in Sweden for 1986 and 1996 is plotted in Figure 15.5. The results from an estimation of the model $\ln(\text{size}) = \alpha + \beta\ln(\text{rank}) + \varepsilon$ are presented in Table 15.3. The slope parameter (β) has decreased from -1.11 in 1986 to –1.22 in 1996. The α effect of rank on the size of the functional regions is more negative in 1996 than in 1986. The α-parameter is 14.1 in 1996 and 13.9 in 1986. The parameter measures the estimated size of the functional region with rank 1, that is $\ln(\text{rank}) = 0$. The regression results indicate that the largest regions are larger in 1996 than in 1986.

One important conclusion that can be drawn is that the number of functional regions has decreased and a majority of them has decreased in size. Only large functional regions have grown in size. One must in this context recognise that in these ten years the number of persons employed decreased by about 500 000 to about 3 820 000.

Table 15.2 Summary statistics on the functional regions, 1986 and 1996

	1986	1996
Number	172	142
Max	860 523	871 733
Min	1 463	1 176
Mean	25 076	26 851
Median	10 048	9 332
Standard deviation	75 117	82 664

Table 15.3 The estimated parameters, when 75 per cent self-sufficiency limit is used, t-values are given in parentheses

	1986	1996
Constant	13.9 (147.1)	14.1 (128.5)
	–1.11 (50.1)	–1.22 (45.4)
	0.936	0.936

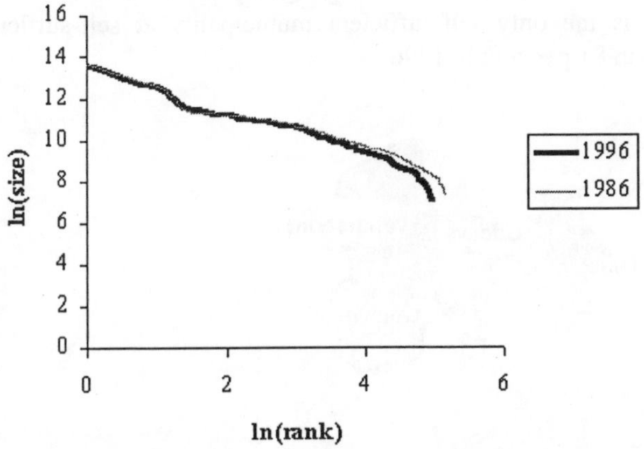

Figure 15.5 The rank–size distribution of the functional regions 1986 and 1996

3.1 Conclusions

The conclusions from this section are that the number of functional regions in Sweden decreased between 1986 to 1996. An implication of the smaller number of regions is that the functional regions have grown in geographic space. We found that the median value of the working population in the functional regions decreased during 1986 to 1996. The functional regions that have increased their working population are the large functional regions. It has to be remembered that the total number of workers decreased by almost 500 000 persons in the period 1986 to 1996.

4 THE FYRSTAD REGION AS A FUNCTIONAL REGION

The purpose of this section is to use the tools from Section 2.2 to analyse the Fyrstad region in Western Sweden.

The Fyrstad region is mostly used as the name for the region formed by four neighbouring municipalities: Uddevalla, Trollhättan, Vänersborg and Lysekil (Figure 15.6). However, if we look upon the Fyrstad region as a functional region it also contains a number of neighbouring municipalities. The location of the core Fyrstad region is shown in a map of the county of Västra Götaland (Appendix, Figure 15A.1). In Table 15.4 we list all municipalities in the larger Fyrstad region and illustrate the situation in 1986 and 1996 in terms of self-sufficiency. The self-sufficiency values are lower in 1996 than in 1986,[4] for all municipalities that belong to the larger Fyrstad region. This is a sign of increasing regional integration.

Trollhättan is the only self-sufficient municipality at self-sufficiency level higher than 81 per cent in 1996.

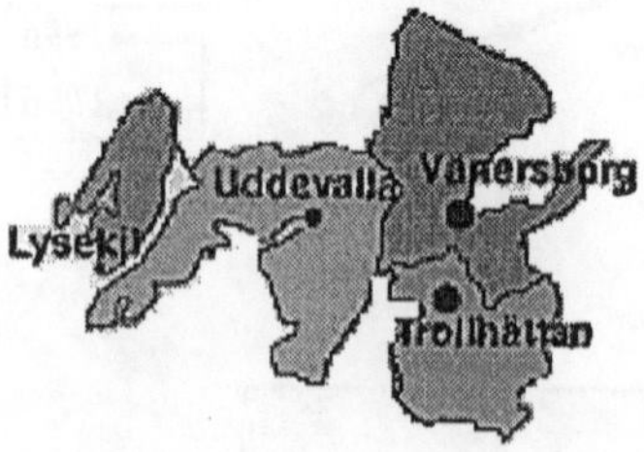

Source: The county administration of Västra Götaland

Figure 15.6 A map of the core of the region.

Table 15.4 The self-sufficiency in 1986 and 1996 in the larger Fyrstad region

Municipality	1986	1996
Trollhättan	0.87	0.84
Lysekil	0.84	0.81
Sotenäs	0.79	0.79
Uddevalla	0.83	0.79
Mellerud	0.78	0.73
Färgelanda	0.69	0.67
Munkedal	0.67	0.62
Vänersborg	0.77	0.61
Essunga	0.64	0.60
Orust	0.60	0.56
Grästorp	0.59	0.51
Lilla Edet	0.56	0.50

Non self-sufficient municipalities with commuter flows greater than 5 per cent to a self-sufficient municipality are added to Trollhättan to form the functional region (with the self-sufficient municipality as the core). According to this definition, the municipalities of Uddevalla, Mellerud, Vänersborg, Lilla Edet, Grästorp and Essunga belong to the functional region of Trollhättan.

Source: The county administration of Västra Götaland .

Figure 15.7 The Trollhättan and Lysekil functional regions (self-sufficiency level = 80 per cent, 1996)

If the self-sufficiency criterion is set at 80 per cent, Lysekil becomes self-sufficient. Sotenäs is added to the functional region of Lysekil as a non self-sufficient municipality with a commuter flow to Lysekil larger than 5 per cent. The larger Fyrstad region now consists of two functional regions: the Trollhättan region and the Lysekil region (Figure 15.7).

Source: The county administration of Västra Götaland.

Figure 15.8 The Trollhättan, Lysekil and Uddevalla functional regions (Self-sufficiency limit = 73 per cent, 1996)

Trollhättan, Lysekil and Sotenäs are self-sufficient municipalities when the limit is set at 79 percent. Sotenäs is excluded from Figure 15.8, since Sotenäs no longer belongs to the Fyrstad region. When the limit for self-sufficiency is lowered to 73 percent, two municipalities: Uddevalla and Mellerud are classified as self-sufficient municipalities. Mellerud is excluded from Figure 15.8, since at this level it becomes self-sufficient and therefore no longer belongs to the Fyrstad region. Munkedal, Färgelanda and Orust have more than 5 percent of the workers commuting to Uddevalla and are therefore included in the Uddevalla functional region. The larger Fyrstad region now consists of the three functional regions: the Trollhättan region, the Lysekil region and the Uddevalla region (Figure 15.8).

If the self-sufficiency criterion is set to 65 per cent, Färgelanda becomes self-sufficient. When the limit is 60 per cent Vänersborg, Munkedal and Essunga are classified as self-sufficient. Färgelanda, Munkedal and Essunga are self-sufficient and do not at this level belong to the Fyrstad region (Figure 15.9). The larger Fyrstad region then consists of four functional regions: the Trollhättan region, the Lysekil region, the Uddevalla region and the Vänersborg region.

If the requirement for self-sufficiency is lowered to 50 per cent then Orust, Grästorp and Lilla Edet become self-sufficient. This is seen in Table 15.4 and the Fyrstad region then consists of the four municipalities Uddevalla, Trollhättan, Vänersborg and Lysekil (Figure 15.6).

The definition of Local Labour Markets (SCB, 1992) can be used to classify the municipalities in the Fyrstad region. The self-sufficient municipalities (close to the Fyrstad region) are Lysekil, Strömstad, Bengtsfors, Trollhättan, Lidköping and Skövde. The result of using the local labour market criterion is that the Fyrstad region consists of two local labour markets: Trollhättan and Lysekil. The municipalities included[5] in these local labour markets are presented in Table 15.5 and Figure 15.10.

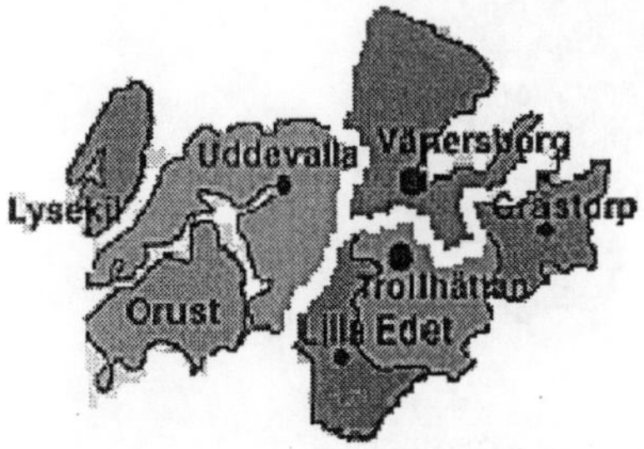

Source: The county administration of Västra Götaland.

Figure 15.9 The Trollhättan, Lysekil, Uddevalla and Vänersborg functional regions (Self-sufficiency limit = 60 per cent, 1996)

Table 15.5 The local labour markets in the Fyrstad region, 1996

Trollhättan	Lysekil
Uddevalla, Vänersborg, Grästorp, Munkedal (through Uddevalla), Färgelanda (Uddevalla), Mellerud (Vänersborg)	Sotenäs

A two-way commuter-flow measure (Section 2.2) has also been calculated for the municipalities in the larger Fyrstad region. The Fyrstad region would then consist of two areas with strong mutual commuter flows (Table 15.6 and Figure 15.11). Lilla Edet is a municipality with interesting characteristics. Lilla Edet sends most of its commuters to Göteborg so Lilla Edet belongs to the Göteborg functional region using a one-way flow measure and, therefore, does not belong to the Fyrstad region (Figure

15.10). Very few people commute from Göteborg to Lilla Edet. Lilla Edet sends almost as many commuters to Trollhättan as to Göteborg but more people commute from Trollhättan than from Göteborg to Lilla Edet. Using a two-way flow measure Lilla Edet would be included in the Fyrstad region (through Trollhättan), because the two-way flow measure between Lilla Edet and Trollhättan was 0.21 which is larger than 0.19 that was the two-way flow measure between Lilla Edet and Göteborg.

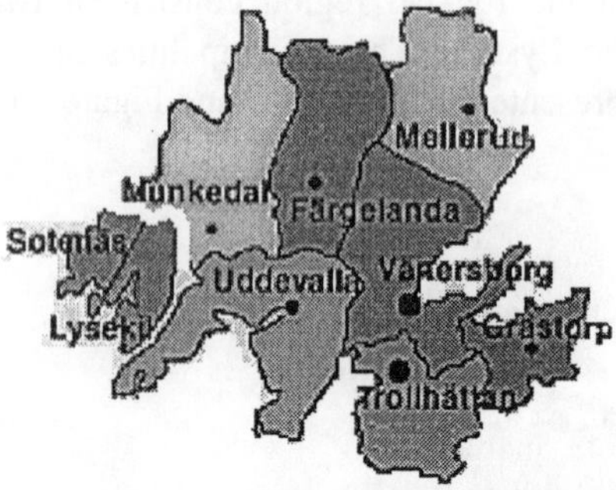

Source: The county administration of Västra Götaland.

Figure 15.10 The Uddevalla and Lysekil local labour markets (1996)

Source: The county administration of Västra Götaland.

Figure 15.11 The Fyrstad region as two functional regions in 1996

We now continue by analysing how the situation has changed between 1986 and 1996 in the larger Fyrstad region.

If the self-sufficiency limit is between 87 per cent and 84 per cent, only Trollhättan was self-sufficient in 1986 (Table 15.4). In 1986, four municipalities (Grästorp, Essunga, Vänersborg and Lilla Edet) had more than 5 per cent commuting into Trollhättan. The Trollhättan functional region in 1986 did not contain Mellerud and Uddevalla, which was the case in 1996 (Figure 15.7).

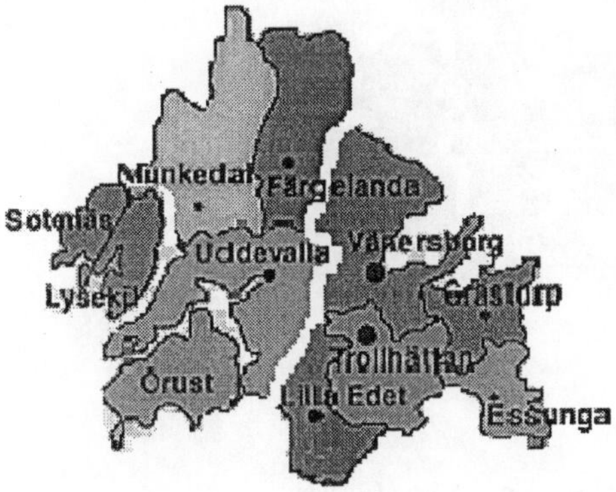

Source: The county administration of Västra Götaland.

Figure 15.12 The Trollhättan, Lysekil and Uddevalla functional regions (self-sufficiency limit = 83 per cent, 1986.

Lysekil becomes self-sufficient at 84 per cent and Uddevalla at 83 per cent. Sotenäs is added to Lysekil and Orust, Munkedal and Färgelanda belongs to the functional region of Uddevalla (Figure 15.12). The larger Fyrstad region at this self-sufficiency level consists of three functional regions: the Trollhättan region, the Lysekil region and the Uddevalla region.

Lowering the limit to 79 per cent makes Sotenäs self-sufficient. When the level is set to 78 per cent Mellerud becomes self-sufficient. Because of that, Sotenäs and Mellerud do not belong to the Fyrstad region. Vänersborg turns self-sufficient at 77 per cent. No municipality is added to the functional region of Vänersborg. The main difference compared to 1996 is that in 1986 Vänersborg is much less connected to the neighbouring municipalities. The larger Fyrstad region then consists of four functional regions: the Trollhättan region, the Lysekil region, the Uddevalla region and the Vänersborg region (Figure 15.13).

As the requirement for self-sufficiency gets lower, more municipalities become self-sufficient and are excluded from the Fyrstad region. Färgelanda is lost at 69 per cent, Munkedal at 67 per cent and Essunga at 64 per cent. Orust becomes self-sufficient at 60 per cent, Grästorp at 59 per cent and Lilla Edet at 56 per cent. The Fyrstad region at this self-sufficiency level consists of the core municipalities (Figure 15.6).

Source: The county administration of Västra Götaland.

Figure 15.13 The Trollhättan, Lysekil, Uddevalla and Vänersborg functional regions (Self-sufficiency limit = 77 per cent, 1986).

In 1996, the Fyrstad region consisted of two local labour markets (Figure 15.10). Repeating the procedure for 1986 shows that in 1986, the region contained three local labour markets. From 1986 to 1996, the region did not change, but the labour markets became more interwoven. The 1986 local labour markets of Uddevalla and Trollhättan are 1996 joined into the Trollhättan local labour market in 1996 (Figure 15.14). Lysekil and Sotenäs were a separate local labour market in 1986.

If the two-way commuter-flow measure used for 1996 is used for 1986 it can be shown that the Fyrstad region has not changed over these ten years. Figure 15.11 is valid for both 1986 and 1996. However, during these ten years, there has been an increase in the connectivity between the municipalities (Table 15.6), but the Fyrstad region has not expanded to include other municipalities.

The Fyrstad region had (in 1996) parts in three counties (now joined into the county of Västra Götaland). In the Fyrstad region the borders of the functional regions tend to follow the county border (Figures 15.11 and

15.15). Municipalities are relatively more connected inside counties than across counties. The exceptional municipalities are Grästorp and Färgelanda. Färgelanda belonged to the county of Älvsborg and to the Uddevalla functional region. Grästorp belonged to the county of Skaraborg and to the functional region of Trollhättan.

Source: The county administration of Västra Götaland.

Figure 15.14 The Trollhättan, Uddevalla and Lysekil local labour markets in 1986

These cross-county functional regions created planning problems and might have been the main reason for the relative stability of the Fyrstad region between 1986 and 1996. This also suggests that barriers to cross-county borders exist. Using local labour markets instead, in principle, leads to the same conclusions, except that Lilla Edet is not included in the Fyrstad region (Figures 15.14 and 15.15).

The Fyrstad region consists of ten municipalities: Färgelanda, Grästorp, Lilla Edet, Lysekil, Mellerud, Munkedal, Sotenäs, Trollhättan, Uddevalla and Vänersborg. We include Lilla Edet, even though Fyrstad seems to gradually lose Lilla Edet to Göteborg. The two-way flow measure between Lilla Edet and Göteborg increased from 0.14 in 1986 to 0.19 in 1996 while the two-way flow measure between Lilla Edet and Trollhättan is unchanged at 0.21 although larger than the 1996 Göteborg index measure (Table 15.6).

Table 15.6 The two-way flow measures in 1986 and 1996

Municipality	Municipality	1986	1996
Vänersborg	Trollhättan	0.26	0.37
Munkedal	Uddevalla	0.19	0.22
Lilla Edet	Trollhättan	0.21	0.21
Färgelanda	Uddevalla	0.17	0.18
Grästorp	Trollhättan	0.15	0.18
Mellerud	Vänersborg	0.11	0.14
Lysekil	Uddevalla	0.08	0.10
Sotenäs	Lysekil	0.07	0.08

Source: The county administration of Västra Götaland.

Figure 15.15 The Fyrstad region had parts in three counties

4.1 Conclusions

We conclude that the main change during the period from 1986 to 1996 is the increased connectivity between municipalities (Table 15.6). The self-sufficiency was lower in 1996 than 1986 (Table 15.4). The increased commuting has extended the Trollhättan region using a 5 per cent in-commuting limit (Figures 15.7 and 15.12). Using measures that take other core municipalities into consideration the Fyrstad region in year 1996 is exactly the same as in 1986. Using the local labour market definition, the Fyrstad region in 1996 (Figure 15.10) is the same area as the Fyrstad region was in 1986 (Figure 15.14). Using a two-way flow measure, the Fyrstad region in 1986 and 1996 is the same (Figure 15.11). For further research, we consider the Fyrstad region to consist of ten municipalities: Färgelanda, Grästorp, Lilla Edet, Lysekil, Mellerud, Munkedal, Sotenäs, Trollhättan, Uddevalla and Vänersborg. We have also found an indication that administrative borders may have acted to create barriers to commuting.

5 CONCLUSIONS AND SUGGESTIONS FOR FUTURE RESEARCH

Between 1986 and 1996 the self-sufficiency of Swedish municipalities has been decreasing. At the national level there are fewer functional regions, and at the same time the size of the median region has decreased, measured by number of workers. This is due to the general decrease in employment in the early 1990s.

A general reflection regarding the municipalities in the Fyrstad region is that their mutual connectivity has increased over the study period. It is noteworthy that this has limited effects on the municipal members of the constructed region. This is in contrast to what has happened in the rest of Sweden. For the Fyrstad region, the commuter flows have become more intertwined among the municipalities, but the geographic extension of the region has not grown. We consider the Fyrstad region to consist of Färgelanda, Grästorp, Lilla Edet, Lysekil, Mellerud, Munkedal, Sotenäs, Trollhättan, Uddevalla and Vänersborg.

This study of functional regions and labour markets suggests a need for further research. This chapter was based on total commuter flows. The commuting distances for men are on average longer than the commuting distances for women and the commuted distance tends to increase with the length of the commuter's education level. Hence, the male functional regions are larger (in geographic space) than the female regions and people with high education have a larger functional region than people with less education do. Since the main motivation for this study is labour market integration and infrastructure planning, it is not enough to have knowledge of the functional regions based only on total flows. It would be of value to perform an analysis of gender differences and to study the connection between commuting behaviour and educational level.

We also found that the functional regions in the Fyrstad region behaved as if they were prevented from growing geographically, because of the prevailing county borders. This matter is serious. To measure the sizes of these apparent barriers to commuting is important, since such barriers contribute to welfare losses. Another issue for future research is to examine how the relative wage levels change in municipalities as they become more connected and form an integrated labour market.

APPENDIX 15A

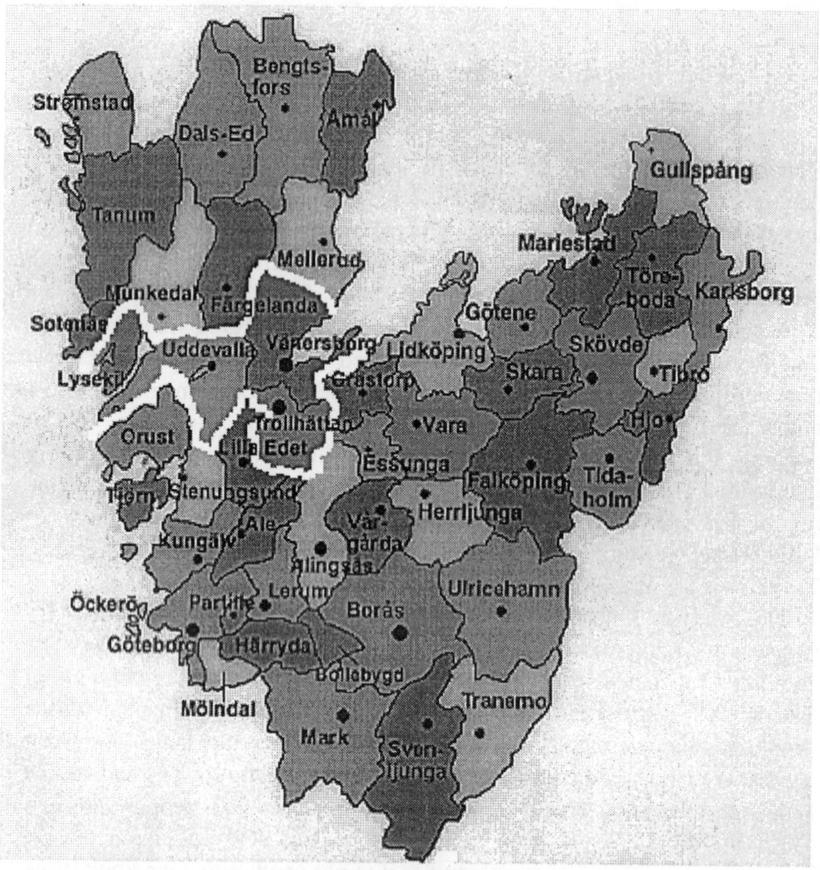

Source: The county administration of Västra Götaland.

Figure 15A.1 The position of the Fyrstad region in the county Västra Götaland.

NOTES

1. A municipality is the smallest civil jurisdiction in Sweden. Counties consist of several municipalities, which include both urban and non-urban areas.

2. The number of municipalities increased from 284 (1986) to 288 (1996). The new municipalities are Bollebygd, Gnesta, Lekeberg and Trosa.
3. Here we define self-sufficiency by choosing the 25 per cent limit as the only criterion. When defining Local Labour Markets (SCB, 1992) the limit is set to 20 per cent, but with additional criteria (and considerations) (Section 2.2). The simple reason for raising the limit from 20 per cent to 25 per cent is that we here just use one criterion and the fact that at the 20 per cent limit, for example, Stockholm is not self-sufficient. To better reflect the reality and to get relevant information using only one criterion, the limit had to be increased (, but the actual level chosen is to some degree arbitrary).
4. Marginally lower for Sotenäs.
5. The other surrounding municipalities, not included in the Fyrstad region are: Orust (largest commuter flow to Göteborg [G]), Tjörn (G), Stenungsund (G), Lilla Edet (G), Ale (G), Alingsås (G), Vårgårda (Alingsås), Herrljunga (Borås), Essunga (Vara), Vara (Lidköping), Falköping (Skövde), Skara (Skövde), Åmål (Bengtsfors), Dals-Ed (Bengtsfors), Tanum (Strömstad).

REFERENCES

Andersson, Å. and U. Strömquist (1988), *K-samhällets framtid*, Värnamo: Prisma.

Bradford, M.G. and W.A. Kent (1981), *Human Geography, Theories and Their Applications*, Oxford: Oxford University Press.

CERUM (1993), *Creating Labour Market Areas and Employment Zones*, Umeå: Umeå University print.

Johansson, B. (1998), *Infrastructure, Market Potential and Endogenous Growth*, Jönköping: JBS.

Karlsson, C. (1994), *Regioner och nätverk i Europa, En forskningsöversikt*, Stockholm: Landstingsförbundet.

Killian, M.S. and C.M. Tolbert (1993), 'Mapping Social and Economic Space: The delineation of local labour markets in the United States', in J. Singelmann and F.A. Desaran (eds), *Inequalities in Labour Market Areas*, Boulder, CO: Westview Press.

Krugman, P. (1991), *Geography and Trade*, Cambridge, MA: MIT Press.

Kullenberg, J. and L.O. Persson (1997), 'Tänjbara räckvidder, lokala arbetsmarknader i förändring', Swedish Institute for Regional Research, Report 101, Stockholm.

NUTEK (1997), *Regioner på väg mot år 2015, Förutsättningar, fakta och tendenser,* NUTEK R 1997:10, Stockholm.

Rouwendal, J. (1998), 'Search theory, spatial labor markets, and commuting', *Journal of Urban Economics* **43**, 1–22.

SCB (Statistics Sweden) (1992), *Local Labour Markets and Employment Regions, A new regional division of labour market areas in Sweden grounded on commuting statistics*, Labour Information 1991: 7, Stockholm.

Vanhove, N. and L.H. Klaassen (1987), *Regional Policy: A European Approach*, 2nd edition, Avebury: Aldershot.

Other Sources

The county administration of Västra Götaland, http://www.o.lst.se.

16. European Integration and International Trade in Manufacturing: Productivity Considerations and Employment Consequences

Kingsley Haynes and Mustafa Dinc

INTRODUCTION

New developments in technology and improvements in telecommunications and transportation have been forcing countries to adjust to the changing social and economic environment. Economic activities in different countries have become increasingly interdependent due to these developments and the resulting dynamics of trade in goods and services and flows of capital and technology. This new 'closeness' has brought increasing competition into the world marketplace. Two new topics have emerged or become reenergized due to these developments: globalisation and regionalisation. Globalisation and regionalisation issues are two of the major economic developments during the post-war period. Globalisation refers to trade liberalisation and increasing factor mobility across the world. Globalisation and liberalised international trade played a major role in the rise of living standards of people by improving the allocation of resources and by exerting discipline on economic policies through exposure to intense competition. Regionalisation, on the other hand, means the formation of regional groups of countries with free internal trade and factor mobility (Walz, 1999; Krugman, 1996).

The most prominent example of such regional integration is the European Union (EU). It is the product of 50 years of movement toward a united Europe. The process has been almost completed and from the initial six countries the Union now reaches 15 members with more than ten applying to join. The building of a united Europe is, no doubt, one of the greatest institutional undertakings of the twentieth century, and both social and economic expectations are high in terms of enhancing economic security and advancing social well being of the people as well as preserving the peace. A united Europe is seen as the only credible answer to the hazards and opportunities posed by the increasing globalisation of the world economy (Fontaine, 1998).

The European integration has some important effects on employment growth (decline). As a result of freer trade, a growth in exports brings more jobs due to increasing national outputs. On the other hand, increasing imports may cause employment decline even as it helps raise living standards and contributes to improving the quality and efficiency of domestically produced goods and services. According to official figures, the unemployment rate in the EU is around 12 per cent, which means 18 million European citizens are officially looking for work (Pelagidis, 1998). There have been different approaches to explaining such high unemployment rates in EU member countries. Some argued that it is a result of skill-biased technological change (Lawrence, 1994; Krugman, 1995; Baldwin, 1997). Some blamed the inflexibility of the European labour market, the high living standard of European working people, welfare programmes and firing costs (Bean and Holden, 1994). Finally, increasing international trade and intensification of international competition has been identified as another source of unemployment (Baldwin, 1997).

These are quite valid arguments and provide useful perspectives, although they cover only parts of a large picture. Estimating the linkages between regional economies and the global economy through international trade and examination of these past developments and their impacts on regional and national employment change are of great value and provide a useful framework for future policymaking. There have been some recent studies addressing these issues (see for examples Markusen, Noponen and Driessen, 1991; Noponen, Markusen and Driessen, 1997; Dinc and Haynes, 1998a, 1998b).

In this chapter, we employ Dinc and Haynes' (1998b) extended international trade and productivity shift–share model to assess the impact of international trade and productivity on regional (national) manufacturing employment change in eight major manufacturing sectors in thirteen EU countries between 1980 and 1995. By limiting the investigation to EU members it will be possible to capture the impact of the economic integration on manufacturing employment change.

The next section provides background information about the EU integration process and its recent employment and trade performance. The following section discusses the methodology and data employed. The findings and analysis are discussed in the fourth section. A concluding section follows.

BACKGROUND

Integration Process

With a proposal by France on 9 May, 1950 the movement toward a united Europe was begun in the form of a jointly managed market for the coal and steel sectors, which would be controlled by an independent authority. Germany, Italy, the Netherlands, Belgium and Luxembourg were the first group of supporters of it. The treaty that established the European Coal and Steel Community (ECSC) was signed in April 1951, and opened up the door to an integrated Europe.

To rebuild the war-tattered Europe and to achieve an economic revival the initial six ECSC member states decided to set up a common market, and on 25 March 1957 they signed the Treaty of Rome, which established the European Economic Community (EEC). Denmark, Ireland and the United Kingdom became members of the Community on 1 January 1973. Later, in the 1980s, more southern members were admitted as Greece, Spain and Portugal joined. Even though objectives of the Treaty of Rome have not yet been fully realised, there was a dramatic increase in trade within the EEC. The EEC's next step was to further liberalise trade and develop the Single European Act (SEA) in 1986. This act aimed at reducing trade barriers – non-tariff as well as tariff barriers – particularly in manufactured goods among member countries. The treaty set 1 January, 1993 as the date by which a full internal market was to be established (Fontaine, 1998). The third wave of admissions, Finland, Sweden and Austria, in 1995, reflected the eagerness of countries in Scandinavia and Central Europe to join the expanding Union.

Growth, Employment and Trade in the EU[1]

Over the last two decades, 1977–97, the European economy's rate of growth has shrunk from around 4 per cent to around 2.5 per cent a year. Unemployment in the member countries has been rising from cycle to cycle and the investment rate has fallen by 5 per cent. The competitive position of EU firms relative to their American and Japanese counterparts has worsened. Parallel to this the EU's shares of export markets, R&D and innovation and its incorporation into goods brought to the market, and in the development of new products have been declining. In spite of all these negative signs during the expansion period of 1986–90, EU enjoyed a continuous pattern of growth and restructuring (EU 1997 *Annual Economic Report*).

However, this growth and restructuring was not enough to make it possible to catch or at least not fall behind its international counterparts (that is, the USA and Japan). Table 16.1 presents an overall picture of the EU economy in comparison with its major international partners from 1974 to 1995. During 1991–96, average GDP growth in the Community has been 1.5 per cent per year. This performance is much lower than the average 3.3 per cent growth rate achieved in the latter half of the 1980s, and it is also lower than the average 2 per cent growth rate registered during the years 1974–85 even though this earlier period was characterised by adverse supply shocks. Low growth has been reflected in disappointing employment trends. Over the years 1991-96, employment in the Community has fallen by an average 0.4 per cent per year, amounting to a total of 4.5 million jobs lost since 1990. As a result, almost half the 10 million jobs created during the growth period 1986–90 have been lost.

Table 16.1 Growth and employment EUR, USA and Japan

	Real GDP growth (average annual percentage change)			Employment growth (average annual percentage change)		
	1974–85	1986–90	1991–96	1974–85	1986–90	1991–96
EUR	2.0	3.3	1.5	0.0	1.3	-0.4
USA	2.3	2.8	2.3	1.8	2.1	1.2
Japan	3.4	4.6	1.7	0.7	1.0	0.7

Source: EU 1997 Annual Economic Report.

Table 16.2 shows the geographical distribution of extra-EU trade. The Community has a comparatively low share of extra-EU exports directed towards the Asian markets, which have been growing, although the recent crisis has put a halt on this growth. In 1995, Community exports to Asia (Developing Asian Economies, DAE, China and the rest of the Asia but excluding Japan) represented only 17 per cent of total extra-EU exports against 20 per cent and 44 per cent for the United States and Japan, espectively. It should be noted that Community exports to these countries have risen strongly since the late 1980s. Furthermore, the share of Community exports directed towards the Central and Eastern European Countries (CEECs), which also constitute high-growth markets, is significantly higher than that of the United States and Japan.

The EU, on the other hand, exhibits a comparatively low degree of specialisation in the strong-demand, high-tech sectors. The share of the high-demand sectors in total extra-EC exports amounted to 30 per cent in 1994,

Table 16.2 Geographical structure of extra-community trade (goods, extra-EC)

	As % of nominal GDP			Annual % change in value			% of total
	1976	1982	1995	82/77	87/82	95/87	1995
Exports to:							
Total	10.9	11.5	9.8	12.5	3.3	8.7	100.0
OECD	4.6	5.0	4.9	13.0	9.3	4.9	49.7
of which:							
USA	1.2	1.7	1.6	17.9	10.9	3.3	15.8
Japan	0.2	0.3	0.5	14.6	15.5	10.2	5.0
Non-OECD	6.2	6.4	4.9	12.1	-2.5	12.9	50.3
of which:							
DAE	0.3	0.4	1.1	17.7	11.3	16.4	10.6
China	0.1	0.1	0.2	10.5	18.7	11.3	2.2
Rest of Asia	0.2	0.5	0.4	25.9	3.7	8.5	4.0
CEECs	0.9	0.7	1.0	5.7	1.4	16.4	10.7
Imports from:							
Total	12.1	12.9	9.6	12.6	0.8	8.2	100.0
OECD	4.9	5.7	5.1	14.3	5.6	5.9	53.2
of which:							
USA	1.9	2.2	1.6	13.5	0.9	7.2	17.1
Japan	0.5	0.7	0.8	18.8	12.4	4.8	8.8
Non-OECD	7.2	7.2	4.5	11.4	-3.9	10.7	46.8
of which:							
DAEs	0.5	0.6	0.9	14.7	10.3	9.3	9.4
China	0.1	0.1	0.4	12.0	14.2	21.5	4.3
Rest of Asia	0.3	0.3	0.4	13.3	5.8	10.0	3.9
CEECs	0.8	1.0	1.0	15.9	0.8	13.2	10.9

Source: EU (1997) Annual Economic Report

which compares with 39 per cent in the United States and 34 per cent in Japan. The share of the high-tech sectors in total extra-EC exports (in 1993) amounted to 23 per cent against about 37 per cent in the United States and Japan (EU, 1997).

Table 16.3 shows that the growth of Asian exports to the Community is not restricted to traditional, low-skilled sectors such as clothing and textiles. High-skilled, capital-intensive sectors such as machinery and transport equipment and high-tech products represent a rising share of Asian exports to the Community. Greater global mobility of financial capital and easier access to technology since the early 1980s have been contributors to this trend. Moreover, restricted market access for 'sensitive' products (for example, textiles and clothing, steel and iron) may have encouraged the shift in Asian countries towards a greater specialisation in more sophisticated market segments. As a result, part of the adjustment burden in the EU has been shifted towards sectors in which EU countries have not until very recently faced direct competition from Asian exports.

Table 16.3 The regional structure of extra-EU imports of manufactured products (% of total imports of manufactured goods from each country or group of countries)

		% of total extra-EC imports	Machinery transport equipment	Chemi cals	Cloth- ing and textile	Hi-tech
USA	1980	22.9	26.4	9.1	4.3	24.3
	1995	21.6	30.8	8.9	2.2	33.5
Japan	1980	8.6	37.6	3.5	3.1	38.9
	1995	12.4	47.4	5.0	1.4	36.1
Developing	1980	27.4	4.7	6.2	23.7	7.4
Countries	1995	36.4	13.7	4.7	23.7	17.3
of which:						
DAE	1980	7.6	3.1	0.4	31.3	20.2
	1995	12.2	30.8	1.7	11.1	34.3
China	1980	0.9	0.8	13.5	44.1	1.9
	1995	5.7	9.6	5.8	23.9	21.3
Other Asia	1980	2.5	1.5	1.1	42.2	2.9
	1995	4.6	4.1	2.9	50.2	8.6
CCEEs	1980	5.2	9.8	12.7	16.9	3.6
	1995	11.6	14.0	7.3	17.5	9.0

Source: EU (1997).

All these developments obviously put constant pressure on the EU member countries to maintain and improve their competitive position. The ultimate policy objective of a country is to improve its citizens' living standards and well being. In the competitiveness context, the external performance of a country is considered very important because it is a useful indicator of the long-term ability to turn external success into domestic jobs. In this respect, a country's competitiveness is often assessed on the basis of trends in its export performance. Table 16.4 shows the export performances of the EU and its international counterparts in terms of their overall gain (loss) of market shares. As shown in this table, the EU has experienced a steady but moderate decline in export market shares since the mid-1980s. As regards the other regions listed in the table, it is noteworthy that Japan also has suffered from continued losses in export market shares whereas the United States (in the second half of the 1980s) and the Asian economies (since the early 1980s) have enjoyed considerable gains.

Table 16.4 Export performance, total goods (% gain or loss of market share, annual average change)

Region	1981–85	1986–90	1991–95	1996
EU	1.6	–1.9	–0.1	–1.6
USA	–2.8	4.3	–0.2	1.7
Japan	1.6	–3.9	–7.8	–5.9
Non-OECD	–1.4	1.0	1.6	1.9
of which:				
DAEs	3.0	3.3	1.7	3.1
Rest Asia	2.5	2.4	5.5	3.6

Source: EU (1997).

As mentioned above it is argued that the ultimate policy objective of a country is to improve its constituencies' well being and the external performance of such a country is considered as an indicator of its long-term ability to turn external success into domestic jobs. If this is the case, then it is worth exploring the linkage between a country's success in international trade and productivity gain and their contribution to employment growth.

METHODOLOGY AND DATA

Methodology

In this chapter, to investigate the impact of exports, imports, output for domestic demand and productivity on manufacturing employment we employ the Dinc and Haynes (1998a, 1998b) international trade shift–share model. This model is an extension of the well-known and widely applied shift–share decomposition method used to examine regional growth and decline, sectoral performance and interregional comparisons. For a detailed discussion of the pros and cons of *shift–share* models, see Loveridge and Selting (1998), Knudsen (2000), Dinc, Haynes and Qiangsheng (1998).

Some traditional assumptions that shift–share models incorporate may not hold in the real world and have been the sources of some of these criticisms. At the same time new compensating extensions of shift–share have been growing. For example, in this model it is assumed that the regional technology is similar to the reference area (nation), and the regional labour force is as productive as its national counterparts. Historically this model has ignored the impact of international and interregional trade on the regional economy.

These assumptions of the model have been implicitly addressed by the Rigby-Anderson (1993) and Haynes-Dinc (1997) extensions by including output and productivity change into the model. However, the international dimension has been developed elsewhere by Sihag and McDonough (1989), Markusen, Noponen and Driessen (1991), Noponen, Markusen and Shao (1996), Noponen, Markusen and Driessen (1996, 1997), Dinc and Haynes (1998a, 1998b). In these later extensions, international trade and its impact on employment change has been explicitly discussed and they are essential for the integration of regional analysis into global dynamics.

In terms of international trade effects, Markusen, Noponen and Driessen (1991) aptly argued that in the traditional shift–share model the sources of (dis)advantages are masked particularly with respect to their link to trade. Hence, Markusen, Noponen and Driessen expanded the traditional shift–share model by disaggregating both the national share and industry mix components into four new components representing trade and productivity effects. They kept the differential (competitive) shift unchanged because of the lack of available and reliable data. Noponen, Markusen and Driessen (1996, 1997) applied this international trade model to different regions of the US.

This extension of the shift–share model provides a useful framework for examining the impact of international trade on regional employment change. To improve their formulation and to ease its interpretation following the Markusen, Noponen and Driessen (1991) framework, Dinc and Haynes (1998a and 1998b) have extended and refined their formulation of the shift–share model one step further. To see the exchange on this issue and the derivation of their models see Dinc and Haynes (1998a, 1998b) and Noponen, Markusen and Driessen (1998).

Dinc and Haynes (1998c) applied the new extension to the European Union to investigate the impact of international trade on employment change in manufacturing sectors. In that presentation, though, they did not include productivity variation into the study. They argued that in a world where there is no international trade then each country most likely will be producing both final goods and intermediate input goods in all industries. In such an environment, total national output of a country, Q, will be equal to its total domestic demand, D:

$$Q = D$$

That means all factors of production will be employed to meet the domestic demand. Hence, employment can be formulated as:

$$ETotal \equiv Edomestic \tag{16.1}$$

When international trade is introduced, they argued, a dollar of exports of a given country will increase the sales of its domestic manufacturers by one dollar. Similarly, a dollar of imports, in this first approximation, will reduce domestic sales by a dollar. The growth accounting identity then becomes:

$$Q = X + D - M \tag{16.2}$$

where Q is total national output, X is exports, D is domestic demand and M is imports. Then, ceteris paribus, they formulated employment as:

$$E \equiv Ex + (Ed - Em) \tag{16.3}$$

Dinc and Haynes (1998a) also argued that exported and domestically consumed goods are produced at the same places by the same workers, hence, they implicitly assumed that in a given sector, imported goods will require the same amount of labour as in exports or domestic demand. Following the above reasoning they set the output to employment ratios as:

$$\frac{Q}{E} = \frac{X}{E_x} = \frac{M}{E_m} = \frac{D}{E_d} \tag{16.4}$$

Since there is no readily available export, import and domestic demand employment data from the above equation, they defined an export, import and domestic demand employment variable as:

$$E_x = \frac{EX}{Q}\ ; \quad E_m = \frac{EM}{Q} \ \text{and}\ E_d = \frac{ED}{Q} \tag{16.5}$$

From equation (16.5), one can write:

$$\Delta E \equiv \Delta E_x + \Delta E_d - \Delta E_m \tag{16.6}$$

In this chapter, we will employ this model with a productivity component in it. It is argued that in a given sector productivity gain will result in a decline in employment, at least in the short run, then employment change resulting from output growth (decline) and productivity variations can be incorporated as:

$$\Delta E \equiv \Delta E_q - \Delta E_p \tag{16.7}$$

where ΔE_q is employment change resulting from output growth (decline), and ΔE_p is employment change resulting from variations of productivity. Equation (16.8) can also be written as:

$$\Delta E \equiv \Delta E_x + \Delta E_d - \Delta E_m - \Delta E_p \tag{16.8}$$

Turning to the traditional shift–share model and following Haynes, Dinc, and Paelinck (1997), Dinc and Haynes (1998b) integrated productivity and output change into shift–share models. In the traditional shift–share model the variable under investigation is decomposed into three additive components: the reference area component, the industry mix and the regional share. The decomposed variable may be income, employment, value added, number of establishments, or a variety of other measurements.

The reference area component refers to the national economy and is called the national share (for smaller regions such as counties it may refer to the province or state economy). The national share, ($NS \equiv E_{ir}\, g_n$) component measures the regional employment change that could have occurred if regional employment had grown at the same rate as the nation. The industrial mix ($IM \equiv E_{ir}\, (g_{in} - g_n)$) component measures the industrial composition of the region and reflects the degree to which the local area specializes in industries that are fast or slow growing nationally. Thus, if a region contains a relatively large share of industries that are slow (fast) growing nationally it will have a negative (positive) proportionality shift. The regional share ($RS \equiv Eir\ (g_{ir} - g_{in})$) measures the change in a particular industry in the region due to the difference between the industry's regional growth (decline) rate and the industry's reference area growth rate. It may result from natural endowments, other comparative advantages or disadvantages, the entrepreneurial ability of the region, and/or the effects of regional policy. In the above identities, the subscript i indexes the industrial sector in region r. E_{ir}, is employment in sector i of region r. The growth or decline in total employment in sector i of region r is g_{ir}. The growth or decline in industry i in the reference area n is g_{in}.

The sum of these three components is called the total shift, (TS) and measures the region's changing economic position relative to the reference area. It is written as:

$$TS \equiv NS + IM + RS \tag{16.9}$$

The equation can be written in terms of employment growth rates as:

$$\Delta \ln E_{ir} \equiv \Delta \ln E + (\Delta \ln E_i - \Delta \ln E) + (\Delta \ln E_{ir} - \Delta \ln E_i) \tag{16.10}$$

This equation corresponds to the traditional shift–share model, and $\Delta\ln E$ represents the national share, ($\Delta\ln E_i$ – $\Delta\ln E$) represents the industry mix, and the regional share is represented by ($\Delta\ln E_{ir}$ – $\Delta\ln E_i$). From equation (16.8) $\Delta\ln E$ is expressed as:

$$\Delta \ln E \equiv \Delta \ln Q - (\Delta \ln \frac{Q}{E}) \tag{16.11}$$

From this equation, national share, industry mix, and regional share components including export, import, domestic demand, and productivity variations are derived as follows:

$$\Delta \ln E \equiv \Delta \ln Q - (\Delta \ln \frac{Q}{E}) \equiv \Delta \ln Q - (\Delta \ln Q - \Delta \ln E) \tag{16.12}$$

$$\Delta \ln E_i \equiv (\Delta \ln Q_{ix} - \Delta \ln \frac{Q_{ix}}{E_{ix}}) + (\Delta \ln Q_{id} - \Delta \ln \frac{Q_{id}}{E_{id}}) - (\Delta \ln Q_{im} + \Delta \ln \frac{Q_{im}}{E_{im}}) \tag{16.13}$$

$$\Delta \ln E_i^r \equiv (\Delta \ln Q_{ix}^r - \Delta \ln \frac{Q_{ix}^r}{E_{ix}^r}) + (\Delta \ln Q_{id}^r - \Delta \ln \frac{Q_{id}^r}{E_{id}^r}) - (\Delta \ln Q_{im}^r + \Delta \ln \frac{Q_{im}^r}{E_{im}^r}) \tag{16.14}$$

Substituting (16.12), (16.13), and (16.14) into equation (16.10):

$$
\begin{aligned}
\Delta \ln E_{ir} \equiv {} & [\Delta \ln Q_x - \Delta \ln \frac{Q_x}{E_x} + \Delta \ln Q_d - \Delta \ln \frac{Q_d}{E_d} - \Delta \ln Q_m + \Delta \ln \frac{Q_m}{E_m}] \\
& + [\{\Delta \ln Q_{ix} - \Delta \ln \frac{Q_{ix}}{E_{ix}} + \Delta \ln Q_{id} - \Delta \ln \frac{Q_{id}}{E_{id}} - \Delta \ln Q_{im} + \Delta \ln \frac{Q_{im}}{E_{im}}\} \\
& - \{\Delta \ln Q_x - \Delta \ln \frac{Q_x}{E_x} + \Delta \ln Q_d - \Delta \ln \frac{Q_d}{E_d} - \Delta \ln Q_m + \Delta \ln \frac{Q_m}{E_m}\}] \qquad (16.15) \\
& + [\{\Delta \ln Q_{ix}^{r} - \Delta \ln \frac{Q_{ix}^{r}}{E_{ix}^{r}} + \Delta \ln Q_{id}^{r} - \Delta \ln \frac{Q_{id}^{r}}{E_{id}^{r}} - \Delta \ln Q_{im}^{r} + \Delta \ln \frac{Q_{im}^{r}}{E_{im}^{r}}\} \\
& - \{\Delta \ln Q_{ix} - \Delta \ln \frac{Q_{ix}}{E_{ix}} + \Delta \ln Q_{id} - \Delta \ln \frac{Q_{id}}{E_{id}} - \Delta \ln Q_{im} + \Delta \ln \frac{Q_{im}}{E_{im}}\}]
\end{aligned}
$$

In equation (16.15) the impact of trade-related output change and productivity variation on employment was taken into account. At the same time, as can be seen, this equation maintains the additivity property of the shift–share model.

Data

We have employed the same data set in this chapter that was presented by Dinc and Haynes (1999), which come from the OECD Statistical Compendium CD (1997). The data set covers total manufacturing (3) and eight major sectors: food, beverages and tobacco (31), textiles, apparel and leather (32), wood products and furniture (33), paper, paper products and printing (34), chemical products (35), non-metallic mineral products (36), basic metal industries (37) and fabricated metal products (38) sectors in 13 EU countries. Finland and Luxembourg were not included because of data problems. Data for Germany were compiled as West Germany before its union with East Germany. After unification the data were compiled as a united Germany. The numbers presented in parenthesis are Standard Industrial Classification (SIC) numbers. In some of these sectors for some countries data were available separately, for example, wood products and furniture. In such cases, based on the SIC number, data were aggregated.

In this data set, manufacturing output is given as manufacturing production in monetary terms in the local currency. The export variable is available as the share of production. The import variable is given as either an export/import ratio or an import penetration rate. From these ratios export and import values have been calculated by Dinc and Haynes. There was no domestic demand variable readily available, hence following the earlier mentioned growth accounting framework they have estimated this variable. The employment variable is given by sector and includes all manufacturing workers, both blue- and white collar. Export, import and domestic demand related employment variables have been estimated based on equation (16.5).

All monetary values have been deflated and converted to 1995 values by using the GDP deflator of the country under investigation. Since all these values were in local currency to maintain consistency and by using the relevant year's average exchange rates, these values have been converted into US dollars.

FINDINGS AND DISCUSSION

We investigated the employment change in EU member countries resulting from international trade and productivity variations in two sub-periods. The first period covers from 1980 to 1986, the second covers from 1986 to 1995. In this way it is possible to better understand the impact of international trade and productivity gain (loss) on employment change, as well as the impact of the integration process on trade and hence on employment. Recall that the Single European Act of 1986 was the turning point in the European integration process in terms of freer international trade within the EU, although 1993 was the first full integration year. It should also be noted that although Austria, Sweden and Finland joined the EU in 1995, Sweden and Austria were included in the analysis. These countries have a relatively small manufacturing base so their inclusion does not affect overall findings of the study, but it may provide some information about these countries' performance.

Aggregate Changes, 1980–95

Aggregated results of the international trade and productivity shift–share model for three different time periods are presented in Table 16.5.[2] During the entire study period, in four countries, Denmark, Germany, the Netherlands and Portugal, the change in manufacturing employment growth rate was positive. The highest change in growth occurred in Portugal followed by the Netherlands and Germany. In terms of negative change, Ireland and Spain were the leading countries. While in Ireland this change was driven by large productivity gains and decreasing exports, in Spain declining outputs and increasing imports were the responsible causes. Sweden, the UK and Belgium were the other large declining countries. The driving force of the employment losses in manufacturing during the investigation period was declining domestic demand and increasing imports; productivity gain also played a significant role. In four countries, Greece, Ireland, Italy and Sweden, declining exports had a negative impact on employment growth.

The results based on the three components of the model are presented in Table 16.6. Note that in this model employment growth rate is the variable, so the EU share and industry mix components are the same for all countries. The sign and magnitude of these sub-components, however, provide some valuable information. The EU share had a positive impact on the export sub-component and a negative impact on the import and domestic demand sub-components. It also contributed to productivity improvements. The industry mix component indicates a declining pattern in all sub-components.

The regional (country) share component provides the most valuable information about the region (country) under investigation because it shows the advantages or disadvantages of the region. During the entire study period, based on this component, six countries had disadvantages in exports while seven countries had advantages. In terms of imports five countries reduced their imports and had positive growth in employment. The domestic demand sub-component had a significant positive impact on employment growth rates in six countries while in the remaining six countries its impact was negative. In France domestic demand had a negligible impact on employment growth. Another important factor that affected the employment growth (decline) was the productivity variation in manufacturing sectors in EU member countries. In the UK, Sweden and France its impact was relatively small while in the remaining countries it was significant.

Sub-Period Changes, 1980–86 and 1986–95

During the first part of the study period two countries, Denmark and Portugal, enjoyed a positive change in employment growth while others had a negative change. During this period Ireland, Spain and the UK suffered the highest negative change. In Spain and Ireland all sub-components contributed to this decline, for example, declining exports, domestic demand and increasing imports accompanied with the productivity gains. In the remaining countries decline was moderate and sub-components had a mixed effect.

After the Single European Act of 1986, in seven countries, France, Germany, Greece, Italy, the Netherlands, Portugal and the UK the manufacturing employment growth rate changed positively. In this period, the declining countries of the earlier period improved their performance in all sub-components, hence the growth rate of manufacturing employment. The three components of the model showed a similar pattern in both periods; bad performance of first period reversed in the second period or vice versa.

Productivity effects across countries, manufacturing sectors and over time are extremely complex and highly variable. In general, the scale of these productivity effects on changes on employment growth rates appear to be significant in many EU member countries, though output growth effects particularly those related to domestic output played the dominant role.

To have a better understanding of the impact of international trade and integration on different size members of the EU it is useful to investigate the largest and smallest manufacturing countries. Among the three largest manufacturing economies Germany averaged a (0.12) rise in employment rates between 1980 and 1995. A loss of (–0.04) in the first period, and a gain of 0.16 in the second period, 1987–95. The latter translated into just under a million new manufacturing jobs led by expansion of the food, beverage and tobacco sector (0.39), wood products and furniture (0.38) and printing, paper and paper products (0.58). Output expansion to meet domestic demand drove these increases together with a decline in domestic productivity. The latter of course is partly related to the absorption of East Germany.

In the UK the average employment rate change was negative (–0.34) for the entire period, with a turn around from negative in the early period (1980–86) to slightly positive (0.03) in the integration period (1986–95) The two positive sectors in the second period resulted from declines in imports and positive employment effects of productivity declines in exports and domestic output. However, the negative sectors, non-metallic mineral products (–0.20) and fabricated metals (–0.23) were both driven by declines in exports and domestic demand rather than productivity changes.

Italy had an average decline (–0.08) for entire period (1980–95) but an increase in the second part of the study period. The two positive sectors in the integration period were food, beverages and tobacco and non-metallic mineral products. Both were affected by productivity decline in exports and domestic production and food, beverages and tobacco sector was also affected by declining imports. Italy's major declining sector (–0.26), textile, apparel and leather was a result of export and domestic demand losses.

Hence, in general for the major manufacturing economies, productivity change played an important but not a dominant role in employment change by sector. Output changes driven by domestic demand and/or exports were the dominant employment change components.

For the three smallest manufacturing economies (Ireland, Denmark and Greece) productivity changes by sector played a more important role in these economies. In Ireland, for example rises in export and domestic productivity accounted for a large part of employment rate decline (–0.98) in fabricated metals in the integration period (1986–95). However, the two growth sectors in this second period in Ireland are a function of output increases to meet domestic demand and import declines. This is true for both the base metal industry's rise (0.50) and the non-metallic minerals sector's rise (0.30).

For Denmark and Greece major sector employment adjustments are more responsive to productivity change than to output changes. Rises in exports and domestic productivity accounted for employment decline in Denmark's three declining sectors, food, beverages and tobacco, textiles, apparel and leather and wood products and furniture sectors, although import rises also affected the food, beverages and tobacco sector. In Greece declines in productivity positively affected printing, paper and paper products (0.32) and chemical products (0.35) during the integration period (1986–95). The negative employment change in textile, apparel and leather (–0.53) was primarily affected by declining output for exports and domestic demand. But declines in wood products and furniture (–0.45) was impacted by decline in output for domestic demand compounded by productivity gains in export and domestic production.

Among the small manufacturing economies changes in productivity by sector played a more important role in terms of its impact on rates of employment change than larger manufacturing economies. These findings suggest that in general the integration process helped large manufacturers more than smaller ones. These large manufacturers particularly improved their position in the second period. This may be interpreted as an indicator of the expansion of integrated markets suggesting that the expanded EU market had a positive impact on countries with a strong manufacturing base.

These results seem convincing because relatively large manufacturing firms are located within these early-industrialised core countries (regions). On the other hand, locally oriented small and medium-size enterprises are concentrated in relatively small countries and less developed regions. These findings suggest, at least in the short run, that integration will favour larger firms and countries. However, the good news for smaller countries with smaller manufacturing bases is that productivity appeared to be improving which has important implications for the future.

CONCLUSION

In this study we have focused on the impact of international trade and productivity variations on the change of manufacturing employment growth in the increasingly integrated market of the EU. By dividing the study period into before and after the Single European Act 1986 and comparing these two periods we have captured some of the contribution of integration to international trade and eventually employment growth (decline) in manufacturing in member countries.

The findings of the analysis have shown that productivity variations had an important impact on employment growth rate particularly in the smallest economies. However, the domestic demand sub-component was the most important force behind employment change in manufacturing particularly in the largest economies. Export and import changes also had a significant but generally a secondary impact. We also found that larger manufacturing countries improved their performance in the second period, while smaller manufacturers did perform better in the first half, which suggests that the early results of economic integration are more beneficial for large and well-established manufacturers in sectors where economies of scale appeared to be important. However, given the productivity improvements of the smaller economies, the future for them looks hopeful.

As a future research strategy the impact of international trade on employment could be examined by distinguishing trade as intra and extra EU. This may provide deeper understandings about the effect of integration on the sectoral structure of international trade.

Table 16.5 Aggregated results

	Exp	Dom	Imp	E Prd	D Prd	I Prd	Change
1980–1995							
Austria	0.52	0.29	0.49	0.36	0.36	0.36	–0.04
Belgium	0.32	0.22	0.45	0.42	0.42	0.42	–0.33
Denmark	0.60	0.28	0.50	0.26	0.26	0.26	0.12
France	0.25	–0.14	0.17	0.10	0.10	0.10	–0.17
Germany	0.63	0.35	0.65	0.21	0.21	0.21	0.12
Greece	–1.34	–1.75	–1.10	–1.97	–1.97	–1.97	–0.03
Ireland	–0.13	0.22	0.40	0.28	0.28	0.28	–0.58
Italy	–0.31	–0.62	–0.39	–0.46	–0.46	–0.46	–0.08
Netherlands	0.57	0.14	0.39	0.24	0.24	0.24	0.09
Portugal	0.09	–0.63	0.28	–1.15	–1.15	–1.15	0.33
Spain	0.31	–0.65	0.64	–0.44	–0.44	–0.44	–0.54
Sweden	–0.19	–0.65	–0.25	–0.09	–0.09	–0.09	–0.49
UK	0.03	–0.36	0.01	0.01	0.01	0.01	–0.34
1980–1986							
Austria	0.21	0.11	0.23	0.14	0.14	0.14	–0.04
Belgium	–0.01	–0.09	0.07	0.07	0.07	0.07	–0.24
Denmark	0.05	–0.09	0.02	–0.28	–0.28	–0.28	0.22
France	–0.16	–0.31	–0.12	–0.13	–0.13	–0.13	–0.22
Germany	0.29	0.01	0.18	0.17	0.17	0.17	–0.04
Greece	–1.09	–1.08	–0.68	–1.45	–1.45	–1.45	–0.05
Ireland	–0.24	–0.17	0.27	–0.17	–0.17	–0.17	–0.51
Italy	–0.34	–0.35	–0.36	–0.17	–0.17	–0.17	–0.16
Netherlands	0.09	0.15	0.22	0.13	0.13	0.13	–0.11
Portugal	–0.49	–0.90	–0.34	–1.15	–1.15	–1.15	0.10
Spain	0.00	–0.48	0.26	–0.36	–0.36	–0.36	–0.38
Sweden	–0.13	–0.36	–0.19	–0.19	–0.19	–0.19	–0.10
UK	–0.11	–0.14	0.07	0.05	0.05	0.05	–0.37
1986–1995							
Austria	0.31	0.18	0.26	0.22	0.22	0.22	0.00
Belgium	0.33	0.32	0.38	0.35	0.35	0.35	–0.09
Denmark	0.55	0.37	0.48	0.54	0.54	0.54	–0.10
France	0.41	0.17	0.30	0.23	0.23	0.23	0.05
Germany	0.34	0.33	0.48	0.04	0.04	0.04	0.16
Greece	–0.25	–0.67	–0.42	–0.52	–0.52	–0.52	0.02
Ireland	0.11	0.40	0.13	0.45	0.45	0.45	–0.07
Italy	0.03	–0.27	–0.03	–0.29	–0.29	–0.29	0.08
Netherlands	0.48	0.00	0.17	0.11	0.11	0.11	0.20
Portugal	0.59	0.27	0.62	0.00	0.00	0.00	0.23
Spain	0.31	–0.17	0.38	–0.08	–0.08	–0.08	–0.16
Sweden	–0.06	–0.30	–0.06	0.10	0.10	0.10	–0.40
UK	0.14	–0.22	–0.06	–0.05	–0.05	–0.05	0.03

Table 16.6 Employment change in the EU countries, shift–share results

	EU Share						Industry mix					
	Exp	Dom	Imp	E	D	I Prd	Exp	Dom	Imp	E	D	I Prd
1980–95												
Austria	0.35	-0.06	0.35	0.15	0.08	0.08	-0.11	-0.07	-0.07	-0.19	-0.13	-0.076
Belgium	0.35	-0.06	0.35	0.15	0.08	0.08	-0.11	-0.07	-0.07	-0.19	-0.13	-0.076
Denmark	0.35	-0.06	0.35	0.15	0.08	0.08	-0.11	-0.07	-0.07	-0.19	-0.13	-0.076
France	0.35	-0.06	0.35	0.15	0.08	0.08	-0.11	-0.07	-0.07	-0.19	-0.13	-0.076
Germany	0.35	-0.06	0.35	0.15	0.08	0.08	-0.11	-0.07	-0.07	-0.19	-0.13	-0.076
Greece	0.35	-0.06	0.35	0.15	0.08	0.08	-0.11	-0.07	-0.07	-0.19	-0.13	-0.076
Ireland	0.35	-0.06	0.35	0.15	0.08	0.08	-0.11	-0.07	-0.07	-0.19	-0.13	-0.076
Italy	0.35	-0.06	0.35	0.15	0.08	0.08	-0.11	-0.07	-0.07	-0.19	-0.13	-0.076
Netherland	0.35	-0.06	0.35	0.15	0.08	0.08	-0.11	-0.07	-0.07	-0.19	-0.13	-0.076
Portugal	0.35	-0.06	0.35	0.15	0.08	0.08	-0.11	-0.07	-0.07	-0.19	-0.13	-0.076
Spain	0.35	-0.06	0.35	0.15	0.08	0.08	-0.11	-0.07	-0.07	-0.19	-0.13	-0.076
Sweden	0.35	-0.06	0.35	0.15	0.08	0.08	-0.11	-0.07	-0.07	-0.19	-0.13	-0.076
UK	0.35	-0.06	0.35	0.15	0.08	0.08	-0.11	-0.07	-0.07	-0.19	-0.13	-0.076
1980–86												
Austria	0.03	-0.18	0.03	-0.01	-0.06	-0.07	-0.08	-0.06	-0.04	-0.09	-0.05	0.004
Belgium	0.03	-0.18	0.03	-0.01	-0.06	-0.07	-0.08	-0.06	-0.04	-0.09	-0.05	0.004
Denmark	0.03	-0.18	0.03	-0.01	-0.06	-0.07	-0.08	-0.06	-0.04	-0.09	-0.05	0.004
France	0.03	-0.18	0.03	-0.01	-0.06	-0.07	-0.08	-0.06	-0.04	-0.09	-0.05	0.004
Germany	0.03	-0.18	0.03	-0.01	-0.06	-0.07	-0.08	-0.06	-0.04	-0.09	-0.05	0.004
Greece	0.03	-0.18	0.03	-0.01	-0.06	-0.07	-0.08	-0.06	-0.04	-0.09	-0.05	0.004
Ireland	0.03	-0.18	0.03	-0.01	-0.06	-0.07	-0.08	-0.06	-0.04	-0.09	-0.05	0.004
Italy	0.03	-0.18	0.03	-0.01	-0.06	-0.07	-0.08	-0.06	-0.04	-0.09	-0.05	0.004
Netherland	0.03	-0.18	0.03	-0.01	-0.06	-0.07	-0.08	-0.06	-0.04	-0.09	-0.05	0.004
Portugal	0.03	-0.18	0.03	-0.01	-0.06	-0.07	-0.08	-0.06	-0.04	-0.09	-0.05	0.004
Spain	0.03	-0.18	0.03	-0.01	-0.06	-0.07	-0.08	-0.06	-0.04	-0.09	-0.05	0.004
Sweden	0.03	-0.18	0.03	-0.01	-0.06	-0.07	-0.08	-0.06	-0.04	-0.09	-0.05	0.004
UK	0.03	-0.18	0.03	-0.01	-0.06	-0.07	-0.08	-0.06	-0.04	-0.09	-0.05	0.004
1986–95												
Austria	0.32	0.12	0.32	0.16	0.15	0.15	-0.04	-0.01	-0.03	-0.10	-0.07	-0.081
Belgium	0.32	0.12	0.32	0.16	0.15	0.15	-0.04	-0.01	-0.03	-0.10	-0.07	-0.081
Denmark	0.32	0.12	0.32	0.16	0.15	0.15	-0.04	-0.01	-0.03	-0.10	-0.07	-0.081
France	0.32	0.12	0.32	0.16	0.15	0.15	-0.04	-0.01	-0.03	-0.10	-0.07	-0.081
Germany	0.32	0.12	0.32	0.16	0.15	0.15	-0.04	-0.01	-0.03	-0.10	-0.07	-0.081
Greece	0.32	0.12	0.32	0.16	0.15	0.15	-0.04	-0.01	-0.03	-0.10	-0.07	-0.081
Ireland	0.32	0.12	0.32	0.16	0.15	0.15	-0.04	-0.01	-0.03	-0.10	-0.07	-0.081
Italy	0.32	0.12	0.32	0.16	0.15	0.15	-0.04	-0.01	-0.03	-0.10	-0.07	-0.081
Netherland	0.32	0.12	0.32	0.16	0.15	0.15	-0.04	-0.01	-0.03	-0.10	-0.07	-0.081
Portugal	0.32	0.12	0.32	0.16	0.15	0.15	-0.04	-0.01	-0.03	-0.10	-0.07	-0.081
Spain	0.32	0.12	0.32	0.16	0.15	0.15	-0.04	-0.01	-0.03	-0.10	-0.07	-0.081
Sweden	0.32	0.12	0.32	0.16	0.15	0.15	-0.04	-0.01	-0.03	-0.10	-0.07	-0.081
UK	0.32	0.12	0.32	0.16	0.15	0.15	-0.04	-0.01	-0.03	-0.10	-0.07	-0.081

NOTES

1. This section heavily draws from EU (1997) *Annual Economic Report: Growth, employment and convergence on the road to EMU.*
2. Individual country results by sector are presented in Appendix 16A.

REFERENCES

Baldwin, R.E. (1997), 'The causes of regionalism', *The World Economy*, **20** (7), 865-889.

Barf, R.A. and P.L. Knight (1988), 'Dynamic shift–share analysis', *Growth and Change*, **19**, 1–10.

Bean, R. and K. Holden (1994) 'Determinants of trade union membership in OECD countries: a survey', *International Journal of Manpower*, **15** (6), 4 .

Dinc, M. and K.E. Haynes (1998a), 'International trade and the shift–share analysis: a specification note', *Economic Development Quarterly*, **12** (4), 337–43.

Dinc, M. and K.E. Haynes (1998b), 'International trade and the shift–share analysis: a specification note, rejoinder', *Economic Development Quarterly*, **12** (4), 351–4.

Dinc, M. and K.E. Haynes (1998c), 'European integration and international trade in manufacturing', paper presented at the 38th European Regional Science Association Conference in Vienna, Austria, August 28 – September 1, 1998.

Dinc, M., K.E. Haynes, R.R. Stough and S. Yilmaz (1998), 'Universal telecommunication service provision in the U.S.: efficiency versus penetration', *Telecommunication Policy*, **22** (6).

Dinc, M., K.E. Haynes and L. Qiangsheng (1999), 'A comparative evaluation of shift–share models and their extensions', *Australasian Journal of Regional Studies*, **4** (2), 275–302.

EU (1997), 'Growth, employment and convergence on the road to EMU', *Annual Economic Report 1997*, http://europa.eu.int/en/record/aer97

Fontaine, P. (1998), 'Seven key days in the making of Europe', http://europa.eu.int/abc/obj/chrono/40years/7days/en.htm

Haynes, K.E. and M. Dinc (1997) 'Productivity change in manufacturing regions: a multifactor / shift–share approach', *Growth and Change*, **28**, Spring, 150–70.

Haynes, K.E., M. Dinc and J.H.P. Paelinck (1997) 'Identifying sources of regional productivity change in manufacturing: alternative productivity measurement approach in a shift–share framework', paper presented at the European Regional Science Association Annual Meeting in Rome, Italy August 27–29, 1997.

Knudsen, D.C. (2000), 'Shift–share analysis: further examination of models for the description of economic change', *Socio-Economic Planning Sciences*, **34** (3), 159–235.

Krugman, P. (1996), '*Pop Internationalism*', Cambridge: MIT Press.

Krugman, P. (1995), 'Technology, Trade and Factor Prices', NBER Working Paper Series No: 5355.

Lawrence, R.Z. (1994), 'Regionalism: an overview', *Journal of the Japanese and International Economies*, **8** (4), 365–87.

Loveridge, S. and A.C. Selting (1998), 'A review and comparison of shift–share identities', *International Regional Science Review*, **21** (1), 27–58.

Markusen, A.R., H. Noponen and K. Driessen (1991), 'International trade, productivity, and U.S. Job growth: a shift–share interpretation', *International Regional Science Review*, **14** (1), 15–39.

Noponen, H., A. Markusen and Y. Shao (1996), 'Is there a trade and defense perimeter? The regional impacts of trade and defense spending in the United States, 1978-1986', *Growth and Change*, **27** (4), 405.

Noponen, H., A. Markusen and K. Driessen (1997), 'Trade and American cities: who has the comparative advantage?', *Economic Development Quarterly*, **11** (1), 67–87.

Noponen, H., A. Markusen and K. Driessen (1998), 'International trade and shift–share analysis: a response to Dinc and Haynes', *Economic Development Quarterly*, **12** (4), 344–50.

Pelagidis, T. (1998), 'European unemployment: myths and realities', *Challenge*, **41** (4), 76–91.

Rigby, D.L. and W.P. Anderson (1993), 'Employment change, growth and productivity in Canadian manufacturing: an extension and application of shift–share analysis', *Canadian Journal of Regional Science/Revue canadienne des sciences regionales*, **XVI**, Spring/ printemps, 69–88.

Sihag, Balbir S. and C.C. McDonough (1989), 'Shift–share analysis: the international dimension', *Growth and Change*, Summer, 80–8.

Walz, U. (1999), *Dynamics of Regional Integration*, Heidelberg, Germany: Physica-Verlag.

APPENDIX 16A.1 SECTORAL RESULTS

AUSTRIA

1980 - 1995

	EU SHARE						INDUSTRY MIX						COUNTRY SHARE						Total
	Exp	Dom	Imp	E Prd	D Prd	I Prd	Exp	Dom	Imp	E Prd	D Prd	I Prd	Exp	Dom	Imp	E Prd	D Prd	I Prd	Change
Total manufacturing	0.35	-0.06	0.35	0.15	0.08	0.08	-0.11	-0.07	-0.07	-0.19	-0.13	-0.08	0.28	0.42	0.20	0.40	0.41	0.36	-0.04
Food, beverages & tobacco	0.35	-0.06	0.35	0.15	0.08	0.08	-0.01	0.01	-0.05	-0.17	-0.11	-0.06	0.37	0.35	0.38	0.21	0.21	0.16	0.16
Textiles, apparel & leather	0.35	-0.06	0.35	0.15	0.08	0.08	-0.24	-0.42	-0.11	-0.24	-0.17	-0.03	0.03	0.21	-0.13	0.20	0.20	0.06	-0.35
Wood products & furniture	0.35	-0.06	0.35	0.15	0.08	0.08	0.02	0.03	0.08	-0.28	-0.21	-0.13	0.44	0.92	0.35	0.64	0.64	0.56	0.42
Paper, p aper products & printing	0.35	-0.06	0.35	0.15	0.08	0.08	0.07	0.15	0.06	-0.24	-0.11	-0.10	0.27	0.39	0.24	0.56	0.50	0.49	0.04
Chemical products	0.35	-0.06	0.35	0.15	0.08	0.08	0.04	-0.02	-0.05	-0.08	-0.14	-0.10	0.28	0.14	0.33	0.04	0.17	0.13	-0.02
Non -metallic mineral products	0.35	-0.06	0.35	0.15	0.08	0.08	-0.32	-0.08	-0.12	-0.27	-0.07	0.05	0.08	0.58	-0.16	0.46	0.33	0.21	0.14
Basic metal industries	0.35	-0.06	0.35	0.15	0.08	0.08	-0.59	-0.38	-0.54	-0.42	-0.41	-0.43	0.36	0.36	0.28	0.67	0.73	0.74	-0.45
Fabricated metal products	0.35	-0.06	0.35	0.15	0.08	0.08	0.12	0.18	0.18	0.18	0.21	0.19	0.44	0.39	0.34	0.44	0.48	0.50	-0.23

1980 - 1986

	EU SHARE						INDUSTRY MIX						COUNTRY SHARE						Total
	Exp	Dom	Imp	E Prd	D Prd	I Prd	Exp	Dom	Imp	E Prd	D Prd	I Prd	Exp	Dom	Imp	E Prd	D Prd	I Prd	Change
Total manufacturing	0.03	-0.18	0.03	-0.01	-0.06	-0.07	-0.08	-0.06	-0.04	-0.09	-0.05	0.00	0.26	0.35	0.24	0.24	0.25	0.20	-0.04
Food, beverages & tobacco	0.03	-0.18	0.03	-0.01	-0.06	-0.07	-0.10	0.02	-0.04	-0.13	-0.03	0.00	0.26	0.34	0.21	0.33	0.28	0.26	-0.03
Textiles, apparel & leather	0.03	-0.18	0.03	-0.01	-0.06	-0.07	-0.01	-0.13	0.08	-0.11	-0.07	0.08	0.14	0.25	0.06	0.11	0.12	-0.02	-0.07
Wood products & furniture	0.03	-0.18	0.03	-0.01	-0.06	-0.07	-0.09	-0.14	-0.10	-0.25	-0.14	-0.05	0.34	0.82	0.36	0.74	0.68	0.60	0.00
Paper, paper products & printing	0.03	-0.18	0.03	-0.01	-0.06	-0.07	0.11	0.14	0.12	0.00	0.05	0.08	0.17	0.28	0.17	0.20	0.20	0.17	0.03
Chemical products	0.03	-0.18	0.03	-0.01	-0.06	-0.07	-0.02	-0.08	-0.07	-0.11	-0.18	-0.13	0.24	0.24	0.30	0.01	0.12	0.08	0.08
Non -metallic mineral products	0.03	-0.18	0.03	-0.01	-0.06	-0.07	-0.23	-0.14	-0.03	-0.07	-0.05	0.05	0.29	0.44	0.11	0.31	0.33	0.25	-0.12
Basic metal industries	0.03	-0.18	0.03	-0.01	-0.06	-0.07	-0.38	-0.27	-0.43	-0.18	-0.15	-0.11	0.41	0.28	0.47	0.27	0.28	0.25	-0.25
Fabricated metal products	0.03	-0.18	0.03	-0.01	-0.06	-0.07	0.09	0.13	0.13	0.13	0.12	0.11	0.26	0.18	0.24	-0.04	0.02	0.05	0.04

1986 - 1995

	EU SHARE						INDUSTRY MIX						COUNTRY SHARE						Total
	Exp	Dom	Imp	E Prd	D Prd	I Prd	Exp	Dom	Imp	E Prd	D Prd	I Prd	Exp	Dom	Imp	E Prd	D Prd	I Pr d	Change
Total manufacturing	0.32	0.12	0.32	0.16	0.15	0.15	-0.04	-0.01	-0.03	-0.10	-0.07	-0.08	0.02	0.06	-0.04	0.16	0.15	0.15	0.00
Food, beverages & tobacco	0.32	0.12	0.32	0.16	0.15	0.15	0.09	-0.01	-0.01	-0.05	-0.08	-0.06	0.11	0.01	0.17	-0.12	-0.08	-0.10	0.18
Textiles, apparel & leather	0.32	0.12	0.32	0.16	0.15	0.15	-0.23	-0.29	-0.20	-0.13	-0.10	-0.11	-0.11	-0.04	-0.19	0.09	0.08	0.08	-0.29
Wood products & furniture	0.32	0.12	0.32	0.16	0.15	0.15	0.11	0.17	0.18	-0.03	-0.07	-0.09	0.11	0.11	-0.01	-0.10	-0.04	-0.04	0.42
Paper, paper products & printing	0.32	0.12	0.32	0.16	0.15	0.15	-0.04	0.01	-0.06	-0.24	-0.16	-0.18	0.10	0.11	0.07	0.36	0.30	0.32	0.01
Chemical pro ducts	0.32	0.12	0.32	0.16	0.15	0.15	0.06	0.06	0.02	0.04	0.04	0.03	0.04	-0.10	0.03	0.04	0.05	0.05	-0.11
Non -metallic mineral products	0.32	0.12	0.32	0.16	0.15	0.15	-0.10	0.06	-0.08	-0.20	-0.03	0.00	-0.21	0.14	-0.27	0.16	0.00	-0.04	0.25
Basic metal industries	0.32	0.12	0.32	0.16	0.15	0.15	-0.21	-0.11	-0.11	-0.24	-0.27	-0.32	-0.05	0.07	-0.19	0.40	0.45	0.49	-0.20
Fabricated metal products	0.32	0.12	0.32	0.16	0.15	0.15	0.02	0.04	0.05	0.05	0.08	0.08	0.18	0.20	0.10	0.48	0.46	0.45	-0.27

BELGIUM

1980-1995

	EU SHARE						INDUSTRY MIX						COUNTRY SHARE						Total
	Exp	Dom	Imp	E Prd	D Prd	I Prd	Exp	Dom	Imp	E Prd	D Prd	I Prd	Exp	Dom	Imp	E Prd	D Prd	I Prd	Change
Total manufacturing	0.35	-0.06	0.35	0.15	0.08	0.08	-0.11	-0.07	-0.07	-0.19	-0.13	-0.08	0.08	0.35	0.16	0.47	0.47	0.42	-0.33
Food, beverages & tobacco	0.35	-0.06	0.35	0.15	0.08	0.08	-0.01	0.01	-0.05	-0.17	-0.11	-0.06	0.36	0.51	0.62	0.54	0.54	0.49	-0.26
Textiles, apparel & leather	0.35	-0.06	0.35	0.15	0.08	0.08	-0.24	-0.42	-0.11	-0.24	-0.17	-0.03	0.06	0.68	0.10	0.66	0.66	0.52	-0.54
Wood products & furniture	0.35	-0.06	0.35	0.15	0.08	0.08	0.02	0.03	0.08	-0.28	-0.21	-0.13	-0.01	0.14	0.03	0.39	0.39	0.31	-0.25
Paper, paper products & printing	0.35	-0.06	0.35	0.15	0.08	0.08	0.07	0.15	0.06	-0.24	-0.11	-0.10	0.17	0.32	0.25	0.59	0.53	0.52	-0.17
Chemical products	0.35	-0.06	0.35	0.15	0.08	0.08	0.04	-0.02	-0.05	-0.08	-0.14	-0.10	0.02	0.20	0.18	-0.08	0.05	0.01	0.06
Non-metallic mineral products	0.35	-0.06	0.35	0.15	0.08	0.08	-0.32	-0.08	-0.12	-0.27	-0.07	0.05	0.36	0.50	0.36	0.69	0.56	0.44	-0.42
Basic metal industries	0.35	-0.06	0.35	0.15	0.08	0.08	-0.59	-0.38	-0.54	-0.42	-0.41	-0.43	0.07	0.19	-0.07	0.71	0.76	0.78	-0.61
Fabricated metal products	0.35	-0.06	0.35	0.15	0.08	0.08	0.12	0.18	0.18	0.18	0.21	0.19	-0.38	0.28	-0.16	0.23	0.27	0.29	-0.44

1980-1986

	EU SHARE						INDUSTRY MIX						COUNTRY SHARE						Total
	Exp	Dom	Imp	E Prd	D Prd	I Prd	Exp	Dom	Imp	E Prd	D Prd	I Prd	Exp	Dom	Imp	E Prd	D Prd	I Prd	Change
Total manufacturing	0.03	-0.18	0.03	-0.01	-0.06	-0.07	-0.08	-0.06	-0.04	-0.09	-0.05	0.00	0.04	0.15	0.09	0.17	0.19	0.14	-0.24
Food, beverages & tobacco	0.03	-0.18	0.03	-0.01	-0.06	-0.07	-0.10	0.02	-0.04	-0.13	-0.03	0.00	0.39	0.31	0.58	0.29	0.25	0.23	-0.26
Textiles, apparel & leather	0.03	-0.18	0.03	-0.01	-0.06	-0.07	-0.01	-0.13	0.08	-0.11	-0.07	0.08	0.01	0.28	-0.01	0.24	0.25	0.11	-0.22
Wood products & furniture	0.03	-0.18	0.03	-0.01	-0.06	-0.07	-0.09	-0.14	-0.10	-0.25	-0.14	-0.05	0.10	0.25	0.35	0.35	0.29	0.21	-0.40
Paper, paper products & printing	0.03	-0.18	0.03	-0.01	-0.06	-0.07	0.11	0.14	0.12	0.00	0.05	0.08	0.03	0.07	0.01	0.12	0.12	0.09	-0.07
Chemical products	0.03	-0.18	0.03	-0.01	-0.06	-0.07	-0.02	-0.08	-0.07	-0.11	-0.18	-0.13	-0.20	-0.12	-0.24	-0.16	-0.04	-0.08	-0.02
Non-metallic mineral products	0.03	-0.18	0.03	-0.01	-0.06	-0.07	-0.23	-0.14	-0.03	-0.07	-0.05	0.05	0.27	0.24	0.21	0.24	0.27	0.18	-0.37
Basic metal industries	0.03	-0.18	0.03	-0.01	-0.06	-0.07	-0.38	-0.27	-0.43	-0.18	-0.15	-0.11	-0.02	0.08	0.02	0.23	0.25	0.22	-0.39
Fabricated metal products	0.03	-0.18	0.03	-0.01	-0.06	-0.07	0.09	0.13	0.13	0.13	0.12	0.11	-0.26	0.08	-0.24	0.07	0.13	0.15	-0.21

1986-1995

	EU SHARE						INDUSTRY MIX						COUNTRY SHARE						Total
	Exp	Dom	Imp	E Prd	D Prd	I Prd	Exp	Dom	Imp	E Prd	D Prd	I Prd	Exp	Dom	Imp	E Prd	D Prd	I Prd	Change
Total manufacturing	0.32	0.12	0.32	0.16	0.15	0.15	-0.04	-0.01	-0.03	-0.10	-0.07	-0.08	0.04	0.20	0.08	0.29	0.28	0.28	-0.09
Food, beverages & tobacco	0.32	0.12	0.32	0.16	0.15	0.15	0.09	-0.01	-0.01	-0.05	-0.08	-0.06	-0.02	0.20	0.04	0.24	0.29	0.27	0.00
Textiles, apparel & leather	0.32	0.12	0.32	0.16	0.15	0.15	-0.23	-0.29	-0.20	-0.13	-0.10	-0.11	0.05	0.40	0.11	0.42	0.41	0.41	-0.32
Wood products & furniture	0.32	0.12	0.32	0.16	0.15	0.15	0.11	0.17	0.18	-0.03	-0.07	-0.09	-0.11	-0.12	-0.33	0.04	0.10	0.10	0.15
Paper, paper products & printing	0.32	0.12	0.32	0.16	0.15	0.15	-0.04	0.01	-0.06	-0.24	-0.16	-0.18	0.14	0.24	0.24	0.47	0.41	0.43	-0.11
Chemical products	0.32	0.12	0.32	0.16	0.15	0.15	0.06	0.06	0.02	0.04	0.04	0.03	0.22	0.33	0.42	0.08	0.09	0.09	0.07
Non-metallic mineral products	0.32	0.12	0.32	0.16	0.15	0.15	-0.10	0.06	-0.08	-0.20	-0.03	0.00	0.08	0.25	0.15	0.45	0.29	0.25	-0.05
Basic metal industries	0.32	0.12	0.32	0.16	0.15	0.15	-0.21	-0.11	-0.11	-0.24	-0.27	-0.32	0.08	0.11	-0.09	0.47	0.52	0.56	-0.21
Fabricated metal products	0.32	0.12	0.32	0.16	0.15	0.15	0.02	0.04	0.05	0.05	0.08	0.08	-0.12	0.21	0.08	0.16	0.14	0.14	-0.23

DENMARK

1980-1995

	EU SHARE						INDUSTRY MIX						COUNTRY SHARE						Total
	Exp	Dom	Imp	E Prd	D Prd	I Prd	Exp	Dom	Imp	E Prd	D Prd	I Prd	Exp	Dom	Imp	E Prd	D Prd	I Prd	Change
Total manufacturing	0.35	-0.06	0.35	0.15	0.08	0.08	-0.11	-0.07	-0.07	-0.19	-0.13	-0.08	0.36	0.41	0.22	0.30	0.30	0.25	0.12
Food, beverages & tobacco	0.35	-0.06	0.35	0.15	0.08	0.08	-0.01	0.01	-0.05	-0.17	-0.11	-0.06	0.32	0.19	0.67	0.02	0.02	-0.03	-0.16
Textiles, apparel & leather	0.35	-0.06	0.35	0.15	0.08	0.08	-0.24	-0.42	-0.11	-0.24	-0.17	-0.03	0.18	0.43	-0.02	0.29	0.28	0.15	-0.17
Wood products & furniture	0.35	-0.06	0.35	0.15	0.08	0.08	0.02	0.03	0.08	-0.28	-0.21	-0.13	0.79	0.99	0.54	1.45	1.44	1.37	-0.18
Paper, paper products & printing	0.35	-0.06	0.35	0.15	0.08	0.08	0.07	0.15	0.06	-0.24	-0.11	-0.10	0.03	0.07	-0.24	-0.13	-0.18	-0.20	0.64
Chemical products	0.35	-0.06	0.35	0.15	0.08	0.08	0.04	-0.02	-0.05	-0.08	-0.14	-0.10	0.19	0.06	-0.10	-0.26	-0.13	-0.17	0.54
Non-metallic mineral products	0.35	-0.06	0.35	0.15	0.08	0.08	-0.32	-0.08	-0.12	-0.27	-0.07	0.05	0.18	0.29	-0.03	0.43	0.29	0.17	-0.14
Basic metal industries	0.35	-0.06	0.35	0.15	0.08	0.08	-0.59	-0.38	-0.54	-0.42	-0.41	-0.43	1.08	0.94	0.83	0.79	0.85	0.86	0.18
Fabricated metal products	0.35	-0.06	0.35	0.15	0.08	0.08	0.12	0.18	0.18	0.18	0.21	0.19	0.11	0.29	0.08	-0.21	-0.17	-0.15	0.25

1980-1986

	EU SHARE						INDUSTRY MIX						COUNTRY SHARE						Total
	Exp	Dom	Imp	E Prd	D Prd	I Prd	Exp	Dom	Imp	E Prd	D Prd	I Prd	Exp	Dom	Imp	E Prd	D Prd	I Prd	Change
Total manufacturing	0.03	-0.18	0.03	-0.01	-0.06	-0.07	-0.08	-0.06	-0.04	-0.09	-0.05	0.00	0.10	0.16	0.04	-0.18	-0.16	-0.21	0.22
Food, beverages & tobacco	0.03	-0.18	0.03	-0.01	-0.06	-0.07	-0.10	0.02	-0.04	-0.13	-0.03	0.00	0.18	0.09	0.28	-0.20	-0.25	-0.27	0.11
Textiles, apparel & leather	0.03	-0.18	0.03	-0.01	-0.06	-0.07	-0.01	-0.13	0.08	-0.11	-0.07	0.08	0.14	0.28	-0.01	-0.05	-0.04	-0.18	0.20
Wood products & furniture	0.03	-0.18	0.03	-0.01	-0.06	-0.07	-0.09	-0.14	-0.10	-0.25	-0.14	-0.05	0.32	0.37	0.18	0.03	-0.04	-0.12	0.43
Paper, paper products & printing	0.03	-0.18	0.03	-0.01	-0.06	-0.07	0.11	0.14	0.12	0.00	0.05	0.08	-0.01	0.13	-0.08	-0.39	-0.39	-0.41	0.54
Chemical products	0.03	-0.18	0.03	-0.01	-0.06	-0.07	-0.02	-0.08	-0.07	-0.11	-0.18	-0.13	0.03	-0.10	-0.19	-0.33	-0.22	-0.26	0.36
Non-metallic mineral products	0.03	-0.18	0.03	-0.01	-0.06	-0.07	-0.23	-0.14	-0.03	-0.07	-0.05	0.05	-0.02	0.31	0.03	0.02	0.05	-0.04	-0.19
Basic metal industries	0.03	-0.18	0.03	-0.01	-0.06	-0.07	-0.38	-0.27	-0.43	-0.18	-0.15	-0.11	0.16	0.03	0.08	-0.21	-0.20	-0.23	0.12
Fabricated metal products	0.03	-0.18	0.03	-0.01	-0.06	-0.07	0.09	0.13	0.13	0.13	0.12	0.11	-0.04	0.14	-0.01	-0.27	-0.21	-0.19	0.17

1986-1995

	EU SHARE						INDUSTRY MIX						COUNTRY SHARE						Total
	Exp	Dom	Imp	E Prd	D Prd	I Prd	Exp	Dom	Imp	E Prd	D Prd	I Prd	Exp	Dom	Imp	E Prd	D Prd	I Prd	Change
Total manufacturing	0.32	0.12	0.32	0.16	0.15	0.15	-0.04	-0.01	-0.03	-0.10	-0.07	-0.08	0.26	0.25	0.18	0.47	0.46	0.46	-0.10
Food, beverages & tobacco	0.32	0.12	0.32	0.16	0.15	0.15	0.09	-0.01	-0.01	-0.05	-0.08	-0.06	0.14	0.09	0.39	0.22	0.27	0.24	-0.27
Textiles, apparel & leather	0.32	0.12	0.32	0.16	0.15	0.15	-0.23	-0.29	-0.20	-0.13	-0.10	-0.11	0.04	0.15	-0.01	0.34	0.33	0.33	-0.37
Wood products & furniture	0.32	0.12	0.32	0.16	0.15	0.15	0.11	0.17	0.18	-0.03	-0.07	-0.09	0.46	0.62	0.36	1.43	1.48	1.49	-0.61
Paper, paper products & printing	0.32	0.12	0.32	0.16	0.15	0.15	-0.04	0.01	-0.06	-0.24	-0.16	-0.18	0.03	-0.06	-0.16	0.26	0.20	0.22	0.10
Chemical products	0.32	0.12	0.32	0.16	0.15	0.15	0.06	0.06	0.02	0.04	0.04	0.03	0.16	0.16	0.09	0.07	0.09	0.09	0.18
Non-metallic mineral products	0.32	0.12	0.32	0.16	0.15	0.15	-0.10	0.06	-0.08	-0.20	-0.03	0.00	0.20	-0.01	-0.06	0.40	0.24	0.21	0.05
Basic metal industries	0.32	0.12	0.32	0.16	0.15	0.15	-0.21	-0.11	-0.11	-0.24	-0.27	-0.32	0.92	0.91	0.75	1.00	1.05	1.09	0.06
Fabricated metal products	0.32	0.12	0.32	0.16	0.15	0.15	0.02	0.04	0.05	0.05	0.08	0.08	0.15	0.16	0.09	0.07	0.04	0.04	0.08

FRANCE

1980-1995

	EU SHARE						INDUSTRY MIX						COUNTRY SHARE						Total
	Exp	Dom	Imp	E Prd	D Prd	I Prd	Exp	Dom	Imp	E Prd	D Prd	I Prd	Exp	Dom	Imp	E Prd	D Prd	I Prd	Change
Total manufacturing	0.35	-0.06	0.35	0.15	0.08	0.08	-0.11	-0.07	-0.07	-0.19	-0.13	-0.08	0.01	-0.01	-0.11	0.15	0.15	0.10	-0.17
Food, beverages & tobacco	0.35	-0.06	0.35	0.15	0.08	0.08	-0.01	0.01	-0.05	-0.17	-0.11	-0.06	-0.01	-0.08	-0.01	-0.07	-0.07	-0.12	0.01
Textiles, apparel & leather	0.35	-0.06	0.35	0.15	0.08	0.08	-0.24	-0.42	-0.11	-0.24	-0.17	-0.03	0.02	0.14	-0.07	0.44	0.44	0.30	-0.73
Wood products & furniture	0.35	-0.06	0.35	0.15	0.08	0.08	0.02	0.03	0.08	-0.28	-0.21	-0.13	0.00	-0.13	-0.47	-0.03	-0.03	-0.11	0.41
Paper, paper products & printing	0.35	-0.06	0.35	0.15	0.08	0.08	0.07	0.15	0.06	-0.24	-0.11	-0.10	0.20	0.17	-0.06	0.29	0.23	0.22	0.31
Chemical products	0.35	-0.06	0.35	0.15	0.08	0.08	0.04	-0.02	-0.05	-0.08	-0.14	-0.10	-0.15	-0.12	-0.09	-0.25	-0.12	-0.16	0.00
Non-metallic mineral products	0.35	-0.06	0.35	0.15	0.08	0.08	-0.32	-0.08	-0.12	-0.27	-0.07	0.05	0.10	-0.01	-0.15	0.26	0.13	0.01	-0.24
Basic metal industries	0.35	-0.06	0.35	0.15	0.08	0.08	-0.59	-0.38	-0.54	-0.42	-0.41	-0.43	-0.02	-0.01	-0.01	0.63	0.69	0.71	-0.89
Fabricated metal products	0.35	-0.06	0.35	0.15	0.08	0.08	0.12	0.18	0.18	0.18	0.21	0.19	-0.05	0.00	-0.01	-0.12	-0.08	-0.06	-0.20

1980-1986

	EU SHARE						INDUSTRY MIX						COUNTRY SHARE						Total
	Exp	Dom	Imp	E Prd	D Prd	I Prd	Exp	Dom	Imp	E Prd	D Prd	I Prd	Exp	Dom	Imp	E Prd	D Prd	I Prd	Change
Total manufacturing	0.03	-0.18	0.03	-0.01	-0.06	-0.07	-0.08	-0.06	-0.04	-0.09	-0.05	0.00	-0.11	-0.07	-0.11	-0.03	-0.01	-0.06	-0.22
Food, beverages & tobacco	0.03	-0.18	0.03	-0.01	-0.06	-0.07	-0.10	0.02	-0.04	-0.13	-0.03	0.00	-0.11	-0.12	-0.11	-0.17	-0.21	-0.23	-0.03
Textiles, apparel & leather	0.03	-0.18	0.03	-0.01	-0.06	-0.07	-0.01	-0.13	0.08	-0.11	-0.07	0.08	-0.16	0.06	-0.11	0.16	0.17	0.03	-0.44
Wood products & furniture	0.03	-0.18	0.03	-0.01	-0.06	-0.07	-0.09	-0.14	-0.10	-0.25	-0.14	-0.05	-0.10	-0.06	-0.14	0.00	-0.06	-0.14	-0.07
Paper, paper products & printing	0.03	-0.18	0.03	-0.01	-0.06	-0.07	0.11	0.14	0.12	0.00	0.05	0.08	-0.05	-0.02	-0.12	0.01	0.01	-0.02	0.00
Chemical products	0.03	-0.18	0.03	-0.01	-0.06	-0.07	-0.02	-0.08	-0.07	-0.11	-0.18	-0.13	-0.16	-0.17	-0.08	-0.20	-0.08	-0.12	-0.15
Non-metallic mineral products	0.03	-0.18	0.03	-0.01	-0.06	-0.07	-0.23	-0.14	-0.03	-0.07	-0.05	0.05	0.06	-0.04	-0.11	0.07	0.09	0.01	-0.37
Basic metal industries	0.03	-0.18	0.03	-0.01	-0.06	-0.07	-0.38	-0.27	-0.43	-0.18	-0.15	-0.11	-0.16	-0.09	-0.12	0.02	0.03	0.01	-0.36
Fabricated metal products	0.03	-0.18	0.03	-0.01	-0.06	-0.07	0.09	0.13	0.13	0.13	0.12	0.11	-0.23	-0.11	-0.09	-0.11	-0.05	-0.03	-0.33

1986-1995

	EU SHARE						INDUSTRY MIX						COUNTRY SHARE						Total
	Exp	Dom	Imp	E Prd	D Prd	I Prd	Exp	Dom	Imp	E Prd	D Prd	I Prd	Exp	Dom	Imp	E Prd	D Prd	I Prd	Change
Total manufacturing	0.32	0.12	0.32	0.16	0.15	0.15	-0.04	-0.01	-0.03	-0.10	-0.07	-0.08	0.12	0.06	0.00	0.17	0.16	0.16	0.05
Food, beverages & tobacco	0.32	0.12	0.32	0.16	0.15	0.15	0.09	-0.01	-0.01	-0.05	-0.08	-0.06	0.09	0.04	0.10	0.09	0.14	0.11	0.04
Textiles, apparel & leather	0.32	0.12	0.32	0.16	0.15	0.15	-0.23	-0.29	-0.20	-0.13	-0.10	-0.11	0.18	0.08	0.04	0.28	0.27	0.27	-0.30
Wood products & furniture	0.32	0.12	0.32	0.16	0.15	0.15	0.11	0.17	0.18	-0.03	-0.07	-0.09	0.10	-0.08	-0.33	-0.03	0.03	0.03	0.48
Paper, paper products & printing	0.32	0.12	0.32	0.16	0.15	0.15	-0.04	0.01	-0.06	-0.24	-0.16	-0.18	0.24	0.18	0.06	0.28	0.22	0.24	0.31
Chemical products	0.32	0.12	0.32	0.16	0.15	0.15	0.06	0.06	0.02	0.04	0.04	0.03	0.01	0.05	-0.01	-0.05	-0.04	-0.03	0.14
Non-metallic mineral products	0.32	0.12	0.32	0.16	0.15	0.15	-0.10	0.06	-0.08	-0.20	-0.03	0.00	0.04	0.03	-0.04	0.19	0.03	0.00	0.13
Basic metal industries	0.32	0.12	0.32	0.16	0.15	0.15	-0.21	-0.11	-0.11	-0.24	-0.27	-0.32	0.14	0.08	0.11	0.61	0.66	0.70	-0.53
Fabricated metal products	0.32	0.12	0.32	0.16	0.15	0.15	0.02	0.04	0.05	0.05	0.08	0.08	0.18	0.10	0.08	0.00	-0.02	-0.03	0.13

GERMANY

1980-1995

	EU SHARE						INDUSTRY MIX						COUNTRY SHARE						Total
	Exp	Dom	Imp	E Prd	D Prd	I Prd	Exp	Dom	Imp	E Prd	D Prd	I Prd	Exp	Dom	Imp	E Prd	D Prd	I Prd	Change
Total manufacturing	0.35	-0.06	0.35	0.15	0.08	0.08	-0.11	-0.07	-0.07	-0.19	-0.13	-0.08	0.39	0.48	0.37	0.25	0.25	0.20	0.12
Food, beverages & tobacco	0.35	-0.06	0.35	0.15	0.08	0.08	-0.01	0.01	-0.05	-0.17	-0.11	-0.06	0.45	0.46	0.42	0.09	0.09	0.04	0.42
Textiles, apparel & leather	0.35	-0.06	0.35	0.15	0.08	0.08	-0.24	-0.42	-0.11	-0.24	-0.17	-0.03	0.45	0.39	0.15	0.31	0.31	0.17	-0.14
Wood products & furniture	0.35	-0.06	0.35	0.15	0.08	0.08	0.02	0.03	0.08	-0.28	-0.21	-0.13	0.50	0.64	0.57	0.18	0.17	0.10	0.43
Paper, paper products & printing	0.35	-0.06	0.35	0.15	0.08	0.08	0.07	0.15	0.06	-0.24	-0.11	-0.10	0.51	0.27	0.23	0.04	-0.02	-0.03	0.68
Chemical products	0.35	-0.06	0.35	0.15	0.08	0.08	0.04	-0.02	-0.05	-0.08	-0.14	-0.10	0.38	0.47	0.32	0.28	0.41	0.37	0.17
Non-metallic mineral products	0.35	-0.06	0.35	0.15	0.08	0.08	-0.32	-0.08	-0.12	-0.27	-0.07	0.05	0.41	0.69	0.41	0.70	0.57	0.45	-0.22
Basic metal industries	0.35	-0.06	0.35	0.15	0.08	0.08	-0.59	-0.38	-0.54	-0.42	-0.41	-0.43	0.17	0.40	0.32	0.18	0.24	0.26	-0.15
Fabricated metal products	0.35	-0.06	0.35	0.15	0.08	0.08	0.12	0.18	0.18	0.18	0.21	0.19	0.28	0.48	0.53	0.21	0.25	0.27	-0.26

1980-1986

	EU SHARE						INDUSTRY MIX						COUNTRY SHARE						Total
	Exp	Dom	Imp	E Prd	D Prd	I Prd	Exp	Dom	Imp	E Prd	D Prd	I Prd	Exp	Dom	Imp	E Prd	D Prd	I Prd	Change
Total manufacturing	0.03	-0.18	0.03	-0.01	-0.06	-0.07	-0.08	-0.06	-0.04	-0.09	-0.05	0.00	0.34	0.26	0.19	0.27	0.29	0.24	-0.04
Food, beverages & tobacco	0.03	-0.18	0.03	-0.01	-0.06	-0.07	-0.10	0.02	-0.04	-0.13	-0.03	0.00	0.37	0.26	0.21	0.31	0.27	0.25	0.02
Textiles, apparel & leather	0.03	-0.18	0.03	-0.01	-0.06	-0.07	-0.01	-0.13	0.08	-0.11	-0.07	0.08	0.37	0.31	0.14	0.43	0.44	0.30	-0.17
Wood products & furniture	0.03	-0.18	0.03	-0.01	-0.06	-0.07	-0.09	-0.14	-0.10	-0.25	-0.14	-0.05	0.38	0.17	0.05	0.40	0.33	0.25	0.05
Paper, paper products & printing	0.03	-0.18	0.03	-0.01	-0.06	-0.07	0.11	0.14	0.12	0.00	0.05	0.08	0.42	0.21	0.20	0.28	0.28	0.26	0.10
Chemical products	0.03	-0.18	0.03	-0.01	-0.06	-0.07	-0.02	-0.08	-0.07	-0.11	-0.18	-0.13	0.29	0.26	0.25	0.12	0.23	0.19	0.10
Non-metallic mineral products	0.03	-0.18	0.03	-0.01	-0.06	-0.07	-0.23	-0.14	-0.03	-0.07	-0.05	0.05	0.45	0.26	0.14	0.25	0.28	0.20	-0.12
Basic metal industries	0.03	-0.18	0.03	-0.01	-0.06	-0.07	-0.38	-0.27	-0.43	-0.18	-0.15	-0.11	0.19	0.25	0.21	0.26	0.27	0.24	-0.23
Fabricated metal products	0.03	-0.18	0.03	-0.01	-0.06	-0.07	0.09	0.13	0.13	0.13	0.12	0.11	0.29	0.32	0.33	0.15	0.21	0.23	-0.07

1986-1995

	EU SHARE						INDUSTRY MIX						COUNTRY SHARE						Total
	Exp	Dom	Imp	E Prd	D Prd	I Prd	Exp	Dom	Imp	E Prd	D Prd	I Prd	Exp	Dom	Imp	E Prd	D Prd	I Prd	Change
Total manufacturing	0.32	0.12	0.32	0.16	0.15	0.15	-0.04	-0.01	-0.03	-0.10	-0.07	-0.08	0.05	0.22	0.18	-0.02	-0.04	-0.04	0.16
Food, beverages & tobacco	0.32	0.12	0.32	0.16	0.15	0.15	0.09	-0.01	-0.01	-0.05	-0.08	-0.06	0.08	0.20	0.21	-0.22	-0.18	-0.20	0.39
Textiles, apparel & leather	0.32	0.12	0.32	0.16	0.15	0.15	-0.23	-0.29	-0.20	-0.13	-0.10	-0.11	0.08	0.08	0.02	-0.12	-0.13	-0.13	0.03
Wood products & furniture	0.32	0.12	0.32	0.16	0.15	0.15	0.11	0.17	0.18	-0.03	-0.07	-0.09	0.12	0.47	0.52	-0.22	-0.16	-0.15	0.38
Paper, paper products & printing	0.32	0.12	0.32	0.16	0.15	0.15	-0.04	0.01	-0.06	-0.24	-0.16	-0.18	0.08	0.06	0.03	-0.24	-0.30	-0.29	0.58
Chemical products	0.32	0.12	0.32	0.16	0.15	0.15	0.06	0.06	0.02	0.04	0.04	0.03	0.09	0.20	0.07	0.17	0.18	0.18	0.08
Non-metallic mineral products	0.32	0.12	0.32	0.16	0.15	0.15	-0.10	0.06	-0.08	-0.20	-0.03	0.00	-0.04	0.44	0.27	0.45	0.29	0.25	-0.11
Basic metal industries	0.32	0.12	0.32	0.16	0.15	0.15	-0.21	-0.11	-0.11	-0.24	-0.27	-0.32	-0.02	0.16	0.11	-0.08	-0.03	0.02	0.08
Fabricated metal products	0.32	0.12	0.32	0.16	0.15	0.15	0.02	0.04	0.05	0.05	0.08	0.08	-0.01	0.16	0.19	0.07	0.04	0.04	-0.18

GREECE

1980-1995

	EU SHARE						INDUSTRY MIX						COUNTRY SHARE						Total
	Exp	Dom	Imp	E Prd	D Prd	I Prd	Exp	Dom	Imp	E Prd	D Prd	I Prd	Exp	Dom	Imp	E Prd	D Prd	I Prd	Change
Total manufacturing	0.35	-0.06	0.35	0.15	0.08	0.08	-0.11	-0.07	-0.07	-0.19	-0.13	-0.08	-1.58	-1.62	-1.38	-1.93	-1.92	-1.97	-0.03
Food, beverages & tobacco	0.35	-0.06	0.35	0.15	0.08	0.08	-0.01	0.01	-0.05	-0.17	-0.11	-0.06	-1.79	-1.30	-1.18	-1.67	-1.67	-1.71	-0.21
Textiles, apparel & leather	0.35	-0.06	0.35	0.15	0.08	0.08	-0.24	-0.42	-0.11	-0.24	-0.17	-0.03	-1.32	-1.49	-0.74	-1.98	-1.98	-2.12	-0.61
Wood products & furniture	0.35	-0.06	0.35	0.15	0.08	0.08	0.02	0.03	0.08	-0.28	-0.21	-0.13	-0.94	-1.58	-0.95	-1.55	-1.55	-1.63	0.02
Paper, paper products & printing	0.35	-0.06	0.35	0.15	0.08	0.08	0.07	0.15	0.06	-0.24	-0.11	-0.10	-2.05	-1.41	-1.40	-2.06	-2.12	-2.13	0.18
Chemical products	0.35	-0.06	0.35	0.15	0.08	0.08	0.04	-0.02	-0.05	-0.08	-0.14	-0.10	-2.21	-1.86	-1.66	-2.31	-2.18	-2.22	-0.17
Non-metallic mineral products	0.35	-0.06	0.35	0.15	0.08	0.08	-0.32	-0.08	-0.12	-0.27	-0.07	0.05	-1.51	-1.69	-1.29	-1.78	-1.92	-2.04	-0.34
Basic metal industries	0.35	-0.06	0.35	0.15	0.08	0.08	-0.59	-0.38	-0.54	-0.42	-0.41	-0.43	-1.62	-1.70	-1.64	-2.27	-2.21	-2.19	0.37
Fabricated metal products	0.35	-0.06	0.35	0.15	0.08	0.08	0.12	0.18	0.18	0.18	0.21	0.19	-1.20	-1.97	-2.18	-1.79	-1.75	-1.73	0.53

1980-1986

	EU SHARE						INDUSTRY MIX						COUNTRY SHARE						Total
	Exp	Dom	Imp	E Prd	D Prd	I Prd	Exp	Dom	Imp	E Prd	D Prd	I Prd	Exp	Dom	Imp	E Prd	D Prd	I Prd	Change
Total manufacturing	0.03	-0.18	0.03	-0.01	-0.06	-0.07	-0.08	-0.06	-0.04	-0.09	-0.05	0.00	-1.04	-0.84	-0.66	-1.34	-1.33	-1.38	-0.05
Food, beverages & tobacco	0.03	-0.18	0.03	-0.01	-0.06	-0.07	-0.10	0.02	-0.04	-0.13	-0.03	0.00	-0.61	-0.65	-0.17	-0.95	-1.00	-1.02	-0.23
Textiles, apparel & leather	0.03	-0.18	0.03	-0.01	-0.06	-0.07	-0.01	-0.13	0.08	-0.11	-0.07	0.08	-0.20	-0.65	0.14	-1.20	-1.20	-1.33	-0.08
Wood products & furniture	0.03	-0.18	0.03	-0.01	-0.06	-0.07	-0.09	-0.14	-0.10	-0.25	-0.14	-0.05	-1.06	-0.89	-0.49	-1.98	-2.04	-2.12	0.47
Paper, paper products & printing	0.03	-0.18	0.03	-0.01	-0.06	-0.07	0.11	0.14	0.12	0.00	0.05	0.08	-1.60	-0.79	-0.97	-1.32	-1.32	-1.34	-0.15
Chemical products	0.03	-0.18	0.03	-0.01	-0.06	-0.07	-0.02	-0.08	-0.07	-0.11	-0.18	-0.13	-1.69	-0.88	-0.83	-1.30	-1.18	-1.22	-0.52
Non-metallic mineral products	0.03	-0.18	0.03	-0.01	-0.06	-0.07	-0.23	-0.14	-0.03	-0.07	-0.05	0.05	-0.95	-0.79	-0.77	-1.12	-1.09	-1.17	-0.29
Basic metal industries	0.03	-0.18	0.03	-0.01	-0.06	-0.07	-0.38	-0.27	-0.43	-0.18	-0.15	-0.11	-0.79	-0.85	-0.74	-1.21	-1.20	-1.23	0.12
Fabricated metal products	0.03	-0.18	0.03	-0.01	-0.06	-0.07	0.09	0.13	0.13	0.13	0.12	0.11	-1.42	-1.23	-1.46	-1.66	-1.60	-1.57	0.27

1986-1995

	EU SHARE						INDUSTRY MIX						COUNTRY SHARE						Total
	Exp	Dom	Imp	E Prd	D Prd	I Prd	Exp	Dom	Imp	E Prd	D Prd	I Prd	Exp	Dom	Imp	E Prd	D Prd	I Prd	Change
Total manufacturing	0.32	0.12	0.32	0.16	0.15	0.15	-0.04	-0.01	-0.03	-0.10	-0.07	-0.08	-0.54	-0.78	-0.72	-0.58	-0.60	-0.59	0.02
Food, beverages & tobacco	0.32	0.12	0.32	0.16	0.15	0.15	0.09	-0.01	-0.01	-0.05	-0.08	-0.06	-1.18	-0.65	-1.02	-0.72	-0.67	-0.69	0.01
Textiles, apparel & leather	0.32	0.12	0.32	0.16	0.15	0.15	-0.23	-0.29	-0.20	-0.13	-0.10	-0.11	-1.12	-0.84	-0.88	-0.78	-0.79	-0.79	-0.53
Wood products & furniture	0.32	0.12	0.32	0.16	0.15	0.15	0.11	0.17	0.18	-0.03	-0.07	-0.09	0.13	-0.69	-0.45	0.43	0.49	0.50	-0.45
Paper, paper products & printing	0.32	0.12	0.32	0.16	0.15	0.15	-0.04	0.01	-0.06	-0.24	-0.16	-0.18	-0.45	-0.62	-0.43	-0.74	-0.80	-0.79	0.32
Chemical products	0.32	0.12	0.32	0.16	0.15	0.15	0.06	0.06	0.02	0.04	0.04	0.03	-0.52	-0.99	-0.83	-1.01	-1.00	-0.99	0.35
Non-metallic mineral products	0.32	0.12	0.32	0.16	0.15	0.15	-0.10	0.06	-0.08	-0.20	-0.03	0.00	-0.56	-0.90	-0.52	-0.66	-0.83	-0.86	-0.06
Basic metal industries	0.32	0.12	0.32	0.16	0.15	0.15	-0.21	-0.11	-0.11	-0.24	-0.27	-0.32	-0.84	-0.85	-0.90	-1.06	-1.01	-0.96	0.25
Fabricated metal products	0.32	0.12	0.32	0.16	0.15	0.15	0.02	0.04	0.05	0.05	0.08	0.08	0.22	-0.74	-0.72	-0.13	-0.16	-0.16	0.27

IRELAND

1980-1995

	EU SHARE						INDUSTRY MIX						COUNTRY SHARE						Total
	Exp	Dom	Imp	E Prd	D Prd	I Prd	Exp	Dom	Imp	E Prd	D Prd	I Prd	Exp	Dom	Imp	E Prd	D Prd	I Prd	Change
Total manufacturing	0.35	-0.06	0.35	0.15	0.08	0.08	-0.11	-0.07	-0.07	-0.19	-0.13	-0.08	-0.37	0.36	0.11	0.32	0.32	0.28	-0.58
Food, beverages & tobacco	0.35	-0.06	0.35	0.15	0.08	0.08	-0.01	0.01	-0.05	-0.17	-0.11	-0.06	-0.86	-0.04	-0.78	0.29	0.29	0.24	-0.38
Textiles, apparel & leather	0.35	-0.06	0.35	0.15	0.08	0.08	-0.24	-0.42	-0.11	-0.24	-0.17	-0.03	-1.77	-0.02	-1.91	0.05	0.05	-0.09	-0.46
Wood products & furniture	0.35	-0.06	0.35	0.15	0.08	0.08	0.02	0.03	0.08	-0.28	-0.21	-0.13	-0.56	0.17	0.13	0.15	0.14	0.07	-0.63
Paper, paper products & printing	0.35	-0.06	0.35	0.15	0.08	0.08	0.07	0.15	0.06	-0.24	-0.11	-0.10	-0.70	0.18	-0.47	0.29	0.23	0.22	-0.16
Chemical products	0.35	-0.06	0.35	0.15	0.08	0.08	0.04	-0.02	-0.05	-0.08	-0.14	-0.10	0.66	1.08	1.97	0.29	0.41	0.38	-0.59
Non-metallic mineral products	0.35	-0.06	0.35	0.15	0.08	0.08	-0.32	-0.08	-0.12	-0.27	-0.07	0.05	-1.42	-0.36	-1.44	-0.16	-0.30	-0.42	-0.40
Basic metal industries	0.35	-0.06	0.35	0.15	0.08	0.08	-0.59	-0.38	-0.54	-0.42	-0.41	-0.43	0.86	0.91	1.82	0.22	0.28	0.29	-0.49
Fabricated metal products	0.35	-0.06	0.35	0.15	0.08	0.08	0.12	0.18	0.18	0.18	0.21	0.19	0.84	0.94	1.60	1.45	1.49	1.51	-1.56

1980-1986

	EU SHARE						INDUSTRY MIX						COUNTRY SHARE						Total
	Exp	Dom	Imp	E Prd	D Prd	I Prd	Exp	Dom	Imp	E Prd	D Prd	I Prd	Exp	Dom	Imp	E Prd	D Prd	I Prd	Change
Total manufacturing	0.03	-0.18	0.03	-0.01	-0.06	-0.07	-0.08	-0.06	-0.04	-0.09	-0.05	0.00	-0.19	0.07	0.28	-0.07	-0.05	-0.10	-0.51
Food, beverages & tobacco	0.03	-0.18	0.03	-0.01	-0.06	-0.07	-0.10	0.02	-0.04	-0.13	-0.03	0.00	-0.35	-0.05	-0.33	0.20	0.16	0.13	-0.35
Textiles, apparel & leather	0.03	-0.18	0.03	-0.01	-0.06	-0.07	-0.01	-0.13	0.08	-0.11	-0.07	0.08	-1.11	-0.19	-1.30	-0.14	-0.13	-0.27	-0.15
Wood products & furniture	0.03	-0.18	0.03	-0.01	-0.06	-0.07	-0.09	-0.14	-0.10	-0.25	-0.14	-0.05	-0.35	0.02	0.39	-0.26	-0.33	-0.41	-0.51
Paper, paper products & printing	0.03	-0.18	0.03	-0.01	-0.06	-0.07	0.11	0.14	0.12	0.00	0.05	0.08	-0.33	-0.16	0.00	-0.13	-0.13	-0.15	-0.41
Chemical products	0.03	-0.18	0.03	-0.01	-0.06	-0.07	-0.02	-0.08	-0.07	-0.11	-0.18	-0.13	-0.17	0.23	0.48	-0.10	0.01	-0.03	-0.41
Non-metallic mineral products	0.03	-0.18	0.03	-0.01	-0.06	-0.07	-0.23	-0.14	-0.03	-0.07	-0.05	0.05	-0.53	-0.12	-0.32	-0.05	-0.03	-0.11	-0.70
Basic metal industries	0.03	-0.18	0.03	-0.01	-0.06	-0.07	-0.38	-0.27	-0.43	-0.18	-0.15	-0.11	0.78	0.32	2.11	-0.23	-0.22	-0.24	-0.99
Fabricated metal products	0.03	-0.18	0.03	-0.01	-0.06	-0.07	0.09	0.13	0.13	0.13	0.12	0.11	0.53	0.50	1.22	0.19	0.25	0.28	-0.58

1986-1995

	EU SHARE						INDUSTRY MIX						COUNTRY SHARE						Total
	Exp	Dom	Imp	E Prd	D Prd	I Prd	Exp	Dom	Imp	E Prd	D Prd	I Prd	Exp	Dom	Imp	E Prd	D Prd	I Prd	Change
Total manufacturing	0.32	0.12	0.32	0.16	0.15	0.15	-0.04	-0.01	-0.03	-0.10	-0.07	-0.08	-0.18	0.29	-0.17	0.39	0.38	0.38	-0.07
Food, beverages & tobacco	0.32	0.12	0.32	0.16	0.15	0.15	0.09	-0.01	-0.01	-0.05	-0.08	-0.06	-0.51	0.01	-0.46	0.09	0.13	0.11	-0.03
Textiles, apparel & leather	0.32	0.12	0.32	0.16	0.15	0.15	-0.23	-0.29	-0.20	-0.13	-0.10	-0.11	-0.66	0.17	-0.61	0.19	0.18	0.18	-0.31
Wood products & furniture	0.32	0.12	0.32	0.16	0.15	0.15	0.11	0.17	0.18	-0.03	-0.07	-0.09	-0.20	0.15	-0.26	0.42	0.47	0.48	-0.12
Paper, paper products & printing	0.32	0.12	0.32	0.16	0.15	0.15	-0.04	0.01	-0.06	-0.24	-0.16	-0.18	-0.37	0.34	-0.47	0.42	0.36	0.37	0.25
Chemical products	0.32	0.12	0.32	0.16	0.15	0.15	0.06	0.06	0.02	0.04	0.04	0.03	0.82	0.85	1.48	0.39	0.40	0.40	-0.18
Non-metallic mineral products	0.32	0.12	0.32	0.16	0.15	0.15	-0.10	0.06	-0.08	-0.20	-0.03	0.00	-0.89	-0.25	-1.12	-0.11	-0.27	-0.30	0.30
Basic metal industries	0.32	0.12	0.32	0.16	0.15	0.15	-0.21	-0.11	-0.11	-0.24	-0.27	-0.32	0.08	0.59	-0.30	0.45	0.49	0.54	0.50
Fabricated metal products	0.32	0.12	0.32	0.16	0.15	0.15	0.02	0.04	0.05	0.05	0.08	0.08	0.31	0.44	0.39	1.26	1.24	1.24	-0.98

ITALY

1980-1995

	EU SHARE						INDUSTRY MIX						COUNTRY SHARE						Total
	Exp	Dom	Imp	E Prd	D Prd	I Prd	Exp	Dom	Imp	E Prd	D Prd	I Prd	Exp	Dom	Imp	E Prd	D Prd	I Prd	Change
Total manufacturing	0.35	-0.06	0.35	0.15	0.08	0.08	-0.11	-0.07	-0.07	-0.19	-0.13	-0.08	-0.55	-0.49	-0.68	-0.42	-0.41	-0.46	-0.08
Food, beverages & tobacco	0.35	-0.06	0.35	0.15	0.08	0.08	-0.01	0.01	-0.05	-0.17	-0.11	-0.06	-0.33	-0.45	-0.52	-0.33	-0.33	-0.38	0.09
Textiles, apparel & leather	0.35	-0.06	0.35	0.15	0.08	0.08	-0.24	-0.42	-0.11	-0.24	-0.17	-0.03	-0.27	-0.18	-0.20	-0.30	-0.30	-0.44	-0.47
Wood products & furniture	0.35	-0.06	0.35	0.15	0.08	0.08	0.02	0.03	0.08	-0.28	-0.21	-0.13	-0.54	-0.74	-1.09	-0.24	-0.25	-0.32	0.09
Paper, paper products & printing	0.35	-0.06	0.35	0.15	0.08	0.08	0.07	0.15	0.06	-0.24	-0.11	-0.10	-0.48	-0.53	-0.58	-0.23	-0.28	-0.29	-0.03
Chemical products	0.35	-0.06	0.35	0.15	0.08	0.08	0.04	-0.02	-0.05	-0.08	-0.14	-0.10	-0.95	-0.25	-0.74	-0.48	-0.35	-0.39	-0.04
Non-metallic mineral products	0.35	-0.06	0.35	0.15	0.08	0.08	-0.32	-0.08	-0.12	-0.27	-0.07	0.05	-0.46	-0.68	-0.71	-0.86	-1.00	-1.12	0.22
Basic metal industries	0.35	-0.06	0.35	0.15	0.08	0.08	-0.59	-0.38	-0.54	-0.42	-0.41	-0.43	-0.58	-0.23	-0.65	-0.02	0.04	0.05	-0.37
Fabricated metal products	0.35	-0.06	0.35	0.15	0.08	0.08	0.12	0.18	0.18	0.18	0.21	0.19	-0.79	-0.88	-0.91	-0.88	-0.84	-0.82	-0.15

1980-1986

	EU SHARE						INDUSTRY MIX						COUNTRY SHARE						Total
	Exp	Dom	Imp	E Prd	D Prd	I Prd	Exp	Dom	Imp	E Prd	D Prd	I Prd	Exp	Dom	Imp	E Prd	D Prd	I Prd	Change
Total manufacturing	0.03	-0.18	0.03	-0.01	-0.06	-0.07	-0.08	-0.06	-0.04	-0.09	-0.05	0.00	-0.29	-0.11	-0.34	-0.07	-0.05	-0.10	-0.16
Food, beverages & tobacco	0.03	-0.18	0.03	-0.01	-0.06	-0.07	-0.10	0.02	-0.04	-0.13	-0.03	0.00	-0.07	-0.07	-0.12	0.04	0.00	-0.03	-0.15
Textiles, apparel & leather	0.03	-0.18	0.03	-0.01	-0.06	-0.07	-0.01	-0.13	0.08	-0.11	-0.07	0.08	-0.13	-0.05	-0.23	-0.02	-0.02	-0.15	-0.21
Wood products & furniture	0.03	-0.18	0.03	-0.01	-0.06	-0.07	-0.09	-0.14	-0.10	-0.25	-0.14	-0.05	-0.16	-0.13	-0.58	0.09	0.03	-0.05	0.14
Paper, paper products & printing	0.03	-0.18	0.03	-0.01	-0.06	-0.07	0.11	0.14	0.12	0.00	0.05	0.08	-0.34	-0.20	-0.30	-0.11	-0.11	-0.14	-0.18
Chemical products	0.03	-0.18	0.03	-0.01	-0.06	-0.07	-0.02	-0.08	-0.07	-0.11	-0.18	-0.13	-0.48	0.12	-0.25	0.03	0.15	0.10	-0.22
Non-metallic mineral products	0.03	-0.18	0.03	-0.01	-0.06	-0.07	-0.23	-0.14	-0.03	-0.07	-0.05	0.05	-0.38	-0.07	-0.49	-0.23	-0.20	-0.29	-0.16
Basic metal industries	0.03	-0.18	0.03	-0.01	-0.06	-0.07	-0.38	-0.27	-0.43	-0.18	-0.15	-0.11	-0.31	-0.16	-0.35	-0.10	-0.08	-0.11	-0.23
Fabricated metal products	0.03	-0.18	0.03	-0.01	-0.06	-0.07	0.09	0.13	0.13	0.13	0.12	0.11	-0.46	-0.33	-0.44	-0.25	-0.19	-0.17	-0.30

1986-1995

	EU SHARE						INDUSTRY MIX						COUNTRY SHARE						Total
	Exp	Dom	Imp	E Prd	D Prd	I Prd	Exp	Dom	Imp	E Prd	D Prd	I Prd	Exp	Dom	Imp	E Prd	D Prd	I Prd	Change
Total manufacturing	0.32	0.12	0.32	0.16	0.15	0.15	-0.04	-0.01	-0.03	-0.10	-0.07	-0.08	-0.26	-0.38	-0.33	-0.35	-0.36	-0.36	0.08
Food, beverages & tobacco	0.32	0.12	0.32	0.16	0.15	0.15	0.09	-0.01	-0.01	-0.05	-0.08	-0.06	-0.26	-0.38	-0.40	-0.37	-0.33	-0.35	0.24
Textiles, apparel & leather	0.32	0.12	0.32	0.16	0.15	0.15	-0.23	-0.29	-0.20	-0.13	-0.10	-0.11	-0.13	-0.13	0.03	-0.28	-0.29	-0.29	-0.26
Wood products & furniture	0.32	0.12	0.32	0.16	0.15	0.15	0.11	0.17	0.18	-0.03	-0.07	-0.09	-0.38	-0.62	-0.52	-0.33	-0.28	-0.27	-0.05
Paper, paper products & printing	0.32	0.12	0.32	0.16	0.15	0.15	-0.04	0.01	-0.06	-0.24	-0.16	-0.18	-0.14	-0.33	-0.28	-0.11	-0.17	-0.16	0.15
Chemical products	0.32	0.12	0.32	0.16	0.15	0.15	0.06	0.06	0.02	0.04	0.04	0.03	-0.47	-0.37	-0.49	-0.51	-0.50	-0.49	0.18
Non-metallic mineral products	0.32	0.12	0.32	0.16	0.15	0.15	-0.10	0.06	-0.08	-0.20	-0.03	0.00	-0.08	-0.61	-0.23	-0.63	-0.79	-0.83	0.38
Basic metal industries	0.32	0.12	0.32	0.16	0.15	0.15	-0.21	-0.11	-0.11	-0.24	-0.27	-0.32	-0.27	-0.07	-0.29	0.08	0.12	0.17	-0.14
Fabricated metal products	0.32	0.12	0.32	0.16	0.15	0.15	0.02	0.04	0.05	0.05	0.08	0.08	-0.33	-0.55	-0.48	-0.63	-0.66	-0.66	0.16

NETHERLANDS

1980-1995

	EU SHARE						INDUSTRY MIX						COUNTRY SHARE						Total
	Exp	Dom	Imp	E Prd	D Prd	I Prd	Exp	Dom	Imp	E Prd	D Prd	I Prd	Exp	Dom	Imp	E Prd	D Prd	I Prd	Change
Total manufacturing	0.35	-0.06	0.35	0.15	0.08	0.08	-0.11	-0.07	-0.07	-0.19	-0.13	-0.08	0.33	0.27	0.11	0.28	0.28	0.24	0.09
Food, beverages & tobacco	0.35	-0.06	0.35	0.15	0.08	0.08	-0.01	0.01	-0.05	-0.17	-0.11	-0.06	0.02	0.37	-0.06	0.36	0.36	0.31	0.12
Textiles, apparel & leather	0.35	-0.06	0.35	0.15	0.08	0.08	-0.24	-0.42	-0.11	-0.24	-0.17	-0.03	0.42	0.36	-0.11	0.78	0.78	0.64	-0.42
Wood products & furniture	0.35	-0.06	0.35	0.15	0.08	0.08	0.02	0.03	0.08	-0.28	-0.21	-0.13	0.70	0.12	0.33	0.13	0.12	0.05	0.40
Paper, paper products & printing	0.35	-0.06	0.35	0.15	0.08	0.08	0.07	0.15	0.06	-0.24	-0.11	-0.10	-0.13	0.21	-0.02	-0.03	-0.08	-0.10	0.30
Chemical products	0.35	-0.06	0.35	0.15	0.08	0.08	0.04	-0.02	-0.05	-0.08	-0.14	-0.10	0.75	0.49	0.57	0.27	0.40	0.36	0.33
Non-metallic mineral products	0.35	-0.06	0.35	0.15	0.08	0.08	-0.32	-0.08	-0.12	-0.27	-0.07	0.05	0.79	0.39	0.15	0.52	0.39	0.27	0.29
Basic metal industries	0.35	-0.06	0.35	0.15	0.08	0.08	-0.59	-0.38	-0.54	-0.42	-0.41	-0.43	0.19	0.17	0.19	0.27	0.33	0.34	-0.33
Fabricated metal products	0.35	-0.06	0.35	0.15	0.08	0.08	0.12	0.18	0.18	0.18	0.21	0.19	-0.08	0.08	-0.21	-0.04	0.00	0.02	-0.02

1980-1986

	EU SHARE						INDUSTRY MIX						COUNTRY SHARE						Total
	Exp	Dom	Imp	E Prd	D Prd	I Prd	Exp	Dom	Imp	E Prd	D Prd	I Prd	Exp	Dom	Imp	E Prd	D Prd	I Prd	Change
Total manufacturing	0.03	-0.18	0.03	-0.01	-0.06	-0.07	-0.08	-0.06	-0.04	-0.09	-0.05	0.00	0.14	0.39	0.23	0.23	0.25	0.20	-0.11
Food, beverages & tobacco	0.03	-0.18	0.03	-0.01	-0.06	-0.07	-0.10	0.02	-0.04	-0.13	-0.03	0.00	-0.04	0.31	-0.06	0.26	0.22	0.19	-0.02
Textiles, apparel & leather	0.03	-0.18	0.03	-0.01	-0.06	-0.07	-0.01	-0.13	0.08	-0.11	-0.07	0.08	0.16	0.33	0.03	0.36	0.37	0.23	-0.19
Wood products & furniture	0.03	-0.18	0.03	-0.01	-0.06	-0.07	-0.09	-0.14	-0.10	-0.25	-0.14	-0.05	-0.19	0.36	0.44	0.32	0.26	0.18	-0.64
Paper, paper products & printing	0.03	-0.18	0.03	-0.01	-0.06	-0.07	0.11	0.14	0.12	0.00	0.05	0.08	-0.09	0.30	0.04	-0.13	-0.13	-0.15	0.26
Chemical products	0.03	-0.18	0.03	-0.01	-0.06	-0.07	-0.02	-0.08	-0.07	-0.11	-0.18	-0.13	0.87	0.85	0.79	0.57	0.69	0.64	0.27
Non-metallic mineral products	0.03	-0.18	0.03	-0.01	-0.06	-0.07	-0.23	-0.14	-0.03	-0.07	-0.05	0.05	-0.02	0.46	0.27	0.39	0.41	0.33	-0.65
Basic metal industries	0.03	-0.18	0.03	-0.01	-0.06	-0.07	-0.38	-0.27	-0.43	-0.18	-0.15	-0.11	0.15	0.18	0.10	0.00	0.01	-0.02	0.03
Fabricated metal products	0.03	-0.18	0.03	-0.01	-0.06	-0.07	0.09	0.13	0.13	0.13	0.12	0.11	0.28	0.33	0.24	0.10	0.16	0.19	0.06

1986-1995

	EU SHARE						INDUSTRY MIX						COUNTRY SHARE						Total
	Exp	Dom	Imp	E Prd	D Prd	I Prd	Exp	Dom	Imp	E Prd	D Prd	I Prd	Exp	Dom	Imp	E Prd	D Prd	I Prd	Change
Total manufacturing	0.32	0.12	0.32	0.16	0.15	0.15	-0.04	-0.01	-0.03	-0.10	-0.07	-0.08	0.19	-0.12	-0.13	0.05	0.04	0.04	0.20
Food, beverages & tobacco	0.32	0.12	0.32	0.16	0.15	0.15	0.09	-0.01	-0.01	-0.05	-0.08	-0.06	0.07	0.07	0.00	0.10	0.14	0.12	0.14
Textiles, apparel & leather	0.32	0.12	0.32	0.16	0.15	0.15	-0.23	-0.29	-0.20	-0.13	-0.10	-0.11	0.26	0.04	-0.14	0.42	0.41	0.41	-0.22
Wood products & furniture	0.32	0.12	0.32	0.16	0.15	0.15	0.11	0.17	0.18	-0.03	-0.07	-0.09	0.89	-0.25	-0.11	-0.19	-0.14	-0.13	1.04
Paper, paper products & printing	0.32	0.12	0.32	0.16	0.15	0.15	-0.04	0.01	-0.06	-0.24	-0.16	-0.18	-0.04	-0.10	-0.05	0.10	0.04	0.06	0.04
Chemical products	0.32	0.12	0.32	0.16	0.15	0.15	0.06	0.06	0.02	0.04	0.04	0.03	-0.12	-0.36	-0.22	-0.30	-0.29	-0.29	0.06
Non-metallic mineral products	0.32	0.12	0.32	0.16	0.15	0.15	-0.10	0.06	-0.08	-0.20	-0.03	0.00	0.82	-0.07	-0.12	0.13	-0.03	-0.06	0.95
Basic metal industries	0.32	0.12	0.32	0.16	0.15	0.15	-0.21	-0.11	-0.11	-0.24	-0.27	-0.32	0.04	-0.02	0.09	0.27	0.31	0.36	-0.36
Fabricated metal products	0.32	0.12	0.32	0.16	0.15	0.15	0.02	0.04	0.05	0.05	0.08	0.08	-0.36	-0.25	-0.45	-0.15	-0.17	-0.17	-0.08

PORTUGAL

1980-1995

	EU SHARE						INDUSTRY MIX						COUNTRY SHARE						Total
	Exp	Dom	Imp	E Prd	D Prd	I Prd	Exp	Dom	Imp	E Prd	D Prd	I Prd	Exp	Dom	Imp	E Prd	D Prd	I Prd	Change
Total manufacturing	0.35	-0.06	0.35	0.15	0.08	0.08	-0.11	-0.07	-0.07	-0.19	-0.13	-0.08	-0.14	-0.50	0.00	-1.11	-1.10	-1.15	0.33
Food, beverages & tobacco	0.35	-0.06	0.35	0.15	0.08	0.08	-0.01	0.01	-0.05	-0.17	-0.11	-0.06	-0.83	-0.37	-0.01	-0.62	-0.62	-0.67	-0.55
Textiles, apparel & leather	0.35	-0.06	0.35	0.15	0.08	0.08	-0.24	-0.42	-0.11	-0.24	-0.17	-0.03	0.20	-0.05	0.47	-0.51	-0.52	-0.65	-0.33
Wood products & furniture	0.35	-0.06	0.35	0.15	0.08	0.08	0.02	0.03	0.08	-0.28	-0.21	-0.13	-0.50	-0.55	0.97	-1.10	-1.11	-1.18	-0.89
Paper, paper products & printing	0.35	-0.06	0.35	0.15	0.08	0.08	0.07	0.15	0.06	-0.24	-0.11	-0.10	-0.34	-0.58	0.09	-1.10	-1.15	-1.16	0.27
Chemical products	0.35	-0.06	0.35	0.15	0.08	0.08	0.04	-0.02	-0.05	-0.08	-0.14	-0.10	-0.44	-0.95	-0.79	-1.78	-1.65	-1.69	1.11
Non-metallic mineral products	0.35	-0.06	0.35	0.15	0.08	0.08	-0.32	-0.08	-0.12	-0.27	-0.07	0.05	0.39	-0.54	-0.29	-0.55	-0.69	-0.81	0.47
Basic metal industries	0.35	-0.06	0.35	0.15	0.08	0.08	-0.59	-0.38	-0.54	-0.42	-0.41	-0.43	0.19	-0.28	-0.05	-2.28	-2.22	-2.20	2.01
Fabricated metal products	0.35	-0.06	0.35	0.15	0.08	0.08	0.12	0.18	0.18	0.18	0.21	0.19	0.18	-0.67	-0.44	-0.90	-0.86	-0.84	0.58

1980-1986

	EU SHARE						INDUSTRY MIX						COUNTRY SHARE						Total
	Exp	Dom	Imp	E Prd	D Prd	I Prd	Exp	Dom	Imp	E Prd	D Prd	I Prd	Exp	Dom	Imp	E Prd	D Prd	I Prd	Change
Total manufacturing	0.03	-0.18	0.03	-0.01	-0.06	-0.07	-0.08	-0.06	-0.04	-0.09	-0.05	0.00	-0.44	-0.65	-0.32	-1.05	-1.03	-1.08	0.10
Food, beverages & tobacco	0.03	-0.18	0.03	-0.01	-0.06	-0.07	-0.10	0.02	-0.04	-0.13	-0.03	0.00	-0.85	-0.56	-0.39	-0.66	-0.70	-0.72	-0.44
Textiles, apparel & leather	0.03	-0.18	0.03	-0.01	-0.06	-0.07	-0.01	-0.13	0.08	-0.11	-0.07	0.08	-0.18	-0.58	-0.15	-1.14	-1.14	-1.27	0.25
Wood products & furniture	0.03	-0.18	0.03	-0.01	-0.06	-0.07	-0.09	-0.14	-0.10	-0.25	-0.14	-0.05	-0.78	-1.01	0.08	-1.70	-1.77	-1.85	-0.22
Paper, paper products & printing	0.03	-0.18	0.03	-0.01	-0.06	-0.07	0.11	0.14	0.12	0.00	0.05	0.08	-0.43	-0.63	-0.34	-0.66	-0.66	-0.69	-0.10
Chemical products	0.03	-0.18	0.03	-0.01	-0.06	-0.07	-0.02	-0.08	-0.07	-0.11	-0.18	-0.13	-0.92	-0.71	-0.82	-1.76	-1.65	-1.69	0.87
Non-metallic mineral products	0.03	-0.18	0.03	-0.01	-0.06	-0.07	-0.23	-0.14	-0.03	-0.07	-0.05	0.05	-0.06	-0.72	-0.29	-0.82	-0.80	-0.88	-0.10
Basic metal industries	0.03	-0.18	0.03	-0.01	-0.06	-0.07	-0.38	-0.27	-0.43	-0.18	-0.15	-0.11	0.15	-0.09	0.08	-0.09	-0.07	-0.10	-0.15
Fabricated metal products	0.03	-0.18	0.03	-0.01	-0.06	-0.07	0.09	0.13	0.13	0.13	0.12	0.11	-0.48	-0.91	-0.76	-1.55	-1.49	-1.46	0.71

1986-1995

	EU SHARE						INDUSTRY MIX						COUNTRY SHARE						Total
	Exp	Dom	Imp	E Prd	D Prd	I Prd	Exp	Dom	Imp	E Prd	D Prd	I Prd	Exp	Dom	Imp	E Prd	D Prd	I Prd	Change
Total manufacturing	0.32	0.12	0.32	0.16	0.15	0.15	-0.04	-0.01	-0.03	-0.10	-0.07	-0.08	0.30	0.15	0.32	-0.06	-0.07	-0.07	0.23
Food, beverages & tobacco	0.32	0.12	0.32	0.16	0.15	0.15	0.09	-0.01	-0.01	-0.05	-0.08	-0.06	0.01	0.19	0.38	0.03	0.08	0.06	-0.11
Textiles, apparel & leather	0.32	0.12	0.32	0.16	0.15	0.15	-0.23	-0.29	-0.20	-0.13	-0.10	-0.11	0.38	0.53	0.63	0.63	0.62	0.62	-0.58
Wood products & furniture	0.32	0.12	0.32	0.16	0.15	0.15	0.11	0.17	0.18	-0.03	-0.07	-0.09	0.28	0.46	0.90	0.60	0.66	0.67	-0.67
Paper, paper products & printing	0.32	0.12	0.32	0.16	0.15	0.15	-0.04	0.01	-0.06	-0.24	-0.16	-0.18	0.09	0.05	0.44	-0.43	-0.49	-0.48	0.36
Chemical products	0.32	0.12	0.32	0.16	0.15	0.15	0.06	0.06	0.02	0.04	0.04	0.03	0.47	-0.24	0.03	-0.01	0.00	0.00	0.24
Non-metallic mineral products	0.32	0.12	0.32	0.16	0.15	0.15	-0.10	0.06	-0.08	-0.20	-0.03	0.00	0.45	0.18	0.00	0.27	0.11	0.07	0.57
Basic metal industries	0.32	0.12	0.32	0.16	0.15	0.15	-0.21	-0.11	-0.11	-0.24	-0.27	-0.32	0.05	-0.18	-0.12	-2.19	-2.14	-2.10	2.16
Fabricated metal products	0.32	0.12	0.32	0.16	0.15	0.15	0.02	0.04	0.05	0.05	0.08	0.08	0.66	0.24	0.31	0.65	0.62	0.62	-0.14

SPAIN

1980-1995

	EU SHARE						INDUSTRY MIX						COUNTRY SHARE						Total
	Exp	Dom	Imp	E Prd	D Prd	I Prd	Exp	Dom	Imp	E Prd	D Prd	I Prd	Exp	Dom	Imp	E Prd	D Prd	I Prd	Change
Total manufacturing	0.35	-0.06	0.35	0.15	0.08	0.08	-0.11	-0.07	-0.07	-0.19	-0.13	-0.08	0.07	-0.52	0.36	-0.40	-0.39	-0.44	-0.54
Food, beverages & tobacco	0.35	-0.06	0.35	0.15	0.08	0.08	-0.01	0.01	-0.05	-0.17	-0.11	-0.06	0.05	-0.36	0.69	-0.36	-0.36	-0.41	-0.62
Textiles, apparel & leather	0.35	-0.06	0.35	0.15	0.08	0.08	-0.24	-0.42	-0.11	-0.24	-0.17	-0.03	0.14	-0.53	0.85	-0.51	-0.52	-0.65	-1.25
Wood products & furniture	0.35	-0.06	0.35	0.15	0.08	0.08	0.02	0.03	0.08	-0.28	-0.21	-0.13	0.02	-0.59	0.07	-0.21	-0.22	-0.29	-0.38
Paper, paper products & printing	0.35	-0.06	0.35	0.15	0.08	0.08	0.07	0.15	0.06	-0.24	-0.11	-0.10	0.03	-0.20	0.59	-0.08	-0.14	-0.15	-0.50
Chemical products	0.35	-0.06	0.35	0.15	0.08	0.08	0.04	-0.02	-0.05	-0.08	-0.14	-0.10	-0.22	-0.67	-0.10	-0.57	-0.45	-0.48	-0.29
Non-metallic mineral products	0.35	-0.06	0.35	0.15	0.08	0.08	-0.32	-0.08	-0.12	-0.27	-0.07	0.05	0.16	-0.46	0.04	-0.03	-0.17	-0.29	-0.52
Basic metal industries	0.35	-0.06	0.35	0.15	0.08	0.08	-0.59	-0.38	-0.54	-0.42	-0.41	-0.43	-0.18	-0.90	0.34	-1.10	-1.04	-1.03	-0.54
Fabricated metal products	0.35	-0.06	0.35	0.15	0.08	0.08	0.12	0.18	0.18	0.18	0.21	0.19	0.57	-0.44	0.40	-0.31	-0.27	-0.25	-0.24

1980-1986

	EU SHARE						INDUSTRY MIX						COUNTRY SHARE						Total
	Exp	Dom	Imp	E Prd	D Prd	I Prd	Exp	Dom	Imp	E Prd	D Prd	I Prd	Exp	Dom	Imp	E Prd	D Prd	I Prd	Change
Total manufacturing	0.03	-0.18	0.03	-0.01	-0.06	-0.07	-0.08	-0.06	-0.04	-0.09	-0.05	0.00	0.05	-0.24	0.28	-0.26	-0.25	-0.29	-0.38
Food, beverages & tobacco	0.03	-0.18	0.03	-0.01	-0.06	-0.07	-0.10	0.02	-0.04	-0.13	-0.03	0.00	0.01	-0.15	0.44	-0.20	-0.24	-0.26	-0.47
Textiles, apparel & leather	0.03	-0.18	0.03	-0.01	-0.06	-0.07	-0.01	-0.13	0.08	-0.11	-0.07	0.08	0.13	-0.36	0.37	-0.35	-0.34	-0.48	-0.53
Wood products & furniture	0.03	-0.18	0.03	-0.01	-0.06	-0.07	-0.09	-0.14	-0.10	-0.25	-0.14	-0.05	0.11	-0.29	0.18	-0.12	-0.19	-0.27	-0.28
Paper, paper products & printing	0.03	-0.18	0.03	-0.01	-0.06	-0.07	0.11	0.14	0.12	0.00	0.05	0.08	-0.09	-0.14	0.25	-0.13	-0.13	-0.16	-0.39
Chemical products	0.03	-0.18	0.03	-0.01	-0.06	-0.07	-0.02	-0.08	-0.07	-0.11	-0.18	-0.13	0.20	-0.31	0.16	-0.30	-0.19	-0.23	-0.05
Non-metallic mineral products	0.03	-0.18	0.03	-0.01	-0.06	-0.07	-0.23	-0.14	-0.03	-0.07	-0.05	0.05	-0.09	-0.23	0.12	-0.14	-0.12	-0.20	-0.73
Basic metal industries	0.03	-0.18	0.03	-0.01	-0.06	-0.07	-0.38	-0.27	-0.43	-0.18	-0.15	-0.11	-0.05	-0.22	0.40	-0.60	-0.59	-0.62	-0.28
Fabricated metal products	0.03	-0.18	0.03	-0.01	-0.06	-0.07	0.09	0.13	0.13	0.13	0.12	0.11	0.15	-0.18	0.32	-0.23	-0.17	-0.14	-0.32

1986-1995

	EU SHARE						INDUSTRY MIX						COUNTRY SHARE						Total
	Exp	Dom	Imp	E Prd	D Prd	I Prd	Exp	Dom	Imp	E Prd	D Prd	I Prd	Exp	Dom	Imp	E Prd	D Prd	I Prd	Change
Total manufacturing	0.32	0.12	0.32	0.16	0.15	0.15	-0.04	-0.01	-0.03	-0.10	-0.07	-0.08	0.02	-0.28	0.08	-0.14	-0.15	-0.15	-0.16
Food, beverages & tobacco	0.32	0.12	0.32	0.16	0.15	0.15	0.09	-0.01	-0.01	-0.05	-0.08	-0.06	0.04	-0.20	0.24	-0.16	-0.12	-0.14	-0.14
Textiles, apparel & leather	0.32	0.12	0.32	0.16	0.15	0.15	-0.23	-0.29	-0.20	-0.13	-0.10	-0.11	0.00	-0.17	0.48	-0.16	-0.17	-0.17	-0.72
Wood products & furniture	0.32	0.12	0.32	0.16	0.15	0.15	0.11	0.17	0.18	-0.03	-0.07	-0.09	-0.09	-0.30	-0.11	-0.09	-0.03	-0.02	-0.10
Paper, paper products & printing	0.32	0.12	0.32	0.16	0.15	0.15	-0.04	0.01	-0.06	-0.24	-0.16	-0.18	0.12	-0.06	0.34	0.05	-0.01	0.01	-0.10
Chemical products	0.32	0.12	0.32	0.16	0.15	0.15	0.06	0.06	0.02	0.04	0.04	0.03	-0.42	-0.36	-0.25	-0.27	-0.26	-0.25	-0.23
Non-metallic mineral products	0.32	0.12	0.32	0.16	0.15	0.15	-0.10	0.06	-0.08	-0.20	-0.03	0.00	0.25	-0.23	-0.08	0.11	-0.05	-0.08	0.21
Basic metal industries	0.32	0.12	0.32	0.16	0.15	0.15	-0.21	-0.11	-0.11	-0.24	-0.27	-0.32	-0.12	-0.68	-0.06	-0.50	-0.46	-0.41	-0.26
Fabricated metal products	0.32	0.12	0.32	0.16	0.15	0.15	0.02	0.04	0.05	0.05	0.08	0.08	0.42	-0.26	0.08	-0.08	-0.10	-0.11	0.08

SWEDEN

1980-1995

	EU SHARE						INDUSTRY MIX						COUNTRY SHARE						Total
	Exp	Dom	Imp	E Prd	D Prd	I Prd	Exp	Dom	Imp	E Prd	D Prd	I Prd	Exp	Dom	Imp	E Prd	D Prd	I Prd	Change
Total manufacturing	0.35	-0.06	0.35	0.15	0.08	0.08	-0.11	-0.07	-0.07	-0.19	-0.13	-0.08	-0.43	-0.52	-0.54	-0.05	-0.05	-0.10	-0.49
Food, beverages & tobacco	0.35	-0.06	0.35	0.15	0.08	0.08	-0.01	0.01	-0.05	-0.17	-0.11	-0.06	-0.19	-0.49	-0.44	-0.15	-0.15	-0.20	-0.07
Textiles, apparel & leather	0.35	-0.06	0.35	0.15	0.08	0.08	-0.24	-0.42	-0.11	-0.24	-0.17	-0.03	-0.71	-0.79	-1.14	-0.06	-0.07	-0.21	-0.82
Wood products & furniture	0.35	-0.06	0.35	0.15	0.08	0.08	0.02	0.03	0.08	-0.28	-0.21	-0.13	-0.48	-0.80	-0.46	-0.13	-0.13	-0.21	-0.65
Paper, paper products & printing	0.35	-0.06	0.35	0.15	0.08	0.08	0.07	0.15	0.06	-0.24	-0.11	-0.10	-0.63	-0.25	-0.19	0.01	-0.04	-0.05	-0.53
Chemical products	0.35	-0.06	0.35	0.15	0.08	0.08	0.04	-0.02	-0.05	-0.08	-0.14	-0.10	-0.30	-0.57	-0.63	-0.33	-0.20	-0.24	0.02
Non-metallic mineral products	0.35	-0.06	0.35	0.15	0.08	0.08	-0.32	-0.08	-0.12	-0.27	-0.07	0.05	-0.71	-0.93	-0.93	0.05	-0.08	-0.20	-0.98
Basic metal industries	0.35	-0.06	0.35	0.15	0.08	0.08	-0.59	-0.38	-0.54	-0.42	-0.41	-0.43	0.11	0.06	0.03	0.52	0.58	0.60	-0.61
Fabricated metal products	0.35	-0.06	0.35	0.15	0.08	0.08	0.12	0.18	0.18	0.18	0.21	0.19	-0.49	-0.40	-0.53	-0.34	-0.30	-0.28	-0.31

1980-1986

	EU SHARE						INDUSTRY MIX						COUNTRY SHARE						Total
	Exp	Dom	Imp	E Prd	D Prd	I Prd	Exp	Dom	Imp	E Prd	D Prd	I Prd	Exp	Dom	Imp	E Prd	D Prd	I Prd	Change
Total manufacturing	0.03	-0.18	0.03	-0.01	-0.06	-0.07	-0.08	-0.06	-0.04	-0.09	-0.05	0.00	-0.08	-0.11	-0.18	-0.09	-0.08	-0.13	-0.10
Food, beverages & tobacco	0.03	-0.18	0.03	-0.01	-0.06	-0.07	-0.10	0.02	-0.04	-0.13	-0.03	0.00	0.01	-0.08	-0.24	0.03	-0.01	-0.04	0.06
Textiles, apparel & leather	0.03	-0.18	0.03	-0.01	-0.06	-0.07	-0.01	-0.13	0.08	-0.11	-0.07	0.08	-0.18	-0.17	-0.41	-0.06	-0.06	-0.19	-0.16
Wood products & furniture	0.03	-0.18	0.03	-0.01	-0.06	-0.07	-0.09	-0.14	-0.10	-0.25	-0.14	-0.05	-0.14	-0.15	-0.14	0.04	-0.03	-0.11	-0.24
Paper, paper products & printing	0.03	-0.18	0.03	-0.01	-0.06	-0.07	0.11	0.14	0.12	0.00	0.05	0.08	-0.17	-0.10	0.04	-0.15	-0.15	-0.18	-0.20
Chemical products	0.03	-0.18	0.03	-0.01	-0.06	-0.07	-0.02	-0.08	-0.07	-0.11	-0.18	-0.13	-0.09	-0.23	-0.35	-0.35	-0.23	-0.27	0.28
Non-metallic mineral products	0.03	-0.18	0.03	-0.01	-0.06	-0.07	-0.23	-0.14	-0.03	-0.07	-0.05	0.05	0.07	-0.05	-0.15	-0.08	-0.06	-0.14	-0.19
Basic metal industries	0.03	-0.18	0.03	-0.01	-0.06	-0.07	-0.38	-0.27	-0.43	-0.18	-0.15	-0.11	0.02	-0.03	-0.05	0.11	0.12	0.09	-0.27
Fabricated metal products	0.03	-0.18	0.03	-0.01	-0.06	-0.07	0.09	0.13	0.13	0.13	0.12	0.11	-0.14	-0.08	-0.10	-0.26	-0.19	-0.17	-0.07

1986-1995

	EU SHARE						INDUSTRY MIX						COUNTRY SHARE						Total
	Exp	Dom	Imp	E Prd	D Prd	I Prd	Exp	Dom	Imp	E Prd	D Prd	I Prd	Exp	Dom	Imp	E Prd	D Prd	I Prd	Change
Total manufacturing	0.32	0.12	0.32	0.16	0.15	0.15	-0.04	-0.01	-0.03	-0.10	-0.07	-0.08	-0.35	-0.41	-0.36	0.04	0.03	0.03	-0.40
Food, beverages & tobacco	0.32	0.12	0.32	0.16	0.15	0.15	0.09	-0.01	-0.01	-0.05	-0.08	-0.06	-0.19	-0.41	-0.19	-0.18	-0.14	-0.16	-0.13
Textiles, apparel & leather	0.32	0.12	0.32	0.16	0.15	0.15	-0.23	-0.29	-0.20	-0.13	-0.10	-0.11	-0.54	-0.62	-0.73	0.00	-0.01	-0.01	-0.66
Wood products & furniture	0.32	0.12	0.32	0.16	0.15	0.15	0.11	0.17	0.18	-0.03	-0.07	-0.09	-0.34	-0.65	-0.32	-0.16	-0.11	-0.10	-0.41
Paper, paper products & printing	0.32	0.12	0.32	0.16	0.15	0.15	-0.04	0.01	-0.06	-0.24	-0.16	-0.18	-0.46	-0.16	-0.23	0.17	0.11	0.12	-0.33
Chemical products	0.32	0.12	0.32	0.16	0.15	0.15	0.06	0.06	0.02	0.04	0.04	0.03	-0.21	-0.34	-0.28	0.02	0.03	0.03	-0.26
Non-metallic mineral products	0.32	0.12	0.32	0.16	0.15	0.15	-0.10	0.06	-0.08	-0.20	-0.03	0.00	-0.78	-0.88	-0.78	0.13	-0.03	-0.07	-0.79
Basic metal industries	0.32	0.12	0.32	0.16	0.15	0.15	-0.21	-0.11	-0.11	-0.24	-0.27	-0.32	0.09	0.10	0.09	0.42	0.46	0.51	-0.34
Fabricated metal products	0.32	0.12	0.32	0.16	0.15	0.15	0.02	0.04	0.05	0.05	0.08	0.08	-0.35	-0.32	-0.42	-0.08	-0.10	-0.11	-0.24

UK

1980-1995

	EU SHARE						INDUSTRY MIX						COUNTRY SHARE						Total
	Exp	Dom	Imp	E Prd	D Prd	I Prd	Exp	Dom	Imp	E Prd	D Prd	I Prd	Exp	Dom	Imp	E Prd	D Prd	I Prd	Change
Total manufacturing	0.35	-0.06	0.35	0.15	0.08	0.08	-0.11	-0.07	-0.07	-0.19	-0.13	-0.08	-0.21	-0.23	-0.27	0.05	0.05	0.00	-0.34
Food, beverages & tobacco	0.35	-0.06	0.35	0.15	0.08	0.08	-0.01	0.01	-0.05	-0.17	-0.11	-0.06	-0.11	-0.12	-0.29	0.28	0.28	0.23	-0.20
Textiles, apparel & leather	0.35	-0.06	0.35	0.15	0.08	0.08	-0.24	-0.42	-0.11	-0.24	-0.17	-0.03	-0.08	-0.04	-0.20	0.14	0.14	0.00	-0.58
Wood products & furniture	0.35	-0.06	0.35	0.15	0.08	0.08	0.02	0.03	0.08	-0.28	-0.21	-0.13	-0.40	-0.37	-0.66	-0.20	-0.21	-0.28	0.13
Paper, paper products & printing	0.35	-0.06	0.35	0.15	0.08	0.08	0.07	0.15	0.06	-0.24	-0.11	-0.10	0.01	-0.14	-0.29	0.13	0.07	0.06	0.20
Chemical products	0.35	-0.06	0.35	0.15	0.08	0.08	0.04	-0.02	-0.05	-0.08	-0.14	-0.10	-0.26	-0.03	0.04	0.15	0.28	0.24	-0.54
Non-metallic mineral products	0.35	-0.06	0.35	0.15	0.08	0.08	-0.32	-0.08	-0.12	-0.27	-0.07	0.05	-0.49	-0.41	-0.19	0.15	0.02	-0.10	-1.08
Basic metal industries	0.35	-0.06	0.35	0.15	0.08	0.08	-0.59	-0.38	-0.54	-0.42	-0.41	-0.43	0.16	-0.24	-0.20	-0.18	-0.12	-0.10	0.07
Fabricated metal products	0.35	-0.06	0.35	0.15	0.08	0.08	0.12	0.18	0.18	0.18	0.21	0.19	-0.50	-0.44	-0.37	-0.10	-0.06	-0.04	-0.77

1980-1986

	EU SHARE						INDUSTRY MIX						COUNTRY SHARE						Total
	Exp	Dom	Imp	E Prd	D Prd	I Prd	Exp	Dom	Imp	E Prd	D Prd	I Prd	Exp	Dom	Imp	E Prd	D Prd	I Prd	Change
Total manufacturing	0.03	-0.18	0.03	-0.01	-0.06	-0.07	-0.08	-0.06	-0.04	-0.09	-0.05	0.00	-0.06	0.11	0.08	0.16	0.17	0.12	-0.37
Food, beverages & tobacco	0.03	-0.18	0.03	-0.01	-0.06	-0.07	-0.10	0.02	-0.04	-0.13	-0.03	0.00	0.07	0.05	0.00	0.27	0.22	0.20	-0.23
Textiles, apparel & leather	0.03	-0.18	0.03	-0.01	-0.06	-0.07	-0.01	-0.13	0.08	-0.11	-0.07	0.08	-0.09	0.22	0.03	0.24	0.24	0.11	-0.42
Wood products & furniture	0.03	-0.18	0.03	-0.01	-0.06	-0.07	-0.09	-0.14	-0.10	-0.25	-0.14	-0.05	-0.14	0.23	0.14	0.20	0.14	0.06	-0.31
Paper, paper products & printing	0.03	-0.18	0.03	-0.01	-0.06	-0.07	0.11	0.14	0.12	0.00	0.05	0.08	-0.06	0.05	0.04	0.11	0.11	0.09	-0.21
Chemical products	0.03	-0.18	0.03	-0.01	-0.06	-0.07	-0.02	-0.08	-0.07	-0.11	-0.18	-0.13	-0.02	0.20	0.23	0.23	0.35	0.31	-0.38
Non-metallic mineral products	0.03	-0.18	0.03	-0.01	-0.06	-0.07	-0.23	-0.14	-0.03	-0.07	-0.05	0.05	-0.22	0.08	0.20	0.10	0.12	0.04	-0.87
Basic metal industries	0.03	-0.18	0.03	-0.01	-0.06	-0.07	-0.38	-0.27	-0.43	-0.18	-0.15	-0.11	0.19	0.15	0.06	0.10	0.12	0.09	-0.02
Fabricated metal products	0.03	-0.18	0.03	-0.01	-0.06	-0.07	0.09	0.13	0.13	0.13	0.12	0.11	-0.25	-0.12	-0.04	0.01	0.07	0.10	-0.53

1986-1995

	EU SHARE						INDUSTRY MIX						COUNTRY SHARE						Total
	Exp	Dom	Imp	E Prd	D Prd	I Prd	Exp	Dom	Imp	E Prd	D Prd	I Prd	Exp	Dom	Imp	E Prd	D Prd	I Prd	Change
Total manufacturing	0.32	0.12	0.32	0.16	0.15	0.15	-0.04	-0.01	-0.03	-0.10	-0.07	-0.08	-0.15	-0.33	-0.35	-0.11	-0.12	-0.12	0.03
Food, beverages & tobacco	0.32	0.12	0.32	0.16	0.15	0.15	0.09	-0.01	-0.01	-0.05	-0.08	-0.06	-0.18	-0.18	-0.30	0.01	0.05	0.03	0.03
Textiles, apparel & leather	0.32	0.12	0.32	0.16	0.15	0.15	-0.23	-0.29	-0.20	-0.13	-0.10	-0.11	0.01	-0.26	-0.24	-0.09	-0.10	-0.11	-0.16
Wood products & furniture	0.32	0.12	0.32	0.16	0.15	0.15	0.11	0.17	0.18	-0.03	-0.07	-0.09	-0.26	-0.61	-0.81	-0.40	-0.34	-0.34	0.44
Paper, paper products & printing	0.32	0.12	0.32	0.16	0.15	0.15	-0.04	0.01	-0.06	-0.24	-0.16	-0.18	0.07	-0.19	-0.33	0.02	-0.04	-0.03	0.41
Chemical products	0.32	0.12	0.32	0.16	0.15	0.15	0.06	0.06	0.02	0.04	0.04	0.03	-0.24	-0.22	-0.19	-0.08	-0.07	-0.07	-0.17
Non-metallic mineral products	0.32	0.12	0.32	0.16	0.15	0.15	-0.10	0.06	-0.08	-0.20	-0.03	0.00	-0.27	-0.48	-0.39	0.05	-0.11	-0.14	-0.20
Basic metal industries	0.32	0.12	0.32	0.16	0.15	0.15	-0.21	-0.11	-0.11	-0.24	-0.27	-0.32	-0.03	-0.40	-0.26	-0.28	-0.24	-0.19	0.09
Fabricated metal products	0.32	0.12	0.32	0.16	0.15	0.15	0.02	0.04	0.05	0.05	0.08	0.08	-0.26	-0.33	-0.32	-0.11	-0.13	-0.13	-0.23

17. Regional Development Potentials and Policy Options for Selected EU Regions

Jan S. Kowalski and Axel J. Schaffer

INTRODUCTION

This contribution is based on current research pursued by the authors within the framework of the 'Scenarios' and 'Scenes' projects funded by the European Commission under the Transport Programme of the 4th Framework Programme (Kowalski et al., 1998). We employ a concept of regional development potentials as immobile input equipment of a region which is combined with attractable inputs. The regional potential approach was applied in numerous studies in the 1970s and 1980s. We attempt to fill it with new content in order to gain insight into the evaluation of regional policy measures in the EU regions. The main idea is that sometimes regions are relatively well equipped with immobile potentials but are using them in a relatively inefficient manner. The thrust of regional policy should be then directed towards enhancing the attraction of mobile inputs into the region.

METHODOLOGICAL REMARKS

Regional development level is normally measured in terms of income, productivity and employment. Besides attraction factors, such as private capital, resources characterised by a high degree of public provision are the main determinants of the regional product levels. These resources do not only influence the current regional income level; they also determine the potential income of the region.

Since future development is dependent on the potential input of a region, and not automatically on its momentary status, the potential regional income seems to be of considerable interest for the conceptualisation and formulation of regional policy prescriptions – maybe of even higher interest than the actual regional product.

Potential analysis is an important approach for the derivation of regional policy instruments. The idea is to identify the weaknesses and the strengths of each region and to simulate the use of appropriate policy instruments.

According to many, development potential approaches to public resources are identified by the following characteristics (for example, Biehl, 1991):

- Indivisibility: Resources with high degrees of indivisibility have large capacities that are normally utilised in different intensities. There is no benefit from a resource, if only parts of the resource are available (for example, a bridge cannot be used if it is not finished, neither by one nor thousands of cars).
- Non-substitutability: Resources that can hardly be replaced by other resources, in particular by attractable factors.
- Immobility: Resources that cannot or can hardly be moved.
- Polyvalence: Resources that can be used as input for a large number of production processes.

In other words the 'potential approach' is based on two constitutive assumptions:

(1) On the regional level of analysis, locational factors, infrastructure capacities, and other immobile inputs, which are not homogeneously distributed over space, are important determinants of production capacities; input factors of this kind are called regional input potentials.
(2) All other input factors, which are called attraction factors, are combined with input potentials in fixed proportions, according to the underlying production technology.

Attraction factors are always fully employed. They are of course hoarded and constitute reserves of unproductive slack, but there are no attraction factors idle and waiting at the market to be bought by some potential producers. Once the capacity of an input potential is exhausted, further growth can be achieved only by increasing marginal costs, if substitution processes with other input potentials are possible. If not, growth will come to a standstill and the input potential is limitating.

In the literature various potential factors can be found. All are based on these characteristics, but as most of the factors do not fit all characteristics exactly, different authors may, or may not, identify the considered resource. While, for example, infrastructure and agglomeration are taken into consideration as potential inputs in almost all approaches, employment or sectoral structure are evaluated differently. After the selection of the potential inputs, the problem of collinearity must be carefully addressed. That means it has to be proved that a potential factor does not explain another of the selected potential factors (for example, potential employment could be explained by potential population and vice versa).

RESULTS

Results at NUTS 3 level (Federal State Baden-Wuerttemberg)

In order to gain some reference results for regions about which there was in-depth expert knowledge, an analysis was conducted for selected regions in the federal state of Baden-Württemberg in Germany.

The following potential inputs are used for this analysis. Some are inputs that have been suggested by Blum (1982) and Biehl (1975):

- Agglomeration (*D*)
- Infrastructure (*I*)
- Accessibility (*A*)
- Education (*E*)
- Nature (*N*)
- Industrial settlement area (*S*)

Density (*D*) was used as an agglomeration indicator. As we know from previous research it is strongly related to employment capacity.

Due to the data availability the infrastructure variable focuses on the regional road network. according to Biehl (1975) the infrastructure indicator may be defined in the following way:

$$\text{Road Infrastructure } (I): \quad 0.5 \quad * \quad \frac{\text{population}}{\text{roadnetwork w.}} + \frac{\text{roadnetwork w.}}{\text{area}})$$

The roads are subdivided into four groups. Motorways, national, interurban and urban roads are taken into consideration with different weights (highest weights for motorways and lowest for urban roads). Much more information, such as rail km, waterway km, communication networks and so on would be interesting, but the data are not available at the regional level.

The third factor is accessibility. At first it seems to be similar to infrastructure, but it is not. While infrastructure describes the internal regional road network, accessibility focuses on the exogenous (road) links of a region. This indicator is generated by the number of persons travelling from the considered region *i* to any region *j* multiplied by the travel time. The result is divided with the total number of travelling persons.

$$\text{Accessibility:} \quad \frac{\sum x_{ij} * t_{ij}}{\sum x_{ij}}$$

Where:
x_{ij} = number of persons travelling from *i* to *j*
t_{ij} = travel time from *i* to *j*
i = considered region
$j = 1, ..., i - 1, i + 1, ..., n$

Contrary to all other indicators the smaller and not the higher values are the 'better' ones. Therefore the reciprocal value is used for the analysis. Concerning education obviously two alternative directions can be followed. At first the indicator could focus on school education. The alternative is to build an indicator with some qualifications. For this approach the indicator is defined as follows:

$$\text{Education:} \quad \frac{\text{employees with university degree}}{\text{total employment}}$$

The fifth indicator is connected with the natural environment. Natural area plays an important role if soft factors, that have become more and more important in recent years, are taken into account. Beside recreation areas, considered in this approach, cultural activities would be an interesting indicator.

$$\text{Nature:} \quad \frac{\text{recreation area + forests + waters}}{\text{total area}}$$

Blum (1982) suggests integrating industrial settlement (measured by sqkm). Actually the availability of industrial area has been a bottleneck in the late 1980s and early 1990s. It is not clear if it can still be seen as a bottleneck factor. On the one hand big parts of industrial estates remain unoccupied and many office buildings are not in use in Germany, but on the other hand new industrial plants are established in emerging regions. In this approach the availability of industrial areal is taken into account as a necessary input which can be seen as a complementary factor to the public resources listed above. Nevertheless, the risk of collinearity is rather small, because industrial land use is not included in any of the other inputs.

Sectoral structure (GVA by sectors) and employment by sectors are not defined as inputs, because in this analysis they are – similar to the regional product – seen as endogenous variables, which will be explained by the exogenous potential factors.

While creating a production function based on the regional input potentials, it is assumed that the already mentioned attractable factors are combined with input potentials in fixed proportions (Blum and Kowalski, 1985). First of all, the regional product (RDP) is analysed. Hence the general form of the production function is as follows:

$$RDP = f(D, I, A, E, N, S)$$

Based on the well-known Cobb-Douglas production function, a quasi-production function is created. Following Biel we called it quasi-production function because it is based on public immobile resources and not on classical arguments of this type of production functions. The specific form is:

$$Y = c * D^{\delta} * I^{\beta} * A^{\alpha} * E^{\varepsilon} * N^{\lambda} * S^{\sigma}$$

A Cobb–Douglas function is characterised by a total sum of the elasticities of one. The applied quasi-production function, however, is in the proper meaning not a production function. Therefore, the sum of elasticities can be different from one.

Due to its high level of data availability the Federal State Baden-Wuerttemberg in the south of Germany has been chosen. It is subdivided into 44 NUTS-3 regions. Comparative data concerning the potential factors mentioned above have been available for all regions. Baden-Wuerttemberg is a rather high-developed 'Bundesland'. In particular the regions around Stuttgart and Karlsruhe can be seen as drivers for prosperous economic development in the south of Germany. Nevertheless, rural areas (for example, Sigmaringen) can be found as well as regions characterised by a high percentage of traditional industries (for example, Mannheim). Regression analysis is used to estimate the following elasticities (the T-Statistics, R^2, and the other standard tests were performed and found satisfactory, with the exception of the equations for value added and employment in agriculture were the number of observations was too low for statistical purposes).

The correlation is rather high for all endogenous variables, except for the variables related to agriculture. In particular the elasticities for employment (agriculture) are not based on sufficiently high correlation. High density obviously is strongly related to GVA and to employment in the service sector. The negative correlation to agriculture is not surprising but seems to be too high for the agricultural GVA.

Infrastructure is often considered as the main indicator for regional development potential. In fact, infrastructure plays quite an important role if industrial GVA and employment are taken into account. However, concerning the service sector it is less important. For the employment situation in the service sector elasticity of infrastructure is even lower than the natural indicator, which is measured by recovery areas.

Table 17.1 Elasticities of the quasi-production function

	Elasticities						
Endogenous variable	Agglomeration	Infra-structure	Access-ibility	Education	Nature indicator	Industrial settlement area	
Y	δ	β	α	ε	λ	σ	Σ
GVA (total)	0.26	0.22	0.08	0.29	0.04	0.77	1.66
GVA (agricult.)	–0.84	0.30	0.09	0.17	–0.73	0.63	–0.38
GVA (industry)	0.18	0.34	0.21	0.16	0.03	0.93	1.85
GVA (service)	0.34	0.16	–0.03	0.35	0.07	0.67	1.56
Empl. (total)	0.28	0.10	0.13	0.21	0.06	0.66	1.44
Empl. (agricult.)	–0.33	0.62	0.42	0.36	0.02	0.57	1.66
Empl. (industry)	0.16	0.28	0.12	–0.05	0.01	0.81	1.33
Empl. (service)	0.38	0.06	0.03	0.41	0.10	0.57	1.55

Similar to infrastructure, accessibility reaches higher elasticities for the industrial parts. For services the influence seems to be of smaller relevance. Infrastructure and accessibility elasticities are probably partly the result of the fact that, due to data availability, only road infrastructure and accessibility by road are taken into consideration. For example, the high standard of communication networks (as part of the infrastructure) could be seen as public resource, which is rather important for many service sectors, but data have not been delivered within the Scenarios project.

A high standard of professional qualifications has become more important in recent years. Hence high elasticities concerning the service sector are not really surprising. It may be a signal that, despite the growing number of low qualified employees in the service sector, the tertiary sector still depends on a highly qualified workforce.

The nature indicator is near zero for the GVA and becomes only a little higher if the employment situation is considered. Nevertheless, the correlation is, except agricultural GVA, positive. For the employment of service sectors sufficient recovery areas seem to be even more important than (road) infrastructure and accessibility (by car) factors.

The availability of land for industrial activities can be seen as a necessary input. It can not be regarded in isolation, but it is taken into consideration as a complementary factor. Therefore, the high elasticities (in particular for industrial GVA and employment) were expected when starting the analysis. It is also known from location choice analyses in the South of Germany that this factor often plays a decisive role in the decisions of many newly establisht enterprises, both in services and in manufacturing.

Results at NUTS 2 level for Regions in Europe

The regional development potential analysis as performed above for the federal state of Baden-Württemberg on the NUTs 3 level is not feasible at the European level. In particular the information about the industrial settlement and the recovery areas are not available in detail. Hence it was planned to focus on agglomeration, infrastructure and education, retaining the results of the more detailed analysis for Baden-Wuerttemberg as a possible frame of reference.

We based our investigation of the European NUTs 2 regions on the clustering classification suggested by the team from the Technical University of Madrid (UPM, 1998), who participated in the Scenarios project. Modifying their work to some extent we identified four main regional clusters (see Figure 17.1) named 'service dominated-regions', 'industrial core', 'relatively rich and rural' or 'rich and peripherial regions' and 'low developed regions' (for details on the derivation of clusters see Kowalski et al., 1998).

In the preceding section we have chosen as endogenous variables the total and sectoral GVA and employment respectively. For our investigation of the European NUTs 2 regions we have decided, due to the availability of the statistical data, to use the GDP per capita as the explained variable. Hence the production function is given by the equation:

$$Y = c * D^{\delta} * I^{\beta} * E^{\varepsilon}$$

with Y = GDP per capita.

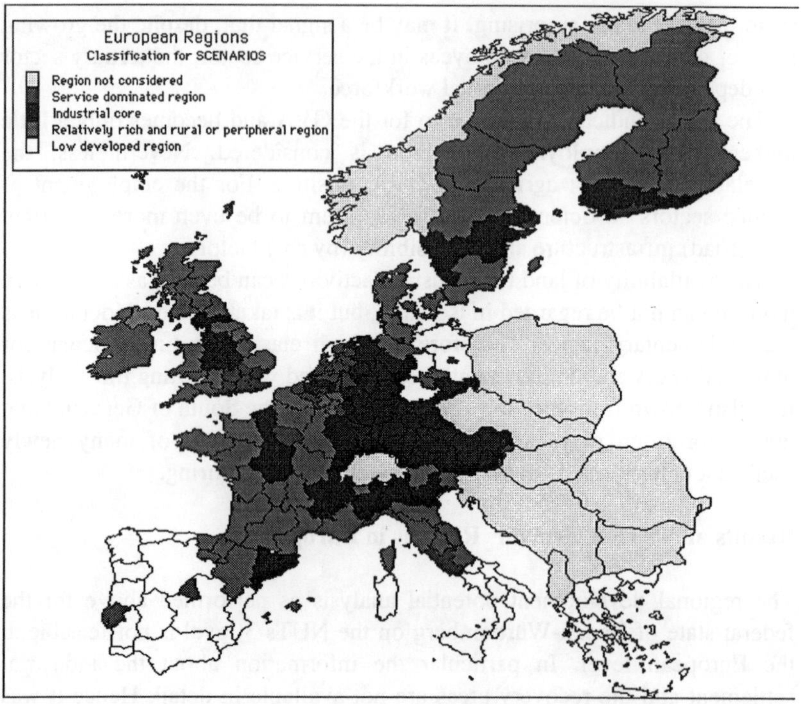

Figure 17.1 Classification of European regions

Based on the NUTS 3 regions of Baden-Wuerttemberg the regression analysis using three explanatory variables and GDP per capita as an endogenous variable results in the following elasticities:

Table 17.2 Elasticities of German regions belonging to the industrial core

Endogenous variable	Elasticities		
	Agglomeration	Infrastructure	Education
Y	δ	β	ε
GDP per capita	0.14	0.15	0.13

Since the quasi production function is based on the Cobb–Douglas production function, the sum of elasticities is of special interest:

$$\delta + \beta + \varepsilon = 0.42$$

That means, that agglomeration, infrastructure and education per capita influence 42 per cent of the GDP. A further 58 per cent is determined by other mobile and immobile inputs, which are not explained in the quasi production function.

Although the 'Industrial core' covers each NUTs 2 (and hence NUTs 3) region of Baden-Wuerttemberg, the elasticities should not be taken unchanged for the new 'Industrial core elasticities'. Austrian, French, Italian and Swedish regions belong to the same cluster and may influence the results. In particular detailed data about road infrastructure is only rarely available for European NUTs 2 level (normally only two categories: motorways and other roads). Hence the motorisation M (cars per 1000 inhabitants) was taken into consideration instead. We are aware that this indicator is not an adequate substitute for an infrastructure indicator suggested by Biehl (1975), but it seems to be a sufficient one for our approach here.

Also, in order to be able to cover all the European NUTs 2 regions we changed the indicator for education in the computations for Europe. In accordance with EUROSTAT (1997) the indicator concerning education is based on the percentage of the highest educational attainment.

The production function for the selected European regions is thus given by the equation:

$$Y = c * D\delta * M\mu * E\varepsilon$$

with Y = GDP per capita.

Table 17.3 shows the elasticities of the functions depending on the type of the region. The numbers for 'betas' in brackets relate to Baden-Württemberg and are computed for this region separately on the NUTs 3 level for an additional comparison between infrastructure elasticties (which we were unable to provide for all European regions) and those for motorisation.

The elasticities do not say anything about the total values. They can be seen as indicators of relative importance of a given immobile input potential for the regional GDP per capita. Regarding 'Service-dominated regions' high density and high levels of educational attainment are more important for the future development of GDP per capita than 'motorisation'.[2] Minor importance of private car ownership can be interpreted as an indicator for the availability and necessity of high quality public transport. On the contrary, the development of the GDP per capita of the other regions is much more correlated with the development of 'motorisation'. In particular the economic situation of the 'Relatively rich and rural or peripheral regions' depends on improved accessibility and infrastructure, which are expressed by 'motorisation'.

Table 17.3 Region-type specific elasticities

Region type		Elasticities		
	Endogenous Variable *Y*	Agglo-meration δ	Motorisation (Infrastructure) μ (->β)	Edu-cation ε
Service-domin.	GDP / capita	0.17	0.14 (0.09)	0.17
Industrial core	GDP / capita	0.12	0.23 (0.15)	0.10
Relat. rich rural or peripheral	GDP / capita	0.01	0.43 (0.28)	0.13
Low-developed	GDP / capita	–0.02	0.39 (0.25)	–0.08

If β (0.23) of the European 'Industrial core' is compared with β (0.15) of the Industrial core based on Baden-Wuerttemberg, it becomes clear, that β is probably too high as an indicator of infrastructure and accessibility. But if this share is taken into consideration, plausible results (in brackets) for the relevance of road infrastructure and accessibility can be given. Since the richer peripheral areas often show high shares of services, the relevance of the educational attainment is, for future development, higher than for members of the 'Industrial core'. The lower elasticity levels for motorisation and infrastructure in 'low developed regions' as compared to 'relatively rich and rural or peripherial regions' can be reasonably explained by backwash effects, namely the first regions often record a large number of commuters going outside of the region to their workplaces, thus diminishing the importance of this potential for the regional level of GDP per capita.

The elasticities are the result of a linear regression analysis. Obviously the 'real' elasticities concerning above- and below-average performing regions differ extremely. But since the regional equilibrium is considered as a main issue of regional politics, below- as well as above-average performing regions are expected to reach approximately the average elasticities in the coming years. As already mentioned, slight changes of the average elasticities will be anticipated. The main assumption is that GDP per capita will be increasingly determined by educational level. On the other side, infrastructure effects are expected to decrease, at least, if infrastructure covers nothing but road and rail infrastructure.

POLICY CONCLUSIONS

Several policy conclusions can be drawn from the regional potential analysis. The elasticities are average values of all considered regions in one cluster. The next step is to compare the potential regional product based on the average elasticicities shown in Table 17.3 with the real actual regional product. After the comparison the regions can be subdivided into three groups:

(i) Above-average performing regions (Real regional product > Potential regional product)
(ii) Below-average performing regions (Real regional product < Potential regional product)
(iii) Average performing regions (Real regional product = Potential regional product)

Above-average performing regions, which are characterised by over-utilisation of their development potential, are relatively better equipped with mobile or private capital than with public resources. This implies that the costs of attracting and using private capital are in high performing regions relatively lower than in low performing ones. In this case public investments should be focused on the public inputs mentioned above. A better endowment with public resources will result in higher growth rates of the regional product. However, these regions run the risk of growing beyond their optimal degree of agglomeration and of increasing their benefits at the cost of pollution and time loss.

Below-average performing regions lack adequate quantities and qualities of private capital and labour. First of all, policymakers should concentrate their efforts on attracting private capital. In the short run it may be helpful to subsidise private investors. Due to the already existing under-utilisation of public inputs it would not be helpful to increase expenditures for resources characterised by a high degree of publicness. If there is a sufficient endowment of public resources, this strategy will succeed. But as long as the costs of attracting private capital are high because of a low potential productivity (as a result of low resource endowment), this strategy will fail in the long term. In this case, as a long term strategy, public resources must be improved. Long- and short-term strategies can be considered as complementary policies, which have to be implemented simultaneously.

The public endowment of above and below average performing regions cannot be automatically considered as high or low, but in fact, most over-utilised regions are characterised by a high level of public inputs, as well as many under-utilised regions show modest levels.

The third group is a more or less theoretical one. However, it may be possible that some regions may generate a real regional product that is near the potential product. As a long-term strategy these regions should improve their public resource endowment, while attracting mobile factors simultaneously.

Table 17.4 gives an overview of the derivation of regional policy conclusions for above and below average performing regions.

Table 17.4 Derivation of regional policy conclusions

Performance of the region	Comparison: Real Regional Product versus Potential Regional Product	Equipment with mobile/ private capital	Equipment with public capital	Regional policy conclusions
Above-average performing	Real Regional Product > Potential Regional Product	Relative high	Relative low	Improving the equipment with public capital
Below-averag performing	Real Regional Product < Potential Regional Product	Relative low	Relative high	Improving the equipment with private and public capital

Though above- or below-average performance results from public resource endowments, different above-average performing regions may show the same degree of over-utilisation with a totally different structure of potential inputs. Due to this fact it is not surprising that different bottlenecks could be identified for different over- or under-utilising regions. One possible way of identification is to calculate the regional marginal rate of substitution (MRS) and to compare it with the average MRS. As the MRS shows the approximate increase of a potential input, which is necessary to compensate for a unit decrease of another input potential, the MRS is suitable to identify regional bottlenecks (Blum and Kowalski, 1985). The calculation of the MRS is beyond the scope of this contribution. Hence the suggested policy tools will be the same for different above-average performing regions of the same cluster, even if different bottlenecks could be assumed. On the other hand the policy instruments will not be applied in isolation, but as a bundle, such that the orientation on a specific bottleneck will hardly correspond to regional policies.

It is obvious that the policy mix for above-average performing regions is different from the policy mix for below-average performing ones. Therefore, by taking into account the performance of the regions, the process of clustering is to be extended: European regions grouped in four clusters are subdivided into above- and below-average performing regions so that the final classification of regions consists of eight region types (see

Figure 17.2) providing much more insight than the original four cluster classification.

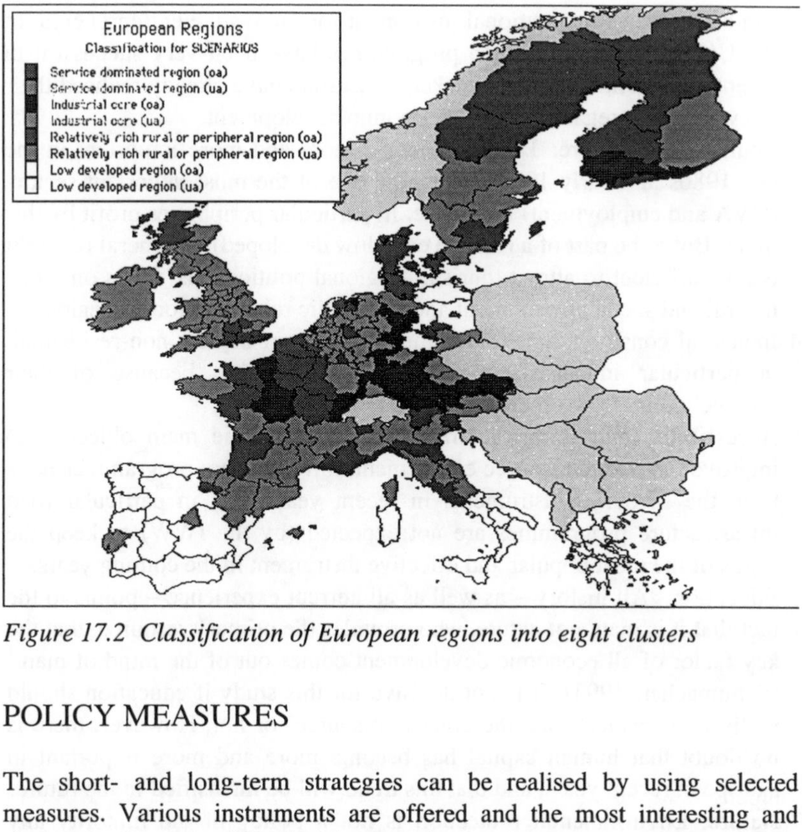

Figure 17.2 Classification of European regions into eight clusters

POLICY MEASURES

The short- and long-term strategies can be realised by using selected measures. Various instruments are offered and the most interesting and obviously the most difficult job is to choose the most appropriate policy mix for the considered region at the considered moment. Due to the regional type, the political willingness and the above – or below – average performance mentioned above, a specified bundle of measures will be applied. It is not possible to list all instruments known and applied in European regional policy. However, seven popular policy instruments are briefly introduced here:

1. SME programmes: A popular measure to strengthen the regional economy is to subsidise small and medium sized enterprises. In most regions GVA and employment are deeply related to the strong presence of these companies. In paticular a too heavy dependence on big companies, maybe even on so-called global players, can be avoided.

2. High-tech programmes: This measure is often used to support young (and therefore small) enterprises. It is part of most of the programmes for establishment of new companies (setting up premium programmes) and can be seen as a motivational instrument for innovative entrepreneurs. In the United States High-Tech programmes have been very successful in recent years, and also policymakers in Europe have already realised their relevance with regard to future economic development.
3. Tourism and culture: Tourism became more and more important in the late 1980s and early 1990s. It is now one of the most important sectors (GVA and employment) in Europe. In particular peripheries profit by this trend. But to be part of a (maybe even low developed) peripheral region it is not sufficient to attract tourism. Regional politics must focus on intact natural and social environment and on 'public relations' for the regions.
4. Industrial construction: Programmes for support of new non-residential, in particular industrial, construction are popular, because of their relatively high flow-on effects on the labour market.
5. Accessibility and infrastructure programmes: If the main object is to improve the public resource endowment, infrastructure programmes have been the favourite instruments in recent years. But in particular road infrastructure programmes are not expected (by the IWW) to keep the status of the most popular and effective instrument in the coming years.
6. Education: 'All history – as well as all current experience – points to the fact that it is man, not nature, who provides the primary resource: that the key factor of all economic development comes out of the mind of man.' (Schumacher, 1993). It is not decisive for this study if education should really be considered as 'the greatest resource' or not. However, there is no doubt that human capital has become more and more important in Europe in recent years, and that this trend will be intensified in the future.
7. Nature: Environmental protection is not a policy of the minority any more. The issue of environmental pollution is often mentioned in polls as one of the most important problems that has to be solved by politics in the coming years. Intact nature is part of the standard of living in particular in highly-developed regions.

SUITABILITY OF SELECTED POLICY MEASURES

As already mentioned the policy measures depend not only on the region type, but also on the performance of the region. Table 17.5 gives an overview of a bundle of three regional policy instruments and their suitability for the different region types subdivided into above- and below-average performing regions. When we write in the table 'policy mix' we mean different weights given to the three selected policy measures. Obviously the suitability of these policy measures for a given region type can only be understood as a very rough approximation. We have therefore not attempted to give more exact weightings to the elements of the policy mixes for various types of regions, but rather, based on expert knowledge reflect on the 'reasonable' composition of policy measures. Other arguments and weightings are obviously imaginable. The preceding analysis of regions with respect to their efficiency of the employment of a combination of fixed and attraction inputs permits the drawing of interesting conclusions, but the analysis of concrete regions should always be confronted with specific expert knowledge.

Table 17.5 Appropriate policy bundles

Performance	Below-average performance			Above-average performance		
Policy measure / Cluster	SME- and high-tech	Accessibility, infrastructure	Education	SME- and high-tech	Accessibility, infrastructure	Education
Service-domin. regions		Policy mix 1			Policy mix 2	
	+	o	++	++	o	+
Industrial core		Policy mix 3			Policy mix 4	
	+	++	++	++	+	+
Relat. rich rural or periph.region		Policy mix 5			Policy mix 6	
	+	++	+	++	++	+
Low-developed regions		Policy mix 7			Policy mix 8	
	++	++	+	++	+	+

Notes: ++: very appropriate measure, +: appropriate measure, o: neither positive nor negative effects are expected

CONCLUSIONS

We are aware of the limitations and weaknesses of the 'regional potential' approach as a tool for the study of regional production systems. Nevertheless we think that by providing very rough approximations about the way regional economic subjects are able to utilise regional 'equipment' in relative comparison to other regions, it is possible to adress very pertinent questions for the evaluation of regional policies. The standard attitude of regional authorities, when confronted with proposals for regional policy projects (especially if they are to be financed generously from the EU and national governments) is never to say no. The idea behind the potential approach is that often the European regions should be forced or motivated to make better use of the existing potentials, to make greater efforts to attract mobile inputs and combine them with what they already have. Particularly with respect to transportation infrastructure the signs of the change in these attitudes are becoming more visible throughout Europe, but we still face a long road ahead of us.

NOTES

1. Industrial area does mean that kind of area, which is available within a short period of time for industrial use (including infrastructure, accessibility, and so on).
2. We are aware that a growing motorization is probably the result of growing GDP per capita and not vice versa, but in this context the regional motorisation is treated as an indicator for accessibility and/or infrastructure.

REFERENCES

Biehl D. (1975), *Bestimmungsgruende des Regionalen Entwicklungspotentials*, Tuebingen: Mohr.

Biehl D. (1991), 'The Role of Infrastructure for Regional Development', in R. Vickerman (ed.), *Infrastructure and Regional Development*, London: Pion.

Blum U. (1982), 'Regionale Wirkungen von Infrastrukturinvestitionen', in R. Funck (ed.), *Karlsruher Beitraege zur Wirtschaftspolitik und Wirtschaftsforschung*, Karlsruhe: IWW.

Blum U. and J. Kowalski (1985), 'On the efficiency of regional production in Poland', Discussion Paper 3, Karlsruhe: IWW.

EUROSTAT (1997), *Education Across the EU*. Brussels.

Kowalski J., W. Rothengatter, A. Schaffer and E. Sziomba (1998), 'Socio-Economic External Developments, Spatial Dynamics and Their Relation to Transport', Report to the European Commission for the Research Project 'Scenarios', IWW, Karlsruhe, December 1999.

Schumacher, E.F. (1993), *Small is Beautiful: Economics as if People Matter*, reissued 8th print, New York: Vintage.

UPM (1998), *Classification of European Regions according to Socio-economic and Accessibility Characteristics*, Madrid, Universida Polytechnica Madrid.

18. Deindustrialisation and Regional Productivity: Swedish Manufacturing Industry, 1970–90

Mats Johansson

INTRODUCTION

Between 1970 and 1990 labour productivity increased 45 per cent in the Swedish manufacturing industry. During these two decades the Swedish economy went through structural transformation and deindustrialisation.

Productivity growth as a consequence of structural change has a key place in the theory of economic growth. This means picking out that part of economic growth which has a connection with a transfer of factors of production from the less productive to the more productive parts of the economy. Of course growth effects of structural change do not have to be a consequence of transfer of production factors in the literal sense but may equally well result from different parts of the economy, with different productivity levels, developing in dissimilar ways.

This means also that the declining, traditionally industrial regions dominated by heavy industry tend to have higher labour productivity than the dynamic, expanding regions where immaterial investments are of greater importance. Thus, a comparison of productivity levels between different branches and regions lacks in many cases meaning. What should rather be done is to examine developments within regions, and analyse the development patterns that are observed. This is the approach taken here, where the focus will lie on the connections that exist between deindustrialisation and the development of labour productivity within different regions.

Thus, as far as productivity trends are concerned, changes in branch structure may have the consequence of bringing 'structural gains' or 'structural losses' depending on the direction in which the branch structure is changed. Two procedures have been employed to estimate the size of structural change and its impacts on productivity development. When estimating structural effects according to the first method, productivity is held constant over time and only the proportions of employment between the various industrial branches are changed. The opposite can be said to apply to the second method. The employment proportions then remain constant – that is the starting year's relations will apply – and are applied to the productivity levels of the closing year. It is implicit in the above argument that different-sized structural effects can be obtained depending on which method is used.

By comparing the results of the various calculations it should be possible to draw certain conclusions concerning the respective changes in productivity and employment. The greater the disparities that emerge according to the different methods, the greater the changes that have occurred between starting year and closing year. If the methods give the same results, the changes in productivity and employment have been similar for the subaggregates included in the study – in this case the industrial subgroups.

FROM GOODS TO SERVICE PRODUCTION

One of the most striking features in the transformation of the Swedish economy during the postwar period is that goods production has shrunk in importance while service production has become much more important. Six of every ten employees in 1950 were involved in goods production and trade, but that figure had dropped to one–third by 1990. The change from an industrial to a service economy has resulted in a redistribution in respect to both production and consumption. The early 1950s saw barely half of the labour force involved in the production of goods and services for the local or regional market – today that figure is over 70 per cent.

The choice of 1970 and 1990 as starting and ending years with regard to the analysis are a consequence of the fact that both years are boom years and that the deindustrialisation process had not begun. Twenty years later, there had been a trend towards deindustrialisation in Sweden – despite business cycles fluctuations – and that year was before the crisis of the 1990s – the deepest crisis since the 1930s.

The increasing importance of the service sector has had a stabilising effect on regional development, as the majority of services are produced where they are consumed. As a result of this expansion of the local market's importance, the regions have become much less vulnerable to external factors either of national or international character. This structural change means that Sweden is on its way into a stage where population settlement patterns determine employment development on the regional level. This change from goods-producing to a service producing society – or from global to local production – has had a major impact upon regional development during the postwar period.

The Swedish industrialisation process was initially a non-urban phenomenon, with the raw-material dependent industry locating near the material (Johansson, 1996). This resulted in, among other things, the development of mill towns and mill villages. It was not until the end of the nineteenth century, with the rapid rise of the engineering industry, that industrial production became an urban activity, which it has remained up to the postwar period. The raw material-based industries are, however, still of great importance in various regions.

Patterns of rapid economic growth have been associated as a rule with the movement of resources between different firms, trades, and industries. These structural changes were an important growth factor in the Swedish economy during the postwar years and especially during the 1960s. The fast growth and the structural transformation of the Swedish economy resulted also in extensive geographical mobility. The latter was especially pronounced during the 1960s, which were characterised in Sweden by high growth, rapid structural transformation, and shortage of labour – the industrial society stood at its zenith. Resources had to be shifted from low-productivity to high-productivity enterprises in order not to inhibit growth. This also formed the foundation of the so-called Rehn/Meidner model, in which a 'wage-solidarity' (that is wage-equalisation) policy was combined with an active labour-market policy. Upward pressure on wage levels in the least productive firms would cause them to go to the wall while at the same time wage increases in the productive firms would be restrained. For this policy to succeed it had to be possible for labour to be shifted swiftly and simply out of low-productivity and into high-productivity firms. (The model took its name from two Swedish trade union economists, Gösta Rehn and Rudolf Meidner, who launched these ideas in the 1950s. However, it was not until the 1960s with its labour shortage that they were translated into practice to form guidelines for labour-market policy.) Because these firms were not evenly distributed geographically the consequence was great geographical mobility during the 1960s. That decade can also be said to be the last – in Sweden at any rate – to be marked by the migration patterns of the industrial society (Bengtsson and Johansson, 1994, 1995).

In the middle of the 1960s the Swedish deindustrialisation process started (ERU 1989a, 1989b; Snickars, 1991; Nilsson, 1995). The first industry that was hit hard by the international competition was the textile industry with a lot of close-downs during the 1960s. The 1970s and 1980s were characterised by great international over-production with falling prices of products from the raw material based-industries. As a consequence, the rather great importance of these industries has led to regional stresses during this period. The mill towns or mill villages, with their one-sided economic structure and great dependence upon a single company, became net out-migration areas. A picture of a 'black Sweden' was painted, with a large proportion of the country experiencing out-migration and stagnation or population decline. However, the problems related to the international over-capacity were not only a problem for the traditional industrial areas with a raw-material based production – especially hard hit by the international over-capacity was the shipyard industry which disappeared between the middle of the 1970s and 1980s.

STRUCTURAL TRANSFORMATION AND DEINDUSTRIALISATION

Deindustrialisation can be interpreted in two ways: either in a broad sense or in a more restricted sense. The broader interpretation comprises the decline in all goods-producing sectors while the more restricted interpretation refers to developments in the manufacturing industry. In this study the term deindustrialisation is interpreted in the more restricted sense, referring to changes in employment, not in production.

Deindustrialisation is regarded as a positive feature of economic change as long as labour and capital are being moved out of low-productive and into high-productive activities. However, in the debate on the effects of deindustrialisation, it is the negative effects that have been emphasised instead. Capital and labour are not moved sufficiently quickly and friction-free from low productive to high-productive activities. The result is thus a stationary rather than an expanding economy. Furthermore, different types of activity are not evenly spread over the country geographically, which means that certain localities and regions are hit harder than others are by deindustrialisation, which gives them an image of crisis, stagnation and apathy.

Deindustrialisation is intimately bound up with structural transformation of the economy (for a discussion of the deindustrialisation debate, see, for example, Rowthorn and Wells, 1987; Rodwin, 1989). However, friction-free economic transformation does not happen as a rule – disharmonies arise by virtue of the fact that resources are not shifted out of stagnating activities into expanding ones. The result instead is a stagnant economy with continually increasing unemployment, which has hit particularly hard in traditional industrial regions with a one-sided labour market. This ought to give rise to increased out-migration from these decaying industrial regions – a migration analogous to the decline of the agrarian society and the rise of the industrial society. A neutralising factor that causes this to happen to only a limited extent, however, is the emergence of the post-industrial society, with its increasing segmentation of the labour market. Today, the consequence is that there is no alternative target-destination for the labour force thrown out of work by deindustrialisation to migrate to, such as there once was for the farmer who had been rationalised out of existence. Instead, stagnation, depression and apathy characterise the districts hit by deindustrialisation that have an inhibiting effect on the in-migration of both people and enterprise.

Simultaneously with deindustrialisation, however, reindustrialisation is going on. What this means is that new industries are replacing old ones and are a natural element of the transformation process. Reindustrialisation, like deindustrialisation, is not a cyclical but a structural phenomenon. Its significance is that new industries are replacing the old, which has always been both a central and a natural element of the process of economic change. However, the term reindustrialisation has assumed an extra dimension when it is coupled together with deindustrialisation and the rise of the service society, and also by virtue of its being associated more with nonmaterial investment than with material investment, while at the same time the labour force has increasingly become a location factor for the new expansive firms and industries. Moreover, change in the concept of industry also affects the interpretation. Much of what is growing in the borderlands between manufacturing industry and service production – industry-related service production – belongs to the reindustrialisation process. Industry-related service production has grown via two processes – first through the sector's 'intrinsic' growth, secondly through the statistical reclassifications occurring when departments and units of industrial firms have become independent businesses and workplaces. The latter means that both deindustrialisation and the expansion of the private service sector are overestimated – according to the official statistics at least.

The problem is, though, that these processes do not coincide spatially; what frequently happens instead is that reindustrialisation occurs in districts quite different from the traditional industrial regions (see for example, Cheshire and Hay, 1989; Commission of the European Communities, 1991, 1993; Hall, 1991; Fothergill and Guy, 1991) This also ties in with the changed alignment of investment. In the traditional industrial regions, productivity, profitability and expansion were associated in high degree with material investments in buildings and machinery – that is the investment pattern of the old industrial society. Today and tomorrow it is the non-material investments instead – R&D, product development, training, and marketing – that form the foundation of profitability, productivity and expansion. The result has been that traditional industrial districts dominated by large-scale companies and with an image of stagnation and apathy have problems to attract knowledge-intensive and dynamic companies (Johansson, 1996).

One element of this transformation process is increasing segmentation of the labour market. Labour and real capital used to be interchangeable to a large extent. Today the picture is different. The introduction of new technology requires labour with certain qualifications and thus also a certain degree of training – labour as a factor of production has become increasingly heterogeneous. Applying a production-theory conceptual apparatus, we can say that there are 'vintages' of both capital and labour. Today, the increased labour market segmentation hampers the transfer of unemployed industrial workers from traditional blue-collar jobs to new jobs in knowledge-intensive activities – neither in the manufacturing industry nor in the dynamic parts of the service sector. This phenomenon has also resulted in a higher structural unemployment today compared to the situation in the 1960s.

This phenomenon can be illustrated by the following story. The unemployment level was roughly three times higher in Northern Sweden than in the Stockholm/Uppsala region during the late 1960s and early 1970s and about twice as high during the 1980s (Swedish Labour Market Board). For the newly unemployed, one choice is to move to the more expansive regions, that is Stockholm. This also happened during the 1960s and the first part of the 1970s. However, as mentioned above, the deindustrialisation started in the Stockholm/Uppsala region, with the effect being that traditional sectors were been pushed out even earlier than in the rest of the country, with employment beginning to decrease as early as the 1960s (Table 18.3). Most of the jobs that were phased out were blue-collar jobs. Between 1965 and 1975 the number of blue-collar jobs diminished by 26 per cent. This figure can be compared by the number of white-collar jobs, which was almost at the same level in 1975 as it was in 1965. This segmentation process has, by the way, been accentuated during the 1980s. By the middle of the 1980s half of those employed in the manufacturing industry in Stockholm County were white collar. The white-collar shares in the northern manufacturing industry were at the same time below 25 per cent in Bergslagen and Northern Sweden.

PRODUCTIVITY DEVELOPMENT AND STRUCTURAL CHANGE

Productivity growth as a consequence of structural change has a key place in the theory of economic growth. This means picking out that part of economic growth which has a connection with a transfer of factors of production – usually labour – from the less productive to the more productive parts of the economy. Of course growth effects of structural change do not have to be a consequence of transfer of labour in the literal sense but may equally well result from different parts of the economy, with different productivity levels, developing in dissimilar ways.

The term 'productivity' can be interpreted in a variety of ways. Sometimes one refers to labour productivity, while other times it is total factor productivity that is discussed. There are also different 'vintages' of capital and labour concealed in the term, which makes measurement of both level and development more difficult. This need for more sophisticated measurement systems has led to increasing problems in interregional comparison. Differing regions have different labour force compositions and production concentrations, even within the same companies or branches. Certain regions have been selected to serve as the sites for headquarters, marketing divisions, and R&D activities, while the actual production has been placed in other regions. An examination of the level of labour force productivity also requires consideration of the region's capital intensity. Today, this means that the declining, traditionally industrial regions dominated by heavy industry tend to have higher labour force productivity than the dynamic, expanding regions where immaterial investments are of greater importance. Thus, a comparison of productivity levels between different branches and regions lacks meaning. What should rather be done is examine developments within regions, and analyse the development patterns which are observed. This is the approach taken by this paper, where the focus will lie on the connections that exist between deindustrialisation and the development of labour productivity within different regions. This means also that productivity here is synonymous with labour productivity.

Thus, as far as productivity trends are concerned, changes in branch structure may, through differences in levels of production per employee, have the consequence of bringing 'structural gains' or structural losses' depending on the direction in which the branch structure is changed. If branches with high value added per employee become more important than branches with low value added per employee, the effect would be higher productivity than if the branch structure had remained constant. The productivity gains through factor allocation have, however, been smaller during the postwar years as a consequence of the transfer from an industrial society to a post-industrial one (Denison, 1967; van der Wee, 1986).

Two procedures – both of shift–share type – can be employed to estimate the size of structural change. When using shift–share analysis, it is important to be aware of its restricted explanation power according to regional development with regard to, for example, employment and production (see for example Richardson, 1978). Instead, the usefulness of the procedure is rather that the method can be seen as indications of differing transformation processes and not so much to identify the factors behind development or transformation. As used in this study – comparing two differing methods – it is, however, possible to get a hint of the structural transformation and the productivity development.

When estimating structural effects according to the first method, productivity is held constant over time and only the proportions of employment between the various industrial branches are changed. The basis, then, is that unless some change takes place within the various subgroups during the period studied, production will follow changes in employment completely. The difference between hypothetical productivity at an aggregated level and the actual productivity at the beginning of the period will then be an effect of the altered employment structure (SE). The rest – that is the difference between actually measured and hypothetical productivity at the end of the period – will be an expression of the altered productivity in the subgroups (PE). This method will in the following be termed Method A.

The opposite can be said to apply to the second method (Method B). The employment proportions then remain constant – that is the starting year's relations will apply – and are applied to the productivity level of the closing year (for a discussion of these two differing estimations, see Kuznets, 1952). By comparing this hypothetical productivity with actual productivity at the end of the period, a measure is obtained of the impact of the structural change (SE). Consequently the remainder – in this case the difference between the magnitude of hypothetical productivity at the end of the period and actual productivity at its commencement – is a result of the altered productivity within the subgroups (PE).

These procedures can be expressed in the following way:

LP_t = labour productivity at the starting year
LP_{t+n} = labour productivity at the closing year
LP_S = productivity development as a consequence of structural changes
LP_P = productivity development as a consequence of changes in branches

$$LP_t = \frac{Q_t}{L_t}\,, \quad \text{Labour productivity at year } t$$

$$LP_{t+n} = \frac{Q_{t+n}}{L_{t+n}} \quad \text{Labour productivity at year } t+n$$

$$LP_S = \frac{\sum_i LP_{t,i} * L_{t+n,i}}{L_{t+n}}$$

According to Method A: $PE_A = TOT - SE_A$,

where $$TOT = \frac{LP_{t+n}}{LP_t} \; ; \; SE_A = \frac{LP_s}{LP_t}$$

and according to Method B: $SE_B = TOT - PE_B$,

where $$TOT = \frac{LP_{t+n}}{LP_t} \; ; \; PE_B = \frac{LP_P}{LP_t}$$

It is implicit in the above argument that different-sized structural effects can be obtained depending on which method is used. If the productivity of a given year – for example, the starting year – is taken as a basis and held constant over time while letting employment be altered, the result will be different compared with the alternative of holding the employment structure constant but letting productivity change over time. Different authors have varying interpretations of how the structural effects should be measured. Some base themselves on a constant productivity trend over time while others keep the employment structure unaltered.

By comparing the results of the various calculations it should be possible to draw certain conclusions concerning the respective changes in productivity and employment. The productivity effects can be compared with one another and so can the structure effects. The greater the disparities that emerge according to the different methods of measurement, the greater the changes which have occurred between starting year and closing year. If the methods give the same results, the changes in productivity and employment have been similar for the subaggregates included in the study – in this case the industrial subgroups. Incidentally, this method is reminiscent of comparing Laspeyre and Paasche price indices in order to discover great shifts in economic activity during periods of sweeping economic transformation (see, for example, Gerschenkron, 1962; Krantz and Nilsson, 1975).

By comparing the structure effects according to the two methods of calculation (SE_A and SE_B, respectively), different cases can be distinguished. The terms ‘expanding’ and ‘contracting’ refer to employment changes and not to production or productivity changes. Moreover, the terms are relative in the sense that the employment trends in the branches will be compared with one another and a positive structure effect occurs even if a branch with high productivity has a decrease in employment; but this decrease is not as large as the decrease in a branch with lower productivity. This phenomenon is of course very relevant with regard to the deindustrialisation process. This means also that the term 'expanding' and 'contracting' shall be taken in a relative way. Even an 'expanding' branch can experience an employment slack between two years, but this decline is less than the corresponding decline in the 'contracting' branch.

Six separate cases can be identified in which the results of the different methods of calculation and the conclusions that can be drawn from them diverge. These can be said to form typical examples and are theoretical constructs of tendencies rather than exact statements of what happened during the period studied. It should be remembered that the figures are based on circa 20 groups of industries. When one speaks of productivity differences having diminished, for example, this obviously does not necessarily mean that the productivity differences between all subgroups have diminished; and when it is stated that the productivity ranking has been reversed, this does not mean that all groups have changed position in the productivity hierarchy. Thus the cases constitute an indicator of the changes rather than a detailed description of the course of events. The less the outcomes of the different methods of calculation differ, the less are the changes which have occurred in the productivity hierarchy between the various years studied.

Case 1. $SE_{A+} > SE_{B+}$, both structure effects are positive. The expanding and high-productive branches have displayed a worse productivity trend than the contracting low-productive ones. The absolute productivity differentials have diminished, but not enough to upset the ranking.

Case 2. $SE_{A+} < SE_{B+}$; both are positive. The high-productive and expanding branches have displayed a better productivity trend than the low-productive and contracting. The absolute productivity differences have increased.

Case 3. $SE_{A+} > SE_{B-}$; SE_A is positive but SE_B is negative. In this case a positive structure effect is ascertained according to Method A. The expanding and at first high-productive branches have had such poor productivity growth compared with the contracting branches that the productivity ranking is reversed. The formerly high-productive branches have become low-productive by the end of the period and vice versa. The expansion in the formerly high-productive branches may thus have led to slow productivity developments in those branches, while contraction in the branches with low productivity in the initial phase may have resulted in a rapid rise in productivity.

Case 4. $SE_{A-} < SE_{B+}$; SE_A is negative but SE_B is positive. The expanding branches have lower productivity than the contracting branches at the beginning of the period. However, the expanding or the slowly contracting branches enjoy faster productivity growth than the fast contracting branches – so much faster, in fact, that the productivity ranking has been reversed. The difference compared with Case 3 is that a rapid rise in productivity goes 'hand in hand' with a rise or a relatively slow retardation in employment, while the branches with a slow rise in employment or a more accentuated decline also have weak productivity growth.

Case 5. $SE_{A-} > SE_{B-}$; both structure effects are negative. The structural effects are, thus, negative independently of which method is employed, but the negative consequences of structural change will be smaller according to Method A than they will with Method B. This suggests that in the early part of the period the high-productive branches have had worse employment but a better productivity development than the low-productive. The productivity differences have thus increased.

Case 6. $SE_{A-} < SE_{B-}$; both are negative. In this case too a negative structure effect arises irrespective of which method is employed, but unlike Case 5 it will be smaller according to Method B than Method A. In this case too the high-productive branches have worse employment growth than the low-productive, but the productivity trend is better for the expanding low-productive branches than for the contracting high-productive branches. The productivity differentials have thus diminished but not to such an extent as to reverse the productivity ranking. Had that been the case, a positive structural effect would arise according to Method B (compare Case 4). The various typical cases are illustrated in Table 18.1.

However, the terms 'structural gains' and 'structural losses' are extremely arbitrary and a symptom of how many parts can be caught up statistically in the whole. It is possible to 'explain' the rise of productivity in a branch of business or industry, or in a firm, by breaking the aggregate down into smaller and smaller units so that all change in the distribution of labour results in 'structural gains'. Of course it is a condition of this line of reasoning that production per employee rises through this redistribution. Regard must then also be had to such factors as expansion of old production lines or adoption of new manufacturing processes, should this lead to a redistribution of the labour force and consequently a change in productivity.

This line of reasoning can be pursued in terms of 'dynamic' and 'static' gains of structural transformation. These gains are quite often static in nature, since they do not account for the developmental possibilities found in the transfer of labour from activities of low productivity to high productivity employment, an act that affects productivity development in both activities. These development possibilities are accounted for in the term 'dynamic gains of structural transformation'. Assume that a highly productive and expansive branch develops more successfully due to resources being placed at its disposal – this is an example of a dynamic gain of structural transformation. The same applies to a declining branch with low productivity, which experiences a productivity boost due to the elimination of the least productive units in the branch. These dynamic gains will – at least in this chapter – be concealed in the branches' internal productivity development. During a deindustrialisation period, it will be the second of the above examples which is the more important. It is often the least productive companies within a branch which are eliminated first during deindustrialisation, which explains the common increase in productivity within declining branches via an increase in the mean productivity of the remaining companies. If these declining branches are within traditional, capital-intensive activities then the deindustrialisation will result in declining productivity, however, since the mean productivity of the industrial sector will decline, it thereby brings with it a net loss attributed to structural transformation.

Table 18.1 A schematic comparison between structure effects according to methods A and B

Case	Productivity (t_1)	Employment change	Productivity change	Productivity (t_2)
1. $SE_{A+} > SE_{B+}$	High	Fast	Slow	High
	Low	Slow	Fast	Low
2. $SE_{A+} < SE_{B+}$	High	Fast	Fast	High
	Low	Slow	Slow	Low
3, $SE_{A+} > SE_{B-}$	High	Fast	Slow	Low
	Low	Slow	Fast	High
4. $SE_{A-} < SE_{B+}$	High	Slow	Slow	Low
	Low	Fast	Fast	High
5. $SE_{A-} > SE_{B-}$	High	Slow	Fast	High
	Low	Fast	Slow	Low
6. $SE_{A-} < SE_{B-}$	High	Slow	Slow	High
	Low	Fast	Fast	Low

If we are content to use the term 'beneficial effects of structural change' or 'structural gains' for those changes that have a connection with differing development phases or redistribution – literally speaking – of the labour force from less productive to more productive parts of the economy, industry or firm, that is that. But it is never possible to go so far as to 'explain' all rises in productivity in terms of the designation 'beneficial effects of structural change'. However, examples such as an expansion of traditional production lines in order to exploit the advantages of large scale, or the introduction of new technologies, manufacturing processes and new skills that result in higher productivity, ought not to be attributed to positive structural effects but to productivity-raising investment and innovations (see, for example, Johansson, 1985). As a rule of thumb we might say that positive structural effects are attributable to an alteration of the employment structure such as to signify that productivity rises at the aggregate level but remains constant at the disaggregated level. But if on the other hand productivity rises at the disaggregated level despite the fact that the employment structure is no longer constant, then this is a 'productivity effect'. It is the transfer of labour from the low-productive to the high-productive unit that causes the beneficial effects of structural change and not the increased productivity arising by virtue of the raising of productivity in the low-productive unit, for example because the labour force remaining now has more capital at its disposal than before. Rather, the latter is a manifestation of the 'productivity effect', even though this may of course have some connection with the transfer of labour between the two production units.

It is evident from the above that the productivity effect is not a pure productivity effect, but that it also includes such structural gains or losses as occur in the various subgroups. In this way the structure effect measures only the gains/losses occurring between different development of the various branches, not those within the branches. Moreover it should be stressed that these unrecorded intra-branch structural changes probably vary considerably between different subgroups because of their varying size – the larger a subgroup is, the greater the importance which this intra-branch structure effect probably has.

However, it is not only the intra-branch structure effects which are influenced by the fact that the subgroups differ in size. The measurable 'structure effects' are influenced as well. If a subgroup dominates a main group because of its size, the scope for structural gains or losses is smaller than if the subgroups are of the same size – provided, of course, that there are productivity differences between the subgroups. The implication is that it may be somewhat meaningless to analyse the impact of the different effects on the trend of productivity for certain of the main groups of industry. Moreover the distribution of productivity between the various subgroups has an impact on the magnitude of the structure effects. The bigger the productivity variances the bigger the chances of structural gains (Johansson, 1985).

REGIONAL CHARACTERISTICS AND REGIONAL DEINDUSTRIALISATION

In order to get a better understanding of possible effects of structural changes and deindustrialisation, and its effects on labour productivity in the manufacturing industry, the country has been divided into eight different regions (see Figure 18.1 and Table 18.2). The criteria for choice of regions were that they had a large enough population to be analytically useful, and that their internal economic structures were as similar as possible, while they remained as unique as possible in relation to other regions. The regions are:

1. Stockholm/Uppsala area; metropolitan area, small goods-producing sector, high-tech industry, densely populated.
2. The corridor Stockholm–Gothenburg; farming and small-scale industry.
3. Småland; forestry and small-scale industry.
4. Southeastern Sweden; small heterogeneous area.
5. Malmö county; dual industrial structure, metro area, densely populated.
6. Western Sweden; engineering industry, metro area, densely populated.
7. Bergslagen; the Swedish 'rust belt', paper and pulp.
8. Northern Sweden; sparsely populated, forestry, and small-scale farming.

Deindustrialisation in Sweden, like deindustrialisation in the rest of the industrialised world, has been an uneven process in terms of regional patterns of development. Certain regions felt the touch of deindustrialisation earlier than others. Regions have also been affected in different ways because of the dissimilar structure of their economies. Localities and regions with a diversified economic life have got off more lightly than localities and regions with a strong dependence on industry – especially if that dependence was on a few large industries. Sensitivity with reference to propensity to migrate is also dependent on whatever possibilities exist for commuting to labour markets nearby. Commuting facilities are dependent not only on distance and communications but chiefly perhaps on how diversified the labour markets are in the potential commuting regions (Carlsson et al., 1993).

There were, thus, some regional time lags in the deindustrialisation process (Table 18.3). This started in the Stockholm/Uppsala region during the first half of the 1960s, where the 'traditional' industrial jobs were phased out. Many of these jobs were relatively highly paid and it was not necessary for them to be localised in the Stockholm/Uppsala region.

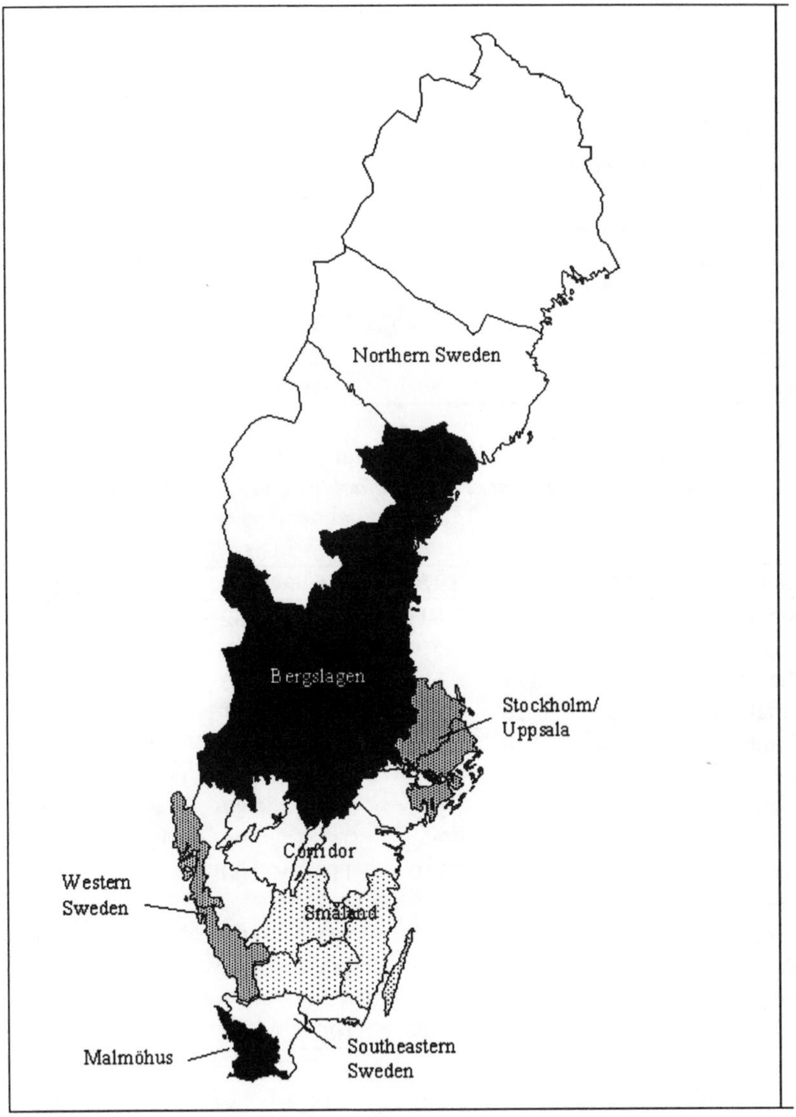

Figure 18.1 Sweden and the eight analysed regions

Table 18.2 Employment in manufacturing industry (SNI3) in Sweden and eight Swedish regions, 1970 and 1990, percentage of total employment

Region	1970	1990
1. Stockholm/Uppsala area	21	13
2. The corridor Stockholm–Gothenburg	38	26
3. Småland	38	29
4. Southeastern Sweden	34	26
5. Malmöhus county	29	20
6. Western Sweden	29	20
7. Bergslagen	36	24
8. Northern Sweden	22	17
Sweden, total	31	21

Table 18.3 Deindustrialisation in Sweden and eight Swedish regions, 1960–90, employment in manufacturing industry (SNI3) 1960=100

Region	1960	1965	1970	1975	1980	1985	1990
1. Stockholm/ Uppsala area	100	108	103	90	82	75	75
2.The corridor	100	113	111	108	96	91	88
3. Småland	100	116	121	117	111	102	104
4. Southeast Sweden	100	118	125	123	114	102	109
5. Malmöhus county	100	109	105	96	87	75	77
6. Western Sweden	100	112	110	110	100	91	92
7. Bergslagen	100	105	103	101	93	80	79
8. Northern Sweden	100	108	123	141	136	119	120
Sweden, total	100	110	109	106	97	87	87

Source: Wibe (1995).

The result was a location shift of the ordinary manufacturing industry from the Stockholm/Uppsala region to other parts of Sweden where the costs in a broad sense – not only the wages – were lower and the preconditions for standardised production the same (Johansson and Strömquist, 1986; ERU, 1989b). One of the results of this process was that between 1970 and 1980 the employment in the manufacturing industry decreased by one-fifth in the Stockholm/Uppsala region. Much of the deindustrialisation in the Stockholm/Uppsala region was, however, a statistical illusion. Many of the activities in the manufacturing sector were shifted to the business-oriented service sector without any changed production (see, for example, ERU, 1989b).

It is obvious that much of the change that would shape the national economy during the 1970s and 1980s had already begun in the Stockholm/Uppsala region by the mid–1960s, so that the capital region was at an advantage when the boom came. The opposite also holds true – much of that which was to be phased out on a national level in the 1970s and 1980s had already been phased out in Stockholm/Uppsala in the 1960s. A result of this 'head start' was that the region expanded powerfully during this period, and its dominance in the Swedish economy was reinforced (ERU, 1989b). The economy came to be more and more characterised by concentrations of knowledge–intensive activities, which affected the labour market through increased demand for highly educated labour (see for example, Johansson and Strömquist, 1986; ERU, 1989b; SOU, 1990: 36). As a result, the education level of employees in the Stockholm area is notably higher than in the rest of the country.

The corridor between the Stockholm/Uppsala region and Western Sweden is characterised by heavy deindustrialisation during the 1970s and 1980s. In the mid-1960s, industry accounted for 41 per cent of employment in the region. The region also features a relatively high proportion of employees in the agricultural sector, where there is a big element of large farms. The structural crisis of the most recent decades has knocked out many firms that were operating in maturated markets. Deindustrialisation hit hard, especially in the eastern districts. Traditional industrial localities ran into serious problems when industries shut down because sufficient new job opportunities did not emerge in the public sector to compensate for the decline in industrial employment. Dependence on industry for jobs is still great, however – only Småland has a higher proportion employed in industry (Table 18.2).

Småland is notable because goods production has been, and still is, a very important factor in regional employment. In 1965, 65 per cent of its labour was involved in goods production, dropping to 45 per cent in 1985. If one excludes those areas which serve as regional service centres the dependence becomes even greater.

Looking at growth potential, Småland was not favourably composed in the mid-1960s. This has been largely corrected by a relatively positive employment development within the different branches. Deindustrialisation did not affect Småland as much as the rest of the country during the 1980s.

Many smaller communities dominated by small-scale industrial production actually saw increases in industrial employment up to the middle of the 1980s (Carlsson et al., 1991).

Low unemployment, high labour force participation, and low educational level characterise the labour market in Småland. Small-scale production and flexible specialisation, and thus less sensitivity to economic fluctuations characterise the economy in this region. The small-scale industries in the region have also shown themselves to be quite resistant to the structural crises that have shaken industry in other parts of the country.

Southeastern Sweden has an economy of dual character in the sense that people in the western parts (Kristianstad County) are relatively very dependent on agriculture for their livelihood. On the other hand the eastern parts (Blekinge County) have a strong element of large industrial firms which have made the region extremely sensitive to changes in the world outside. During the 1970s and 1980s, also, many localities experienced various types of structural crisis. The dependence on large firms has manifested itself in the establishment of branch manufacturing companies in the region – branches, which have functioned as buffers against variations in demand. This has also had the consequence of reducing industrial employment. The decline in jobs was particularly drastic between 1975 and 1985. Because of the enclave character of industry, with little diversification of the economy, these industrial crises struck particularly hard at a number of big industrial districts – districts usually dominated by a single firm.

Developments in Malmöhus County are more reminiscent of developments in Sweden as a whole than of the Stockholm/Uppsala region with respect to deindustrialisation and reindustrialisation. Malmöhus County has a dual character to its economic structure. It has an expansive area around the university in Lund, and then it has a traditional, mature economy in the rest of the county (Olander, 1989; ERU, 1989b). This situation has influenced the development over the past decades. Deindustrialisation has been extensive, with a decrease in employees in the manufacturing industry of about one-third from 1965 to 1985, which was greater than that in the other metropolitan areas. In contrast to the other metro areas, the Malmö region (with the exception of Lund) has not restructured its economy towards a more knowledge-intensive direction (Olander, 1989). This region has remained to a great degree dependent upon the food processing industry, and there has not been the same demand for highly educated employees that is present in the Stockholm/Uppsala region.

Western Sweden has been, and still is, highly dependent upon the development of the engineering industry. This industry has also undergone significant structural changes since the beginning of the 1960s. The shipyards have been practically eliminated while employment in the automotive industry and its sub-contractors has increased dramatically to become Sweden's major industry. Deindustrialisation in Western Sweden has not been as sweeping as in Malmöhus County or the historic central industrial belt of Bergslagen. However, this does not mean that the region was exempt from the process.

Dependence on international economic development is great in Western Sweden, with the result that international economic swings strongly affect regional development. This dependence has become accentuated by the increasing importance of the automotive industry in the region. Despite the structural crises brought about by the extinction of the shipyards and textile industry, the transportation industry has gained importance during the 1980s due to the development of the car industry, that is Volvo. Volvo has come to dominate Western Sweden's economy, and through its cyclical nature increased the region's vulnerability.

Bergslagen – the Swedish 'rust belt' – is characterised by goods production and large-scale industry dominated by iron and steel and a small service sector (see, for example, Vinell and Ohlsson, 1987; Lundmark and Malmberg, 1988; ERU, 1989a; Carlsson et al., 1991). The structural changes during the past decades have thus strongly affected employment in Bergslagen. Its regional problems are directly connected to its industrial problems, with deindustrialisation and the decline in manufacturing accounting for much of the region's weak employment development. For the same period we have also noted a population decline in most of the Bergslagen communities, which is mainly a product of net out-migration.

Despite deindustrialisation, Bergslagen continues to be dependent upon large-scale industry and is thus extremely sensitive to international trends and fluctuations. The structural crises of the past decades have hit the labour force hard, with long-term unemployment and early retirement as results.

In this chapter, Bergslagen includes – not correctly – Västernorrland County. The reason for this is that this region is also dominated by raw material-based industries – sawmills, paper and pulps – and shows the same dependence on international economic fluctuations as the Bergslagen counties.

In Northern Sweden one finds, despite many similarities, large regional differences in economic features. Some of the cities are old administrative centres, which traditionally have had large public sectors which have consistently grown. Other cities have, however, a larger share of the total labour force employed in manufacturing. These cities can be seen as the industrial base of Northern Sweden, where raw material-based industries have had a considerable impact on employment. Unfortunately, these industries have exhibited weak growth capacity since the mid-1970s.

The development of the economy and labour market in the interior of Northern Sweden – which is extremely sparsely populated – is closely tied to developments in the natural resource and raw material-based industries – that is forestry, ore and hydroelectric power – and small-scale industry. The development of the interior has been influenced by the structural rationalisation of, primarily, agriculture and forestry which occurred mainly during the 1960s and 1970s. It was at this time that out-migration began to pick up speed. In Northern Sweden, however, there was still an expansion of the manufacturing industry, which can partly be explained by the small share of the manufacturing industry. Industrial employment in Northern Sweden reached its top level in the middle of the 1970s. After that, even this region took part in the deindustrialisation process. New jobs have been created in recent years, mainly due to the growth of the public sector from the mid-1970s. The public sector, and public transfers, is more important for employment in the interior of Northern Sweden than in any of the regions studied above (Beckman and Lenntorp, 1989; Holm and Tapper, 1990; Nyström, 1994).

INDUSTRIAL TRANSFORMATION AND REGIONAL PRODUCTIVITY CHANGE

Deindustrialisation in Sweden has led to a relative decline in the importance of natural resource-based and capital-intensive industries. Knowledge-intensive industries, on the other hand, have developed in a more positive direction – at least in the respect that employment there has not declined as dramatically as in the capital-intensive industries. This aspect of Swedish development coincides with experiences from the development patterns exhibited by other mature industrial countries.

The absence of correlation between employment development and productivity development is a well-known phenomenon. Branches in the beginning of the product cycle take advantage of new technologies and expand at the same time as their productivity increases, while other branches are phased out, resulting in employment decline and productivity increase. Between 1970 and 1990, industrial employment in Sweden declined by 20 per cent while productivity of labour increased by nearly 50 per cent. This entire increase was largely due to the fact that productivity increased within the different branches (Tables 18.4 and 18.5). It is possible to discern a trend towards weak development of employment and productivity for those branches which displayed high productivity in 1970 – so much so that there is a tendency for these branches to be classified as low productivity branches at the end of the period (Case 4, $SE_{A-} < SE_{B+}$).

Differences in structural effects in Method A and Method B are not large, however, even though the signs are different.

The reason for choosing the years 1970 and 1990 is the similarity with regard to the phases in the business cycle and labour market conditions – both years are characterised as peak years in the demand for labour.

Regarding regional productivity development, we find opposite examples of rates of increase in the cases of the Stockholm/Uppsala region and Northern Sweden. The Stockholm/Uppsala region has the highest rate of productivity increase of all Swedish regions (68 per cent), while Northern Sweden has the lowest rate (25 per cent). The interesting fact here is that the only regions which come near to Stockholm/Uppsala's rate of productivity increase are two regions with very different economic structures: Malmöhus county (64 per cent) and Bergslagen (67 per cent). The common denominator for these three regions is that they have all undergone significant structural change and deindustrialisation between 1970 and 1990. Northern Sweden, on the other hand, has seen very little change in the share employed in industry during this period. This supports the arguments that deindustrialisation itself prompts productivity increases through the elimination of the least productive companies. All three of the regions displaying high rates of productivity increase also exhibit quite positive productivity effects within the individual branches. This is especially true in Malmöhus County that shows a very strong productivity effect according to Method B.

Table 18.4 *Labour productivity – thousands of SEK – within Swedish industry and in eight Swedish regions, 1970–90; 1990 prices*

Region	1970	1990
1. Stockholm/Uppsala area	291	489
2. The corridor Stockholm–Gothenburg	129	182
3. Småland	248	370
4. Southeastern Sweden	261	373
5. Malmöhus County	201	330
6. Western Sweden	278	396
7. Bergslagen	247	413
8. Northern Sweden	305	381
Sweden, total	271	403

Source: Estimations based on Wibe (1995).

Table 18.5 Productivity development (%) 1970–90 according to Method A and Method B

Region	Total change	Productivity change (A)	Structural change (A)	Productivity change (B)	Structural change (B)
1. Stockholm/ Uppsala area	68	67	1	60	8
2. The corridor Stockholm–Gothenburg	41	51	–10	44	–4
3. Småland	49	56	–7	47	–2
4. Southeastern Sweden	43	45	–2	43	0
5. Malmöhus County	64	34	30	102	–38
6. Western Sweden	42	42	0	36	6
7. Bergslagen	67	61	6	50	17
8. Northern Sweden	25	38	–13	19	6
Sweden, total	49	52	–3	45	4

A look at the effects of structural transformation shows a somewhat different picture. Here, Stockholm/Uppsala also shows positive, albeit small, effects, with the interesting fact being that those branches which were highly productive in 1970 developed fairly well in terms of both productivity and employment (Case 2, $SE_{A+} < SE_{B+}$). This implies that the branches that were phased out had low productivity and lacked competitiveness, an observation which is supported by other studies of the capital region's structural transformation during recent decades (see, for example, Johansson and Strömquist, 1986; ERU, 1989a, 1989b).

Even Bergslagen – as with Western Sweden – belongs to Case 2. Western Sweden is quite similar to Stockholm/Uppsala in terms of the size of structural effects. These structural effects have been of greater importance to Western Sweden, however, since it is a generally weaker region. In the case of Bergslagen, the typical deindustrialisation phenomenon should have occurred with much greater effect. Here, the branches exhibiting high productivity in 1970 appear to have fared well during the industrial restructuring which occurred between 1970 and 1990, with its wide-scale eradication of the weaker, low productive companies.

An analysis of the effects of structural change shows that Malmöhus County was the region which experienced the most widespread industrial restructuring during this 20-year period. As mentioned above, the county has had both a significant deindustrialisation and strong productivity increases within industry. A comparison of the structural effects shows a consequential industrial transformation (Case 3, $SE_{A+} > SE_{B-}$). The branches with high productivity in the beginning of the period show a slow productivity development and a relatively good employment development, while those branches with low initial productivity display rapid productivity development, but slower employment progress. Productivity development within the various branches in Malmöhus County has been so varied that the branch productivity rankings have been all but reversed, with high productivity branches moving to the bottom of the scale during the period and vice versa. This suggests that the low productivity branches from 1970 have been eliminated to a greater degree than the highly productive ones, and that those companies which remain in the former low productivity category are companies with fairly high productivity, a finding supported by other studies (see, for example, Olander, 1989). The dual character of the region's industry in 1970 thus resulted in a significant structural transformation and renewal – processes not unusual in a deindustrialisation phase.

In the case of Northern Sweden, the region displayed the lowest productivity increase of any region during the period 1970-90. The region is characterised by the extremely low importance of the industrial sector for employment, with only Stockholm/Uppsala showing a lower employment share within industry (Table 18.1). An examination of structural effects places the region in Case 4 ($SE_{A-} < SE_{B+}$). Those branches with high productivity in 1970 developed poorly in regard to both productivity and employment. Those branches with low productivity in 1970 performed much better during this period, so much so in fact that the productivity rankings between branches was reversed. The structural transformation within Swedish industry was felt in Northern Sweden through the rationalisation of many of the region's large, forest-based companies. Unfortunately, this did not have positive structural effects for Northern Sweden, as it did in Bergslagen. Here it was rather the more flexible small companies which have developed the best, with one result being that deindustrialisation was not felt as much in Northern Sweden as in the rest of the country.

Småland, with a high share of its labour force employed within industry and a large number of small companies, is an interesting case of structural transformation (Case 6, $SE_{A-} < SE_{B-}$). Those branches with high productivity in 1970 showed both a slow productivity and employment development. This implies that deindustrialisation in this region has resulted in employment losses in big companies with high productivity. In Småland, it is rather the more flexible small companies that have kept up employment.

These companies have demonstrated themselves to be particularly resistant to crises and bankruptcies and they also seem to have had a good productivity development. Instead of investing in new technology and increased capital intensity, these companies have expanded largely through the utilisation of labour. This has led to Småland having unusually low unemployment figures, relative to the country as a whole.

The two other regions – the corridor between Stockholm and Gothenburg and Southeastern Sweden have far too diffuse economic structures, which make any analysis meaningless. Both cases have economic structures that are too dual in character to allow for an analysis of structural transformation from a deindustrialisation perspective.

In conclusion, it can be said that it is primarily productivity developments with branches that have affected the overall productivity patterns. Structural transformation within the industrial sector has only in exceptional cases – Malmöhus County – had any significant influence. It is plausible, however, to argue that an increased disaggregation of industry would yield greater effects of structural change. Deindustrialisation has not resulted in any notable gains or losses attributed to structural change through developments in the various branches influencing industrial productivity. Deindustrialisation has, however, led to the elimination of companies with low productivity as well as renewal within branches, which has had significant positive effects on productivity.

REFERENCES

Beckman, B. and B. Lenntorp (1989), 'Staten i geografin', *SOU 1989:65,* Stockholm: Allmänna Förlaget.

Bengtsson, T. and M. Johansson (1994), 'Internal Migration', in T. Bengtsson (ed.), *Population and Welfare in Sweden,* Berlin: Springer Verlag.

Bengtsson, T. and M. Johansson (1995), 'The New Migration Transition – The Case of Post-Industrial Sweden', in C. Lundh (ed.), *Population, Economy and Welfare,* Scandinavian Population Studies, Vol. 10, Lund: Lund University Press.

Carlsson, F., M. Johnsson, L.O. Persson and B. Tegsjö (1991), *Lokala arbetsmarknader och förvärvsregioner. Nya geografiska indelningar för regionala analyser,* Örebro: SCB.

Carlsson, F., M. Johansson, L.O. Persson and B. Tegsjö (1993), *Creating Labour Market Areas and Employment Zone,* Umeå: CERUM Report.

Cheshire, P.C. and D.G. Hay (1989), *Urban Problems in Western Europe: An Economic Analysis,* London: Unwin Hyman.

Commission of the European Communities (1991), *Europe 2000,* Luxembourg.

Commission of the European Communities (1993), *Regional Studies,* Luxembourg.

Denison, E.F. (1967), *Why Growth Rates Differ. Postwar Experience in Nine Western European Countries*, Washington, DC: Brookings Institution.

ERU (1989a), 'Den regionala problembilden', *SOU 1989:12,* Stockholm: Allmänna Förlaget.

ERU (1989b), 'Storstadsregioner i förändring', *SOU 1989:69,* Stockholm: Allmänna Förlaget.

Fothergill, S. and N. Guy (1990), *Retreat from the Regions. Corporate Change and the Closure of Factories,* Regional Studies Association, London: Jessica Kingsley Publishers.

Gerschenkron, A. (1962), *Economic Backwardness in Historical Perspective: A Book of Essays,* Cambridge, MA: Belknap Press.

Hall, P. (1991), 'Structural transformation in the regions of the United Kingdom', in L. Rodwin and H. Sazanami (eds), *Industrial and Regional Transformation: The Experience of Western Europe,* Boston: Harper Collins.

Holm, E. and H. Tapper (1990), 'Geografin i den ekonomiska politiken', *Ds 1990:74,* Stockholm: Allmänna Förlaget.

Johansson, B. and U. Strömquist (1986), *Teknikspridning och importsubstitution. Stockholmsregionens teknikförnyelse,* Stockholm County Council, Stockholm.

Johansson, M. (1985), *Svensk industri 1930–1950. Produktion, produktivitet, sysselsättning,* Lund: Studentlitteratur.

Johansson, M. (1996), 'Flexibility, Rigidity, and Innovation Diffusion – The Case of Northern Sweden', in M. Johansson and L.O. Persson (eds), *Extending the Reach. Essays on Differing Mobility Patterns in Sweden,* Stockholm: Fritzes.

Krantz, O. and C.A. Nilsson (1975), *Swedish National Product 1861-1970. New Aspects on Methods and Measurements,* Lund: Gleerup.

Kuznets, S. (1952), 'Long-Term Changes in the National Income of the United States of America since 1970', *Income and Wealth, Series II,* New York: NBER.

Lundmark, M and A. Malmberg (1988), *Industrilokalisering i Sverige – regional och strukturell förändring,* Kulturgeografiska institutionen, Uppsala Universitet. Uppsala.

Nilsson, Jan-Evert (1995), *Sverige i förnyelsens Europa: En industrinations uppgång och fall,* Stockholm: Liber.

Nyström, H. (1994), 'Stadsbudgetens regionala fördelning', *NUTEK B 1994:3,* Stockholm: Gotab.

Olander, L.O. (1989), 'Skånskt näringsliv i förvandling', *ERU-rapport 57,* Stockholm.

Richardson, H.W. (1978), *Regional and Urban Economics,* London: Penguin.

Rodwin, L. (1989), 'Deindustrialisation and regional economic transformation', in L. Rodwin and H. Sazanami (eds), *Deindustrialisation and Regional Economic Transformation: The Experience of the United States,* Boston: Harper Collins.

Rowthorn, R.E. and J.R. Wells (1987), *De-industrialisation and Foreign Trade,* Cambridge: Cambridge University Press.

Snickars, F. (1991), 'Regional Perspectives on the Deindustrialisation of Sweden', in L. Rodwin and H. Sazanami (eds), *Industrial and Regional Transformation: The Experience of Western Europe,* Boston: Harper Collins.

SOU (1990:36), *Storstadsliv. Rika möjligheter – hårda villkor,* Stockholm: Allmänna Förlaget.

van der Wee, H. (1986), *Prosperity and Upheaval. The World Economy 1945–1980,* London: Penguin.

Vinell, L. and L. Ohlsson (1987), *Tillväxtens drivkrafter,* Stockholm: Industriförbundets Förlag.

Wibe, S. (1995), 'Struktur och produktivitetsutveckling inom svensk industri 1970/90', *SIR Rapport 93*, Supplements, Stockholm: Fritzes.

PART FOUR

New Concepts and Perspectives

19. Place Surplus, Exit, Voice and Loyalty

Roger E. Bolton

INTRODUCTION

A common tool of evaluation in economics is consumer surplus. It offers a theoretically sound measure of benefits of various public actions. It is widely taught and widely understood by professional planners as well as regional and urban economists. This chapter is an effort to show how one variety of consumer surplus can be used as an evaluation tool in regional policymaking.

My thoughts here were inspired originally by Albert Hirschman's discussion, in *Exit, Voice, and Loyalty* (1970) of the 'surplus' that people enjoy as members of an organisation. Hirschman saw that surplus as a straightforward extension of consumer surplus, and felt that it strongly affected people's choice between exit and voice in coping with an organisation's decline.

> Consumer surplus measures the gain to the consumer of being able to buy a product at its market price: the larger that gain the more likely is it that the consumer will motivated to 'do something' to have that gain safeguarded or restored. In this way it is possible to derive the chances for political action from a concept that has dwelt so far exclusively in the realm of economic theory. (Hirschman, 1970, p. 50)

By 'do something' Hirschman was referring to voice as opposed to exit, to staying in a declining organisation and attempting to change its ways, as opposed to leaving it. A person who has a high surplus from being a member of a group stands to lose the surplus if the organisation deteriorates further, so he or she is reluctant simply to sit back and watch the surplus dissipate. He stands to lose all the surplus instantly if he exits, so that's not an attractive alternative either. If she stays and participates – utilises 'voice' – she has some chance of reversing the decline and preventing the loss of surplus.

In addition to helping explain individuals' choice between exit and voice, the notion of surplus offers a tool for planning by decisionmakers responsible for the organisation in question. It offers one way of measuring the benefits of group action, to be set against the costs of group action.

This chapter explores an analogous concept that I call 'place surplus'. I suggest the concept has utility for public policy, local planning and urban/regional research, and show how it is founded on microeconomic theory. I then elaborate some of Hirschman's ideas and try to recast them in a form that relies on place surplus instead of the traditional consumer surplus he had in mind.

It is not helpful simply to define a good, called 'place', draw a compensated demand curve for 'place', and then measure the area under the demand curve above the price. That seems way too artificial: what does a 'good' called 'place' mean? What would the demand curve for such a good mean? The better approach is to attribute the surplus to the combination or package of goods that the consumer buys in a place, and also to unpriced goods he consumes, in the context of spatial differences in prices of some goods and spatial differences in the quantities available of unpriced goods.

Including unpriced goods is essential for at least two reasons: first, some of the most important applications of consumer surplus in welfare economics are to non-market goods, and there is an advantage to linking the analysis of place surplus to previous work on consumer surplus in welfare economics; second, many of the most important characteristics of a place are nonmarket goods that one can enjoy without having to pay for them. Indeed, the common notions of a 'sense of place' and 'social capital' presumably refer in part to intangible and unpriced characteristics of a place that affect people's behaviour (Bolton, 1992, 1995, 1998; Bolton and Jensen, 1995).

Of course, a full consideration of place surplus should take into account surplus arising from one's production activities. In other words, producer surplus also contributes to place surplus. Surplus from labour participation seems most important as a form of producer surplus that varies from place to place, but surplus from the provision of capital is probably not negligible as an additional factor. For example, a small business owner may earn more on a given amount of capital in one place than in another. I shall ignore these aspects of surplus in this present chapter, and will use the term 'place surplus' to refer to the consumer surplus alone. I shall assume that the monetary income of a household does not vary from one place to another. Admittedly, this is oversimplified, because it means essentially that I am ignoring some real income differences that are due to place-specific characteristics – and that means ignoring a major area of concern in regional economics. Furthermore, theory and empirical evidence implies that producer surplus varies systematically in a way that partially offsets consumer surplus, as for example when money wage rates are bid down or land rents bid up in response to advantages in lower goods prices and/or amenities (see Blomquist, Berger and Hoehn, 1988; and Stover and Leven, 1992). But for now I want to concentrate on the links between place surplus and the older concept of consumer surplus, so I will limit the analysis to cases where monetary income does not vary between places.

THE BASIC IDEA

Start with the traditional notion of consumer surplus. It is a concept in the economic theory of the consumer relating to the consumer's reaction to temporal changes in price. Imagine the following sequence: in an initial situation, denoted by T_*, a consumer does not have the opportunity to buy some good, X. He attains the utility level U_*. Then the situation changes, to one denoted by T_0 : he has an opportunity to buy X at a price, p_0 , and he buys the quantity x_0 . He also buys other goods and services, and his total utility = U_0. U_0 exceeds U_*, the utility being higher than if he did not have an opportunity to buy X, and the monetary measure of the difference in utility is consumer surplus. Now, the situation changes again, to one denoted by T_1 : the price of X changes to p_1, other prices remaining unchanged, and the consumer responds by buying some different quantity, x_1 . He will likely also change his purchases of other goods and services as well. The new utility level is U_1 If the price of X decreases, the consumer's utility will increase above U_0 ; if the price increases, it will decrease. We are interested in the monetary measure of the change in utility, $U_1 - U_0$, which is the change in consumer surplus.

All through this sequence, T_*, T_0, T_1, we assume the consumer's preference function does not change.

In this chapter I am interested in a sequence of 'situations', T, that are different places. I shall also assume that the market 'goods' in the model are so aggregate in their definition that all goods are available in all places, though of course some prices will vary by place. This is as required by applied work comparing consumption behaviour across space. Therefore, we need not consider a place analogous to T_*, rather we will simply compare two places T_0 and T_1 From now on, I shall limit comparisons to two such places.

To return to the temporal analysis, one can find in the microeconomics literature several different monetary measures of a temporal change in price – several varieties of change in consumer surplus – depending on whether the price rises or falls and on some other assumptions (Mas-Collel,

Whinston, and Green, 1995, pp. 80–3; Freeman, 1993, pp. 46–70; and Jehle, 1991, pp. 272–81 are excellent sources; Layard and Walters, 1978, pp. 143–54 and Silberberg, 1990, pp. 396–405 discuss price changes in more than one good at a time). In this chapter, however, I shall confine myself to the compensating variation measure. For a price decrease, it is defined as the maximum amount of money income the consumer could lose, given p_1, and still be able to achieve utility level U_0, the utility level he would have if he had to pay p_0. For a price increase, compensating variation (CV) is the amount of income he would have to receive to make him as well off as if the price had remained at p_0 and not increased. Again, the amount of income transfer is determined by the criterion of leaving utility unchanged at U_0.

It is easy to see that CV is the difference in the consumer's cost of achieving the utility level $U = U_0$ in the two situations, where 'consumer's cost' is the minimum expenditure needed by the consumer assuming he optimises perfectly in the two situations.

Although the CV is more soundly based in theory than the simple Marshallian consumer surplus – the area under an ordinary demand curve – the simple Marshallian consumer surplus is very often an excellent approximation of the CV (Willig, 1976; Jehle, 1991, pp. 271–82). The CV can be defined for a simultaneous change in the prices of more than one good, as discussed in a later section. It can also be defined for situations in which some goods are not priced in the market, but which are available to the consumer in a fixed quantity – which may vary from one situation to another. Public goods and environmental or cultural amenities are obvious examples.

One important advantage of using CV as a measure is that it can be aggregated across individuals, being a monetary measure. An important disadvantage is that the aggregation loses information on the distribution of effects. Another important disadvantage is that it is a valid measure only if the consumer's preferences are unchanged from one situation to another. This is potentially a rather significant limitation in analysis of place differences, because it seems likely that preferences are actually somewhat endogenous to location change. These disadvantages are familiar ones in benefit-cost analysis, and intelligent planners understand them.

Now, for place surplus. The place surplus analogue arises when there are spatial differences in prices and quantities rather than temporal changes. Assume there is a place where the consumer might consume – a benchmark place, as it were – denoted by T_0, and some other place where he might consume, denoted by T_1. The consumer's utility is higher or lower in T_1 than in T_0, and we seek a monetary measure of that difference in utility. Just as in the temporal case, the difference depends on the benchmark situation.

The place surplus in Williamstown is measurable, even in principle, only against some benchmark alternative, say Cleveland. Of course, if we use place surplus in an analysis explaining exit versus loyalty, it makes sense to use as the benchmark the alternative place the person would move to if he exited the place where he lives now.

In the case of temporal change, described above, it may make sense to analyse a change in only one good's price at a time, and indeed that is the prevailing practice in most textbook discussions. In the spatial application, however, it seems essential to assume that quite a few prices differ in the two places. Formally, if one wishes to calculate the compensating variation version of consumer surplus, one can work with expenditure functions. Define the expenditure function for a place as a function giving the minimum expenditure the consumer must make in order to attain some specified utility level given the prices he faces. The specified level of utility is U_0, the maximum utility attainable in the benchmark place. The expenditure function assumes the consumer optimises in the sense of choosing quantities of goods so as to achieve U_0 at the minimum possible expenditure. Therefore, compensating variation is the difference between the expenditure function values in two different situations. Formal analysis shows that the minimum is a function of U_0, the prices of all market goods, and the quantities of all nonmarket goods consumed in fixed quantities. The expenditure function is sometimes referred to as the consumer cost function.

Formally, the expenditure functions for T_0 and T_1 are as follows, now denoting different market goods by superscripts and the quantities of unpriced amenities or disamenities by *A* (a vector):

$$E_0 = E(p_0^1, p_0^2, p_0^3, p_0^4, \ldots, A_0, U_0)$$

$$E_1 = E(p_1^1, p_1^2, p_1^3, p_1^4, \ldots, A_1, U_0)$$

where p_i^j = price of good j in place i.

Note that utility is the same level, U_0, in both E_0 and E_1. For each good *j*, we may have any of three possibilities: $p_1^j = p_0^j$; $p_1^j > p_0^j$; $p_1^j < p_0^j$. That is, a good may have the same price in Williamstown as in the benchmark place, or a higher price, or a lower price. A_0 and A_1 may or may not be different; if different, they affect E_0 and E_1 directly and also by affecting the optimal quantities of market goods the consumer buys in order to reach U_0 at the lowest possible cost.

Place surplus for T_1 is defined as: $\Delta E_1 = E_0 - E_1$

If positive, the cost of achieving the specified utility is lower in T_1 by the amount ΔE_1, so if the consumer moves from T_0 to T_1 that is the amount of income we could take away from him and leave him just as well off as in T_0. If negative, it is the amount by which the cost of achieving the specified utility is higher in T_1, so if the consumer moves from T_0 to T_1 it is the extra income we would have to give him to keep him just as well off as in T_0. Unless stated otherwise, assume $E_0 - E_1$ is positive so that T_1 has positive place surplus.

A numerical example with a CES preference function is in the Appendix; it is primarily pedagogical in value. It has the merit of having three different market goods and one unpriced amenity, but is somewhat simplified by fixing the quantity of the latter that the consumer consumes (rather than merely setting the upper limit on the quantity, which would be more realistic).

DIFFERENT KINDS OF GOODS

It may be helpful to think of several classes of goods. The classification will be helpful when we turn to the diagrammatic analysis below.

First, there is housing, a big ticket item that typically is a large proportion of E and also has significantly different prices in different places, certainly for many consumers and many pairs of places. It is highly likely the quantities consumed will be different. Second, there are other goods that have different prices in the two places and which the consumer will consume in different quantities there. Examples are fuel, commuting and other personal travel, various types of entertainment, and recreation and other activities that depend heavily on environmental amenities or public services. Some of these may be goods that are priced in one place and unpriced in the other. Third, there are market goods whose prices are the same in the two places, but which are consumed in different quantities, because they are substitutes or complements to housing, other market goods, or to amenities. In some pairs of places, fuel, various types of recreation and personal travel are examples. Fourth, there are market goods for which neither price nor quantity consumed differs in the two places. Many common mass-marketed foods, clothing (if the two places happen to have roughly the same climate), computers, books and magazines, are plausible examples. The existence of this group of goods of course eases empirical analysis, though it does not make empirical analysis easy. Fifth, and finally, we have unpriced goods that are 'free' in both places, but are limited in quantity, and the degree of quantity rationing to the consumer differs in the two places. If the quantity available equals or exceeds the quantity the consumer would desire to consume at a zero price, then there is no quantity rationing. But if the quantity available is less than that, then there is an additional constraint in the consumer's optimisation problem and the levels of E_0 and E_1 will reflect that. Environmental and public amenities are prominent examples.

USEFUL DIAGRAMS IN PLANNING EDUCATION

Although the discussion of place surplus in terms of the expenditure function may be quite satisfying to many, clearly some diagrams will help to popularise the concept. For the multitude of economics undergraduates and city and regional planning students, and indeed even for many professional economists over a certain age, the 'area under a demand curve' is a much more intuitively appealing way of talking about traditional consumer surplus, and something like that is helpful here. There is, however, a fundamental problem of exposition. The traditional analysis usually has only one good's price changing, or two goods' prices at most. But place surplus makes the most sense when we compare places in which many prices, not just one or two, are different in two places. Furthermore, the quantity rationing of some unpriced goods is important. All that makes any diagrammatic analysis very cumbersome. There is no single diagram that easily captures the essence of the idea, unlike in the more familiar traditional case when only one good's price changes.

Figures 19.1–19.4 are meant to be illustrative and pedagogical. They show demand curves for various kinds of goods, and the shapes are very generalised ones meant to remind us of the variety of shapes in the real world (and to remind us that linear demand curves are seldom used in empirical work). They are not meant to be consistent with the numerical example in the Appendix, which is for a CES preference function. All the demand curves are compensated (or 'Hicksian') demand curves, meaning that they show how quantity responds to price assuming the consumer's money income is decreased (increased) enough to offset the utility effect of the price decrease (increase). It is the area under the compensated or Hicksian demand curve that shows CV, and thus a component of the total ΔE_1 magnitude referred to above.

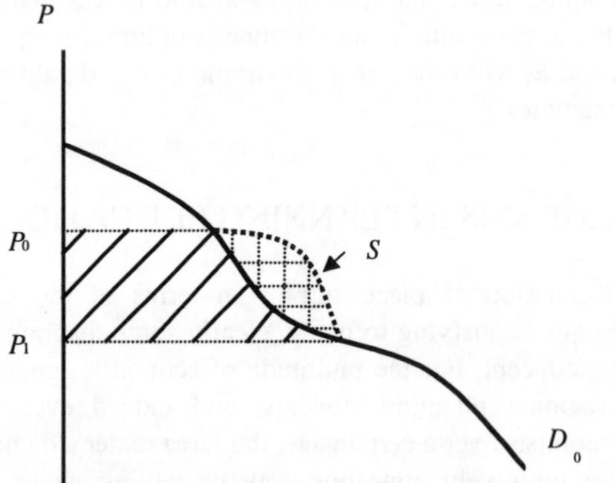

Figure 19.1 Good L

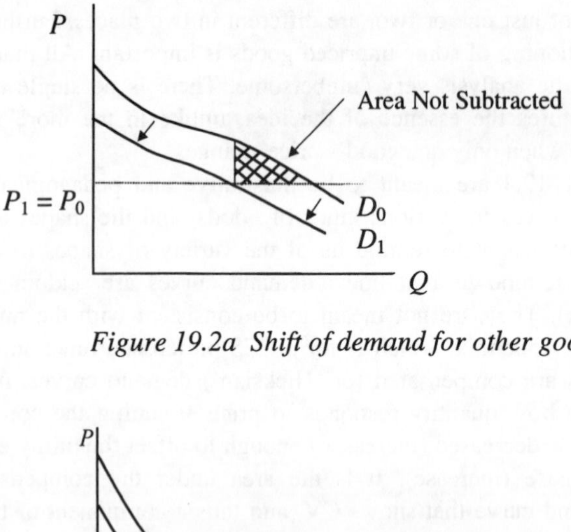

Figure 19.2a Shift of demand for other goods (a)

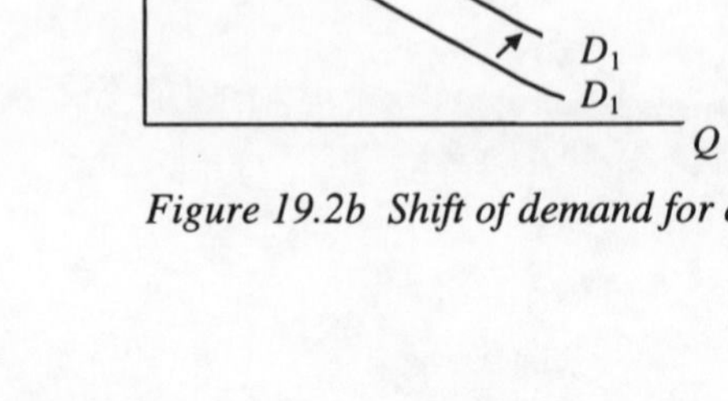

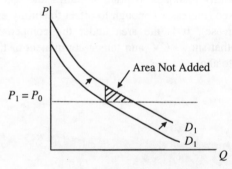

Figure 19.2b Shift of demand for other goods (b)

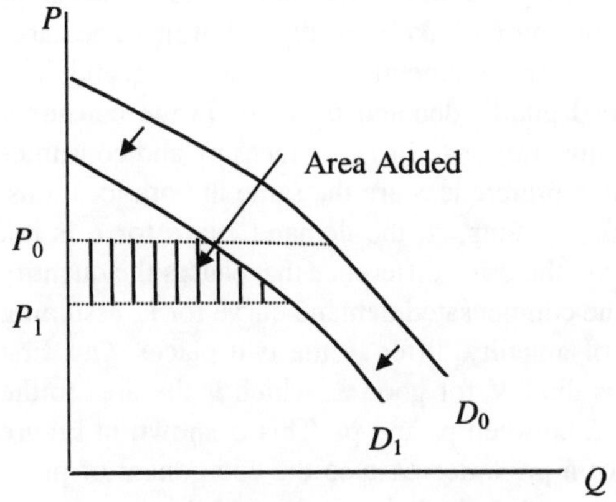

Figure 19.3 Demand curve shifts right

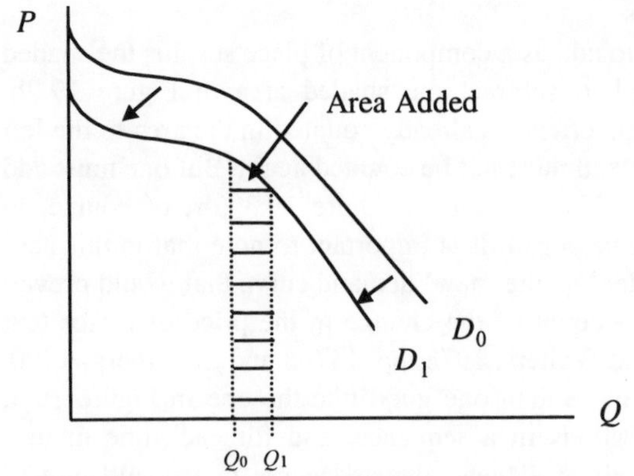

Figure 19.4 A case of a fixed quantity but zero-priced good

It is perhaps desirable to start with the demand curve for some especially important good that accounts for a good bit of expenditure and for which p_0 and p_1 differ significantly. Housing is a likely example, but in some cases another good, perhaps even an unpriced amenity, may be a better candidate. Refer to this good as the 'lead good,' denoted by *L*. In T_0 the consumer faces p_0 and consumes some quantity of *L*; in T_1 he faces p_1 and consumes a different quantity. We assume preferences are the same in both locations, and we measure goods in quality units, so the demand curve for *L* is not different in T_1 from T_0: it is only the price difference that causes the quantity to differ. Figure 19.1 shows the compensated demand curve for L, assuming no other prices or the level of amenity differ in the two places. Our first component of place surplus is the CV for good *L*, which is the area to the left of the demand curve for *L* between p_0 and p_1. This is shown in Figure 19.1, which shows the case of a price decrease so the component of place surplus is positive. If $p_1 > p_0$ the shaded area would be a negative component. Ignore the dotted line S and the shaded area between it and the demand curve for the moment; I will return to it below.

But L is not the only good to consider. The consumer's optimisation is a general equilibrium problem, so demand curves for other goods will shift due to the change in price and quantity of *L*. Figures 19.2 and 19.3 show examples: in Figure 19.2a, $p_1 = p_0$ and the demand curve shifts left; in Figure 19.2b, $p_1 = p_0$ and the demand curve shifts right; in Figure 19.3, $p_1 < p_0$ and the demand curve shifts left. To save space I omit the other obvious possible examples.

One might be tempted to add as a component of place surplus the shaded area in Figure 19.2a, and to subtract the shaded area in Figure 19.2b. However, the value of these effects is already counted in the area to the left of the demand curve for L and must not be counted again. But one must add the shaded area in a case like the one in Figure 19.3 (or, of course, to subtract the counterpart if $p_1 > p_0$). It is important to note that in this case one must add the area under D_1, the 'new' demand curve that would prevail after the consumer takes account of the change in the price of *L* (for text discussions, see Layard and Walters, 1978, pp. 147–8 and Silberberg, 1990, pp. 396–405). If there is more than one good like the one in Figure 19.3, then one must array the goods in a sequence, and for each one in turn calculate the area to the left of a 'new' demand curve that would prevail after the consumer takes account of the price differences in all the goods preceding it in the sequence. This is what is necessary in order for the area in Figure 19.1 plus the areas in all cases like Figure 19.3 to add up to ΔE, which is place surplus. Again, the numerical example with a CES preference function in the Appendix is helpful in understanding this point. If one analyses the sequence correctly, the areas will add up to ΔE, no matter what sequence is used, but unfortunately – for pedagogy – the shaded area for any one good will depend on where in the sequence it is analyzed (this would be true even if there were only two goods, the lead good in Figure 19.1 and one as in Figure 19.3). This is a shortcoming of the graphical analysis, and cannot be helped, being caused by the impossibility of showing more than a few things changing at a time. But the order in which the goods are diagrammed does not affect total ΔE_1, total place surplus.

Finally, Figure 19.4 shows the case of a fixed quantity but zero-priced good, an amenity, which is greater in T_1 than in T_0. (An analogous diagram, omitted here, could show the case where the quantity is less in T_1. The reader can easily extend the analysis to the case of a disamenity, for which the height of the 'demand' curve is the willingness to pay to avoid an increase in the quantity.) The shaded area in Figure 19.4 is also a component of place surplus. Note that although the amenity has zero monetary price, there is a shadow price or willingness to pay, and its value in T_1 compared to T_0 is the result of two kinds of forces: differences in the quantity; shifts in its demand curve caused by differences in prices of other goods. Again, the size of the shaded area in Figure 19.4 is dependent on where the amenity comes in the sequence of goods, and again this is an unavoidable problem of the graphical depiction, but if D_1 is drawn correctly the order of the sequence does not affect the total ΔE.

Finally, I suggest a new – I think – pedagogical device. On Figure 19.1, draw a new curve *S* such that the area between *L*'s demand curve and S is the amount of CV arising from all the other goods other than *L*. *S* is the dotted line, and the added CV is shown by the different shading pattern. The precise shape of *S* is arbitrary. Figure 19.1 shows a case where all goods other than *L* have, in aggregate, a positive effect on place surplus, so total place surplus is the sum of the two shaded areas. It is important to note that S is not any kind of demand curve, but simply a graphical device to allow areas on a diagram to show total compensating variation – total place surplus.

Of course, as is typical in benefit–cost analysis the depiction of aggregate consumer surplus in this graphical way does not show the important aspect of the distribution of the surplus among the community's members.

HIRSCHMAN'S *EXIT, VOICE, AND LOYALTY*

Few scholars in urban and regional economics have delved deeply into Albert Hirschman's provocative distinctions between 'exit, voice, and loyalty' (1970). His analysis suggests connections between place surplus, including surplus from intangible characteristics of a place, and individuals' choices between exit and voice when they must adjust to a decline in the quality of a community. Exit is outmigration, voice is persistence and participation in public discussion. Exit and voice sometimes compete, sometimes are complementary. Loyalty is a characteristic of a person that conditions a person's choice between exit and voice.

The decline in community quality might begin as a result of external forces beyond the place's control, but even so residents must decide how to respond. I suggest that in places with a strong sense of place more people will opt for voice and fewer for exit, *ceteris paribus*. Indeed, the relative balance of these two responses in a declining community, or in any community undergoing major change, might be taken as an a priori indicator of the sense of place, and a suitable quantifiable proxy for the sense of place, although much remains to be done to operationalise that notion.

Hirschman himself is not very helpful in this respect, since he refers to firms, political groups, specialised local governments like school districts, and social groups, but not to 'places' explicitly. However, a review of his basic analysis may help one extend it in the right direction.

Hirschman points out that for the individual or small group, exit and voice are alternatives to improve one's personal situation, but at the social level they are alternatives to help organisations recover stability and recuperate after they are stressed, this recuperation saving valuable capital for society. Hirschman pays considerable attention to recuperation – a dynamic notion, he notes, that traditional economics slights compared to static equilibria and compared to two other dynamic processes, namely sustained growth and liquidation (Hirschman, 1970, p. 22; all further citations of page numbers alone are to this source).

In an empirical analysis of the intangible features of places, case studies of successful recuperation in the face of stress should offer important insights. An example might be a large plant closing or a natural disaster. An important task for research is to model just how recuperation is related to successful voice activity.

One of Hirschman's points is that the contrast between exit and voice reflects the difference between economics and political science as disciplines. I think one can rephrase this as the difference between economics and other social sciences generally. Economics has tended to see exit and acquiescence as the two main options for disaffected customers of a firm, for example, and political science has tended to see voice and acquiescence as the two main options of disaffected citizens of a government. Hirschman felt that neither discipline has framed the critical choice as one between voice and exit (31).

One reason economics pays so much attention to exit is that exit is neater than voice, being a zero–one variable as opposed to a finely graduated one; exit is impersonal and its efficacy in forcing change is an example of the working of the invisible hand, while voice is personal and direct and often confrontational (15–16), and, indeed is essentially an 'art constantly evolving in new directions' (43, italics in original).

Hirschman's analysis is rich in dynamics. He notes that in the case of both exit and voice, recuperation is more likely if the response to declining quality is neither too rapid (or strong) nor too slow (or weak). Exit responses must be fast enough to signal clearly to leaders that action is needed, but if too fast they will kill the organisation before it has time to organise for recovery. In Hirschman's words, referring to customers of a firm, 'it is generally best ... to have a mixture of *alert* and *inert* customers. The alert customers provide the firm with a feedback mechanism which starts the effort at recuperation while the inert customers provide it with the time and dollar cushion needed for this effort to come to fruition' (24, italics in original). Analogously, voice best serves recuperation if it is quick and strong enough to force action, but is not so harassing that it hamstrings effective action (31–3).

Of course it goes without saying that it is the possibility of exit that gives voice its force.

Hirschman notes that some traditional concepts of economics are relevant. One is the difficulty of collective action in large groups, which raises the cost of voice. Another is the importance of development of new institutions in response to social need. Society needs inventions of ways that can increase the effectiveness of voice. 'the possible *discovery* of lower cost and greater effectiveness is of the very essence of voice. The presence of the exit alternative can therefore tend to *atrophy the development of the art of voice*' (43, italics in original). One can add that the newer institutional economics – not yet so prominent at the time Hirschman wrote – should be helpful on this score.

And, as mentioned at the beginning of the chapter, another relevant concept is consumer's surplus (49–50). I believe that the relevant consumer's surplus in this connection is the place surplus defined and elaborated in this chapter. People who get the greatest place surplus, relative to the place they would move to if they exited, will lose the most if they exit quickly. Thus they are the persons most likely to speak up, employing voice over a prolonged period and delaying exit until the surplus is essentially dissipated completely by the organisation's decline. Thus a clearer understanding of 'place surplus' would help us predict much better the social dynamics of decline and attempted recuperation in geographically defined communities. A goal of local planning should be the generation of substantial place surpluses for a large number of citizens, thus giving many residents a motive for effective voice but also delaying exit so as to give breathing space for recuperation. An interesting empirical question is whether persons with large surpluses are also ones who function as especially important nodes in the social networks that build and maintain social capital in the community.

Hirschman offers the empirical hypothesis that in cross-sections of organisations there will be a positive correlation between the level of surplus, and thus the propensity to use voice, and 'quality' (51–4). His examples include neighbourhoods and school districts: in the higher quality ones parents and other residents are likely to use voice, whereas in the lower quality ones they are more likely to exit. This seems to me a reasonable proposition as long as one recognises that one important dimension of 'quality' is a sense of place, which residents value along with more tangible things like test scores, low crime rates, clean streets, and other amenities. These intangibles are important determinants of place surplus.

The characteristics of the social network clearly affect an individual's choice between voice and exit, and then, if he/she chooses voice, it affects the particular forms voice takes. On the one hand we have the basic fact that the possibility of exit is what ultimately gives voice its power; on the other hand, the possibility of exit may facilitate voice sufficiently so as to make exit unnecessary.

What about 'loyalty'? Of Hirschman's three concepts, this is the hardest to define in an abstract sense. Loyalty is a characteristic of a member of a group that affects his or her choice between voice and exit. The person choosing must make a judgement on the effectiveness of continued voice compared to the benefits of immediate access to some better situation elsewhere. Continued voice has costs and benefits, the latter especially being quite uncertain; exit gives immediate access to a new situation but also implies abandoning the possibility of continued voice. A person's optimism on the effectiveness of voice, both by oneself and by one's fellow members, is relevant, and presumably the degree of optimism depends in part on the quality of the social network.

Hirschman does not actually define loyalty in any abstract sense; he says merely it is a 'special attachment' (79). But he does define it operationally. It is a 'special' attachment in the sense that it works in addition to or as a substitute for the force of a large consumer surplus. Surplus is the amount of satisfaction a person would lose on exit and thus is one of the costs of exit. Loyalty is a subset of personal characteristics that favour voice over exit even when the surplus is small, that is when the cost of exit is small. Loyalty becomes critical when the surplus is small, for then loyalty augments the weak incentives to stay. This will often be the case when the organisation has reasonably close substitutes and its 'quality' is low (81).

However, I think Hirschman is inconsistent when he says that loyalty induces people to stay even when the surplus is small. If it is loyalty that leads people to stay, it must be because exit would be very costly psychologically. Therefore, a high degree of loyalty necessarily implies that the surplus is large, if we measure surplus to include intangible value. Loyalty automatically is evidence of a large surplus. Hirschman's argument would be valid if we measure surplus in a narrow way, perhaps focusing on quantifiable dimensions of quality – test scores in the school situation, for example.

Whatever it is, loyalty makes members more tolerant of uncertainty that their voice will be effective; it makes them more confident of the efficacy of their voice 'loyalty holds exit at bay and activates voice... it can neutralize within certain limits the tendency of the most quality-conscious customers or members to be the first to exit ... [and] pushes men into the alternative, creativity-requiring course of action from which they would normally recoil' (78–80).

CONCLUSION

The extension of the traditional concept of consumer surplus to the aggregate surplus enjoyed by residents of a geographical community seems a promising idea in urban and regional evaluation and research. The preceding analysis demonstrates how some of the 'softer' concepts that recent theorists have been discussing (see Bolton, 1998) can be put on a sound microeconomic footing. The creation and maintenance of place surplus can be an important goal of local and regional public policy. Of course, policymakers must take full account of the distribution of surplus, not just the aggregate amount, and also must recognise all the various costs of creating and maintaining it. And they must be careful to encourage voice.

APPENDIX: NUMERICAL EXAMPLE

Assume a CES (constant elasticity of substitution) preference function:

$$U = [b_x X^\rho + b_y Y^\rho + b_z Z^\rho + b_A A^\rho]^{1/\rho}$$

where X, Y, and Z are goods chosen by the household in response to fixed prices, P_x, P_y, and P_z, with the constraint that total expenditure = M; A is an

amenity available in fixed quantity at zero price; the b's are constants. The elasticity of substitution = $s = 1/(1 - \rho)$. In discussions of CES functions, it is also convenient to define the parameter $r = \rho/(\rho - 1)$.
Define the units for each of the four goods such that: $b_x = b_y = b_z = b_A = 1$. Also, define: x = vector of X, Y, Z; p = vector of P_x, P_y, and P_z. Then we have:

Preference Function: $U = U(x,A) = [X^\rho + Y^\rho + Z^\rho + A^\rho]^{1/\rho}$
Indirect utility function: $V(\text{p},A,\text{M}) = [(\text{P}_x{}^\rho + \text{P}_y{}^\rho + \text{P}_z{}^\rho) -{}^{\rho/r} M^\rho + A^\rho\,]^{1/\rho}$
Expenditure function: $E(\text{p},A,U) = (\text{P}_x{}^\rho + \text{P}_y{}^\rho + \text{P}_z{}^\rho\,)^{1/\rho}\,(U^\rho - A^\rho)^{1/\rho}$

The indirect utility function and the expenditure function are derived in a straightforward way from the first order conditions for constrained optimisation problems (the indirect utility function from the first order conditions of the utility maximisation problem; the expenditure function from the first order conditions of the expenditure minimisation problem). Details are available on request. The derivations for the two good case can be found in Jehle (1991).

Initial Situation: Consumer is in T_0

Assume:

$\rho = 0.2$; $\sigma = 1.25$; $r = -0.25$; $M = 1000$;
$P_x = 2$, $P_y = 4$, $P_z = 6$; $A = 10$.

The Marshallian demand functions show the optimal quantities of X, Y, Z:

$$X^M = (P_x{}^{\rho-1}M)(P_x{}^r + P_y{}^r + P_z{}^r)^{-1} = 192.254$$
$$Y^M = (P_y{}^{r-1}M)(P_x{}^r + P_y{}^r + P_z{}^r)^{-1} = 80.833$$
$$Z^M = (P_z{}^{r-1}M)(P_x{}^r + P_y{}^r + P_z{}^r)^{-1} = 48.694$$

The level of utility = U_0 = 60.041, which can be calculated from either the preference function $U(x_0, A_0)$ or the indirect utility function $V(p_0, A_0, M)$. Note that $E_0\,(p_0, A_0, U_0) = 1000 = M$, as we expect: the minimum expenditure, E_0, necessary to reach U_0 is M, the level of expenditure that allowed the household to reach U_0 in the usual consumer optimization problem.

The marginal willingness to pay ('shadow price') of $A = (1/\lambda)[\delta U/\delta A]$ = 21.29, where λ = Lagrangian multiplier, which is the marginal utility of income in the constrained maximisation process.

The Consumer in Alternate Location, T_1

Now, consider the consumer in T_1. The preference function and all its parameters (ρ, σ, r), and M remain unchanged. Assume that P_x is unchanged, P_y is lower, P_z is higher, and A is higher. Specifically, in the new situation:

$P_x = 2$; $P_y = 3.60$; $P_z = 7$; $A = 15$.

The new optimal quantities are: $X^M = 192.719$; $Y^M = 92.434$; $Z^M = 40.257$; and the new level of utility = $U_1 = 64.118$. These however, are not relevant to the present purposes. Rather, we use the expenditure function to show the cost of reaching U_0 in this new location: $E_1 = E(p_1, A_1, U_0) = 922.17$. Therefore place surplus = $\Delta E_1 = E_0 - E_1 = 77.83$.

The marginal willingness to pay ('shadow price') of $A = (1/\lambda)[\delta U/\delta A] = 15.42$.

Hicksian Demands: The Hicksian demand functions and Hicksian quantities are:

$$X^H = \delta E/\delta P_x = (U^\rho - A^\rho)^{1/\rho} (P_x^r + P_y^r + P_z^r)^{(1/r)-1} P_x^{r-1} = 177.720$$
$$Y^H = \delta E/\delta P_y = (U^\rho - A^\rho)^{1/\rho} (P_x^r + P_y^r + P_z^r)^{(1/r)-1} P_y^{r-1} = 85.240$$
$$Z^H = \delta E/\delta P_z = (U^\rho - A^\rho)^{1/\rho} (P_x^r + P_y^r + P_z^r)^{(1/r)-1} P_z^{r-1} = 37.124$$

(We could have got the same results by maximising U subject to a hypothetical income equal to $E_1 = 922.17$. Note also that the sum $\Sigma X^H P_j = 922.17 = E_1$, using prices of T_1)

The place surplus in location T_1 is the result of various interaction effects of the three variables that are different from T_0 : P_y, P_z, and A. The following tables show examples of these interaction effects. The example illustrates two points in the main text: (a) one must analyze the goods in a sequence, and measure each one's contribution to place surplus after taking account of price differences in all goods preceding it in the sequence; (b) each one's contribution will depend on where in the sequence it is analysed. Not every possible sequence is shown (omitted are: $Y \rightarrow A \rightarrow Z$; $Z \rightarrow Y \rightarrow A$; $A \rightarrow Z \rightarrow Y$).

SUMMARY

Component	Place Surplus ($= \Delta E = E_0 - E_1$)
I. Effects ignoring interactions	
Effect of decrease in P_y alone, without changes in P_z and A	33.78
Effect of increase in P_z alone, without changes in P_y and A	– 45.43
Effect of increase in A alone, without changes in P_y and P_z	86.71
This Sum is Not Meaningful; Not = 'Place Surplus'	75.06
II. Effects improperly allowing for interactions	
Decrease in P_y, already allowing for changes in P_z and A	32.61
Increase in P_z, already allowing for changes in P_y and A	– 39.73
Increase in A, already allowing for changes in P_y and P_z	87.58
This Sum is Not Meaningful; Not = 'Place Surplus'	80.46
III. A meaningful decomposition in sequence Y = 'Lead Good'; Sequence = $Y \rightarrow Z \rightarrow A$	
Effect of decrease in P_y alone, without changes in P_z and A ($E_1 = 966.22$)	33.78
Incremental effect of increase in P_z but without change in A ($E_1 = 1009.75$)	– 43.53
Incremental effect of increase in A ($E_1 = 922.17$)	87.58
Total Place Surplus	77.83
IV. Another meaningful decomposition in sequence Z = 'Lead Good'; Sequence = $Z \rightarrow A \rightarrow Y$	
Effect of increase in P_z alone, without changes in P_y and A ($E_1 = 1045.43$)	– 45.43
Added effect of increase in A, without change in P_y ($E_1 = 954.78$)	90.65
Added effect of decrease in P_y ($E_1 = 922.17$)	32.61
Total Place Surplus	77.83

V. Another meaningful decomposition in sequence
A = 'Lead Good'; Sequence $A \rightarrow Y \rightarrow Z$

Effect of increase in A alone, without changes in P_y and P_z (E_1 = 913.29)	86.71
Added effect of decrease in P_y but without change in P_z (E_1 = 882.44)	30.85
Added effect of increase in P_z (E_1 = 922.17)	– 39.73
Total Place Surplus	77.83

ACKNOWLEDGEMENT

I read an earlier version of this chapter, except for the section on Hirschman's ideas, at the Meeting on Analytical Economic Geography and Regional Change, sponsored by the National Science Foundation, Storrs, Connecticut, March 1998, and also at the Meeting of the North American Regional Science Association, Santa Fe, New Mexico, November 1998 (session in honour of Ben Stevens). The section on Hirschman's ideas is taken from an earlier paper: ''Place' as 'Network': Applications of Network Theory to Local Communities', Paper Read at North American Regional Science Meetings, Arlington, Virginia, November 1996.

For helpful comments, I especially thank participants in the Uddevalla conference, especially Bjarne Madsen and Kiyoshi Kobayashi, and also Jonathan Conning, Antoine Bailly, Hans Westlund, Eric Sheppard, Andrew Haughwout, Marlon Boarnet, Ron Miller, Michael Lahr, Walter Isard, and many of my colleagues at Williams for helpful comments. Any remaining errors are mine alone.

REFERENCES

Blomquist, Glenn C., Mark C. Berger and John P. Hoehn (1988), 'New estimates of quality of life in urban areas', *American Economic Review,* **78** (1), 89–107.

Bolton, Roger (1998), 'Some Thoughts on the Concept of Social Capital'(revised version of paper read at meeting of Regional Science Association International, Buffalo, New York, November 1997, and at meeting of Association of American Geographers, Boston, March 1998).

Bolton, Roger (1992), ''Place Prosperity' vs. 'People Prosperity' Revisited'', *Urban Studies*, **29** (2), 185—203; shortened version reprinted in R.D. Norton (ed.)

(1993), *Structuring Direct Aid: People versus Places*, vol. 9 of *Research in Urban Economics* series, Greenwich, CT.: JAI Press, pp. 79–98.
Bolton, Roger (1995), 'New regional science and new economics', *Australasian Journal of Regional Studies,* **1** (1), 31–48.
Bolton, Roger and Rodney C. Jensen (1995), 'Regional science and regional practice', *International Regional Science Review,* **18** (2), 133–45.
Freeman, A. Myrick III (1993), *The Measurement of Environmental and Resource Values: Theory and Methods,* Washington, DC: Resources for the Future.
Hirschman, Albert (1970), *Exit, Voice, and Loyalty: Responses to Decline in Firms, Organisations, and States,* Cambridge, MA.: Harvard University Press.
Jehle, Geoffrey A. (1991), *Advanced Microeconomic Theory,* Englewood Cliffs, NJ: Prentice-Hall.
Layard, Richard and Alan Walters (1978), *Microeconomic Theory*, New York: McGraw-Hill.
Mas-Collel, Andreu, Michael D. Whinston and Jerry R. Green (1995), *Microeconomic Theory*, New York: Oxford University Press.
Silberberg, Eugene (1990), *The Structure of Economics: A Mathematical Analysis,* second edition, New York: McGraw-Hill.
Stover, Mark E. and Charles L. Leven (1992), 'Methodological issues in the determination of the quality of life in urban areas', *Urban Studies,* **29** (5), 735–53.
Willig, Robert D. (1976), 'Consumer's surplus without apology,' *American Economic Review,* **66** (4), 589–97.

20. Capital and the Regions: Other Concepts in Need of Evaluation

John Rees

INTRODUCTION

Successful regional development reflects successful means of capital formation. As regional scholars we tend to define four types of capital: physical, financial, human and social. While we have good information about the role of physical infrastructure and financial capital on regional development, we need to know much more about the role of human and social capital. This chapter explores the role of universities and community colleges as agents of human capital formation. It also examines non-profit organisations as generators of social capital and as variables whose impact remains unknown on the process of regional development.

TYPES OF CAPITAL

As regional scholars we tend to differentiate between four types of capital:

A. physical capital or infrastructure, ranging from roads to the information highway;
B. financial capital;
C. human capital, and, more recently,
D. social capital.

Physical capital is the most studied as it relates to regional development. In the United States this includes the role of the Tennessee Valley Authority (TVA) in accelerating Southern Economic Development as part of President Roosevelt's New Deal Program in the 1930s. The focus on infrastructure as opposed to direct subsidies to industry was an explicit part of the Public Works and Economic Development Act of 1965 and the Appalachian Regional Commission, at a time that marked the heyday of regional policy in the US. Since then the Interstate Highway system of the 1950s and the Information Highway of the 1990s has and will have a major impact on regional development in the United States. Regional development in the US today is the result of the indirect impact of other government policies like defence spending more than direct regional policy (see Rees, 1980). While the influence of Keynesian approaches is evident in the story of American regional policy, it is much more evident in the evolution of European regional policy. The history of European regional policy and its focus on physical capital is well known and will not be repeated here. Even the recent economic success of the first Celtic Tiger, Ireland, can be interpreted as a function of the European Union's Structural Funds and their focus on infrastructure development as opposed to the influence of either foreign direct investment (FDI) or indigenous growth.

The role of *financial capital* and financial institutions in regional development (as opposed to direct investment in plant and equipment by the private sector) has been a more elusive variable for regional scholars to pin down. This is partly because of the difficulty in undertaking empirical studies of financial flows as their speed and complexity increases, whether it is the role of the Arab petrodollar in Europe or America's regions, or the pending impact of the Euro on regional development. We still know very little about the impact of banking deregulation on regional development in the US, or the impact of venture capital on the new industrial regions there. The secret world of financial capital will not be pursued further in this chapter.

This brings us to the role of *human capital* on regional development and to differentiate this from its conceptual stepbrother: *social capital*. Whereas the impact of human capital has long been familiar to economists, the concept of social capital is a newer one, and the distinction between the two is important. Drawing upon the classic work of Coleman (1988), Putnam (1993) and Fukuyama (1995), we can differentiate between human capital as an individual attribute related to skill, expertise and educational achievement, and social capital as a collective attribute related to trust, values and networks as features of the social life of a community. In a regional context Cooke (1998) sees social capital as an important but missing ingredient in explaining successful regions while Malecki (2000) sees social capital and embeddedness as some of the softer variables in need of further research in regional science.

Fukuyama (1995, p. 306) makes an important point relative to this chapter: that the concept of social capital clarifies why capitalism and democracy are so closely intertwined. 'A healthy capitalist economy is one in which there will be sufficient social capital in the underlying society to permit businesses, corporations, networks and the like to be self organizing'

(Fukuyama, 1995, p. 356). It is this voluntary and self-organizing characteristic of social capital that makes it so important for the formation of democratic political institutions. Putnam (1993, p. 167) also argues that voluntary cooperation is much easier in a community and region that has inherited a substantial amount of social capital. In his in-depth empirical investigation of civic traditions in modern Italy, Putnam (1993) sees clear regional differences between Northern and Southern Italy, where the Mezzogiorno appears lacking in social capital and 'spontaneous sociability' as measured by a small number of voluntary organisations. An Italian trend is also seen by Putnam in a larger European context, where Italy has a much smaller number of large corporations than other European countries of a comparable size. Before we explore the role of voluntary and non-profit agencies as an integral part of a region's social capital, we need to discuss two agents of human capital formation.

HUMAN CAPITAL AND REGIONAL DEVELOPMENT

Human capital is generally defined as an individual attribute of people related to their skill, expertise and educational achievement. And by today 'the importance of investing in human capital, especially education for economic growth and household welfare is recognised worldwide' (World Bank, 1995, p. 3). The role of education in generating human capital involves a number of path-dependent stages: elementary and secondary education, higher education and continuing education. While recognising the importance of building a strong foundation for human capital at the elementary and secondary levels, this part of the chapter will focus on universities and community colleges.

Role of Universities

Over the past twenty years, universities have been recognised as engines of regional development as well as centres of learning (Schmandt and Wilson, 1990). At the Uddevalla 98 conference, we were told that proximity to major universities and research centres should be an integral part of a scientific infrastructure that will ensure a region's economic development in the future. Feldman and Florida (1994) showed a positive connection between the propensity to innovate and a region's supply of university and industry R&D. The issue of the university as an engine for regional growth has been caught up in a wider debate about the role of universities in general.

Reflecting on an Academy in Crisis, Sommer (1999) laments on the contradictions implicit in the number of directions the modern American university is pulled: as an extended childcare centre (helping students 'find herself or himself'), as a place for remedial education (for students given 'social passes' through elementary and secondary levels), as a regional entertainment centre (particularly for athletics) and as a real estate developer. These types of pressures are particularly prevalent in metropolitan universities which some see in danger of becoming job training centres as opposed to centres of learning.

Those in favour of universities having a broader mission see regional development as one of the more worthy goals (Mazey 1991). Johnson, Farrell and Henderson (1998) document how a major research university, the University of North Carolina at Chapel Hill, has got directly involved in community revitalisation. Its Urban Investment Strategies Center engages Business School and other faculty in their core missions related to the revitalisation of inner cities: entrepreneurship and community development, child and family development, and education and literacy training. Business School alumni support these activities as ways of helping their future labour pool. The Urban Enterprise Corps promotes entrepreneurship and local economic development by linking minority businesses with emerging market opportunities. One outreach programme, the Durham Scholars Program, seeks to foster college access among at-risk youth in distressed areas within Durham and other North Carolina cities. In this way the university is directly involved in generating social as well as human capital.

The European university may not be quite as far down the regional development path as its American counterpart, but the political pressures are bound to increase.

Role of Technical and Community Colleges

America's community colleges may be the most under-appreciated factor in the country's regional development successes. In a useful review of technical colleges and regional development for OECD, Rosenfeld (1998) compares the American system with its European counterparts. Though each reflects its own national differences, America's community and technical colleges are similar to Denmark's technical colleges, Britain's further education colleges, Belgium's and Austria's polytechnics. What they have in common is technical education that usually succeeds a country's compulsory years of secondary education. Europe also has another set of institutions that also operate in the gap between secondary and higher education: *Fachhochschulen* in Germany, *Hoge* schools in

Holland and the former polytechnics of the UK. These usually teach more advanced levels of education than the two-year community colleges of the US or the technical colleges of Denmark.

A great deal of variation clearly exists in the structure of educational systems across OECD countries. One major difference lies between colleges that offer formal education, usually to national standards, and those that are also responsible for workforce development and customised training for industry. This factor has increasingly become a major point of strength for community colleges in the USA and particularly the southern states. From the 1960s onwards, states in the American south considered regional (mostly county based) vocational schools and technical colleges as an essential part of regional economic development. The Public Works and Economic Development Administration Act of 1965 contained funding for vocational and technical schools, as did the Appalachian Regional Commission. North and South Carolina were the first states to adopt a statewide strategy to establish a large system of regional vocational schools and community colleges mainly to provide customised training to new industry.

'The major effect of this strategy was to shift the target of training from the individual to the company' (Rosenfeld, 1995, p. 8). The emphasis on technical training at these colleges has since spread nationally, shifting much of their curriculum from college transfer to occupational training programmes.

This technical/community college system then became much more responsive to the needs of industry, and many courses are actually taught at company factories. Conceptually, what this represents is the American community college providing a post-Fordist educational opportunity tailored to the needs of specific companies. And this has generally been received with great enthusiasm. In turn, community colleges have experienced increased visibility and responsibilities in many state education systems. In addition to improving the skill levels of the entering workforce, these colleges also had to compensate for the past failures of elementary and secondary education as well as retrain workers in a technical world of fast-paced changes. While more of these colleges are located in metropolitan counties, their mission is proving particularly important to rural areas of the US.

Rosenfeld's (1998) study for OECD shows that the regional technical college model has important commonalities: they are more applied than universities, they target occupations classified as technicians and engineers, and function mostly for the benefit of companies and people residing within their regions (usually counties in the US). Most salient to this author is their flexibility in a post-Fordist sense that allows them to respond to the changing demands of an inherently complex technological workplace. Success stories are heard not only from the US, but also from the further education colleges of the UK, and the technical colleges of Ireland and Denmark. Given the relative newness of many of these college activities, more evaluation is clearly needed, and will undoubtedly come. Because of the public sector nature of funding, we can only hope that accountability in this context will not stifle creativity. Not only do these enterprises add value to the human capital of specific regions, but the way they facilitate learning among individuals in different organisations also makes a valuable contribution to the development of social capital.

THE THIRD SECTOR AS REGIONAL SOCIAL CAPITAL

Because the voluntary and self-organising characteristics of social capital are important foundations of democracy in any region, we need to examine these characteristics and how they evolve institutionally. The voluntary, non-profit or third sector tends to be the *terra incognita* of development at the national and regional level. Yet Salamon (1997) reminds us that in the US alone over one million non-profit organisations had operating expenditures close to $400 billion in 1989, equal to 7 per cent of GDP. This third sector then can play a significant if unknown role in a region's economic and social development. In this section of the chapter we will explore the characteristics of this third sector: how they differ between Europe and the United States, and how they have a regional dimension.

The American Non-profit Sector

In economic issues alone the non-profit sector tends to be far more important than is commonly recognised. In the US, this sector accounts for over half the hospitals, half of the colleges and universities, most social services and almost all of the cultural activity. While scholarly attention has recently focused more on this sector, Salamon and Anheier (1997) remind us that much more attention needs to be given to how this third sector is defined and what it contains. They note the important distinction between philanthropy and the non-profit sector. Philanthropy is the giving of gifts for public purposes, but it is just a part of the non-profit sector defined as a set of private, often self-organising groups that provide a wide variety of information, advocacy and services.

According to Salamon (1997) the United States has a more clearly defined non-profit sector than most other countries. While still complex, the non-profit sector is explicitly recognised by American jurisprudence where organisations are allowed to incorporate under state laws and to secure exemption from federal income taxes, and most state and local taxes. As Figure 20.1 shows, non-profit organisations fall into two groups: one including member-serving organisations (like labour unions, business and academic organisations, social clubs); and the other including organisations that serve public needs in a broad array of ways. These public serving institutions are defined by section 501.c.3 of the IRS code and provide religious, charitable, scientific, literary and educational services. They are tax exempt because their activities are likely to relieve the public sector of burdens it would otherwise have to bear. They are agents of social capital formation because they are grassroots organisations involved in the nurturing of literacy and education, family and community development and in crime prevention.

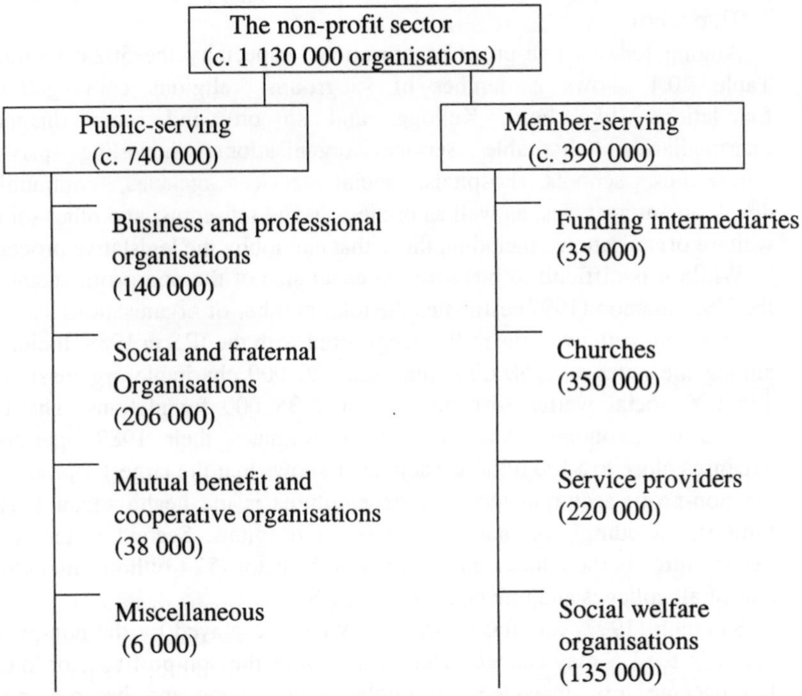

Source: Adapted from Salamon (1997, p. 13). Data on member-serving organisations from US Internal Revenue Service, *Annual Report,* 1990. All data for 1989.

Figure 20.1 Major types of US non-profit organisations

A strong non-profit sector based on volunteerism and self-organisation might be expected in an American context that values individualism, a relative hostility towards centralised control and the public sector in general and the separation of church and state. Salamon (1997) reminds us, however, that a separate non-profit sector did not really emerge in the US until the late nineteenth century, not coincidentally related to the arrival of new immigrants with needs of communal identity and mutual aid (a Tocquevillian recognition of the important link between democracy and association). In this process of American social evolution, the time-honoured practice of relying on voluntary organisations to meet community needs was transformed from a practical necessity into a political ideology which later (including the 1980s) become a rallying point for conservatives to oppose public sector-based social welfare policies. 'Non-profit organisations came to be defended not simply as useful supplements to public action, but as superior vehicles for meeting public needs' (Salamon, 1997, p. 286).

Among today's non-profit organisations, especially the 502.c.3 group, Table 20.1 shows a number of subgroups: religious congregations, foundations (like Ford, Kellogg, and so on) and other financial intermediaries: charitable service organisations, including private universities, schools, hospitals, social service agencies, community development agencies, as well as orchestras and museums; and other social welfare organisations, including those that can lobby the legislative process.

While it is difficult to measure the exact size of the non-profit sector in the US, Salamon (1997) estimates the total number of organisations as over two million, with over one million registered with the IRS in 1989. Included among the latter are 350 000 churches, 220 000 charitable organisations, 135 000 social welfare organisations and 35 000 foundations. The US Bureau of Economic Analysis (BEA) estimates their 1989 operating expenses close to $400 billion. Table 20.1 shows that the largest segment of the non-profit sector in terms of expenditures is the health sector ($165 billion), including over half of America's hospitals. Second in terms of expenditures is the educational and research sector ($77 billion), including half of all colleges and universities in the US.

Salamon (1997) reminds us that the vital role played by the non-profit sector in the US may change. During the 1980s the non-profit sector in the US became less dependent on public sector funds and became more commercial, with paying customers, and faced increasing competition from the private sector.

Table 20.1 Current operating expenditures of US non-profit organisations, by type of organisation, 1989

Type of organisation	Amount ($ billion)	% of total
Member serving	62.0	16
Public serving	327.1	84
Foundations	1.4	–
Religious	31.1	8
Health	165.2	42
Education/Research	76.9	20
Social and legal	35.8	9
Civic and fraternal	10.2	3
Arts and Culture	6.4	2
International	–	–
Total	389.1	100

Sources: US Bureau of Economic Analysis, Survey of Current Business; Hodgkinson et al. (1992).

Ryan (1999) reminds us of the new landscape for non-profits, typified by the decision of Lockheed Martin (the big defence company) to bid for the management of $563 million of welfare operations in Texas. In the 1990s the 'Reinventing Government' policy of the Clinton administration has meant the growth of outsourcing from the public to the private sector. Furthermore, the tax-exempt status of non-profits has also been questioned, particularly by local governments. This implies that a careful reexamination of the role of the non-profit sector in American life is now taking place, some of this in a comparative, international context.

The European Context

The status of the third sector is different in Europe because the common law countries of the US (and the UK) make distinctions between private and public institutions that are not done in the civil law countries of Europe. There, non-profit organisations often have the status of public law corporations largely because the state is considered the best guardian of the public good. According to European Commission estimates, the non-profit sector accounts for 2–4 per cent of GDP, depending on the member state, and has created 1 in 17 of all jobs in some countries. This reflects the different levels of public social welfare spending in member states, ranging from 20 per cent in the UK, 23 per cent in Germany and Italy, 29 per cent in France to 36 per cent in Sweden. A June 1997 communication of the

European Commission drew the attention of political decision makers to voluntary organisations and foundations as a group whose social and economic importance had been underestimated in the past and may make an important contribution to the development of Europe in the future. The Commission proposed research programmes to enhance their knowledge of the third sector, setting up a clear and useful legal framework for non-profits, and giving the sector better access to other European financial programmes in the context of European citizenship.

In Sweden, the status of non-profits seems to reflect the complex mixture of continental and Anglo-Saxon law. Because of the highly developed nature of social welfare policies in Sweden, it has been assumed that little or no third sector exists. In fact, a sizable and important non-profit sector does exist in Sweden, but it is far less involved in the provision of services and more involved in promoting social integration and political participation. Ideal associations (serving ideal purposes), popular movement organisations (*folkrÖrelserna*), cooperatives, trade unions and recreational organisations are examples. Lundstrom and Wijkstrom (1997) see Swedish non-profits as essential for keeping contact between government and citizens that forms part of the foundation for the Swedish model of social democracy, though little is included in law. Contrary to widespread belief, therefore, the Swedish population seems to be actively engaged in a variety of non-profit organisations and the growth of the welfare state has not obliterated them. Indeed the Swedish model reflects Fukuyama's concept of voluntary and self-organising associations that form the basis of social capital and in turn plays such an important role in the continuous nurturing of a liberal democracy.

4.3 Regional Implications

One of our premises as regional scholars is that inter-country differences can also be reflected at the intra-country or interregional scale, as in Putnam's 1993 study of social capital within Italy. Just as at the national level, however, the scope and impact of the third sector is little known at the regional level.

Julian Wolpert (1977) was one of the first regional scholars to examine geographical variations in the voluntary sector and indeed to use the term 'social capital' in this context. In 1988 Wolpert asked whether 'regional values' can account for spatial differences in the expressions of generosity in the United States and whether some regions are more generous and supportive of their own residents. His findings are surprising since moderate (not high) income levels, a low level of distress and relatively smaller community size appear related to higher levels of generosity. 'The regional patterns are not as clear-cut as had been expected...the recent rapid urbanization of the Old South and Sunbelt has been accompanied by an accelerated "catch up" in the quality of their service institutions and organisations. Houston and Denver may now be experiencing the same stage of service development in the arts as nineteenth century Philadelphia and early twentieth century Chicago' (Wolpert, 1988, p. 677). Our Swedish colleagues will not be surprised to find that Minneapolis-St. Paul is widely cited as the 'generosity capital of the US'.

Wolpert's pioneering work is an exception on a topic that we still know very little about at the urban and regional scale. That is one of the reasons for an ongoing project in the US on non-profits, social capital and regional development (Johnson and Rees, 1999). One of our hypotheses is that the philosophy and methods of a non-profit organisation reflect the regional culture and context where it is based. Consider research on the high-tech regions of Boston's Route 128 and California's Silicon Valley. Saxenian (1994) tells us that one of the major differences between these regions is that Route 128 has a regional culture based on a hierarchical, authoritarian and rigid form of Puritanism whereas Silicon Valley has a culture based on a more pioneering spirit where individuals emphasise experimentation and entrepreneurship. Our findings to date suggest that such traits of regional culture also influence approaches taken by foundations and other non-profit organisations. Many foundations in California define philanthropy as a form of social venture capital, where a new generation of philanthropists is increasingly committed to using market-based approaches to solve social problems. This process has also been called 'social entrepreneurship' and includes business ventures with an explicit social purpose such as for-profit community development banks and hybrid organisations that mix profit and non-profit ventures such as homeless shelters that start businesses to train and employ residents (Dees, 1998). Social entrepreneurs can be compared to the pioneers described by Schumpeter, but with a social mission. This link between venture capital and virtuous capital appears to be a California trend that differs from the more traditional, grant-giving traits of foundations in the Eastern US.

The ongoing research in North Carolina views non-profit organisations as community assets, a form of social capital that can ensure a solid foundation for future regional development through investments in education and literacy training, family and child development, crime prevention, entrepreneurship and local community development initiatives. Figure 20.2 reflects the preliminary stage of this research, involving the identification and classification of non-profit organisations in the Piedmont Triad region of Greensboro, High Point and Winston-Salem, North Carolina. Some functional specialisation can be seen in Figure 20.2 such as the concentration of education and literary programmes in Greensboro. This and other sectors like family and child development show a relatively large number of services in each of the three cities, identifying a potential for more collaboration and less duplication of efforts. A multinodal metropolitan area may be expected to have more duplication and less economic efficiency in its social capital base than a uninodal metro area. All Figure 20.2 does is start to uncover the mysteries of the non-profit sector in one metropolitan area. Further research will focus on policies that may increase the efficiency and outreach of the social capital base in the region and how it can enhance regional development.

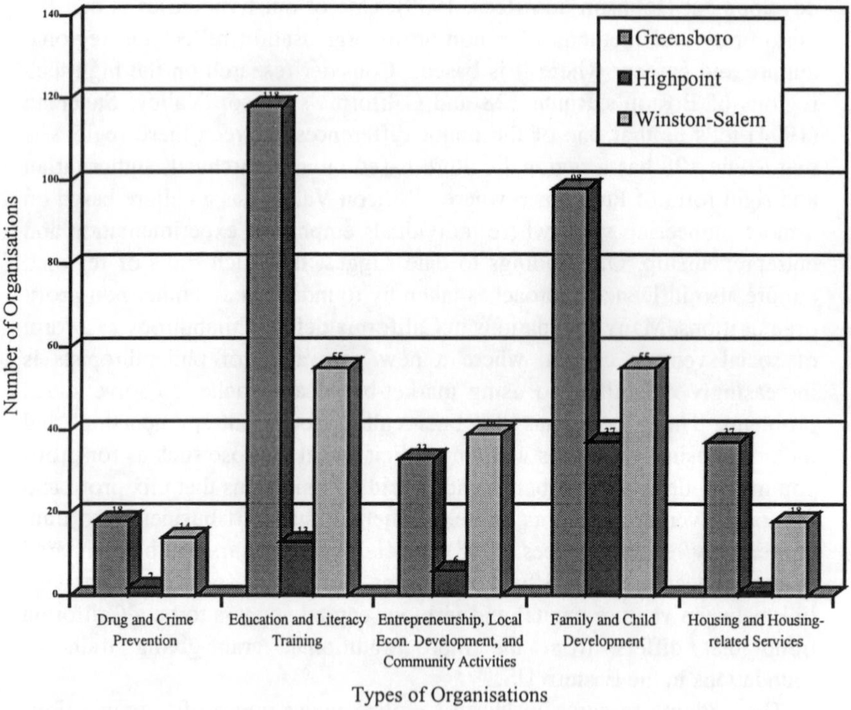

Source: Johnson and Rees (1999).

Figure 20.2 Non-profit organisations by type and city, Piedmont Triad, Inc.

CONCLUSION

This chapter has shown concern for variables that still remain missing in our analysis of regional development and regional policy: human and especially social capital formation. Universities have developed as agents of human capital in a number of different ways. Their role in the regional development process remains a controversial one, given the opportunity costs involving their traditional roles as centres of learning. Other educational institutions have also developed as valuable generators of human capital. Community colleges in the US and related institutions in Europe have emerged as prominent instruments of local development based on their roles as flexible, post-Fordist developers of labour skills.

Successful regional policy usually involves a partnership between the private and public sectors. The third or independent sector tends to be left out of many analyses at the national as well as the regional scale. This paper makes a case for non-profit organisations as important agents in the nurturing of social capital. No regional policy analysis can be complete without a full accounting of the role of this third sector.

REFERENCES

Coleman, J. (1988), 'Social capital in the creation of human capital', *American Journal of Sociology*, **94**, 595–621.

Cooke, P. (1998), 'Social capital in the learning region', Paper, International symposium on skills for the information economy, Chapel Hill, NC.

Dees, J.G. (1998), 'The meaning of social entrepreneurship', Working Paper, Kauffman Center for Entrepreneurial Leadership, Palo Alto, CA.

Feldman, M.P. and R. Florida (1994), 'The geographical sources of innovation: technological infrastructure and product innovation in the US', *Annals. Association of American Geographers*, **84**, 210–29.

Fukuyama, F. (1995), *Trust: the Social Virtues and the Creation of Prosperity*, New York: Free Press.

Johnson, J.H., W.C. Farrell and G.R. Henderson (1998), 'Mr. Porter's competitive advantage for inner city revitalization, exploitation or empowerment', *Review of Black Political Economy*, **24**, 259–84.

Johnson, J.H. and J. Rees (1999), 'Non-profits, Social Capital and Regional Potential', Research Project, University of N. Carolina.

Lundstrom, T. and F. Wijkstrom (1997), 'Sweden', in Salamon and Anheier, op. cit., pp. 215–48.

Malecki, E. (2000), 'Soft variables in regional science', *Review of Regional Studies*, **30**, 61–9.

Mazey, M.E. (1991), 'The Role of a metropolitan university in facilitating regional cooperation', *Metropolitan Universities*, 7–16.

Putnam, R. (1993), '*Making Democracy Work*', Princeton: Princeton University Press.

Rees, J. (1980), 'Government policy and industrial location in the United States', *Special Study on Economic Change*, Joint Economic Committee, US Congress, **7**, 128–79.

Rosenfeld, S. (1995), *New Technologies and New Skills*, Chapel Hill, NC: Regional Technology Strategies.

Rosenfeld, S. (1998), *Technical Colleges, Technology Deployment and Regional Development*, Paris: OECD.

Ryan, W.P. (1999), 'The new landscape for non-profits', *Harvard Business Review*, **77**, 127–36.

Salamon, L.M. and H. Anheier (ed.) (1997), *Defining the Non-profit Sector: a Gross National Analysis,* New York: Manchester University Press.

Salamon, L. M. (1997), 'The United States', in Salamon and Anheier op. cit., pp. 280–320.

Saxenian, A. (1994), *Regional Advantage*, Cambridge, MA: Harvard University Press.

Schmandt, J. and R. Wilson (eds) (1990), *Growth Policy in the Age of High Technology,* London: Unwin Hyman.

Sommer, J. (1999), 'Six lamentations on higher education', Paper, Annual meeting of Association of Private Enterprise Education, Orlando, FL.

Wolpert, J. (1997), 'Social income and the voluntary sector', *Papers, Regional Science Association*, **39**, 217–30.

Wolpert, J. (1988), The geography of generosity: metropolitan disparities in donation and support for amenities', *Annals, Association of American Geographers*, **78**, 665–79.

World Bank (1995), *The Development Report*, Washington, DC: World Bank.

21. How can Regional Policies Influence the Location Advantages of a Region?

Börje Johansson

INTRODUCTION

At several stages in this book the reader is confronted with a classical problem in economic geography and regional science. It may be restated in the following form: how should one delineate regions such that the resulting areas serve the purpose of analysis, and such that results are not completely misleading? With the long tradition of regional science that we have, one may ask: have we not come any further? In fact, the contributions in this book show that one can provide some important answers to how regions should be defined and how contextually meaningful observables can be constructed.

In general, the contributions in this book emphasise the importance of using a concept of region that can refer in a precise way to the processes or phenomena being studied and, for example, 'functional' refers to the functioning of a region's economy. However, there is a competing prime notion, namely the notion of place that corresponds to very durable and possibly very local phenomena. Its extension may be the same as a functional (urban) region. If not, one may expect that place is related to an area inside a functional region.

What, then, is a functional region? As a first step one may consult the idea of forming statistical clusters. From this point of view a region is characterised by having much more intense non-mediated interactions (face-to-face) inside the region than with any other area outside the region. In this perspective, a functional region may be pretty much the same as a labour market region. Empirically it remains to show that the provision of firm and household services has (approximately) the same extension as the labour market. These considerations may lead to workable definitions. However, regions evolve due to changes in transport systems and interaction technologies in general. In contemporary Europe a functional region has a much larger geographic extension than it had 50 years ago. In the case of Sweden it has been shown that the intensity of labour market interaction has a rather sharp border about 45 minutes away from any spatial concentration inside the region. Similar observations are also reported in this book, although experiences from Japan indicate that time distances may be longer there.

Having come this far in making conclusions from the composite knowledge presented in the book, we have to realise that economic geography can (and should, I believe) be depicted as a partly hierarchical structure. There are frequent short-distance interactions that take place inside a region. But we also observe less frequent long-distance interaction, where economic actors make direct contacts to develop, realise and maintain business opportunities. Also in this case we may refer to cluster techniques as a means to identify interaction network patterns that define 'interaction regions', consisting of groups of functional regions. This perspective can be applied to studies inside a country and would comprise concepts such as urban hierarchy networks and models of central place systems. Widening the perspective one may also contemplate a grouping of countries in trade regions, where each country's trade is much more intense with regard to regions (and countries) inside the group than with regions outside the group.

The picture of region complexes presented above implies that there is a corresponding but not congruent map of geographic areas for regional policymaking. That lack of congruency is caused by the unfortunate fact that administrative regions rarely correspond to the places, functional regions or trade regions. In this context we can, for example, identify geographical areas of a local, a regional and a national government – and in several countries an even richer set of (administrative) territorial subdivisions. The mismatch of functional and administrative areas cause problems for policymaking, because the mismatch will imply that there are both positive and negative spillovers from a given policy effort. Secondly, for the analyst the same problem arises when attempts are made to assess the outcome of different policy strategies or approaches. This problem is further aggravated by the fact that we also have statistical regions. For example, in the US we have MSA regions and in the EU so-called NUTS regions, a label that some researchers have found very appropriate. In comparison, the MSA concept is closer to that of a functional region than are any of the different NUTS definitions.

The latter problem is stressed in the contribution by Cheshire and Magrini when they conclude that unless the boundaries (of a functional region) are defined so that they identify regions which are self-contained in labour market terms – that is there is minimal across-boundary net commuting – records of GDP per capita will be misrepresented and misleading. One may especially note that a NUTS region with a significant net inflow of labour commuters will also tend to get a higher GDP per capita than income per capita.

What, then, are the conclusions, what is a region? First, there is a clear message from the different chapters of the book. One cannot get around this problem. The evolution of mobile as well as Internet communication will continue to disturb and change the 'functional borders' of regions. Changes in transport systems will have similar impacts. Hence, in research and model building methods have to keep pace with the changing 'reality' and this requires more stringent theory, purposeful and well-organised statistical information and further developments in spatial econometrics.

FROM RICARDO TO ENDOGENOUS COMPARATIVE ADVANTAGES

The concept of comparative advantage has been central in economics for a very long time. It has remained an important but uncomfortable idea in regional economics, partly because the dynamics behind the advantages are not the same in an interregional context as in standard models in international economics. In a setting where each country has an individual and adjustable exchange ratio, a set of countries can easily exploit productivity differentials. In an interregional context the price mechanisms are different and, from our perspective, more complex with wage and price of floorspace differences that induce migration of labour, capital and techniques. This may imply that a modified concept should be contemplated. Before discussing this we may just emphasise the ingenious nature of comparative advantage by restating the definition of Ricardo's notion:

Consider a region, A, that is specialised in producing good 1. Let x_2 denote the number of units of other goods that have to be given up in order to produce one extra unit of good 1. Region A has a comparative advantage in producing good 1, if x_2 is smaller in A than in other regions with which A has trade relations.

Of course this definition involves an implicit pricing of good 1 and good 2 (other goods), a problem that Ricardo solved by referring to the size of labour input into the production of each type of good. In Ricardo's original model there is no capital and regions (countries) differ, because they have different techniques (different labour productivity) in the production of different goods. Ohlin initiated a discussion of how such differences arise.

His message was that patterns of comparative advantage are based on the availability of different durable characteristics (resources) in the trading regions. With another terminology, each region is assumed to have a specific supply of trapped resources, that is, resources that change on a slow time scale. A region will then have an incentive to specialise in production that uses intensively such resources that are abundant in the region. The output from such production is the source of the regions' exports.

How, then, are comparative advantages of a region explained in the contributions to this book? The basic idea of Ricardo is not changed much, but the focus is on location and one may then suggest a shift in terminology from comparative advantage to 'location advantage'. This corresponds to saying that a certain location (notably a functional region) has a pattern of slowly changing characteristics that determine its advantages. However, this is not all. The Ricardo and Ohlin ideas identify the advantage entirely with supply factors and resource conditions. In the models of this book the demand side has an equally prominent role to play. For example, advantages can be caused by a particular demand profile of region. The latter may be related to deliveries between firms. Secondly, it may be related to the households' demand pattern that depends on the income per capita of consumers and other regional demand idiosyncrasies. Thirdly, it may simply be related to the size of the region, recognising that certain goods and services have low demand intensity, that is, for certain goods potential buyers constitute a small share of the entire population. When this is the case demand will be sufficiently large only in large regions. In summary, location advantages can be classified into

- Resource-based or supply-based advantages
- Market-based or demand-based advantages

Among resource-based advantages, the contributions in the previous chapters emphasise the following supply factors in a region:

- Supply of labour categories or firms' accessibility to labour supply
- Firms' accessibility to input suppliers, venture capital and production factors other than labour inputs (localisation economies)
- Capacity and quality of infrastructure
- Institutions and entrepreneurship traditions, the existence of firm clusters, R&D and knowledge resources
- Sense of place

Some of the above factors may be more important in contemporary economies than ever before. This is emphasised in the chapter on nomadic firms, where it is observed that the location behaviour of modern multi-establishment firms display an increasing tendency towards being footloose. With the above list in mind, which are the demand-based advantages? They should include factors that attract households to stay and move into the region and in particular properties of the following kind:

- Urbanisation economies and associated diversity of purchasing opportunities
- Size and density of the region and its income per capita
- Household milieu and accessibility to household services, place surplus
- Households' accessibility to jobs

The list of supply-based as well as that of demand-based advantages includes partly overlapping attributes. There is also a clear intersection between the two lists, which is a natural consequence of public or collective phenomena. Still, this indicates that the categories in the two lists could be considerably improved to satisfy stronger criteria of theoretical consistency. This may be further illustrated by observing that entrepreneurship institutions of a region often are identified by properties such as a large share of family businesses, sectoral diversity, a community with financial resources and leadership in both the private and public sectors.

The chapter by Bolton presents the concept of place surplus, which includes aspects such as place-specific quality and prices of housing and other goods, consumption profile, and public, non-priced goods. He stresses that many of the most important characteristics of a place are non-market goods the inhabitants can enjoy without having to pay for them.

DYNAMICS OF LOCATION ADVANTAGE

Location advantages may be slowly changing, but they are developing over time and the evolution is path-dependent. An example of the latter is given in the description of industrial regions dominated by heavy industry. In their process of decline, it is not reduced labour productivity that causes the cumulating problems, but the opposite. In such regions increasing productivity together with an insufficient entry of new activities tend to gradually reduce the total employment and make the regions shrink in size.

The observation that regional characteristics are dynamic brings two messages. One is that the development of a region's attributes can have the form of a self-organised, cumulative and path-dependent change process. The second message is that location advantages can be created on the basis of conscious decision making by private and public policymakers, and this constitutes the core of this book.

One approach suggested in the book is to focus on capital formation in a region as the main source of its dynamics. Four specifications of capital are considered: physical, financial, human and social capital. The challenge is to improve the understanding of how the latter two influence regional economic development. Universities and university colleges are typical agents of human capital formation, while various non-profit organisations and similar institutions are assumed to build up social capital. In a development perspective there should be sufficient social capital in the underlying society to provide an arena for business, corporations, networks and the like to be self organising. The overall observation here is of course that the focus on capital is a focus on created resources – and on the capacity to improve the resource supply in a temporal perspective. One may say that it is a focus on dynamic location advantages.

A particular aspect of regional dynamics is exit and entry processes referring to firms and industries, to labour and knowledge/skill resources, and to financial capital. A related phenomenon is exit and voice processes. Structural change and decline in a region usually includes exit processes, in which qualified labour may move to other regions, firms shut down or move to locations away from the region. Such a development may also trigger voice, here recognised as processes in which resources are being mobilised by subgroups of a region's population, and where private and public leaders organise a 'fighting back' spirit. Local voice capacity may be based on local neighbourhood capacities and social capital in general.

What more is recognised in the preceding chapters? The following change phenomena influence the emergence and development of location dynamics of a region:

- Technology development as an internal process, including education and retraining of the labour force, as well as R&D and patent development, and other forms of process and product developments of firms that generate renewal and growth.
- Technology development as an externally generated process, comprising diffusion in the form of knowledge spillovers and start-up incentives as well as inward direct investments.
- Attraction of households embodying skills, experiences and knowledge. An important part of these dynamics is a region's capability to retain individuals who get their university education in the region.
- Regional specialisation as a self-reinforcing process that generates external scale economies and clusters, but also in the form of

decline processes that narrow down the diversity of economic activities.

- Cumulative change based on the interdependence between interaction-intensive transactions and various forms of scale economies, where economic expansion brings about growth of regional population and demand. Cumulative development of this kind may require a complementary development with infrastructure formation and land-use planning.

WHAT REGIONAL ECONOMIC POLICIES CAN WE OBSERVE?

Do regional policies make a difference? In what areas and in what ways can policy influence the economic performance of a region? These questions are vital, since during recent decades influential opinions have stressed that less policy is to be preferred. Such statements have been accompanied by strategies of deregulation and privatisation of previously publicly produced services, for example in areas such as electricity supply, telecommunication services and mail distribution.

As a starting point we may observe that deregulation also requires political decisions and other forms of policymaking. Moreover, deregulation does not really mean taking away rules and regulation. It rather means a change of the regulation framework. However, there is a more important observation to be made, and that has to do with the adjustment speed of political decisions and decisions by suppliers and buyers in the market place. Political decisions and regional policies adjust as a rule on other time scales than market decisions. Policy decisions tend to be delayed and mismatched for several reasons, notably because of observation lags, decision making lags and implementation lags. As a consequence, there is a great risk that political decision-making is mismatched *vis-à-vis* market processes and thus may aggravate problems rather than solve them.

What are the implications of the above observations? Are there any areas for regional policies? A short-cut answer would be tangible and intangible infrastructure. By definition infrastructure is slowly changing and durable. Hence, there is time to think and assess in advance, but it is also necessary to compare alternatives, discuss and plan when the consequences are lasting and more or less irreversible. These types of decisions comprise structural and systems decisions, the architecture of rules and organisation, but also long-term balance of interests.

The above may seem simple as guidance, but things are a little bit more complicated. First, observe that in general terms urban infrastructure may represent the built environment as a whole, which includes the spatial distribution of premises and floorspace as well as land for exploitation. Second, economic life in a region involves repetitive desires from existing firms to change the capacity, quality and location of their premises in response to technique and market changes. The latter may imply both more and less capacity. Third, similar arguments are equally important for firms that enter the market. Certain research results indicate that regional policy has an important role to play in these interregional allocation activities. The crux is then that many of the relocation adjustments referred to above require fast decisions. As a consequence, it becomes necessary to build up an organisation that can handle the allocation problems based on long-term rules. The latter have to be created and developed over time by the political system, but the very day-to-day operation has to be decoupled from the time-consuming elements in political decision making. To develop specific decision systems of the described kind is again part of the slow dynamics.

How should the above be interpreted? In the contributions of this book, the interpretation is that regional development policies are directed towards creation, renewal and maintenance of a region's location advantages. Moreover, in this context we have recognised that there are resource-based and demand-based advantages. The latter advantages arise when a region is large and dense enough that the size of demand and purchasing power provide opportunities for a wide variety of activities to be profitable in the region. For small regions this issue requires creative ways to get around their predicament of being small. In general, infrastructure and land-use policies are basic instruments for making a region dense such that it offers accessibility in a variety of respects. However, the fundamental problem in this area of policymaking is to make the region attractive so that existing and new inhabitants will be attracted to the region and not stimulated to leave it. The relevant policies include a spectrum of household milieu characteristics, and many of these are related to resource-based policy issues.

Resource-based advantages relate to durable characteristics of a region. They have already been presented in this concluding chapter and they are discussed through the book and could be organised as follows:

- *Facility policies*, comprising built infrastructure for urban life, transport, Internet and telecommunications, property development, transport demand and urban management, including land value mechanisms.
- *Household milieu policies*, comprising life conditions and opportunities of households, formation of human and social capital, job accessibility and natural environment attributes.

- *Firm milieu and adjustment policies*, comprising stimulation of technology diffusion, facilitating supply of venture capital, stimulation of firm start-ups and direct investments by external firms, stimulation of cluster formation, reduction of the friction of spatial allocation inside the region and labour market adjustments of various kinds.

In addition to this, special attention is also given to rural regions and small functional regions, which are both more demand and contextual than larger regions from a regional policymaking perspective.

THE ASSESSMENT OF REGIONAL POLICIES

Why should resources be spent on monitoring and evaluating regional policies? First, regional policies consume resources and hence they should satisfy efficiency criteria, just like all other activities. Second, assessments are a necessary part of a region's learning process, and of the learning process that one would hope that states and supra-state decision makers also take part in. For the European Union this may be especially important. Thus, there are good reasons for conducting regular and systematic assessments.

Assessments of regional policies have often been of the case study type. What value do these studies have? One possible attitude, which is promoted here, is that case studies generate ideas and hypotheses, and they make problems obvious. But they do not settle matters. To improve knowledge in a consistent way we need sets of observations, through time and across many cases. This attitude is also reflected in this book.

One recurrent message is that in a lot of cases systematic evaluation is missing or of a very ad hoc nature. In the chapter by Rees there is a plea for systematic analysis and evaluation of social capital formation, and this would include policies to strengthen the development of regional institutions.

The assessment studies and discussions in the book may be grouped into three basic categories:

- Model-based assessment and methods for contrafactual approaches
- Econometric studies
- Policy and market interdependencies

What are the advantages of using a formal model in assessment processes? A major feature to be considered here is that with a model one may carry out simulations of alternative paths, and this could be seen as method to solve the contrafactual dilemma in evaluation activities. One of the chapters presents simulation experiments to investigate path dependence in the evolution of a city's systems through time in response to network formation policies. In these experiments the role of cost–benefit rules is examined. The focus is on improvements in railroad networks. According to the results in the chapter, cost–benefit criteria will stimulate development paths such that the population will concentrate in certain dominant locations.

The background for these experiments is that agglomeration economies introduce multiple and indeterminate development possibilities, and cost–benefit criteria support paths that lead to further concentration. The model framework is a general equilibrium model that tries to highlight the impacts of increasing returns, based on agglomeration economies. The contextual background is regional policies in Japan.

Still one chapter employs a Computable General Equilebrium (CGE) model as a means to reveal effects of policy decisions. The model exercises are carried as an alternative to standard UK approaches, where the direct policy impact is calculated on the basis of questionnaires to and interviews with companies. The focus of assessment is the strategic objective of business competitiveness. The presentation addresses two specific challenges: (i) to capture in the model qualitative changes that occur due to changes of model parameters, which are assumed to be perturbed by policy measures, and (ii) to calibrate the size of the perturbations (shocks) to generate the scale of the direct effects.

This contribution observes that it is difficult to identify the employment gains associated with each improvement of supply-side efficiency. First, increased efficiency expands output, a phenomenon that stimulates employment growth. Second, the resulting reduction of labour input per unit output works in the opposite direction. It is argued that the model can help to get clear insight into the trade-off described above. Moreover, it allows for a discussion of effects on the regional and the national level, which amounts to a deliberation of zero-sum and variable-sum policies.

The two CGE approaches are framed by Moennesland's discussion about the need to generate contrafactual paths in the assessment of how policy programmes (of the EU type) are carried through. This contribution demonstrates the importance of reliable and transparent methods to generate reference scenarios, against which the observed or projected path is measured and evaluated. For large programmes this becomes accentuated, since for such programmes secondary side-effects become important.

Econometric estimations generate another type of model that can be used to assess the development consequences with and without a certain policy programme or a specific policy measure. Once estimated such a model can also be used in ex ante planning. The focus in the contributions in this book has been primarily to use statistical estimation in ex post assessment. One chapter offers a broad examination of different techniques for evaluation of regional policy in the UK. The examined policies have been designed to create jobs in areas suffering from persistently high unemployment. Historically in Europe this policy has dominated over policies that facilitate migration from unemployment areas to areas with better job opportunities. Distinctions are made between a whole set of approaches. Regressions based on aggregate employment trends in assisted areas are compared with regression results based on panel data. In a similar way time-series and cross-sectional regressions are compared with regard to effects in the form of interregional movements of industry. A third category of consideration concerns inward investments. In view of this evaluation of assessment methods progress is recognised in several respects such as:

- Estimates of additionality, displacement and multiplier effects have become more accurate.
- There has been a development of large-scale models of the regional economy to reveal system-wide effects.
- Policy impacts on regional competitiveness get more attention.

Another chapter argues that it is often unclear what policy interventions have actually been employed. This chapter presents a model of how functional regions grow. By estimating such a model across European urban regions, the model-predicted and the observed growth patterns may be compared. Residuals may then reveal for which regions one should expect that effective regional policies have been in operation, and this provides a platform for further and more detailed comparison between regions with positive and negative residuals. Such analyses indicate the importance of how local government is organised and the formation of 'clubs' and leadership capacity to promote regional growth.

In this chapter it is made obvious that regional policy and self-organised market adjustments usually combine and may be hard to separate. This includes assessments of labour market adjustments, capital formation, technology diffusion and many other processes.

BIBLIOGRAPHY

Batey, P.W.J. and P. Friedrich (eds), *Regional Competition,* Berlin: Springer-Verlag.

Cheshire, P. and I. Gordon (eds) (1995), *Territorial Competition in an Integrating Europe*, Aldershot: Avebury.
Johansson, B., C. Karlsson and R. Stough (2001), *Theories of Endogenous Growth – Lessons for Regional Policies*, Berlin: Springer-Verlag.
Nijkamp, P., R. Stough and E. Verhoff (eds) (1998), 'Symposium "Endogenous growth in a regional context"', *Annals of Regional Science*, **32** (1).

Index

accessibility 5–9, 13, 31, 77–80, 90, 96, 140, 163–4, 167, 216–18, 427–38, 506–7, 510
agglomeration 5, 20, 25–6, 29–33, 48, 50, 56, 64–8, 103–8, 114, 186, 212, 218, 370, 426–35, 512
Alonso, W. 107
Anderson, W.P. 103, 398
Arthur, W.B. 104–5
AT&T 51–5

bandwith 49
Batten, D.F. 20, 103–4
benchmark 115, 117, 120, 124, 155
benefit–cost analysis *see* cost–benefit analysis
Bolton, Roger 20, 470, 483, 507
broadband 49, 52–5, 63
Brussels 227, 230, 232
Button, Kenneth 78, 98

calibration 274
Camagni, R. 327, 334
Canada 138, 254
capitalism 131, 147, 490
Castells, Manuel 50, 78, 79
central place system 7, 16–17, 25–9, 31–3, 504
CGE *see* computable general equilibrium
Cheshire, Paul 18, 211, 214–25, 232, 445, 504
Chicago 59–61, 137, 499
cluster 7, 14–15, 26, 64, 67–8, 17, 262, 431–9, 503–8, 511
communication infrastructure 81, 140
commuter-flow 381–2, 387
commuting 96, 107–11, 161–4, 212–14, 339–41, 344–6, 351, 367–76, 382–7, 445, 474, 505
competitive advantage 1, 10–11, 64, 159, 188
competitive efficiency 79–80
competitiveness 65, 69, 127, 143, 145, 157, 169, 254, 262–73, 329, 397, 462, 512–13
computable general equilibrium 18, 196–7, 254–5, 512
computer-integrated manufacturing 65
correlation 35, 193, 215, 218, 249–33, 460, 482
cost–benefit 103, 193, 195
cost–benefit analysis 154, 193–4, 472, 479, 512
costs
  fixed 14, 26–34, 37
  interaction 4–9, 11, 26, 32, 35, 371–2
  opportunity 154, 194
  transaction 4, 14, 25, 28, 78, 82
counterfactual 18, 154, 156, 175, 209–11, 239, 244–51
cross-sectional data 164, 180, 513
customisation 64–5

Dallas 52, 59–61, 137
decomposition 324, 326, 323, 336–40, 344, 349–57, 398–402, 486–7
deindustrialisation 136, 441–7, 450–64
Dinc, Mustafa 20, 392, 398
disparities 127, 141–3, 147, 159–62, 165, 169, 442, 449

disposable income 324–42, 349–56
dynamic specialisation
economic development 1, 144, 221–2, 332, 3349, 391, 249, 438, 459, 489–93, 508
economies of scale 2–6, 8–12, 14, 17, 25–42, 82
economies,
external 6, 8, 11–12, 26, 116
internal 3–6, 8–12, 14, 26, 30–31, 40–41
efficiency 64–6, 78–80, 120, 124, 158, 160, 176, 188, 210, 247, 262–7, 271–3, 288, 392, 439, 500, 511–12
elasticity 39, 262, 277, 429–35, 483
embeddedness 83, 490
endogenous growth theory 211, 218
enterprise zone 19, 301–15, 318–19
entrepreneurship 15, 52, 303–309, 315, 492, 499–501, 506–507
environment 13, 65, 68, 84–5, 143, 156, 199, 391, 399, 428, 438, 510
equilibrium 18, 103, 111, 164, 478
see also general equilibrium model
EU *see* European Union
European Commission 20, 198, 425, 497–8
European integration 215–17, 220–21, 392, 403
European regions 80, 211–12, 432–40
European Union 20, 159, 174, 198–203, 210–14, 217, 221, 490, 511
evaluation 1–2, 15–20, 112–18, 120–24, 132, 153–60, 169–70, 173–4, 190–93, 198–203, 209–10, 225, 239–54, 269–73, 324
evolutionary pattern 105
ex-ante evaluation 193, 98
export-base model
ex-post analysis 329, 323, 336

factor mobility 7, 159, 391
FDI *see* foreign direct investment
flexible automation 65
foreign direct investment 67, 490
foreign inward investment 182–3, 188–9
fragmentation 142–7
France 90–91, 393, 404, 408, 497
Frankfurt 221–35
Fujita, M. 104
Fukuyama, F. 490–91, 498
functional region 4, 7–12, 14, 19, 26–39, 42, 367–88, 503–6, 511–13
FUR 212–36

GATT 159
GDP 130, 212–16, 219–20, 236, 267–9, 277, 324–5, 344–6, 352
general equilibrium model 18, 104–8, 115, 512
geographical
distribution 137, 179, 394
sourcing 17, 128–30, 138
geography 1–3, 13–15, 50, 52, 59, 69, 78, 82, 104–8, 371, 487
Gillespie, A. 18, 53–6, 59, 197, 254, 276
globalisation 66, 81–2, 130, 391–2
glocalisation 66
Gordon, I. 18, 159, 162–5, 169–70, 211, 218, 222, 225
Gorman, S. 50, 60–62
Göteborg 381, 385, 388
government research labs 68
Gramlich, E.M. 140
gravity model 111, 163
Griliches, Z. 129–30
gross domestic product *see* GDP

Haggett 59
Hall, P. 129
Hansen, F. 324–8, 357
Haynes, K.E. 20, 142, 392, 398–402
heartland 81, 130–38, 143, 147
Henderson, J. 103, 108
Hicks 263–5, 73, 475, 485
Hippel, E. 64
Hirschman, A. 469–70, 479–83
home market effect 3, 8–11

human capital 1, 13, 17, 139, 142–3, 147, 216–18, 438, 489–94, 508
immobility 426
increasing returns 1–3, 5–6, 15–16, 66, 104–8, 512
indivisibility 426
industrial
district 65, 441, 458
policy 159
sectors 20, 104, 167, 356, 400, 452, 463–4
industries,
high-order 32, 36–43, 47
low-order 30–32, 35–40, 43
medium-order 36–43, 47
information age 63
innovation 10, 13, 32, 53, 64–9, 79, 81, 127–30, 148, 262, 358, 393, 453
innovative capacity 132–5
inout–output
multiplier 271
model 196–7, 210, 337
international trade 1, 20, 78, 262, 391–2, 397–9, 403–407
Internet 17, 31, 49–55, 59–66, 505, 510
invention 60, 127–38, 144–7, 481

Johansson, B. 21, 367, 371
Johansson, M. 20, 443, 446, 453

Karlsson, C. 16–19, 141, 367
Keeble 32, 217
Keynesian 158, 253, 271–2, 338, 490
Klaasen, L.H. 368
Kobayashi, K. 20, 103–4, 110, 487
Krugman, P. 6, 25, 35, 104, 221, 367, 391–2

labour
productivity 346, 356–7, 441, 447, 458, 461, 505, 507
migration 161–3
supply 13, 158, 162–4, 506
large-scale models 196, 203, 272, 513
location advantage 7, 9, 12, 21, 26, 506–10
lock-in effect 17, 105, 107, 124–5
logit analysis 91
London 169, 184, 213, 222–9, 234
Los Angeles 59–61, 136–7
loyalty 20, 469, 473, 479–83

Maillat, D. 65, 68
Malecki, E. J. 17, 49–53, 65, 130, 144–5, 490
market
incentives 127, 145, 147, 504
potential 1–2, 5–6, 8, 13, 35, 56
marketing 65, 129, 188, 202, 445–7
Markusen, A.R. 145, 392, 398–9
Marshall, A. 12, 26, 104, 472, 484
methodology 18, 20, 98, 198, 221, 239, 241, 244, 324–6, 349, 392, 398
microeconomic 67, 81, 177, 254, 273, 470–71, 483
Midwest 130–37, 140, 143–4
monopoly 52, 54, 130
Mulligan 26

net benefits 20, 195, 224
network
economy 17, 77–9, 85, 97
evolution 108, 112, 115–24
structure 59, 63, 78, 86–9, 104, 106, 111, 114, 122–3
new economic geography 1–3, 13–15, 221
New York 52, 59–61, 135–7
Nijkamp, P. 17, 77–81, 91, 98
Nilsson, R. 16–17
nomadic firm 17, 77, 81–92, 506
non-linear 4, 8, 215
non-profit 111, 489.91, 494–502, 508
non-substitutability 426
NUTs region 20, 212–16, 225–6, 235, 427–33, 504–505

OLS model 212
Olson, M. 222
Oosterhaven, 325–6

Paelinck, J. 400
Parr, J. 30–31
patents 131–2, 136–7, 508
performance indicators 153, 155, 159, 193, 298
peripheral 65, 80, 130, 133, 139, 325–9, 335–6, 356–60, 431–9
Phoenix 140
place surplus 20–21, 470–75, 478–87, 507
polycentric 136
polyvalence 426
potential analysis 20, 426, 431, 435
present value 175, 194, 197, 269, 370
private sector 9, 66, 68, 141, 145, 262, 272, 276, 490, 496–7
product life cycle 4, 32, 50
profitability 14, 66, 80, 88, 90, 202, 262, 445
purchasing power 5–7, 35, 37, 216, 510
Putnam, R. 490–91, 498

R&D 1, 9, 13–16, 29, 32, 82, 128–9, 144, 190, 216, 219, 228, 393, 445–7, 491, 506, 508
rank–size distribution 376–7
real wage 255, 369–71
Rees, John 20–21, 144, 490, 499–500, 511
regeneration 18, 253, 272, 276, 315–22
regional change 130, 139, 147, 507
Regional Development Grant 175–6
regional growth 1, 5, 13, 104, 211–16, 221, 232, 398, 400, 513
regionalisation 391
regulatory change 51
reindustrialisation 20, 445, 458
Research Triangle 59
residuals 211, 218, 221–3, 228–36, 337, 513
Ricardo 505–6
Richardson, H.W. 26, 448
Rigby, D.L. 398
Romer, P.M.104
Rosenfeld, S. 68, 592–3
rough set analysis 17, 77, 81, 91–100
rural 19, 50, 53–6, 80, 323–4, 329, 323–9, 350–62
San Francisco 59–60, 136–7
self-sufficiency 375–88
shift–share analysis 210, 336–8, 447
Silicon Valley 60, 136, 499
Single European Act 221, 393, 403–6
SME 68, 198, 437–9
Smelser, Neil 142
social capital 20, 65, 158, 470, 482, 489–95, 498–501, 508–11
social security 19, 45, 47, 325, 327, 339, 359
socioeconomic 80, 127, 341–6
Southern California 140–43
start-up 3, 19, 191, 301–6, 310, 508, 511
Stigler, G. 38
Storper, M. 65, 79
Stough, R. R. 142, 236
strategic objective 18, 170, 254, 262–73, 277, 512
Suarez-Villa, L. 17, 129–32, 136, 140, 145–6
Sunbelt 130, 47, 499
supply chain 189, 194–6
sustainable development 80
Sweden 17–20, 34–6, 325, 367–78, 387, 393, 403–9, 442–6, 454–64, 497–8, 504
switches 51–60

technological change 17, 32–4, 47, 49, 130, 392
technological sourcing 128, 130
telecommunications 17, 31, 42, 50–56, 88, 66–8, 391, 509–10
Telecommunications Act of 1996 52, 55
territorial competition 209–10, 225
total factor productivity 447
tourism 327, 438
transmission 49, 51–55, 58, 61, 63

transportation 4, 9, 25, 29, 59, 67–8, 78, 80, 87, 96, 103–107, 111–15, 306, 371, 391, 440, 459

UK 54, 158–9, 173–7, 181–93, 202–4, 253–8, 261–74, 301–10, 325, 362, 403–9, 493–7, 512–13
unbundling 55
university 142, 216, 219, 228, 431, 489–96, 501, 508
urban
  core 321, 331, 9, 374
  region 5–9, 27–9, 210–14, 227, 232–3, 236, 513
  system 28–34, 43–4, 103, 105
urbanisation 12, 26, 29–30, 36, 41, 507
US Bureau of the Census 131, 139, 167
US Patent and Trademark Office 129, 132, 134–7

Vanhove, N. 368
venture capital 262, 490, 499, 506, 511
vintage index 28, 33

Washington, DC 59–60, 143
welfare state 19, 80, 323–32, 498
Wildavsky, A. 155
wireless 54, 62
Wolpert 498–99